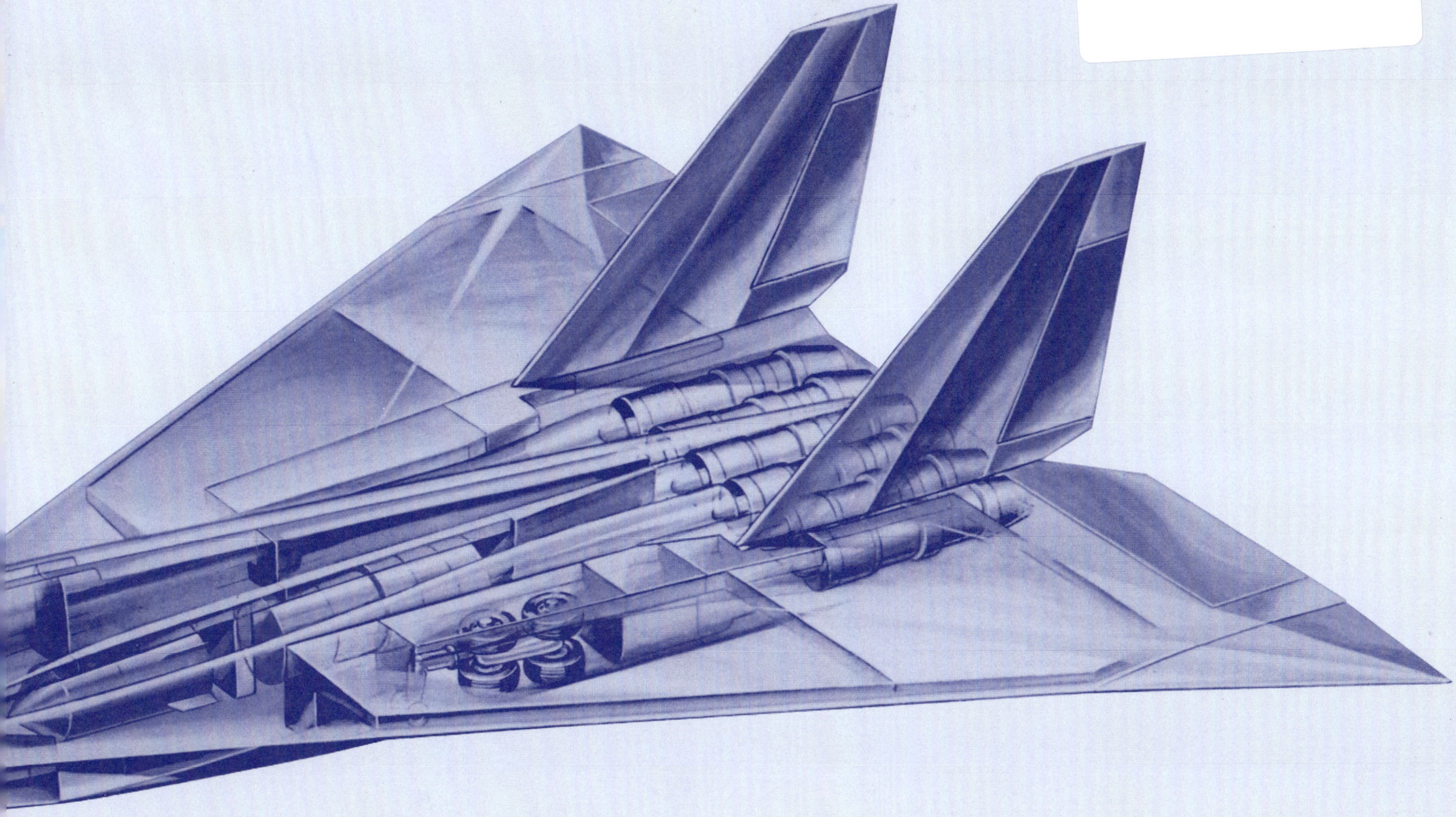

specialty press
PUBLISHERS AND WHOLESALERS

VALKYRIE
NORTH AMERICAN'S MACH 3 SUPERBOMBER

Dennis R. Jenkins and Tony R. Landis

© 2004 by Dennis R. Jenkins and Tony R. Landis

All rights reserved. No part of this publication may be reproduced or utilized in any form or by any means, electronic or mechanical, including photocopying, recording, or by any information storage and retrieval system, without prior written permission from the author. All photos and artwork are the property of the owners as credited.

The information in this work is true and complete to the best of our knowledge. However, all information is presented without any guarantee on the part of the author or publisher, who also disclaim any liability incurred in connection with the use of the information.

ISBN 1-58007-072-8
Item #SP072

specialty press
PUBLISHERS AND WHOLESALERS

39966 Grand Avenue
North Branch, MN 55056 USA
(651) 277-1400 or (800) 895-4585
www.specialtypress.com

Printed in China

Distributed in the UK and Europe by:

Midland Publishing
4 Watling Drive
Hinckley LE10 3EY, England
Tel: 01455 233 747 Fax: 01455 233 737
www.midlandcountiessuperstore.com

Library of Congress Cataloging-in-Publication Data

Jenkins, Dennis R.
　Valkyrie : North American's Mach 3 superbomber / by Dennis R. Jenkins and
Tony R. Landis.
　　p. cm.
　ISBN 1-58007-072-8 (hardcover)
　1. B-70 bomber--Design and construction--History. 2. High-speed aeronautics--United States--History. 3. Aeronautics, Military--Research--United States--History. I. Landis, Tony. II. Title.
TL685.3.J46 2004
623.74'63--dc22
　　　　　　　　　　　　　2004001278

In Memory of

Mrs. Mary E. Jenkins

On the Front Cover: **Al White taxies A/V-1 into position for her first flight from the manufacturing site in Palmdale to Edwards AFB on 21 September 1964.** (Boeing Historical Archives)

On the Front Dust Jacket Flap: **A female model dressed as a Valkyrie holds a model of the B-70 bomber. Although not politically correct today, this was considered good publicity in the mid 1960s.** (Boeing Historical Archives)

On the Front Endsheet: **An early B-70. Note the nuclear weapon in the bomb bay, and the four person crew. The folding wingtips were still small at the point, and the rudders and elevons were more traditional than those ultimately built. Also note the position of the canard relative to the crewmembers.** (Boeing Historical Archives)

On the Front Page: **Both Valkyries together; A/V-1 is in the distance.** (Boeing Historical Archives)

On the Title Page: **The first Valkyrie during an engine run prior to her maiden flight. Note the large sound abatement chamber attached to the engine exhaust so that the noise did not disturb Palmdale-area turkey farmers.** (Boeing Historical Archives)

On the Back Endsheet: **The cockpit of Air Vehicle 1 (the escape capsules are not shown).** (Jim Tuttle Collection)

On the Back Cover: **The second Valkyrie soars above the Southwestern desert. The easiest way to tell the two airplanes apart was that the radome on A/V-2 was black instead of white. The airplane is configured for high-speed flight – windshield ramp up and wingtips full down.** (AFFTC History Office Collection)

TABLE OF CONTENTS

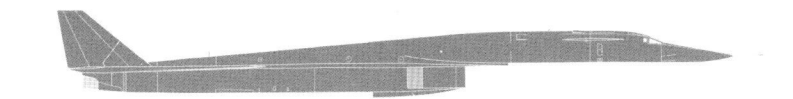

FOREWORD	ALVIN S. WHITE	VI
FOREWORD	FITZHUGH L. "FITZ" FULTON, JR.	VII
AUTHORS' PREFACE	THE ULTIMATE BOMBER	VIII
CHAPTER 1	AN EXPENSIVE DIVERSION – THE ATOMIC POWERED AIRPLANE	1
CHAPTER 2	TECHNICAL VOODOO – HIGH HOPES FOR WS-110A	13
CHAPTER 3	THE ELUSIVE MACH 3 FIGHTER – XF-103 AND XF-108	43
CHAPTER 4	ANOTHER DIVERSION – HIGH-ENERGY FUELS	77
CHAPTER 5	POLITICS – AND CONTINUED RESTRUCTURING	91
CHAPTER 6	THE FLIGHT PROGRAM – HALF A MILLION POUNDS AT MACH 3	121
CHAPTER 7	1960s STATE-OF-THE-ART – CONSTRUCTION AND SYSTEMS	183
CHAPTER 8	NO APPARENT THREAT – MILITARY SYSTEMS	211
APPENDIX A	129 FLIGHTS OF THE MAIDENS	237
APPENDIX B	THE VALKYRIE PILOTS	245
APPENDIX C	A PILOT'S PERSPECTIVE	246
APPENDIX D	LESSONS FOR A SUPERSONIC TRANSPORT	249
APPENDIX E	INTERESTING FACTS	253
APPENDIX F	NOTES AND CITATIONS	255
APPENDIX G	INDEX	261

FOREWORD

Alvin S. White

In 1955, North American Aviation, Incorporated, and The Boeing Company were requested by the United States Air Force to submit competitive bids for Weapons System 110A. Both proposals were rejected by the Air Force, and the companies were "sent back to the drawing board." With a completely new design, in December 1957 North American was finally selected as the winner and awarded a contract to build the B-70. The proposal was for an airplane capable of flying from bases in the United States to any target in the Soviet Union at Mach 3 and 70,000 feet, carrying a 25,000 pound payload, with the ability to recover to a base in friendly territory. It was a proposal that required the designers to use concepts that were at the extremes of aircraft technology. At that time, I was chosen to be the project pilot for the flight test program.

After the contract was awarded by the Air Force, it was the task of engineering and manufacturing personnel to coordinate with the designers to build this remarkable airplane. At a time when aluminum was used extensively in the construction of airplanes, stainless steel and titanium had to be used for most of the XB-70 to withstand the temperatures that aerodynamic heating would generate at Mach 3. Stainless steel honeycomb panels were used for most of the skin of the airplane. The task was enormous, but it was only one of many to be accomplished so that this airplane could meet its speed, altitude, range, and payload requirements. The result was a magnificent airplane. Originally, it has been intended as the next generation of heavy bomber for the Strategic Air Command, but was ultimately relegated to use as a research aircraft.

Four years before the first flight of the airplane, a fixed-base simulator was built and the first task was to optimize the flight control system. Simulators are used in engineering departments primarily as development tools, not as pilot training devices, but in this case, I learned a lot about the handling qualities of the airplane while participating in these development tests.

When construction was completed, the airplane was towed to the run-up pad for systems checkout. The pilots had attended a ground school on aircraft systems provided by the engineering departments at North American, and had flown the fixed-based simulator for many hours. Now we would run the engines and participate in the system checkout programs as final preparation for the first flight. The maintenance and engineering personnel were faced with many new problems, but worked around the clock to get the airplane ready to fly.

Flying the airplane was probably the easiest job of all. The pilots were well prepared. Granted, there were some unknowns, and some surprises that required quick decision-making, but that is not unusual in the initial test flights of any aircraft. The first takeoff went as planned, but was followed by failure of the landing gear to retract properly, a runaway engine, and a failure of the brake system causing a couple of blown tires. In spite of that, the flight was deemed successful. It was the beginning of a flight test program that was successful. Ship #1 (20001) flew at Mach 3 for the first time on its 17th flight – the largest and heaviest aircraft to have ever flown that fast. The final milestone for the program was to fly at Mach 3 for 30 minutes since it was predicted that all of the temperatures in the airplane would have stabilized at that time. Ship #2 (20207) flew at Mach 3 for 32 minutes on its 39th flight.

Considering all of the new concepts in the airplane – folding wingtips, huge variable area inlet ducts, canard surface with flaps, 4,000-psi hydraulic systems, a moveable windshield, and a variety of frustrating problems that arise in an airplane this complex – it was remarkable that it accomplished the goals of the program without any optimization. It continued to fly at a rate of about one flight per week for all the time I was on the program. That is a testimony to the maintenance and engineering people who had to solve the problems and get it ready to fly again.

The airplane was awesome when first viewed, but in my judgment, it was an easy airplane to fly – and an experience I will never forget.

Alvin S. White
Pilot, first flight of the XB-70A
North American Chief Test Pilot/XB-70 Project Pilot

FOREWORD

Fitzhugh L. "Fitz" Fulton, Jr.

I was privileged to be assigned to the XB-70 program about two years prior to the first flight. Al White, Colonel Joe Cotton, Van Shepard, and I went to XB-70 ground school, flew engineering simulators, and participated in all kinds of engineering studies and tradeoffs. We (the Air Force) felt that it was very important for all of the pilots to have large airplane experience and that we flew together as much as possible. The two airplanes that were selected as training airplanes for the XB-70 pilots were the B-52 and B-58. The B-52 was used to get recent big airplane experience and the B-58 was used to get supersonic experience. The B-58 that was assigned was a TB-58, which had tandem cockpits with dual controls. The B-58 had near identical takeoff and landing speeds to the XB-70. We were able to develop crew coordination and practice some of the maneuvers and tests planned for XB-70 missions.

White and Cotton flew all the early XB-70 flights with Shepard and myself flying as chase pilots. We used the B-58, F-104, and T-38s as chase airplanes. The B-58 was an excellent supersonic chase airplane. It could stay with the XB-70 us to Mach 2 and had long flight duration. The B-58 was used as a chase airplane for about the first 30 flights. It never missed a takeoff. My first XB-70 mission was as copilot on the sixth flight. My next mission was on the 12th flight where we had a structural failure of the wing apex while accelerating past Mach 2.60 for the first time. That resulted in severe damage to engines numbers 4, 5, and 6. One of my most enjoyable missions was when I piloted the number two airplane to Carswell AFB at Fort Worth for an "Air Force Convention" meeting. We cruised at Mach 2.60 at 64,000 feet. The time from takeoff to over the field at Carswell was 59 minutes.

I would not consider the XB-70 to be a difficult airplane to fly, but it did require the pilots to be very knowledgeable of all the systems and the emergency procedures. Landing gear, brakes, and hydraulic systems were a cause of some concern up through the end of the program. The steel honeycomb structure required many repairs, especially when exposed to the high temperatures that resulted from flying at or near Mach 3. The maintenance and engineering personnel working on the program were the cream of the crop. The North American Aviation, General Electric, Air Force, and NASA personnel were some of the best I have ever worked with.

The two-airplane program went on to complete 129 flights, and I was fortunate to fly on 63 of them. Most of the flights resulted in "happy times" but the loss of Major Carl Cross and Joe Walker when the F-104 and number two XB-70 collided was a sad day for the program. Another sad day was when a defueling truck exploded, due to static electricity, while under the XB-70 wing. One North American mechanic was killed and another had his life greatly shortened because of severe injuries. There were some heroic actions taken by North American Aviation and Air Force mechanics to prevent further injuries and the loss of that XB-70.

NASA took over the test program after the accident of the number two airplane and the F-104. Lt. Colonel Emil "Ted" Sturmthal and NASA pilot Don Mallick were trained on the XB-70 and participated in the 34 flights flown during the remainder of the program. The last flight was flown from Edwards AFB to Dayton, Ohio, with Sturmthal as my copilot. Mallick, in the B-58, escorted us all the way. The final flight was flown at Mach 0.92 (about 600 mph) and 29,000 feet. We were being very conservative since the test program was over and our only objective was to deliver the airplane to the Air Force Museum. We did not want to run the risk of having to land some other place.

We arrived at Dayton and made a flight down the runway. I made the last landing in the airplane, taxied to the ramp, and shut down the engines. I then presented the airplane paperwork to the museum director. He signed the receipt for the airplane, and the delivery was complete.

Fitzhugh L. Fulton, Jr.
Pilot, last flight of the XB-70A
Lieutenant Colonel, USAF (Ret.)/NASA Flight Research Center

Authors' Preface

The Ultimate Bomber

For a while during the 1950s, it seemed that all types of aircraft – fighters, bombers, airliners, and maybe even general aviation – were going to fly at three times the speed of sound in the near future. Magazines and newsreels were full of a very fast-flying future. As it turned out, of course, Mach 3 was a lot harder than it first appeared. In fact, there has only been a single Mach 3 production design – the Lockheed Blackbirds. Although the MiG-25 is widely considered a Mach 3 aircraft, most credible sources show its non-destructive top speed to be limited to Mach 2.8 or thereabout.

However, there was another Mach 3 design, one that was a good deal larger and four times heavier than the Blackbird. Perhaps even more futuristic looking, the North American Aviation B-70 Valkyrie was the culmination of General Curtis LeMay's quest for the ultimate strategic bomber. During the 40 years since it first appeared, the airplane has developed an almost-cult following all out-of-proportion to its ultimate use.

The building of the XB-70A ranks as one of the most convoluted processes in modern defense procurement. The beginning of the B-70 story was intermixed with the development of the WS-125A atomic-powered bomber – a concept that could only have been imagined during the 1950s – and a new Mach 3 interceptor, the F-108 Rapier. Largely as a cost-cutting measure, all three were intended to share subsystems, and the funding nightmare soon unraveled as first the atomic-powered bomber, then the F-108, were cancelled.

Today, the popular conception of a heavy bomber is the Boeing B-52 Stratofortress. A product of the 1950s, the B-52 recently made the nightly news supporting the "regime change" in Iraq. What is often overlooked, especially 50 years later, is that the B-52 was the second in a line of "interim" bombers. The first had been the Convair B-36, a program begun when it was feared that World War II would need to be conducted entirely from bases within North America. The resulting aircraft was something of a technical triumph, but it was a piston-powered aircraft born into the beginning of the jet age. Almost as soon as the aircraft appeared, the Strategic Air Command (SAC) began planning to replace it.

The B-52 was also born at an awkward time. Although the aircraft that eventually emerged was blessed with swept wings and jet engines – resulting in a bomber that cruised almost twice as fast as the B-36 – it was still a subsonic aircraft at a time when the Air Force desperately wanted to go faster. The first supersonic bomber – the Convair B-58 Hustler – was an outgrowth of the preliminary studies that ultimately led to the B-70. Sleek looking and fast, it was, at best, a medium bomber. As events turned out, the B-58 – magnificent as it was – became a maintenance nightmare, pushing the state-of-the-art a little too far. Its tenure was very short.

What Curtis LeMay wanted was an aircraft with the range and payload capabilities of the B-36 (or even the B-52) and the speed of the B-58. Initially, the replacement for these bombers was to be split between the futuristic atomic-powered WS-125A and a more conventional chemically powered WS-110A that used a new boron-derived high-energy fuel. When these programs began to lag due to technical challenges and funding difficulties, the "interim" B-52 was supplemented with an "improved" B-52 that emerged as the B-52G/H.

There was, however, a dark horse that had been largely dismissed by the user command (SAC), but was highly prized by the development commands (ARDC and AMC) and the politicians. In 1954, the intercontinental missile was thought to be decades from operations, but it promised a significant reduction in sustainment costs, quicker reaction times, and did not put pilots at risk; it was a politician's dream come true. At first, it was not obvious whether the resulting weapon would be a large cruise missile or a ballistic missile. In fact, it was not readily apparent that the concept would work at all. Ultimately, breakthroughs in building smaller thermonuclear weapons and accurate guidance systems allowed the development of the Atlas and Titan intercontinental ballistic missiles (ICBM) as well as the Navy's Polaris submarine-launched ballistic missiles (SLBM). Manned bombers appeared – at least to some – to be redundant.

Not surprisingly, the entire atomic-powered aircraft program soon ran into a variety of technical and political problems. The eventual demise of the WS-125A was a mixed blessing for the B-70 program. It left the Valkyrie as the only manned strategic system under development, helping it gain priority. However, the loss of a second funding source for shared systems made the B-70 appear to overrun its budget. The cancellation of the F-108 exacerbated this situation. The deployment of workable ICBMs was the deathblow.

The changing political and budgetary climates at first killed the B-70 program, briefly resurrected it, and then reduced it to a two-vehicle test program. Nevertheless, with a great deal less fanfare than has surrounded the Lockheed Blackbirds, North American created an amazing airplane. New materials and manufacturing techniques had to be developed, and the aerodynamics of getting a 500,000-pound airplane to fly at over 2,000 miles per hour pushed the available theories to the limit. When the Valkyrie finally flew, it was truly awe-inspiring. Minor technical glitches plagued the program early on, but eventually the aircraft routinely flew at its Mach 3 design speed, by far the largest and heaviest aircraft to ever fly that fast.

Then tragedy. A midair collision caused the loss of Air Vehicle 2 during a staged photo shoot after returning from a test flight. Pilot Al White survived, but copilot Carl Cross, along with legendary test pilot Joe Walker in an F-104, died in the accident. The program would continue to fly for a while using Air Vehicle 1, but the end was in sight. Today, the single remaining aircraft is housed at the Air Force Museum at Wright-Patterson AFB, Ohio – just as awe-inspiring as the day she was rolled out in Palmdale 40 years ago.

ACKNOWLEDGEMENTS

The authors would like to thank the many people that assisted in preparing this history: the AFFTC History Office, everybody at the Dryden Flight Research Center, Tony Accurso, Louie Alley at the Air Force Safety Center, Gerald H. Balzer, Tom Barrows, Lieutenant Colonel Richard J. Burgess at the Air Force Safety Center, Randy Cannon, Joel Carpenter, Tony Chong, Joseph E. Cotton, C. Roger Cripliver, Archangelo (Archie) Difante at the Air Force Historical Research Agency, Jim Eastham, Bill Elliott, Colin

The first Valkyrie shows the tall access stand that was required to reach the cockpit door; this would not have been very practical for nuclear bombers sitting on alert. Note A/V-2 on the engine runup pad in the background. (Boeing Historical Archives)

Fries at the NASA History Office, Fitzhugh "Fitz" Fulton, Steve Garber at the NASA History Office, Dr. Michael H. Gorn at DFRC, Matt Graham, SSgt Robert Hoffman, Dr. Roger D. Launius at the National Air and Space Museum, Tom Lubbesmeyer at the Boeing Historical Archives, Christian Ledet, Steven Levin, Denny Lombard at Lockheed Skunk Works, Michael J. Lombardi at the Boeing Historical Archives, Mrs. Betty J. Love, Scott Lowther at Aerospace Projects Review, Jerry McCulley (special thanks), Mike Machat at Wings/Air Power, Yancy Mailes, Donald L. Mallick, Frank Mastrovita at the Mitre Corporation, Peter Merlin at the DFRC History Office, Jay Miller, Mike Moore at Lockheed, Claude Morse at AEDC, Doug Nelson at the AFFTC Museum, Ken Neubeck, Jane Odom at the NASA History Office, Terry Panopalis, Jeannette Remak, Charles E. Rogers at AFFTC, Tom Rosquin, Mick Roth, Alan Shoemaker at the Mitre Corporation, Erik Simonsen, Susan M. Stacey, Dawn Stanford at the IBM Archives, Ronald Stephano, Quentin Schwinn at Glenn Research Center, Tom Tullis, Jim Tuttle, Emma Underwood at AEDC, Joseph A. Ventolo, and Dr. James Young in the AFFTC History Office.

A special thanks goes to Alvin S. White, the North American Chief Test Pilot and XB-70 Project Pilot, who graciously walked the authors through many of the early years of the program.

FROM JENKINS

The B-70 has long been a source of amazement for me. Strikingly gorgeous and incredibly fast, there has always been the question of whether the airplane could have performed its intended role had the politicians not intervened. After a lot of research the answer is – maybe. There is little doubt the aircraft would have lived up to its advertising brochure performance specifications, able to cruise for long distances at more than 2,000 miles per hour and above 70,000 feet. Whether this would have protected it from the burgeoning Soviet surface-to-air missile threat is unclear. The airplane would most likely have survived during the early years, before communications and electronics enabled the Soviet Union to build a truly integrated air defense network. After that, it is anybody's guess. It is ironic that the Soviets were more afraid of the airplane than the American government was sure of it – the MiG-25 and several surface-to-air missiles were designed largely in response to the prospect of SAC fielding the B-70.

This book was a long strange road. Finding source material proved harder than expected, mainly because of the various mergers and buyouts that what was once North American Aviation has gone through. And although the people we talked to were proud to have been associated with the program, there was clearly not the level of emotional attachment that had been evident when we were doing our X-15 research. Perhaps it's that the B-70 program always had a cloud hanging over it, unsure of its funding, its future, or even what was expected of it. The tragic loss of Air Vehicle 2 and two pilots certainly could not have helped. Regardless, the people involved have a lot to be proud of. They built, maintained, and flew one of the most remarkable aircraft ever built, even if nobody in Washington appreciated it.

The person I have to thank most – for my interest in aviation, writing, the B-70, and life in general – is my mother, Mrs. Mary E. Jenkins. She always provided encouragement and constructive criticism for all my projects. The Valkyrie was her favorite airplane, but unfortunately, she passed away before this book was finished. I hope that she would approve.

Four of the XB-70A pilots and the Chief Engineer got together at the 30th Anniversary Celebration at Edwards AFB in September 1994. From left are Joe Cotton, Al White, Walt Spivak, Fitz Fulton, and Don Mallick. (Photo by Tony Landis)

The XB-70 Joint Test Force at Edwards was made up of General Electric, the Air Force, and North American Aviation. The Edwards Instrument Shop used the B-70 on their patch, and there was a patch for the first Mach 3 flight. (right: Jerry McCulley; others: Tony Landis Collection)

Air Vehicle 2 banks over Edwards AFB, California. The two B-70s each made a single trip to someplace other than their homes at Palmdale (where they were built) and Edwards (where they were tested). A/V-1 made her final trip to Wright-Patterson AFB, Ohio, and A/V-2 made an appearance at an airshow at Carswell AFB, Texas. Note the Lockheed Blackbird on the ramp in front of the hangar. (Boeing via the Jay Miller Collection)

From Landis

From the first time I saw a photo of the Valkyrie, I was intrigued with this beautiful vehicle – it possessed graceful beauty and unmatched power. It just seemed to embody all that was exciting in aviation design. I feel very privileged to once again be working with Dennis on this detailed history of such a wonderful aircraft.

While researching this book it was evident that the Valkyrie had touched everyone who worked with it. A debt of thanks must once again be given to the kind folks at NASA Dryden Flight Research Center and the AFFTC History Office at Edwards AFB for allowing us access to their incredible collections.

As with any project of this size, it is a combination of effort of many individuals who have given of their time and materials. Much of what is within these pages came from the personal collections of those individuals who cared enough to keep this material for the last 40+ years. With the downsizing and merging of aircraft companies, much of the historical archives needed for such a project have disappeared. Although people like Mike Lombardi at The Boeing Company have done their best to save much of that history, most of the archives disappeared long before they had an opportunity to save them. We are indebted to those who cared enough about the program to save these materials from destruction and kindly shared them with us.

Chapter 1

The Convair NB-36H carried an operating nuclear reactor as part of a test program to define the possible characteristics of an atomic-powered airplane. In this case, the reactor did not provide any power to the airplane. (San Diego Aerospace Museum Collection)

The NX-2 – this is Convair's design – would have been powered by a first-generation production airborne reactor. (Lockheed Martin)

VALKYRIE – NORTH AMERICAN'S MACH 3 SUPERBOMBER

AN EXPENSIVE DIVERSION

THE ATOMIC-POWERED AIRPLANE

The mid-1950s were a time of great promise, and the Air Force was pursuing perhaps the most unlikely concept for the next manned strategic bomber – the atomic-powered aircraft program. Although it may seem strange in today's nuclear-phobic society, during the 1950s there were proposals for atomic-powered cars, ships, rockets, and airplanes. It was, after all, the Atomic Age. Conceptually, it all seemed so simple. Reality proved somewhat different.

What follows is not an exhaustive, or even particularly balanced, look at the nuclear-powered aircraft programs, but it gives some sense of what was involved in one of the more bizarre undertakings in recent memory.[1]

ATOMIC POWER

As early as 1942, Enrico Fermi and his associates involved with the Manhattan District (usually described as the Manhattan Project) discussed the use of atomic power to propel aircraft, although the necessity of developing weapons occupied their immediate interest. Things began to change after the war when Colonel Donald J. Keirn, an Army Air Corps powerplant specialist at Wright Field in Dayton, Ohio, began planning a program to develop nuclear propulsion for aircraft.[2]

A study during 1946 by the Johns Hopkins Applied Physics Laboratory defined the likely benefits and challenges associated with using atomic power for aircraft propulsion. The most obvious benefit was the potential of nearly unlimited range without refueling. Chief amongst the problems was the lack of data on the effects of radiation on the various materials that would be used to construct such an aircraft, the possible release of radioactive products during normal operation or due to an accident, and the difficulties of shielding the crew and persons on the ground.

Although the full effects of radiation were not completely understood, the desired requirements for an operational nuclear aircraft were to not materially increase the general background radiation levels, and that all harmful radiation would be restricted to within the aircraft or a pre-designated exclusion zone. But the greatest challenges were in reactor development. Aircraft would require a reactor much more compact than then available.[3]

Nevertheless, given the seemingly immense potential benefits, in May 1946 the Air Force initiated the Nuclear Energy for the Propulsion of Aircraft (NEPA) program to support developing long-range strategic bombers and other high-performance aircraft. A $5.25 million contract, W-33-038ac-14801, was awarded to the Fairchild Engine & Airplane Company for preliminary studies. The program, which Fairchild was required to conduct at Oak Ridge National Laboratory in Tennessee, was intended to lay the groundwork for the eventual development and flight testing of aircraft.[4]

The president of Fairchild, J. Carlton Ward, Jr., had begun imagining the possibilities of atomic-powered aircraft during 1945, and assembled a consortium of companies that included Allison, Continental Aviation, Flader, General Electric, Lycoming, Menasco Manufacturing, Northrop, United Aircraft, Westinghouse, and Wright Aeronautical. The group produced a variety of reports and conducted some crude experiments, such as placing radium in the bomb bay of a B-29 and measuring the radiation field in the cockpit with Geiger counters, but made little real progress toward defining an actual nuclear-powered airplane. Nevertheless, the commander of the Strategic Air Command, General Curtis E. LeMay, was enthusiastic about the prospects of an atomic-powered bomber, although everyone involved realized that the work was highly speculative in nature.[5]

When the Atomic Energy Commission (AEC) was created in January 1947 to oversee all U.S. nuclear activities, the fate of the military-only NEPA effort became uncertain, and the program was continued mainly to allow time for the AEC to devise its own strategy. On 1 January 1948, the President's Air Policy Commission produced a report, *Survival in the Air Age*, that heavily favored the development of an atomic-powered aircraft. The Air Force had estimated that it would only take five years to design and build an atomic-powered aircraft once the effort began in earnest.[6]

On the other hand, physicists who understood reactor development felt that such a schedule – and perhaps the entire concept of atomic-powered flight itself – bordered on science fiction. The physicists thought that the state of reactor physics and materials science was far too primitive and believed that applied research should come before any flight plans. They proposed that an orderly technical program be integrated into the rest of the AEC reactor research, where high-temperature materials and safety concepts would evolve in due course. Applying the lessons to an actual flight vehicle might take decades.[7]

This conflict prompted the AEC to call for a review by a group of 40 non-government scientists at the Massachusetts Institute of Technology (MIT) during 1948. The effort was headed by Professor Walter G. Whitman, chair of the Department of Chemical Engineering. The resulting "Lexington Report" surprised some opponents when it concluded that a nuclear-powered aircraft was indeed feasible, provided that there was an overriding national commitment to building it and an investment of nearly $1,000 million spread over 15 years. The report also postulated, as future events were to prove correct, that such a long development time meant that some other technology (such as the intercontinental missile) could render the atomic airplane obsolete by the time it was finally completed.[8]

By the end of 1948 the Air Force had invested approximately $10 million in the NEPA program with little to show. On 27 April 1949, a conference was held at Oak Ridge National Laboratory, Tennessee with the NEPA contractors along with AEC, Air Force, and Navy personnel to define a follow-on program. Despite the apparent lack of results from NEPA, the conference agreed that the conceptual work and early experiments had progressed to a point where a real hardware development program could begin. The Aircraft Nuclear Propulsion (ANP) program, a joint effort between the AEC and the Department of Defense to develop a full-scale aircraft propulsion system, was born.[9]

One of the factors that was instrumental in the creation of the ANP program was a section of the Lexington Report that had concluded that "… nuclear aircraft (manned) were likely less difficult than nuclear ramjets, which, in turn, would be less difficult than nuclear rockets to develop." Ironically, this proved to be the opposite of how events came about. Although nuclear ramjets (Project Pluto) and nuclear rockets (Project Rover) were successfully tested at the levels necessary for operational use, an operational-level atomic aircraft powerplant was never developed.[10]

On 19 March 1951, the Air Force initiated a letter contract with the General Electric Aircraft Gas Turbine Division in Evendale, Ohio, for "a development program and the manufacture and ground testing of a nuclear power plant suitable for testing at the earliest feasible date." The ultimate goal of this effort was to develop the P-1 powerplant and to support Convair's development of the X-6 test aircraft.[11]

The definitive contract, AF33(038)-21102, was signed on 30 April; a separate contract with the AEC for the development of the flight reactor was signed on 29 June 1951. At the time, the AEC and Air Force estimated that a ground-based test powerplant would be available in mid-1954, with the first flight-worthy reactor being installed in the X-6 during 1956. General Electric was also tasked with investigating advanced nuclear propulsion systems for future supersonic aircraft.[12]

DIFFERENT STROKES

Two different powerplant concepts were investigated as part of the ANP program – the direct-cycle and indirect-cycle. In the direct-cycle engine, air from the compressor stage of a turbojet was directed through a reactor core to be heated instead of burning chemical fuel (kerosene) in a combustor like a normal jet engine. The air, also acting as the reactor coolant, was then directed to the turbine section and discharged through the exhaust nozzle. The hot air spinning the turbine ran the compressor, and the cycle continued indefinitely.[13]

The competing indirect system directed the air through a heat exchanger instead of passing it through the reactor itself. The heat generated by the reactor was carried by a working fluid (either pressurized water or liquid metal) to the heat exchanger (basically an efficient radiator) where the heat was imparted to the air-stream flowing through the engine. Theoretically this allowed more heat energy to be transferred and thereby increased the efficiency of the system.[14]

Most of the proposed atomic turbojet configurations included a combustor section just upstream from the turbine that allowed the engines to be started on chemical power and then switched over to atomic heat as the reactor was brought up to operating temperatures. Operational aircraft were expected to use the chemical combustor during takeoff and landing, and possibly during target penetration when the relatively slow response time of the reactor could be a disadvantage.

In addition to the two different powerplant concepts, there were two types of reactors that held promise. The first, and most widely used in other applications, was the "slow" model where neutrons were slowed by a bulky moderating substance, such as graphite or water, to a low enough speed for a self-sustaining chain reaction to take place. This type of reactor was relatively easy to design and operate, and had gained general favor in the United States. However, the shielding usually consisted of 5 to 10 feet of concrete that weighed about 200 tons – obviously impractical for an aircraft. The "fast" model ran on higher-speed neutrons, the same kind that activate atomic bombs. Such a reactor could be built in a 3- to 4-foot sphere weighing approximately 50 tons. However, this design ran at temperatures approaching 2,000 degrees Fahrenheit – four times as hot as the slow reactor. Unless the engineers could develop materials that could withstand such heat, the reactor would simply melt.[15]

The reactor was not the only component requiring extensive research since much of the weight came from reactor shielding. Compactness here would be especially critical and ceramic materials would become one of the important avenues of research. Two methods were proposed to shield the airframe, the unit shield and the divided shield. The unit shield, which surrounded the reactor itself, provided the greatest reduction in radiation exposure. Unfortunately, it was also the heavier option. A divided shield would split the shielding between the reactor and the crew compartment. It was, however, feared that leakage of radiation into the components of the plane would reduce reliability, increase maintenance requirements, and shorten the life of the aircraft. The more susceptible organic materials, such as rubber, hydraulic oil, and lubricants, would need to be replaced with inorganic substances or with entirely new systems that did not require organic materials.[16]

The approach chosen by General Electric on 28 August 1951 was to design a large, air-cooled "slow" reactor that had a core using 143 pounds of uranium dioxide fuel elements riddled with air passages and sandwiched between rings of stainless steel. Four X40 turbojets (based on the conventional J53) were attached using manifolds to the front and rear of the reactor. The all-up weight of the powerplant came to about 128,000 pounds, of which 60,000 pounds was shielding.[17]

While General Electric was working on the direct-cycle concept, Pratt & Whitney had a contract to investigate the indirect-cycle design. Early-on, Pratt had decided that the best working fluid was liquid sodium.[18] Work was also begun on the new Connecticut Aircraft Nuclear Engine Laboratory (CANEL) to provide research and test facilities, mainly for the benefit of Pratt & Whitney. Progress on the indirect-cycle design, however, was much slower than expected and Pratt & Whitney never ran a practical test system. In fact, their work was limited mainly to component testing, although significant progress was made in liquid metal cooling loops, corrosion prevention, and heat exchanger design.[19] In the long run, the indirect cycle showed more promise, but it also required a great deal more development work and was never seriously in contention for an operational system.[20]

NB-36H

The ANP program spawned plans for two derivatives of the B-36 heavy bomber modified by Convair under contract AF33(038)-2117 as part of MX-1589. The first was referred to as the Nuclear Test Aircraft (NTA), while the second was assigned the formal X-6 designation.

The construction of the Nuclear Aircraft Research Facility at the Convair plant in Fort Worth to support MX-1589 was carried out under contract AF33(600)-6216.[21] In addition, the AEC awarded General Electric contract AT(11-1)-171 on 29 June 1951 to support operation of the reactors at Convair. Fort Worth division manager August C. Esenwein made the first public announcement of MX-1589 (called NEBO – Nuclear Engine Bomber – by Convair) on 5 September 1951, and the contracts were signed on 11 November.[22]

The decision to use the B-36 for the experiments was largely because the big bomber could be easily modified to carry the reactor and its associated shielding. Performance would not be outstanding given the speed limitations of the B-36, but it would serve as an adequate proof-of-concept. There was never any intention of producing more than the single NTA and two experimental X-6 aircraft. No tactical requirements were levied on either design, and they were to be optimized for their test functions with no regard to future operational utility.[23]

In preparation for the NTA experiments, Convair installed a small Ground Test Reactor (GTR) at the Nuclear Aircraft Research Facility during 1953. The GTR went "critical" on 17 November 1953, although the initial public announcement of the reactor – the first in Texas – did not come until 20 August 1954. The Aircraft Shield Test Reactor (ASTR) that would be carried aboard the NTA first went critical on 17 November 1954.[24]

The NB-36H provided the first experience with an airborne nuclear reactor, even if it did not provide any power for the aircraft. Convair built a special facility in an isolated corner of the Fort Worth plant to service the NTA, and also modified ground support equipment with shielding and remote controls. (San Diego Aerospace Museum Collection)

The Aircraft Shield Test Reactor from the NB-36H in its storage pit at the Nuclear Aircraft Research Facility in Fort Worth. The reactor could be hydraulically raised into the NB-36H for flights. (Jay Miller Collection)

This is what the Convair X-6 would have looked like. The four X40 engines were mounted under what had been bomb bay No. 3, with the reactor located in the former bomb bay No. 4. (Jay Miller Collection)

The entire powerplant – reactor and engines – could be removed for servicing. This also allowed the remainder of the airframe to be maintained without radiological safeguards. (Jay Miller Collection)

The NTA was an effort to more fully understand aircraft shielding requirements using a small operating reactor. The ASTR reactor would not provide any power to the aircraft, but both the reactor and its associated radiation levels would be carefully monitored during a series of flight tests. This would give designers actual flight data to use in determining the characteristics of the shielding needed for future designs, as well as insight into various operational factors.[25]

The NTA began its life as a B-36H-20-CF (51-5712) that had been damaged during a tornado at Carswell AFB on 1 September 1952. The estimated cost to restore the aircraft to an operational configuration was over $1,000,000 – almost 50 percent of the cost of a new aircraft (minus the government-furnished equipment). The aircraft was formally assigned to MX-1589 in early 1953. By the beginning of 1955, the aircraft had received its new forward fuselage, and the wiring, tubing, instrument capsule, and crew compartment cooling systems had been completed and installed. The aircraft was designated XB-36H on 11 March 1955 but was redesignated NB-36H on 6 June 1955. The name *Convair Crusader* was painted on each side of the forward fuselage during the early portion of the test series but was inexplicably removed later.[26]

The NB-36H was modified to carry the 1,000-kilowatt air-cooled ASTR and to provide protection for the crew. The ASTR was not representative of either the direct- or indirect-cycle concept, but was simply a reliable source of radioactivity to evaluate shielding concepts in an actual flyable aircraft. The NTA incorporated shielding around the reactor itself and there were also water jackets in the fuselage behind the crew compartment to absorb radiation. A 4-ton lead disc shield was installed in the middle of the aircraft. The ASTR weighed 35,000 pounds and was installed in a container that could be carried in bomb bay No. 4. A number of large air intakes and exhausts were installed in the sides and bottom of the rear fuselage to cool the reactor. The reactor could be removed from the aircraft while on the ground using special equipment installed at the Nuclear Aircraft Research Facility.

The first flight of the NB-36H was on 17 September 1955, with Convair pilot Arthur S. "Doc" Witchell, Jr. at the controls. Flying alongside the NB-36H on every flight was a C-97 carrying a platoon of armed Marines ready to parachute down and surround the test aircraft in case it crashed. An instrumented B-50D (48-058) also accompanied the NTA on most flights to gather data. The flight program continued through March 1957 and included 47 flights, although the ASTR reactor was critical on only 21 of them. The NB-36H was decommissioned in late 1957 and was scrapped at Fort Worth in September 1958.[27]

The flight program showed that the "aircraft normally would pose no threat, even if flying low." The principal concern was an accident that would cause the release of fission products from the reactor. It was subsequently decided that the risks caused by radiation under normal circumstances were no greater than the risks that had been incurred during the development of steam and electric power, the airplane, the automobile, or the rocket. The consequences of an accident, however, were orders of magnitude more severe.

X-6

The second flight vehicle envisioned by the ANP program would actually use the reactor to provide power for flight. The B-36 was also the basis for the X-6 since it was the only existing airframe large enough to carry the expected engine and shield weight.[28]

The P-1 propulsion system for the X-6 included an R-1 reactor and four X40 turbojets. The system weighed 165,000 pounds, including a 10,000-pound reactor, 60,000 pounds of reactor shielding, 37,000 pounds of crew shielding, and a total engine weight of 18,000 pounds plus an additional 40,000 pounds for ducts and accessories. The complete X-6 was expected to have a gross takeoff weight of 360,000 pounds, somewhat less than a fully loaded B-36. The reactor shield was 60 feet long and 12 feet in diameter, extending basically the entire length of the normal B-36 bomb bays, and a 4-inch thick lead gamma shield was installed directly in front of the reactor. Additional side shielding around the reactor was provided by a 2.5-inch thick layer of polyethylene sandwiched between two sheets of aluminum, one of which was the exterior skin. An additional shield was located on the back of the crew compartment, about 65 feet forward of the reactor. This shield was designed to allow an exposure of 0.25 Roentgen per hour – considerably less than the 1 Roentgen considered safe in 1951.[29]

The four X40 engines were arranged in a horizontal bank under the fuselage slightly forward of the reactor itself. Each engine was positioned so that air from its compressor stage could be ducted straight into the reactor, then be discharged through an S-duct into the engine turbine section. The R-1 reactor was air-cooled and water-moderated, but the water could also serve as additional core coolant if necessary. The core was 5.25 feet in diameter and weighed 4,000 pounds.

By mid-1952, the powerplant had been significantly refined. The most significant change was that the airflow through the reactor was now back-to-front (compressor air would enter the rear of the reactor), allowing a better center-of-gravity location in the X-6 airframe. The entire propulsion package, including the necessary shielding, now weighed only 140,000 pounds and 26,000 lbf would propel the X-6 up to 300 mph at 15,000 feet. Ground testing of the complete powerplant was scheduled for 1954 with initial flight tests beginning in 1957.[30]

THE NAVY'S INVOLVEMENT

The Navy and Air Force had begun working together on atomic-powered aircraft during May 1949 when the Navy transferred $1.5 million to the Air Force for research.[31] According to an agreement between now-Brigadier General Keirn and Rear Admiral James S. Russell, chief of the Bureau of Aeronautics, the Navy's interest would be limited to keeping track of the program's progress with no specific development plans, "Navy participation was not to generate into a competition to fly first."[32]

However, in August 1953 the Navy informed the AEC that it was interested in a low-power reactor for a subsonic seaplane. At the same time, the Navy awarded study contracts to several seaplane manufacturers to "assess the significance of nuclear power for aircraft design." The Navy argued that the remarkable endurance envisioned for an atomic-powered aircraft – the figure of a thousand hours was commonly used – would be better suited to an antisubmarine warfare seaplane than to long-range bombers.

In February 1955, the Navy released Operational Requirement CA-01503 and Developmental Characteristic CA-01503-3 followed in April. Oddly, given the earlier comments, these documents defined the mission of the aircraft primarily as long-range attacks against naval shore targets, warships, and shipping; secondary missions included mining and forward-area reconnaissance. The Navy hoped to have a prototype by 1961.[33]

The proposed airframe was based on the P6M-1 Seamaster, built by the Glenn L. Martin Company of Baltimore, Maryland. The Seamaster, according to Vice Admiral Thomas S. Combs, Deputy Chief of Naval Operations (Air), "seem[ed] ideally suited for eventual nuclear propulsion, due to its size and configuration, combined with [the] practically unlimited takeoff and landing areas water provides." The Seamaster would have four modified turbojet engines powered by a single reactor and would be used initially for antisubmarine warfare and radar early warning. Experience with aircraft nuclear propulsion, the Navy predicted, would eventually lead to the desired high-speed attack aircraft. The Navy argued that atomic power made more sense in a seaplane than in a bomber, since accidents would expose fewer civilians and the weight of the reactor would cause the wreckage to sink quickly.[34]

However, scientists within the AEC were skeptical of the seaplane, on which the Navy was spending several million dollars for preliminary designs. In December 1955 the AEC postponed certain Navy-related contracts to determine whether additional research and development was necessary or if existing programs could be adapted for Navy use. The AEC concluded that no specific Navy program was necessary, and the Department of Defense concurred.[35]

Despite this finding, the Navy's interest in having its own nuclear-powered aircraft grew during early 1956, and the Chief of Naval Operations, Admiral Arleigh A. Burke, stated that the Navy would continue to work on independent studies. As a result, in July the Department of Defense impounded $7.4 million of Navy funds earmarked for the ANP program until such time as the service was able to orient properly its programs. Although the Navy was loathe to give control of the ANP program entirely to the Air Force, it was becoming obvious the effort would not produce an operational system in the near future and the Navy backed off.

THE IDAHO CONNECTION

In November 1951, the government had contracted with an architectural and engineering firm – Parson-Macco-Liewit – to recommend a remote site for ground tests of the P-1 powerplant. If possible, the site was also to be capable of supporting flight tests of the eventual X-6 aircraft. A month later Parsons recommended Arco, Idaho, where the government already operated a nuclear reactor test site. This location would become home to the Flight Engine Test Facility. The land assigned to the ANP program was known as Test Area North, some 30 miles northeast of the existing NRTS facilities.[36]

When Leonard E. "Bill" Johnston, the director of the National Reactor Test Site (NRTS),[37] was told that an atomic-powered airplane might be coming to Idaho, he had his staff research what hazards would come with it. Some of what they discovered was not news to the aeronautical community. For instance, the Idaho staff discovered that test aircraft crashed most often during takeoff or landing. What would happen to the nuclear fuel in a crash involving fire, and what kind of emergency response would be needed? In 1957, the staff at the NRTS organized a pair of fuel element burn tests – soon dubbed Operation Wiener Roast by the participants – to determine the effects.[38]

The idea was to take a known reactor fuel element, and see what would happen if it was placed in a raging fire, typical of an aircraft crash. John Horan was working at the Naval Reactors Facility at the time and observed the tests. "The key idea was to burn it. For the first test, a pool of [500 gallons of jet fuel] was used and part of an aluminum fuselage … The [fuel] element was suspended directly over the center of the fuel and then [the jet fuel was] ignited. … Movie cameras were operating [when] they set the thing on fire. Basically, there was no release. That was Wiener Roast No. 1." The fuel element had reached 2,250 degrees Fahrenheit, but after the fire burned for 2 hours, the element was essentially intact. This seemed to indicate that the effects of an accident might not be as bad as had been feared, but further tests seemed desirable. Horan continues, "The second time, they used an induction furnace to supply higher heat to the fuel element. This time … a release was attained. The fuel [element] melted within 90 seconds." Still, the reality was that there appeared to be little direct danger of fire damaging a nuclear fuel element.[39]

The first phase of the General Electric program in Idaho was called Initial Engine Test, and the idea was simple: prove that nuclear heat could run a turbojet engine. The tests involved a modified J47 engine – designated X39 by General Electric – using thermal energy provided by the purpose-built Heat Transfer Reactor Experiment (HTRE-1) reactor. This was a direct air-cycle reactor using nickel-chromium-plated, uranium-oxide fuel elements, with water serving the combined function of moderator and structural coolant.[40]

The HTRE-1 – Heater One to those who worked around it – went critical on 4 November 1955, not yet attached to any engines. This was a year after the NB-36H had begun flight tests in Fort Worth. The unit generated the equivalent of 20 megawatts of heat energy, and the engineers had made no attempt to restrict the size or weight of the reactor or to approximate a flight version. In fact, the reactor was deliberately large so that crews could easily install monitoring devices and instrumentation. Testing progressed relatively quickly.[41]

On 31 January 1956, HTRE-1 sat on its dolly at the test pad. The X39 engines were mounted vertically above the reactor, an unusual configuration, but one that simplified various systems for the initial tests. The X39 turbojet began operating on chemical fuel, and operators gradually withdrew the control rods from HTRE-1, taking the reactor critical. As the temperature rose to a predetermined level, the chemical fuel valves were closed. Almost surprisingly, everything worked. For the first time, the heat of fissioning uranium powered a jet engine. The General Electric test team cheered, buttoned up, and went off to celebrate at the nearest bar, which was 10 miles away in Mud Lake.[42]

With this initial success, however, it was time to plan the next phase of the Idaho program: an airplane hangar, a runway, and most obviously, an airplane. The new hangar – called the Flight Engine Test Facility – was needed to learn how to service a nuclear aircraft on the ground after it returned from its mission. The powerplant inside the airplane would have to be removed from the airframe and taken to the "hot shop" where it would be disassembled, studied, repaired, or replaced. In addition to the specific nuclear concerns, hangar crews would have to handle the ordinary maintenance of a radioactive airplane. Problems such as extracting crewmembers from their shielded cockpit without exposing them to gamma radiation also had to be solved.[43]

Meanwhile, the experiments continued, and HTRE-1 eventually accumulated 150.8 hours of operating time. Separately, General Electric wanted to irradiate fuel elements in one of the other Idaho facilities, but they were too large to fit in any of the existing reactor cores in Idaho. Therefore, General Electric cut a hexagonal hole, 11 inches across flats, in the center of the HTRE-1 to accommodate the

Operation Wiener Roast tested whether reactor fuel rods could withstand a simulated aircraft accident by burning them. (INEEL)

Right: **The HTRE-2 reactor – complete with the plumbing for its X39 engines – being moved to the INEEL visitor's center in 1985.** (INEEL)

Above: **The General Electric X40 engine was derived from the conventional J53. A pair of X40s was connected to a single reactor.** (INEEL)

This shielded locomotive was used to shuttle the HTRE-1/2 reactor from its maintenance area to the test pad. (INEEL)

The hangar in Idaho was built to support the X-6 test aircraft. Note the dirt-covered control room beside the hangar. A 23,000-foot-long runway was planned nearby but was never built. The hangar was completed in 1959, and finally torn down in 2004. (INEEL)

fuel elements. The modified reactor was called HTRE-2 and went critical in July 1957, eventually accumulating 1,299 hours of operation. Physicists inserted various metals and fuel elements, subjecting them to neutron flux and temperatures up to 2,800 degrees Fahrenheit for sustained periods of time. The materials tested included metallic fuel elements combined with air-cooled hydrided zirconium moderators, and beryllium oxide fuel elements for use in ceramic reactors. It was a necessary step toward creating a flight-weight powerplant.[44]

POLITICAL REALITIES

The first serious setback to the ANP program was political rather than technological. In 1953, the Eisenhower administration was looking for ways to fulfill its campaign promise to trim the federal budget and the ANP was a prime target. Secretary of Defense Charles Wilson claimed that even if the X-6 could be built, it would be no more than a flying platform to prove that nuclear flight was feasible – it would not be a militarily useful aircraft. He neglected to mention that this had always been the plan. To emphasize his point, Wilson did not include the ANP in the FY54 budget. After several weeks of negotiation and compromise, the ANP program avoided complete cancellation, but the X-6 flight vehicle was history.

Surprisingly, the question of military usefulness had always eluded the ANP program. The Air Force began to more clearly articulate that an atomic-powered aircraft would be the first true intercontinental bomber, able to travel supersonically from an inland base in the United States to strike any place on Earth without the need for politically uncertain foreign bases or vulnerable aerial refueling. This remained a compelling argument, and despite the uncertainties surrounding the ANP program, the Air Force began seriously considering the development of an atomic-powered bomber under Weapons System 125A (WS-125A). Oddly, the studies performed by the ANP program seemed only loosely connected to the planning for a nuclear-powered bomber at SAC, and even less connected to the preliminary studies being performed by the airframe contractors. However, the new-found direction apparently satisfied the politicians, who began releasing funding for the program.

The fortunes of the ANP program reached their crest in June 1955 when the AEC and DoD agreed that the program should be accelerated, with the objective of flight testing by 1959. Authorized expenditures increased dramatically and the Air Force now had airframes under study by three contractors – Convair, Douglas, and Lockheed. All were called NX-2, although only the Convair aircraft is generally referred to under that designation, and were remarkably similar, suggesting the Air Force provided a "point design" for the contractors to work with. The subsonic aircraft would be nearly the same size as a B-52 and weigh 450,000 pounds. There were slightly different variants being investigated for the General Electric direct-cycle and Pratt & Whitney indirect-cycle approaches.[45]

To the consternation of both the Air Force and the Navy, in August 1956 the Eisenhower administration again reduced the budget. The ANP program was redirected to research and development applicable to a broad spectrum of potentially useful military propulsion systems, although development of the P-3 propulsion system continued at a low level. The applied research developed the basic materials and engineering analysis methods used in a series of subsequent reactor designs. The materials program encompassed the development of metallic and ceramic fuel elements, hydrided metallic moderators, and various shields, controls, and structural materials for use in both subsonic and supersonic aircraft. These activities were supported by a strong experimental program including the reactor experiments in Idaho, aerothermodynamic tests, and mechanical testing in simulated environments.[46]

The ANP program was waning when a new motivation rocketed onto the scene, quite literally: the Soviets launched *Sputnik I* on 4 October 1957. This event not only started the space race, but also a general technology race. President Eisenhower was urged to accelerate the ANP program to produce an operational atomic-powered aircraft in answer to the Soviet's space endeavors. The new "Fly Early" concept was to rush some kind of atomic-powered airplane into service within three years. However, the opposing "Go Slow" option advocated a policy of concentrating more on basic research rather than racing the Soviets for what might be a militarily useless aircraft. Not surprisingly, the Navy advocated a "Fly First" seaplane program.[47]

Washington was still debating Fly Early when the Air Force came up with another proposal for a militarily useful atomic-powered mission. This was the CAMAL (continuously airborne missile-launcher and low-level) system, in which a nuclear bomber carrying ballistic missiles would remain aloft for weeks at a time, patrolling just outside the Soviet radar and thus supplementing the proposed submarines and land-based missiles. Such an aircraft also could be flown on low-level, below-radar sorties, carrying conventional bombs deep into enemy territory. This was – more or less – a production proposal for the NX-2 design that had been under study for several years.[48]

Opponents of the program were receiving support from the President's Scientific Advisory Committee and a report issued in February 1958 held little good news for advocates of aircraft nuclear propulsion. The report began with review of previous studies, in order to preclude criticism that yet another committee with no experience in the subject area had produced an unfair judgment.[49] It did not directly confront the basic issue of whether a nuclear-powered aircraft could be built but moved quickly to the enormous projected expense of bringing the idea to reality: "Total costs of the project from the present up to the achievement of first nuclear powered flight are estimated by the Air Force to be $1,357 million. This program would require somewhat greater annual expenditures than the present limit of $150 million." The report also emphasized the hazards of nuclear-powered flight in general. It specifically criticized the Navy's approach, on technical grounds. The report recommended "that neither Air Force nor Navy accelerated programs for early manned nuclear flight be implemented at this time."[50]

More bad news came when the AEC announced that it would not allow flight operations at the Idaho test site. The $8 million hangar in Idaho was finished in July 1958 and provided a clear space of 320 feet by 234 feet. By this time, the X-6 had been cancelled for five years; the B-36s had all been scrapped, so some other airframe would be required if a flyable aircraft were to occupy the hangar. The AEC decided in December 1958 that the NRTS could not be used as an ANP flight test site because of safety considerations. Despite the millions of dollars invested in the hangar and its shielded control room, the money was "more than outweighed by the potential risks involved." The AEC told the Air Force that nuclear test flights would have to originate from an island or coastal location and fly only over the ocean.[51]

Despite the politics, the design of the flight reactor for the P-3 propulsion package was progressing, and to support the effort General Electric built another experimental reactor. The HTRE-3 was built as a full-scale aircraft reactor prototype using nickel-chromium fuel elements and an air-cooled hydrided zirconium moderator. The X40 engines and reactor were arranged horizontally, more typical of an aircraft installation. The HTRE-3 produced enough thrust to theoretically sustain flight of an X-6-type aircraft at 460 mph for about 30,000 miles. However, radiation levels were still a problem; at one point during the tests, a minor failure resulted in the release of radioactive products that contaminated 1,500 acres around the site. Nevertheless, just before the experiment was terminated, another milestone was reached

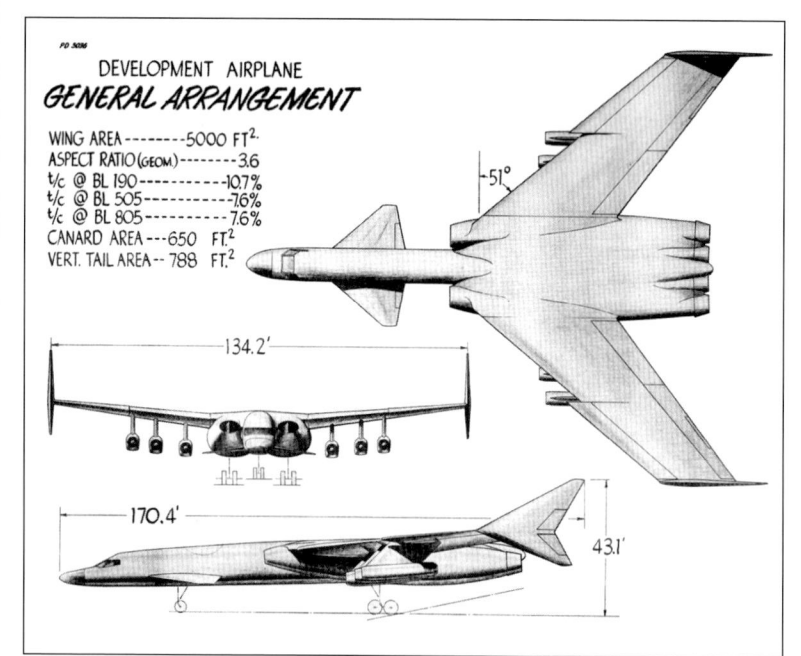

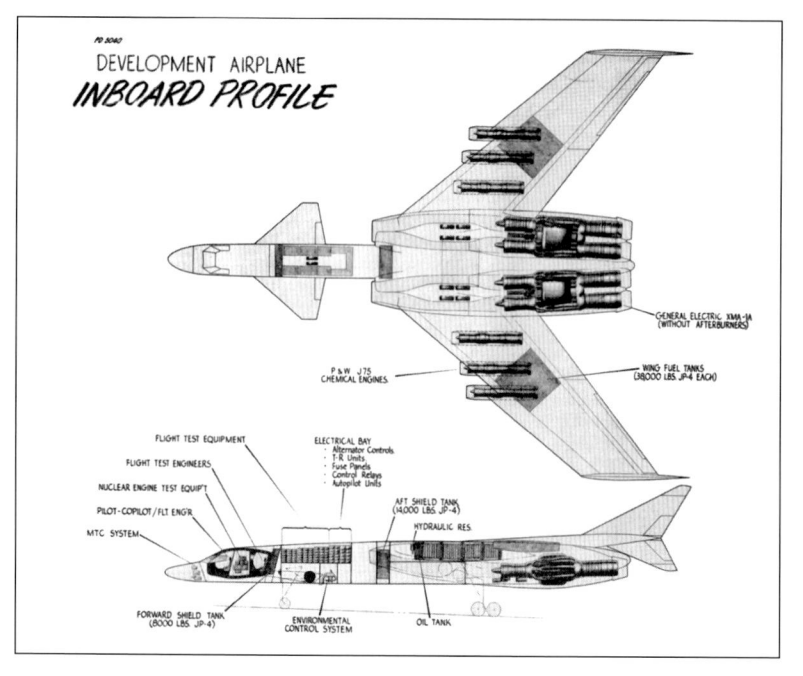

This was the general configuration of the subsonic NX-2 atomic-powered aircraft. Variants of this design were studied by Convair, Douglas, and Lockheed, although the Convair design is the best known. The number of chemical turbojets under the wing varied considerably, with some designs having none (usually associated with the Pratt & Whitney indirect-cycle powerplants) while others had up to six (shown above). (Lockheed Martin)

when the reactor started the X40 engines without the help of any chemical fuel. The HTRE-3 operated between September 1959 and December 1960, accumulating 126 hours of operation.[52]

By the beginning of 1961, General Electric was well into preliminary development of the XNJ140E nuclear powerplant for CAMAL. This powerplant was capable of 1,000 hours of operation at 500 mph before refueling. At this point the 450,000-pound CAMAL was being designed for the "airborne alert and counterstrike mission" where it would remain airborne for five days at a time with a load of air-launched ballistic missiles. The XNJ140E powerplant used a pair of X211 turbojet engines (designated J87) that were not directly based on any production chemical-fuel engine (unlike the earlier X39 and X40). The entire powerplant weighed 43,390 pounds (not including shielding) and produced 55,000-lbf at sea level.[53]

Advanced versions of the XNJ140E were to be capable of propelling a B-70-size aircraft to Mach 2.5 at 45,000 feet. It was beginning to appear that an airborne nuclear powerplant might actually work. However, politics and funding constraints soon intervened, and HTRE-3 was the closest to a flight article the program would come.[55]

WS-125A

Despite the general confusion surrounding the NEPA/ANP program, in October 1954 SAC had issued a mission requirement for an advanced heavy bomber to replace the B-52 beginning in 1965. General LeMay wanted a bomber that had the range and payload capability of the B-52, combined with the supersonic speed of the B-58 medium bomber. The Air Research and Development Command (ARDC) responded by issuing requirements for two new bombers during February 1955. The WS-110A was to use chemical fuels, while the WS-125A was to be nuclear powered. Although it was recognized that developing two advanced bombers simultaneously would be expensive, it was initially believed that having the two aircraft share major subsystems, such as the bombing and navigation equipment, would mitigate some of the cost. This concept faded fairly quickly when it was realized that the nuclear-powered WS-125A could not be developed as quickly as the less-sophisticated WS-110A.

On 21 June 1955, the Deputy Chief of Staff for Development approved a competitive Phase I development program for WS-110A and a formal study program for WS-125A. Six airframe contractors – Boeing, Convair, Douglas, Lockheed, Martin, and North American – were invited to participate in a bidders conference held at Wright Field on 27 July. Convair and Lockheed were soon awarded WS-125A contracts and elected not to compete for the seemingly less-challenging WS-110A contract.[56]

Additional impetus to develop the new aircraft came from a spreading rumor that the Soviets had already flown an atomic-powered aircraft. Senator Richard B. Russell from Georgia issued a statement saying: "The report [that] the Russians have test-flown an atomic-powered aircraft is an ominous new threat to world peace, and yet another blow to the prestige and security of our nation and the free world. It follows in tragic sequence the Russian success of last fall in launching the first earth satellite." On 1 December 1958, *Aviation Week* announced that the Soviets had flown an atomic-

The General Electric XMA-1A was going to be used in the NX-2 development airplane, and was a prototype of the XNJ140E specified for CAMAL and, later, WS-125A. (Lockheed Martin)

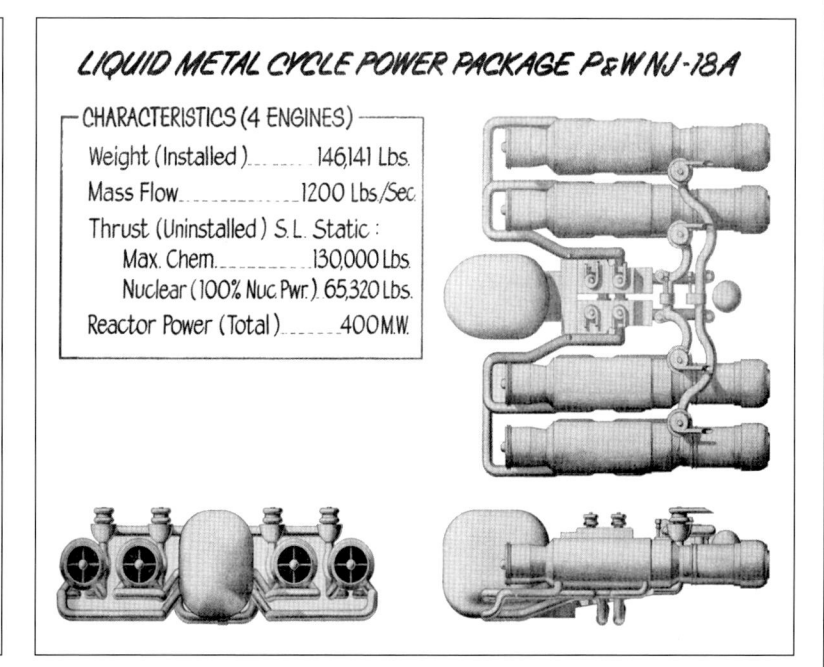

The Pratt & Whitney NJ-18A would have been a much more powerful engine than the General Electric XMA-1A, but Pratt never built anything resembling a workable prototype. (Lockheed Martin)

powered bomber prototype: "A nuclear-powered bomber is being flight tested in the Soviet Union. Completed about six months ago, this aircraft has been flying in the Moscow area for at least two months. It has been observed both in flight and on the ground by a wide variety of foreign observers from Communist and non-Communist countries." The article further claimed that the aircraft was "not a flying test bed in the sense that earlier U.S. Air Force and Navy programs had called for installing a nuclear powerplant in a conventional airframe such as the B-36 … solely for test purposes. The Soviet aircraft is a prototype of a design to perform a military mission as a continuous airborne alert warning system and missile launching platform …" Sketches, complete with large red stars, and speculative data on the aircraft, accompanied this article.[57]

During early 1959, Representative Melvin Price from Illinois, Chairman of the Joint Committee on Atomic Energy, declared that the Russians were three to five years ahead of the United States in the

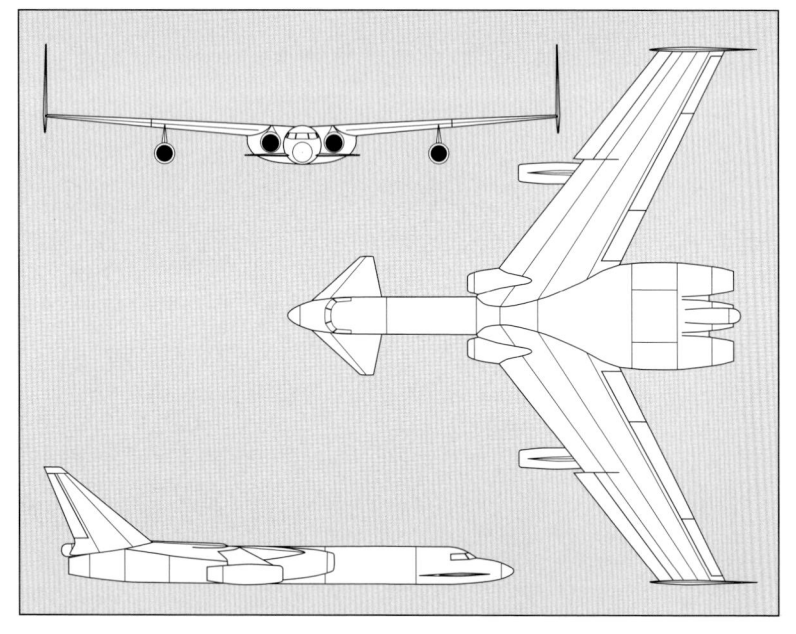

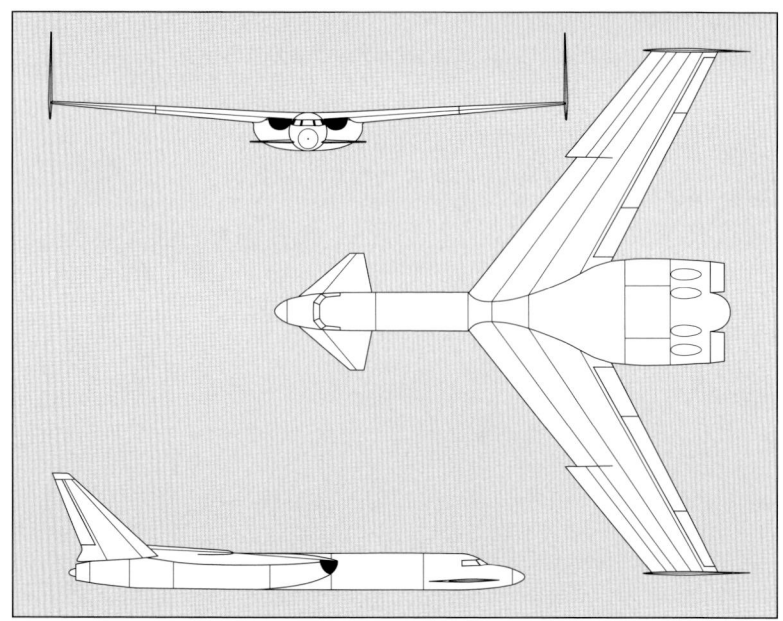

The Convair NX-2 design is the one that has received the most publicity over the years, although all of the companies proposed similar configurations. These two final variants show the differences between the General Electric-powered airplane (left) and the Pratt & Whitney-powered version. Because the indirect-cycle atomic powerplant could spool up faster, there was no need to carry auxiliary turbojets under the wings. (Art by Tony Landis; photos courtesy of Lockheed Martin)

field of atomic aircraft engines and that they would move even further ahead unless the United States pressed forward with its own program. Hindsight shows that his information was incorrect, but was part of the general hysteria surrounding the American perception of the Soviet Union at the time. The Soviets did, however, modify a Tupolev Tu-95 to carry a small reactor for airborne tests much like the NB-36H. A later version was to have been flown using nuclear-powered Kuznetsov turboprop engines, but this never took place.[58]

THE END OF THE LINE

The last chapter for ANP would be written by a civilian scientist raised to a new and powerful post in the Department of Defense – Herbert F. York of the University of California's Radiation Laboratory at Livermore. The Director of Defense Research and Engineering was a particularly powerful position, and York had an excellent reputation in the Department of Defense and at the White House. York made a convincing argument against any nuclear powered flight, expressing the opinion that no such aircraft with any useful military application could be developed before 1970.

In January 1961, John F. Kennedy became president. It had been 15 years since the end of World War II, and as the Lexington Report had predicted, $1,000 million had been spent on atomic-powered aircraft research, but the program was no closer to actually building an airplane. Additionally, Eisenhower's years of budget cutting had eroded conventional defense capability to the point that the Army had only 11 combat-ready divisions, a shortage of ammunition, and little airlift capacity.

The new administration wanted to rectify this situation. Kennedy also wanted more flexibility to respond militarily; to conduct so-called "limited war" instead of the strictly nuclear response associated with the mutually assured destruction concept. This required rebuilding the conventional force structure and tactical airpower instead of concentrating so heavily on strategic deterrents. A nuclear airplane might be possible, but the investment in time and money was prohibitively high, and the environmental dangers remained controversial.[59]

On 28 March 1961, President Kennedy cancelled the ANP program in its entirety. Kennedy wrote, "Nearly 15 years and about $1 billion have been devoted to the attempted development of a nuclear-powered aircraft; but the possibility of achieving a militarily useful aircraft in the foreseeable future is still very remote." It was the end of the line.[60]

No results from either the Convair or Lockheed WS-125A studies could be found other than a few conceptual drawings of the NX-2. It is known that the Convair work was performed in Fort Worth, and somewhat surprisingly, the Lockheed effort was quartered in Marietta, Georgia. At the time of cancellation, $1,040 million had been spent on the various atomic-powered aircraft programs, broken down as $839 for research and development, and $201 million for facilities and equipment. Funding was provided by the Air Force, AEC, and Navy, supplying $518 million, $508 million, and $14 million, respectively. The government had invested $41 million into the Idaho ANP facilities through 1961. The hangar built in the Idaho desert was never used by an aircraft, although both it and the shielded bunker were used later by a variety of other experiments before being demolished in 2004. The two HTRE reactors are on display at the INEEL visitors' center.[61]

The Douglas (left) and Lockheed NX-2 aircraft looked very much like the Convair design that is normally shown. All three companies designed aircraft using both powerplants. (Lockheed Martin)

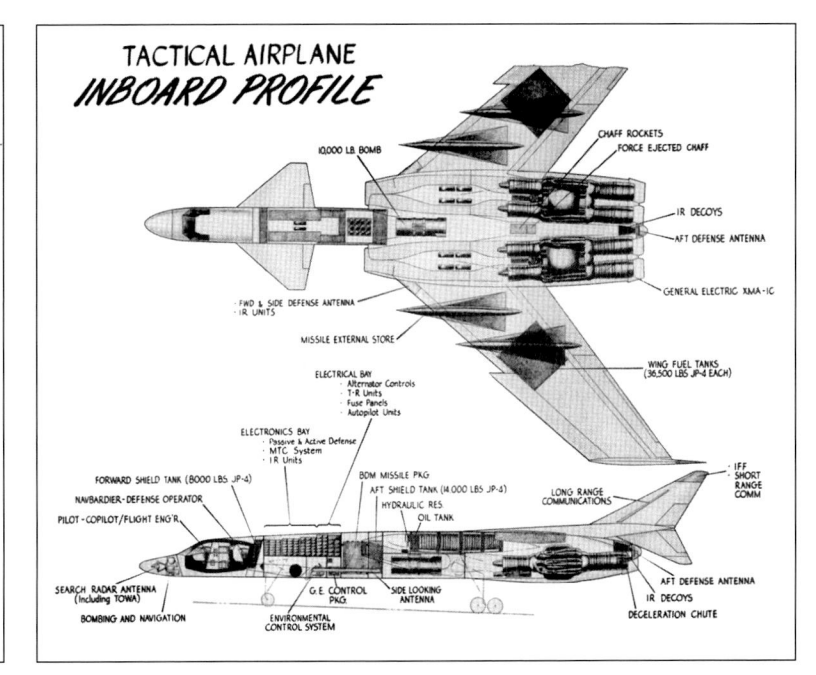

The Convair concept for the CAMAL stand-off missile carrier included provisions to carry a single 10,000-pound nuclear bomb for a direct low-level attack. (Lockheed Martin)

Chapter 2

Left: *One of many highly speculative renditions of a possible new bomber that appeared in the popular press during the 1950s.* (Fort Worth Star-Telegram via the Jeannette Remak Collection)

Below: *Although still highly speculative in nature, this drawing has a little more basis in fact since it was released by the artists at North American Aviation and bears a slight resemblance to the design that ultimately became the B-70. Note the missile being fired.* (Boeing Historical Archives)

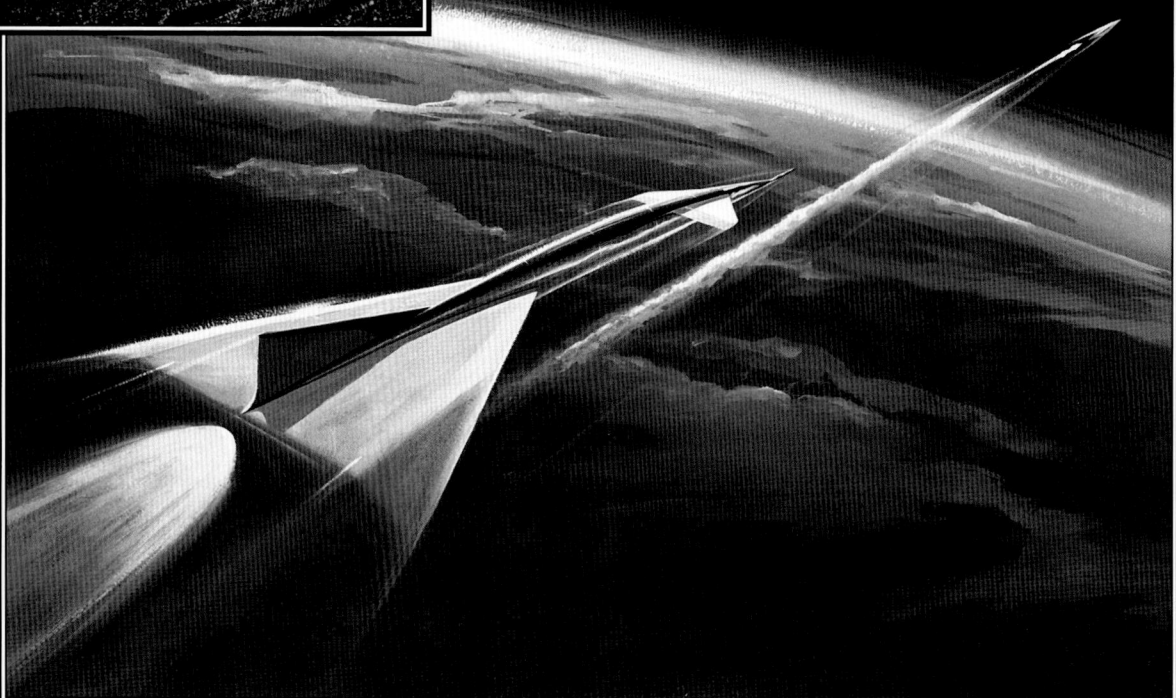

TECHNICAL VOODOO
HIGH HOPES FOR WS-110A

Even before the outbreak of World War II, the Army Air Corps had recognized that it might need to fight a global war without the benefit of bases outside the North American continent. These concerns gave rise to the development of the Convair B-36, which made its maiden flight in 1946 and represented the first true "intercontinental" bomber to enter the U.S. inventory.[1] However, the five years between the aircraft being designed and its first flight saw the beginnings of a revolution. Jet power was the wave of the future, relegating the B-36 to the role of an "interim" bomber pending the development of the all-jet-powered Boeing B-52 Stratofortress.

The B-36 – like all long-range American bombers at the time – was operated by the Strategic Air Command. This was seemingly the private domain of General Curtis Emerson LeMay.[2] Although his first assignments had been in pursuit (fighter) aircraft, LeMay transferred to bombers in time to participate in the first mass flight of early Boeing B-17 Flying Fortresses to South America in 1938, winning the MacKay Trophy for the 2nd Bomb Group.[3]

One of the great thinkers of his time, LeMay saw bombers as the key to modern warfare. He was largely responsible for developing the formation procedures and bombing techniques that were used by B-17 units throughout Europe during World War II. These were later adapted to the Boeing B-29 Superfortresses which fought the war to its conclusion in the Pacific. At the end of the war, LeMay returned to the United States, piloting a B-29 on a non-stop record flight from Hokkaido, Japan, to Chicago, Illinois.[4]

The general's first post-war assignment was at the Headquarters of the Air Materiel Command, followed by a tour at the Pentagon as the first deputy chief of staff for research and development. After a brief

The legendary commander of the Strategic Air Command, General Curtis Emerson LeMay. (Jeannette Remak Collection)

The Convair B-36 was the first aircraft capable of carrying thermonuclear weapons, and was the mainstay of SAC for the first ten years of the Cold War. The aircraft was capable of striking the Soviet Union from North America without refueling. (San Diego Aerospace Museum Collection)

Technical Voodoo

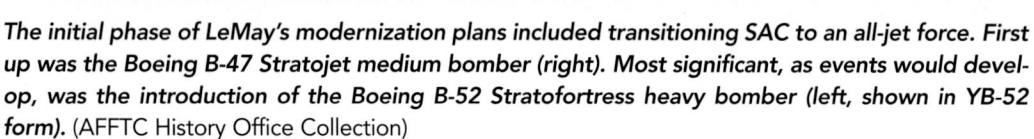

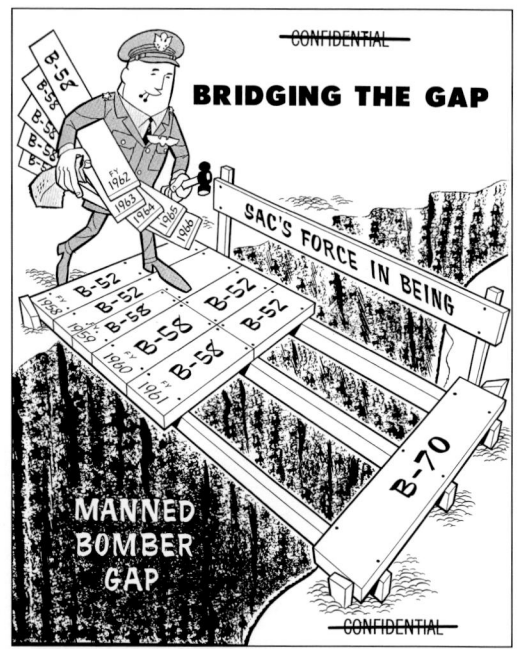

The initial phase of LeMay's modernization plans included transitioning SAC to an all-jet force. First up was the Boeing B-47 Stratojet medium bomber (right). Most significant, as events would develop, was the introduction of the Boeing B-52 Stratofortress heavy bomber (left, shown in YB-52 form). (AFFTC History Office Collection)

A cartoon showing the gap between the B-52 and the B-70. As it turned out, the B-52 would serve for about 40 years longer than expected. (U.S. Air Force via C. Roger Cripliver)

stint in Europe, LeMay assumed command of the newly formed Strategic Air Command (SAC), where he would come to fame as one of the most dynamic leaders the Air Force has ever seen. LeMay's first priority was for SAC to become a nuclear force to ensure the peace and security of the United States. This was accomplished with the new B-36 and an improved version of the B-29 called the B-50. His next priority was to field an all-jet force, retiring the piston-powered B-36 bombers and KC-97 tankers. This saw the introduction of the Boeing B-47, B-52, and KC-135. The ultimate step – one that was never completed – was the deployment of an all-supersonic bomber force. LeMay commanded SAC for nearly 10 years before being appointed Vice Chief of Staff of the Air Force. In July 1957, he became Chief of Staff, serving for eight years before he retired on 1 February 1965.[5]

Although it was much faster than the B-36, the B-52 was still a subsonic design in a time when the Air Force desperately wanted to go supersonic. It was widely believed that going higher and faster was the only way to survive. The concept had several problems, however. The B-36 could fly from one continent to another while carrying a militarily useful bomb load; it was just terribly slow at doing so. The B-52 showed that a much faster aircraft could be built, but it had relatively short legs. Although an excellent aircraft, it was still not supersonic and required a large fleet of aerial tankers to support it. Early estimates for a supersonic bomber required even more refuelings, while carrying much smaller loads. Unfortunately, the advanced nuclear weapons under development at the National Laboratories were getting larger, not smaller.

Nevertheless, as early as 1947, Air Force planners had begun developing requirements for a supersonic intercontinental bomber. Boeing and Consolidated-Vultee (later called Convair) began studying the possibilities of a supersonic bomber in early 1948, concentrating on what technical advances would be needed to support the development of such aircraft. Given that no operational supersonic aircraft of any type had yet been developed, it was a very speculative effort.[6]

As these studies were concluding in late 1951, Colonel Michael N. W. McCoy[7] was accepting the first operational B-47 Stratojet medium bombers at MacDill AFB near Tampa, Florida, marking the beginning of SAC's transition to an all-jet force. At the same time, however, Brigadier General John W. Sessums, Jr., the deputy for development at the Air Research and Development Command (ARDC), noted that the United States had not initiated the development of a new manned strategic weapon system since the B-52 in 1946. He remarked that the Soviets had been making steady progress upgrading their defensive systems during the intervening five years, a situation that would soon lead to the obsolescence of the entire SAC bomber force.[8]

In support of Sessums' contentions, the Wright Air Development Center (WADC) – part of the ARDC – released a technical directive (52-14) on 7 May 1952 estimating that Soviet defensive capabilities would make American strategic bomber losses prohibitive sometime between 1955 and 1960. This assumed the force would be composed of subsonic all-jet B-47 and B-52 bombers, supported by KC-135 tankers. To counter this trend, the WADC believed that at least two new strategic weapons systems needed to be developed during the coming decade.

The contracts at Boeing and Convair were revised to place an emphasis on defining an aircraft capable of penetrating the defenses that the WADC envisioned being in place during the 1960s. The unspoken goal was to conceive a supersonic bomber capable of carrying nuclear weapons. However, early jet engines were not efficient at any speed, and even less so at very high speeds, so it was assumed that it was essentially impossible to fly the entire mission at supersonic speeds. Early analysis had indicated that the fuel flows necessary to support sustained supersonic flight were as much as 70 percent higher than subsonic requirements.[9]

Still, supersonic flight in the immediate vicinity of the target was considered crucial. The radar installations of the time were largely unautomated – human operators stared at cathode ray tubes and tried to pick targets out of the clutter. Computers that would have sophisticated moving target indicators and anti-clutter filters were still years in the future, especially in the Soviet Union. The technology of the radar and its display meant that fast moving targets often appeared as ghosts on the display rather than bright, well-defined blips. So the faster the interdicting aircraft, the fainter the target on the display and the less time an operator would have to make a positive identification. The radar sites communicated with each other via simple voice lines and radio, resulting in minimal coordination between the various assets of the air defense system. Fast and high-flying bombers also operated above the reach of most contemporary fighters, and the surface-to-air missile had not yet developed into a truly workable weapon. Correctly given the circumstances, high-speed and high-altitude flight was seen as a panacea for the attacking force.

To support this concept, the Boeing MX-1022 study centered on an aircraft that was capable of supersonic dashes near its target but otherwise flew at subsonic speeds. This subsonic-cruise/supersonic-dash profile became known as the "split-mission" scenario and would dominate early efforts. The study lasted 18 months and confirmed the feasibility of a large supersonic aircraft.[10] This part of the study included wind tunnel tests that had originally been scheduled as part of the cancelled XB-55 bomber program.

Between February 1951 and August 1952, the Boeing study continued under the auspices of Project MX-1712. During this time the proposed aircraft was more clearly defined: a bomber-reconnaissance vehicle capable of performing medium- and long-range strategic missions at maximum speeds between Mach 1.6 and Mach 1.8. The aircraft would be refueled – often – by airborne tankers in order to achieve intercontinental range. This basic concept would evolve further as part of the follow-on Project MX-1965.[11]

At Convair, Air Force contract AF33(038)-2664 began in June 1949 and lasted for three years. The outcome was a concept for a semi-expendable parasite bomber that would be carried close to its target by a B-36, and then released. The parasite would be capable of supersonic speeds over the target while delivering a nuclear weapon; the B-36 carrier returned to base. The parasite would, it was hoped, be able to fly to the Soviet coast where the pilot would be recovered by friendly naval forces. It was hardly an ideal solution, but one that seemed within the technical realm.

Perhaps more significantly, in February 1951 Convair received contract AF33(038)-21250 for an 18-month study of a supersonic bomber with the same general characteristics as the one studied by Boeing under Project MX-1712. The concept was designated MX-1964 and would soon go head-to-head with the Boeing MX-1965 for a production contract.

In evaluating the two bomber studies, the WADC concluded that either design would meet the general requirements for a new strategic weapon. Both designs were powered by the General Electric J47-X24A, which developed into the outstanding J79 turbojet engine. There were, however, significant differences between the two designs, and the WADC believed that the Convair team had come closer to meeting the spirit of the development planning objectives. The WADC recommended that Boeing be eliminated from the program, and the Convair concept was selected for development as the B-58 Hustler medium bomber. Nevertheless, the WADC suggested that, because of its accumulated experience, Boeing receive another contract to study

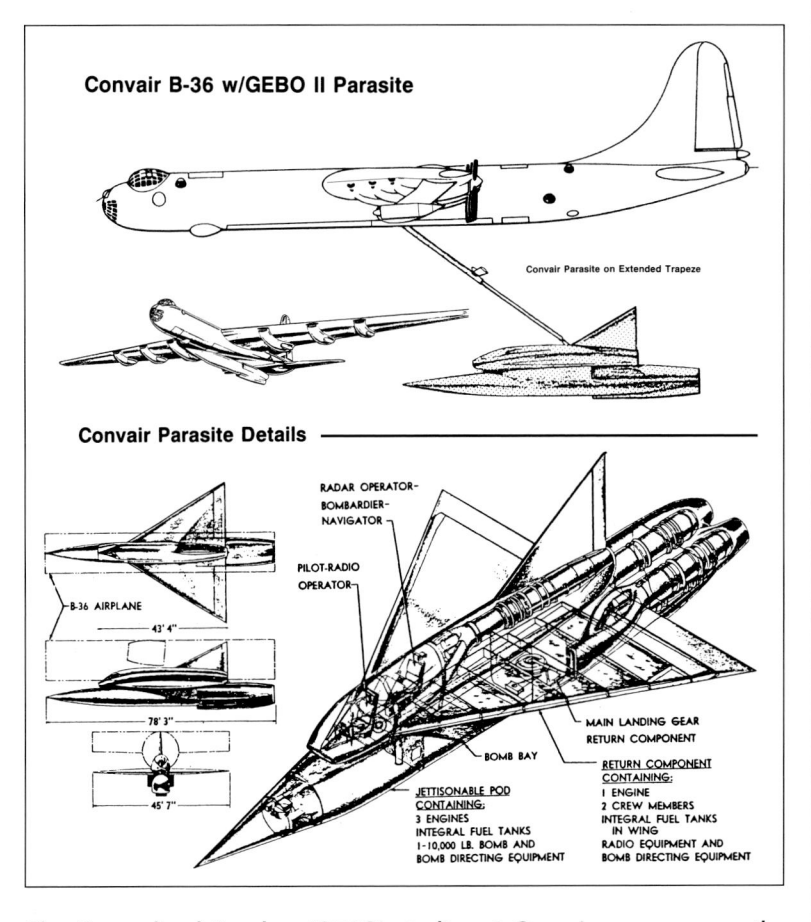

The Generalized Bomber (GEBO) studies at Convair were among the more bizarre attempts to create a supersonic intercontinental bomber. A small two-part parasite would be "towed" by a B-36 to a location off the Soviet coast and the parasite would make a supersonic dash to the target. Assuming the aircraft survived, the pilot would bail out over the ocean to be recovered by friendly naval forces. (Jay Miller Collection)

an optimized thermonuclear delivery system, new propulsion concepts, high-energy fuels, and other advanced developments.[12]

Independently, on 30 March 1953, SAC defined its anticipated future requirements in a letter to Air Force Headquarters. SAC continued to believe that manned flight to high altitudes and long ranges should be "… at all times a priority objective of the Air Force development program." The on-going intercontinental missile efforts were not expected to yield a reliable and capable weapon for the foreseeable future, due in large part to the anticipated size and weight of the thermonuclear warhead. Therefore, SAC called for the initiation of studies leading to the design and production of a high-performance long-range bomber to follow the B-52 and meant specifically to deliver thermonuclear weapons from bases within the continental United States into the heart of the Soviet Union. The projected bomber was to employ "… the longest range, highest altitude, and greatest speed (in that order of priority), capable of attainment in the time period under consideration and consistent with requirements for military payload and defensive systems."[13]

The bureaucracy was apparently much more responsive in 1953, and on 1 May contract AF33(616)-2070 was issued to Boeing for a one-year study of an advanced strategic weapons system to meet the SAC requirements. Boeing's very broad mandate was for a manned intercontinental bomber to be operational in 1960–1965. Boeing presented preliminary information on 22 January 1954, pointing out the possibilities of an aircraft powered by a chemically augmented nuclear powerplant, similar to the ones being developed by the ANP program.[14] For the first time, it appeared feasible to develop a weapons system of a reasonable size possessing the unlimited range characteristics of nuclear propulsion, plus a high-altitude, supersonic dash capability. In March 1954, Boeing presented more promising data on a chemically augmented, nuclear-powered aircraft.[15]

Then the unexpected occurred. Work on a thermonuclear fusion weapon had begun at the Los Alamos Laboratory in 1942, but continued on a very limited basis due to the wartime pressure to develop the fission bombs ultimately used against Japan. The first large-scale U.S. fusion explosion occurred on 1 November 1952 when the "Mike" device was exploded on Eniwetok atoll as part of Operation Ivy. This liquid deuterium-triggered device was 6 feet in diameter, 20 feet tall, and weighed approximately 130,000 pounds – hardly a deliverable weapon. However, the designers were already working on ways to replace the liquid deuterium trigger with solid lithium-6. By May 1954, the National Laboratories had managed to reduce the size and weight of the so-called "H-bombs" to the point that they no longer represented a daunting payload. The first "emergency capability" weapons available to the Air Force were 10-megaton-yield TX-14 devices that were roughly the same size as Mike but weighed less than 30,000 pounds, mostly because they did not need large quantities of cryogenic liquid deuterium. Within a few years, the weight had decreased (for the 1 megaton-yield Mk 28) to just over 2,000 pounds. This technical advance provided a strong impetus to accelerate serious planning for a new manned strategic bomber. Perhaps unfortunately, it also provided the breakthrough that was necessary for the development of workable

The Convair B-58 medium bomber was an outgrowth of early studies along the way to WS-110A. The Hustler was the first operational supersonic bomber, but would prove to be very maintenance intensive and was retired after only ten years in service. (U.S. Air Force)

The B-58 was powered by four General Electric J79 turbojet engines. This engine would also power such notable aircraft as the F-4 Phantom II and F-104 Starfighter. The experience gained with the J79 allowed GE to successfully develop the J93 for the B-70. (NASA Glenn Research Center)

intercontinental ballistic missiles (ICBM), which would eventually replace the manned bomber as the deterrent system of choice.[16]

Since this development largely invalidated most of the concepts investigated by Boeing for the previous year, a one-year extension was awarded as Project MX-2145. The primary goal was to determine the optimum means to deliver the smaller thermonuclear weapons being developed at the National Laboratories. During these studies, Air Force Headquarters requested that the study program be expanded to include additional trade-off information; for example, the potential results of trading weight for speed, weight for range, or speed for range. Boeing's tentative parameters were 20,000- and 40,000-pound payloads, an operational radius between 3,000 and 5,000 miles, refueling (if necessary) outside the Soviet early-warning system, and a cruise altitude above 50,000 feet while over enemy territory.

On 21 July 1954, Brigadier General Benjamin S. Kelsey at Air Force Headquarters issued a letter directive to the ARDC to expedite the development of a successor to the B-52 by developing a strategic intercontinental bomber with a nuclear-powered cruise and chemically augmented dash capability. This split-mission scenario was considered an attractive compromise since it was believed that the ability to build a nuclear-powered subsonic aircraft was well in hand, and using modified conventional turbojet ("chemical") engines would surely allow at least a short distance to be covered at supersonic speeds. The message directed an operational date in the 1960–1965 period. The WADC recommended that five contractors – Boeing, Convair, Douglas, Lockheed, and Martin – receive contracts to study chemically augmented nuclear propulsion systems and high-energy fuels. In contrast with the $5 million budgeted to study nuclear-only concepts, each of the five contractors received only $100,000 for the new study.[17]

The letter directive from Air Force Headquarters also called for the immediate development of a subsonic intercontinental bomber with chemical power only, and an evaluation to determine whether the nuclear-cruise chemical-dash aircraft would be flexible enough to operate without the nuclear components aboard. Because of the risk involved in depending completely on the development of a safe and reliable nuclear-powered aircraft, the chemically powered bomber was viewed as a "hedge" against possible failure to develop the nuclear aircraft. Nevertheless, the nuclear-powered aircraft would remain at the core of the strategic bomber studies for some time to come.[18]

Kelsey's letter was the impetus behind the creation of an aircraft that could operate from bases within the continental United States and deliver a 10,000-pound thermonuclear weapon against the Soviet Union. According to the preliminary development plan drafted in May 1954, the minimum required radius of action for the new bomber was 4,000 nautical miles, preferably without aerial refueling. The desired radius was 5,500 nautical miles, with aerial refueling being allowed outside of enemy territory. The specified cruise speed of Mach 0.9 would be accomplished at a minimum altitude of 40,000 feet. The aircraft would be capable of a dash speed greater than Mach 2.0 at altitudes of 60,000 feet; a minimum of 2,000 nautical miles at this speed was required while over enemy territory. High speed and high altitude alone were regarded as inadequate defense, so the bomber would also be

Lighter thermonuclear warheads and reliable inertial guidance systems allowed the development of workable intercontinental ballistic missiles, dealing a deathblow to the manned bomber. This is an early Atlas A test launch on 3 June 1958. (45th Space Wing History Office)

equipped with an array of passive and active defensive systems. Given the state-of-the-art at the time, these were ambitious requirements.

On 14 October 1954, the Air Force published GOR-38, "General Operation Requirement for an Intercontinental Bombardment Weapon System Piloted Bomber." The document was brief; essentially, it called for an intercontinental piloted bomber that would replace the B-52 in 1965 and be operational until 1975.[19]

To this end, on 28 October 1954, the ARDC presented General LeMay with four possible advanced strategic bombardment system concepts. The first was a conventional chemically powered bomber available in 1963 with a radius of action of 3,000 nautical miles, of which 750 to 1,000 would be flown at supersonic speeds. This bomber was to cruise at Mach 0.9 and penetrate enemy territory at speeds between Mach 1.5 and Mach 2.5 at an altitude of 50,000 to 60,000 feet. The second alternative was the nuclear-cruise and chemical-dash split-mission concept. This aircraft had a 4,000-nautical-mile radius of action with at least 1,000 nautical miles at supersonic speeds. Although this bomber was projected to also be available in 1963, it was felt that it carried a much higher level of development risk than the first concept. The third idea was the same as the second, except the operational date was slipped to 1965, somewhat easing the development risk. The last alternative was a nuclear-cruise aircraft with nuclear-dash capability. This aircraft would not be available until 1968–1970, but was believed to be vastly superior in terms of speed and altitude capabilities.[20]

In choosing the second alternative, LeMay reaffirmed the urgency of the 1963 date. This was a year after the last B-52 was expected to be manufactured, and was the scheduled retirement date for the earlier model B-52s. Preliminary studies by Boeing, Convair, and Lockheed had all shown that a chemically augmented nuclear-powered aircraft could be designed and built, although the supersonic dash capability would likely be limited to less than 750 nautical miles. Nevertheless, it would be a tremendous improvement over the B-52.

However, LeMay was nothing if not a realist. To guard against a possible slip in the nuclear power program, he wanted a separate chemically powered bomber developed in parallel. Although sound from a military perspective, LeMay's proposal was expensive; the cost of developing both aircraft was estimated at $3,900 million, about 30 percent more than the nuclear aircraft alone. To free up development resources, on 9 December 1954 the WADC recommended deleting the chemically powered bomber and concentrating all efforts on the nuclear program. Lieutenant General Thomas S. Power, the Commander of the ARDC, reluctantly accepted the logic of this course, although a lack of complete confidence in the ultimate success of the nuclear development program lurked in the background. The recommendation went forward to LeMay at SAC Headquarters and Air Force Headquarters.

Despite the ARDC position, on 29 December 1954 the Air Council decided to pursue two simultaneous but independent development programs for a nuclear-powered bomber designated Weapons System 125A (WS-125A) and a chemically powered bomber (WS-110A). Both aircraft were to be operational by 1963. It was what LeMay wanted, and the general was not to be ignored.

In light of the Air Council decision, and in response to GOR-38, on 15 April 1955 the ARDC issued System Requirement No. 22 (SR-22) for the chemically powered WS-110A "Piloted Strategic Intercontinental Bombardment Weapon System." This document set a target date of 1963 for an operational wing, designated this aircraft as the B-52 successor, and assigned an IA priority to the program. To meet the target date, a mockup was required by October 1957, a first flight by September 1960, and initial SAC inventory aircraft by November 1962. The aircraft was to be "a conventionally powered bombardment system capable of intercontinental nuclear weapon delivery … thereby permitting maximum freedom from political, logistical, and security problems." Based within the United States, the WS-110A system was to have the capability to strike and destroy three types of targets within the Soviet Bloc:[21]

"… the military, logistic, and control strengths associated with strategic, tactical, and defensive air weapons; the military, logistic, and control strengths associated with land and naval weapons; and the industrial and economic strengths of the enemy that enable him to sustain or increase the expenditures of warfare, to advance the technology of warfare, to outlast or compete with our corresponding strengths as they become strained or exhausted in warfare. Destroy additionally, as required, the control and psychological strengths of the enemy that enable him to direct and organize his strengths in warfare or to adhere to any course of action involving warfare."

The requirements also reflected a refined strategic concept by saying that "winning the air battle by destroying the enemy's air bases is the most important initial task of a war." Under this thinking, other "highly resistant targets" such as nuclear weapon storage sites and missile launching installations were considered secondary. The desired bomber was to "be capable of reacting quickly," meaning that aircraft "in a combat alert status must be capable of taking off on a combat mission within 3 minutes after the crew takes stations." Aircraft not on alert had to be capable of launching within 30 minutes. This was a very stringent requirement for the era and would have a serious impact on the design of the bombing and navigation system.[22]

The aircraft was also to be capable of operating day or night in all weather conditions. It was to overcome what the requirement termed the "limitations of present systems" in terms of range, combat altitude, speed, and defensive capability. Of equal importance to the desired performance was the requirement that called for 85 percent of the available (in commission) aircraft to undertake a defined mission "with no component failures." This was also an extremely stringent requirement.[23]

The target was to be attacked using free-fall bombs (conventional or nuclear) and a new air-to-surface missile. The missile was included as an "alternate load" intended to increase "survival probability" against "intense local defenses or weapons effects." The missile was to have a range of 300 nautical miles, with 700 nautical miles desired, at speeds greater than Mach 3 and an accuracy of 1,500 feet CEP.[24] The bombing and navigation system was to take advantage of the "inherent flexibility" of a manned system and employ automatic features "only to the extent necessary for mission success."[25]

SR-22 specified a minimum unrefueled radius of 4,000 nautical miles, with 5,500 nautical miles desired. The aircraft was to cruise at a minimum of Mach 0.9 "unless a significant increase in maximum radius of action or in combat dash zone performance could be attained by a slower speed." This generally reflected the preference SAC had always shown for range over high speed.[26] In the combat zone, a "maximum possible supersonic dash [speed] was required" for at least 1,000 nautical miles, with 2,000 nautical miles desired. A minimum combat ceiling of 60,000 feet was required, with 70,000 feet desired. The "capability of this weapon system for low altitude operations" was also to be investigated.[27]

Around the same time, the Air Force released GOR-96 for an intercontinental reconnaissance system with requirements that were very similar to WS-110A. This followed LeMay's practice of procuring a reconnaissance version of each post-war strategic bomber (there had been RB-36s, RB-45s, RB-47s, and even some early RB-52s). The reconnaissance system was identified as Weapon System 110L. Logically enough, the two systems were soon combined, becoming WS-110A/L.[28]

A number of engines were under consideration. Wright had come up with an improved J67 called the TJ32C4. Pratt & Whitney offered an improved J75. General Electric proposed at least two advanced versions of the J79 – the company-designated X207, which raised the engine's thrust from about 15,000 to 18,000 lbf, and the 20,700-lbf X275. However, the Allison J89 and the Pratt & Whitney J91 were the only two candidates actively under development by the Air Force. By early 1956, the field was narrowed to the J89, J91, and X275, mostly because those engines seemed to offer the correct thrust levels and fuel consumption, and appeared to stand a chance of being available at the appropriate time.

On 22 March 1955, the Air Force superceded GOR-38 by issuing GOR-82, "Piloted Strategic Intercontinental Bombardment Weapon System." SR-22 was revised to match the new GOR on 15 April. The requirements lowered the radius of action to 3,000 nautical miles and the dash distance to 750 nautical miles in an effort to preserve the 1963 operational date. Still, the goal was an extremely advanced aircraft given the available technology.[29]

On 6 April 1955, a Weapon System Program Office was formed as part of the Bombardment Aircraft Division, Directorate of Systems Management, Detachment 1, Headquarters ARDC, at Wright-Patterson AFB. Between 6 May and 12 July 1955, the Program Office presented a briefing to various headquarters within the Air Force outlining its proposed program to develop and deliver the new bomber at wing strength by 1963. The briefing included a requirement for 20 pre-production aircraft to conduct the flight test program and a single static test airframe. At the time, the estimated cost to develop and field an operational wing of the new aircraft was $2,500 million. This estimate assumed that the nuclear-powered bomber would also be developed, that the new engine for the chemically-powered bomber would be paid for by the normal Air Force engine program, and that certain subsystem development costs would be shared by the WS-125A program.[30]

When both bomber programs had been initiated, a concerted effort had been made to keep development costs to a minimum. Since many major systems – bombing-navigation, defensive, electronics – had very similar requirements, it had been decided they could be shared between the two designs, therefore saving the effort of developing two substantially similar systems. Since the WS-125A effort was the preferred long-term aircraft, it was programmed to pick up the majority of the development costs. This created the appearance that WS-110A cost less and this raised fewer objections within political circles about initiating two new manned bomber programs simultaneously. In addition, at the time the Air Force usually developed engines independently of specific aircraft programs, meaning that these costs were also "hidden" from the WS-110A line item.

By the summer of 1955, the WS-110A program had begun to take on a more definitive character that set it apart from the planning for WS-125A. On 21 June, the Deputy Chief of Staff for Development approved a competitive Phase I development program for WS-110A. Still, the two programs progressed in tandem, if somewhat offset in time. Six airframe contractors – Boeing, Convair, Douglas, Lockheed, Martin, and North American – were invited to bid on the preliminary WS-110A and WS-125A studies on 16 July, and a bidders conference was held at Wright Field on 27 July. Convair and Lockheed were soon awarded WS-125A contracts and elected not to compete for the seemingly less-challenging WS-110A contract. Convair, Douglas and Martin were busy developing ballistic missiles and did not want to dilute that effort.[31] Therefore, the WS-110A competition narrowed to two companies, Boeing and North American Aviation.[32]

On 1 July 1955, the ARDC released SR-56 in support of the GOR-96 issued a year earlier for a reconnaissance version of WS-110A. The matter was further complicated on 11 October when the ARDC issued a revision to SR-22 that slipped the operational date of the bomber from 1963 to July 1964. Nevertheless, in mid-December 1955, the Air Force awarded letter contracts to both Boeing and North American for the Phase I development of Weapon System 110A/L, although the contracts were back-dated to 8 November to cover work begun earlier. Each contractor had to provide models, drawings, specifications, reports, conduct wind tunnel tests, and construct a mockup within two years. Boeing signed contract AF33(600)-31802 on 15 March 1956; North American followed on 16 April with contract AF33(600)-31801. At the same time, IBM was awarded a contract for preliminary studies into a new bombing and navigation system (see Chapter 8), and General Electric received a contract to study advanced propulsion systems (see Chapter 4).[33]

On 27 April 1956, everybody was directed to stop-work on WS-110L pending a review of the requirements by the Air Force. Although work never resumed, the requirement was not formally cancelled until February 1958, the same time that President Dwight D. Eisenhower authorized the CORONA reconnaissance satellite program. The ICBMs had become powerful enough to place meaningful payloads into orbit; although nobody recognized it at the time, it was a deathblow to the manned bomber.[34]

By mid-1956 Boeing and North American had not established specific engine requirements, but both had decided that the optimum powerplant should incorporate four specific features: the highest feasible turbine inlet temperature, to give low supersonic fuel consumption; the highest practicable pressure ratio, to obtain low specific fuel consumption at subsonic cruise; high thrust and low specific fuel consumption for supersonic dash; and a minimum high altitude speed of Mach 3 for Boeing and Mach 2.7 for North American.[35]

Both companies believed that any of the major engine manufacturers could build an engine that met these specifications, but by mid-1956, both airframe contractors had largely settled on versions of the proposed General Electric X275. However, each airframe contractor had different thrust and specific fuel consumption requirements. Engine selection was thus complicated by the different sizes and varying installation features requested by the airframe contractors; the fact that neither improved X275 model was being funded by the government further hampered a decision.[36]

In July 1956 Air Force Headquarters ordered the ARDC to conduct a source selection for the bomber, and on 24 August General Estes decided that one of the airframe contractors would be eliminated and the development contract awarded to the other. Boeing and North American were told to submit proposals based on their work to date.[37]

Floating Panels

Not surprisingly, the preliminary designs submitted by Boeing and North American in mid-1956 were quite different, but at the same time very similar. Both aircraft would weigh some 750,000 pounds and use "floating wing panels" (a term coined by Boeing but ultimately applied to both designs) to house additional fuel. Each of the 190,000-pound (loaded) panels was the size of a B-47 medium bomber and would carry fuel for the trip to the target. When the fuel was exhausted, the panels would be jettisoned – without them, the main aircraft would be capable of dash speeds in excess of Mach 2.[38]

The theory behind using the floating wingtips had originated with Dr. Richard Vogt, a German scientist who had come to America after World War II. Vogt proposed increasing the range of an aircraft by attaching two "free floating" panels to the wingtips to carry extra fuel. He believed this could be accomplished without undue structural weight penalties if the extensions were free to articulate and self-supported by their own aerodynamic lift. In addition, the panels would effectively increase the aspect ratio of the overall wing (while they were attached), providing a significant reduction in wing drag. Therefore, as the theory went, the extra fuel was being carried "for free" by the more efficient wing and the additional fuel increased the range of the aircraft.

Other potential uses for this concept quickly became apparent. The one that sparked the most interest was for a bomber to carry two escort fighters, one on each wingtip. The Germans had apparently experimented with the idea during late 1944 and early 1945.[39]

Wingtip coupling experiments with two EF-84Ds and an EB-29A proved difficult and eventually led to the loss of all three aircraft and their crews. The designers of WS-110A did not believe they would have the same problems since there were no plans to ever link-up during flight. The proposed WS-110A bombers would take off with the "floating panels" already attached to each wingtip, and simply jettison them when the fuel was depleted. (Peter M. Bowers Collection)

During 1949, initial U.S. experiments had used a Douglas C-47A and Culver PQ-14B. These tests involved a very simple coupling device: a single-joint attachment that permitted three degrees of freedom for the PQ-14. A small ring was placed on a short boom attached to the right wingtip of the C-47. Only local structural reinforcement was required since the PQ-14 would be supported by its own lift. A rearward lance was mounted on the left wingtip of the PQ-14, and the PQ-14 would position itself slightly ahead of the C-47 and essentially "back" the lance into the ring. No locking mechanism was required since drag would keep the aircraft in place. To uncouple, the PQ-14 would simply speed up. The first attempt at coupling was made on 19 August 1949 over Wright Field. Problems with wingtip vortex interference were encountered, forcing the engineers to reevaluate the concept. The solution was to move the ring further away from the C-47's wingtip, and on 7 October 1949, a successful coupling was made with Major Clarence E. "Bud" Anderson at the controls of the PQ-14B.[40]

At the same time as the C-47/PQ-14 experiments took place, a full-scale program was initiated using a B-29 to "tow" two straight-wing F-84 fighters. Republic Aviation Corporation was awarded a contract to design, build, and evaluate the combination under Project TIP TOW. Two F-84D-1-REs (serial numbers 48-641 and 48-661) were modified for the initial TIP TOW tests under the designation EF-84D. The wingtips of the EF-84Ds were modified so that they could be attached to flexible mounts fitted to the wingtips of a specially modified EB-29A (44-62093). This idea proved to be highly dangerous, although several successful linkups were made. Tragically, midway through the planned test series, the entire three-plane array crashed as a unit on 24 April 1953, killing everybody on all three aircraft. TIP TOW was immediately cancelled. The cause was subsequently traced to one of the EF-84Ds going out of control during the link-up and flipping over onto the wing of the B-29.[41]

A parallel project was undertaken using a pair of swept-wing RF-84F-5-REs (51-1848 and 51-1849) attached to wingtip hook-up assemblies on the JRB-36F (49-2707 – the initial FICON testbed). The B-36 was formally assigned to the Tom-Tom project on 8 May 1954. Interestingly, the Tom-Tom moniker was derived from the first names of two men, Major General Tom Gerrity and Convair contract manager Tom Sullivan, which is why it is not written in all caps.

The B-36 system included provisions to launch and retrieve the fighters in flight, and to provide fuel, pressurization, and heating air to the parasites while coupled. The wing structures of the B-36 and F-84s were substantially strengthened to tolerate the stress of coupled flight. The Thieblot Engineering Company accomplished the actual design of the Tom-Tom mechanisms under subcontract to Convair. A fixed mockup of the coupling mechanism was attached to the wing of the JRB-36F and one RF-84F, and 7 hours of proximity flight tests were completed by 30 September 1954. Each of the F-84s was equipped with an articulating jaw that was designed to firmly clamp onto a retractable member on the wingtip of the B-36. Once a firm attachment was made, the B-36 would retract the member into a streamlined fairing where fluid, electrical, and air connections would automatically be made to allow the F-84 to shut down its engine.[42]

After the TIP TOW crash, tests continued for a few months with the RF-84F/JRB-36F/RF-84F array. Only a few hookup attempts[43] were made, and wingtip vortices and turbulence made this operation considerably more dangerous than the average operational pilot could accomplish. The first hookup, using only the left-hand fighter, was made on 2 November 1955. In what became the final Tom-Tom flight, on 26 September 1956, Beryl Erickson found the F-84 he was piloting oscillating violently up and down while attached to the B-36 wingtip. Fortunately, part of the attachment mechanism broke and the F-84 fell away from the bomber before any serious damage was done. Since experiments with in-flight refueling techniques seemed to offer greater promise for increased fighter ranges with far less risk to the lives of aircrews, the Tom-Tom experiments were cancelled.

Nevertheless, the floating wingtip concept was strongly supported by the ARDC during 1956 as a likely method of achieving the desired range for WS-110A. It should be noted that the WS-110A concepts took off with the wing panels attached – and there were no plans to reattach after the separation during flight – so many of the difficulties encountered during TIP TOW and Tom-Tom would not have been encountered. In September 1956, an ARDC study group reported that floating wingtips appeared to be a "very promising means of extending the subsonic range of aircraft from 30% to 100%."[44]

However, the floating wingtip design was not where either contractor began, so a quick look at the design evolution is in order.

The Boeing Design, Take 1

Boeing, of course, had a long history of developing strategic bombers for the U.S. Air Force and its predecessor organizations. The B-17 Flying Fortress and B-29 Superfortress from World War II were legendary; the B-47 Stratojet and B-52 Stratofortress were examples of the post-war technological explosion that introduced swept wings and podded jet engines, allowing high-speed flight for large aircraft.

Boeing began work on what would become WS-110A very early, with the conceptual design performed at Plant II in Wichita, Kansas. Oddly, the first related effort was the MX-1847 study of nuclear-powered aircraft for logistic and air defense missions. Unfortunately, nothing could be found describing the results of the study, other than that it was a catalyst for the MX-2145 study that investigated intercontinental strategic bombers. This study confirmed the desirability of a Mach 3 bomber, but predicted that its combat radius would be too short to be operationally useful. Subsequent studies concentrated on the development of advanced fuels and aerodynamics, and resulted in significant enough performance gains that Boeing engineers believed a useful high-altitude Mach 3 bomber could be designed.[45]

The first design to be drafted was the Model 713 series, beginning in August 1954 under the direction of Benjamin F. Ruffner and J. M. Wickham. In December 1954, the study was divided into two projects, the nuclear effort led by Ruffner and the chemical side led by Lloyd T. Goodmanson. This continued until early December 1955.

The 713 model numbers consisted of three parts. Each model number had the 713 prefix followed by a –1 for chemical configurations or a –2 for nuclear configurations. This was followed by a second dash number that began at –101 and ran consecutively. Floating wingtips were designated using –1xxx after the basic airplane model number. In July 1955, after Model 713-1-208, all nuclear airplanes became Model 722 and the chemical airplanes remained Model 713 with no intermediate dash number. The last dash number continued consecutively regardless of chemical or nuclear configuration. In October 1955, the project organizations were physically separated, with the nuclear program moving to Harbor Island near Seattle, while the chemical program remained in Wichita. At this time, the files were also separated and each project's model numbers ran consecutively from –230 on. In mid-November 1955, the nuclear effort was cancelled, although further study continued under an internal Boeing work order until the end of December.[46]

A family of eight chemical and nuclear airplanes was designed around a 400,000-pound gross weight with a 7,500-pound bomb load. Performance, weight, and design details for these airplanes were published in August 1954. Typical of the early designs was the Model 713-1-101; this chemically powered aircraft was 170 feet long with a high-mounted swept wing spanning 116 feet. A single ducted fan engine was mounted under each wing, with an additional engine on each side of the fuselage just below the trailing edge wing root. Bicycle landing gear was located in the fuselage, with outrigger gears located in fairings that extended ahead of the wing near the tips. The Model 713-2-102 was generally similar except nuclear engines replaced the fuselage-mounted ducted fan engines with the reactor located just behind the weapons bay where the chemical airplane carried additional fuel.[47]

The study continued during late August 1954 with the Model 713-1-113, the first concept that was thought to have the range and payload capability necessary of an intercontinental bomber. This design was pursued in great detail and was used as a basis for parametric studies that included engine size and location, landing gear type, wing planform and size, body shape, nose configuration, and structural materials. The final configuration was a sleek swept-wing aircraft that was 177 feet long and spanned 121.5 feet. The wing provided a gross area of 4,000 square feet and had a leading edge sweep of 45 degrees. Gross weight was again estimated at 400,000 pounds, and four ducted fan engines were mounted in individual pods under the wing. A small weapons bay could carry a 7,500-pound "package" while five MX-601 air-to-air defensive missiles were carried in the aft fuselage. Performance was estimated to include a subsonic radius of 4,000 nautical miles, with a dash speed of Mach 2 at 60,000 feet.[48]

Models 713-1-114 through 713-1-168 were designed with varying gross weights, engine arrangements and sizes, wing planforms and sizes, wing loadings, and types of engines, both chemical and nuclear. The Model 713-1-169 was the final design proposed as the Boeing Model 713 to the Air Force in April 1955. This swept-wing airplane was powered by four low-pressure ratio turbojet engines with afterburners and could carry a bomb load of 10,000 pounds. A crew of four operated equipment that allowed attacking targets while the airplane was dashing at Mach 3 and 60,000 feet altitude after a long-range subsonic cruise.[49]

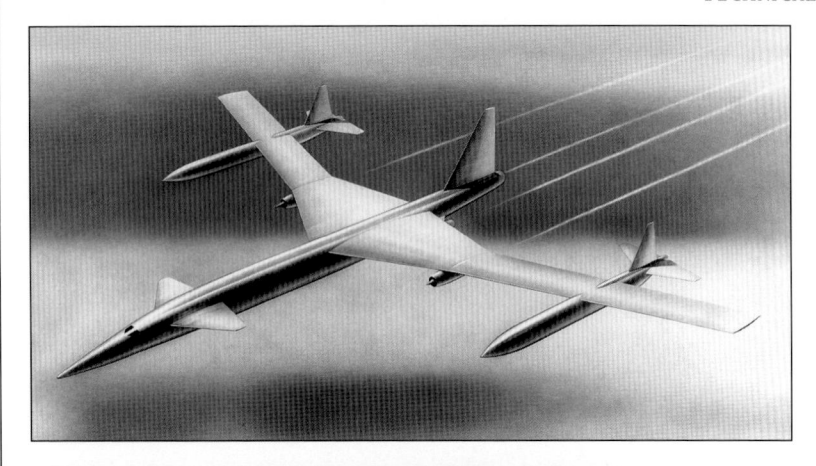

TECHNICAL VOODOO

The mostly stainless-steel Model 713-1-169 was 200 feet long and spanned 118 feet. The four engines were located in individual pods very far outboard on the wings. The fuselage was unusually slender, with the wings mounted near the mid-point. A largely conventional tricycle landing gear was used, although its retraction sequence was particularly complicated since both main gear were stowed in the fuselage. Large fuel tanks dominated the fuselage and wing. A crew of four was seated in individual ejection capsules. It appears the MX-601 defensive missiles were deleted from this design, but an unidentified "sophisticated" ECM system was included.[50]

Interestingly, Boeing continued looking at alternative configurations under the Model 713 designation even after submitting the "final" design. The first was the Model 713-1-229, generated in October 1955. Whereas the –169 had been a steel Mach 3 dash airplane, the –229 was constructed from aluminum and limited to Mach 2 dash speeds, although the general configuration was similar.[51]

In December 1955, attention turned to a new concept, intended mainly to increase the radius of action of the new bomber. The Model 724 study began in December 1955 with –1 and ran through February 1957 with the –16. The study was under the direction of Lloyd Goodmanson and Douglas E. Graves. The Model 724-1 was the first Boeing design to use floating wingtips for range extension. The basic airplane was very similar to the Model 713-1-169, although it was 209.5 feet long with a wingspan of 118.3 feet. The primary external difference was the addition of an outrigger landing gear in a streamline fairing projecting behind the wing between the two engine nacelles. The defensive missiles made a comeback, this time looking more like the Falcon missiles they would ultimately evolve into. What really made the design different, however, was the addition of two large fuel tanks carried on their own wing section outboard of the basic aircraft. Each of the fuel tanks was 8 feet in diameter and 62 feet long, and housed a landing gear to support it during taxi and takeoff. The dedicated wing section spanned 55 feet, but was mounted obliquely on the fuel tank to continue the sweep of the main wing. The bomber would take off with the floating wingtips attached, using the fuel contained within their tanks during the first part of the journey. The extensions would be jettisoned before the bomber entered enemy airspace and were not recoverable.[52]

The next Boeing design using the floating wingtips was a radical departure from the comparatively normal-looking Model 724-1. Boeing documentation in March 1956 described the Model 724-13 as "a straight wing, canard type airplane weighing 300,000 pounds powered by four turbojet engines with afterburners carrying a bomb load of 10,000 pounds and a crew of four." However, the overall design was very unusual. Although described as "straight wing," in reality the design featured a trapezoidal planform spanning 70.6 feet with a General Electric X275 engine mounted under each wingtip. Two other engines were mounted on the sides of the fuselage under the trailing edge of the wing. No conventional horizontal tail surfaces were fitted, the design relying totally on the canard for pitch control.[53]

The fuselage was 156.6 feet long, with the wing mounted about two-thirds of the way back. The basic airplane had an empty weight

During March 1956 Boeing began investigating the Model 724-13, and this is the model that is usually – incorrectly – shown as the Boeing entry in the competition. The airplane was 156.6 feet long and weighed 300,000 pounds. Each of the Model 724-1001 floating wingtips was nearly 76 feet long and had an all-up weight of 131,000 pounds. The airplane used four General Electric X275 turbojet engines; one under each wing and two mounted on the lower corners of the fuselage under the wing root. (Boeing via Terry Panopalis Collection)

of 106,710 pounds, with a maximum takeoff weight of 225,000 pounds and a maximum flight weight of 300,000 pounds. The fuselage had a diameter of 12.5 feet, and a 10,000-pound weapon could be carried in the single bomb bay. Four crewmen sat in an unusual arrangement; the pilots were side by side, the bombardier-navigator behind the co-pilot and the "battle director" behind him. Comparatively large areas inside the fuselage were dedicated to electronics, primarily ECM equipment, and the bomb-nav system. Conventional chaff and flare dispensers replaced the defensive missile system.[54]

The Model 724-1001 fuel tanks were fairly good-sized aircraft themselves. The floating wingtips had a span of almost 81 feet, and the fuel tanks were 6.6 feet in diameter and nearly 76 feet long. Each fuel tank had a horizontal and vertical stabilizer, and was fitted with a tricycle landing gear. Each had an empty weight of 24,500 pounds and an all-up weight of 131,000 pounds. Again, the tanks were not recoverable, the landing gear being provided to facilitate takeoff only. Operationally the floating wingtips would be empty at takeoff and filled during the first aerial refueling. The fuel in the wingtips would then be used first so that they could be jettisoned before entering enemy airspace.[55]

By July 1956, Boeing had progressed to the Model 724-15, which was the design presented to the Source Selection Board Evaluation Team on 24-26 July. This 370,000-pound airplane returned to the basic concepts explored in the Model 724-1, with a conventional empennage instead of a canard and a more conventional wing planform. A crew of four and up to 10,000 pounds of bombs, along with another 10,000 pounds of ECM equipment, and expendable countermeasures (the defensive missiles again being deleted).[56]

The Model 724-15 was 156.6 feet long and spanned 93.5 feet. The airplane was powered by four 26,425-lbf General Electric X275A turbojet engines in individual pods under the outer portion of the wing. The four-man crew sat behind a retractable ramp that was installed ahead of the windshield to provide better aerodynamics at high speeds. The same offset crew arrangement used in the Model 724-1 was retained. An air-to-air refueling receptacle was located just ahead of the retractable windshield ramp. The main landing gear

The Model 724-15 was the airplane presented to the Source Selection Board on 24-26 July 1956. Oddly, it is not the design that is usually shown when talking about the first part of the competition, and very few illustrations of the airplane exist. It was generally similar to the 725-16 shown in model form at the bottom of the page but was slightly smaller and lighter. (Boeing Historical Archives)

The Model 724-16 was submitted as an alternate design to the Source Selection Board. This version had four more-powerful X279A engines mounted in individual pods under the wings and weighed 425,000 pounds. The forward 30 feet of the nose articulated downward to provide visibility during landing. (Boeing via the Terry Panopalis Collection)

Boeing records the history of each design in the "Boeing Model Records D-4500" book that includes basic data and three-view drawings of each concept investigated by the company. The following pages show selected designs from the first phase of the WS-110A competition, including some nuclear-powered versions. Boeing evaluated a wide range of options, from designs that looked like enlarged B-52s to some futuristic concepts that would have been interesting to behold. The drawings are not the same scale. (Boeing Historical Archives)

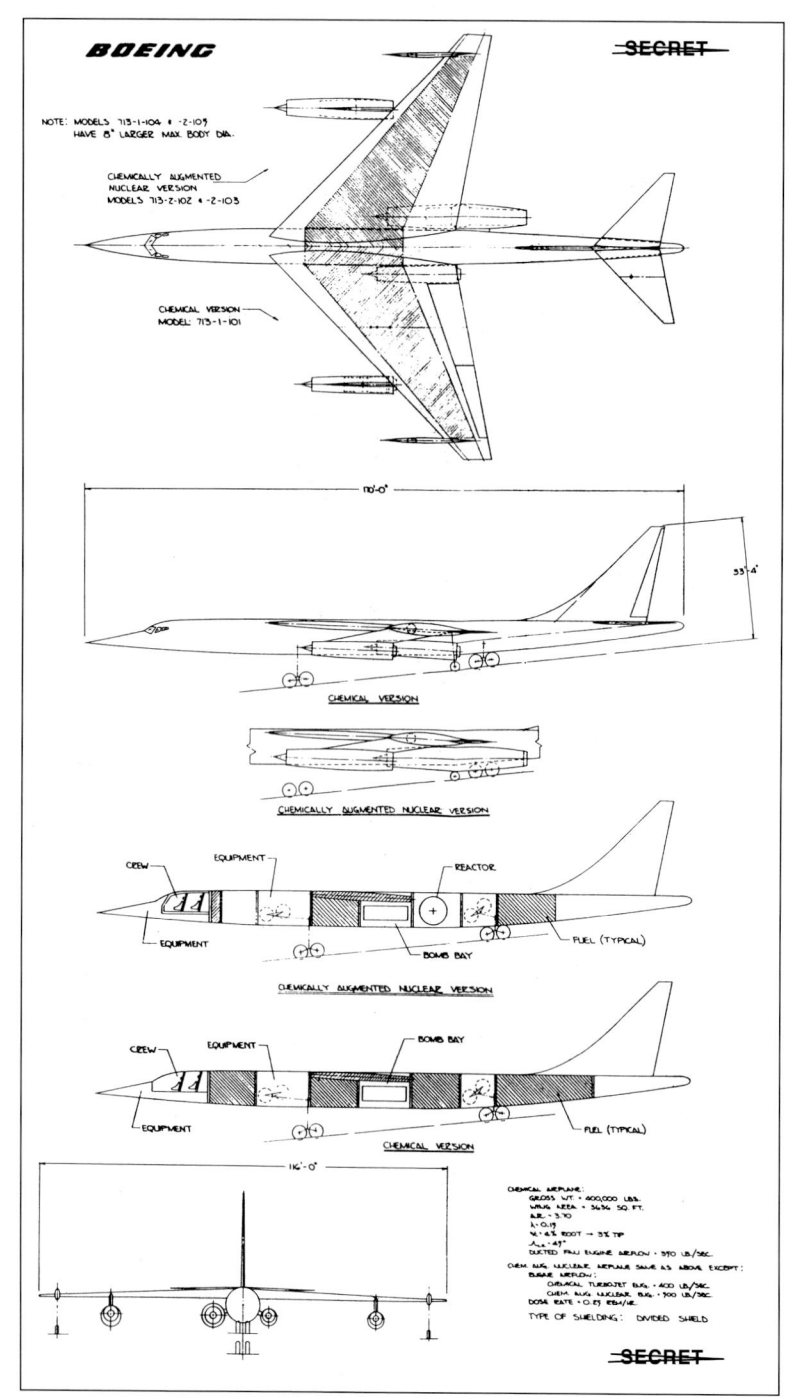

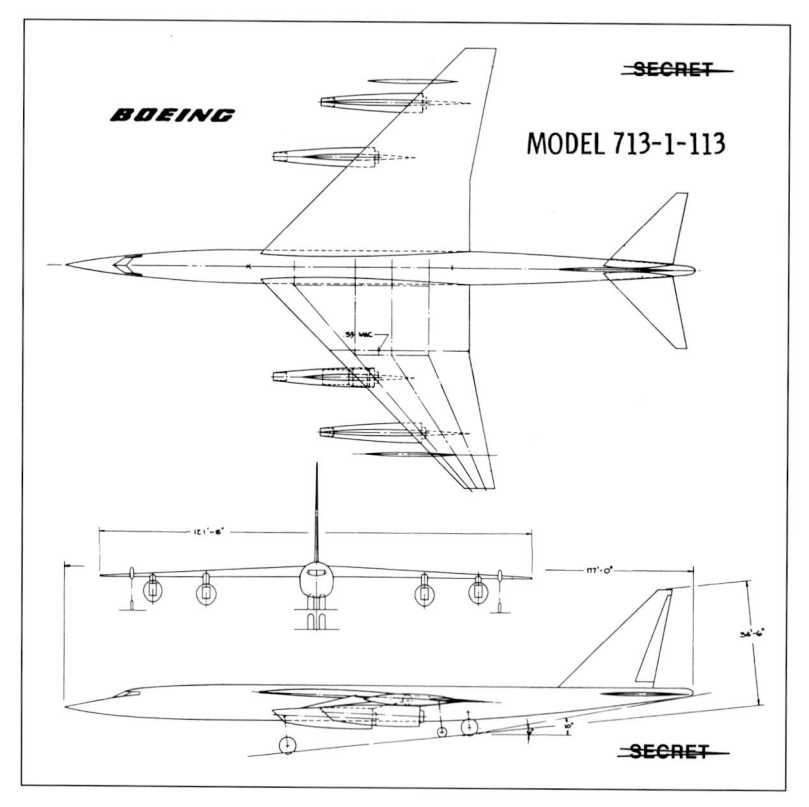

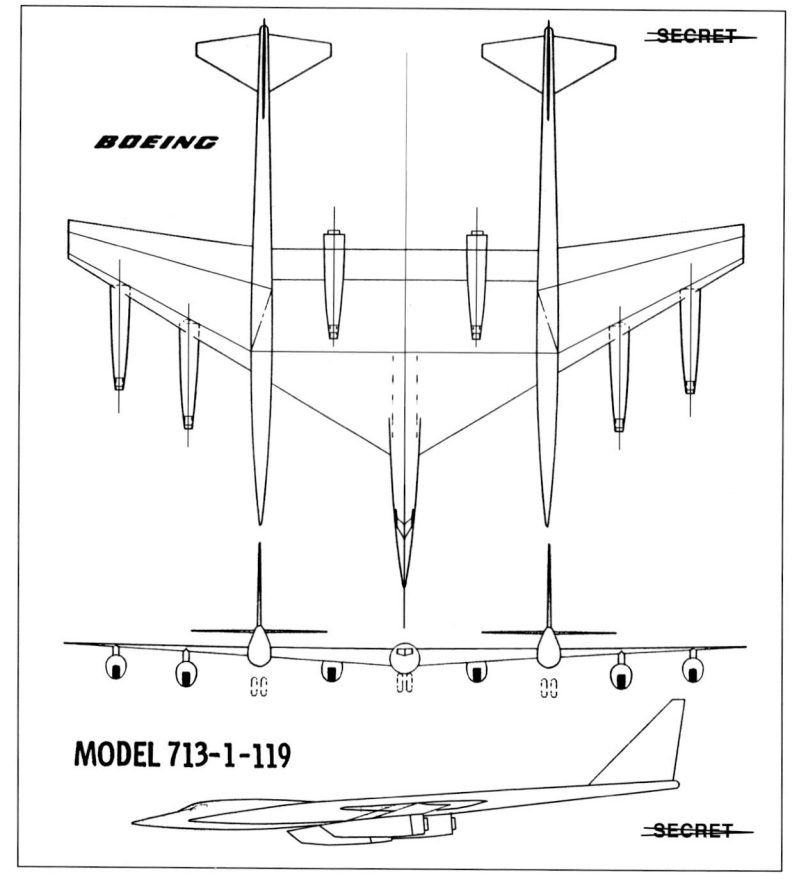

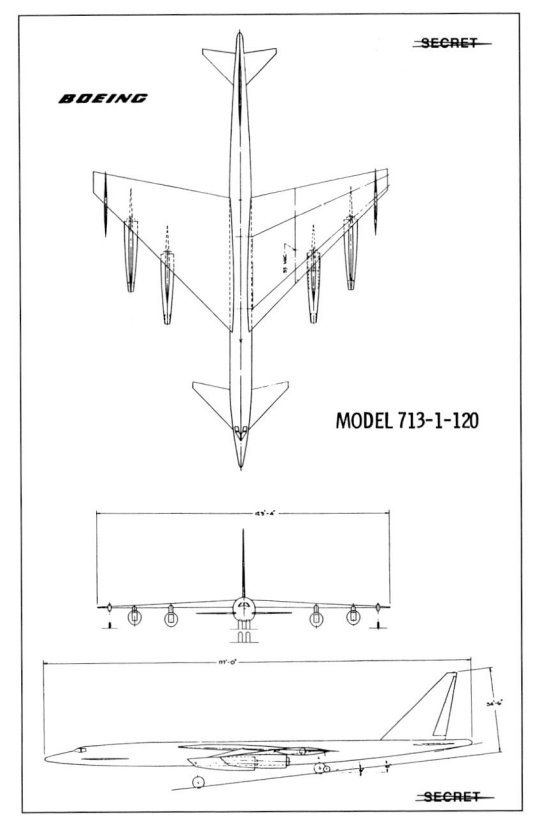

Technical Voodoo

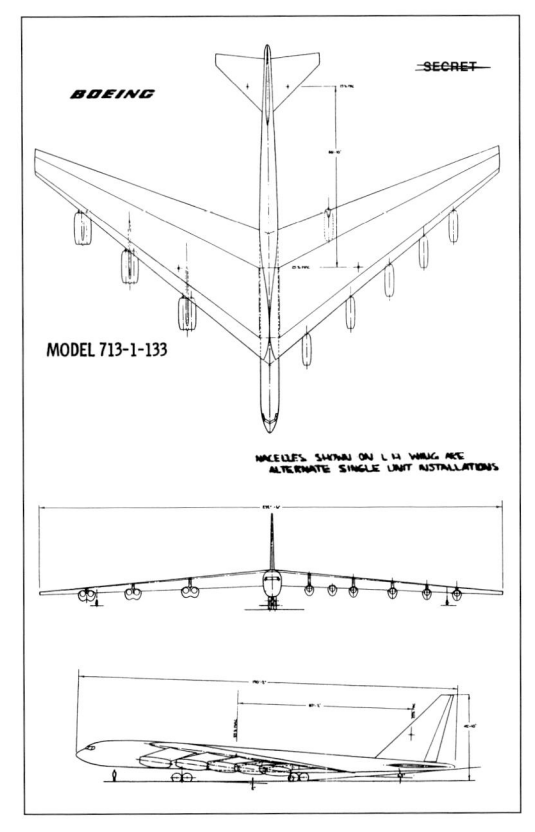

MODEL 713-1-120

MODEL 713-1-133
NACELLES SHOWN ON L.H. WING ARE ALTERNATE SINGLE UNIT INSTALLATIONS

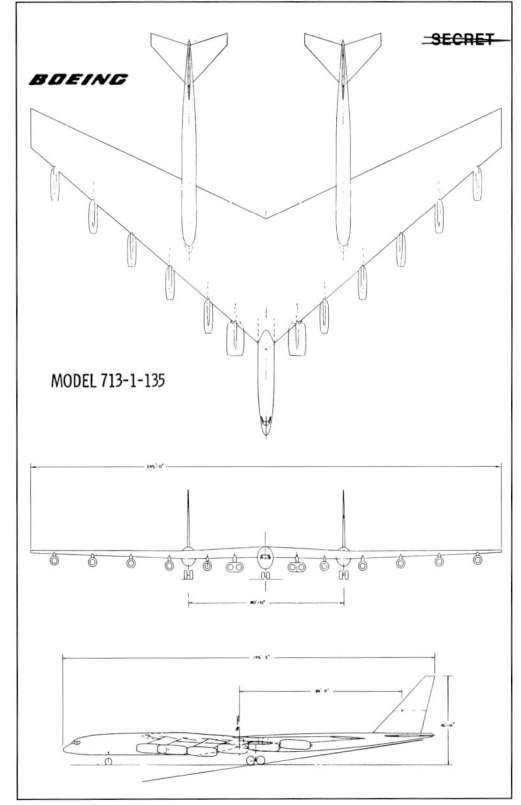

MODEL 713-1-135

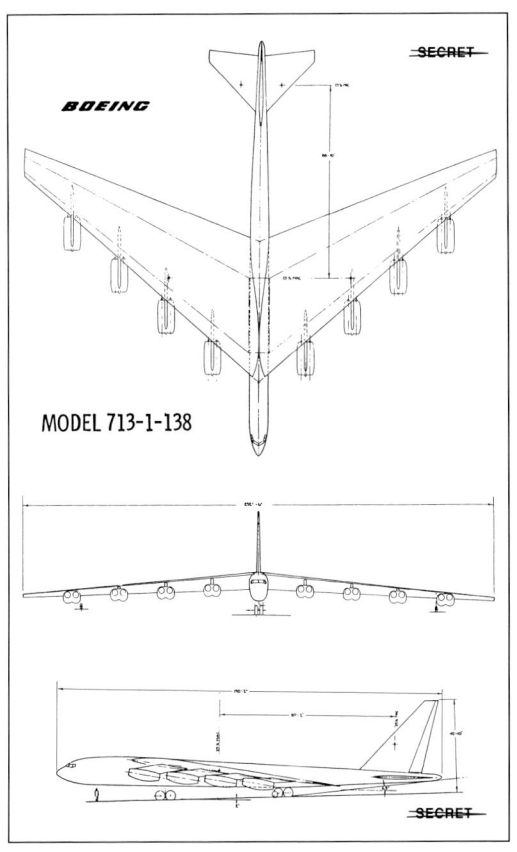

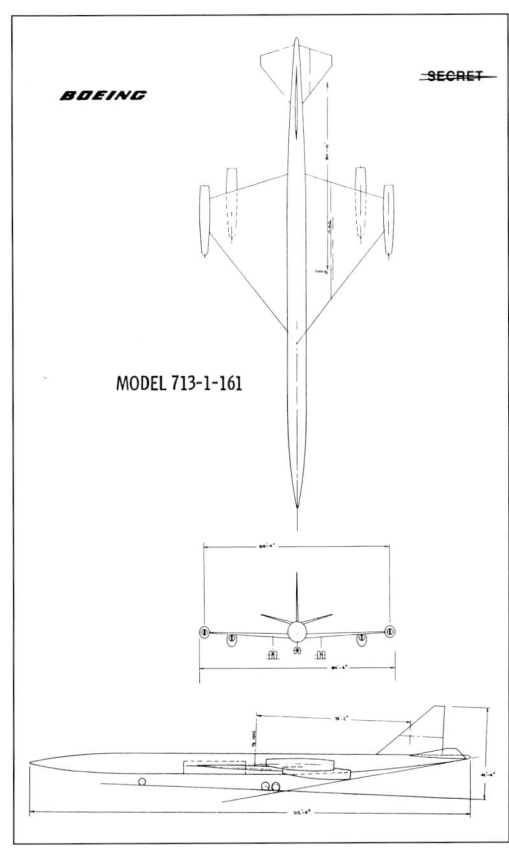

MODEL 713-1-138

MODEL 713-1-161

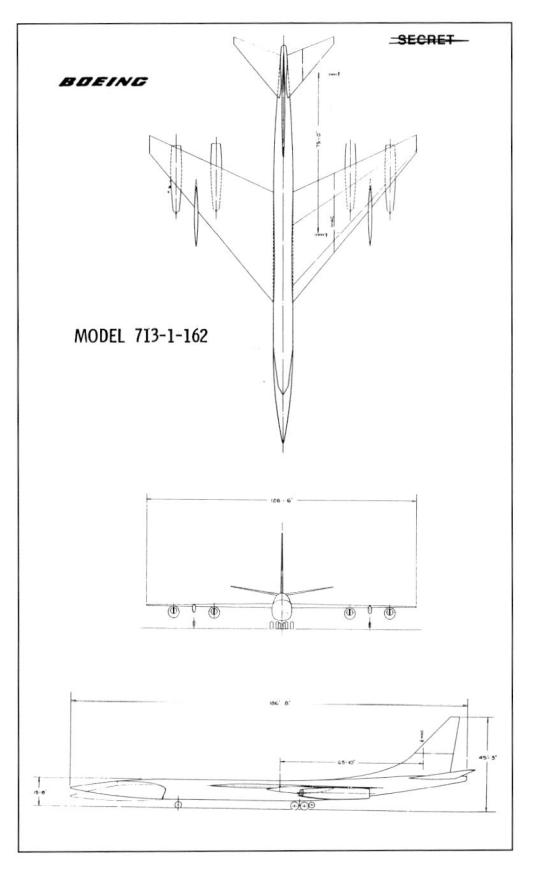

MODEL 713-1-162

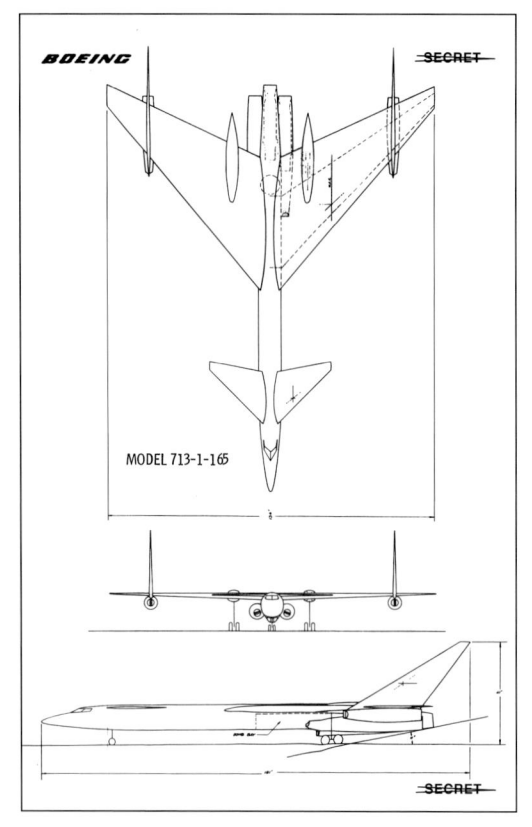

Technical Voodoo

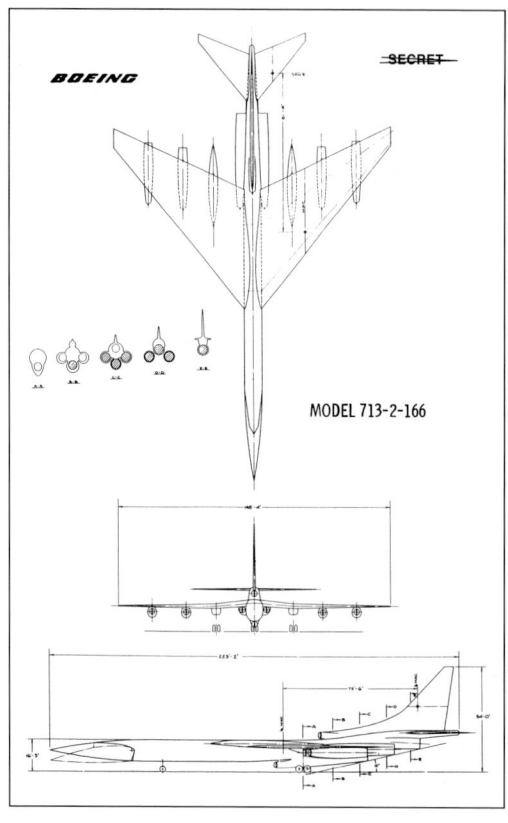

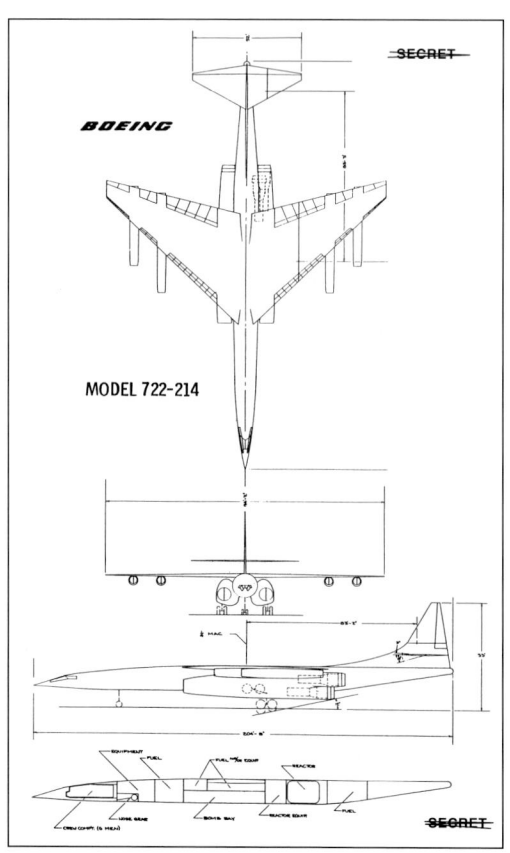

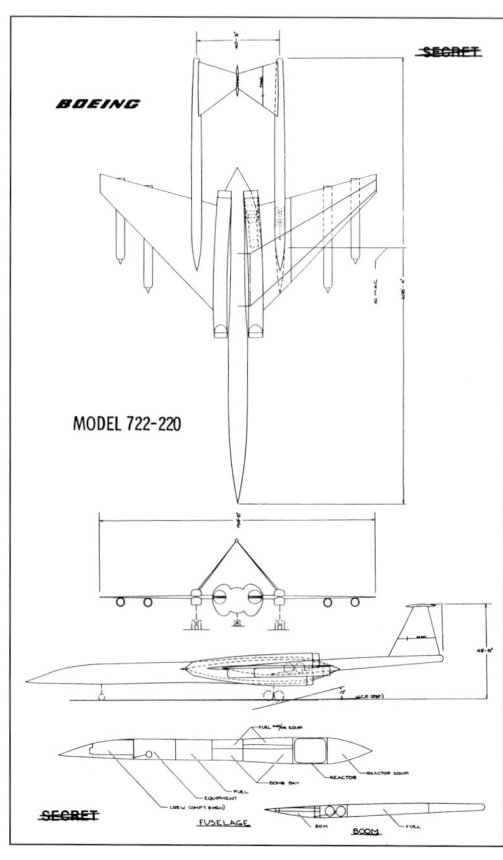

MODEL 713-1-165

MODEL 713-2-166

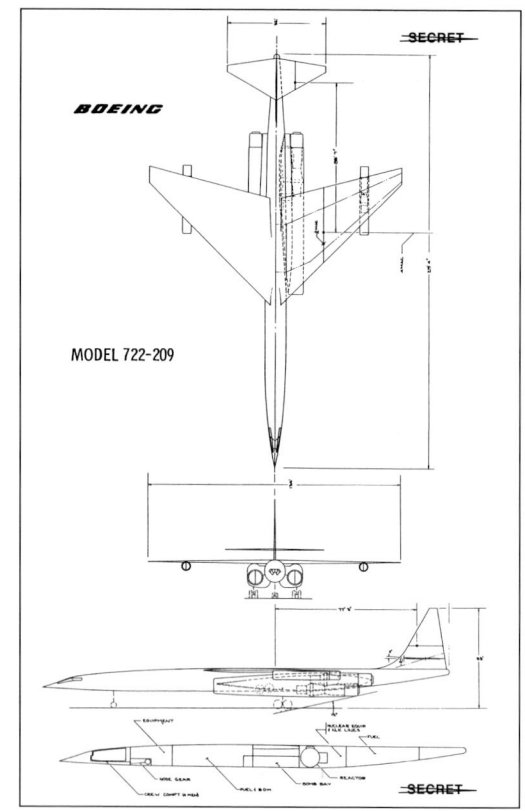

MODEL 722-209

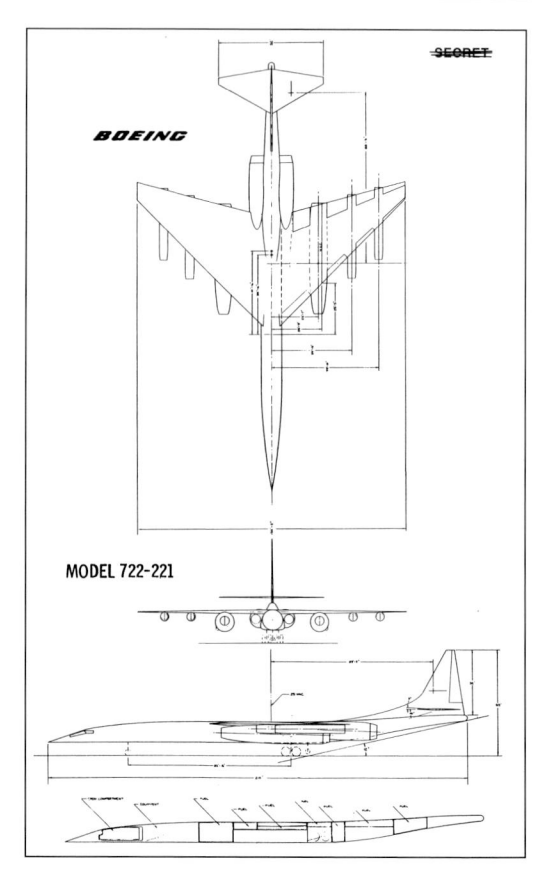

MODEL 722-214

MODEL 722-220

MODEL 722-221

Technical Voodoo

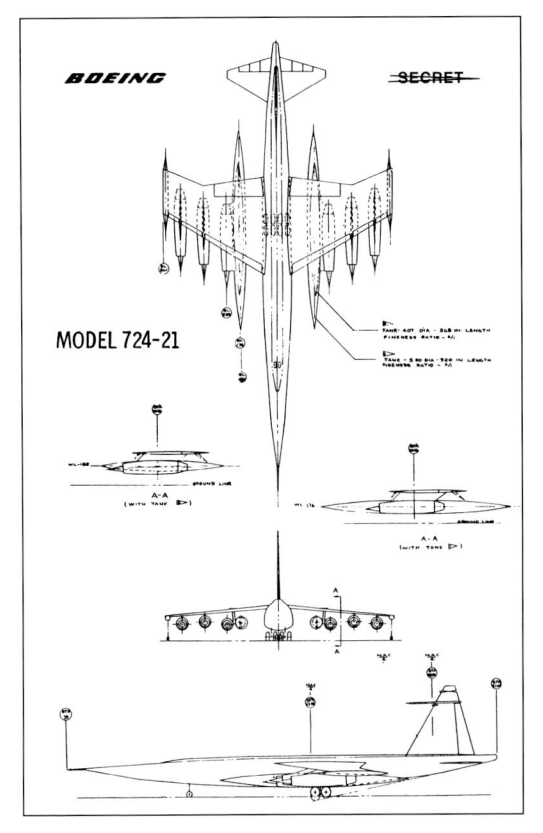

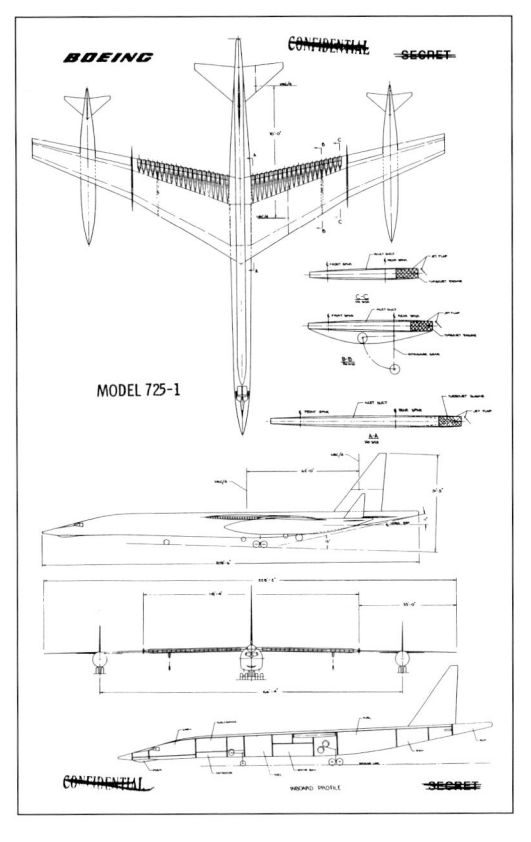

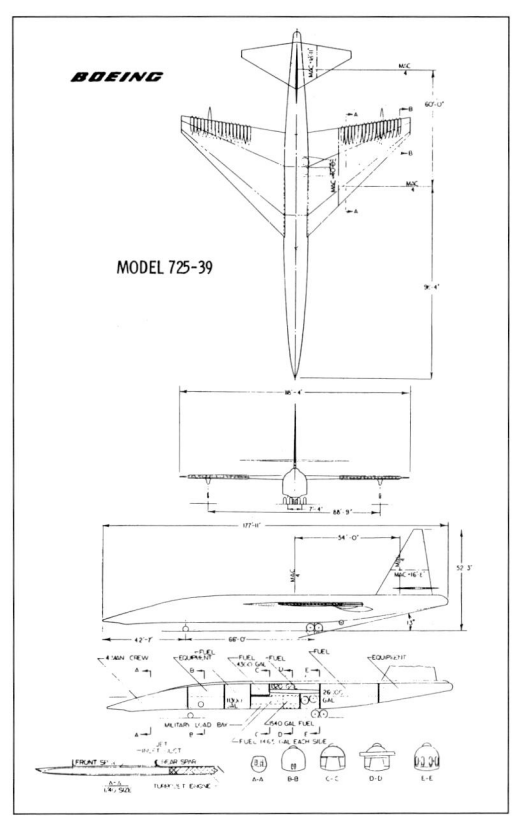

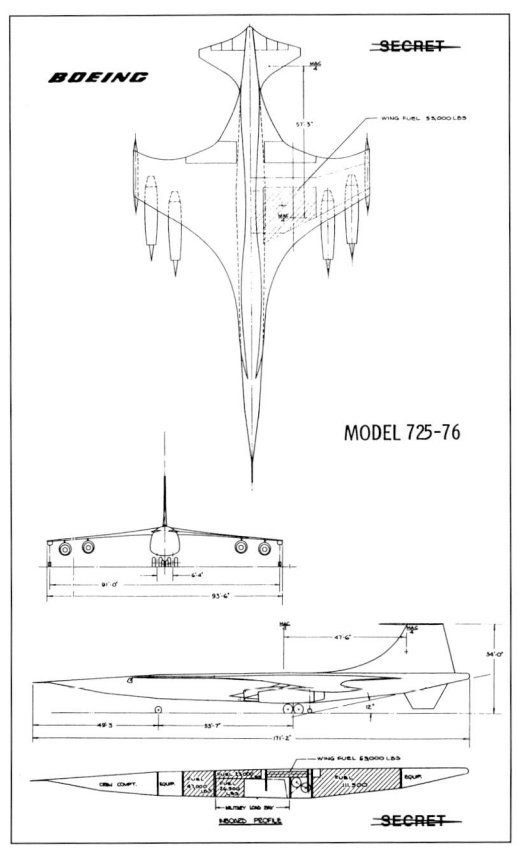

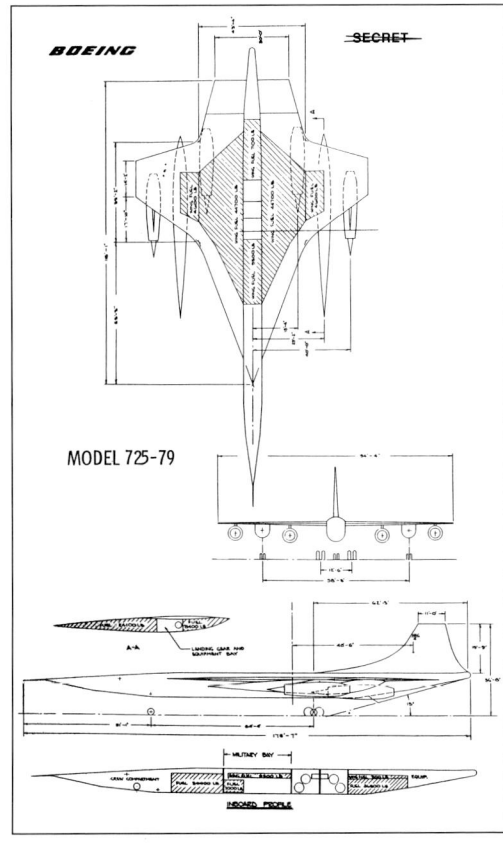

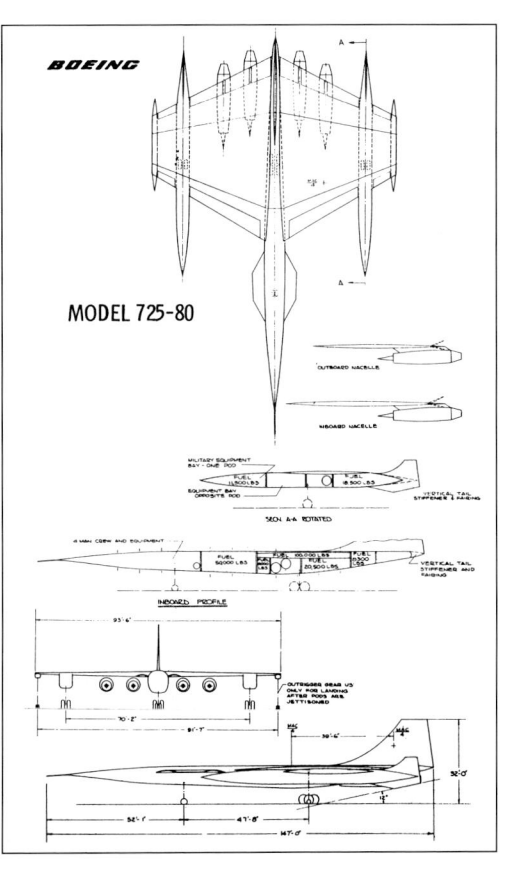

Chapter 2

27

Technical Voodoo

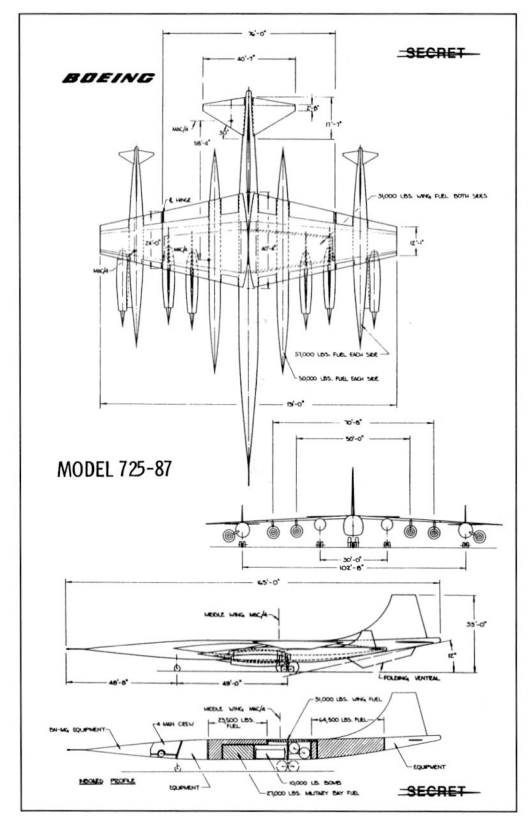

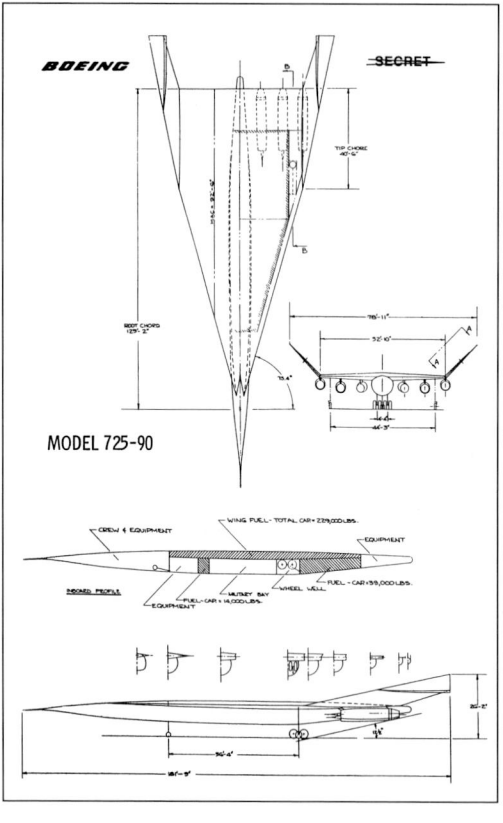

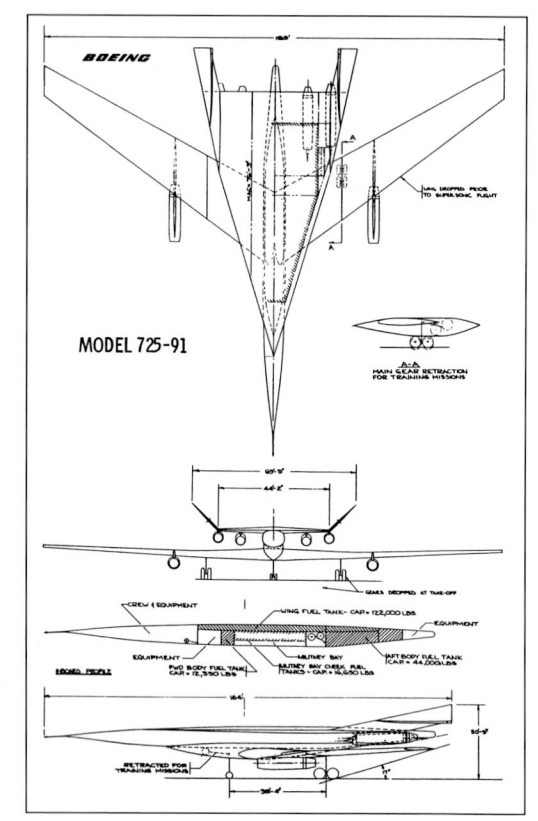

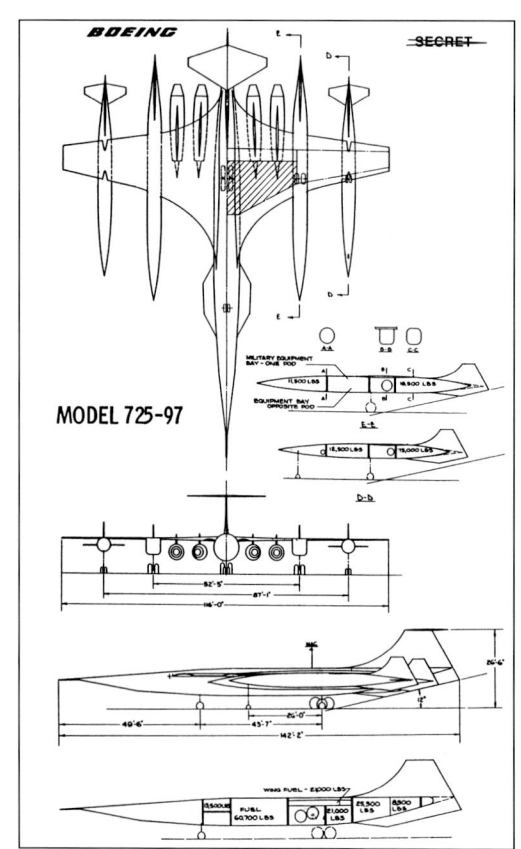

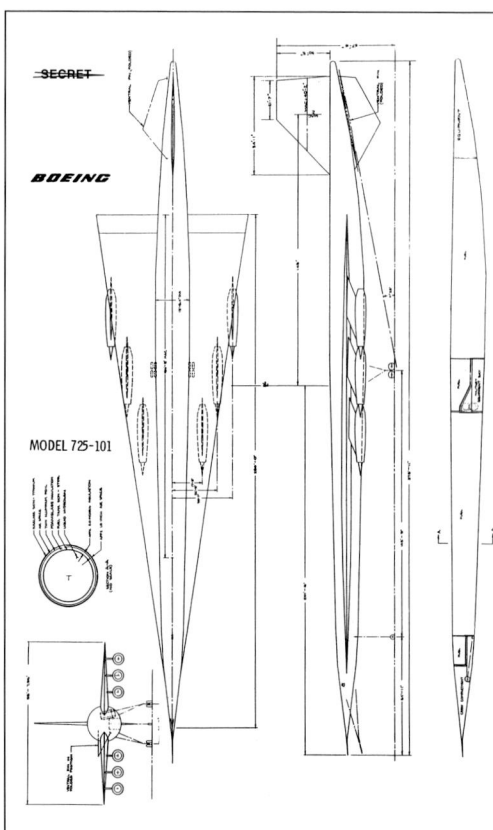

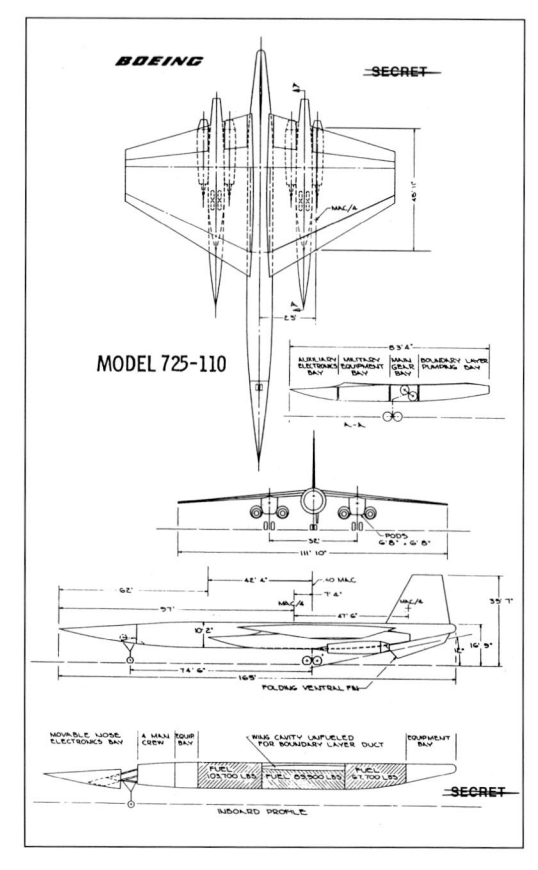

retracted into the fuselage just behind the weapons bay. The airplane had an empty weight of 135,500 pounds and a maximum takeoff weight of 350,000 pounds.[57]

Each of the Model 724-1003 floating wingtips was 75.8 feet long and had an oblique wing that spanned 90.8 feet. Since the wing continued the same sweep as the main airplane, each wingtip panel was different, although the fuel tanks themselves were identical. Each had an empty weight of 31,000 pounds and an all-up weight of 180,000 pounds. The wingtip panels were not reusable, did not have an engine, and were meant to be dropped prior to the airplane entering enemy airspace. They were equipped with landing gear to make ground handling easier, and to support themselves during taxi and takeoff.[58]

Boeing also proposed an alternate design to the Source Selection Board. The Model 724-16 had more powerful General Electric X279A engines, different floating wingtips, a higher flight weight (425,000 pounds), and a 4,000-pound increase in useful military load. This airplane was 175.25 feet long and had a wingspan of 93.5 feet. Instead of the retractable ramp of the Model 724-15, the –16 had an articulating nose: the forward 30 feet could swing down approximately 15 degrees to provide pilot vision during low-speed operations – shades of the supersonic transport a decade later. The articulating nose held the aerial refueling receptacle, all of the radar antennas, and some of the electronic equipment. The crew arrangement was also different, with the two systems operators facing backward directly behind the two pilots, all in individual escape capsules.[59]

While the Model 724 study was in progress, another effort was initiated that resulted in the Model 725. This study began in January 1956 with –1 and ran through December 1957 with the –143 under the direction of Benjamin Ruffner and D. W. Thurlow. The first concept was a chemically powered vehicle and looked at parameters such as variations in the bomb load and gross weight, afterburning versus non-afterburning engines, engine size and location, high-energy fuels, range extension vehicles, and canard and tail-less configurations. Models 725-41 through –45 were tail-less airplanes of various gross weights using a delta planform. The most developed of the Model 725 designs was the –44 configuration. This design had a 4,500 square foot delta wing that spanned 92.3 feet and a fuselage that was 150.6 feet long. Four X275 engines were located in individual pods on the outer wings. This part of the study concluded in April 1956.[60]

THE NORTH AMERICAN DESIGN, TAKE I

A note of caution is needed when discussing North American designs. The oft quoted "model numbers" were, in reality, internal tracking numbers. They simply defined tasks that the engineers and others charged their time against so that the company could bill the government. Unlike Boeing, where the model numbers indicated a specific design, North American also used its "model numbers" to track things like flight test efforts and advanced studies. From a historical perspective this makes it much harder to track the evolution of the WS-110A (or any other) design through the process since immediate derivatives were seldom uniquely identified. This is com-

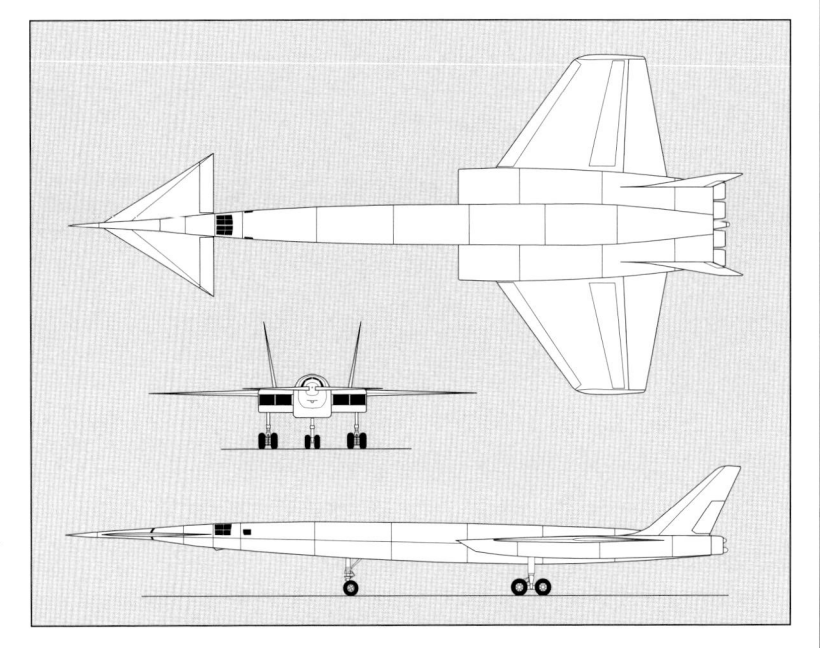

North American investigated this concept powered by high-energy fuels, and without the floating wing panels found on later designs. The shape would carry over to subsequent concepts. (Art by Tony Landis)

plicated by the fact that very few records survived the various reorganizations, mergers, and buyouts that plagued North American over the years. Nevertheless, here is what we know.

An intermediate version of the North American floating panel design. Compare the canards and the wingtip fuel tanks with the version on the following page. Also note that the fuselage "neck" extends further rearward, similar to the eventual B-70. (Boeing Historical Archives)

TECHNICAL VOODOO

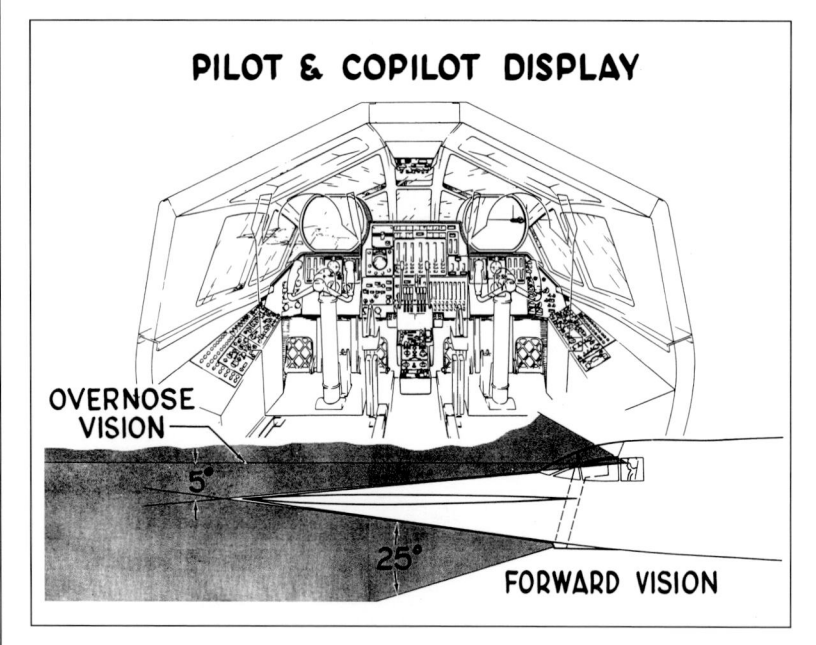

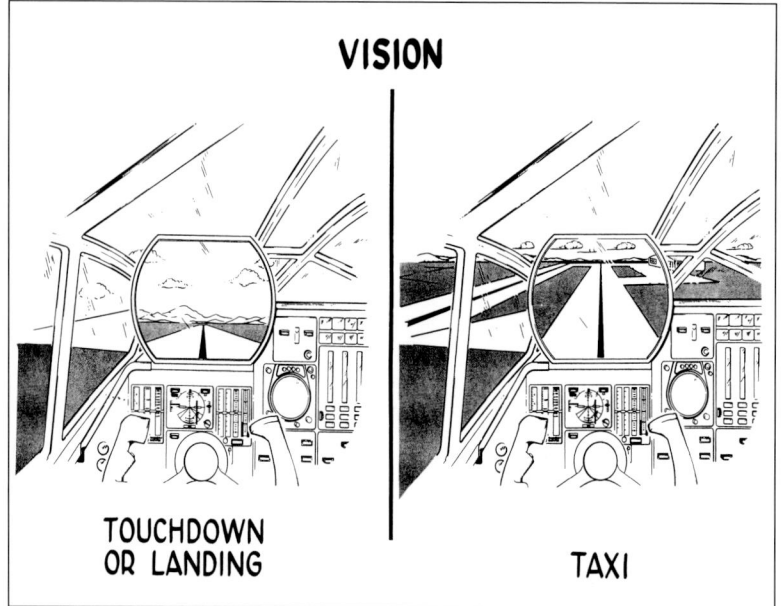

PILOT & COPILOT DISPLAY

OVERNOSE VISION
5°
25°
FORWARD VISION

VISION

TOUCHDOWN OR LANDING

TAXI

The engineers at North American attempted to explain that the far-forward canards did not create a major visibility problem. This set of drawings showing that the pilots had reasonable vision at all times, but the Air Force was not convinced. The drawings also indicate how the cockpit was expected to look, with round-dial and tape-style instrumentation. (Boeing Historical Archives)

The initial proposal effort for WS-110A was NA-239, called simply "SAC Bomber." This task was begun under Air Force contract AF33(600)-31801 and covered both Phase I and Phase II studies. The official North American model number log describes this effort as "Engineering design proposal and mockup for WS-110A/L. WS-110L cancelled on 7 June 1956."

This was the North American floating wingtip concept that was presented to the Air Force. Note the position of the canard, directly in front and below the pilots; the Air Force was concerned that this would present operational problems by restricting visibility during landing and takeoff. The twin vertical stabilizers that would ultimately appear on the B-70 were already present, although the inlets for the four X275 engines look much like those used on the A-5 Vigilante. (above: Boeing via the Gerald H. Balzer Collection; below: Boeing via the Terry Panopalis Collection)

Technical Voodoo

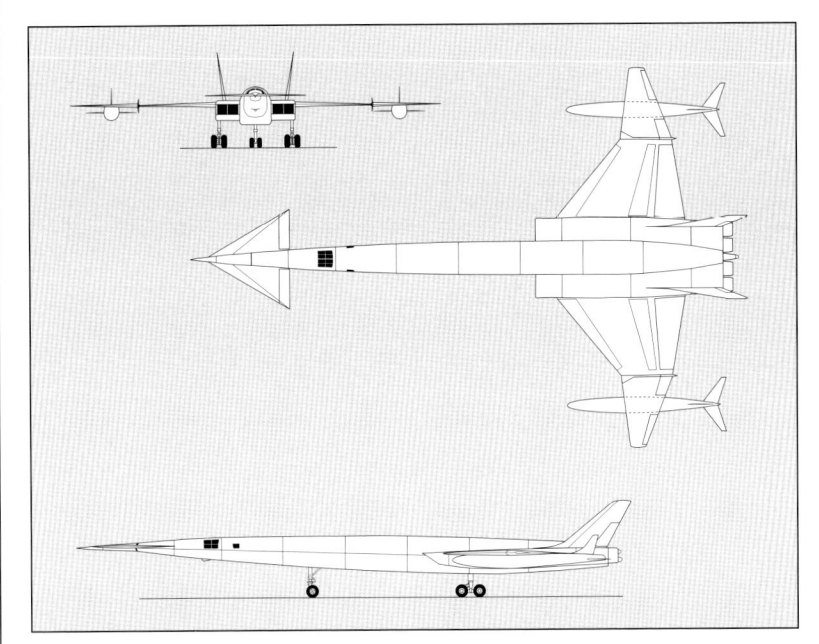

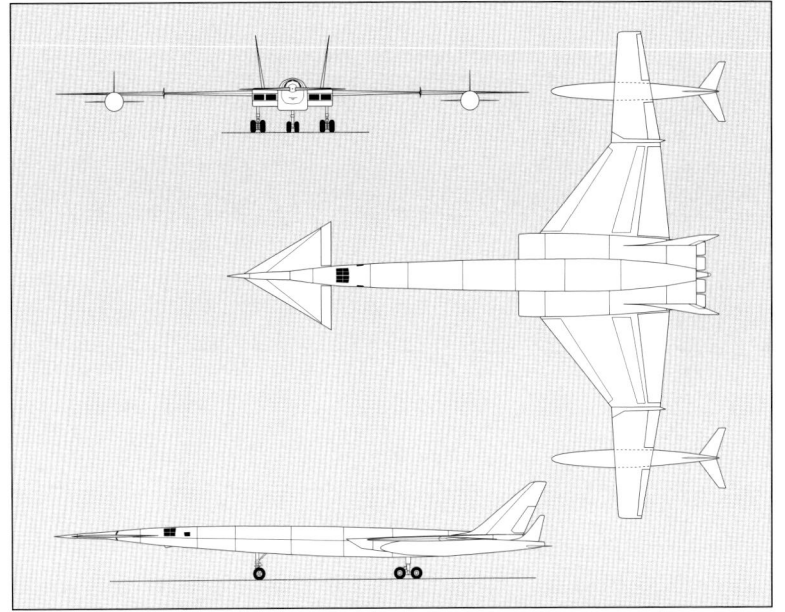

The evolution of the North American design shows that the floating wingtips kept getting larger. The first design (upper left) was meant to run on high-energy fuel, but this approach was abandoned in favor of conventional JP-4 for the other designs. The two versions at top used four engines each, while the final version (below) used six engines. The canard also changed shape, although it remained in the same unsatisfactory location. Note the drop tanks located under the wings of the design below left. As with the similar Boeing design, the Air Force was not particularly excited by the prospects of these "three ship formations" and sent the manufacturers back to the drawing boards. (Art by Tony Landis)

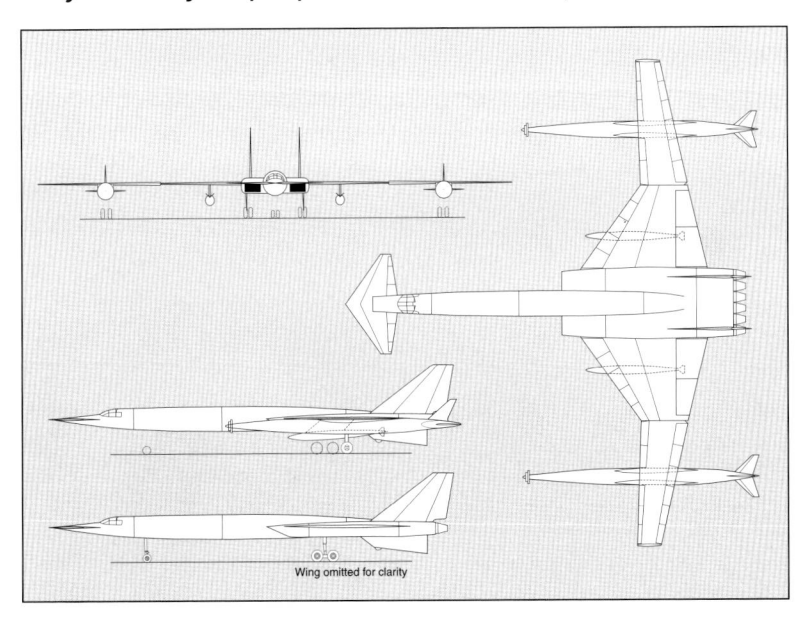

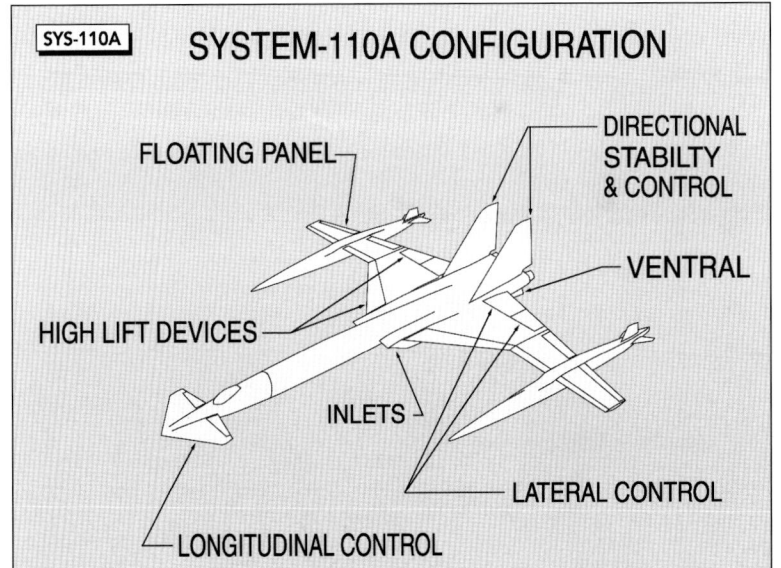

In March 1955 the North American design had a gross takeoff weight of over 450,000 pounds, was 182 feet long, and spanned 88 feet. The airplane would cruise at subsonic speeds to the target, and then accelerate to its Mach 2.75 dash speed for the final penetration. The airplane burned a high-energy chemical fuel in four General Electric X275 engines located in the aft fuselage, fed by an intake on either side of the fuselage ahead of the wing. Twin vertical stabilizers and a large nose-mounted canard provided directional stability. The crew sat in a flush cockpit and used a periscope for visibility. Interestingly, documentation indicates that the design had cannon mounted in a tail turret for defense.[61]

By April 1955, the design had evolved considerably. The same basic airplane was fitted with a set of floating wingtips to carry additional fuel, resulting in a gross weight of over 650,000 pounds. The

Technical Voodoo

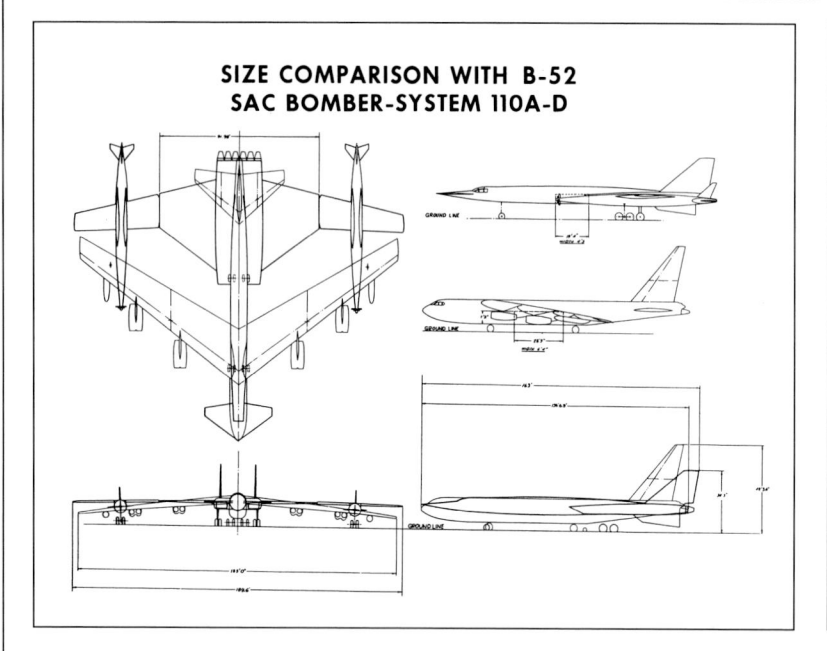

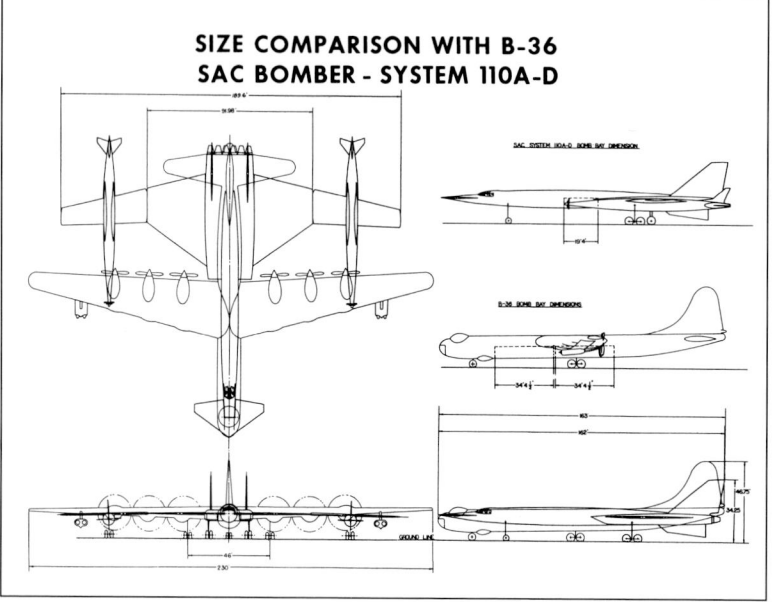

North American produced these two charts to compare the proposed WS-110A with the B-36 and B-52. The overall size of the three airplanes was comparable. The runway footprint of the WS-110A was very similar to the B-52 with its outrigger gear, and both the WS-110A and B-52 had much larger footprints than the more conventional landing gear on the B-36. (Boeing Historical Archives)

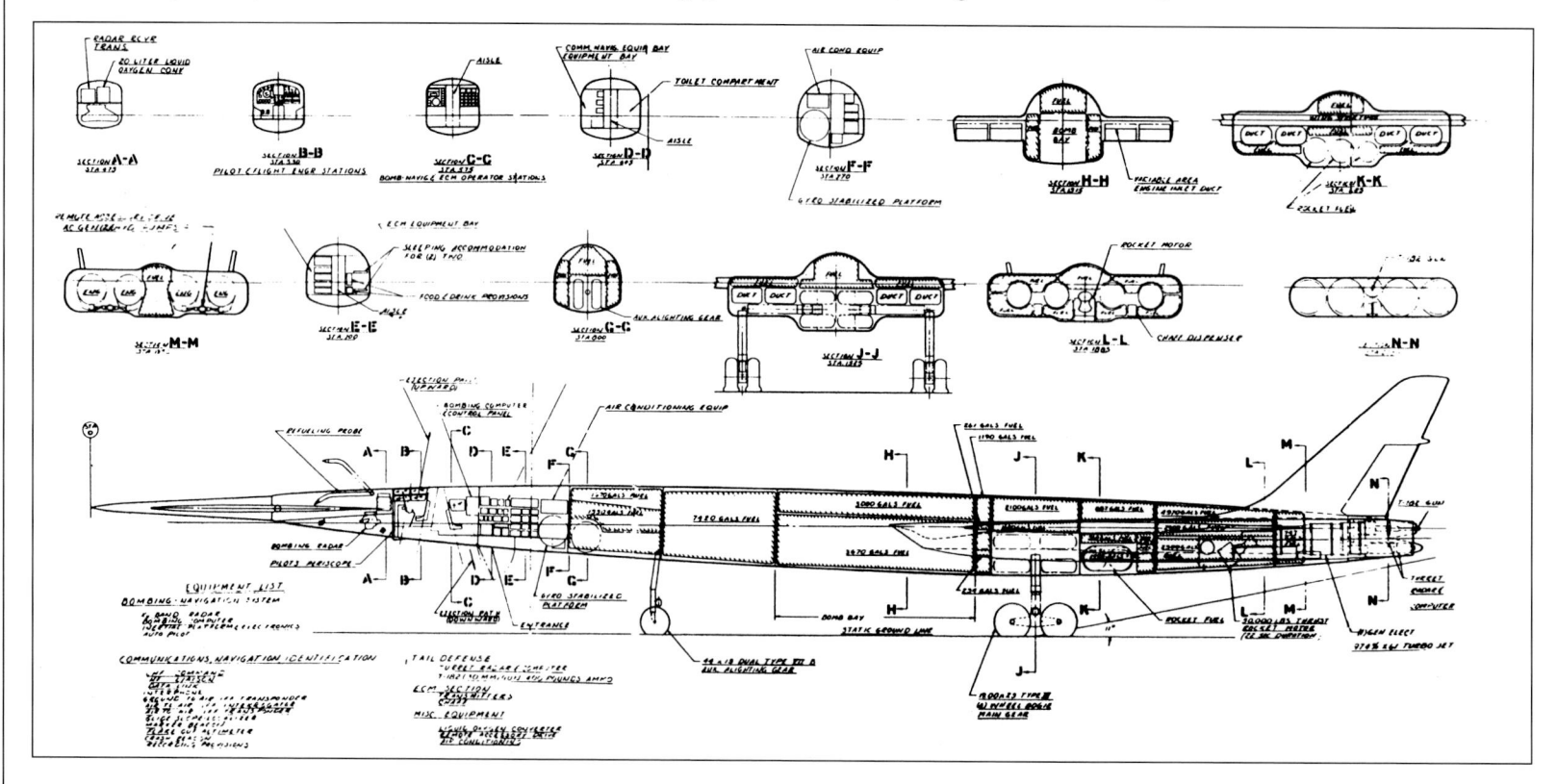

This particular variant of the North American design was meant to use high-energy fuels (see illustration on page 29), but is still representative of the general design. Note the rocket fuel and 22,000-lbf takeoff assist rocket just behind the main landing gear, the tail turret, and that the backseat crewmen faced rearward. The weapons bay is at section H-H with a fuel tank on each side of it. (Boeing Historical Archives)

fuel was specified as JP-4 instead of the high-energy fuel used previously. The basic airplane was essentially the same size, and each fuel tank was just over 61 feet long with a 40-foot wingspan.[62]

The design continued to evolve and by July 1956, the floating wingtip idea had increased in gross weight to approximately 700,000 pounds. At this point, the airplane was only 162 feet long, with a basic wingspan of 92 feet. Two 1,500-gallon drop tanks could be carried under the wing at mid-span in addition to the floating wingtips. By now, six General Electric X279A engines of 27,070-lbf each were required for power, but JP-4 fuel was still being specified. The floating wingtip panels were each 92 feet long with a span of almost 49 feet, resulting in a complete airplane spanning 190 feet. A large canard was located in front of the cockpit, severely hindering the forward visibility at high angles of attack (such as landing and take-off). This is generally the design that is depicted when discussing the early North American concepts.[63] North American compared the design with both a B-36 and a B-52, with some interesting results. For instance, the B-36 had four bomb bays that totaled 69 feet in length and could accommodate 84,000 pounds of bombs; the new design had a weapons bay somewhat less than 20 feet long that could accommodate only 10,000 pounds. The B-52 fell somewhere in the middle with a 29-foot-long bomb bay that could accommodate 25,000 pounds. The B-36 had a far greater wingspan than either of the others (230 feet versus 185 for the B-52 and 190 for the new design), but unlike the others the B-36 did not have outrigger landing gear and could operate off of much narrower runways. (The B-36 had a track of 46 feet, compared to 135 feet for the floating wingtip airplane and the outrigger-gear on the B-52.)[64]

BACK TO THE DRAWING BOARD

Besides the floating wingtips, the preliminary Boeing and North American designs had another factor in common – both were rejected by the Air Force. Upon seeing the concepts, Curtis LeMay is reported as saying, "These aren't airplanes, they are three-ship formations." At roughly 750,000 pounds fully loaded, 300,000 pounds more than the B-36 or B-52, there were no runways in the world that could support either proposed aircraft. Additionally, many in the Air Force had grown wary of the floating panel concept after the 1953 TIP TOW crash. In September 1956, a disappointed Air Staff recommended that both contractors "return to the drawing board."[65]

However, by that time both North American and Boeing were practically out of funding and had been authorized to continue the study "on a sustaining basis" only. On 18 October 1956 Air Force Headquarters directed that the Phase I development efforts be discontinued and the contractors return to preliminary studies. The disappointing designs and fiscal problems led to the entire WS-110A effort being extended 14 months, delaying the first flight date of the aircraft from April 1960 until June 1961. Matters were further complicated in January 1957 when the Air Force dictated another 11 month schedule slip – caused by more funding concerns – pushing first flight out to May 1962 and the first delivery to SAC to November 1964.[66]

Returning to a "preliminary study" status allowed both contractors to seriously reconsider their design approach. Technology was advancing at a rapid pace and all concerned were getting smarter. New developments included turbojet engines with reduced supersonic fuel consumption, and basic research in aerodynamics at the NACA Ames Aeronautical Laboratory allowed the contractors to refine their airframe configurations to varying degrees. During late 1956 and early 1957, both contractors realized that if the entire aircraft was optimized for a single flight condition – as opposed to the split mission configuration designed to accommodate two conditions – the combat radius of an all-supersonic vehicle could be competitive with subsonic ones. The engine contractors seemed to support this theory. Both airframe contractors also concluded that, as suggested by the Air Force, a boron-based high-energy fuel used in the engine afterburner would provide a 10- to 15-percent increase in range over conventional JP-4. North American had already briefly toyed with this idea during 1955. This extra range, however, would come at a significant cost in terms of fuel system complexity and engine design. (See Chapter 4 for a history of the HEF program.) By March 1957, it seemed almost certain that the new weapon system could be an all-supersonic cruise vehicle instead of one using the split-mission scenario. Both contractors quickly abandoned the floating wingtip concept and each began investigating the use of high-energy fuel to allow for smaller aircraft or significantly longer ranges or greater payloads in some combination.[67]

During the spring of 1956, there had been three engines under active consideration: the Allison J89, General Electric X275, and Pratt & Whitney J91. The race became a two-way contest after the all-supersonic mission model was adopted, effectively ruling out the J89 that was optimized for subsonic cruise. The two remaining engines were gradually tailored to the anticipated needs of the advanced bomber. The giant J91 was scaled down and transformed into a Mach 3 engine; as a Navy-sponsored project it became the J58 that would go on to power the Lockheed Blackbirds. The General Electric X275, which began as a scaled-up J79, became the X279 when it was optimized for Mach 3 cruising and eventually became the J93.[68]

Since both of the airframe contractors favored the General Electric engine over that from Pratt & Whitney, on 26 July 1957 the Air Force issued a letter contract for the development of the X279E (the fifth major variant studied). This engine was officially designated XJ93-GE-1 on 25 September 1957 and the definitive contract, AF33(600)-35824, was signed on 14 May 1958. The new engine – the most powerful ever conceived – was a medium-pressure-ratio turbojet with a mass airflow of approximately 220 pounds per second and a potential speed of more than Mach 3. Interestingly, the engine contract made no mention of high-energy fuels.[69]

On 30 August 1957, the Air Force – having acquired funding and assuming the concept had been studied sufficiently – told the airframe contractors that a winner would be selected after a short competitive design period. On 18 September, the Air Force issued a final request for proposals that called for a cruise speed of Mach 3.0 to Mach 3.2, an altitude of 70,000 to 75,000 feet, a range of 6,100 to 10,500 nautical miles, and a gross weight between 475,000 and 490,000 pounds. The bomber was to be capable of operating in accordance with the "SAC alert concept" where one third of a unit's aircraft were to be airborne "within 15 minutes after receipt of the order" to launch. The final Boeing and North American proposals would be due in 45 days.[70]

The resulting designs were for much more realistic aircraft. They were about the same length as the B-52, but had slightly less wingspan, were a little taller, and weighed about 10 percent more. Both aircraft were designed to use existing B-52 bases and to be maintained by existing skills available to SAC. Although delayed, it appeared that WS-110A was finally on a more realistic track.

THE BOEING DESIGN, TAKE II

Despite the fiscal problems being experienced on WS-110A, during November 1956 Boeing made a concentrated effort to achieve a technical breakthrough in airplane performance to meet more nearly the WS-110A requirements. During an in-house program known as "Tea Bag" Boeing went back and reevaluated all of the design studies that had led to the floating wingtip concept to determine if any of them offered promise. Led by Edward Z. Gray, this effort studied no less than 28 basic concepts, with many parametric excursions from each. The ideas included all-supersonic profiles, subsonic-cruise, supersonic-dash profiles, floating wingtip designs, hydrogen-powered designs, and one design that used an innovative approach to boundary layer control to extend its range. These designs all carried either Model 724 or Model 725 designations; the results of the study were published in December 1956.[71]

The investigation of the all-supersonic configuration seemed to yield the most promise, so Boeing started to concentrate on that

The second round of aircraft from both manufacturers were much more reasonable than the floating wingtip idea had been. This is the Boeing Model 801-1, showing an obvious resemblance to some of the original Boeing SST concepts. Note the individual engines with three-dimensional inlets (like the Lockheed Blackbird) and the lack of a canard. (Boeing Historical Archives)

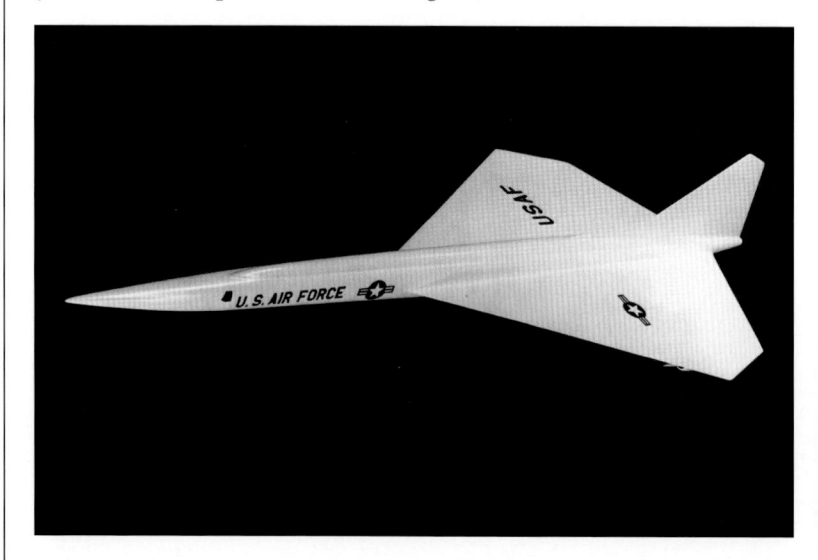

The Model 804-1 was exceptionally clean-looking, with very few external bumps or control surfaces other than a large vertical stabilizer and a small fixed ventral fin. This was the first Mach 3-cruise design presented to the Air Force by Boeing. (Boeing via the Terry Panopalis Collection)

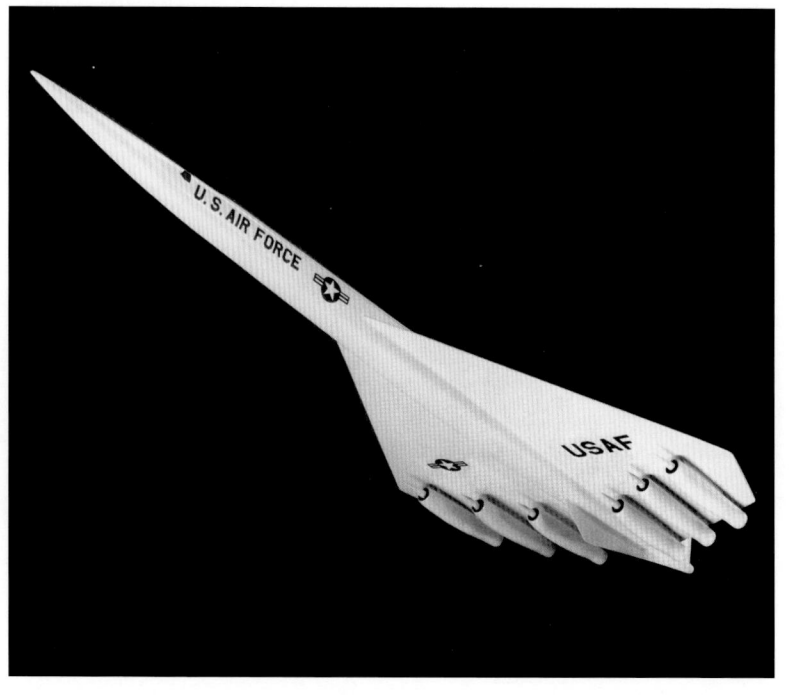

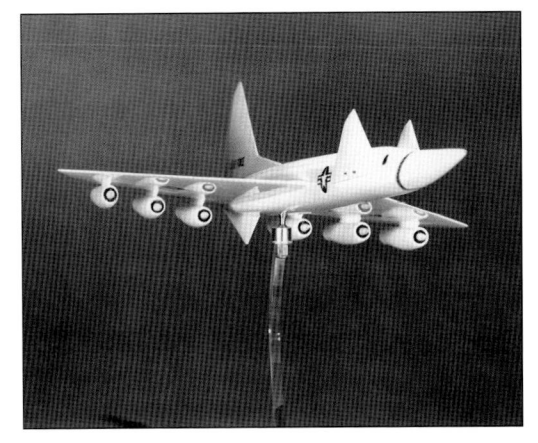

This is the Model 804-4 that was presented to the source selection board and ultimately lost to the North American design. It was substantially similar to the earlier Model 804-1 except for the large folding canard (which had been added to the Model 804-1A). (Boeing Historical Archives)

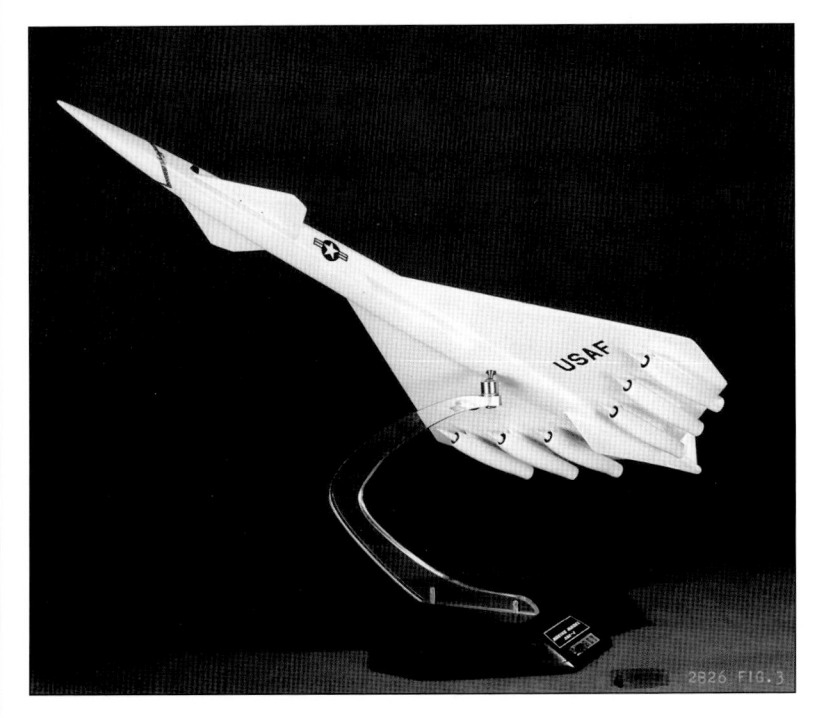

idea. The Model 804 began with the –1 in February 1957 and ended on 23 December 1957 with the –10 derivative. H. W. "Bob" Withington and Lloyd Goodmanson led the study. The Model 804-1 was a development of the Model 725-115 and tailless delta wing configurations studied during Tea Bag.[72]

The Model 804-1 was a sleek, delta-wing airplane that was 201.1 feet long with a 94.5-foot wingspan. The wing planform, although described as a delta, was actually a large trapezoid with clipped wingtips. No canard or horizontal control surfaces were used. A large dorsal vertical stabilizer and smaller ventral stabilizer provided directional stability. Six X279E turbojets were arranged in individual pods under the trailing edge of the wing. The airplane had a maximum taxi weight of 499,500 pounds with a 24,200-pound military load (weapons and defensive systems).[73]

The crew of four was arranged with the offensive and defensive systems operators facing rearward behind the pilots, each in individual escape capsules. The complex articulating nose used on some Model 724/725 configurations was abandoned, leaving the pilot with no forward visibility during low-speed operations except via a television system. The single weapons bay was offset to the left side of the fuselage (a fuel tank occupied the other side).[74]

Technical Voodoo

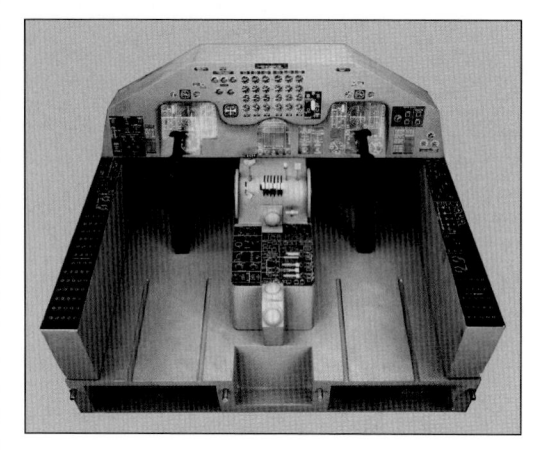

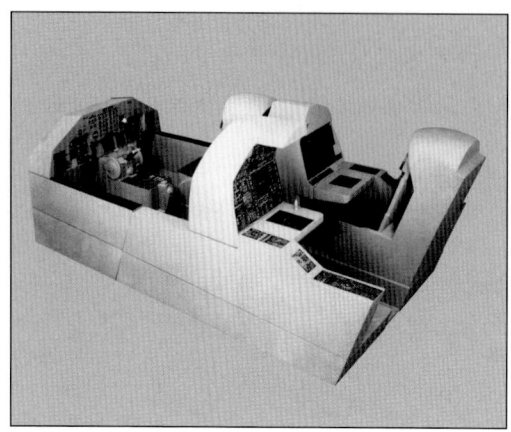

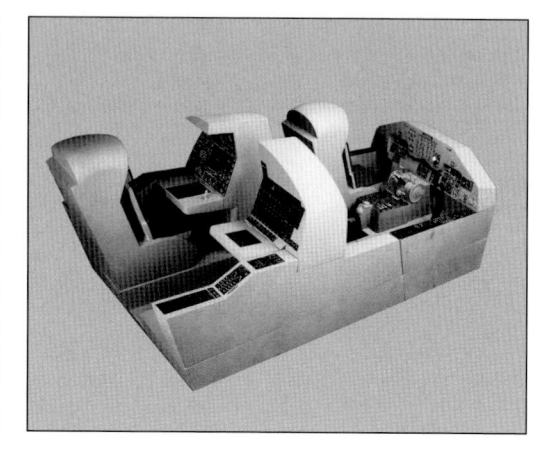

The proposed cockpit of the Model 804-4 was conventional, with the offensive and defensive operators sitting behind the two pilots facing forward. Each crewmember had an individual escape capsule very similar to the ones ultimately used on the B-70. (Boeing Historical Archives)

Further study into the aerodynamic characteristics of this airplane resulted in the addition of a large (350 square foot) canard surface on the Model 804-1A in July 1957. Externally, this revised configuration was almost identical – excepting the canard – to the basic airplane, although it grew to 208.6 feet long. Internally, the crew compartment was rearranged so that all four crewmembers faced forward.[75]

The Model 804-2 used a different fuselage shape and increased wing sweep with slightly larger engines, but was not pursued very far. The Model 804-3 had a greater wing sweep, and a short life. The Model 804-5 used larger engines, while the Model 804-6 had a 650,000-pound gross weight. Neither was considered satisfactory.[76]

This left the Model 804-4, which was submitted to the Source Selection Board evaluation team during a meeting of 4–6 November 1957. This design had a gross weight of 542,000 pounds and a large canard surface that folded to an upright position during subsonic flight and lowered to horizontal during supersonic flight. Exactly why this complicated approach was adopted was not explained. Externally, the airplane – excepting the odd canard – did not differ significantly from the Model 804-1A although the wing planform was a little less trapezoidal.[77]

The Model 804-4 was just over 206 feet long with a 94.5-foot wingspan and the six X279J (a later version of the X279E) turbojets were still in individual pods under the back of the wing. Small windows allowed limited forward vision from the cockpit, although they were recessed into the fuselage and would probably have provided next to no visibility during the high-angle-of-attack landings that are normal of a delta-wing airplane. Once more the crew faced forward, still seated in individual escape capsules. The weapons bay was enlarged to occupy the entire fuselage cross-section and could carry a single 10,000-pound or single 25,000-pound weapon. A large VLF antenna, characteristic of many of the Boeing designs, projected rearward from the trailing edge of the vertical stabilizer. A drag chute was provided to help slow the airplane, allowing it to operate from any runway capable of accommodating the B-52.[78]

Although the Model 804-4 was the final design entered into the WS-110A competition, Boeing continued to evaluate several other

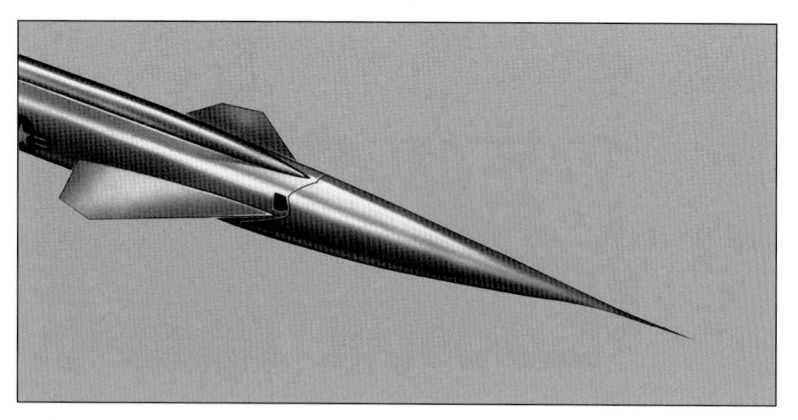

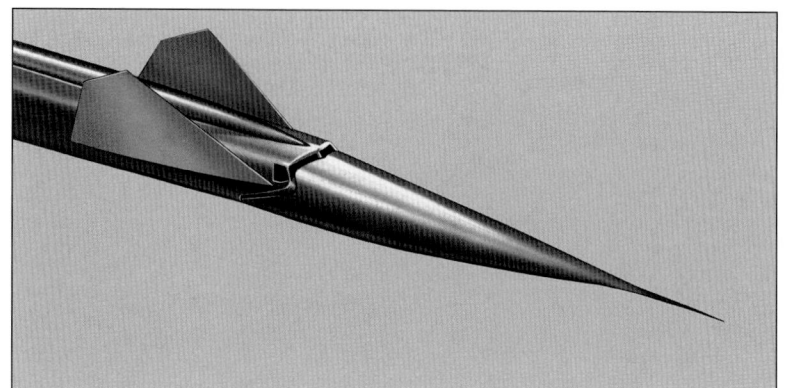

The nose section of the Boeing Model 804-4 was certainly odd. A large canard folded upright during subsonic flight, lowering to horizontal as the airplane went supersonic; no explanation for this design concept could be found. Similar to the future Concorde and Boeing SST designs, the entire nose articulated downward to provide better visibility during landing and takeoff. (Boeing Historical Archives)

Technical Voodoo

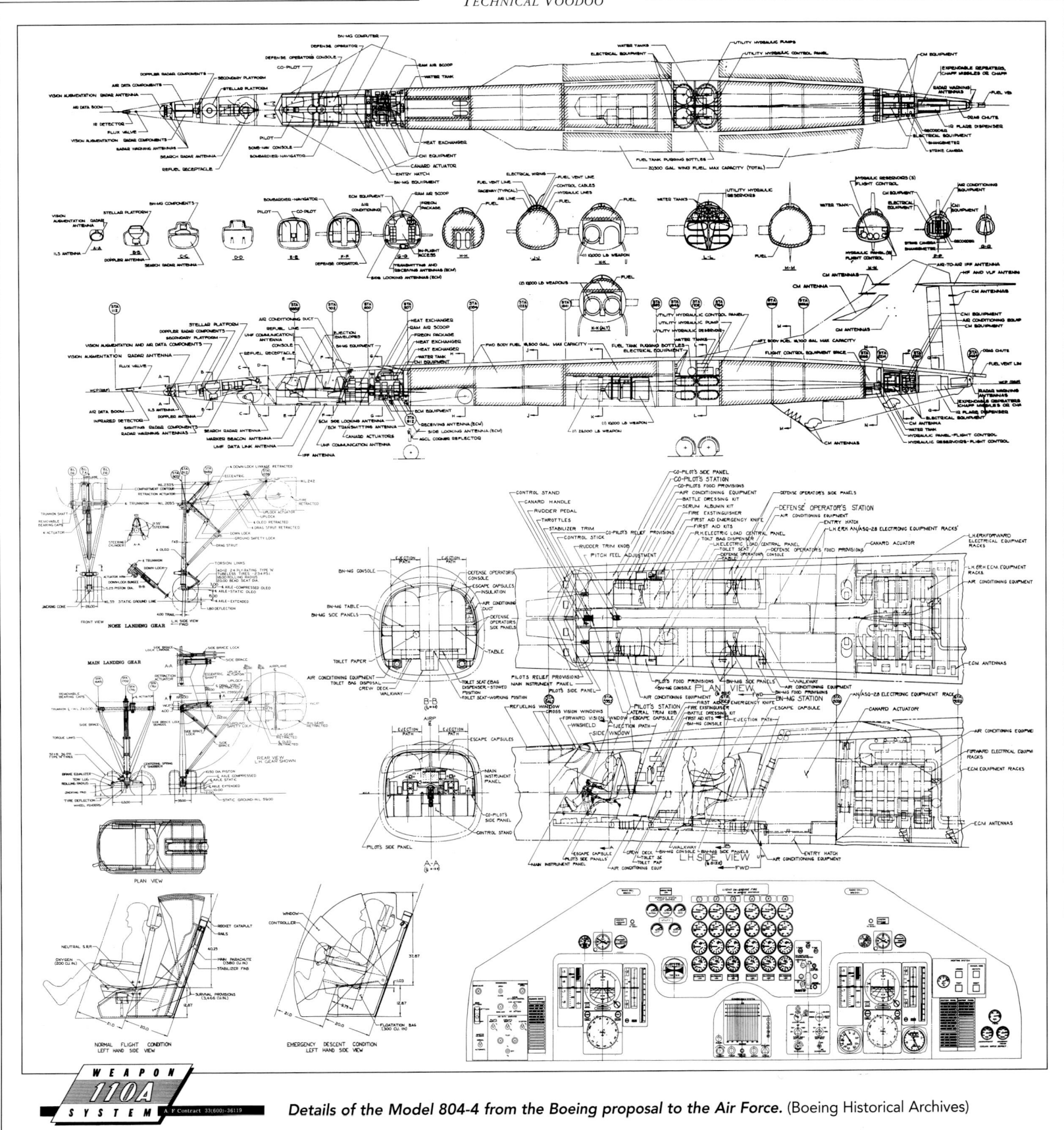

Details of the Model 804-4 from the Boeing proposal to the Air Force. (Boeing Historical Archives)

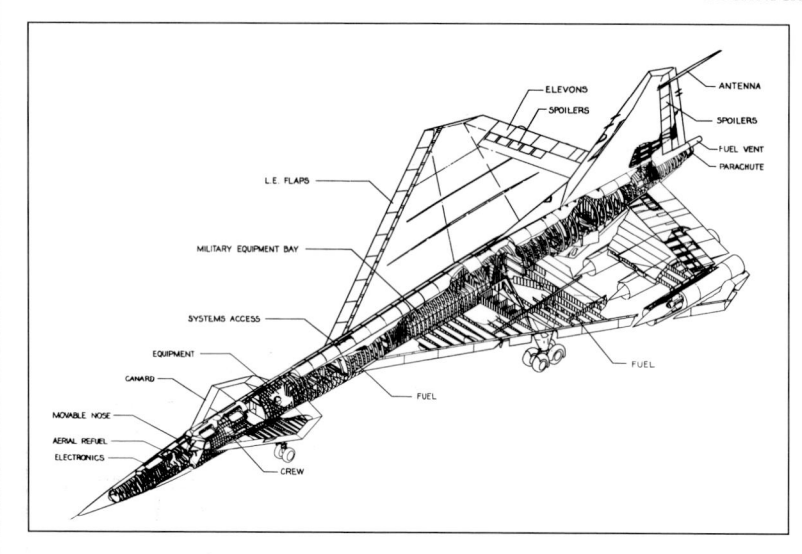

The Model 804-4 had several features that would have been welcomed during the B-70 flight program, such as the much more straightforward landing gear. However, the Air Force did not believe the aircraft would perform as well as the North American entry and the 804 would get no further than these drawings. (Boeing Historical Archives)

concepts. The Model 804-7 used six Pratt & Whitney J58 turbojet engines, the Model 804-8 had six dual-cycle J58s and could cruise at Mach 4, the Model 804-9 used six dual-cycle X279 engines for Mach 4 cruise, and the Model 804-10 had six dual-cycle Curtiss-Wright DC-36 engines. None were submitted to the Air Force.[79]

THE NORTH AMERICAN DESIGN, TAKE II

After being told to go back to the drawing board things began to come together fairly quickly at North American, with the legendary Harrison Storms heading the design team. Unfortunately, little documentation exists to trace the progress of the effort. In early 1957, the design had taken on the general look of the eventual B-70 with a large aft-mounted delta wing, a canard mounted behind the cockpit on a long fuselage that resembled a bird's neck, and a conventional windscreen with no moving ramps. A gross weight of 450,00 pounds was envisioned, with power coming from six X279 engines burning either JP-4 or high-energy fuel buried in the fuselage. Small folding wingtips were provided for additional directional control at high speeds; oddly North American referred to these as variable-geometry wings, although they were very different from the swing-wings the world later thought of as variable-geometry. This design was intended to cruise at Mach 3 and had a projected range of 5,200 nautical miles. A single 13-foot long weapons bay was located at the front of the lower fuselage.[80]

North American went somewhat out on the limb and included a bit of aerodynamic voodoo in the proposal. Without the floating wingtips to provide additional range, North American engineers had pored through every aerodynamic study they could find, looking for anything that could be applied to the new bomber. What they "dis-covered" during the literature search was a report written by NACA[81] researchers Alfred J. Eggers and Clarence A. Syverston on 5 March 1956. The paper, *Aircraft Configurations Developing High Lift/Drag Ratios at High Supersonic Speeds*, suggested that a high-speed aircraft could be designed such that the lift-over-drag ratio could be increased in supersonic flight by relying on pressure from the shock wave impinging on the lower surfaces of the wings.[82]

In general, "compression lift" is achieved by positioning the wing in a manner to take advantage of the pressure field behind the shock wave generated by the fuselage body. Since a supersonic air inlet for the engines must create a disturbance in the form of a shock wave in order to compress and slow the incoming air and make it available to the engines, North American already had a ready source of a large pressure field. The first shock of that compression was generated by the fixed-wedge at the front of the inlet. At Mach 3 this shock wave was bent back about 65 degrees and there was a 0.3-Mach reduction from in front of the shock wave to just aft of it. This resulted in an average pressure rise of 40 pounds per square foot (psf). By shaping the underbody at the same angle, the compression field was maintained for most of the length of the fuselage. Superimposing the wing on top of the shock system exposed nearly the entire undersurface of the wing to the pressure rise. Since there was no equivalent pressure wave on top of the wing to cancel it out, roughly a 30-percent increase in lift was available with no drag penalty. Actually, the concept reduced drag, at least indirectly. A more conventional airplane would likely need to cruise at an angle-of-attack of about 4 degrees; the shock-riding design could cruise at 2 degrees. Since the drag due to lift at Mach 3 is essentially

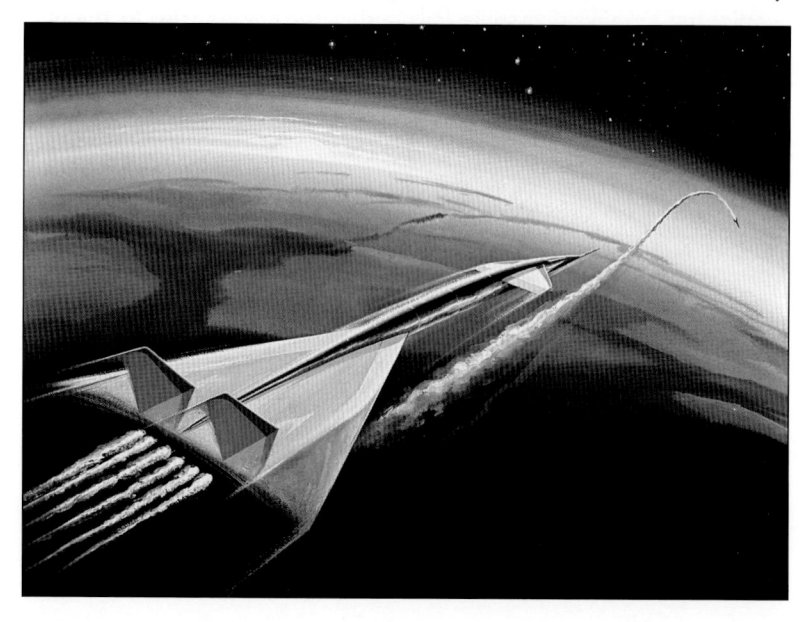

It is hard to date this North American concept since it does not truly resemble any of the proposals. Note the general similarity to the drawing on page 12, although it now has twin vertical stabilizers and the missile is taking more of an arc toward its target. Oddly, this concept seems to have large folding wingtips. (Boeing Historical Archives)

proportional to angle of attack, the improvement was considerable. All of this would substantially increase the range – if it worked.[83]

It should be noted that compression lift did not depend on the wingtips folding downward as they did in the ultimate North American design, although that feature did help capture some of the shock under the wing. Instead, North American folded the wingtips primarily to increase directional stability and minimize drag by allowing smaller vertical stabilizers.

The North American design was unique. A main underbody fuselage housed two large two-dimensional air intakes for the six General Electric engines. The leading edge of the inlets were swept at 65 degrees to correspond to the first shock wave and maximize the compression lift effect. A large delta wing sat over the underbody fuselage with two large vertical stabilizers mounted just outboard of the engines. A long "neck" protruded forward from the top of the wing with the cockpit at the extreme front and a delta-shape canard just behind and over the crew compartment. It appears that even at this point, small portions of the outer wings could be folded downward at high speeds to provide additional directional stability. Surprisingly, very little documentation shows the actual North American submittal to the Source Selection Board.

Designing a Mach 3 inlet was complicated, and North American took a unique approach with a two-dimensional variable-geometry inlet that fed multiple engines instead of the single three-dimensional inlet per engine used by Boeing on most of its designs and Lockheed on the Blackbird. There was a great deal of debate over the single-engine-per-inlet versus grouped engine concepts. When a podded engine employing a translating spike fails (either the engine fails, or the inlet unstarts), the air essentially "piles up" in front of the engine, forming a natural shock wave and greatly increasing drag. The loss of thrust, compounded by the increased drag, further compounded by the distance from the aircraft centerline, causes excessive yaw. If there are multiple podded engines on one wing, it is conceivable that the yaw will be great enough to blank the airflow to the other engines, causing even more problems. By grouping the engines together near the centerline and sharing intakes, North American had hoped to minimize this concern. However, as Flight 1-12 would later prove, having a common air intake could lead to damage to multiple engines from a single FOD event.[84]

At low supersonic speeds, oblique shocks formed on the external ramps, slowing the air to the subsonic speeds required by the engines. North American kept the terminal shock outside the inlet because the internal area contraction was too great to swallow the normal shock at low supersonic speeds. Bypass doors were provided that allowed excess air to spill overboard. As flight speed increased, the external normal shock could be swallowed and the inlet "started." At the design Mach 3 cruise speed the external shock decelerated the flow at about Mach 2.3 at the cowl lip and internal oblique shocks further reduced flow at about Mach 1.3 at the inlet throat. The normal shock at the throat increased the static pressure by a factor of two and the subsonic diffuser further raised the pressure. North American predicted that the inlet would provide ten times more compression than the engines.[85]

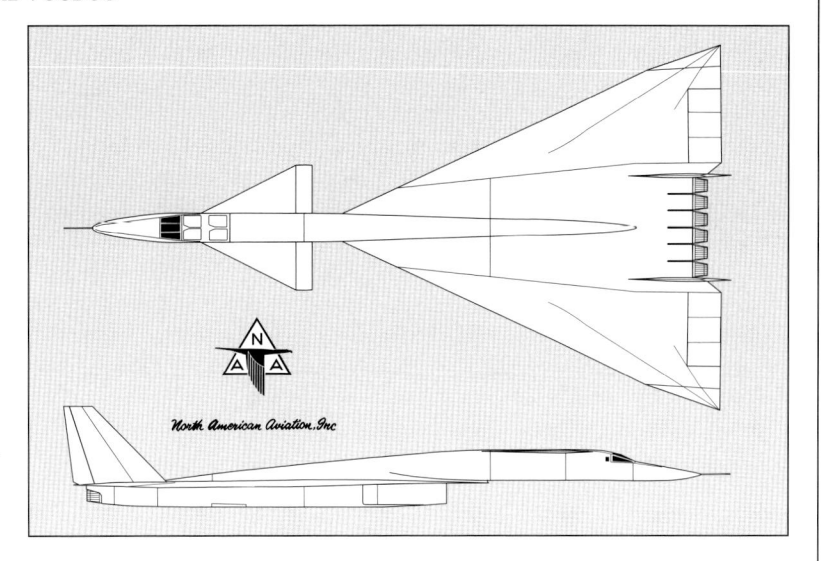

This was the design that North American submitted to the Source Selection Board the second time. It is clearly a Valkyrie, although many details would be refined before the two air vehicles were eventually built and flight tested. (Art by Tony Landis)

COMPRESSION LIFT ULTIMATELY WINS

The Air Force Source Selection Board evaluation team,[86] numbering about 60 members, reviewed the North American proposal during the last week of October 1957; Boeing had their turn during the first week of November.[87] On 27 November, the lead officers from each of the commands (AMC, ARDC, and SAC) reported their findings in a formal briefing to their commanders. The North American proposal was unanimously found to be superior, and the results were presented to the Air Staff on 11 December and the Air Council on 12 December. Secretary of the Air Force James H. Douglas was briefed the following day and concurred with the selection. The Air Force formally announced North American's selection on 23 December 1957.[88]

In support of the WS-110A effort, on 7 January 1958, the ARDC published a comprehensive statement that outlined the current thinking about manned bombers. It stated that although "surface-to-surface strategic bombardment missiles [e.g., ICBMs] having widely different characteristics will be operational as a vital portion of the strategic air arm" during the operational period of the WS-110A:[89]

> "...total dependence cannot be placed on these missiles due to uncertainties about their reliability, accuracy, flexibility of employment and relative immobility. Because of these uncertainties, the use of missiles in this era will be limited, initially at least, to unhardened accurately located targets. Such targets comprise only part of the strategic target system.
>
> "A second part of the strategic target system is composed of smaller targets, some of which may be hardened to the extent they can be destroyed only by accurate bombing with high yield weapons. For such tasks, a manned bomber is the only known system possessing the

such tasks, a manned bomber is the only known system possessing the needed and proven capabilities. In addition, man provides discretionary capabilities for target discrimination, malfunction correction or override, timely evasive maneuvers and judgment in selection and employment of penetration aids. These attributes, coupled with bomber flexibility of employment … are important considerations to the probability of success in a strategic campaign.

"A third important consideration requiring the continued use of manned weapon systems is related to the roles which the strategic air arm may be expected to play and kinds of wars in which it may be employed. In some instances, physically demonstrable presence may be sufficient. Alternately, it may be required to engage in a major conflict or in a limited war which may also mean limited weapons. Such possibilities attach decisive importance to the economic values associated with heavy payloads, high accuracies, recallability, and, in particular, recoverability."

With these elements in mind, the WS-110A was to operate from bases in the United States and be capable of striking anywhere in the world, in all types of weather, under the SAC alert concept. A 90-percent reliability factor became a requirement. The minimum unrefueled range was 6,000 nautical miles, with 11,000 desired. Bombing altitude was to be 60,000 feet, with 75,000 or higher desirable. For the first time, a low altitude (500 feet) bombing capability was also required. A speed of at least Mach 3 was required at high altitude, and Mach 0.9 for the low altitude penetration.[90]

Eight weapons loads were listed for the new bomber. For the "design mission," a 10,000-pound thermonuclear weapon was required, or alternately, a pair of 10,000-pound thermonuclear weapons for a shorter combat radius. Other possible loads included multiple units of small bombs, one 10,000-pound bomb along with a reduced load of small bombs, a single 20,000-pound bomb, a yet-to-be-developed air-to-surface missile and a 10,000-pound thermonuclear bomb, two missiles and one smaller bomb, or biological and chemical weapons. The missile – at this point part of the WS-110A development effort – was to have a range of at least 300 nautical miles with 700 nautical miles being desirable; accuracy (CEP) was to be 5,000 feet at 300 nautical miles, with 2,500 feet desirable.[91]

One of the most challenging problems faced by the engineers was designing and building an airplane that could operate in the thermal environment caused by aerodynamic heating; the total temperature at Mach 3 could reach 630 degrees Fahrenheit. In an industry that was using aluminum as the primary metal in airplane structure and surfaces, it now meant that stainless steel and, in some cases, titanium, would have to be used. New – and in many cases innovative and expensive – manufacturing techniques had to be developed for these heavier metals in order to keep the weight of the airplane at a usable level.[92]

North American signed contract AF33(600)-36599 for the Phase I development of WS-110A/L on 24 January 1958 and assigned the NA-259 internal reference number to the effort. At the time, the Air Force was expecting that the first operational wing of 30 aircraft could be available in late 1965. The aircraft component of WS-110A was designated B-70 on 14 February 1958. The WS-110L would likely have been RB-70, but it never got that far.[93]

Less than a month after contract award, in February 1958, the Air Force formally cancelled the development of WS-110L since it believed that "other systems" could better satisfy the reconnaissance requirements in the 1965 time frame. Contrary to popular opinion, the "other system" was the CORONA satellite program that was approved by President Eisenhower at the same time. Lockheed's Blackbird (A-12) was still a year or two in the future. There would

This is the design that won the B-70 competition. Note the large delta-shaped canard, very similar to the one on early F-108 designs – in fact, the entire aircraft looks like an enlarged version of the first F-108 design. Small folding wingtips provided additional directional stability at high speeds and were not related to the compression lift theory. (Boeing Historical Archives)

be no reconnaissance version of the B-70.[94]

At the same time that the reconnaissance requirement was being deleted, an acceleration of the B-70 program was being planned. On 7 March 1958, a revised GOR-82 was published for the B-70, and a tentative operational concept appeared six days later. The latter document called for the first test aircraft in January 1962, the initial delivery to SAC by October 1963, and the 45th inventory aircraft in August 1964. The revision also raised the unrefueled range requirement by 500 nautical miles (to 6,500), increased the cruise altitude to 80,000 feet, and specified a capability to deliver bombs from altitudes between 500 and 80,000 feet. Another revision, in April 1958, called for an unrefueled range of 6,873 nautical miles. Where the initial concept required the air-to-surface missile "concurrently with the introduction of the aircraft into the inventory," the latter revision added that this development was not to "delay the progress or procurement of the basic aircraft." Although this would bring the aircraft closer to the 1963 date desired by LeMay, the change would add an additional $165 million to the development cost. Nevertheless, the Air Staff approved the accelerated plan in principle on 19 March 1958.[95]

With a contract in hand, North American began issuing subcontracts for major portions of the B-70. Westinghouse was to design the defensive electronics system that would include advanced infrared and radar warning receivers, as well as sophisticated jamming equipment. General Electric would be responsible for the jam-resistant radars that would eventually be hooked up to the IBM AN/ASQ-28 offensive bombing-navigation subsystem (which was originally under separate Air Force contract, but later came under North American's purview). The airframe was divided between Boeing (wings), Chance-Vought (tail and elevons), Lockheed (aft fuselage), and various North American divisions. Sperry was providing a twin-gyro star tracker while Sundstrand designed the secondary power system. Cleveland Pneumatic provided the landing gear and Oster the engine instrumentation. And on it went – North American was well aware that spreading the wealth ensured that every Congressman and Senator would want to continue funding the program.

Although the General Electric engine had been conceived for the B-70, North American and the Air Force also intended to use the initial J93-GE-1 on the F-108 interceptor. On 13 January 1958, General Electric suggested a growth version of the –1 engine for the B-70 that featured higher internal and exhaust temperatures and used air-cooled turbine blades. This engine would produce slightly more thrust at Mach 3 and provide better specific fuel consumption, something more important to the B-70 than to the F-108. On 18 April 1958, the growth version of the engine was officially designated XJ93-GE-3 and programmed for the B-70. However, planning was also underway for a –5 engine using high-energy boron fuels.

By July 1958, General Electric reported that development would be greatly simplified if the –3 engine was used in the F-108 and early B-70 aircraft, pending availability of the boron burning –5 engine. Notable logistics support savings could also be achieved by using one engine, since a number of major components in the –1 and –3 were not interchangeable. As far as the F-108 was concerned, North American believed that the improved thrust and specific fuel consumption performance of the –3 engine compensated adequately for its 240 pounds of extra weight. The Air Force made the idea official on 8 September 1958; only the four –1 engines already being manufactured would be built, mainly to provide an early testing opportunity. All further effort would concentrate on the –3 engine. Interestingly, there was still no authorized –5 development effort, although General Electric and North American continued to plan around the high energy fuel engine.[96]

Like most combat aircraft of the period, the name for the B-70 was decided by a contest, not by a corporate advertising agency. In this case, SAC held an Air Force-wide contest that attracted 20,000 entries. The winner was an Air Force Sergeant who proposed Valkyrie, from the Maidens in Norse mythology.[97] The name became official on 3 July 1958.[98]

In the summer of 1958, the Air Force again considered the possibility of supporting the Pratt & Whitney J58 as a backup engine for the J93, but elected not to. It was decided, however, to contribute a small amount of funding to the Navy's J58 program during FY59 just to keep the door open. By late 1958, General Electric was making good progress on the J93 engine. The Air Force had finally issued a contract amendment for the high-energy fuel version, and now two different engines were officially being developed; the J93-GE-3 burned JP fuel and was intended for the F-108 and prototype B-70s, and the J93-GE-5 burned HEF-3 boron fuel in the afterburner and was intended for production B-70s.

Just as everything seemed to be falling into place, during the fall of 1958, the B-70 program received a severe jolt when Air Force Chief of Staff General Thomas D. White announced that the planned acceleration was no longer viable because of funding limitations. The first flight was still in January 1962, but the first operational wing would not appear before August 1965 at the earliest. White also told his staff that the Eisenhower Administration believed that no large sums of money should be committed to the B-70 program before the proto-

CHANGING OPERATIONAL DATES FOR THE B-70

	First Flight	First Inventory	First Wing
SR-22 (15 April 1955)	September 1960	November 1962	Late 1963
SR-22-I (11 October 1955)	September 1960	November 1962	July 1964
April 1956	April 1960	November 1962	November 1963
October 1956	June 1961	November 1962	November 1963
January 1957	May 1962	November 1964	March 1965
January 1958	May 1962	November 1964	Late 1965
7 March 1958	January 1962	October 1963	August 1964
Late 1958	January 1962	—	August 1965

Between 1955 and 1958, the expected dates for the first B-70 flight and its entry into operational service changed eight times as shown here.

Chapter 3

Above: *Artist concept of a late North American F-108 design.* (Boeing Historical Archives)

Right: *This was as far as the Republic XF-103 got – a detailed metal and wood mockup. Note the extended Falcon air-to-air missiles and the flush canopy. The F-103 was an outgrowth of the competition that eventually fielded the Convair F-102 Delta Dagger.* (Republic Aviation)

THE ELUSIVE MACH 3 FIGHTER
XF-103 AND XF-108

With 40 years of hindsight, it is obvious that the Convair F-106 Delta Dart was destined to be the last dedicated interceptor ever fielded by the United States Air Force. But it was not so apparent at the time, and a great deal of time and money would be spent trying to build something better than the Ultimate Interceptor.[1]

The concept of dedicated interceptors had come to fruition during World War II – the Messerschmitt Me163 Komet rocket plane being an early example of an aircraft intended solely to shoot down enemy bombers over its home territory. After the war it seemed that all things became more specialized, furthering the concept of dedicated interceptors. This was helped in the U.S. Air Force by the fact that there were two operating commands – the Air Defense Command (ADC) and the Tactical Air Command (TAC). Each wanted its "own" aircraft, and so defense interceptors and tactical fighters began to diverge in design and capabilities. Even the weapons carried by each began to diverge: the ADC pressed the development of the Falcon family of air-to-air guided missiles, while TAC fielded the Sparrow and Sidewinder, both ironically developed by the Navy.

In early 1949, the Air Force issued a Request for Proposals (RFP) for an advanced interceptor capable of attacking the new Soviet intercontinental bombers that were expected to enter service soon. The interceptors being developed at the time, the North American F-86D Sabre, Northrop F-89 Scorpion, and Lockheed F-94 Starfire, were all subsonic aircraft, and the Air Force did not believe that they had sufficient growth potential to meet the anticipated threat. This program came to be known as the "1954 Interceptor," after the year that the new aircraft was scheduled to enter operational service.

At the time, the Air Force recognized that the increasing complexity of modern weapons meant it was no longer practical to develop the airframe, electronics, and engines in isolation and then expect them to work properly when they were put together. In response, the Air Force introduced the "weapons system" concept where a single prime contractor would be selected to manage the entire development effort, making sure that the various systems would be compatible with each other when they were incorporated into the final aircraft. (The highly touted "system-of-systems" concept from the

The Hughes Falcon family of air-to-air missiles has a long and strange history. The program began as a bomber defense missile, but ultimately became the primary armament for all American interceptors. The missiles were available with semi-active radar homing or infrared seekers, and different variants used conventional or nuclear warheads. (Hughes Aircraft via the Tony Landis Collection)

first part of the twenty-first century is hardly a new idea.) The 1954 Interceptor was assigned the first "fighter" moniker in the new scheme – WS-201A.[2] As originally conceived, WS-201A consisted of a new air-to-air guided missile, an all-weather fire control system, a new engine, and an airframe optimized for supersonic flight.

The weapons system concept notwithstanding, the Air Force had begun studying a new advanced electronics package in February 1949, with a goal of having it ready to equip the 1954 Interceptor. In January 1950 the Air Force solicited bids from 18 electronics contractors for the system: only Bendix, General Electric, Hughes Aircraft Company, North American Aviation, Sperry Gyroscope, and Westinghouse responded. On 7 July 1950, it was announced that Hughes had won the MX-1179 contract to develop what would become the MA-1 fire control system. The MX-1179 was intended to "direct some type of air-to-air guided missile," although the exact nature of this weapon was unknown during the bidding. Separately, Hughes had already won the MX-904 competition to develop the GAR-1 Falcon, and this missile was subsequently selected for use with the MX-1179 mainly because it seemed to be the only one that could be ready in time to meet the 1954 operational date. The MX-904 was an outgrowth of the MX-798 Subsonic Air-to-Air Missile program, which itself was a follow-on to the first serious study of an "unmanned interceptor" – the MX-601.[3]

The airframe for WS-201A was Project MX-1554, and a request for proposals was issued by the Air Force on 18 June 1950; the winner would also become the "weapons system integrator." (Another concept that has found renewed interest in the twenty-first century, although nobody will admit it is a 50-year-old idea.) By the January 1951 deadline, nine different proposals were submitted by six airframe manufacturers – Republic had three separate designs, North American two, and Chance-Vought, Convair, Douglas, and Lockheed each submitted a single design. On 2 July 1951, the Air Force announced that Convair, Lockheed, and Republic had been selected to continue development through the mockup stage, with the design deemed most promising at that time being awarded a production contract. A short while later, the Air Force decided that it also needed a lightweight fighter to combat the new MiG day-fighters that were being encountered over Korea. The Lockheed effort was redirected toward a day superiority fighter that ultimately became the F-104 Starfighter; with Convair and Republic continuing on MX-1179. Without waiting for the mockups, on 11 September 1951 the Convair design was selected as the MX-1554 airframe and was designated F-102.[4]

The F-102 was closely related to the XF-92A that Convair had built in 1948 as a testbed for a possible Mach 1.5 fighter. The revolutionary design had been developed in consultation with Dr. Alexander Lippisch, who had done pioneering work on delta-winged aircraft in Germany during World War II. Convair had become convinced that the delta configuration provided a viable solution to the problems of supersonic flight, and the company would eventually produce a family of delta-wing aircraft, including the first supersonic bomber. The XF-92A was the first powered delta-winged aircraft in the world to actually fly.

Almost as soon as the development of the F-102 began, it was obvious that the design would not meet the original performance requirements, and a revised aircraft – the F-102B "Ultimate Interceptor" – began to be studied. The MX-1179 also ran into problems, forcing a "universal computer fire control system" (originally the MG-3; later the MG-10) to be substituted in the F-102A. Not surprisingly, there were any number of problems encountered during the development and early operational service with the F-102 and its electronics and weapons. Nevertheless, the Delta Dagger would go on to a fairly long, if undistinguished, career in the air forces of several countries. The Ultimate Interceptor eventually emerged as the Convair F-106 Delta Dart.[5]

THE REPUBLIC XF-103

Always at the forefront of innovation, Republic chief engineer Alexander Kartveli had begun designing the Mach 3 AP-44A all-weather high altitude defense fighter in early 1948 – less than a year after the first supersonic flight of Chuck Yeager in the XS-1. When the Air Force first saw the preliminary data, they were greatly intrigued, at least partly explaining why Republic was selected to continue in the WS-201A competition. But, like many visionaries, Kartveli was "on the fringe."

During 1951, the Republic design evolved into the AP-57 that was estimated to be capable of Mach 4 at altitudes up to 80,000 feet. By September 1951, when the Air Force made the WS-201A selection, it was obvious that the Kartveli design was far too advanced to become operational in the near term, but at the same time, it promised such a leap in performance that the Air Force felt the project had to continue.

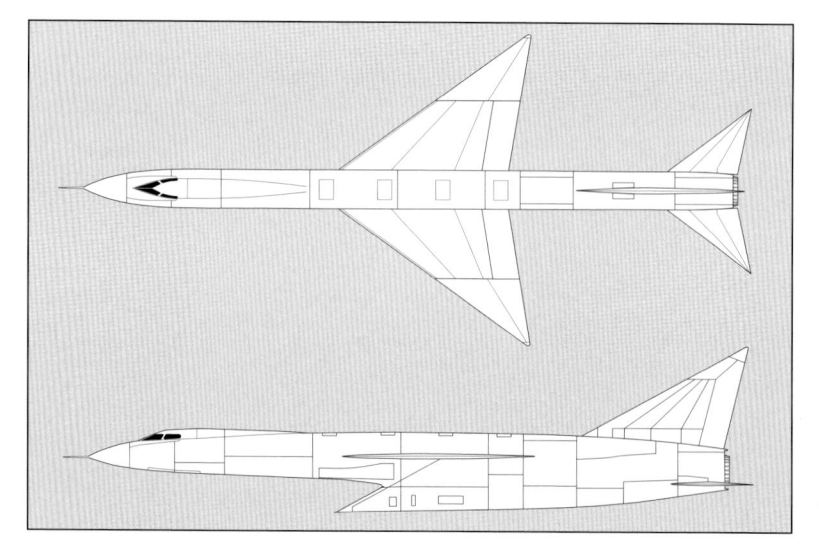

Kartveli wanted a conventional canopy on his interceptor, and the initial design included a streamlined raised canopy. The Air Force insisted on the flush cockpit that is usually shown, but Republic always maintained a second mockup with the canopy favored by the chief designer. (Art by Tony Landis)

The Elusive Mach 3 Fighter

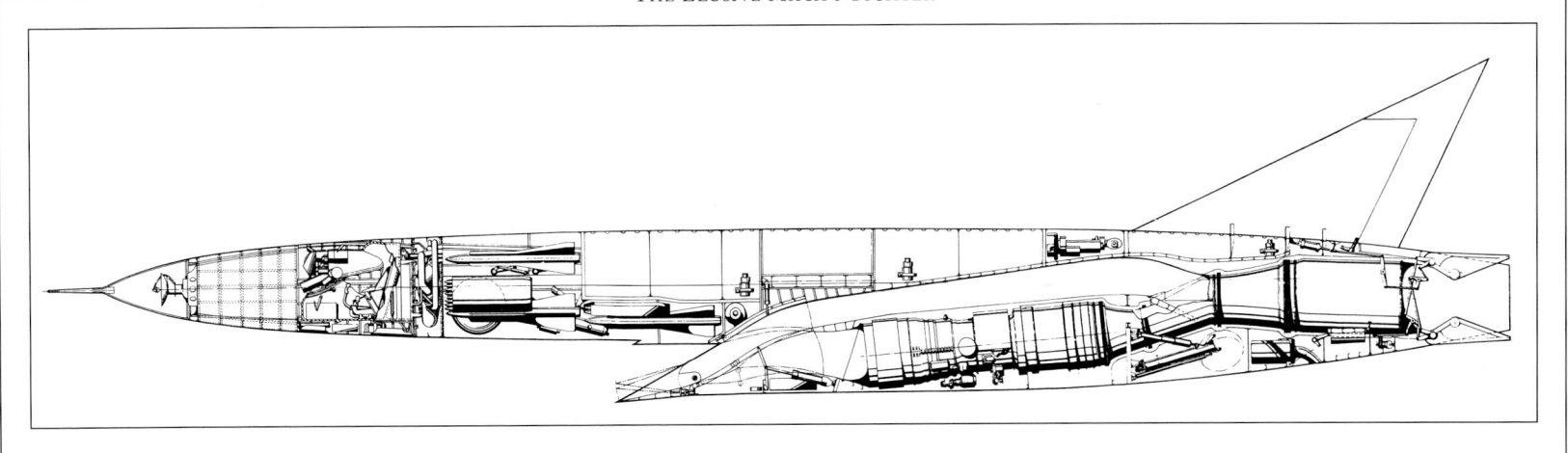

Alexander Kartveli designed his Mach 3 fighter around an engine concept where the afterburner was physically separated from the Wright J67 turbojet. At speeds above Mach 2.5, inlet air was routed around the J67 directly to the afterburner, fuel was added, and the unit became a ramjet. This eliminated the temperature restrictions inherent in turbojet engines. As initially envisioned, the fire control system and Falcon missiles would have been identical to those installed in the Convair F-102 Delta Dagger. (Republic Aviation via Charles E. Rogers)

Concurrently with the Convair design being selected for further development as MX-1554, Republic received a Phase I development contract for WS-204A, with the airframe designated XF-103. It would use the same Hughes MX-1179 fire control system and MX-904 missiles intended for the F-102. It was also scheduled to use a variation of the Wright J67 engine that was initially selected for the Convair design.[6]

Although the entire XF-103 was extremely futuristic, perhaps its most notable feature was the dual-cycle propulsion system developed as Project MX-1787.[7] There was nothing particularly noteworthy about the Wright Aeronautical Corporation XJ67-W-1 turbojet engine itself, being a license-built version of the Bristol Olympus. What was notable was its installation. The engine is usually described as being equipped with an afterburner, but this is not truly the case for the XF-103, at least not in the conventional sense. The afterburner was a separate unit (eventually designated XRJ55-W-1) located several feet behind the engine itself. The XRJ55 could be used as a traditional afterburner – hot exhaust gas from the J67 was ducted into it, mixed with fresh fuel, and ignited. It could also be used as a ramjet where the turbojet was shut down and all incoming air was ducted directly into the XRJ55, fuel was injected, and the mixture ignited.[8]

This was a novel approach to a propulsion system. The turbine inlet (compressor output) temperature of the J67 was limited to about 1,500 degrees Fahrenheit, a figure corresponding to just under Mach 3, because that was the limit of the materials used to manufacture the engine. It would be difficult to maintain Mach 3 for any length of time, or to achieve higher speeds, without destroying the engine. The dual-cycle approach eliminated this problem by removing the J67 from the propulsion system at high speeds.[9]

At this point in time, the metal mockup still had the raised canopy (right). The drop tanks looked much like those used on the F-105, and the nose gear was completely conventional. The unique air inlet may be seen just behind the nose gear. (Republic Aviation via Ken Neubeck)

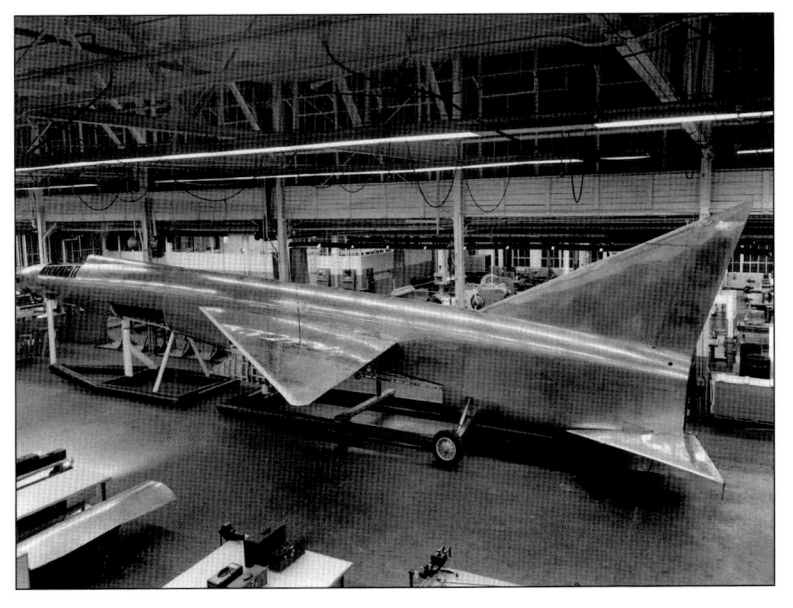

Chapter 3

45

This is a somewhat confusing wind tunnel model since it shows an early-style raised canopy with the late-model large-diameter fuselage, air intake, and ventral stabilizer. (Republic Aviation via the Tony Landis Collection)

It should be noted that the ramjet provided somewhat less thrust than the J67, and used more fuel while doing it. This was not, however, considered a major liability. The F-103 would take off and climb using the J67 with the XRJ55 functioning as an afterburner, and as the aircraft approached Mach 2.25, the combination was generating approximately 19,500 lbf. At this point, the pilot opened the exhaust nozzle, disengaged the turbojet, and bypassed all incoming air to the XRJ55. In less than one second the thrust fell off to about 14,000 lbf – the XRJ55 was now using bypass air, but it was doing so less efficiently than it had been using engine exhaust. About 6 seconds later the airflow and temperature had stabilized, the fuel flow into the XRJ55 was increased, and thrust came up to about 16,000 lbf. The entire transition took about 10 seconds and the aircraft continued to accelerate to its Mach 3 design speed. Thrust reportedly increased to 18,800 lbf at 55,000 feet. The concept was successfully demonstrated several times in test cells at the Air Force Arnold Engineering Development Center.[10]

A Ferri-type two-dimensional air intake with a sharply forward-swept lip was located under the fuselage. The intake divided into two separate ducts; the lower one fed the J67 during turbojet operations and the upper bypass duct fed air directly into the remotely located XRJ55. The two-dimensional exhaust nozzle had variable throat and exit surfaces moving within fixed side plates. The nozzle employed a combination of film and convective cooling using bypass air from the intake and discharge air from the aircraft cooling system. The exhaust nozzle incorporated dive brakes at the sides and was designed to be the outer structure of the aft fuselage. Fuel was located in five pressurized fuel cells, and a single drop tank could be carried under each wing. Like the F-105 (also a Kartveli design) drop tanks, the pylon was an integral part of the tank and was jettisoned at the same time.[11]

Despite the initial Mach 4 estimate, as the concept progressed Kartveli came to realize that the structural design of the aircraft – or more precisely, the materials being used in its construction – would limit the XF-103 to just over Mach 3 due to aerothermal concerns. An independent performance evaluation conducted by the Air Materiel Command (AMC) showed a sustained speed of just over Mach 2.5 (1,438 knots), still a fast airplane for the time. The rate of climb at 45,000 feet was projected to be almost 70,000 feet per minute, equal to Mach 1.2 straight up, using the ramjet. Even at lower altitude while using the normal afterburner, the initial rate of climb would be over 40,000 feet per minute. Total time-to-climb to 60,000 feet was just over 7 minutes from brake release. A service ceiling in excess of 75,000 feet was expected using the ramjet.[12]

The XF-103 escape capsule was tested at Edwards AFB by dropping it from the bomb bay of a Boeing B-47 bomber (left). Several drops were made, and were considered successful except for the parachute being deemed slightly too small. (via WINGS & AIRPOWER Magazine Archives)

A full-scale metal mockup of the XF-103 was inspected on 2 March 1953 with encouraging results. An 18-month extension of the Phase I contract was used for further studies of titanium fabrication, high-temperature hydraulics, escape capsules, and periscopic sights. Although development money was hard to come by, the Air Force decided that the Mach 3+ interceptor held so much promise that the program continued to be funded despite a variety of technical problems. By July 1954, the design had advanced to the point that the Air Force awarded Republic a contract to manufacture three prototypes.[13]

As was his style, Kartveli had designed an airplane that was certainly unique. The main wing used a delta planform with a leading edge sweep of 55 degrees; the horizontal stabilizer also used a delta planform, this time with a leading edge sweep of 60 degrees. A rather odd-looking tricycle landing gear retracted into the fuselage – odd because the main gear were located very far back on the fuselage, retracting into wells on the sides of the fuselage between the trailing edge of the wing and the leading edge of the horizontal stabilizer. This arrangement was dictated because the wheel wells were located between the J67 and XRJ55. The J67 could be removed through large access doors located under the main wing and the XRJ55 was removed through the rear of the fuselage.

The cockpit of the XF-103 has always been the subject of discussion since it was very different from contemporary fighters. At least one version of it was. Kartveli had designed the XF-103 with a

The XF-103 was the first fighter designed with an escape capsule. A single sliding door was stowed over the lower section of the capsule and slid upward as the capsule ejected out the bottom of the airplane. The capsule also acted as an elevator, allowing the pilot to get into the airplane with the use of access stands (there was no other hatch or canopy). (Republic Aviation via Ken Neubeck)

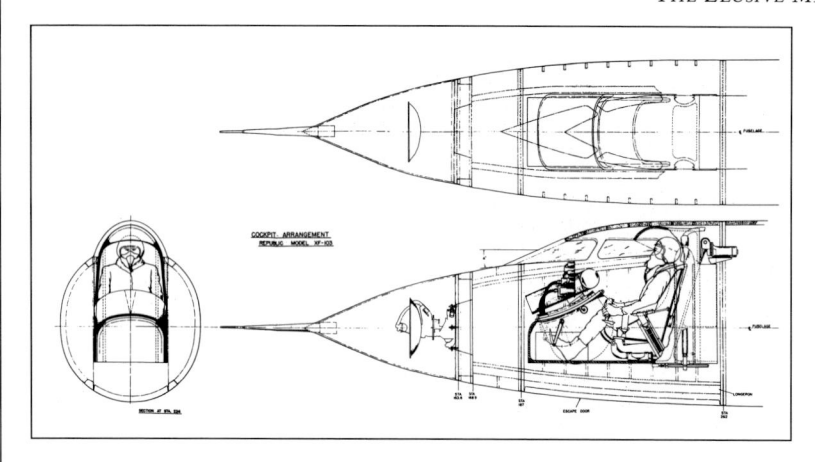

The Elusive Mach 3 Fighter

The original cockpit had a conventional canopy with front and side glass that provided adequate, but not great, visibility forward and to the sides. (Republic Aviation via Charles E. Rogers)

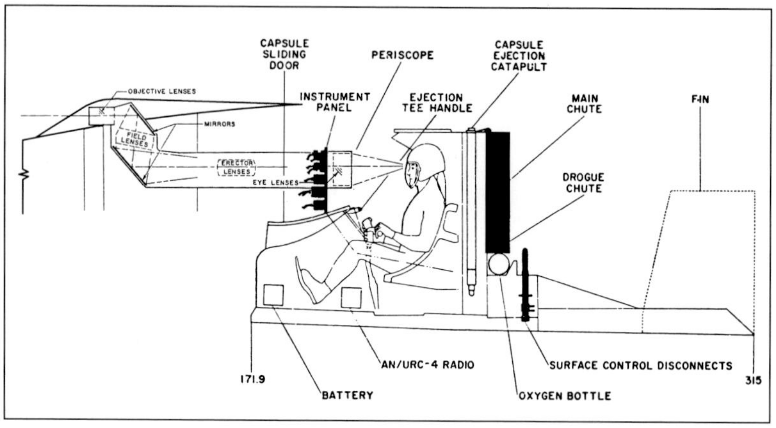

Just before the program was cancelled, a fixed periscope looking through a small sapphire window in a fairing on top of the nose was added. (via WINGS & AIRPOWER Magazine Archives)

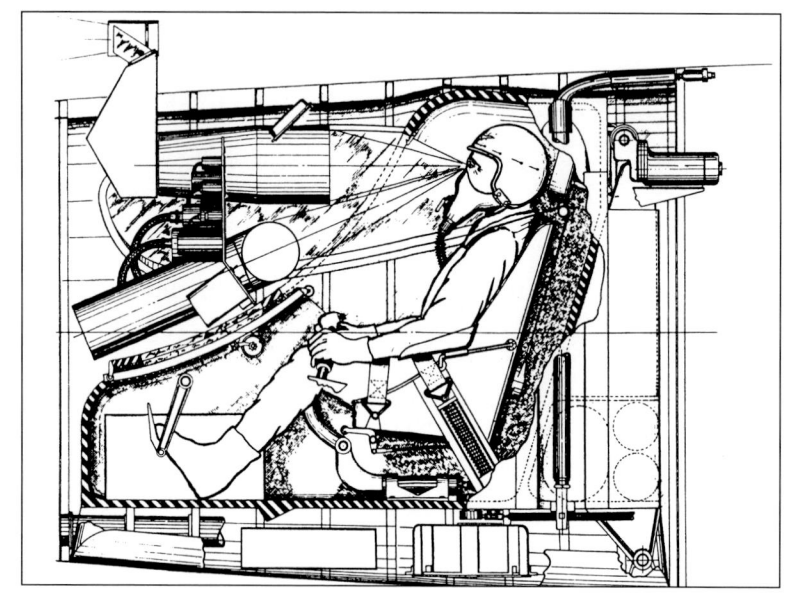

The concept that was carried for most of the development period was a retractable periscope to be used for takeoffs, landings, and taxi. Large side windows gave excellent visibility to the sides, and allowed some oblique forward vision. (Republic Aviation via Charles E. Rogers)

Republic used an F-84G Thunderjet as a testbed for various periscope systems for the XF-103. Ultimately, a unit developed by Bausch & Lomb was selected. The F-84 accumulated nearly 50 hours of flight time during the tests. (via WINGS & AIRPOWER Magazine Archives)

conventional windscreen and canopy and the mockup was constructed with this arrangement. Concerns were raised at the mock-up review about the drag associated with the canopy, and over aerothermal problems with the plexiglass windscreen. The Air Force ordered Republic to change the design, although Kartveli continued to refine the original concept as an alternative. The mockup was revised with a cockpit that was completely flush with the fuselage, although a second full-scale forward fuselage was maintained with the original design. In the new design, two large side windows provided a relatively good view for takeoff and landings, and a retractable periscope could be used for forward vision at high speeds if necessary. Late in the development effort, a fixed periscope was added under a fairing on top of the nose, a less than ideal solution but one that provided at least a little forward vision during all phases of flight. Tracking the target during combat was accomplished using the MX-1179 radarscope positioned in front of the single pilot, although an optical sight was also provided.[14]

To evaluate the visibility from the revised configuration, Republic built a full-scale cockpit section and mounted it on a truck in an attitude and elevation simulating the XF-103. The truck then

The left and center photos show the XF-103 cockpit mockup – conventional by 1950s standards. The right photo shows the MA-1 fire control system installed in the XF-103 escape capsule; this was essentially identical to the installation in the F-102. (via WINGS & AIRPOWER Magazine Archives)

taxied around the ramp and runways at Farmingdale, New York (where Republic was located), while an engineer took photographs through the periscope and windows for evaluation. At the same time, photos were taken from an F-84G with an A-1 gunsight installed as a basis of comparison. The periscope and large side windows of the XF-103 offered slightly better vision directly ahead (no windscreen frames interfered as on the F-84) and adequate vision to the front quarters. Vision to the sides was excellent, but there was essentially no rearward vision. In all, everybody agreed the concept appeared to be workable, if slightly less than ideal.[15]

Another innovative feature of the XF-103 was its escape capsule. Kartveli believed that in order to survive a Mach 3 escape, some sort of capsule was necessary – a view not universally shared in the aircraft industry, although the use of a capsule in all new aircraft was briefly codified by the Air Force during the late 1950s. The use of a capsule also addressed another problem – how to get into the XF-103, which sat fairly high off the ground. The solution was to have the capsule lower on a rail to ground level where the pilot got in. Escape was also from the bottom, making it useless at low level or during takeoff and landing (much like early F-104s). The capsule itself had a forward door that was stowed in a down position. When the pilot wanted to encapsulate, the door slid upward between the instrument panel and the pilot, sealing along the top edge of the capsule. The flight controls and throttle were located inside the capsule; exactly how they would have been connected to the aircraft systems was never completely explained. Two large windows in the capsule allowed the pilot to see the instrumentation and fly the aircraft while encapsulated.[16]

Six GAR-1 Falcon missiles were carried on retractable launchers inside the fuselage. There was an upper missile bay and two lower missile bays on each side of the fuselage, just behind the cockpit, each with separate quick-action doors. A retractable rocket pod was also located on each side of the fuselage, just above the lower missile bays. Each pod contained eighteen 2.75-inch "Mighty Mouse" folding fin aerial rockets (FFAR).[17] The Air Force had some concerns about the lower missiles and all of the rockets since their motor exhaust would likely be ingested by the XF-103 engine air intake.[18]

Most of the fire control system electronics were located in a compartment adjacent to the radar equipment in the nose. Maintenance access was deemed less than ideal since a ladder was required for access to all components. This limited the use of test equipment and made minor adjustments difficult. However, the entire nose compartment and its collection of rack-mounted components were designed to be removable for major servicing.

The XF-103 was one of the first programs be investigate the widespread use of titanium, paving the way for the Lockheed Blackbirds and North American XB-70 later in the decade. Actually, four different construction techniques were investigated by Republic: all Ti-150B titanium, all 4130 steel, a combination that used Ti-150B titanium alloy

The large rectangular object above the radar screen is the forward vision periscope. Note the early partial pressure suit and helmet being worn by the pilot. (via WINGS & AIRPOWER Magazine Archives)

The Elusive Mach 3 Fighter

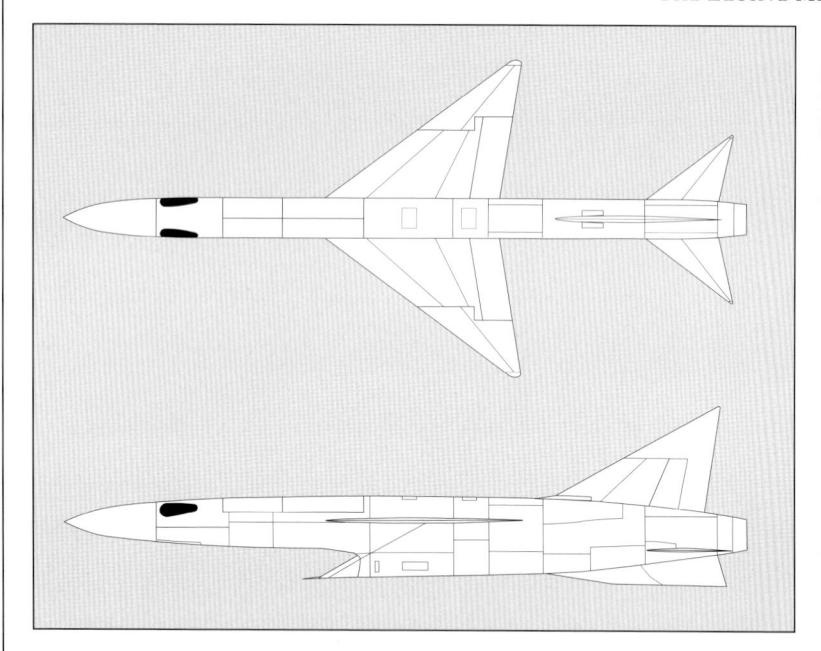

Above and Below: *The final version of the XF-103 represented a major change, driven at least partially by Hughes. The MA-1 fire control system was gone, replaced by the ASG-18 with its 40-inch antenna and the GAR-9 missile being developed for the F-108. The forward fuselage was greater in diameter to support the new radar and larger missiles, and a large ventral stabilizer was added to regain the directional stability lost by the changes. There was a last-ditch proposal to use the XF-103 as a test aircraft for the F-108, but the Air Force did not approve the idea.* (Art by Tony Landis)

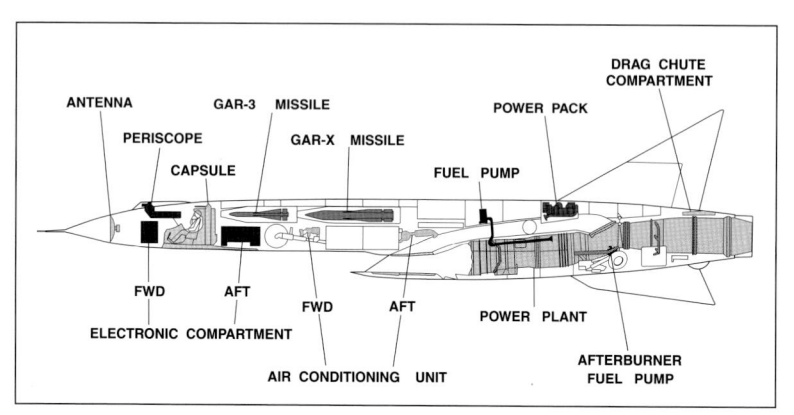

The addition of the ASG-18 required a major revision of the forward fuselage. Here, the original raised-canopy cockpit mockup is shown next to the final ASG-18 nose; the greater diameter is clearly evident. Even the escape capsules (below) were changed to accommodate the new system. (via WINGS & AIRPOWER Magazine Archives)

outer skins and a 4130 stainless steel inner structure, and an all-aluminum (24S-T86) structure. The aluminum aircraft was limited to Mach 2.8 (375 degrees Fahrenheit), and also turned out to be the heaviest at 10,250 pounds (empty airframe weight); it was quickly dropped from consideration. Not surprisingly, the all-titanium structure was deemed the lightest (8,750 pounds), with the combination structure being second (9,400 pounds). The all-steel structure was 100 pounds lighter[19] than the all-aluminum design. Both the steel and titanium aircraft were capable of sustained Mach 3 operation. A great deal was learned about the manufacture of high-strength titanium alloy and the fabrication of aircraft parts out of it during the course of the XF-103 program, although neither Lockheed nor North American ever acknowledged the contribution to their later programs.[20]

Despite a low priority and little funding, the program continued to advance, albeit slowly. A few major subcontracts for the three prototypes were issued, primarily for the landing gear and various pieces of titanium tooling. However, it was becoming obvious that the XF-103 was never going to fly. The effort was experiencing serious difficulties

XF-103 Specifications and Performance at Mockup Review

Span:	35 feet 10 inches	Maximum Speed:	Mach 3+
Length:	75 feet 2 inches	Combat Speed:	Mach 2.2 at 75,000 feet
Height:	18 feet 4 inches	Combat Radius:	Approximately 450 miles
Maximum Weight:	Approximately 40,000 pounds	Service Ceiling:	Approximately 80,000 feet
Armament:	36 2.75-inch "Mighty Mouse" FFAR unguided rockets; 6 MX-904 (GAR-1) Falcon guided missiles		
Engine:	Wright XJ67-W-1 turbojet / XRJ55-W-1 ramjet		
Fuel Capacity:	Approximately 1,800 gallons		
Crew:	One, in an escape capsule		

Comparison of Flush Cockpit with Raised Cockpit Canopy [23]

	No Canopy Ramjet Operative	No Canopy Ramjet Inoperative	With Canopy Ramjet Operative
Gross Weight (general air defense): (pounds)	40,000	38,254	41,982
Gross Weight (local air defense): (pounds)	26,663	26,223	26,810
Combat Altitude: (feet)	60,000	55,000	60,000
Speed at Combat Altitude: (knots)	1,725	1,190	1,725
Time to Combat Speed and Altitude: (minutes)	7.1	5.4	9.0
Max Sea Level Rate of Climb: (feet per minute)	38,200	39,000	35,900
Max rate of Climb @ 35,500 feet:			
With Ramjet: (feet per minute)	73,000	–	62,000
Only afterburner: (feet per minute)	37,000	37,500	30,000
Combat Ceiling: (feet)	73,000	63,000	70,500
External Fuel: (gallons)	450	217	723
Takeoff Distance (over 50-foot): (feet)	4,300	3,800	4,950
Landing weight: (pounds)	24,958	24,958	24,981
Landing Distance (over 50-foot): (feet)	4,130	4,130	4,130

by 1955, but the Air Force still felt a need for an interceptor with higher performance than the upcoming Ultimate Interceptor. On 6 October 1955, the Air Defense Command released GOR-114 for the Mach 3 Long-Range Interceptor, Experimental (LRI-X) program.[21]

In anticipation of the LRI-X program entering development, during early 1957, the XF-103 was cut back to a single prototype and two flight engines. In this role, the Republic aircraft was to be an advanced research vehicle for the LRI-X program, but was no longer considered a possible operational aircraft. The design evolved considerably during this period, with more than a little assistance from Hughes, which intended to use it as a demonstrator for its long-range radar and Super-Falcon missile. External changes included a more slab-sided shape for the rear fuselage, a refined variable-geometry inlet, and a rearrangement of the armament. Hughes proposed a weapons load of four GAR-1 Falcons in individual bays (two on each side, one above the other) and two GAR-9 long-range missiles, located in bays behind the upper GAR-1s. Little progress had been made by 21 August 1957 when the XF-103 and Wright engine were cancelled entirely. The program had cost $104 million over 9 years.[22]

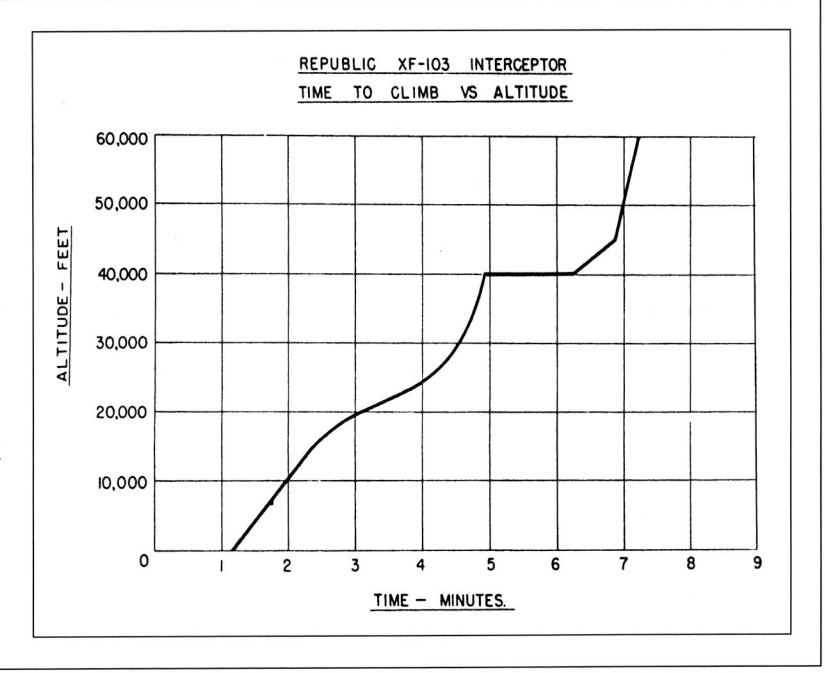

THE ELUSIVE MACH 3 FIGHTER

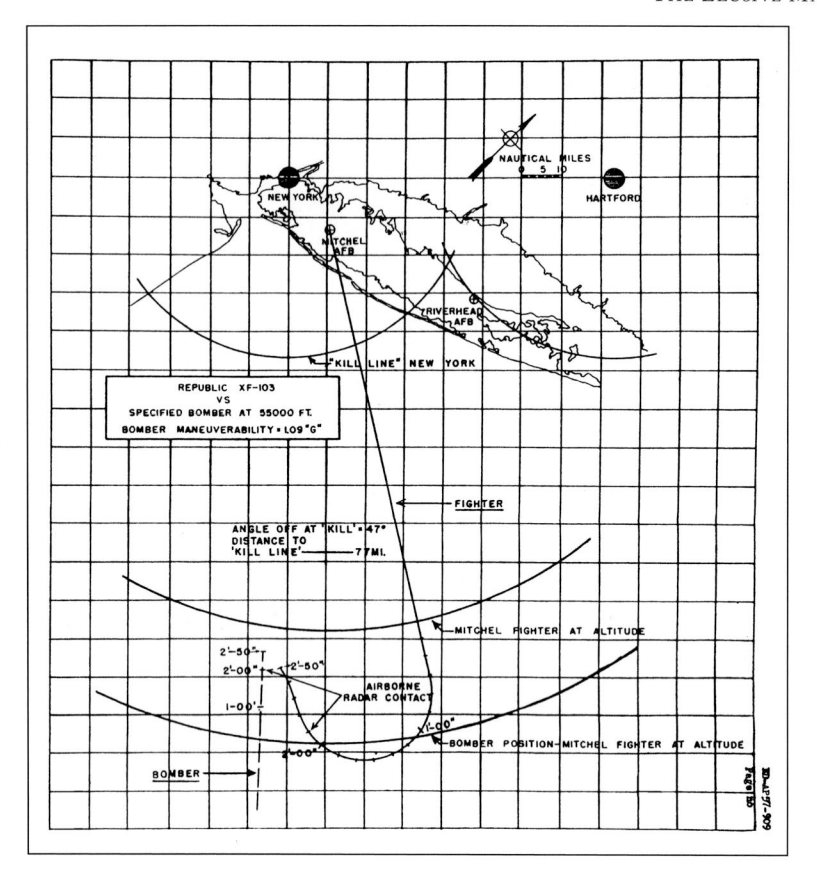

This was a typical air defense mission envisioned for the F-103. The threat was a bomber capable of 770 knots at 40,000 feet (Mach 1.34). It was assumed that New York City was the target, and that defensive fighters were based at Riverhead AFB and Mitchel AFB in up-state New York. Detection range by air defense radars was limited to 255 nautical miles at 55,000 feet. The F-103 would be guided by ground controllers until its own radar could acquire the target at a range of approximately 20 nm. The fighter would fly past the bomber and turn in order to get on its tail to ease the computations necessary for a missile launch. This also simplified launching rockets as needed. At Mach 3, the F-103 was more than fast enough for a tail-chase on the bombers. However, the Falcon had a maximum speed of just under Mach 4, complicating high-speed launch. It is interesting to note that Mitchel AFB had only two 5,000-foot runways with no overruns – just barely adequate for the needs of the F-103. (Republic Aviation via Charles E. Rogers)

Below: *Given the state-of-the-art for the 1950s, the XF-103 provided fairly decent maintenance access. The major problem would be the sheer size of the airplane – the nose was more than 15 feet above ground level, meaning that access stands would be required to reach most of the electronics in the nose. At least the engine was at a convenient level for the mechanics.* (Republic Aviation via Charles E. Rogers)

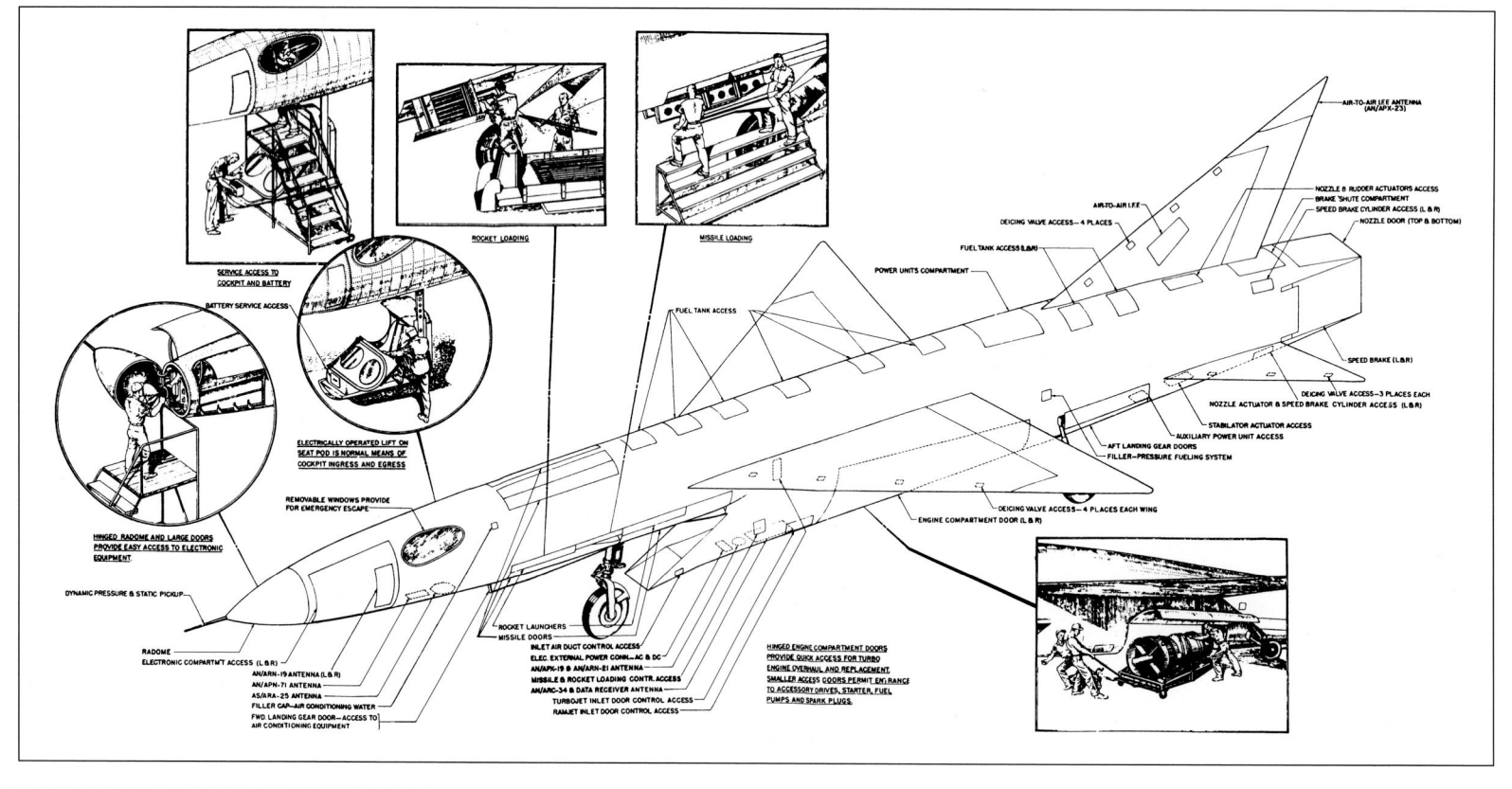

SAGE

Although not directly part of the story, another development of the 1950s played a peripheral role in the history of the elusive Mach 3 interceptor. With the advent of radar during World War II, the concept of ground-controlled intercepts was brought almost to an art form. After the war, the United States intended to raise that art form to a science. To this end, in 1948 the Massachusetts Institute of Technology (MIT) Lincoln Laboratory proposed a radical improvement to continental air defense, but the basic technology to implement the plan did not yet exist. Nevertheless, a seed had been planted.

Finally, in October 1952, the Air Force initiated a project to develop the Semi-Automatic Ground Environment (SAGE) to protect the airspace over the United States and Canada. SAGE was an integrated set of radar, surface-to-air missiles, and interceptor aircraft all tied together by digital computers and long-distance communications. This was by far the most technologically demanding project ever attempted, surpassing even the development of the atomic bomb in size and complexity. When the program began, there was only a single digital computer in the world – the *Whirlwind* at MIT. As the major development effort associated with SAGE, the International Business Machines Corporation (IBM) won a contract in April 1953 to design and build the Whirlwind II, designated AN/FSQ-7 by the military.[24]

The FSQ-7 was, for all practical purposes, the first "production" computer ever manufactured and weighed 275 tons, used 919 miles of cables, had approximately 50,000 vacuum tubes, 7,300 pluggable units, and 170,000 diodes. It consumed 3 megawatts of power, enough for a city with 15,000 inhabitants. Over the next eight years, SAGE would employ over 800 programmers, 20 percent of the world's supply, to design and test the largest real-time (over 500,000 lines) computer program written at the time. The program processed radar and other data, and then presented the information to 100 operators on cathode ray tubes: one of the first uses of this device to display computer-generated data. Light pens were used to interact with the data on the CRTs.[25]

At the heart of the system that eventually emerged were 24 hardened-concrete "Direction Centers" across the United States and Canada. An extensive series of radar sites scattered around the periphery of the continent would detect Soviet bombers and guide friendly fighters or Bomarc and Nike missiles to intercept them. The fighters were connected to SAGE by a radio data link, allowing them to fly intercepts with only minimal action from the pilot.[26]

Each Direction Center was linked to more than 100 air defense elements by long-distance telephone lines, requiring system integration on a scale previously unimagined. It is estimated that SAGE cost between $5,000 million and $12,000 million in 1964 dollars – the single most expensive defense project until the development of the intercontinental ballistic missile (ICBM). The first SAGE Direction Center came online at McGuire AFB, New Jersey, in November 1956; the last was completed in 1962. They would operate continuously until SAGE was formally decommissioned in 1983. Today, only a few remnants of the Direction Centers remain, most having been torn down to make room for newer facilities.[27]

SAGE was a marvel of technology and the FSQ-7 computers proved remarkably reliable. In an era when analog computers were frequently out of service over 10 percent of the time, the IBM system was seldom down for more than one day per year. Almost unbelievably, given its 275 tons of electronics, the FSQ-7 did not have the raw processing power that is currently available in a Palm Pilot that weighs less than a pound. Nevertheless, the system showed the way to the future. The basic computer and communications architecture of the system was reused by the FAA air traffic control system and the SABRE airline reservation system. What had been learned in developing the FSQ-7 itself was instrumental in the design of the IBM System/360, the most successful large computer architecture of all time (over $100 billion worth of systems sold). The communications system laid the groundwork for the internet; the cathode ray tubes and their light pens showed the way to modern displays and input devices such as mice.[28]

Because of the processing power provided by SAGE, it was possible to extend the defensive perimeter further toward potential enemies,

One of the technical marvels of the 1950s – SAGE. At left is the 275-ton FSQ-7, the first production digital computer. In the center is the Direction Center at McGuire AFB. At right is an operator using a "light pen" pointing device. (The Mitre Corporation)

allowing more time to counter whatever hostile advances they might make. This led directly to placing radars and surface-to-air missiles in remote locations, and for a desire to have a manned interceptor that could destroy the enemy bombers further from the populated areas of North America. The search for a Mach 3 interceptor continued.

LRI-X

The commander of the Northeast Air Command, Major General Lyman P. Whitten, suggested the development of a truly long-range interceptor in 1952.[29] Whitten felt that the interceptors then under development could not fully exploit the SAGE network that was then being planned. In his opinion, the warning time available from SAGE should be used by a long-range interceptor to attack incoming bombers well before they threatened the key industrial targets of the United States and Canada. To Whitten, the logical platform was a modified Boeing B-47 Stratojet medium bomber armed with dozens of air-to-air missiles.[30]

However, this proposal for a "very long-range, high speed, high-armament-capacity interceptor" did not go far toward defining the character of the vehicle that would eventually be developed. In April 1953 Major General Frederic H. Smith, Jr., vice commander of the Air Defense Command (ADC),[31] expanded on the concept by calling for a twin-engine aircraft with a combat radius of 700 to 1,900 nautical miles, a combat ceiling of 60,000 feet, and a speed of between Mach 1.4 and Mach 1.9 at 35,000 feet. To meet these requirements, the ADC favored improved versions of either the Northrop F-89 Scorpion or the McDonnell F-101 Voodoo.[32]

Although the Pentagon apparently agreed with the need for a long-range interceptor, no development program was immediately forthcoming. The ADC was insistent, however, and in October 1953 again attempted to gain formal Air Force approval for such a program. In doing so, the ADC added some important requirements to the characteristics of the new aircraft. The command emphasized that the long-range interceptor had to be capable of executing an attack based on both the lead pursuit (behind the bomber) and lead collision (in front of the bomber) techniques, and should carry weapons armed with nuclear warheads. The radar needed to include an airborne moving target indicator (to find targets in ground clutter) and an "anti-chaff synchronizer" (to counter enemy countermeasures). Since the ADC wanted "the equivalent of three bomber kills" per mission, it estimated that each aircraft should carry "270 2.75-inch rockets, 18 Falcons, and 3 atomic rockets of the 10 to 20 kiloton variety." Apparently, the command had little faith in either the reliability of the weapons or the aim of the pilots.[33]

For the next six months, various Air Force organizations debated the need for the aircraft, with the ADC supporting the request with great vigor. The command felt that time was *the* most critical factor and wanted to proceed in the most expeditious manner possible. In the view of the ADC, this meant eliminating an industry competition and selecting either an unsolicited proposal from Northrop for the "Delta Scorpion" or an idea from McDonnell to build a two-seat variant of the F-101 Voodoo. For unexplained reasons, the ADC thought the Northrop aircraft would come closest to meeting their requirements in the shortest possible time.[34]

At this point, the Pentagon envisioned an open 6- to 10-month industry competition leading to an operational capability in mid-1958. General Smith objected to this procedure and reiterated that the choice should be limited to the Delta Scorpion or the two-seat F-101 with an operational date no later than January 1958. The matter of an early operational date would continue to be a point of contention between the ADC and nearly everybody else.[35]

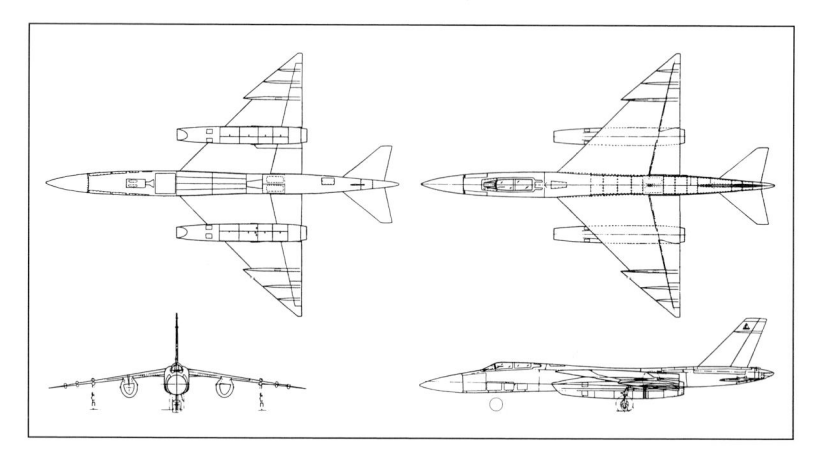

The Northrop N-126 Delta Scorpion bore absolutely no resemblance to the F-89 that it was supposedly derived from. Power came from a pair of Allison J71 engines slung under the wings provided an estimated Mach 1.9 top speed. Northrop invested a good deal of time and effort into defining the Delta Scorpion, but ultimately the Air Force opted for a two-seat F-101 variant. (Gerald H. Balzer Collection)

No matter what the selection process, Air Force Headquarters established that the eventual long-range interceptor needed to be an all-weather, two-seat, twin-engine aircraft with a radius of 1,000 nautical miles. The search radar was to have a range of at least 100 nautical miles and needed to be immune to enemy jamming. Speed was defined as at least 25 percent greater than the best expected enemy bomber, with the required altitude being at least 10 percent greater. The interceptor would be designed to work inside the SAGE network, but would also be capable of operating independently as necessary.[36]

The armament load was to provide "the highest possible kill probability on a minimum of three bombers" and, if possible, was to include a "type of guided missile which can be launched at a great distance to keep the interceptor out of the enemy defensive fire or warhead damage area." Nuclear warheads were to arm the primary missiles, but secondary conventional weapons were also required. Finally, the interceptor was to be equipped with the "best possible" communication and navigation system for operation "in the higher latitudes," acknowledging the problems associated with operating in the arctic.[37]

Despite the ADC pleas for an early availability, the idea of a full-scale industry competition gained considerable support in the Pentagon. As a result, General Benjamin W. Chidlaw, the ADC commander, appealed directly to General Nathan F. Twining, the Air Force Chief of Staff. In a rather long letter of 6 March 1954, backed by various attachments, Chidlaw said he was dismayed over the lengthy delay. With all due respect, to his superior, he emphasized, in no uncertain terms, that the ADC still considered an early operational date to be the single most critical requirement. Chidlaw emphasized that an industry competition would result in a delay "we cannot tolerate in the face of the known and growing Russian threat of air attack."[38]

The letter seemed to have the desired effect. Five days later, the ARDC directed the Wright Air Development Center (WADC) to evaluate the Delta Scorpion and two-place F-101 proposals – concentrating on the former – to provide the Pentagon with a "conclusive answer" for a long-range interceptor. The WADC immediately began the evaluation, but quickly advised ARDC Headquarters that they were "apprehensive of the apparent assumption that the Delta Scorpion and the two place F-101 interceptor are the only fighter aircraft possible for the LRI problem in the stipulated time period." They did not, however, list any alternatives.[39]

Delta Scorpion

Generally portrayed as a "derivative" of the Northrop F-89, the Delta Scorpion actually bore absolutely no resemblance to, and shared very few parts with, the production aircraft. The final configuration for the Northrop Model N-126 showed an airplane that was 85 feet long with a span of 62.25 feet and a height of 22 feet. The planform of the main wing was indeed a delta that provided 1,050 square feet of area, but the airplane also had a conventional horizontal stabilizer mounted on the aft fuselage. The trailing edge of each side was made up of three control surfaces: an "altitude flap" located inboard, with an aileron in the middle, and a split speed brake located outboard.[40]

A single pod under the mid point of each wing held one of two potential powerplants. The Allison J71-A-11 was an advanced derivative of the J35 that provided between 10,200 lbf and 11,000 lbf; similar engines would later power the Douglas B-66 Destroyer and McDonnell F3H Demon. The Wright J67-W-1 was a license-built version of the Bristol Olympus and provided 13,200 lbf. The Wright engine – also proposed for the XF-102 and XF-103 – was generally favored and resulted in an aircraft with an empty weight of 41,671 pounds and a maximum gross takeoff weight of 75,830 pounds.[41]

The streamlined fuselage housed a crew of two and the same Hughes E-9 fire control system used on the F-89H. A bicycle landing gear was retracted into the fuselage, and outriggers – made from modified F-89 nose gear – were housed in the engine pods. The armament consisted of eight GAR-1 Falcon missiles carried in a 20-foot-long weapons bay, along with two packs containing twenty-four 2.75-inch rockets each that retracted into the bottom of the fuselage just behind the forward landing gear. Alternate loads included swapping the Falcons for 203 more FFARs, or installing two T-171 (later M61) 20-mm rotary cannon in the weapons bay. The airplane had an estimated top speed of Mach 1.9 and an operating range of 800 nautical miles on internal fuel.[42]

Double Voodoo

The development of the McDonnell Voodoo had begun with the XF-88 in 1947 and progressed to the single-seat F-101A escort fighter for the Strategic Air Command in 1952. The F-101A was the first production aircraft capable of flying 1,000 miles per hour. McDonnell was convinced that the big supersonic fighter would make a good interceptor and had submitted an unsolicited proposal for a two-seat version to the Air Force during early 1953. Later in the year, the Air Force finally began paying more attention to the concept. It was not until November 1954, however, that McDonnell was finally authorized to proceed with the development of a two-seat F-101, and a letter contract for WS-217A was issued on 25 February 1955. The gestation period was remarkably short, and sufficient numbers of F-101Bs were on hand to equip four interceptor squadrons by the end of June 1959.[43]

The aircraft that finally emerged looked like a two-place F-101, and was equipped with an MG-13 fire control system along with two MB-1 Genie unguided rockets with atomic warheads or two GAR-1 Falcon missiles. A pair of Pratt & Whitney J57s allowed the airplane to reach Mach 1.5 at 35,000 feet. The combat ceiling was 44,000 feet and the airplane needed only 195 seconds to climb to 40,000 feet. The F-101B was just over 71 feet long, spanned almost 40 feet, and had a maximum take-off weight of 52,350 pounds. McDonnell manufactured 398 F-101Bs and 72 dual-control F-101F trainers. On 12 June 1961, the United States transferred 56 F-101Bs and 10 F-101Fs to the Royal Canadian Air Force in return for Canada assuming responsibility for a number of Pinetree radar sites that were part of the SAGE system. In Canadian service the aircraft were designated CF-101.[44]

More Proposals

It seemed that all the pressure to select from the existing proposals was coming from inside the Air Force, but it appears that might not have been the case. On 16 March 1954 Brigadier General Floyd B. Wood, ARDC Deputy Commander for Technical Operations, told the WADC commander, Major General Albert Boyd, that the long range interceptor affair had turned into a "political problem … because of the efforts of one particular contractor [Northrop] to sell its airplane to the [Air] Defense Command." The reference was in response to a Congressional inquiry, a relatively rare occurrence in those days. Still, the McDonnell and Northrop airplanes appeared to offer the most expedient solution.[45]

Although the original direction had expressly excluded evaluating any contractor material not already on-hand, both McDonnell and Northrop submitted additional material at the request of the WADC, and that material was evaluated in due course. In the end the WADC drew the "very broad conclusion that … neither proposal specifically meets the stated operational requirements" but cautioned that the hurried evaluation was only a "best estimate of realism."[46]

The two-place F-101 offered the correct speed and altitude, but lacked the desired radius of action. It did, however, enjoy the advantage of being largely a derivative aircraft and could be "obtained sooner than the Delta Scorpion." The Northrop proposal fell somewhat short of the desired speed and altitude, but could achieve the required radius of action. A review by the Air Materiel Command (responsible for production) showed that Northrop was overly optimistic in its schedule given that the airplane was largely a new design. The schedule proposed by McDonnell was considered achievable, if only barely.[47]

At this point Air Force Headquarters began to stiffen in the face of the pressure from the ADC on behalf of the Northrop proposal. The fact that neither proposal was truly satisfactory only compounded the problem. General Twining responded to General Chidlaw on 30 March that he felt that the selection must "await the completion of a formal, but expedited, competition and evaluation." Twining continued that "I am most reluctant to take action which will involve us in a blitz development of another brand new aircraft with built-in compromises and subsequent headaches," especially because the Air Force was already "confronted with too many projects snarled up as a result of precipitous action in similar cases in prior years." The stage was finally set for a formal competition.[48]

By the end of April, the ARDC had published a set of military characteristics in preparation for an industry competition. These included the ability to operate under the control of the SAGE as well as being able to operate autonomously outside the network. The aircraft was to be capable of point defense and area coverage as well as long-range interception. Other important features included an ability to use runways as short as 5,000 feet (6,000 feet in the arctic) and to be airborne 2 minutes after the scramble signal while on 24-hour alert status. The combat radius remained 1,000 nautical miles with a speed of Mach 1.7 at 40,000 feet, or 25 percent greater than the "best enemy threat." The combat ceiling was to be 60,000 feet. Other requirements included two engines, a two-man crew, a data link, an automatic instrument landing system, TACAN, and a UHF command radio set.[49]

The interceptor was to use an integrated electronics system, and the Air Force felt that it "would be most desirable for this to be a completely automatic system that encompasses the entire aircraft operation from a point immediately after take-off to a point immediately before touch down." A separate competition would be held to select a fire control system that could detect a target the size of a B-47 at a range of 100 nautical miles. Each fighter was still expected to engage three enemy bombers on each mission, but the total weapons load had been reduced to three unguided atomic rockets or eight Falcons, along with forty-eight 2.75-inch rockets.[50]

Air Force Headquarters recognized that "a solution which fully meets each of these military characteristics could probably not be operational before 1959–1960 at the earliest," and the Pentagon established January 1959 as the target date for the production of early versions of the airplane. In order to expedite the competition, requests for proposals were to be issued by 10 May 1954 and the evaluation would begin by 16 July. The winner would be announced by 17 September 1954 with a first flight 30 months later.[51]

Seven proposals were received, but none were really satisfactory. The WADC rated them in order of Northrop, Lockheed, Douglas, Martin, Boeing, McDonnell, and Republic. Thirteen fire-control system proposals were also received, but again, none met the specifications. The systems proposed by Hughes and Sperry used 40-inch-diameter antennas with a 40-nautical-mile range, and were rated first and second. The evaluators judged, however, that none of the fire-control systems could be available before mid-1961. A year could be saved if the Air Force decided to accept a system based on the MX-1179 effort that was already underway at Hughes with the addition of a 40-inch antenna.[52]

All of the evaluating organizations agreed that none of the aircraft or fire-control systems met the requirements. Several possible courses of action were suggested, including relaxing some or all of the specifications, accepting an interim aircraft pending the development of one that could meet the specifications (the same tact taken by the F-102/F-106), or terminating the procurement and trying again later. General Chidlaw was not happy with any of these alternatives and requested that Air Force Headquarters approve development of the two-seat F-101 to serve as an interim long-range interceptor. This request was apparently taken more seriously than previous ones, and the F-101B program was initiated in November 1954. The Delta Scorpion concept finally faded from the scene; the competitors were thanked for their input and sent home empty handed.[53]

Whatever the final decision on the long-range interceptor, the competition had pointed out that fire-control system development was lagging behind airframe concepts. In June 1955, it was decided to have Hughes and Sperry undertake preliminary development of a new fire-control system that would be applicable to any future interceptor. After the Air Force had "validated test demonstrations" from both firms, it would decide which would enter final development, with an operational system desired in early 1962.[54]

At this point, the long-range interceptor became involved in another round of discussions. Things became more complicated when General Earle E. Partridge succeeded General Chidlaw as the commander of the ADC, and when an unsolicited proposal to use the Convair B-58 as a long-range interceptor appeared. At the same time, the ADC was beginning to realize it needed a medium-range interceptor even more than a long-range one. Additional pressure was coming from the Pentagon, which was pressing for an overall reduction in the cost of operating the Air Force. Despite all of this, Air Force Headquarters formally approved the development of a new long-range interceptor on 20 July 1955.[55]

In response, the ARDC released GOR-114 on 6 October 1955 for the Long-Range Interceptor, Experimental (LRI-X) program. The aircraft was to have a service ceiling of 60,000 feet (65,000 desired), a speed of Mach 1.7 at 40,000 feet, a 1,000-nautical-mile radius, a two-man crew, at least two engines ("at least" so as not to exclude variants of the B-58 Hustler), an integrated fire-control system capable of detecting a B-47-size target at 60 nautical miles (100 desired), and the ability to kill three bombers per mission. On 11 October 1955, study contracts were issued to Lockheed, North American, and Northrop that included fabricating wooden mockups of their proposed designs. One of the contractors would be eliminated from competition after the mockup review, with the other two manufacturing prototype aircraft for a fly-off.[56]

By early 1956, each company had completed its preliminary study, and the results were being evaluated by the WADC. It was expected that each company would begin building their mockups after incorporating the comments generated during the WADC review, but it would never get that far. The original plan notwithstanding, funding constraints forced the Air Force to down-select to a single contractor, and the Source Selection Board believed the North American NA-236 design offered the most promise.[57]

In the meantime, however, the ADC requested that the Pentagon cancel the long-range interceptor program and replace it with a new medium-range aircraft with a 350-nautical mile radius. The North American selection was put on hold while this new wrinkle was sorted out. General Partridge further complicated the matter by introducing the concept of a lightweight interceptor modeled after the Lockheed F-104 Starfighter. It now appeared that both the medium- and long-range interceptors might fall by the wayside. On 9 May

North American won the initial Long-Range Interceptor competition with this design, but the program was cancelled before a formal contract was awarded because the Air Defense Command was changing its mind on the type of aircraft needed most. (Art by Tony Landis; photos courtesy of the Boeing Historical Archives)

1956, the Pentagon formally cancelled the long-range interceptor due to "questions which had arisen regarding the utility and desirability" of such a weapon system.[58]

Despite the confusion over what type of aircraft the ADC really wanted, the termination order allowed the two fire-control system development efforts to continue. Sperry had signed their development contract in December 1955, and Hughes followed two months later. Each company was to develop preliminary designs for an advanced fire-control system for the now-cancelled long-range interceptor. Although the Pentagon termination order had allowed the ARDC to continue the development of both systems, a lack of progress at Sperry led to that contract being cancelled by the end of May 1956. The Hughes design seemed to be progressing well, and the company was working with Ramo-Wooldridge (which later became TRW) to further define the required capabilities, with special consideration being given to using the system on an unlikely production version of the Republic F-103. Despite the seemingly good progress at Hughes, the Air Force awarded a similar development contract to RCA during September 1956 to replace the cancelled Sperry effort.[59]

With the entire matter of what type of interceptor was needed still undecided, the ADC proposed yet a different set of requirements during the summer of 1956. This time the command wanted a Mach 2.5 aircraft capable of 70,000 feet altitude with a 300 nautical mile radius flown by a single pilot operating a modified MX-1179 fire control system. Interestingly, this aircraft was called a "long range" interceptor, although its radius was less than the previous "medium range" requirements.

Amid this confusion, the Pentagon intervened, deciding that the original long-range interceptor really was what the Air Force needed in the near term, but that it should now be equipped with an advanced GAR-X air-to-air missile in addition to the new fire control system. This decision was confirmed by a special "generals board" chaired by Major General Albert Boyd, the commander of the WADC.[60] The board reported its results directly to the Air Force Chief of Staff, concluding that a "two-place manned interceptor, capable of attaining a speed of Mach 3, altitudes of 70,000 feet plus, and a radius of action of 1000 miles … is essential to the defense of the United States." The fire control system envisioned by the board had an 80- to 100-nautical-mile range and would be able to operate with or without the SAGE network. The GAR-X missile would have a range of 15 to 25 nautical miles with interchangeable nuclear and high explosive warheads.[61]

Heeding this guidance, the Pentagon reinstated the long-range interceptor program on 11 April 1957. Fifteen days later, the ARDC published the requirements for the fire control system and radar, essentially echoing the earlier recommendations by Boyd. It was decided that a single contractor would be responsible for the design and development of the fire control system and missile, eliminating many of the problems that had been encountered when integrating the Falcon with the various fire control systems in earlier interceptors. A "weapon system" contractor would build the airframe and oversee the fire control system and missile contracts, much like the earlier Convair F-102 effort but with increased responsibility and authority.

F-108

The result of the previous LRI-X competition was reaffirmed, and on 6 June 1957 North American was issued contract AF33(600)-35605 for two prototypes of a long-range, high-performance interceptor to be designated F-108A as part of WS-202A. North American assigned the NA-257 control number to the effort, although the aircraft was essentially identical to the earlier NA-236.[62] An additional 31 YF-108As were also ordered, but apparently, no serial numbers were allocated. The stated Air Force requirement was for 480 production aircraft. There was some confusion over whether the aircraft should be designed strictly for the long-range mission, or if it should also tackle the medium-range mission now highly prized by the ADC. The final answer was that while the F-108 was to be designed "primarily for the long-range interceptor mission," it was also to contain "provisions … to perform the medium range and scramble-from-loiter missions." These considerations appear to have been largely ignored during the actual development. Reports that the F-108 was intended to be a long-range "escort fighter" for the soon-to-enter-development B-70 appear to be unfounded, although the aircraft would certainly have been capable of such missions.[63]

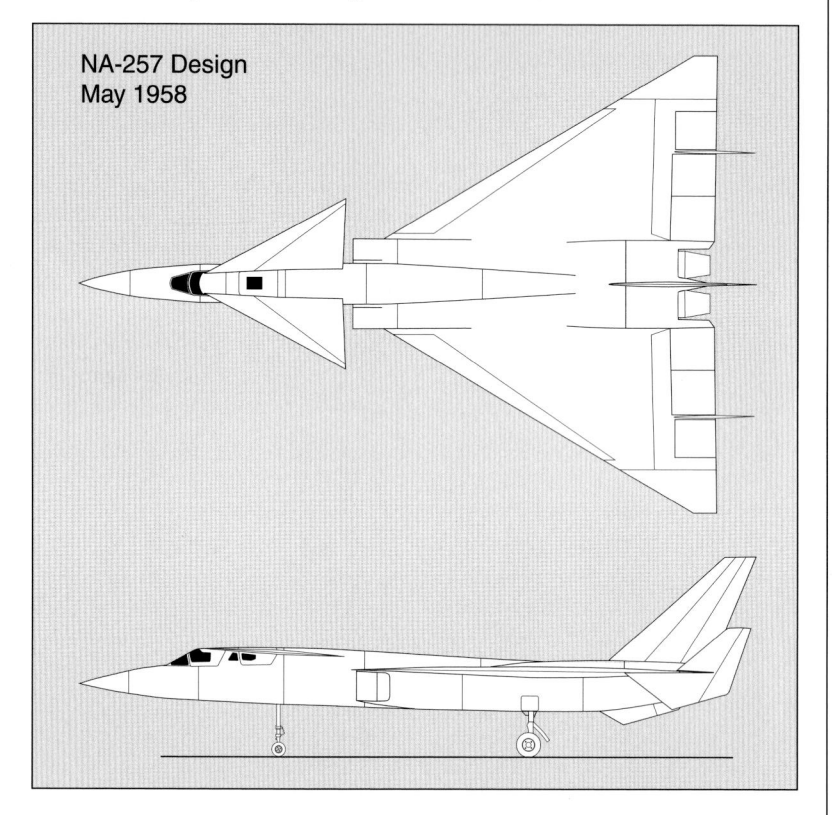

NA-257 Design
May 1958

When the Air Force finally decided to proceed with the Long Range Interceptor, they simply reaffirmed the results of the earlier competition. The internal control number used by North American changed from NA-236 to NA-257, but the aircraft was almost identical to the earlier version. (Art by Tony Landis)

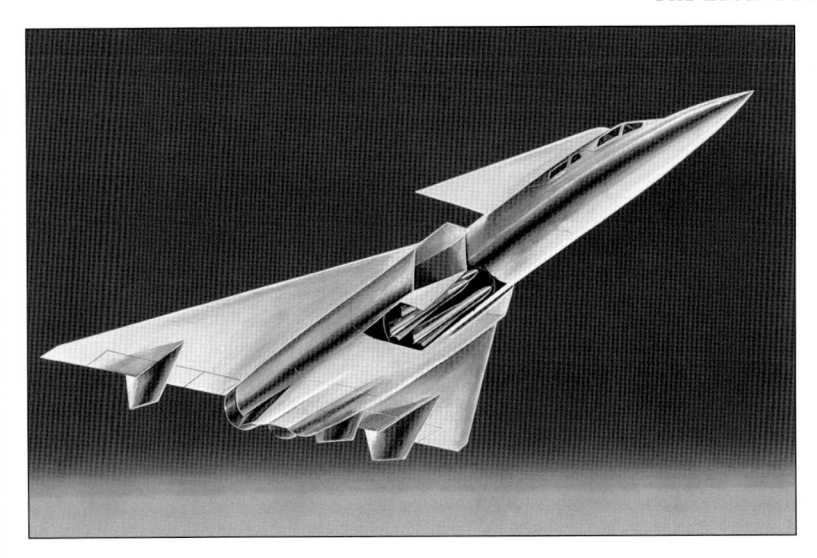

Three GAR-X missiles were carried on a rotary launcher and ejected through doors in the bottom of the fuselage. The air intakes on this design were odd, with horizontal plates extending forward above and below the intake face. (Boeing Company Archives)

The original design for the F-108 featured a large canard directly over the weapons systems operator and in many ways resembled the winning WS-110A proposal from North American (see pages 39 and 40). (Boeing Company Archives)

One of the first tasks performed by North American as the weapons systems contractor was to evaluate the competing Hughes and RCA fire control systems. The Hughes system was believed to be slightly superior in countermeasures, but the RCA design seemed more flexible, if somewhat more complex. Most importantly, however, the Hughes system was thought to be more reliable. This swung the decision to Hughes, and the RCA contract was subsequently cancelled. Almost immediately, however, there were issues between North American and Hughes. The weapon system contractor felt that the F-108 would require a radar search range of 30 to 40 nautical miles against a target traveling at Mach 1; 45 to 65 nautical miles against a Mach 2 target; and 90 to 110 nautical miles against a Mach 3 target. The Air Force generally supported these estimates. The Hughes radar, however, had a limit of about 50 nautical miles. Hughes was ordered to redesign its radar to accommodate the North American requirements, underscoring the authority of the weapons system contractor.[64]

As originally defined, the interceptor was to be highly automated, requiring human intervention primarily for takeoff and landing. This led, naturally, to a very complex vehicle. Surprisingly, developing reliable autopilots, especially for high-speed vehicles, was a major problem before small, reliable digital computers were available. Many within the ARDC favored simplifying the requirements in an effort to achieve higher reliability, a view shared by North American. General Partridge had long expressed his displeasure at the growing complexity of Air Force weapons systems, and he fully supported simplifying the vehicle. The ARDC completed a study on 17 May 1958 that concluded it would be possible to delete most of the autopilot functions because they were "not essential to successful completion of the F-108 combat mission ... and are detrimental to ... reliability." Everybody seemed to concur.[65]

Despite this simplification, the North American effort did not come cheaply. By the beginning of 1958, the company was burning more than $3 million per month, and this did not include the effort by Hughes on the fire control system and missile. In May 1958, the NA-257 design had an empty weight of 48,193 pounds and a gross takeoff weight of 99,400 pounds. The aircraft was 84.9 feet long and spanned 52.9 feet across a large delta wing that had a leading-edge sweep of 53.5 degrees and provided 1,400 square feet of area. A large canard that spanned 19.8 feet was located far forward, directly over the cockpit area. The vertical surfaces were many and varied: a large central dorsal stabilizer was flanked by smaller vertical surfaces that extended above and below the wing at mid-span, and a large ventral stabilizer was located under the fuselage. The crew of two sat in tandem in individual ejection capsules. Three GAR-X missiles were carried on a rotary launcher and fired through doors in the bottom of the fuselage.[66]

Two General Electric J93-GE-1 engines each provided 22,500 lbf at maximum power and 14,100 lbf without the afterburner. A total of 7,100 gallons of JP-6 fuel was carried in two wing and five fuselage tanks. At this point the performance estimates were still very rough, but encouraging. For the design long-range intercept mission, the aircraft needed a takeoff roll of 3,100 feet and would take 6.2 minutes to reach 40,000 feet. The combat radius was estimated at 1,002 nautical miles, and the top speed was 1,721 knots at 72,800 feet or 1,525 knots at 50,000 feet.[67]

The first part of 1958 also saw a new complication added to the F-108 program. As part of its bid for the WS-110A (B-70) competition, North American had proposed "sharing" components between the F-108 and B-70 development efforts. In theory, this would lower the cost of both aircraft, much as the anticipated sharing of subsystems between the WS-110A and WS-125A lowered the cost of those programs. Items to be shared included the basic engine design, ejection systems, some electronics, construction techniques, displays, and a myriad of minor parts. It was a brilliant move, since it allowed North American to reduce the cost of its WS-110A proposal, something that undoubtedly contributed to the company winning that program on 23 December 1957. It was, however, a decision everybody would come to regret.

One of the major resources from the F-108 that was to be tapped for the B-70 program was not hardware per se, but rather expertise. The F-108 program was spending a great deal of time and money testing materials and developing methods of fabricating aircraft from advanced alloys. In addition to the stainless-steel honeycomb panels that would come to fame on the B-70, the F-108 investigated various hardened steels, beryllium, titanium, and René-41, as well as cloth laminates and other composites. The F-108 also invested heavily into research on welding and brazing techniques, forging and casting, machining, and the technology for radiological testing of welds. Many of these technologies would benefit the aerospace industry as a whole, although they apparently did not come soon enough to significantly help Lockheed during the development of the Blackbird.[68]

North American was designing an escape capsule for the F-108 that it also wanted to use in the B-70. This was not unusual since, at the time, most aircraft manufacturers designed their own escape systems. However, in an effort to reduce development costs, the Air Force directed North American to investigate capsules being designed by Convair, Goodyear Aircraft Corporation, Martin Aircraft, and the Talco Engineering Company. The study concluded, perhaps unsurprisingly, that the North American design was the best suited for the F-108 and B-70, and the other systems were no longer considered.[69]

During the first part of 1958, North American unveiled a fixed-base mission simulator that was hosted on analog computers. The initial mission situation was an F-108 being vectored against a number of enemy bombers in a massed raid. The mechanization (programming) incorporated the ability to lock the fire control radar on a target and launch missiles at any range. The heading of the interceptor could be varied through all aspects in the horizontal plane, but was initially limited to the same altitude as the bombers. The preliminary results reported in April 1958 showed that a safe escape margin existed at a 20-mile launch range during a head-on attack using a GAR-X equipped with a nuclear warhead.[70]

Another study conducted during 1958 evaluated the effects of installing an aerial refueling capability in the interceptor, something that the Air Defense Command had traditionally shunned. Little benefit was found when only the baseline long-range intercept mission was considered, but the capability would vastly improve the "remote loiter" mission. The radius for this mission was 1,429 nautical miles, and included 150 minutes of loiter time with two refuelings. By the end of 1958, it had been decided to include aerial refueling in the baseline configuration, and a standard receptacle was added to the top of the fuselage just behind the aft canopy.[71]

The studies were never-ending. North American evaluated using the boron-based high-energy fuel proposed for the WS-110A in the

The early fixed-base simulator was not much to look at, but gave engineers a good tool to refine the F-108 design. The front seat simulator is at the left, with a television screen on the wall just ahead of the cockpit to present imagery. The back-seat simulator on the right has ASG-18 displays in the cockpit. (Boeing Company Archives)

As was common practice at the time, North American developed their own escape system for the F-108. The company intended to use the same capsule in its WS-110A design. The original F-108 capsule was designed around a 95th percentile male wearing an anti-g suit. The Air Force later decided that the capsule should be made six inches wider to allow pilots of the B-70 to wear full pressure suits when necessary. The early, narrow units already built were used for test purposes and were called Type-A capsules. (Boeing Company Archives)

F-108 instead of JP-6 and determined that HEF-3 resulted in a 6 percent increase in radius. Separately, a concern over landing distances – particularly at Arctic bases – resulted in North American recommending that a thrust reverser be installed on each engine since it offered better braking performance than drag chutes.[72]

The Air Force had asked about the feasibility of substituting Pratt & Whitney JT9-5A (early J58) engines for the General Electric J93s originally proposed, and the initial study results were available in April 1958. Maximum takeoff weight would decrease a bit, from 99,400 to 99,226 pounds, hardly enough to matter. The combat radius increased 4 nautical miles (from 1,002 to 1,006), but the area intercept mission radius decreased from 877 to 820 nautical miles. All other performance figures remained the same. The study concluded that switching did not materially affect performance, but would "cause a substantial delay" in the WS-202A program. This did not appear to settle the issue, however, and the J58 was carried as an alternate engine through at least March 1959. This effort went so far as to maintain two sets of engine installation drawings, one for the J58 and another for the J93.[73]

The mockup inspection of the radar and missile was held at the Hughes plant in Culver City, California, on 15-17 April 1958, and the Air Force concluded that the design approach was both "feasible and acceptable." After successfully passing this milestone, the Hughes XY-1 fire control system was designated AN/ASG-18 and the GAR-X missile became the GAR-9. At the same time, it was decided that Hughes would provide an infrared search and track (IRST) system as a secondary sensor for the F-108. The IRST would provide a field of view of 70x140-degrees and have an angular resolution accuracy of 1 degree. Similar, but less sophisticated, systems were being installed on the F-101 and F-102 interceptors. Exactly why an IRST was specified is uncertain since the only weapons carried by the aircraft were radar-guided (not IR) missiles that could not take cues from the optical system.[74]

North American received the first mockup of a J93-GE-1 on 7 October 1958, allowing engineers to further refine the engine compartment of the new fighter. This "engine" would also be presented at the mockup inspection early the following year. By now, the aircraft design had evolved considerably. The most obvious change was the elimination of the forward canard to improve the low-speed stall characteristics, lower trim drag, and reduce the fuselage boundary layer ahead of the inlet. The vertical surfaces above each wing had also been deleted, with an equivalent amount of area added to the stabilizers under the wing. This improved the handling characteristics and directional stability at high angles of attack and low speeds. The wing itself had changed shape slightly, spanning 56.1 feet and providing 1,865 square feet of area with a 58-degree sweep on the leading edge.[75]

The fuselage was slightly longer (89 feet), mostly to accommodate a larger weapons bay – the GAR-9 missiles were longer than previously thought. The variable-geometry air intakes on either side of the fuselage had taken on the shape used by the A3J (A-5) Vigilante and many subsequent designs both in the United States and the Soviet Union. Power was still provided by two J93-GE-1s, but the total fuel capacity was increased to 7,200 gallons, mainly because of the larger wing that contained two of the seven fuel tanks. Maximum gross takeoff weight was 101,800 pounds, and the expected radius of action was 1,005 nautical miles. Top speed was still estimated at 1,721 knots at 72,800 feet. The airframe was stressed for +5.33/-3.00-g at 80-percent internal fuel, the Air Force standard for fighters at the time.[76]

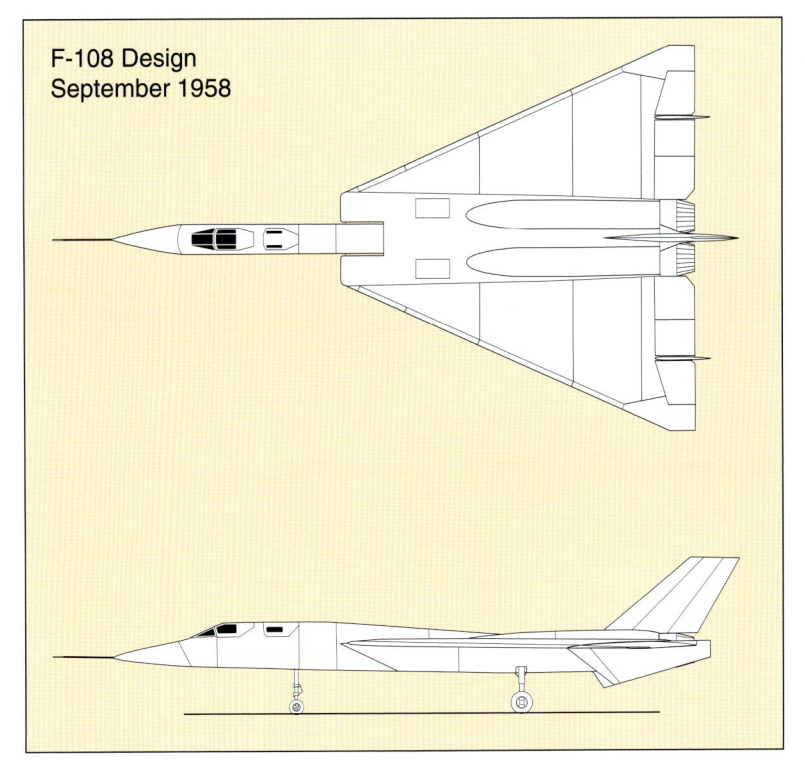

F-108 Design September 1958

The first major revision to the F-108 saw the elimination of the canard to improve the low-speed stall characteristics. The vertical surfaces above each wing were also gone, but the ventral stabilizers were larger. The airplane could be powered by J58s or the baseline J93s. (Art by Tony Landis; drawing courtesy of the Terry Panopalis Collection)

A good view of the ASG-18 and IRST installation in Snoopy. The 40-inch radar antenna allowed the system to detect bomber-size targets over 100 miles away, and provided a look-down, shoot-down capability for the F-108. Limited computer power meant only a single target could be tracked at a time. The IRST sensors are mounted on the side of the fuselage just behind the radome, and approximate the relationship between the radar and IRST on the later YF-12A. (Tony Landis Collection)

On 19 November 1958, the operational date for the F-108 was pushed back to mid-1963 due to budgetary issues. Just over a month later, on 30 December, the number of prototypes was cut from 31 to 20 and the first flight date was delayed three months to April 1961.[77]

Despite this, the year ended with some good news since the ASG-18 and GAR-9 subsystem testing in a B-25J and T-29 was progressing well. Earlier in the year, Hughes had requested that a B-58 be made available for integrated testing of the new systems, although some thought had briefly been given to using an F-106 because it was less expensive to operate. Air Force Headquarters agreed with the request for a B-58, and actually suggested that four aircraft be provided for the use of the F-108 and B-70 test programs. There was some debate over the need for so many aircraft, but two early test B-58As (55-660 and 55-665) were finally allocated in October 1958.

The ASG-18 was the first coherent pulse-Doppler radar developed in the United States. From a nominal 70,000-foot altitude, the weapon system was to be able to launch missiles "without the need for precise interceptor pre-launch maneuvers" against "any air-breathing target flying at altitudes from sea level to 100,000 feet." The fire control system was built around a 40-inch-diameter antenna and could detect B-47-size targets at a range of over 100 nautical miles at all altitudes. The radar was capable of look-down or look-up operation, but could only track a single target at a time because of limited computer power. The ASG-18 employed a liquid-cooled transmitter consisting of two traveling wave tube amplifiers in tandem to provide the desired gain, and analog circuitry for generating and processing the coherent high-pulse repetition frequency waveform. The radar consisted of 41 separate units weighing nearly 2,100 pounds that occupied most of the nose of the F-108. The entire package included a solid-state digital computer for navigation and firing solutions, an analog-attack steering computer, and an infrared search–and-track system capable of being slaved to the radar.[78]

The new radar included an inherent self-test capability, both on the ground and in flight. Prior to takeoff, circuits in each electronics bay would test the equipment and display a "readily visible go-no-go" indicator to the maintenance crew. This was a tremendous improvement over the MX-1179 and earlier systems where large and cumbersome ground test equipment was required. The in-flight self-test would be initiated by the weapons system officer, who would perform a final check of the system before the F-108 entered combat. If the results were negative, this information could be automatically relayed to the SAGE network so that a "substitute F-108" could be vectored to the battle. All of the equipment would also have time-in-service clocks and would be removed at predetermined intervals corresponding to its demonstrated mean-time-between-failure rate (in spite of its apparent operating condition). North American believed this would "help maintain confidence level and mission reliability" of all the systems.[79]

Tests of the ASG-18 continued using the B-25 and T-29 surrogates against a variety of targets, including a B-57, DC-3, and Aero Commander. All of the targets were "augmented" to provide an "equivalent reflecting area of 343 square feet" which apparently corresponded to the anticipated Soviet threat. The prototype radar was demonstrating a decent ability to find the targets, but the ranges were usually less than 40 nautical miles, substantially less than the actual requirement. The testing included an ability to find and lock onto a target dropping chaff, plus look-down acquisitions of targets in ground clutter. Flights were made over various terrain features around Southern California to collect clutter data to improve the algorithms being used.[80]

The IRST system was to be capable of detecting a tail-aspect B-47-size target at a range of 34.8 nautical miles at 45,000 altitude. From directly ahead of the bomber, the detection range was to be 10.3 nautical miles. A Mach 3 bomber – a very large target because of heat from skin friction – was to be detected at 76.5 nautical miles from any aspect. This convinced North American that lowering the infrared signature of the B-70 was essential, since it was known that the Soviets included IRST systems on virtually all of their interceptors. The prototype Hughes IRST (called X-2, with later systems being X-3) was to be installed in a C-131B transport for initial testing against a B-57 target, but this fell by the wayside due to budget cuts. Instead, the system was mounted in a turret atop the Hughes Culver City facility and a B-57 flown through the rather dense Los Angeles airspace as a target; the results were mixed mainly due to the uncontrolled target environment.[81]

Initially the IRST used a multi-element telescopic lens composed of silicon and sapphire elements and a 7-inch hemispherical silicone irdome (a term seemingly unique to Hughes) to protect the detection

An artist concept of the September 1959 version of the F-108 operating above the arctic. (Gerald H. Balzer Collection)

This is what a testbed F-106 equipped with the ASG-18 would have looked like had the Air Force opted to pursue that option. A pair of F-106As (57-239 and 57-240) were modified to test a 40-inch-diameter radar housing and were redesignated F-106C. Only 57-239 actually flew, and made ten flights during 1959 before the Air Force abandoned the effort. (Terry Panopalis Collection)

The Elusive Mach 3 Fighter

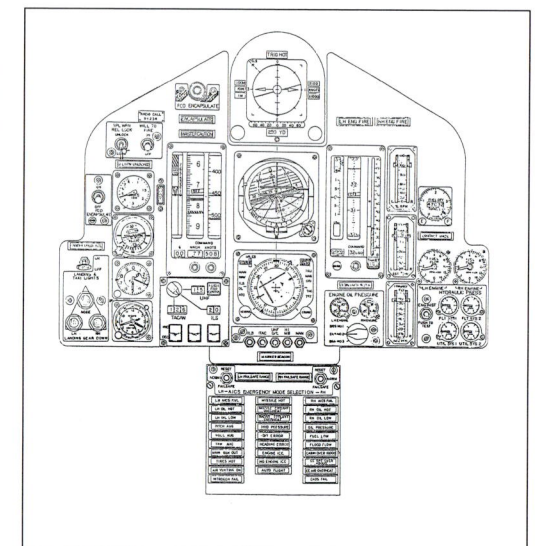

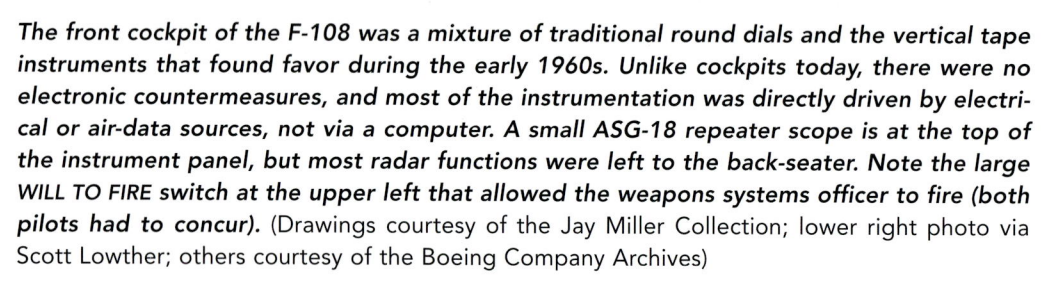

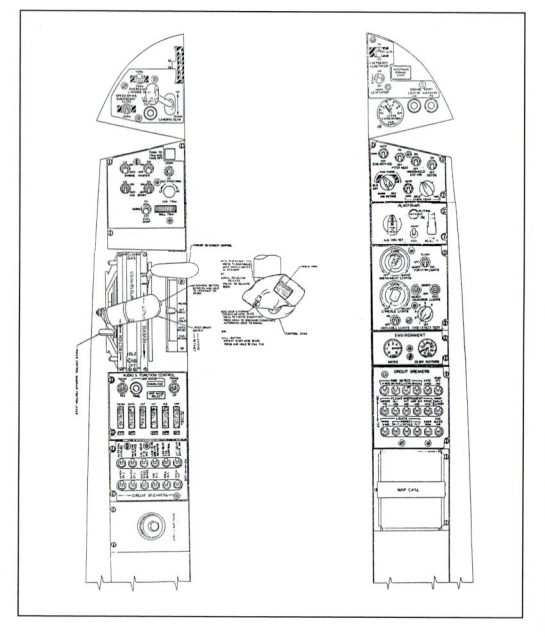

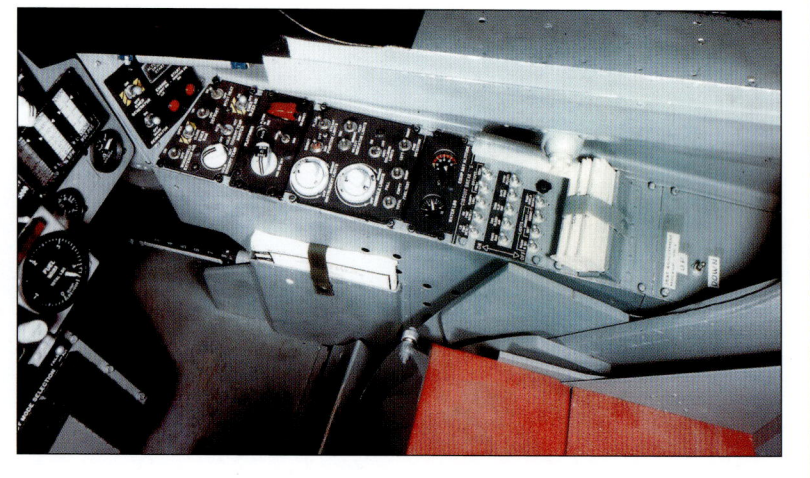

The front cockpit of the F-108 was a mixture of traditional round dials and the vertical tape instruments that found favor during the early 1960s. Unlike cockpits today, there were no electronic countermeasures, and most of the instrumentation was directly driven by electrical or air-data sources, not via a computer. A small ASG-18 repeater scope is at the top of the instrument panel, but most radar functions were left to the back-seater. Note the large WILL TO FIRE switch at the upper left that allowed the weapons systems officer to fire (both pilots had to concur). (Drawings courtesy of the Jay Miller Collection; lower right photo via Scott Lowther; others courtesy of the Boeing Company Archives)

The Elusive Mach 3 Fighter

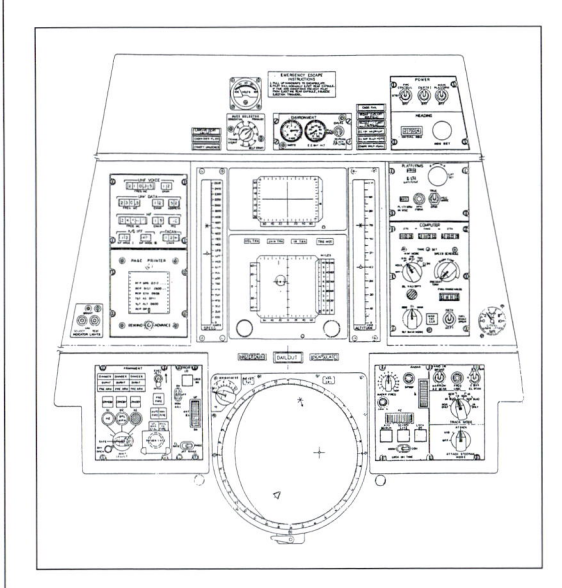

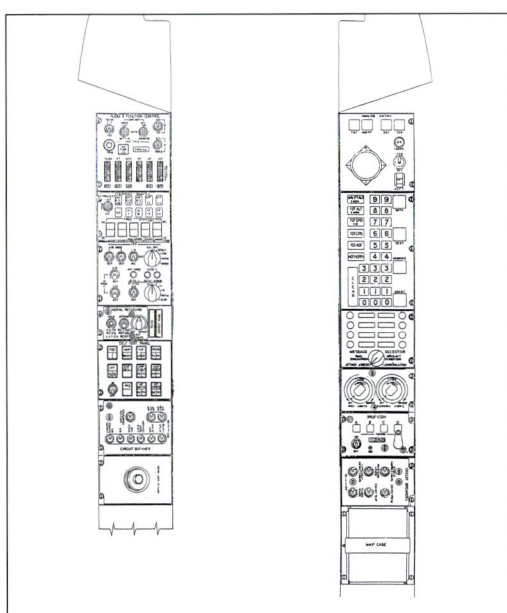

The back cockpit of the F-108, unsurprisingly, looked much like the Lockheed YF-12A would later when it began flight testing the ASG-18 and AIM-47. In the F-108, the armament controls are at the lower left side of the instrument panel and contain lights and switches for three missiles. The radar and infrared controls are at the lower right, with the computer and navigation system just above them. Data was entered into the computer using the keyboard on the right console. The back seater did not have flight controls or throttles, and had very limited visibility outside the airplane. (Drawings courtesy of the Jay Miller Collection; lower photos via Scott Lowther; main photo courtesy of the Boeing Company Archives)

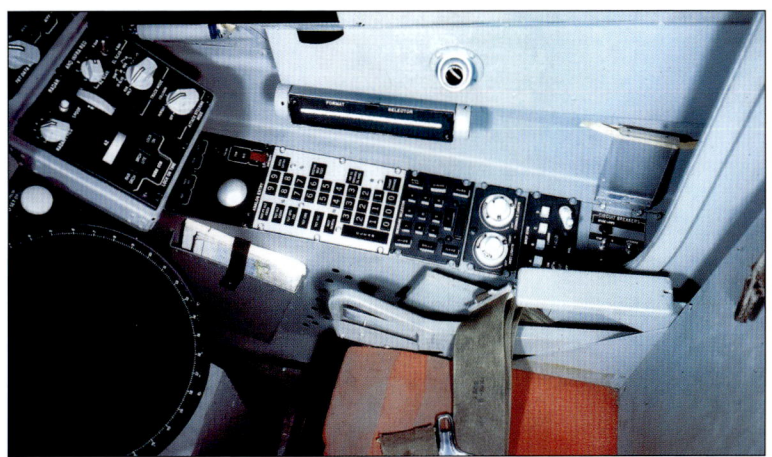

The artists showed the F-108 operating out of austere arctic bases with a minimum of ground support equipment. Given the sophistication of the ASG-18 and J93s, it is doubtful this is what the maintenance scene would have looked like. (Terry Panopalis Collection)

array. A single IRST receptor would be located on the leading edge of each F-108 wing root near the junction with the air intake. This location was determined to offer adequate viewing coverage, but wind tunnel testing revealed that the location imposed a drag penalty equal to 30 nautical miles in range. A variety of other locations were evaluated, with the two most promising being a pair of retractable sensors located on the top and bottom of the forward fuselage, or a single sensor located in the extreme nose of the radome. The former seemed overly complicated, while the latter restricted the ASG-18 antenna coverage directly ahead. In the end, it was decided to use a pair of 6-inch elliptical (ogive) shaped irdomes in the original location on the wing leading edges. This reduced the range penalty to a couple of miles and still offered reasonable fields of views without any mechanical complications. The IRST sensors were slaved to point in the same direction as the ASG-18 radar antenna.[82]

As conceived, the GAR-9 was to be powered by an Aerojet-General XM59 solid-propellant rocket that provided a maximum speed of Mach 6 and a range of 100 nautical miles. As originally conceived, the missile relied exclusively on semi-active radar homing (SARH) guidance. The missile was designed to lock onto a 343-square-foot radar cross-section target at a range of 38 nautical miles, having flown the first 62 nautical miles on autopilot based on prelaunch programming. By the end of 1958, it was estimated that the seeker had the ability to lock onto a 100-square-foot radar cross-section target at a range of 63 nautical miles. The improvement was primarily due to changes in the signal-to-clutter ratio algorithms.[83]

For reasons that are not readily apparent from the available documentation, the Air Force was not happy with the progress on the SARH seeker for the GAR-9. The first approach to correcting the perceived problem was to develop a "dual mode" missile that used SARH for the initial portion of flight (instead of the preprogrammed autopilot) and then switched to infrared homing for terminal guidance. This presented many problems for Hughes, since the missile had not been designed to accommodate both seekers and their processing equipment. Early estimates were that the missile would need to grow 2 inches in diameter, something that would have serious repercussions for the F-108. By December 1958, the Air Force had directed Hughes to concentrate on the development of an infrared-only seeker, but to continue an operational analysis of the dual-mode concept. It was a confusing time.[84]

Preliminary planning showed that the missile would conduct its early unguided flight tests from one of the auxiliary bomb pylons under a B-58. It was expected that the missiles would be free-dropped from the pylon at Mach 1.5 and 50,000 feet, then be boosted to approximately Mach 3 and 70,000 feet by the Aerojet-General solid-rocket motor. These tests would be conducted from an essentially unmodified B-58A (some wiring would need to be changed, as well as the suspension hooks) while Convair was building the special pods that would be used during the guided flights later in the program.[85]

By late 1958, the Aerojet-General solid rocket motor was running into problems. The initial test motors were deemed unsatisfactory because of "spots and streaks of fuel unmixed with the oxidizer" during the loading process. Two later motors, however, were considered satisfactory, and one of these was fired in a test cell at –65 degrees Fahrenheit; the other was fired at +200 degrees Fahrenheit. Both experienced some mechanical problems, but the overall ballistic performance was considered satisfactory. In January 1959, a test motor overheated during a full-duration test, but this was attributed to a unique motor case configuration. By May 1959, environmental testing of XM59 motors had revealed a tendency to crack during temperature cycle, rendering the motors unusable. Unfortunately, temperature cycles are a fact of life for fast, high-flying aircraft such as the F-108. Continued problems would lead Hughes to abandon the Aerojet-General motor in favor of a Lockheed-developed storable liquid propellant rocket engine for a short time before the program switched to a Lockheed Propulsion Company XSR13-LP-1 solid rocket motor by the time the GAR-9 was actually built. The new motor had a great deal less power, providing only a Mach 4 top speed instead of the anticipated Mach 6 capability.[86]

North American, Air Force, and Navy personnel had conducted a study during early 1958 to determine if the development of the GAR-9 and the Bendix AAM-N-10 Eagle air-to-air missile could be combined. The Eagle was the primary armament for the Douglas F6D Missileer fleet defense fighter that was under development for the Navy. The study indicated that the GAR-9 and Eagle requirements were not compatible; this is probably just as well, since the Missileer program was soon cancelled. Interestingly, much of what was to be learned while developing the GAR-9 was later used for the Navy AIM-54 Phoenix, which armed the Grumman F-14 Tomcat that effectively replaced the F6D concept.[87]

The issue of polar navigation was still critical during the late 1950s before the advent of reliable inertial platforms and star trackers. For the F-108, it was decided that the moving map display would switch from its normal true North orientation to a hybrid grid that was oriented to the Greenwich meridian. A suitable chart showing this polar grid would be included in the horizontal tactics display film magazine. Upon switching to the polar navigation mode, the heading indications in the aircraft would be rotated through the appropriate angle to relate them to Greenwich. The Air Force had wrestled with this problem since the late 1940s and had yet to find a truly acceptable answer. It would take a few more years for the electronic systems to solve the problem for good.[88]

The December 1958 configuration mostly represented the F-108 that would be reviewed at the mockup inspection the following month. The fuselage was 89.2 feet long and the wing had taken on a "cranked arrow" shape, spanning 57.4 feet and providing 1,865 square feet of area. The basic wing was unchanged except for wingtip extensions that improved "stability at higher lift coefficients." A less noticeable change was the addition of a slight twist to the leading edge of the wing to reduce transonic drag. The single dorsal stabilizer was now all-moving, with only a small forward piece being fixed (much like the final XB-70A design) with the hinge line canted forward. This design proved lighter due to an inherently stiffer load path. Fixed ventral stabilizers were still mounted under the wings at mid span and under each outer corner of the rear fuselage. A pair of J93-GE-1 engines provided power, but they were now rated at 24,800 lbf in afterburner and 16,900 lbf without. Six fuel tanks provided 7,109 gallons of JP-6 fuel.[89]

Empty weight was up to 50,544 pounds, with a maximum take-off weight of 102,234 pounds. North American stated "this high performance air vehicle cruises and combats at Mach 3 with a 1,000-nautical mile radius on internal fuel. It has a [combat] ceiling in excess of 77,000 feet and a zoom-climb ceiling in excess of 100,000 feet. Under normal loading and weather, the air vehicle requires runway lengths of only 3,200 feet for takeoff and landing. It can be operated from 6,000-foot runways in all weather conditions. From a nominal 70,000-foot combat altitude, missile launch can be accomplished against any air-breathing target flying at altitudes from sea level to 100,000 feet." The accompanying charts showed a maximum speed of 1,721 knots at altitudes up to 81,800 feet.[90]

As with any large development effort, the number of details that must be considered during design are never-ending. For instance, a study was conducted to evaluate the effect of the landing gear doors being open or closed during takeoff and acceleration. It was determined that the performance effects were negligible due "to the very favorable thrust-to-weight ratio of the F-108A." Therefore, North American opted to leave the doors open whenever the gear was down since this reduced the retraction time and enhanced reliability since the doors would not cycle as often. Similarly, there was a study to determine if separate landing and taxi lights were required. The result was that two landing lights would articulate and have a low-power setting to provide appropriate illumination while taxiing.[91]

The escape capsules presented a unique challenge for designers since they were a relatively new technology. One of the more interesting items was how the pilot could control the aircraft after he had encapsulated (certain emergencies might force a pilot to encapsulate, but not eject from the aircraft). In the B-70, this would be accomplished by providing an "electric throttle retard" capability, but a different tack was selected for the F-108. Although it had been scaled down considerably from its original "fully automated" concept, the automatic flight control subsystem in the F-108 was the most advanced yet designed. It was decided that the F-108, being a fighter, was more likely to be in an unusual attitude when the pilot encapsulated than the B-70, hence the extra effort.[92]

The pilot could observe the main instrument panel through the window in the escape capsule, but could not manipulate any controls. However, when the pilot closed his capsule, a "descent button" inside the capsule was armed. If the pilot depressed this button, the throttles were automatically retarded to the idle position, the roll attitude hold mode was engaged, and the aircraft was driven to a wings-level attitude. When the roll attitude reached less than 7 degrees, the heading hold mode was engaged, and the pitch atti-

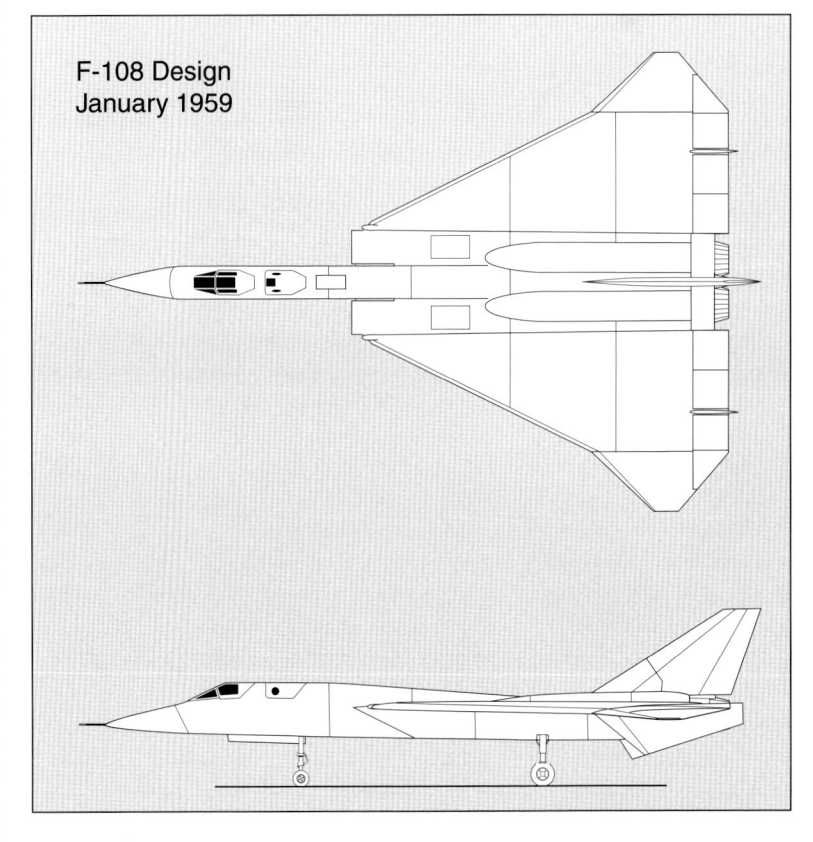

F-108 Design
January 1959

A cranked-arrow wing was incorporated onto the F-108 at the end of 1958. The basic structure of the wing did not change, but the shape was altered by a pair of wingtip extensions that improved stability under certain flight conditions. The leading edge of the wing also received a slight twist to reduce drag. (Art by Tony Landis)

The Elusive Mach 3 Fighter

The F-108 mockup under construction, probably sometime in December 1958 just prior to the development engineering inspection. The canopies could be raised and lowered, and the yellow cover on the irdome for the IRST can be seen at the wing root. The other side of the mockup did not have any skin, allowing the inspectors to view the structure and subsystem installation. (Boeing Historical Archives)

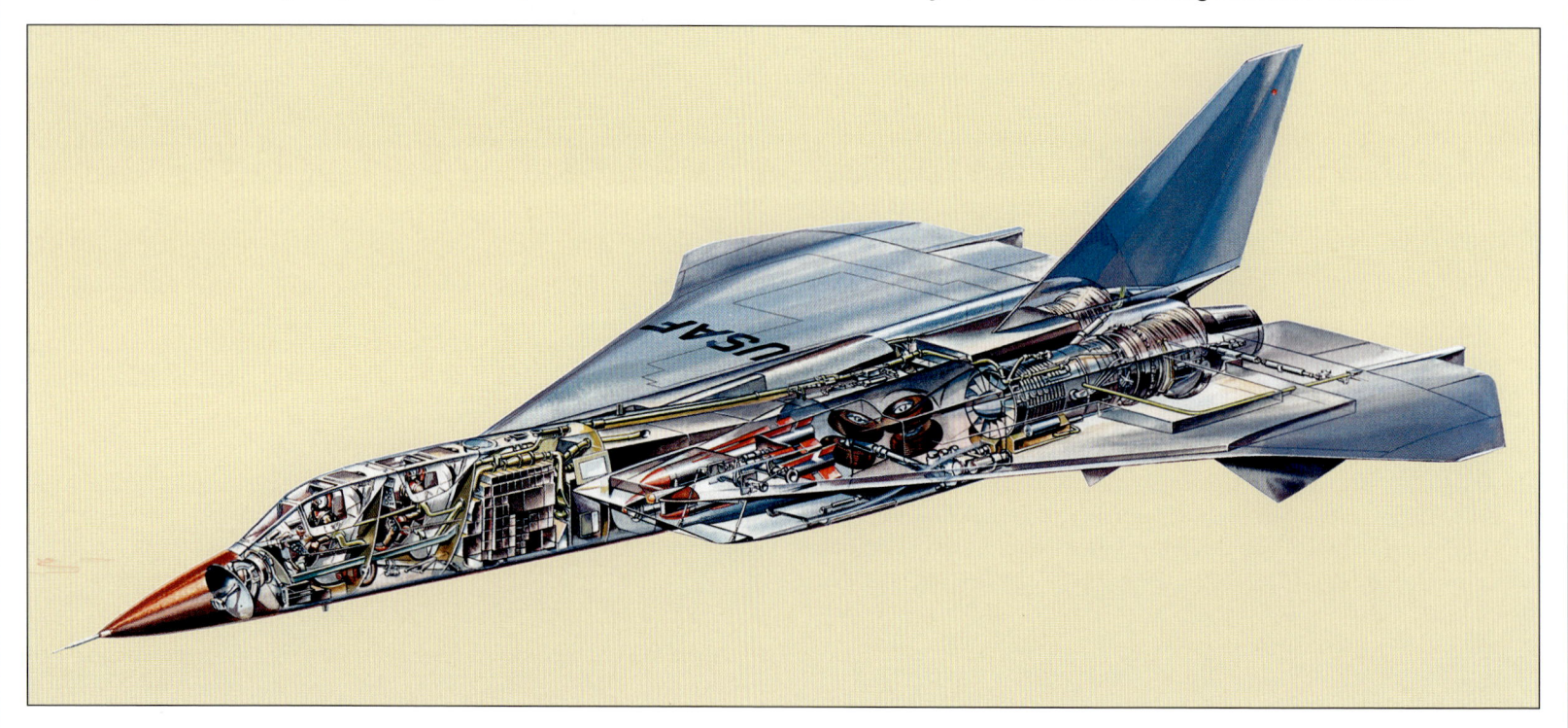

This cutaway gives a good look inside the planned F-108. The three GAR-9 missiles are on a rotary launcher in the center of the airplane. Like the B-70, the F-108 had a complicated landing gear folding sequence to allow the gear to fit into the fuselage. The large electronics compartment just behind the cockpit held equipment for the ASG-18 and navigation systems. The thrust reversers shown on the drawing do not match the engineering description, and its hard to see how they would have worked as drawn. (Boeing Historical Archives)

This is how the mockup looked during the inspection. Standard Air Force markings had been added, and various exhibits had been set up around the mockup. (Terry Panopalis Collection)

The mockup continued to evolve, and sometime after the inspection it was given a coat of gloss white paint and a painted backdrop. Note the back canopy window has changed shape. (Boeing Historical Archives)

tude was driven slightly nose-up. The aircraft would decelerate and descend at a predetermined rate until it reached 40,000 feet, then it would level off and fly straight and level until it exhausted its fuel. During the time, the pilot (and back-seater) could elect to eject, or they could open their capsules and retake control of the aircraft.[93]

A detailed presentation was made to the Air Force development engineering inspection (DEI) team the week of 5 January 1959, and the F-108 mockup was inspected the week of 26 January. The chairman of the inspection team was Colonel Linus F. Upson, Jr. from the ARDC, and a notable member was double-ace (at the time, later a triple ace) Lieutenant Colonel Robin Olds. In addition to a full-scale mockup of the entire aircraft, a metal mockup of the forward fuselage was provided to demonstrate the fitment of the ASG-18, and a wooden "vision" mockup was constructed to show the view from the cockpit. A notable item briefed to the inspection team was the use of semi-conductor (solid-state) relays instead of the reed-relays that had been used to switch electrical power in all previous aircraft. The use of this advanced technology was expected to significantly increase the reliability of the electrical system. It was also decided that the first five aircraft would use metal noses instead of composite radomes and would not be equipped with fire control systems, mainly to allow 12-foot-long flight test booms to be installed. First flight was expected in March 1961, and the Air Force still had a stated requirement for 480 of the aircraft.[94]

The major change between the December 1958 configuration and that presented at the mockup inspection was the powerplant. The J93-GE-1 engines that had been carried as a baseline since the beginning of the program were replaced with J93-GE-3R variants that

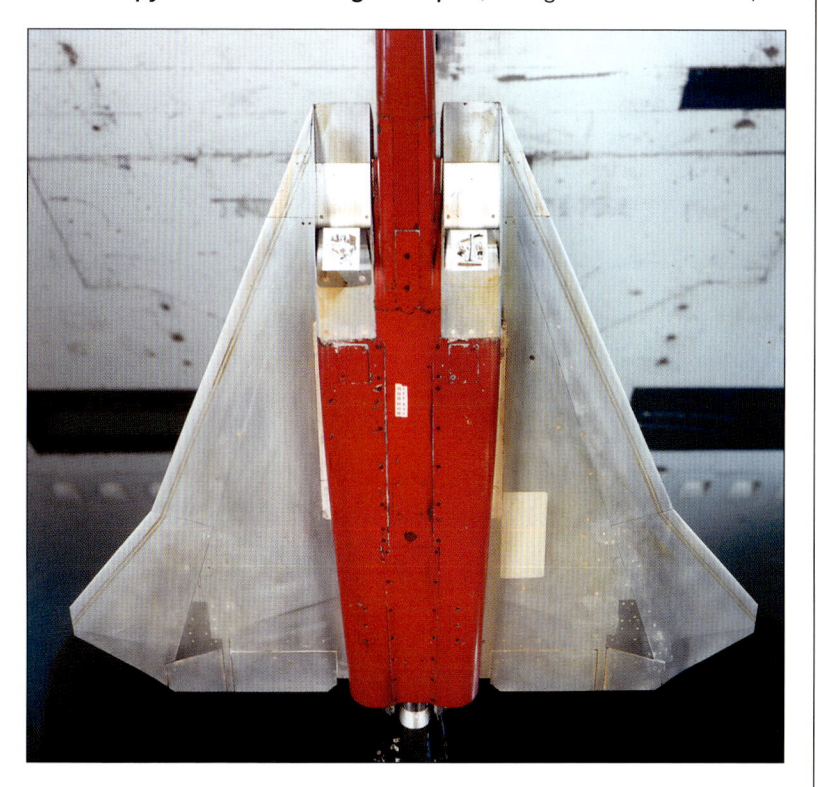

The new wing planform was extensively tested in a variety of wind tunnels. This brightly-painted model gives a good view of the shape of the wing and air intakes. (Boeing Historical Archives)

produced 27,200 lbf at maximum thrust and 17,500-lbf normal thrust. These finally included the thrust reversers that had long been desired, adding 345 pounds to each engine. Testing of the thrust reverser had begun at Edwards in January 1959 using a scaled-down reverser attached to a J79 engine; these tests indicated that the design would meet the performance requirements.[95]

The decision to use a thrust reverser was creating some problems in addition to the extra 690 pounds. The installation of the J93-GE-1 (no reverser) with a convergent-divergent nozzle used a seal between the airframe and nozzle to guide air flowing around the engine to cool the afterburner. The J93-GE-3R was equipped with a translating-type reverser that stowed within the airframe above and below the engine and slid to the aft end of the convergent-divergent nozzle for thrust reversing. This made it difficult to design a seal since the space had to allow the reverser to deploy as needed. Also, there was a great deal of debate over whether the thrust reverser could be deployed in flight to enhance maneuverability; the final decision was that this placed too much stress on the engine and airframe and the reverser was limited to under 180 knots airspeed.[96]

The escape capsule concept was coming along well by January 1959, and nine weighted capsules had been completed for the initial series of aircraft drop tests and high-speed sled tests that were scheduled between June and October 1959. An additional five capsules were being manufactured for additional sled tests, aerial tests, water tests, and pressure chamber tests. The first of these capsules was to be delivered in November 1959 to support a second series of high-speed sled tests. This program would be dealt a blow during the mockup inspection when it was decided that the capsule should be 6 inches wider than North American had expected. This was mainly to allow the pilot to wear the soon-to-be-developed David Clark A/P22S full-pressure suit, although the baseline concept of operations showed a shirtsleeve environment with the pilots in just a flight suit and helmet. The early narrow capsules were subsequently called "Type A" capsules, while the wider ones were called "Type B" units.[97]

As could be expected, the F-108 was being looked at to fill roles other than the long-range interceptor it had been designed as. Perhaps the most important was as a gap-filler for the Distant Early Warning (DEW) radars. If a few aircraft were based at remote arctic airstrips, a sufficient number of them could be constantly airborne to eliminate the gaps that existed in radar coverage. Each F-108 could scan about 210,000 square nautical miles – an area a little larger than Texas – per hour. In addition to basic radar coverage, the F-108 would also provide positive identification of targets and act as a radar and communications relay for other F-108s scrambled to intercept the bombers. It was noted that the ambient temperatures encountered by the F-108 at the arctic (ZI) bases would "not last longer than 36 hours below –25°F or 2 hours below –40°F." Separately, it had already been decided that the performance of the F-108 was sufficient to allow it to intercept any known target well outside the air defense identification zone with the exception of a small area of the southern United States where there was very limited radar coverage, hence preventing early detection of possible targets.[98]

By the time of the mockup inspection, the escape capsules were undergoing tests. Here is a dummy capsule with the stabilization booms and parachutes deployed. The impact attenuator bag is on the bottom, and various other waffle-pattern airbags are around the capsule to provide floatation in the event of a water landing. (Jim Tuttle Collection)

THE ELUSIVE MACH 3 FIGHTER

**F-108 Design
June 1959**

**F-108 Design
1960 Evolution**

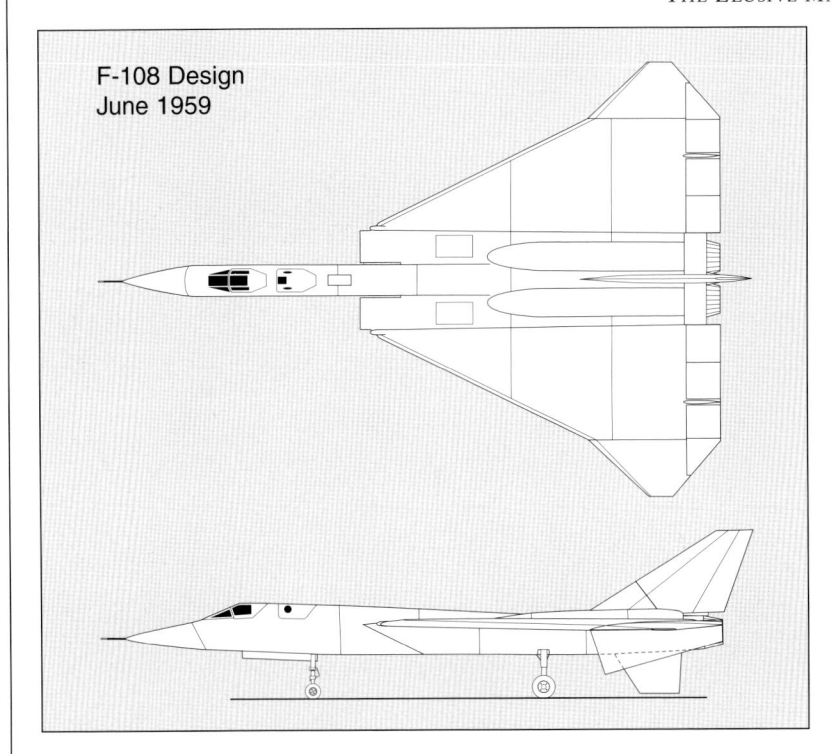

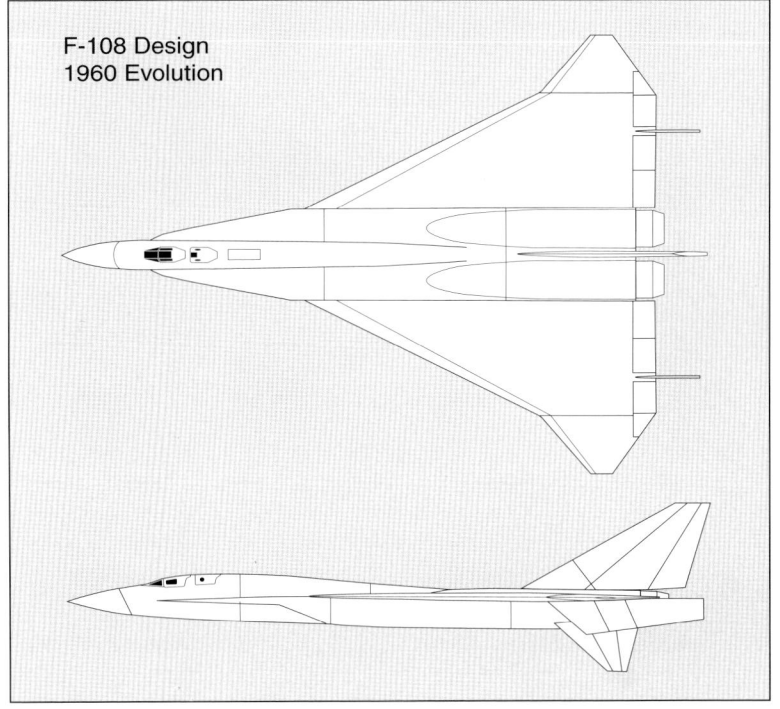

Continued concerns over directional stability led North American to add large folding ventral stabilizers on the lower fuselage corners. The hinge line for the dorsal rudder also changed slightly. (Art by Tony Landis)

Hughes and North American continued to refine the basic F-108 design even after the program was cancelled, since there was still a requirement for a Mach 3 interceptor. (Art by Tony Landis)

The long-range interceptor was gathering support during early 1959 based on its apparent successful development, but this was outweighed by an increasing funding problem. The Air Defense Command opposed any further delay in the operational service date (as they had opposed the previous delays), and the Air Force Scientific Advisory Board also supported the program. The Joint Chiefs of Staff evaluated the F-108 against yet-another B-58 interceptor concept, and substantiated the value of the F-108. It was pointed out that the F-108 program was paying for the development of systems for the B-70 bomber, and that these costs would not go away even if the F-108 were eliminated. However, the politicians did not seem to care; development continued at least for the time being.[99]

During May 1959, Hughes finalized the design of the dual-mode GAR-9. It was noted that the infrared system provided "an improved capability under certain ECM and clutter conditions when radar guidance may be degraded. It also provides a standby capability in the event of radar failure." This seems to indicate that the missile could be launched in full-IR mode without using the SARH feature. The length and wingspan of the two versions were the same: 150.5 and 33.0 inches, respectively. The dual-mode version was, however, 2 inches greater in diameter (15.5 instead of 13.5 inches) and its prelaunch gross weight was 180 pounds heavier (998 versus 818 pounds).[100]

The increased diameter and weight of the dual-mode missile meant that North American would need to redesign the weapons bays on the F-108, costing several hundred miles in range. This was unacceptable to the Air Force. Fortunately, improvements in the design of the SARH seeker seemed to eliminate the need for the IR component, and ultimately the Air Force decided to cancel the development of the dual-mode seeker and its revised airframe. It appears that none of the dual-mode missiles were actually constructed.

Both versions of the missile had a tail-control configuration with the control surfaces hinged near the center of pressure in a "gapped" arrangement to provide high-altitude maneuverability. The fuzing antennas were mounted on the leading edge of the wings, like all earlier versions of the Falcon. Both missiles shared the same construction: a semi-monocoque stainless steel fuselage with solid cast magnesium wings. An ethylene glycol and water cooling system – provided by the F-108 – was required for both missiles while they were carried in the aircraft.[101]

The National Laboratories began developing a 0.25-kiloton W-42 nuclear warhead for the GAR-9 during early 1958, but it was soon cancelled. Note that the W-42 was a 0.25-kiloton device (250 pounds), *not* 250 kilotons as generally reported. An unspecified alternate nuclear warhead was selected, but its test record prior to the moratorium on nuclear testing was not considered satisfactory, so it too was cancelled. Other nuclear warheads were investigated, and several fit into the GAR-9 without major modification, but no final decision was forthcoming. As late as February 1959, "special" warheads were still being investigated, but attention had also turned toward conventional high explosive warheads. In the end, the idea of using a nuclear

The Elusive Mach 3 Fighter

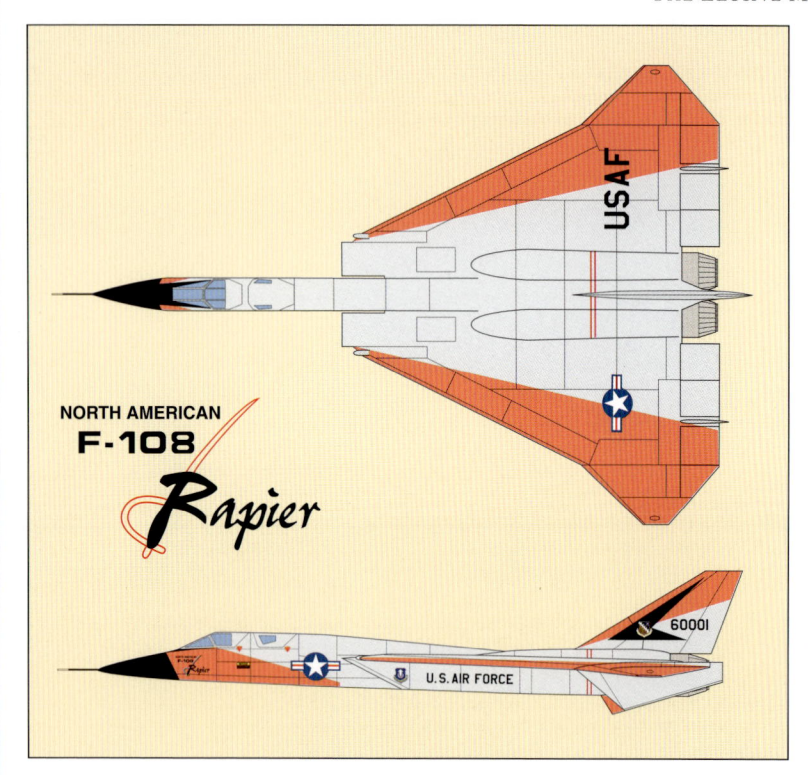

Speculative version of what an F-108 assigned to the Air Force Flight Test Center at Edwards AFB might have looked like in the markings of the period. The logo was used by North American. (Art by Tony Landis)

A slight variation on the same theme by artist Craig Kodera. (Original artwork by Craig Kodera, ©2004)

warhead was dropped and a 100-pound conventional warhead with a proximity fuze used.[102]

The aircraft was named Rapier on 15 May 1959, continuing a short-lived tradition of naming North American fighters after swords. A revised aircraft configuration was issued on 12 June where the basic external appearance of the aircraft had not changed, but many details had been refined. The wing leading edge had been changed from a relatively rounded shape to a "sharp" airfoil with an included angle of 4 degrees. Directional stability had become an issue during the latest round of wind tunnel tests, and a couple of changes were made to fix the problem. The ventral stabilizers under the wing were larger with slightly less leading edge sweep, and their leading edge was extended forward and the lower edge downward to provide 88.5 versus the original 75 square feet. The hinge line on the vertical stabilizer was changed again, this time remaining canted all the way to the fuselage. The wing gained 4 degrees dihedral to provide adequate ground clearance for the larger wing ventral stabilizers. The fixed ventral stabilizers under the fuselage had been replaced with much larger units that now folded to either side when the wheels were down to provide runway clearance. This increased their area from 10.9 square feet each to 37 square feet.[103]

The forward fuselage was slightly modified by decreasing the forebody camber. This reduced drag at supersonic speeds and provided a small increase in range that could be used to compensate for a growth in weight. The aircraft now had an empty weight of 50,907 pounds and a maximum takeoff weight of 104,320 pounds. The increase in gross weight resulted from the addition of a tail bumper under the rear fuselage, the larger escape capsules, improvements to the air intakes, the larger ventral stabilizers, a higher-capacity environmental control system, heavier missiles, and stiffening the rudder, wing, and fuselage. Two J93-GE-3AR engines with thrust reversers provided power, fed 7,109 gallons of JP-6 from four wing tanks and five fuselage tanks. Maximum thrust was rated at 29,300 lbf, and normal thrust was up to 20,900 lbf. Surprisingly, the estimated performance did not change. A study showed the aircraft would require 3.6 maintenance hours for each flight hour.[104]

The cost of the program, however, would eventually overshadow all of the technical progress. In June 1959, the anticipated peak production rate was cut, and on 21 August, the program was placed in the "strictest austerity" category. A variety of schedule slips, technical changes, production efficiencies, and other techniques were considered. It did not matter; the Air Force could not come up with the funds to continue, and the F-108 was officially cancelled on 23 September 1959. North

American had issued an internal reference number – NA-268 – for the flight test effort 12 days earlier which would go unused.[105]

At the time of the cancellation, the major subcontractors involved in the F-108 program included AiResearch (central air data subsystem), Autonetics (automatic flight control system), Cleveland Pneumatic Industries (landing gear), Columbus Division of North American (intermediate fuselage), Convair (wing), the Electronic Specialty Company (antennas), the Federal Division of the International Telephone & Telegraph Company (ASG-41 mission and traffic control subsystem), Hamilton Standard (air conditioning and pressurization), and Marquardt (air induction control subsystem).

The Pentagon did, however, continue development of the ASG-18 fire control system and GAR-9 missile. The design of the ASG-18 was to be frozen after 104 flight test hours in the B-58 (it had accumulated more than 1,000 in the B-25), while the design of the GAR-9 would be frozen after 24 flight test hours and the firing of two unguided and six guided prototypes. Since the requirement for a long-range interceptor had not gone away, the Air Force investigated using the ASG-18 and GAR-9 on another aircraft. In the end, they found that only the F-108 could do the job, and recommended that the North American effort be reinstated, or that the fire control system be cancelled also. The Pentagon disagreed, and funds were provided to continue the Hughes effort through 30 June 1960.[106]

The cancellation of the F-108 pushed approximately $180 million worth of development effort onto the B-70 for subsystems that had been intended to be common. There were some further unrecognized cost increases because the size of orders for raw materials was less than expected, resulting in smaller discounts. More importantly, the most likely candidate for a Mach 3 interceptor faded from the scene.[107]

LATER TESTING

On 17 October 1958, Convair had received a contract to modify two B-58As (55-660 and 55-665) and to manufacture three specially configured pods for ASG-18 and GAR-9 testing. A shortage of funds resulted in this being cut back to a single B-58A (55-665) and two pods. The first pod was completed on 28 May 1959 and the second on 15 July 1959. They each featured a large internal bay for a single GAR-9 missile, a cooling system, telemetry equipment, and tracking flares.[108]

The B-58A was transferred from the Air Force Flight Test Center (AFFTC) to Convair (on the B-58 contract) on 14 February 1959, and accepted by North American on a bailment agreement AF33(600)-3702 on 18 February. The aircraft was subsequently transferred from North American back to Convair, then to Hughes as government-furnished property. Nothing in the government is simple.[109]

Beginning on 23 February 1959, the forward fuselage of the B-58 was extensively reconfigured to accept the ASG-18 radar and its 40-inch antenna. The new radome was almost 7 feet longer and slightly larger in diameter, and earned the aircraft the name *Snoopy*. The second and third crew stations of the B-58 also received substantial alterations to accommodate the ASG-18 displays and controls, while the front cockpit received minor changes to accommodate a small ASG-18 scope. The B-58 modifications began on 2 March 1959 and were completed on 2 August after which the aircraft was delivered to Hughes where the ASG-18 and its hydraulically actuated antenna were installed.[110]

Snoopy *in 1961 or 1962 ...* (Jim Eastham)

Initial ground tests with the complete system included dummy GAR-9 launches into a Styrofoam-lined pit. The first flight of the modified B-58 was on 11 March 1960, although problems with the aircraft prevented the fire control system from being operated. On 22 March, after repairs, the B-58 flew for 1 hour 40 minutes and the ASG-18 operated for 50 minutes. The radar successfully detected a B-57 target at 14 nautical miles.[111]

In August 1961 the first GAR-9 missile was launched from the ground to verify the performance of its Lockheed XSR13-LP-1 rocket engine. By January 1962, three unguided ground-launches had been

... Snoopy in 2003. After the AN/ASG-18 testing was completed, the B-58 was stripped of all usable components and placed on the photographic calibration range at Edwards AFB. Years of sitting in the desert sun on the open range, as well as vandals looking for souvenirs, have taken their toll on this rare airplane. (Tony Landis)

conducted, and on 15 January, the first guided missile came within 55 feet of a QF-80 target drone flying at 13,500 feet. On 25 May 1962, the first GAR-9 air-launch was conducted from *Snoopy* while flying at 36,000 feet over the Edwards range. The missile passed within 6 feet of a QF-80 target drone that was approximately 15 nautical miles from the B-58. A similar test on 17 August 1962 resulted in the missile grazing the side of the QF-80 target. However, a launch on 21 February 1963, against a Vought Regulus II target resulted in the GAR-9 breaking up in-flight. Testing was halted while Hughes attempted to understand the failure. By July 1963, both the GAR-9 and the B-58 had been modified and flight-testing continued.

The original 7-inch diameter IRST system was also installed on the B-58 testbed, one sensor on each side of the forward fuselage, in about the same relative position to the radar as they would occupy on the later Lockheed YF-12A. These were chosen instead of the newer (and more sensitive) 6-inch ogive units simply because they were finished and ready for testing.[112]

Although it would not benefit the now-cancelled F-108 program, it had been decided to use the ASG-18 and GAR-9 in three interceptor versions of Kelly Johnson's fabled Lockheed Blackbirds. Hughes completed the first ASG-18 system for the YF-12A in late 1961 and it was installed and ground-tested during early 1962. The GAR-9 was redesignated AIM-47 in 1962, and ultimately, about 80 missiles were manufactured. By late 1963, the YF-12As were capable of conducting fully guided launches of the AIM-47 and the use of the B-58 began to decline. The last launches from *Snoopy* were during February 1964,

Rarely seen image of an AIM-47 missile launch from the B-58. The image is from a frame of movie film, explaining its quality. (Jay Miller Collection via 'Coz' Mallozzi Collection.)

and the aircraft was retired shortly thereafter. The ASG-18 was removed to support the YF-12A program, and the B-58 airframe was moved to the Edwards photo range where it still languishes.

Eventually the YF-12A program proved the worthiness of the ASG-18 and AIM-47. On 28 September 1965, an AIM-47 was fired from a YF-12A flying at Mach 3.2 and 75,000 feet. Telemetry

Two specially configured pods were manufactured by Convair to house a single AIM-47 missile and its associated support hardware and cooling system. Note the missile hanging from the extended launch rack. (Hughes Aircraft)

The first YF-12A (60-6934) during a test flight in late 1963. All three YF-12s were initially flown with only the nose and chine areas painted black, and were painted black overall just prior to their delivery to Edwards AFB in March 1964. The YF-12A was a minimal adaptation of the CIA-developed A-12 reconnaissance aircraft equipped with the ASG-18 radar and GAR-9 missile originally intended for the F-108. (Lockheed Martin)

showed that the missile missed its intended target – flying 36 miles away at 40,000 feet – by less than seven feet. After that, the Air Force was ready to test the system against more realistic targets, and the first and third YF-12As were flown to Eglin AFB, Florida, for firing trials. On 25 April 1966, Lockheed test pilot Jim Eastham fired an unarmed AIM-47 against a QB-47 flying 60,000 feet below the Blackbird (which was flying at 75,000 feet and Mach 3.2). The missile passed through the forward root of the QB-47's horizontal stabilizer, right where the radar reflection was greatest. If the missile had been armed, the bomber would have been destroyed. Instead, the controllers managed to land the crippled aircraft; it was repaired and later suffered the indignity of being hit by another AIM-47 over White Sands Missile Range. Altogether, the weapon system scored an impressive six "kills" out of seven attempts. The single miss was attributed to a defective missile gyro system.[113]

The YF-12 program itself was cancelled on 1 February 1968, and along with it, the ASG-18 and AIM-47. The Air Force had finally found the elusive Mach 3 interceptor, and built exactly three of them. Nevertheless, the ASG-18 provided Hughes with much of the technology later used to design the Navy AN/AWG-9 installed in the Grumman F-14 Tomcat and the AIM-47 would form the basis for the AIM-54 Phoenix.

The AIM-47 was a big missile by air-to-air standards, and even aircraft as large as the F-108 and YF-12A could only carry three of them. Here a missile is being loaded into a YF-12A (60-6935). (Lockheed Martin)

Lockheed test pilot Jim Eastham brings the first YF-12A in for a landing after a successful first flight on 7 August 1963. The Air Force had finally found its elusive Mach 3 interceptor. (Lockheed Martin)

Chapter 4

Left: *Plans to test the General Electric J93 in-flight using a Convair B-58 Hustler never materialized. Nevertheless, a special pod was apparently manufactured to hold the J93 under the centerline, and the airplane was displayed at an Edwards air show with the pod. Flight tests of the J93 under the B-58 never took place.* (Terry Panopalis Collection)

Below: *The General Electric J93 did, however, undergo considerable testing in the facilities at the Air Force Arnold Engineering Development Center in Tullahoma, Tennessee.* (Arnold Engineering Development Center)

ANOTHER DIVERSION
HIGH-ENERGY FUELS

The official Air Force history states, "the development of an engine for the new chemically-powered bomber was complicated by the need for development of new materials, Air Force indecision in choosing an airframe contractor, costs, and 'other non-technical factors.' " Viewing the process from 40 years later, it is difficult to imagine that an engine was built at all, let alone one that proved to be remarkably trouble-free given its prototype status.[1]

One of the major problems in creating a Mach 3 engine was the development of new materials to withstand high inlet temperatures. The inlet temperature for a Mach 0.8 engine operating between 36,000 and 82,000 feet altitude is about 0 degrees Fahrenheit, but the airflow at Mach 2 raises this to about 230 degrees Fahrenheit; the comparable figure for a Mach 3 engine is 630 degrees Fahrenheit. The effects of the compressor stage raise the Mach 3 inlet temperature to more than 1,200 degrees Fahrenheit.

In addition to the materials problem, there was the task of developing an engine with sufficient thrust to push a large aircraft to three times the speed of sound. The most powerful operational engine during the late 1950s, the Pratt & Whitney J75, was capable of limited Mach 2 operation, but it was too heavy for satisfactory performance in sustained supersonic flight due to a poor thrust-to-weight ratio. Higher specific thrust and lower specific fuel consumption were needed in any new engine to meet the range and speed requirements of any future strategic bomber.

Previously, the Power Plant Laboratory[2] of the Wright Air Development Center had developed a number of advanced engines with no immediate aircraft application, of which the J57 turbojet was an outstanding example. At its inception, the J57 was not designated for any specific program, but over 18,000 engines were eventually produced for use on the B-52, KC-135, B-57D, F-100, F-101, F-102, U-2, and the Snark missile, as well as several Navy aircraft such as the A-3, F4D, and F-8. Similarly, the J75, which originated as a back-up for the stillborn Wright J67, found application in the F-105 and F-106, as well as the cancelled F-107 and P6M.[3]

There was little doubt that American industry could develop a Mach 3 engine, given sufficient time and resources. However, along the way, there was a major diversion.

HIGH-ENERGY FUELS

Since the creation of the internal combustion engine, hydrocarbons had been the chosen fuels because of cost, availability, and convenient physical properties. The search for fuels with more energy per given weight found the improvement potential of existing fuels exhausted, or apparently so. In any case, adapting piston powerplants to use something other than hydrocarbon fuels was judged too difficult. The jet engine, however, seemed to offer new possibilities.

The use of boron dates back at least to the times of ancient Egypt where a salt known as natron, so named because it came from the Natron Valley in Egypt, was used in the mummification process. Natron contained borates as well as other common salts such as sodium bicarbonate and sodium chloride. History records many other uses of boron through the ages including its infusion into Roman glass and as a welding flux in China. Marco Polo introduced the compound to Italy where it was used by the artisans of the time.[4]

In 1869, boron was discovered in what is now Southern California. One of the original sources of borate was the mining company known as the Harmony Borax Works, located in Death Valley. The now famous 20-mule teams were used to transport the borate ore 165 miles to a railroad line in Mojave, where it was loaded onto rail cars and distributed to industries throughout the United States.[5]

Boron is the fifth entry in the Periodic Table, the chart that illustrates the organization of the known elements. The nearest neighbor to boron is carbon, which combines with hydrogen to form hydrocarbons such as gasoline. Around 1910, German scientist Alfred Stock began exploring the possibility of creating boron-hydrogen compounds, none of which are naturally occurring. He was somewhat successful in making small quantities, but the process was expensive and yielded little of these rare compounds, which, in any case, had no known use. It was not until the 1930s that their potential began to be understood when it was discovered that these materials produced a high heat when they burn, making them an excellent candidate for fuel.[6]

Pentaborane and other borane compounds were initially manufactured during the early 1930s but found few applications. At the conclusion of World War II, the U.S. Army organized a program to

The Air Force and Navy were not alone in their interest in high-energy fuels. The National Advisory Committee on Aeronautics (NACA) built this high-energy fuel research facility at the Lewis Flight Propulsion Laboratory near Cleveland, Ohio. (NASA Glenn Research Center)

produce boron hydrides in large quantities with the idea of using them as rocket fuel. The synthesized boron hydrides were capable of producing 30,000 BTUs per pound, compared to about 18,000 BTUs that was generated by typical hydrocarbon fuels.

General Electric began research into boron hydride production at a plant in Malta, New York, ultimately being successful in producing several hundred pounds of diborane, pentaborane, and decaborane. These were the combinations of boron hydrides pioneered by Alfred Stock. By the late 1950s the Callery Chemical Company had been contracted to operate a government-owned manufacturing facility in Muskogee, Oklahoma, to produce pentaborane as an experimental high-energy fuel for the Air Force and Navy. This plant ultimately produced approximately 300,000 pounds of the fuel.[7]

Engine manufacturers began considering the use of high-energy fuels (HEF) in air-breathing turbojets and evaluated numerous special fuels including metal slurries and liquid hydrogen. Alkylborane fuels, however, were believed to offer greater promise.[8] Weighing approximately the same as hydrocarbon fuels and occupying about the same volume, the boron-based fuels produced roughly 40 percent more energy than the available jet fuels. Because the physical properties were so similar, the HEF products could serve as the only propellant or as supplements to petroleum fuels.

The primary advantage of high-energy fuels was a 16-percent range improvement over an all-JP-fuel mission when the new fuels were used only in the afterburners. With engines using boron fuels in both the primary combustor and afterburner, an improvement of 30 percent seemed feasible. In terms of world realities, use of these fuels meant that aerial refueling could take place at points far removed from Soviet areas, and that longer penetration routes could be chosen to deceive an enemy and avoid defenses.

Also significant, from a military perspective, was that as much as 95 percent of the world's boron oxide, the basic material used to produce these fuels, was located outside Soviet-controlled areas, mostly in the dry lake regions of California and Utah. The potential benefits of these fuels likely explained Russia's attempts to purchase rights to boron deposits in South America.

In mid-1955, the WADC did not have a specific program directed toward the use of high-energy fuels. In fact, the laboratory recommended against the use of high-energy or special-purpose fuels, at least in preliminary designs, due to a lack of specific knowledge about the risks and effects of the fuels. At the same time, despite a need to improve the performance of afterburners, the lack of fuel in sufficient quantities for useful testing led the Power Plant Laboratory to discount high-energy fuel afterburner development. This position was bolstered by a near-unanimous lack of interest among the engine companies. Only General Electric had expressed any interest in high-energy fuel afterburner development, and it was minimal.[9]

Nevertheless, the interest in boron fuels spurred work in a relatively unknown field of chemistry. Boron was very complex and differed considerably from other fields of chemistry, particularly the silicon and carbon families. General Electric had begun investigating boron compounds as special fuels during the mid-1940s with no specific development plans. About the same time, the Navy Bureau of Aeronautics also began studying boron hydrides, but the Bureau did not launch an active boron fuel program until 1952 when two Project ZIP contracts were awarded to the Callery Chemical Corporation and Olin Mathieson Chemical Corporation. Boron derivatives would become known as "zip fuels" because of this program. Callery began producing small amounts of an alkylated borane – called ethyl decaborane (later designated HEF-3) – in November 1953. Meanwhile, General Electric was continuing its research as a subcontractor to Olin Mathieson.

During 1955, the Air Force took over the General Electric program and awarded a $178,000 contract (AF33(616)-2961) for a small-scale fuel evaluation known as Project DASH to determine the thermodynamic characteristics of boron oxide exhaust products. The first major effort to extrapolate these small-scale laboratory studies to an actual engine was Project ZOOM, conducted by General Electric under contract AF33(616)-3367. This included modifying a J79 afterburner to run on either JP-type fuel or HEF-3 during ground tests. The American Potash and Chemical Corporation, AFN Inc.,[10] Aerojet, Stauffer Chemical Company, Ethyl Corporation, and the Vitro Corporation also engaged in high-energy fuel research.

Although General Electric's early research was somewhat hampered by a lack of fuel (only small laboratory-produced quantities were available), by the end of 1957 the contractor concluded that the use of high-energy fuel in the afterburner of an engine was feasible. This early work contributed considerable advances in useful materials, definition of design problem areas, fuel properties, and new data on exhaust products and thermodynamics.

The tactical and strategic values of the new fuels were apparent, but serious problems such as the production of fuels, predicted handling difficulties, and high production costs impeded their full and immediate use. On the basis of heating value, flame propagation speed, reactivity, and thermal stability, the properties of HEF-3 were considered superior to those of JP-type fuels. The solid and liquid exhaust products, however, could be quite deleterious to the working components of high-performance engines and could greatly reduce operating efficiency. Basic research also revealed that one of the most critical problems in burning boron fuels was the formation of boron oxide[11] deposits. These deposits were an excellent flux for certain metal oxides that limited the construction materials that could be used in the engines.

The WS-110A program had been reoriented in October 1956 in part because ranges of the proposed aircraft configurations were inadequate without resorting to extraordinary measures such as the floating wingtips. By this time, in-flight refueling no longer seemed a practical means of range extension since tankers were becoming too unwieldy and expensive to satisfy mission requirements. As part of the WS-110A reorientation, Boeing and North American studied the use of high-energy fuel in both the afterburner and main combustion chamber. It appears, however, that high-energy fuels never became a firm requirement during any of the studies.[12]

In March 1957, the WADC presented a high-energy fuel evaluation program to Air Force Headquarters that emphasized creation of a turbojet engine with an afterburner that used the new fuel. Significantly, WS-110A received top priority in this program. The WADC expected to create a qualified afterburner in 1962 and a main combustor in 1963.[13] Air Force Headquarters approved the program but stressed that the application of high-energy fuel to a particular weapon system engine (even WS-110A) was not a requirement.[14]

Soon after North American was selected as the weapon system contractor in December 1957, the B-70 Program Office reiterated its belief that HEF-3 was the most economical method to achieve the desired 15-percent range increase over an all JP mission. Largely to satisfy this desire, GOR-82 was revised on 7 March 1958 to include a study of "all methods of range extension" to achieve an unrefueled range of WS-110A to 6,500 nautical miles.[15] The tentative operational concept alluded that the use of high-energy fuels in the J93 engine could extend the B-70's range and target coverage well beyond the performance specified for the new bomber. The B-70 Program Office promptly suggested that the application of high-energy fuels should become a requirement instead of a mere study. However, high-energy fuel never became a specific requirement for the B-70 bomber, although the use of HEF-3 in the afterburner and the resultant dual-fuel capability to handle JP and HEF-3 did become an integral part of the B-70 design.

General Electric ran a modified J79 afterburner using HEF-3 in test facilities at the NACA Lewis Flight Propulsion Laboratory. A similar engine was flight tested in the prototype McDonnell F-101A. The F-101A was bailed to General Electric in 1958 as a testbed for the J79-GE-1 turbojet, and the aircraft was test flown with two J79s in 1958-59 before being modified to test boron-based fuels. (NASA Glenn Research Center)

On 12 February 1959, contract amendment No. 16 was issued to General Electric to authorize the development of the J93-GE-5 engine with the same basic airflow and speed characteristics as the –3 but using an afterburner capable of burning either JP-4 or HEF-3. In addition to the estimated $150 million required for the –3 engine, another $30.2 million would be needed for –5 development.[16]

Air Force Headquarters agreed that the new fuel was potentially the best method of providing a significant range improvement and directed that the basic B-70 airframe would incorporate, to the maximum degree feasible, the necessary provisions for using the J93-GE-5 engine. The Pentagon, however, withheld approval of –5 engine production, pending a thorough evaluation of the operational advantages of high-energy fuels.[17]

The development of new alloys or resistant coatings was imperative and numerous meetings were held to solve this fundamental problem. Participants included Allison, Curtiss-Wright, Fairchild, Firth Sterling, General Electric, the International Nickel Company, Johns Hopkins University, Marquardt, the Materials Laboratory at the WADC, the Navy's Bureau of Aeronautics, the NASA Lewis Research Center, Pratt & Whitney, Reaction Motors, and two divisions of the Union Carbide Corporation (the Haynes Stellite Company and the Linde Company). The results of these consultations indicated that an alloy could probably be developed for unstressed engine components operating at temperatures up to 2,300 degrees Fahrenheit, and a silicate refractory coating for temperatures over 2,300 degrees Fahrenheit.[18]

This B-58A was displayed at the Edwards air show in 1960 with the special pod that had been built to test the J93 in supersonic flight. When the B-70 production program was cancelled, so were the flight tests that had been intended as part of the production certification program. (Color photo by Robert Cooper via Tony Chong; others courtesy of Terry Panopalis Collection)

Speculative artist concept of a possible WS-110A concept using high-energy fuels. The painting was created based on original North American drawings that were too poor to reproduce here. (Original artwork by Tom Tullis)

While petroleum fuels required relatively simple refining operations, crude boron mixtures first had to be manufactured from basic chemicals before they could be refined. These extra steps imposed a substantial cost penalty on production of high-energy fuels, and the need for additional electric power further increased costs. One estimate held that a 10-tons-per-day production facility to support one B-70 wing with high-energy fuels would cost about $35 million to construct. By the time the B-70 became operational, high-energy fuel production costs could be reduced to about $1.50 per pound (about $10 per gallon, in 1957 dollars, or $50 dollars today), still several orders of magnitude higher than JP fuels.[19]

The heating value of the HEF-3 fuel was more than 25,000 BTUs per pound, as compared to the 18,000 of JP-4 fuel. The spontaneous ignition temperature of the high-energy fuel was about 2,600 degrees Fahrenheit, against 4,550 for JP-4. It appeared that most metallic materials had little effect on HEF-3, although some lead and copper alloys could catalyze fuel decomposition. The fuel's effects on metallic materials presented no problems, but nonmetallic materials – particularly elastomers – were another question, and closely coordinated programs between the WADC and contractors sought a solution. The HEF-3 fuel was more toxic than cyanide, necessitating the development of special handling and storage techniques and would have greatly complicated air base support. The low spontaneous ignition temperature required a nitrogen inerting system in the fuel tanks and a leak-proof fuel system. HEF-3 tended to solidify after a time at high temperatures, and the presence of moisture or oxygen accelerated this decomposition; however, bulk fuel in airframe tanks would probably not reach temperatures high enough for thermal decomposition to become a problem. Little additional thermal decomposition would occur when the fuel passed through high temperature zones in the fuel system, but residual fuel that remained in tanks or stood idle in fuel systems could easily reach solidification temperature in a short time. In-flight flushing of tanks, pumps, and fuel systems with JP fuel was one answer that required only that the two fuels be compatible.

Several companies were investigating high-energy fuels but were receiving little direction, and this impeded the focusing of research on problems most pertinent to the B-70 program. This led to the creation of the "HEF Guidance Committee" in September 1958. Chaired by the WADC and composed of representatives from the Directorate of Systems Management, Command Headquarters, Olin Mathieson, General Electric, North American, and NASA. This was not a policy-making committee; its purpose was to guide the high-energy fuel technical development program and insofar as possible, keep it in line with B-70 developments.

However, a continuing lag in high-level decisions on the fuel program led the Air Materiel Command at the end of April 1959 to notify North American of a six-month slip in the J93-GE-5 engine program.[20] After studying feasibility and cost data, in late May SAC recommended that first allocations of high-energy fuel should aim at qualification of the J93-GE-5 engine, that the first B-70 operational wing should have the –5 (rather than the –3) engine to prevent costly future modifications, and that high-energy fuel should not exclude other means of range extension. Noting that the B-70 should exceed minimum range requirements even with conventional JP fuels, SAC emphasized that the new fuel would allow greater target coverage, heavier payloads, better penetration routes, a choice of recovery bases, and more adequate landing reserves.[21]

The changes added 1,620 pounds to each aircraft – the dual-fuel system added 300 pounds and a heavier afterburner would add 220 pounds to each engine – but the change was still thought to be advantageous. When both engine sections used JP fuel, this weight penalty would result in a range reduction of 75 miles. Moreover, properly metered high-energy fuel flow rates would provide the same exhaust gas temperature as JP fuel. In the dual-fuel configuration, high-energy fuels would require between 30 and 40 percent of the total fuel capacity. Finally, the two types of fuel would have separate sequencing, pressurization, and venting systems that could be integrated, as desired, for all-JP missions.[22]

With prior endorsements from North American and the B-70 Program Office, on 16 June 1959 General Electric suggested to the Air Force an 18-month feasibility program looking to an all-high-energy-fuel engine. Approximately $3.75 million would launch the effort, but development of such a powerplant would require an estimated $52.75 million through FY64. North American called this project the "most significant potential range improvement factor in sight for later versions of the B-70," improving the bombers' range by about 19 percent over the unrefueled range of an aircraft using JP fuel. The B-70 Program Office, however, noted that sufficient funds were not available.[23]

On 8 July 1959, the ARDC, AMC, and SAC made a joint presentation on high-energy fuels to the Air Force Weapons Board. The board chairman, Colonel J. C. Jennison, recommended a continued authorization of J93-GE-5 engine development, inclusion in the FY61 budget of funds for the first 10-tons-per-day fuel facility, an allocation of $3.75 million for an all-HEF engine development feasibility study in FY60, and the provision of $27.6 million in FY60 for fuel purchases to support the current engine developmental program. There were no recommendations, however, to commit the B-70 to high-energy fuels. On 16 July 1959, Air Force Headquarters authorized purchases of the new fuels in FY60, but on 10 August, the Pentagon unexpectedly reduced the over-all scope of the high-energy fuel endeavor and cancelled the J93-GE-5 engine program.[24]

The impact and ultimate extent of this fuel program cutback were not immediately clear. As might have been expected, there were murmurs of a Congressional investigation, and the official Soviet press was portraying the move as a major blow to the American military. Cancellation of the –5 engine definitely limited B-70 planning to using only JP-type fuels, and this restriction in turn forced North American to embark upon a redesign of the B-70 fuel system.[25]

In explaining the decision to a Congressional committee, the Assistant Secretary of the Air Force for Research and Development, Dr. Joseph V. Charyk, maintained that technical considerations had loomed larger than budget problems in the decision. He cited growing evidence that the boron fuels could not provide their theoretical advantages as early or as economically as first believed. In addition, demonstrated increases in JP-type fuel efficiency – including the development and production of JP-6 – and improvements in the efficiency of conventional turbojet engines made the boron fuels a less critical goal. John B. Macauley, Deputy Director of Defense Research and Engineering, reiterated that high-energy fuel production costs were not coming down as rapidly as expected, and that most recent studies showed the expected performance gains were significantly below previous predictions.

A major technical obstacle, which certainly contributed to the official decision even though there was little public discussion of it, continued to arise from the harmful boron oxide deposits resulting from combustion of the high-energy fuels. Despite some progress in 1959 in eradicating this annoyance, the problem remained. Finding materials that could withstand the heating load imposed by the formation of boron oxide deposits was proving to be difficult. There was only relative consolation for the hard-pressed fuel engineers in intelligence reports that indicated that the Russians were plagued by the same problems.

The use of pentaborane as a jet fuel was ultimately abandoned by the military, although research continued on the use of boron hydrides as rocket fuel. During the early 1960s, pentaborane was explored as a rocket propellant at Edwards AFB, but extensive testing failed to achieve the expected high performance while simultaneously maintaining acceptable combustion stability. The hazardous aspects of the compound also contributed to the decision to discontinue the research.

Selecting an Engine

In the fall of 1954, when the future bomber was still contemplated as a subsonic aircraft with supersonic dash ability, the Power Plant Laboratory at Wright Field launched several programs to develop powerplants with airflow between 380 and 400 pounds per second. Two engines were especially promising: the Allison J89 turbojet, and the Pratt & Whitney J91 (JTN9) turbojet being developed for the Aircraft Nuclear Propulsion (ANP) program. The J89 provided an airflow rate of 380 pounds per second and 10:1 pressure ratio, while the J91 handled a 400-pound-per-second airflow and had a 7:1 pressure ratio. Two other engines were less seriously considered: the General Electric TF31 (X84) turbofan[26] proposed for the Lockheed Blackbirds, and the ambitious dual-cycle Wright J67 turbo-ramjet being developed for the Republic XF-103 interceptor.

The number of engines under consideration grew in 1955 and 1956. Wright had come up with an improved J67 that the company called the TJ32C4. Pratt & Whitney offered an improved J75. General Electric proposed at least two advanced versions of the 15,000-lbf J79: the company-designated X207 that increased thrust to 18,000 lbf, and the 20,700-lbf X275, designed more specifically to meet the early requirements of the future strategic bomber. Still, the Allison J89 and the Pratt & Whitney J91 were the only officially funded efforts.

Most of these engines promised desirable thrust-to-weight ratios and fuel consumption characteristics during subsonic cruise, but none measured up in all respects to the powerplant needs of the advanced bomber. Indeed, by the spring of 1956 the informal propulsion competition had narrowed to a choice between the J89, J91, and X275.

Two of the engines gradually morphed into powerplants specifically tailored to the needs of the advanced bomber. The giant Pratt & Whitney J91 was scaled down and transformed into a Mach 3 engine; as a Navy-funded project it became the J58 turbojet that would go on to power the Lockheed Blackbirds. The General Electric X275 evolved into the X279 and, in time, became the J93 that was chosen for the F-108 and B-70.[27]

By mid-1956 Boeing and North American had not established specific engine requirements, but both had decided that the powerplant should incorporate four specific features: the highest feasible turbine inlet temperature, to minimize supersonic fuel consumption; the highest possible pressure ratio, to obtain low specific fuel consumption at subsonic cruise; high thrust and low specific fuel consumption for supersonic dash; and a minimum high-altitude speed of Mach 3 for Boeing and Mach 2.7 for North American.[28]

Since the engines currently under development by the Powerplant Laboratory did not meet the new bomber requirements and a proliferation of new programs was financially impossible, the Air Force decided on a formal solicitation. On 14 September 1956, the Air Materiel Command asked interested engine companies to submit two bids each, one for the Boeing proposal and one for the North American concept. The request for bids spelled out the performance required for each variant. The Boeing engine needed to provide

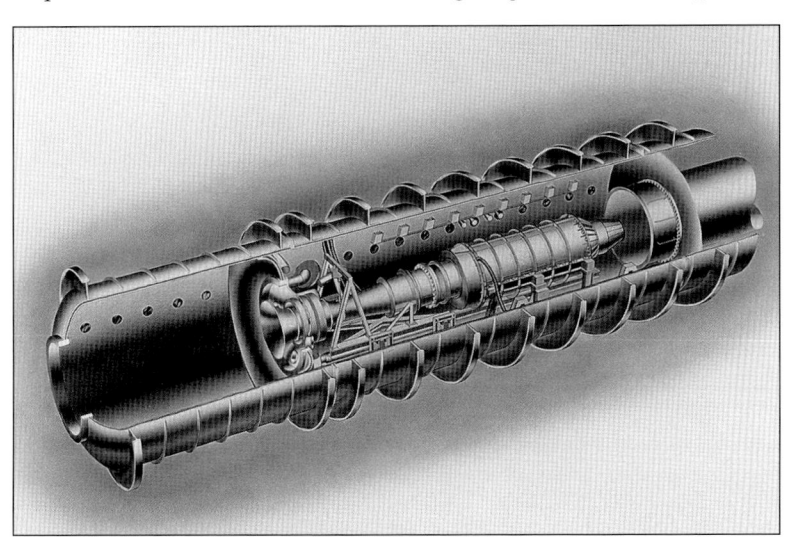

Future B-70 pilots observe a test of the J93 at the Air Force Arnold Engineering Development Center. (Arnold Engineering Development Center)

The test cells at the Arnold Engineering Development Center are enclosed and can be used to simulate a variety of temperature and pressure conditions. This allows realistic testing of large jet engines without the expense and risk of flight testing. Here an early J93 undergoes evaluation in Test Cell J-1 prior to the first flight of the XB-70A. (Arnold Engineering Development Center)

ANOTHER DIVERSION

The Pratt & Whitney J58 was frequently evaluated as a replacement for the General Electric J93, but was never selected for the F-108 or B-70. The engine did, however, go on to a successful career powering the Lockheed Blackbirds. (Pratt & Whitney)

26,425-lbf and a specific fuel consumption rate of 2.13 at Mach 3 and 60,000 feet while the engine for North American needed 27,070-lbf and a specific fuel consumption of 2.10. In both instances, subsonic cruise performance was still the order of the day.[29]

The predicted cost of this engine program more than justified the careful, formal approach. In July 1956, the Air Force estimated that the program would require $120.5 million between FY57 and FY60. For this the Air Force expected to secure a fully qualified engine 4.5 years after the contract was awarded.[30]

Allison, General Electric, and Wright submitted proposals. Pratt & Whitney did not, mainly because the Navy had already awarded the company a contract to develop the J91 into the J58. The WADC and AMC unanimously favored the Allison proposal, and the results of the evaluation were forwarded to Air Force Headquarters on 10 January 1957. This decision was somewhat odd given that both airframe contractors had already expressed their preference for the General Electric engine.[31]

Since this did not evoke any reaction from Air Force Headquarters, a follow-up letter sent on 21 February 1957 emphasized that a quick decision was required to prevent a significant delay in the program. This letter pointed out the superiority of Allison's Model 640 (J89) engine proposal and the company's "excellent job in increasing their capability as a prime engine development source." Assuming that Allison was going to win the engine competition, this letter warned that unless a decision was forthcoming by 15 March, Allison would have to cut back research and development activities and release many of the engineers working on the program. Still no response.[32]

Almost six months later, on 7 May 1957, Air Force Headquarters directed the ARDC and the AMC to award the engine contract to General Electric and to immediately stop all support of the Allison engine, except as an insurance against the failure of the General Electric program. Development and procurement officials were also to monitor the Pratt & Whitney J58 to determine whether it offered more favorable performance characteristics for the new strategic bomber. No explanation for this decision was forthcoming, although it was likely related to the fact that both airframe competitors favored the General Electric engine.

The J93 was a remarkably advanced engine for its day. One innovative feature was moving the hydraulic pumps and generators off the engine. The power takeoff that was used to drive the accessory gearbox is in the box below the engine at left. The engines at right are upside down, a transportation method used to protect the accessory drive. (left: General Electric via the Terry Panopalis Collection; right: Boeing Historical Archives)

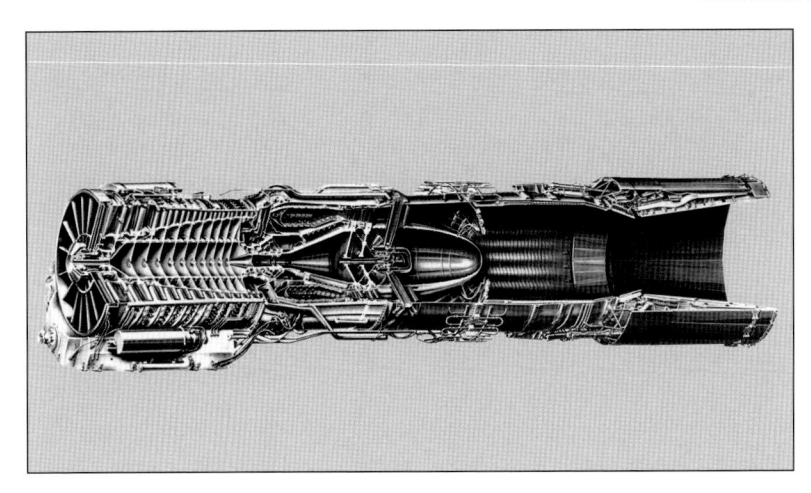

Cutaway and external view of the General Electric YJ93-GE-3 engine. (General Electric via the Terry Panopalis Collection)

Authorizing $10 million for initial work, in May 1957 the Air Force directed that final engine configuration for the new bomber (WS-110A) and interceptor (WS-202A) be postponed until common requirements could be firmly established. General Electric began work on the X279E on 1 June 1957, received Letter Contract AF33(600)-35824 on 26 July, and signed a definitive contract on 14 May 1958. This powerplant was officially designated XJ93-GE-1 on 25 September 1957.[33]

Although both airframe contractors had long contemplated using General Electric engines in their proposals, Air Force Headquarters – before and after the 1957 selection of North American – called for a long series of comparisons between the J93 and other engines. This re-evaluation process finally prompted the B-70 Program Office to comment that further dilution of its engineering effort in such studies would hinder development work on the basic J93 design. Nonetheless, a distracting, intermittent consideration of other engines continued.

The Pratt & Whitney J91 remained under active consideration for a considerable time, although an analysis in the summer of 1957 concluded that the J93 was superior for the needs of the new bomber. The study found that using four J91 engines would degrade takeoff performance and might limit the bomber's future growth. Moreover, the study predicted an increase in fuel flow under almost all conditions with the J91: 8 percent on takeoff, 20 percent at 60,000 feet and Mach 3, and about 10 percent at 75,000 feet.[34]

But not everybody was happy about the selection of the General Electric engine. Lieutenant General Samuel E. Anderson, commander of the ARDC, noted in September 1957 that the Air Force had already invested $25 million and three years of work in the J91. This had resulted in a Mach 3 engine with over 20 hours of test time and a two- or three-year development advantage over the J93. The General Electric engine, theoretically, was superior to all others under development, but was considered a high-risk program.[35]

With seeming finality, Air Force Headquarters on 6 November 1957 selected the J93 as the only engine for the new bomber. Since the budget permitted only one Mach 3 turbojet project in FY58, all support of the Pratt & Whitney J91 was to cease. In the meantime, the Navy had contracted with Pratt & Whitney to develop a scaled-down version of the J91 called the J58. Instead of a second development effort, the Air Force would monitor the Navy program with special attention to a modified J58 designed to be almost interchangeable with the J93 powerplant.[36] The annoyance of informal competition continued, however. At the end of 1957, the J93 was challenged again, this time by the Allison PD24 and Wright DC36, plus two new versions of the J58.

The nuisance value of these distractions was far greater than the possibility that the Air Force might actually drop the J93. The Allison engine was never a serious competitor, and the Wright DC36 proposal was unacceptable on several counts: it would increase the gross weight of the aircraft, would require a revision of the fuel control and engine fuel system, and installing DC36s would also necessitate redesign of the aircraft itself. The only real claim of the advanced Wright engine was the suggestion that it could power a future, improved version of the bomber at speeds approaching Mach 4.[37]

On 17 February 1958, Air Force Headquarters envisaged just such an advanced model of the strategic bomber and directed the ARDC to start a competition for an advanced propulsion system. The Pentagon limited this endeavor by specifying that the improvement should be accomplished without major changes in the aircraft configuration and without affecting the current J93 development program. In response, the B-70 Program Office listed some arguments against further dilution of its engineering effort. The engine currently in development could propel the bomber to the temperature and Mach-number limits of the airframe, and major changes would be necessary to push performance any further. Moreover, the proposed Wright engine, based on a dual turbojet-ramjet cycle, was competitive with the J93 turbojet only when speed considerations reached Mach 4; since that point was somewhere in the future and required a highly-modified airframe, an immediate decision on advanced propulsion was unnecessary.[38]

The J93-GE-1 was intended to first be used on the F-108 interceptor, mainly because it was further along in development. In a 13 January 1958 letter to the Air Materiel Command, General Electric suggested a growth version of the –1 engine in which the inlet temperature would increase to 2,000 degrees Fahrenheit and the maximum afterburner temperature to 3,310 degrees Fahrenheit. This engine also differed from the –1 in having a fixed area exit nozzle and air-cooled turbine blades. The Air Force was receptive, and on 18 April 1958 the growth version of the engine was officially designated XJ93-GE-3. On 8 April 1958, General Electric received Amendment 10 to the engine contract to begin development of the XJ93-GE-3 engine. The use of high-energy fuel had also been discussed, but no mention of it was incorporated in this amendment, although there were already plans for a –5 engine using the advanced fuels.

During the summer of 1958, the Air Force again considered the possibility of supporting the J58 as a backup engine for the J93. Progress at General Electric had significantly reduced the perceived risks, but the Air Force nevertheless decided to invest $2 million in the Navy J58 program during FY59 just to keep the door open. This seed money was, apparently, also used to help develop the version of the J58 that would ultimately power the Lockheed Blackbirds.

North American was selected to build the B-70 in December 1957, meaning the same airframe contractor was responsible for both aircraft destined to receive the J93. Although the Air Force had always desired to use the same engine in the F-108 and B-70, North American had specifically structured their proposal that way to keep the cost of the B-70 as low as possible. After reviewing the –1 and –3 engine programs, General Electric concluded in July 1958 that a significant simplification could be achieved by using the –3 engine in both of the advanced aircraft, pending availability of the –5 engine. General Electric believed that as much as $30 million could be saved during the development phase. Notable logistics support savings could be achieved by using one engine, since a number of major components in the –1 and –3 were not interchangeable. Moreover, if the –1 effort was cancelled, then development of the –3 engine could be accelerated to meet the –1 schedules without compromising performance, engine weight, or the general configuration. North American believed that the decreased time and fuel required to accelerate and climb, the result of improved thrust and specific fuel consumption performance, compensated adequately for the 240 pounds of extra weight per –3 engine.[39]

North American "strongly recommended" adopting this revised engine program. Accordingly, work on the –1 program was redirected, excepting four test engines and spare parts already being manufactured. These would be used for initial testing. On 8 September 1958, the –1 engine contract was formally redirected to provide –3 models. Oddly, a development engineering inspection of the J93-GE-1 engine took place at the General Electric plant in Evendale, Ohio, on 9–11 September 1958 – a day after the engine was officially cancelled.[40]

Developing an engine for two separate aircraft presented a complex coordination problem in satisfying the requirements of both aircraft, in resolving conflicting requirements, and in ensuring airframe-engine compatibility. For instance, the F-108 designers wanted a thrust reverser, although the B-70 did not; the best compromise here was to provide a thrust reverser that was readily removable. In an attempt to expedite matters and clarify procedures, on 12 September 1958, the ARDC and AMC decided that the F-108 Program Office should serve as the focal point for control of the J93 engine program.[41]

However, there was no end to reexamination of the engine program. In late October, Lieutenant General R. C. Wilson, Deputy Chief of Staff for Development at Air Force Headquarters, indicated that the ARDC and AMC should be prepared to make a thorough technical comparison of the J58 and J93 engines. In conjunction with North American, the ARDC was to estimate the cost of adapting the J58 to the two new aircraft without affecting the latter's development schedule. This time Department of Defense budget considerations inspired the review, since both engine programs were entering the high-cost phase of development and it seemed unlikely that the defense establishment could justify continuation of both endeavors. Further, the Navy still had no specific application for the J58 and the choice of an engine for the new strategic bomber would thus depend on Air Force requirements. This seemingly ignored the CIA's interest in the J58 for the Lockheed Blackbirds.[42]

THE MODULE CONCEPT

Representatives of the WADC, AMC, SAC, the B-70 Program Office, General Electric, and North American met on 13 November 1958, and again on 31 March 1959, on the subject of applying the "module concept" to the J93 turbojet. With but one exception, they found the plan promising and definitely worth pursuing.

The module concept was an answer to past instances where severe engine damage had resulted from failures of such engine-mounted accessories as hydraulic pumps and generators. Under the module concept, the basic propulsion unit was a separate entity without extraneous attachments. An auxiliary shaft, mechanically driven from a gearbox on the front of the engine, transmitted the necessary power to accessories (hydraulic pumps, generators, etc.) mounted on the airframe itself. Delivered to operational units, module-type engines would be completely assembled and ready for installation without further run-up or testing. The module concept coincided with existing jet engine field maintenance procedures and required no alteration of facilities. The concept also fitted the earlier plan for engines interchangeable between the F-108 and B-70 since the engine bays could be identical but the accessory mountings could be tailored for each airframe type.

North American believed that the engine module concept would save time in maintenance, result in a better engine, require fewer engines to support the F-108 and B-70 programs, reduce engine pipeline time, and decrease required supply support. In addition, the concept should reduce ground support equipment requirements and increase engine reliability, the latter gain offsetting an anticipated initial increase in costs. There would also be reductions in the time required for routine maintenance and engine inspection.

The Strategic Air Command viewed the idea as a vital aid to its global mission and maintained that modular engines were essential to its proposed B-70 dispersal plan. Recognizing that the technical feasibility of pre-trimming an engine at a General Electric or major overhaul depot for direct installation into an air vehicle had not been proved, SAC agreed that replacement engines shipped to its major jet engine field maintenance bases could be modified module engines. SAC suggested the engine module concept be used during Category I and II flight-testing to verify its feasibility.[43]

The lone dissenter was the AMC's Oklahoma City Air Materiel Area which concluded that North American's idea was but a modified version of the "true module concept," and that no appreciable savings would accrue to the Air Force. Emphasizing the increased initial cost, the AMC recommended against adopting the module concept for the J93 engines in F-108 and B-70 aircraft. They were overruled.

Another Comparison

The WADC completed its comparative technical appraisal of the J58 and J93 in January 1959, according Pratt & Whitney a "slight edge" in factors such as meeting specification guarantees and development schedules, high-Mach flying experience, facilities, personnel, and overall management of development work. On the other hand, the General Electric engine rated higher in such engine-performance considerations as acceleration time, low-speed operation, specific fuel consumption at Mach 3, ease of maintenance, and the fact that General Electric had already accomplished full-scale testing with a high-energy fuel afterburner. In these "hardware" considerations, the J58 scored notably only on its relative mechanical simplicity and predicted easier production.

The WADC found both engines technically suitable for the F-108 and B-70, concluding that the differences between the J58 and J93 were so minor as to preclude selecting one over the other "from a technical standpoint." Additional considerations also tipped the balance back and forth without creating an absolute preference for either engine. Adoption of the J58 would impose delays on first flight dates – by two to eight months for the interceptor and three to six months for the bomber. The Air Force would also have to have different models of the J58: a nine-stage-compressor engine for the bomber but only eight compressor stages for the interceptor.

There was one other significant mechanical-component consideration. Cruise performance of the aircraft depended on the efficiency of the convergent-divergent exhaust nozzle, and small differences could produce disproportionate variations in the aircraft's cruise range. General Electric had already proved, on the J79, a mechanically actuated nozzle similar to that intended for the J93. On the other hand, the aerodynamically controlled nozzle Pratt & Whitney proposed for the J58 had not been thoroughly tested and thus had to be counted as an additional development risk.[44]

Even program cost claims tended to balance out, although the continuing reappraisals derived in part from Pratt & Whitney assertions that it could produce a Mach 3 engine more cheaply than General Electric. To study this disputed area more accurately, the Air Materiel Command examined cost predictions for development and production of varying numbers of engines. On a purchase of engines for 500 interceptors (20 squadrons of 25 aircraft) and 62 bombers (1 operational wing and 12 test aircraft), the Air Force could save $100 million by buying the J58 turbojet. When the contemplated order shrank to 150 interceptors (6 squadrons) and 62 bombers, the predicted savings dropped to $75 million. This was largely because it appeared that the J58 would be easier (and hence, less expensive) to manufacture. These theoretical savings largely vanished, however, when the cost of adjusting the bomber airframe to J58 engines (including the added expenses from schedule slippage caused by the switch) was taken into account. If the change were made with a minimum disruption of program schedules, the Air Force might still save some $15 million; but slip-

North American had an engine test site at Santa Susana, outside Los Angeles, that has long been associated with rocket engines. However, the company also tested the J93 there prior to the first flight of A/V-1 – note the elaborate test facility! (Boeing Historical Archives)

The B-70 pilots at the General Electric Large Jet Engine Facility in Cincinnati, Ohio, on 11 October 1962. Shown are B. W. Bruckman, J93 engine project manager (extreme left), Lieutenant Colonel Fitz Fulton (center), Lieutenant Colonel Joe Cotton (center), Al White (center foreground), O. E. Deal, North American Aviation (near right), and Colonel Guy Townsend, XB-70 joint test force director (far right). The photo was taken during an orientation course by General Electric that included throttle operation at a simulated 2,000 mph in the General Electric Ram Jet Test Facility. (General Electric via the Jeannette Remak Collection)

page of six or eight months would tip the scales far in the opposite direction, adding as much as $120 million.[45]

The ARDC and AMC, therefore, jointly recommended that development and procurement of the J93 continue. By March 1959, some $84.35 million had already been allocated for procurement of the basic General Electric engine. A configuration review of the XJ93-GE-3 engine was conducted at Evendale on 28–30 July 1959. The first –3 began its test series in July 1959, and General Electric had three –3 units and one –1 on the test stands by December 1959.

The HEF program had been losing support for several years, and both the F-108 and B-70 programs had been making plans to use standard JP fuel. Not unexpectedly, on 10 August 1959, the Department of Defense cancelled the high-energy fuel program. By default, this ended the –5-engine development program since an engine is of little use without a fuel. As of 10 July 1959, the –5 high-energy fuel afterburner engine had been tested for 3 hours and 10 minutes at the Peebles Proving Ground in Ohio. The Arnold Engineering Development Center and the National Aeronautics and Space Administration (NASA) also conducted 3 hours and 1.5 hours of testing, respectively, on the –5 engine. In addition, five flights using high-energy fuel in the afterburner of a modified J79 engine successfully demonstrated the utility of the new fuels. These flights use the first McDonnell F-101A (53-2418) that had been used as a testbed for the J79 engine since early 1958. The aircraft was retired after the high-energy fuel tests, becoming a ground maintenance trainer at Amarillo AFB, Texas.

Despite their prototype status, the engines were extensively tested. One was installed in the Rocketdyne Santa Susana engine test facility in the mountains west of the San Fernando Valley. The future XB-70 pilots were invited to see the engine in operation at Santa Susana and at the General Electric engine plant in Evendale, Ohio. Engines were also tested in a thermal and altitude chamber at the Air Force Arnold Engineering Development Center near Tullahoma, Tennessee.[46]

By the beginning of December 1959, the –3 engines had accumulated 363.5 hours of sea-level static operation and 102 hours of testing under heated inlet air conditions. North American believed the status of the J93 in December 1959 represented a promising level of achievement for this stage of engine development. Plans were made to test the J93 in-flight using a B-58 and a special pod was built to carry a single J93 on the centerline station of the Hustler. These plans came and went with the shifting fortunes of the B-70 program and ultimately were not carried out.[47]

New Fuels

During 1956, the Air Force had asked the petroleum industry to develop an improved jet fuel for possible use on the F-108 and B-70. The resulting Mil-J-25656 fuel was called JP-6. Essentially JP-6 was a development of a high-flash-point kerosene (JP-5) developed for the U.S. Navy in 1952, but featured a lower freezing point and improved thermal oxidative stability. The production of JP-6 was ultimately cancelled along with the B-70 program. Nevertheless, the development of JP-6 significantly influenced the JP-TS (JP – thermally stable) fuel used in the Lockheed U-2. JP-TS is an extremely thermally stable jet fuel with a low freezing point to support the high-altitude missions flown by the U-2 and is still used today.[48]

Since the B-70 never entered production, the amount of JP-6 that was produced was limited. Interestingly, the program did not turn to JPTS when it appeared the stocks of JP-6 might be depleted. During mid-1966 General Electric ran a series of tests to validate the YJ93 could run on standard JP-5 fuel. After reviewing the test data, the Air Force approved the use of JP-5 for the XB-70A. When the program resumed flying after the loss of A/V-2 there was sufficient JP-6 for 12 additional flights; it appears that the last 20 or so flights of A/V-1 used JP-5.[49]

It should be noted that the other Mach 3 engine (J58) used a completely different fuel with extremely low vapor pressure and excellent thermal oxidative stability necessary for extreme high altitude operations and use at arctic bases. JP-7 was not a distillate like most other jet fuels, but was composed of special blending stocks to produce a very clean hydrocarbon mixture low in aromatics (typically 3 percent), and nearly void of the sulfur, nitrogen, and oxygen impurities found in other fuels. The combustion characteristics were also tightly specified to ensure adequate combustor life. The production of JP-7 was cancelled when the SR-71 was retired.

Salient Features of the General Electric J93 Turbojet engine

	J93-GE-1	J93-GE-1	J93-GE-3	J93-GE-3R	J93-GE-5
Fuel	JP-4	JP-4	JP-6	JP-6	HEF-3
Thrust Reverser?	No	Yes	No	Yes	No
Maximum Thrust (lbf)	24,800	24,800	29,300	29,300	30,200
Military Thrust (lbf)	16,900	16,900	20,900	20,900	21,900
Specific Fuel Consumption					
@ Maximum Afterburner	1.92	1.92	1.87	1.87	1.84
@ Military Power	0.97	0.97	1.04	1.04	1.06
Airflow (cfm)	242	242	260	260	260
Compressor Ratio	8.0:1	8.0:1	8.7:1	8.7:1	8.7:1
Turbine Inlet Temperature (degreesF)					
< Mach 2	1,800	1,800	2,100	2,100	2,200
> Mach 2	1,850	1,850	1,990	1,990	1,990
Mach Limit	3.2	3.2	3.2	3.2	3.2
Altitude Limit (feet)	95,000	95,000	95,000	95,000	95,000
Afterburner Temperature (degreesF)	3,140	3,140	3,310	3,310	3,310
Engine Weight (pounds)	4,530	4,875	4,770	5,115	4,990
Engine Length (inches)	218.00	218.00	233.00	233.00	234.00
Engine Diameter (inches)	50.60	50.60	52.75	52.75	52.75

After cancellation[50] of the –5 engine and the HEF program, the Air Force and North American considered ways of using JP-6 to obtain the same performance in range, in-flight refueling altitude, takeoff distance, and rate-of-climb-at-takeoff from a modified –3 engine. The most critical item for the B-70 – the rate of climb on a hot day with one engine inoperative at takeoff – was resolved by incorporating an overspeed facility to develop a higher turbine inlet temperature on takeoff and thereby provide the necessary higher rate of climb. The overspeed provision had much to recommend it: greater reliability and economy, and approximately the same rate of climb promised for the –5 engine. Degradations in range and refueling altitude were negligible.

When the B-70 program underwent a drastic alteration on 1 December 1959, the engine project, included in the restrictive budget ceilings of $150 million and $75 million for FY60 and FY61, was redirected toward obtaining a minimum engine to furnish the minimum propulsion requirements of the single XB-70 aircraft. As a result, the qualification tests usually required for an operational "J" engine were eliminated, leaving only the preliminary flight-rating test for an experimental "XJ" powerplant. Although the decision involved accepting a weight penalty, General Electric was allowed to use a 12-stage compressor for this preliminary flight-rating test. Instead of refining the design and reducing weight wherever possible, which would have increased costs, General Electric was allocated an extra 150 pounds per engine over the weight specified for an operational powerplant. The 38 "production" engines were officially designated YJ93-GE-3 throughout their careers.

Despite their prototype status, the engines were extensively tested. One was installed in the Rocketdyne Santa Susana engine test facility in the mountains west of the San Fernando Valley. The future XB-70 pilots were invited to see the engine in operation at Santa Susana and at the General Electric engine plant in Evendale, Ohio. Engines were also tested in a thermal and altitude chamber at the Air Force Arnold Engineering Development Center near Tullahoma, Tennessee.

A YJ93-GE-3 engine being towed past A/V-1. (Terry Panopalis Collection)

Chapter 5

Right: *An early artist concept of the new B-70. Note the shape of the vertical stabilizers and the lack of folding wingtips.* (Boeing Historical Archives)

Below: *Air Vehicle 1 nearing completion at the North American facility in Palmdale, California. The outer wing is in position to be attached to the main wing stub – note the people in the gap between the two structures preparing them to be joined. The lack of production tooling made the job much more difficult than expected.* (Boeing Historical Archives)

POLITICS
AND CONTINUED RESTRUCTURING

The configuration of the North American WS-110A design was controversial given the long – and generally unsuccessful – history of canards on modern aircraft. Nevertheless, North American believed the canard was beneficial because of the long moment arm it provided forward of the center-of-gravity. All aircraft suffer some instability in the transonic regime as the center-of-pressure moves rearward, and this is usually countered by trimming with the elevators (or elevons, in the case of a delta wing). This, however, increases the angle-of-attack and results in higher drag and a decrease in range (or speed, or both). In the North American design, small flaps on the trailing edge of the canard could be used to counter the center-of-pressure shift without changing the angle-of-attack of the main wing. In theory, this allowed trimming without a penalty in range or speed.[1]

The canard also helped minimize the extreme nose-up attitude most delta-wing aircraft use on landing, although this would not be readily apparent when watching the aircraft during its ultimate flight tests. As originally planned, the canard flap could be deflected downward 25 degrees in 1-degree increments; when the flap was lowered in preparation for landing, the aircraft nose pitched up. Moving the control column forward compensated for this change by drooping the elevons on the main wing to act as trailing-edge flaps without subtracting from the basic wing lift. Thus, the landing attitude was shallower and the lift-to-drag ratio higher, permitting landing speeds comparable to other large high-performance aircraft.[2]

Detractors pointed out that canard designs generally had pitch and directional stability issues at high angles-of-attack, plus various flow disturbances around the engine inlets and wing. North American engi-

Note the open weapons bay on this model of the B-70 at the Air Force Arnold Engineering Development Center. The odd upper-aft fuselage shape is simply an attachment point for the "sting" that supports the model in the wind tunnel. (Arnold Engineering Development Center)

B-70 engine and inlet tests were conducted in the 16-foot supersonic wind tunnel at the Air Force Arnold Engineering Development Center. This model of the lower fuselage weighed 210,000 pounds and was 75 feet long. (Arnold Engineering Development Center)

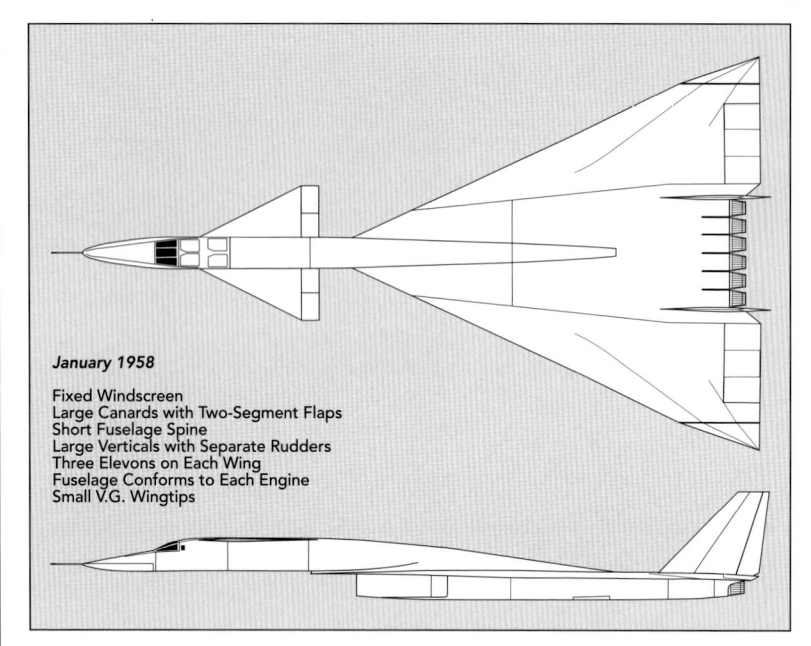

January 1958
Fixed Windscreen
Large Canards with Two-Segment Flaps
Short Fuselage Spine
Large Verticals with Separate Rudders
Three Elevons on Each Wing
Fuselage Conforms to Each Engine
Small V.G. Wingtips

March 1958
Fixed Windscreen
Rounded Side Windows
Reshaped Canard Further Aft and Lower
Single Segment Canard Flaps
Rounded Forward Fuselage
Large Verticals with Separate Rudders
Three Elevons on Each Wing
Rounded Air Inlet
Raised Fuselage Extends Rearward and Ends Vertically
Small V.G. Wingtips

The January 1958 airplane was not much different than the design that had won the competition. The largest external difference was the use of two-segment flaps on the canard versus the original single-segment units and small folding wingtips to improve directional stability. The fuselage neck terminated fairly far forward. (Art by Tony Landis)

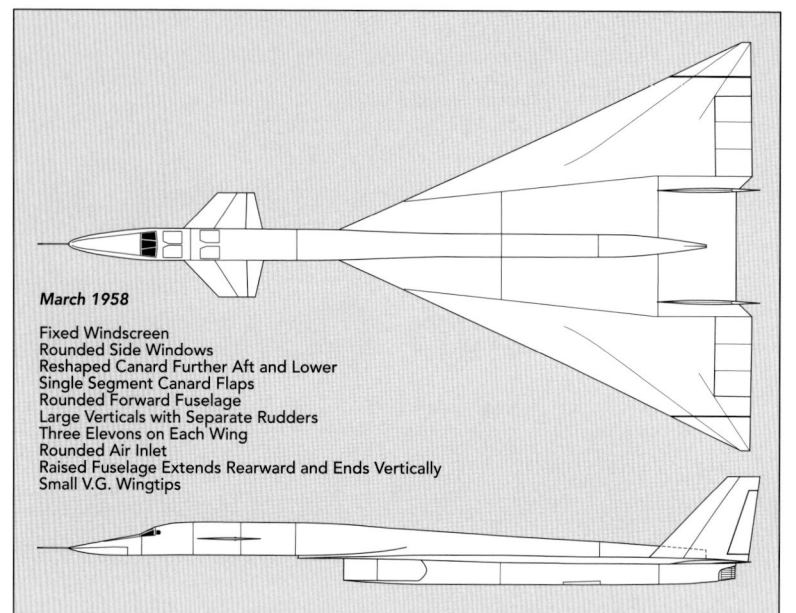

By March 1958 the canard had lost its delta shape and had moved from the top of the fuselage to the middle. The fuselage neck was extended aft and ended vertically instead of being faired into the aft fuselage, which was redesigned around the engines to minimize base drag. This design also saw a large increase in gross weight. (Art by Tony Landis)

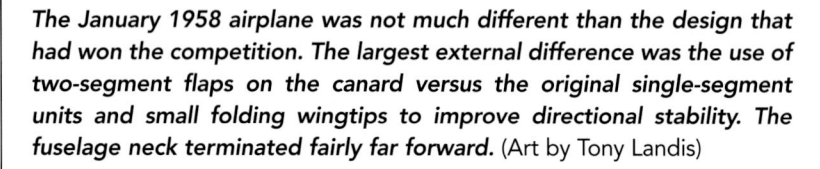

neers countered that unlike most designs – which used the canards as a horizontal stabilizer – the canard on the B-70 was only a trimming device; pitch and roll control was exclusively the province of the elevons and directional stability was handled by the vertical stabilizers and drooped wingtips. As for flow disturbances, given the extreme distance between the canard and air intake (which was at least partially protected by the wing) the engineers believed this was a non-issue. Some 14,000 hours of wind tunnel time backed up this assertion.[3]

Evolution

By March 1958, the North American design had evolved considerably. The canard became much smaller, was moved aft somewhat, and was mid-mounted on the forward fuselage instead of sitting on top of it. The aft end of the fuselage terminated in a vertical "wedge" just behind the leading edges of the vertical stabilizers. The folding wingtips were still small, but their trailing edges had been swept forward, forming triangular sections. The gross takeoff weight increased slightly to 470,000 pounds, and would continue to increase until early summer.[4]

Another major configuration change came during the summer of 1958. The gross weight increased from 483,000 to 537,109 pounds mainly to accommodate a second weapons bay located behind the original one. Each weapons bay was also slightly longer (14 feet) than before. As a result, the airframe structure, landing gear, and tires had to be strengthened accordingly. Extra fuel was added – largely – because it was becoming obvious that the high-energy fuel program was not going to materialize, at least not in the short term. This would force the use of conventional JP fuel in the –3 engine, and the accompanying 10-percent range penalty compared to HEF-3. Nothing could be found that indicated the high-energy fuels were ever a specific requirement for the B-70 program. Still, it is obvious that the Air Force and North American certainly considered its use and the resultant dual-fuel capability to handle JP-4 and HEF-3 were an integral part of the original B-70 design.[5]

The dual-fuel capability added 1,620 pounds[6] to the total weight of the aircraft, 300 pounds for the separate sequencing, pressurization, and venting systems required for the HEF-3, and 220 pounds for each J93-GE-5 engine because of their heavier afterburners. The high-energy fuel would continue to be carried as a baseline until late 1959, but all future range estimates would be calculated using conventional petroleum fuels (JP-4, and later JP-6).[7]

The canard was again redesigned but remained in the same relative position. The largest external change was that the wedge shape on the aft fuselage had given way to a smooth blending into the upper surface of the wing. At the same time, the overall lift-over-drag ratio was significantly improved by a reduction in the wing and canard thickness ratios. The result of these changes was a range improvement of 500 nautical miles (from 5,200 to 5,700 nautical miles).[8]

By the end of 1958, more changes improved the range to 6,539 nautical miles without increasing the gross weight of the aircraft from the previous 537,109 pounds, bringing the design into conformance with the revised GOR-82 that had been issued on 7 March

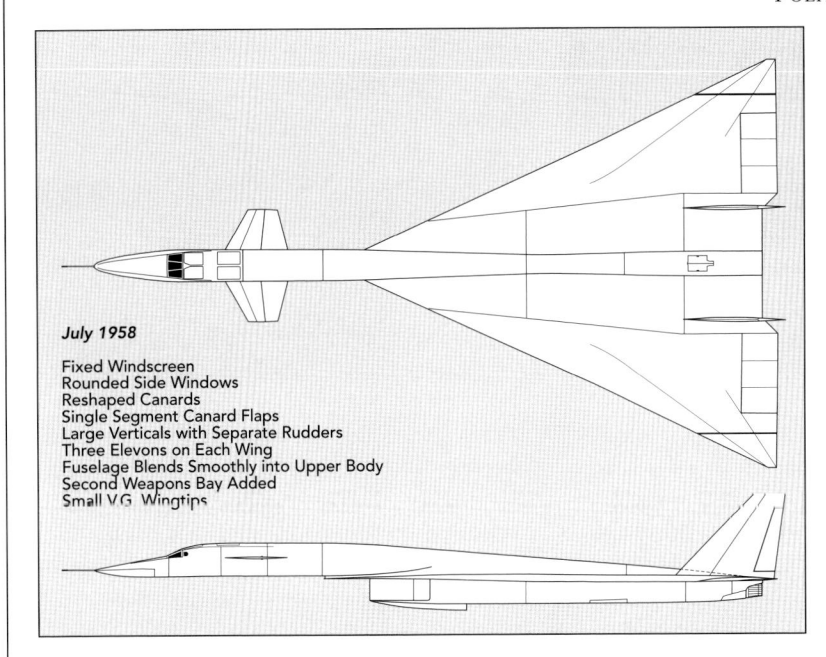

July 1958
Fixed Windscreen
Rounded Side Windows
Reshaped Canards
Single Segment Canard Flaps
Large Verticals with Separate Rudders
Three Elevons on Each Wing
Fuselage Blends Smoothly into Upper Body
Second Weapons Bay Added
Small V.G. Wingtips

December 1958
Movable Windshield Ramp
Square Side Windows
Canards Moved Higher on Fuselage
Large V.G. Wingtips
All-Moving Vertical Stabilizers (Except Wedge Hinge)

The redesign in the summer of 1958 saw the airplane take on nearly its final shape. The canards were again redesigned, but were still located at mid-fuselage and the neck was now faired smoothly into the upper rear fuselage. A second weapons bay was also added. The airplane still had large vertical stabilizers and small folding wingtips. (Art by Tony Landis)

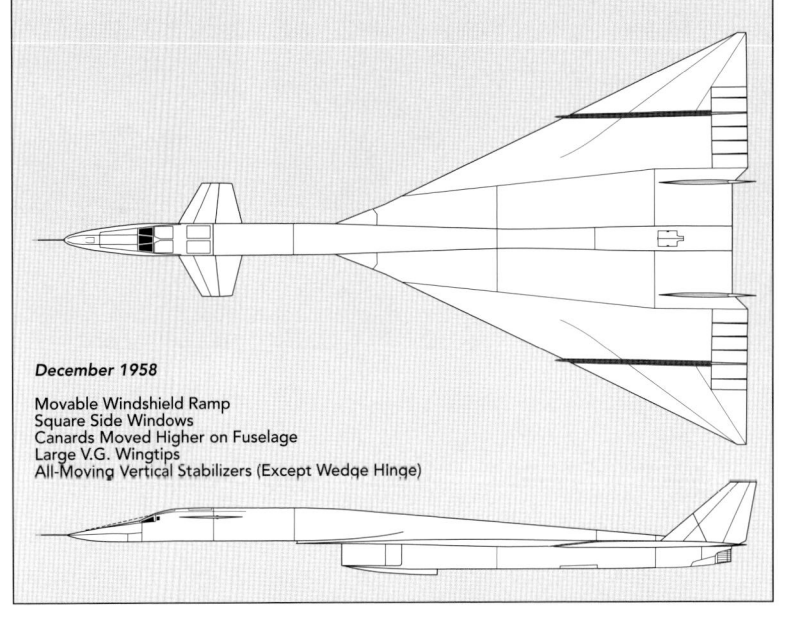

The design that was reviewed at the mockup inspection was very close to what was ultimately manufactured. The canard had moved to the top of the fuselage, the fold line on the wingtips had changed to 60-percent of the semispan instead of 80-percent, and the vertical stabilizers had gotten much smaller and were all-moving. (Art by Tony Landis)

1958. Among the modifications, the fold line of the wingtips was changed to 60 percent of the semispan instead of the original 80 percent, resulting in a folding surface roughly the size of a B-58 wing. This alteration improved directional stability to such an extent that it allowed the vertical stabilizer area to be reduced by half, significantly lowering drag and slightly reducing structural weight. Deflecting the wingtips also reduced the effective area of the wing near the trailing edge, shifting the aerodynamic center forward, helping to reduce the trim drag. The separate rudders shown on the earlier designs gave way to a mostly-all-moving surface (a small wedge at the bottom forward edge was fixed to provide a pivot point).[9]

At the same time, a movable windshield and ramp and trimmable canard were also introduced. Wind tunnel testing had revealed that the conventional canopy originally proposed created a great deal of drag during supersonic flight. Switching to a movable ramp that could be lowered during takeoff, tanking, and landing significantly reduced this, and still allowed the pilots sufficient visibility to operate the aircraft. The change to the canard resulted in the entire surface being infinitely positionable between zero and 6 degrees to provide high-speed trim. Previously moving the trailing edge flap had provided trim. The flap now had just two positions, zero and 20 degrees down and was used strictly as a landing aid.[10] The wing area increased slightly from 6,100 to 6,297.15 square feet. The wing was also cambered by twisting the leading edge downward inboard of the folding tip hinge line to enhance subsonic handling characteristics, primarily for in-flight refueling. Increased turbine inlet temperatures in the J93 engines allowed a slightly reduced fuel flow during supersonic cruise, mostly compensating for the increased drag of the larger wing.[11]

On 31 December 1958, the Air Force authorized North American to proceed with construction of the mockup as part of contract AF33(600)-38669, with North American switching to the NA-264 internal tracking number. This was the beginning of Part 1 of the Phase II development effort. The B-70 development engineering inspection (DEI) was conducted at North American's Inglewood plant on 2 March 1959, and the mockup was reviewed between 30 March and 4 April 1959. A total of 159 participants represented the various Air Force commands and their support contractors. The DEI provided the Air Force with a detailed analysis and theory of operation for each B-70 subsystem, while the mockup review was oriented more toward operational characteristics and suitability of the aircraft configuration.[12]

The Air Force issued 761 "requests for alterations" (the name of the form used to document comments) during the two reviews. One of the most significant was to incorporate provisions to carry air-to-surface missiles and provisions for external fuel tanks, a change that cost 17,500 pounds (including the missiles). No specific information could be ascertained about the missile (probably the GAM-87 Skybolt),[13] but its inclusion can be found in the fact that the IBM offensive system was now officially called the "bombing-navigation, and missile guidance subsystem." In order to keep the gross weight constant, North American deleted internal fuel to compensate for the additional structure needed for the hardpoints, causing the projected range to decrease 202 nautical miles to 6,327 nautical miles.

POLITICS

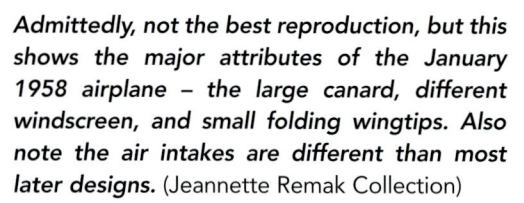

Admittedly, not the best reproduction, but this shows the major attributes of the January 1958 airplane – the large canard, different windscreen, and small folding wingtips. Also note the air intakes are different than most later designs. (Jeannette Remak Collection)

This drawings does not represent any specific design, but still clearly shows an operational B-70 complete with the SAC band on the fuselage. Note the forward extensions on the vertical stabilizers and the lack of folding wingtips. (AFFTC History Office Collection)

A very similar design, again with the vertical stabilizer extensions and no folding wingtips. It is possible the Air Force was discouraging showing the wingtips as a security precaution, or perhaps the artist was just unfamiliar with the concept. (Jeannette Remak Collection)

The Air Force directed North American to recoup the lost range without increasing the gross weight beyond 554,609 pounds, not including external stores. The range estimate using JP-4 increased to 6,500 nautical miles when the missiles and external tanks were not installed, essentially equaling the pre-missile estimates. One aerial refueling extended the total range to 7,901 nautical miles, permitting effective coverage of 96 percent of the desired targets.

After the successful review of the mockup, the Air Force authorized North American to proceed into Phase II Part 2 – which was called detailed development – under the same 38669 contract. North American assigned a new NA-267 internal control number to the effort on 27 July 1959, although the basic design of the aircraft had not changed. By 3 December 1959, work on approximately 95 percent of the requests for alterations had been completed.[14]

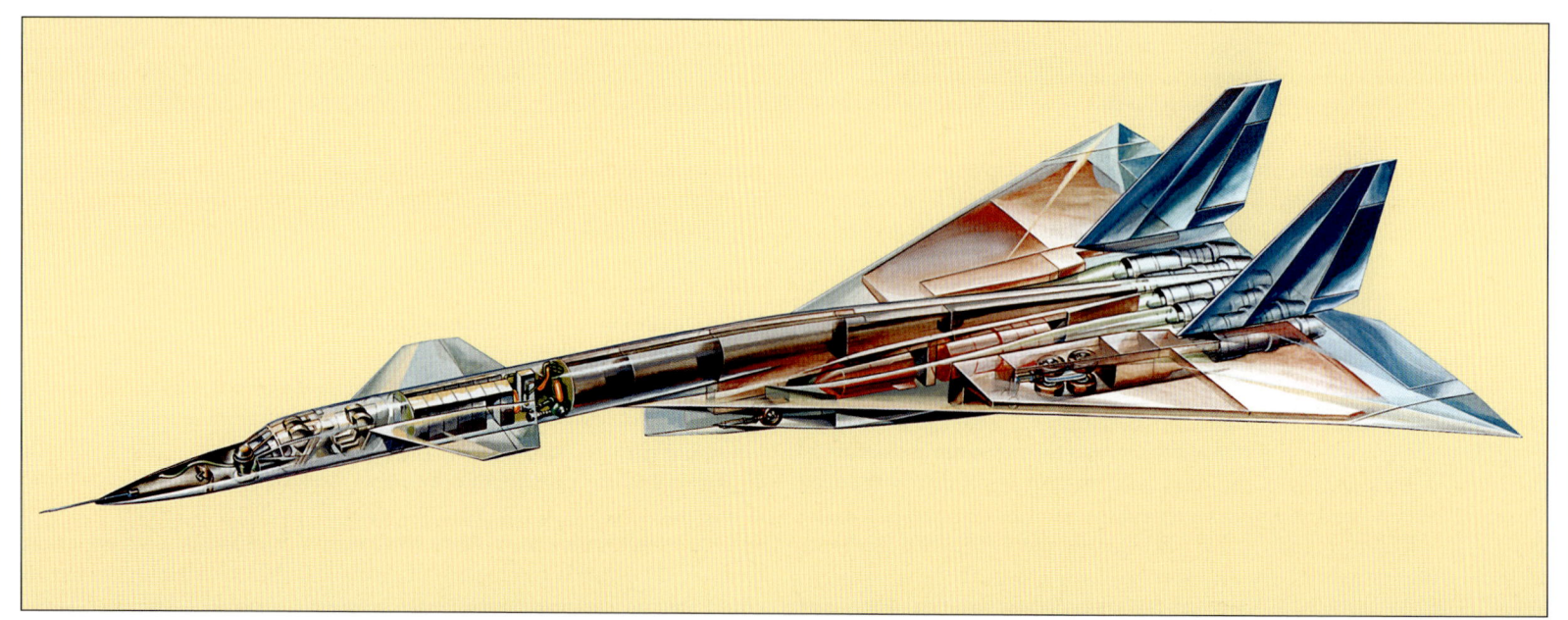

This cutaway of the March 1958 concept shows the location of most of the major systems. Note the single elevon per wing, the rudder on the vertical stabilizer, and the small folding wingtips. There is a thermonuclear weapon in the weapons bay, and two permanent fuel tanks behind it; these were later deleted to make room for the second weapons bay. This drawing shows all four crewmembers sitting ahead of the canard, but most engineering documentation says the backseaters were located under the canard. The attack radar, star tracker, and refueling receptacle are shown in the nose. The electronics compartment is under the canard with the environmental control system equipment immediately behind it. The large reddish areas in the wings and center fuselage are fuel tanks. (Boeing Historical Archives)

POLITICS

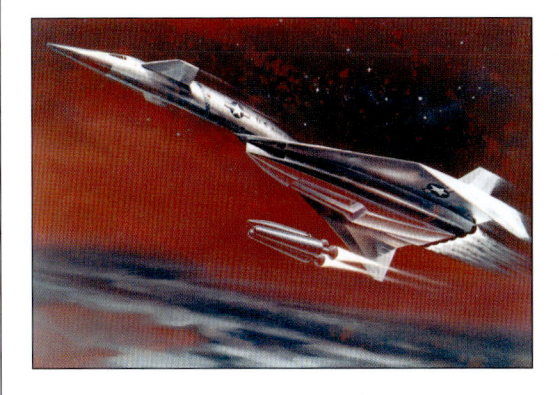

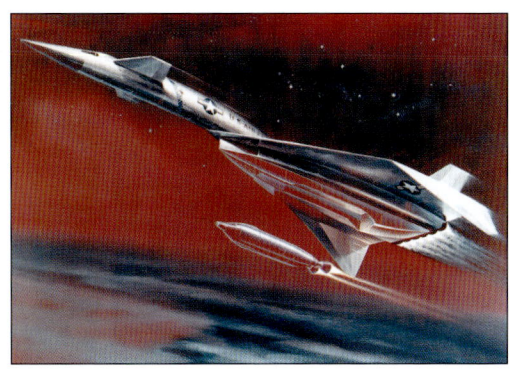

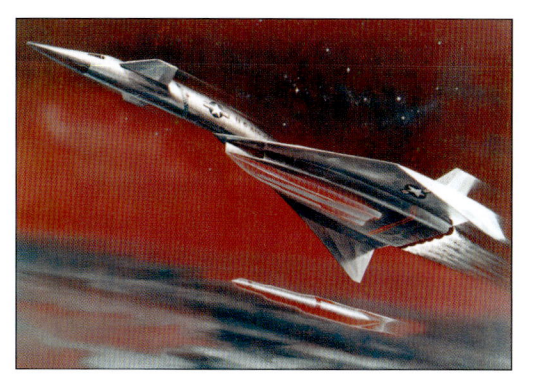

An odd series of artist concepts dated February 1966 showing the B-70 as a first stage booster for various space payloads. The drawing at left is labeled "Agena," although the vehicle being launched does not much resemble any known Agena. The center drawing shows a Gemini space capsule being launched, while the drawing at right shows the firing of a Minuteman ICBM. (Boeing Historical Archives)

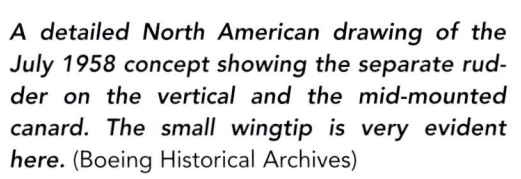

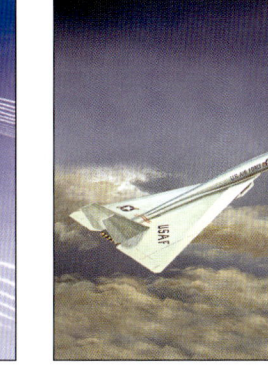

A detailed North American drawing of the July 1958 concept showing the separate rudder on the vertical and the mid-mounted canard. The small wingtip is very evident here. (Boeing Historical Archives)

One of the few drawings that acknowledges the B-70 would have had an in-flight refueling capability. The low-speed characteristics of the B-70 would have made this a challenge for the KC-135. (Boeing Historical Archives)

The near final airplane showing the high-mounted canard and large folding wingtip. The only discrepancy is that the hinge-line on the all-moving vertical is still not quite the final design. (Boeing Historical Archives)

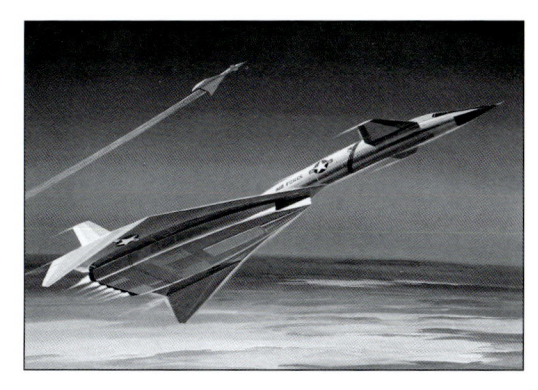

Despite the fact that the production program had been cancelled, North American was very proud of the B-70 and produced a fair amount of art for both public and military consumption. It is interesting to note that almost all of the art showing operational scenarios had more than one aircraft in them. Given the lack of precision altitude control at high altitudes, it is unlikely they would ever have flown in formation. (Boeing Historical Archives)

The final design shown in the expected operational markings. Note the U.S. AIR FORCE was on the lower fuselage instead of on the neck like the prototypes, and the SAC band behind the canard. (Boeing Historical Archives)

New Setbacks

During January 1959, the Pentagon had ordered the B-70 Program Office to reevaluate the engine program – again. This review gave Pratt & Whitney a "slight edge" in various management and contractual factors. On the other hand, the General Electric engine rated higher in most technical areas. In addition, General Electric had already accomplished full-scale afterburner testing with high-energy fuel, which was still carried as the baseline. The J58 scored points for its relative mechanical simplicity and predicted easier production. The evaluation found both engines technically suitable, concluding that the differences between the J93 and the J58 were so minor as to preclude selecting one over the other "from a technical standpoint." In the end, it was decided to proceed with the J93 as the only engine for both the F-108 and B-70s. Nevertheless, although it was technically a Navy program, the J58 would go on to power the CIA and Air Force Lockheed Blackbirds.[15]

Decisions made in the second half of 1959 hampered several Air Force development efforts but seemed to affect the B-70 more so than most.[16] As had been expected, the Department of Defense cancelled the high-energy fuel program on 10 August 1959. Consequently, the J93-GE-5 engine destined for the B-70 was also cancelled, since an engine without fuel is not terribly useful.[17]

The cancellation of the –5 engine and its exotic fuel caused a great deal of concern within the B-70 program but had little real impact. The fuel had been counted upon to provide the intercontinental range required for the primary strike mission although the official range estimates were already being computed using JP-4 as the base fuel. However, the increased aerodynamic efficiency had already provided a significant range boost to the B-70 design. The weight saved by not incorporating the dual-fuel capability (the ability to use either HEF or JP fuels) saved some weight and complexity. At the same time, the petroleum industry had developed a new fuel – JP-6 – that offered significant efficiency improvements over JP-4, but was essentially interchangeable with the old fuel from an engine technology perspective. Unlike the boron-based fuels, JP-6 did not require special metals in the engine or fuel system. It was also no worse environmentally than standard jet fuel, and was perhaps a bit better since it burned more completely.

Analysis showed that the –3 engine burning JP-6 could provide essentially the same range as had been expected with the –5 engine burning HEF-3. There were some compromises, however. The engine produced slightly less thrust, meaning takeoff distances would increase and refueling altitudes would be a little lower. The most critical item – the rate of climb on a hot day with one engine inoperative at takeoff – was resolved by incorporating an overspeed capability into the –3 engine to develop a higher turbine inlet temperature on takeoff and thereby provide the necessary rate of climb. The use of this feature would have a negative impact on engine life, but provided a necessary safety margin for the aircraft and crew.

Far more consequential to the B-70 program than the demise of the high-energy fuel program, on 24 September 1959 the F-108 was cancelled. The F-108 had used many of the same subsystems and technologies as the B-70; the J93 engine was managed and partially funded by the F-108 program, as were the escape capsules and several lesser subsystems. The loss of the second funding source would impact B-70 cost estimates by at least $180 million – a political liability the program would never recover from.[18]

A pair of Schlieren photographs showing the shock waves generated by the B-70 at Mach 3. This model is somewhat of a hybrid design, showing the March 1958 canard shape, but the larger folding wingtips of the late 1958 design. Understanding the shock waves was particularly important for North American, partially because the B-70 performance estimates depended upon the compression lift principle, but mostly because an unexpected shock wave impingement on the airframe could lead to it melting. (Boeing via the Gerald H. Balzer Collection)

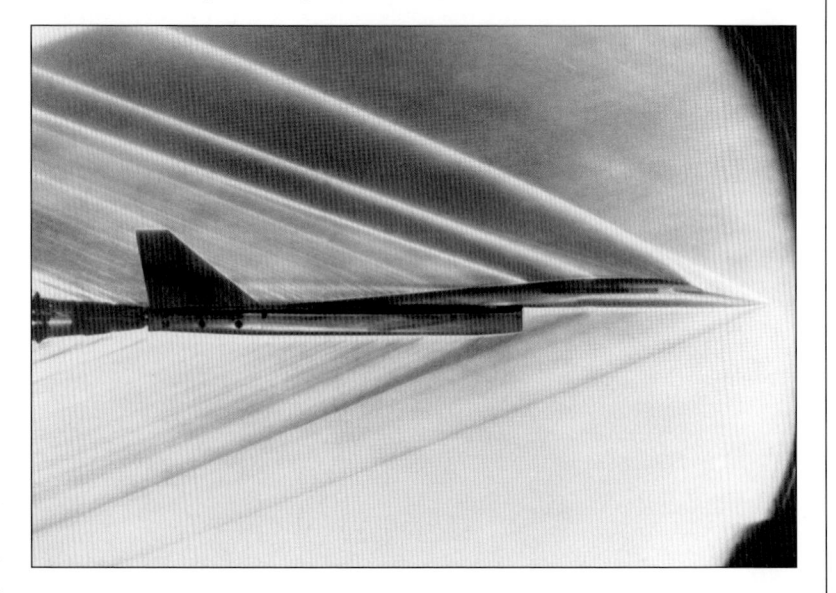

POLITICS

ON THE ROPES

In early November 1959, President Dwight D. Eisenhower told the Air Force Chief of Staff, General Thomas D. White, that the "B-70 left him cold in terms of making military sense." The President was hardly impressed with the many pro-B-70 arguments put forth by White. Eisenhower stressed that at anticipated funding levels the B-70 would not be operational for 8 to 10 years, and by that time, the major strategic retaliatory weapon would be the intercontinental missile. The President finally agreed to take another look at the B-70, but pointed out that speaking of manned bombers in the missile age was like talking about bows and arrows in the era of gunpowder.[19]

Apparently, the B-70 still did not make sense to Eisenhower after another look. On 1 December 1959, the Air Force announced that the B-70 program would be reduced to a single prototype and that the development of most subsystems would be cancelled. The exception was that development of the IBM bomb-nav system would continue as a very modest effort. The program's near-demise was generally attributed to the budget, although it was more directly linked to the anti-bomber sentiment that was prevalent within the Administration at the time. The FY60 funding level was reduced from the approved $345.6 million to only $150 million; FY61 went from $456 million to $75 million. The WS-110A program had already cost over $360 million. This expenditure had bought 8,250 hours of wind tunnel testing of various airframe configurations, and 100 hours of test stand operation for the J93. Over 695,000 engineering man-hours had been expended on the propulsion system, and another 195,000 man-hours on the bomb-nav system.[20]

Despite the dire situation, the Air Force had not given up on the program. On 14 January 1960, the Chairman of the Joint Chiefs of Staff, General Nathan Twining, testified before Congress "A missile is very inflexible. Once you push a trigger, it is gone and you cannot stop it and it is going to be a very serious decision to push that button." This had always been one of the prime arguments in the missile versus manned aircraft debate – a manned aircraft is recallable. "A nation can use a manned aircraft much the same as the ancients rattled their saber. By sending a bomber to a point just outside another

This model shows the March 1958 canards, but the rear portion of the fuselage neck where it meets the wing has some interesting features. North American changed this area several times during development in an effort to find the configuration that offered the least drag and the best airflow over the vertical stabilizers. (Boeing Historical Archives)

North American used numerous wind tunnels around the country during their development program. These photos are of a late B-70 model in the facilities at the NASA Ames Research Center, near Palo Alto, California. (NASA Ames Research Center)

Politics

An unusual angle of the B-70 mockup. Note the yellow alert pod "special power device" in the background. See Chapter 8 for more information on this unique item of ground support equipment. (Boeing Historical Archives)

Rear view of the mockup shows the six J93 engine exhaust nozzles, plus two small fairings for defensive system sensors (one inboard of the elevons, the other outboard of the control surfaces). The mockup was fairly representative of the aircraft as-built. (Boeing Historical Archives)

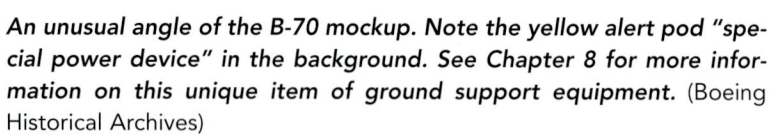

Two legends from North American: Harrison "Stormy" Storms on the left, and Alvin S. White on the right. Storms was chief engineer for the company, and White was chief test pilot and the B-70 project pilot. (Boeing Historical Archives)

Future B-70 pilots Al White and Joe Cotton in the cockpit mockup with project engineer Walt Spivak looking on. The instrument panel and center console fairly represent how the two prototypes would look when they were built. (Boeing Historical Archives)

Politics

country's airspace, there is little doubt about your intent; yet you can still stop at any point until you cross the border, or indeed, until you drop the bombs. A missile on the other hand either sits in its silo, or destroys a city. There is no in-between."[21]

Lieutenant General Bernard A. Schriever, the commander of the ARDC, agreed, "My own feeling is, and it is very strong, that we must maintain manned aircraft in our retaliatory force as well [as ICBMs] … you need, first of all, the flexibility of an aircraft and a man in it – you can never put all your eggs in one basket. You have to have a diversified capability in this job of deterring total war." General White concurred, adding, "We have got to establish that the manned bomber is a requirement." All of the arguments fell on deaf ears.[22]

While the politics were being debated in Washington and elsewhere, North American was proceeding with certain aspects of development. The Columbus Division of North American had a crude g-chair simulator and during early 1960, North American project pilot Al White spent about 10 hours investigating the fuselage bending characteristics of the B-70 design. Although not widely acknowledged, at this point in the program, some thought was given to using the airplane

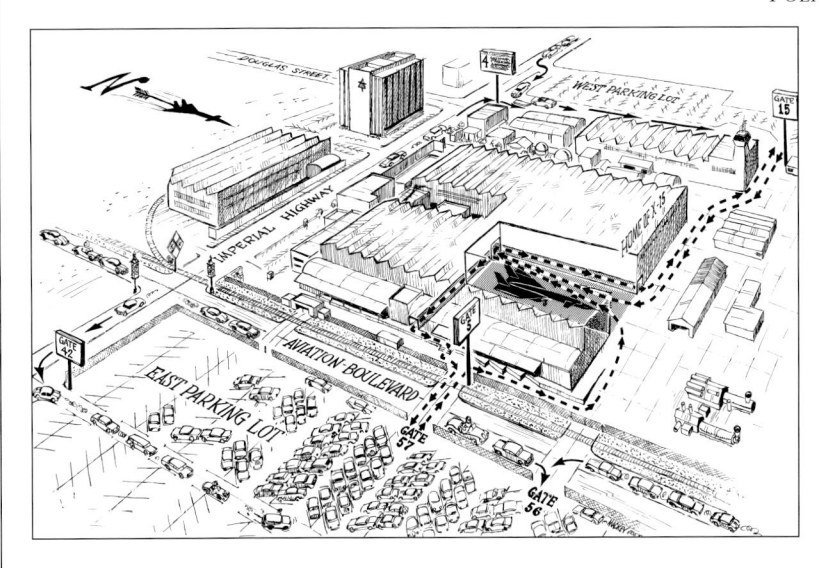

The location of the B-70 mockup at the North American plant next to the Los Angeles International Airport. (Mike Machat Collection)

The B-70 mockup was painted in the expected military markings, including a soon-to-be-obsolete "buzz number" on the back of the fuselage under the wing. The nose of the mockup shows the entry door, star tracker window (just ahead of the windscreen), and aerial refueling receptacle (between the four support wires near the front of the nose). (Boeing Historical Archives)

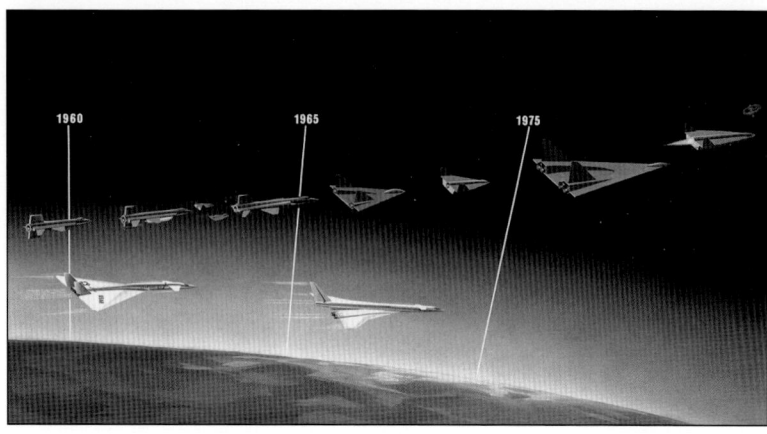

North American clearly saw the B-70 program as a stepping stone to its future, much the same as the X-15 was. This chart shows the X-15 evolving into a series of space vehicles, while the B-70 was expected to lead to a supersonic transport. (Boeing Historical Archives)

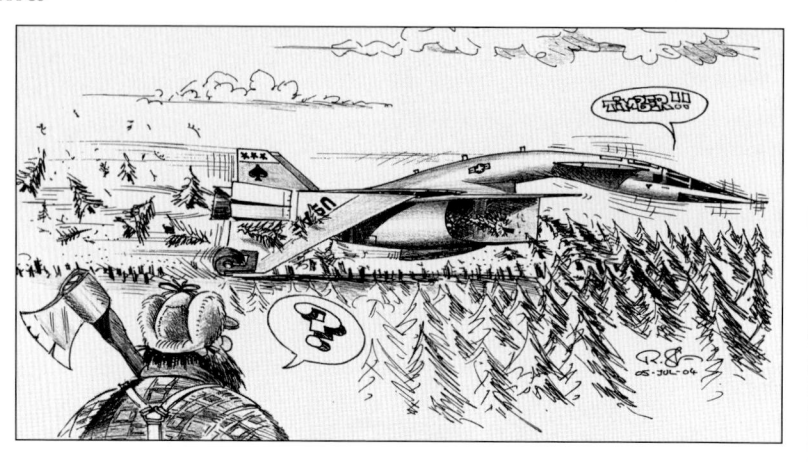

We asked artist Ronald Stephano for his impression of nap-of-earth flight in a B-70, and this is what he came up with. The concept of using a high-altitude bomber for low-level missions seems odd, but it worked for the B-52. (Original artwork by Ronald Stephano, ©2004)

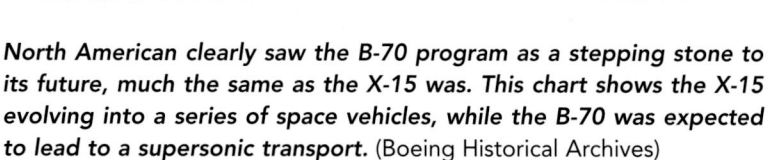

in a low-level, terrain avoidance mode. A year or so later, North American built a dynamic simulator which continued investigating fuselage bending at g-loads from 1 to 7 during simulated low-level missions. White managed to find a structural harmonic frequency that was very painful to his chest, and other frequencies that bothered his ability to read the instruments. North American pilot Van H. Shepard, although not formally assigned to the B-70 program yet, went through the entire series of tests without any major complaints, but later indicated that he could hardly get out of bed the next morning. Although the Air Force continued investigating the use of the B-70 as a low-level interdiction aircraft, this series of tests seemed to have put the issue on the back burner for the duration of the program.[23]

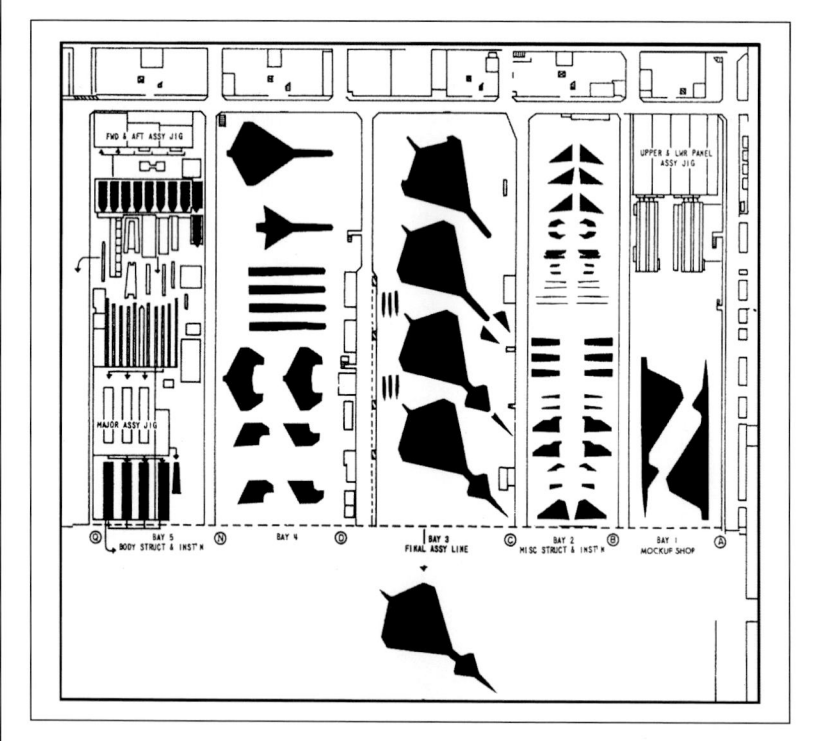

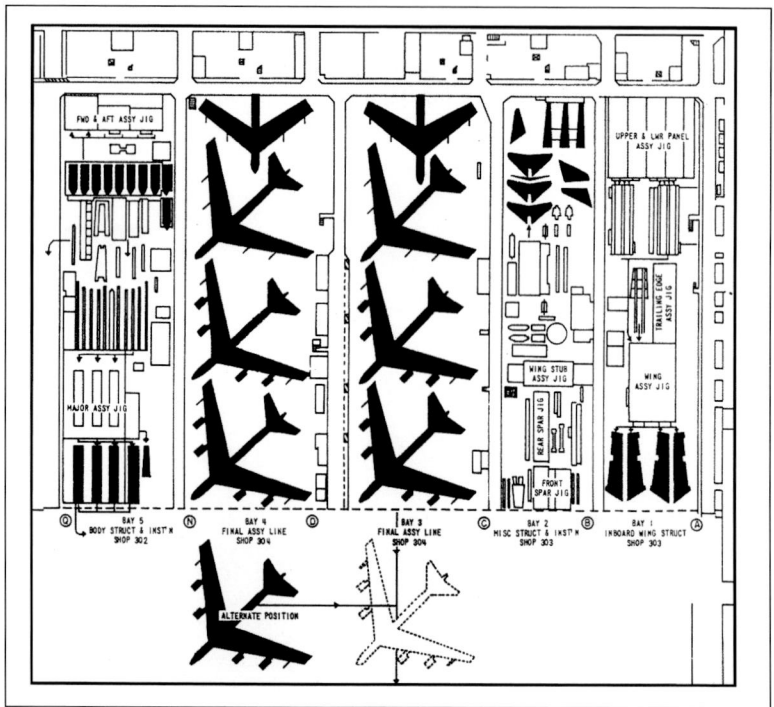

As part of the Boeing proposal, the company showed how it would convert the existing Boeing Plant 2 production line from manufacturing ten B-52s per month to building five Model 804-4 aircraft per month. North American, on the other hand, would need a new final assembly facility since they had never built an aircraft as large as the B-70. The Boeing argument was apparently not persuasive. (Boeing Historical Archives)

The politics of the 1960 presidential campaign sparked renewed interest in the B-70 from both political parties. Thus, with the approval of the Department of Defense, in August 1960 the Air Force directed that the XB-70 prototype effort be changed once again to a full-scale development program. A letter contract for the YB-70 weapon system was signed on 1 August to provide a single XB-70 prototype, eleven YB-70 service test aircraft, and to demonstrate the combat capability of the bombers. This directive, coupled with a congressional appropriation of $365 million for FY61, seemed to restore the B-70 to the status of a weapon system headed for production. The definitive contract, AF33(600)-42058, was signed on 21 September 1960 and was assigned the NA-274 moniker by North American.[24]

By August 1960, the B-70 flight control simulator was ready. Called an "iron cross" because of the layout of its framework, the device consisted of a steel beam the length of the fuselage mounted on support legs with a simulated cockpit at one end. At the other

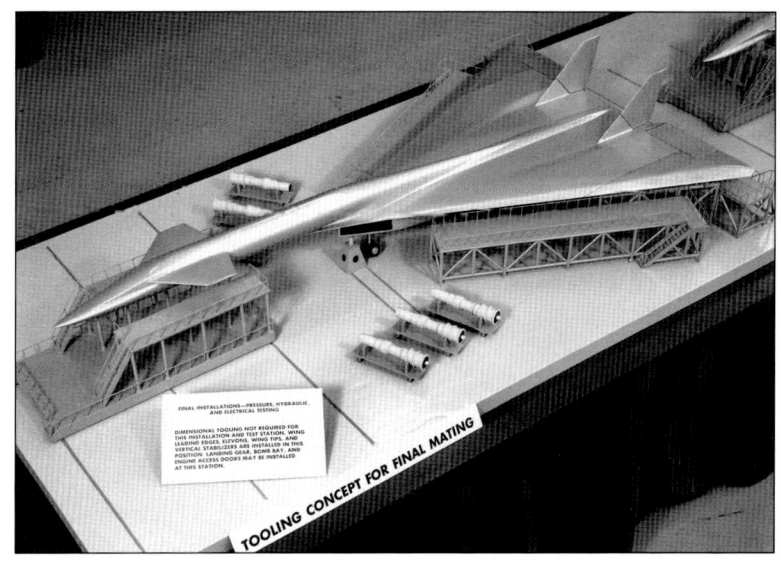

North American built a 1/40th-scale model of the final assembly line to show the production tooling they would need to manufacture the B-70. The last model in line in the left-hand photo is shown in detail at right. Along the back wall are models of the four new production buildings and the final checkout ramp. The models of the airplanes are interesting in that they show a humpback short fuselage neck, the March 1958 canards, but the later all-moving vertical stabilizers. (Boeing Historical Archives)

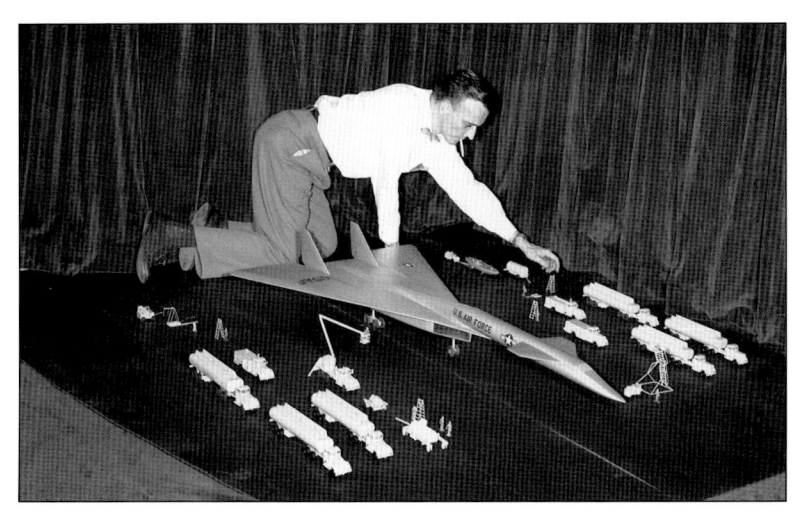

An engineer places models of ground support equipment around the B-70 to depict the expected servicing arrangement. Note the large number of fuel trucks required, plus a cherry-picker to allow access to the upper wings and vertical stabilizers. (Boeing Historical Archives)

This is how the B-70 would look undergoing maintenance in an Air Force B-52 hangar. North American pointed out that the B-70 required less floor space than the Stratofortress. Note the canard has been removed from the model and placed in a cradle. (Boeing Historical Archives)

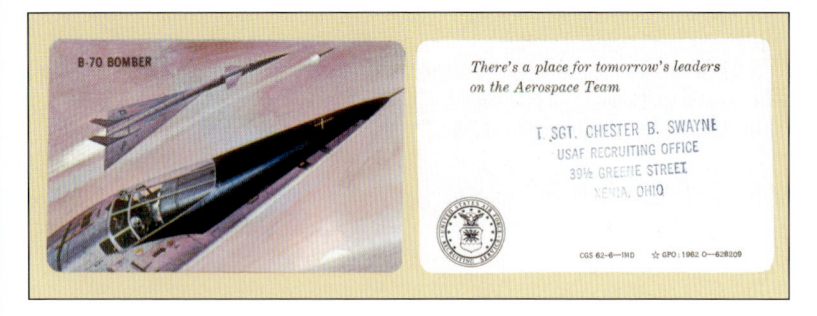

Not surprisingly, the Air Force used the B-70 in many publicity campaigns, including passing them out as recruiting cards. What is a little odd, however, is that this card is dated 1962 – B-70 production had already been cancelled a year earlier. (Jerry McCulley Collection)

end, another beam was mounted across the "fuselage" to hold the hydraulic actuators for the flight control system. Electric motors drove hydraulic pumps, and flight control actuators were loaded to represent the airplane in various flight regimes. This seemingly crude device could fairly accurately duplicate the flight control system being proposed for the airplane, and allowed pilots and engineers to work out many problems before the first aircraft was built. Similar devices were used on many other programs of the era, notably the rocket-powered X-15 research airplane.[25]

The connection from the flight controls in the cockpit to the actuators at the control surfaces was a series of metal-clad cables running through a tube down the length of the fuselage. The cables were supported by fittings inside the tube, and a "feel" system was built in to give the pilot the normal feel of the controls in an airplane in flight. For all intents, the iron cross was a fixed-base simulator. This was not a procedures trainer, but was used as a design tool to optimize the flight control system. Initially, the cockpit was equipped with control wheels, rudders, trim system, and only those instruments that were required to "fly" the simulator. Eventually the cockpit became more complete, but never truly resembled the B-70 layout. This simulator would continue to be used even after the flight program began; actual flight data would be entered into the simulator computers and would then extrapolated to the next point in the envelope expansion program. That mission would then be flown in the simulator, giving the pilots and the engineers some idea of what to expect on the next flight.[26]

It should be noted that when the term "computer" is used in this context, it meant a room-size analog device that was "mechanized" (programmed) using patch cords and cables. The widespread use of general-purpose digital computers was still a decade in the future.

For the rest of 1960 and most of 1961, the flight control system, instrument displays, and trim systems were tested, adjusted, and optimized. Many areas were being evaluated, including the control harmony between longitudinal and lateral forces, trim rates, friction and break-out forces, stick forces throughout the Mach-number range and airplane responses to control input, and so on. Al White insisted on using the "position trim control" that had been developed for the F-107 for longitudinal trim instead of the "coolie hat" control that was used to adjust the longitudinal and lateral trim in most airplanes. This control was a small wheel that could be operated by the pilot's left thumb, and White felt the concept was superior to the other system. Since White was the project pilot, he got his way.[27]

With a new contract in hand, during September 1960, North American was authorized to proceed with the design and manufacture of the 12 aircraft and to restart the development of all subsystems. In mid-October the defensive subsystem contract with Westinghouse was reinstated, with the Motorola mission and traffic control system contract following in November. The Air Force and North American also fully funded the IBM offensive avionics development effort. Unfortunately, the B-70 program's recaptured importance was to be short-lived.[28]

THREE STRIKES ...

Once in office, it did not take long for President John F. Kennedy to take a critical look at the B-70 program. Like his predecessor, Kennedy doubted the aircraft's reason for being, in no small part because the new Secretary of Defense Robert S. McNamara did not support any manned bomber program. On 28 March 1961, Kennedy recommended that the program be reoriented to exploring the problems of flying at three times the speed of sound with an aircraft "potentially useful" as a bomber. Kennedy underscored that this should only require the development of a small number of B-70s and the continued development of the IBM bomb-nav system.[29]

Kennedy's words gave the Air Force no choice but to again redirect the B-70 program to a prototype development effort. The change

When the production program was cancelled, General Electric was relieved of the obligation to certify the J93 as an operational engine, and it spent the entire flight program as the YJ93-GE-3. Nevertheless, the engine proved to be remarkably trouble free during the 129 flights of the Valkyries. Here, the first YJ93 to arrive in Palmdale is installed in A/V-1. (General Electric via the Gerald H. Balzer Collection)

The first YJ93-GE-1 arrives at Palmdale in a C-119 transport. The note on the engine container says "Bill Birdsall: Another milestone met. Courtesy of the SPO. Please keep on schedule." The engine would be installed shortly (see facing page). (Boeing Historical Archives)

The extreme aft fuselage for A/V-1 is hoisted out of its assembly jig. The exhaust nozzles for the J93 engines will be at the left, the engine faces will be a few feet to the right. The H-11 steel and René 41 structure was covered with titanium skins. (Boeing Historical Archives)

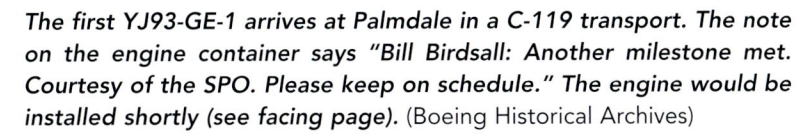

became official on 10 April 1961, when the North American contract was cut to only three XB-70 prototypes and most subsystem development efforts put on hold. In response, North American assigned yet another new internal tracking number, NA-278, to the effort.[30]

Air Vehicle No. 1 (A/V-1)[31] was assigned Air Force serial number (62-0001) which had originally been allocated to the single XB-70 prototype under the December 1959 restructured program. The two additional aircraft were assigned serial numbers 62-0207 (A/V-2) and 62-0208 (A/V-3). There is no record that the 11 short-lived YB-70s ever were allocated serials numbers.[32]

The first two aircraft would be aerodynamic and propulsion system test vehicles, and would not be equipped with weapons bays or any operational systems. According to some sources, the third air vehicle was to be designated XB-70B; others called it YB-70A, which is more likely. This aircraft was to be equipped with a prototype IBM bombing-navigation system and an operable weapons bay in order to demonstrate its military mission. A crew of four would have been accommodated in the forward fuselage, with the defensive systems operator sitting behind the pilot and the offensive systems operator sitting behind the copilot, each in their own ejection capsules. As far as can be determined, the defense operator would have had no equipment to operate since the defensive avionics program had been cancelled. The hydraulic, electrical, and environmental control systems would all have required substantial changes from those installed in the first two airplanes to support the additional crew and electronics to be carried by A/V-3. It appears that the

The canard for A/V-1 being manufactured in its jig. The program would build five canard structures – one for each flight vehicle, two for the structural test program, and the one for A/V-3 that was used by NASA in a thermal laboratory experiment. (Boeing Historical Archives)

canard would also have been slightly reshaped to minimize a minor problem that was discovered with spanwise flow – the Russians would simply have installed a fence on the upper surface, but North American would undoubtedly have found a more elegant solution.[33]

As a consequence of the latest restructuring, the General Electric engine program was also substantially reduced. The qualification tests for an operational "J" engine were eliminated, leaving only the preliminary flight-rating test for an experimental "XJ" powerplant. Instead of continuing to refine the design and reducing weight wherever possible, which would increase development costs, General Electric was allocated an extra 150 pounds per engine over the weight specified for the operational powerplant. A plan to use a B-58 to test the J93 in flight also disappeared, although it would briefly return later.[34]

Since it now appeared very unlikely that the B-70 would ever enter production, the Air Force immediately began to consider various alternatives. In May 1961, there was talk of an improved B-58 armed with air-launched missiles; specially designed, long-endurance, missile-launching aircraft; transport aircraft modified to launch ballistic missiles; resurrected nuclear-powered aircraft; and again of a reconnaissance B-70 that would also be capable of strike missions. In August 1961, the U.S. Senate attempted to rescue the B-70 and asked that a production program be outlined to introduce the aircraft into the operational inventory at the earliest possible date. Undaunted, McNamara expressed his thorough dissatisfaction with any future manned bombers and refused to support the initiative. Surprisingly, the Senate backed down.[35]

Nevertheless, in March 1962 Congress directed the Air Force to begin planning for a reconnaissance-strike version of the B-70, usually referred to as the RS-70.[36] In April, a group headed by General Bernard A. Schriever, Commander of the newly formed Air Force Systems Command, developed several approaches to the proposed RS-70 system. The preferred development plan would cost $1,600 million and estimated that the first flight of an RS-70 prototype could

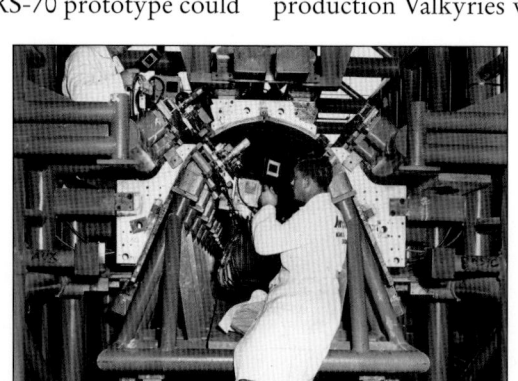

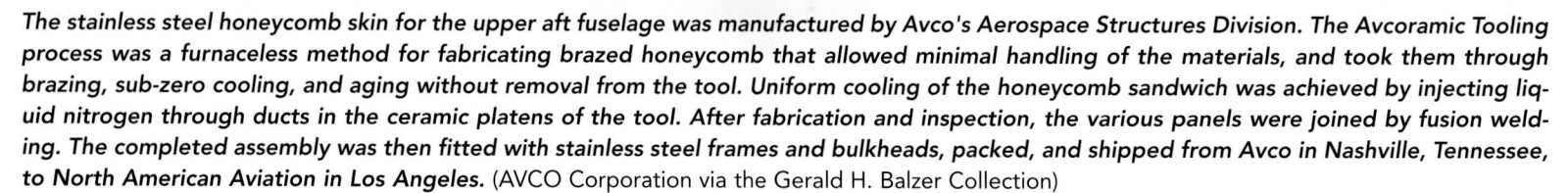

The crew compartment for A/V-1 on 3 February 1962. The rear bulkheads in both the front and rear compartments appear to be configured to accept ejection seats, although only the forward pair was installed in the airplane. (Boeing via the Tony Landis Collection)

occur within two years, assembled from pieces intended for A/V-3. The basic plan called for the first 60 RS-70s to enter service in 1969 and a further 150 the year after. The total cost of the production program was estimated at more than $10,000 million. In addition to the capabilities originally envisioned for the B-70, the RS-70 featured additional stand-off capability (probably in the form of a SRAM-like missile carried in the missile bay), an advanced side-looking radar, and intelligence gathering systems. Although the RS-70 concept languished for some time, ultimately the idea faded as Robert McNamara refused to release the funds Congress had authorized. Any dreams of production Valkyries vanished.[37]

The stainless steel honeycomb skin for the upper aft fuselage was manufactured by Avco's Aerospace Structures Division. The Avcoramic Tooling process was a furnaceless method for fabricating brazed honeycomb that allowed minimal handling of the materials, and took them through brazing, sub-zero cooling, and aging without removal from the tool. Uniform cooling of the honeycomb sandwich was achieved by injecting liquid nitrogen through ducts in the ceramic platens of the tool. After fabrication and inspection, the various panels were joined by fusion welding. The completed assembly was then fitted with stainless steel frames and bulkheads, packed, and shipped from Avco in Nashville, Tennessee, to North American Aviation in Los Angeles. (AVCO Corporation via the Gerald H. Balzer Collection)

POLITICS

The crew compartment being mated with the nose and electronics compartment on 6 February 1962. Note the large crew access door that entered the compartment just behind the forward seats, but ahead of where the systems operators' consoles would have been in production airplanes. The assembly jig is rather crude compared to what would have been used on production airplanes, and required a great deal of manual alignment of the subassemblies. Most of the forward fuselage structure and skin was made of titanium alloy. (Boeing via the Tony Landis Collection)

GETTING READY – ON A MUCH SMALLER SCALE

Despite the setbacks, North American continued preparing for the flight program. Alvin S. White, who had been Scott Crossfield's back-up pilot on the X-15, was assigned as the primary program pilot, with Al "Blacky" Blackburn as his backup. However, once Blackburn finished the F-100 ZEL program he took a leave of absence and went to work for the Department of Defense, never officially joining the B-70 program. Shortly thereafter, his connection with North American was considered a conflict of interest and he had to resign from the company. Zeke Hopkins took his place as backup pilot on the XB-70 program. During late 1961 and early 1962, White and Hopkins attended a 10-week B-52 pilot training course at Castle AFB so that they could better understand how the Air Force operated operational heavy bombers. The two pilots conducted numerous simulations in the iron cross and continued working with the engineers.[38]

In early 1962, Hopkins decided to take the job of chief of North American test operations at Edwards AFB. Van Shepard was selected to replace him as White's backup pilot on the XB-70 program, especially appropriate since Shepard had already participated in many simulations. During the summer of 1962, White and Shepard went to Carswell AFB for the Senior Officer Course in the Convair B-58. This

The nose of the airplane was largely empty since neither the in-flight refueling receptacle or star tracker were installed in the prototypes. (Boeing via the Tony Landis Collection)

The intermediate fuselage for A/V-1 arrived in Palmdale on 1 April. This section was constructed with an H-11 steel structure and stainless steel honeycomb skins. (Boeing via the Tony Landis Collection)

CHAPTER 5

The nose section for A/V-2 is lowered into the mating jig. The assembly order for A/V-2 was a little different than for A/V-1 – note the crew compartment is already in the jig. (Boeing Historical Archives)

The pilot's escape capsule being installed in A/V-1. Note the small window that allowed the pilot to see the instrument panel after he encapsulated. (AFFTC History Office Collection)

provided an introduction into how the Air Force operated a supersonic bomber, albeit one with a relatively limited range. Around this same time, Major Joseph E. Cotton was assigned as the Air Force project pilot for the B-70 program, with Major Fitzhugh "Fitz" L. Fulton (later to be NASA's chief test pilot) designated as his backup.[39]

The use of computers to aid in designing aircraft was just coming into fashion. North American had pioneered the idea during the X-15 program, eventually accumulating 1,235 hours of run-time on IBM 7094 mainframes while designing the small rocket-powered research airplane. For the B-70, North American engineers used more than 18,000 hours of 7094 time, including over 5,000 flight simulations to help define the flight control system. A press release pointed out that the company had used more than 50 million punched cards, and that every day over 20 miles of magnetic tape was input to the mainframes, resulting in a stack of printouts over 10 feet tall. The B-70 was also one of the first applications of numerically-controlled milling machines to fabricate parts. Again driven by IBM 7094 mainframes, approximately 5 percent of the aircraft was manufactured using this process.[40]

The construction of the two XB-70As went remarkably smoothly given how far they were pushing the state-of-the-art. Not unexpectedly, the engineers and technicians had to overcome numerous small problems on an almost daily basis. However, two major problems soon cropped up. The first involved manufacturing and assembling the stainless steel honeycomb skin panels.

The early 1960s saw the appearance of two Mach 3 aircraft in the United States – the XB-70A and the Lockheed Blackbirds. Each used a highly unique approach to develop an airframe capable of withstanding the temperatures created during high-speed flight. Lockheed decided to manufacture the Blackbirds almost exclusively of titanium alloys, and to accept a relatively hot structure and its implications. North American chose a different approach. Or, perhaps the approach was forced upon them by the Air Force; available documentation does not give much insight into the process. It is known that the amount of high-grade titanium available to the industry at the

The forward fuselage (nose, crew compartment, and electronics compartment) being moved into the final assembly hangar in Palmdale on 31 March 1962. (Boeing via the Tony Landis Collection)

Part of the lower aft fuselage being lowered into the assembly jig. The six engine bays are clearly visible. Note the tail of a T-39 in the background at right. (Boeing via the Gerald H. Balzer Collection)

The nose strut sitting in its shipping crate. The landing gear was a major technical achievement since the B-70 was the heaviest aircraft in the world at the time of its first flight. (Boeing Historical Archives)

The intermediate fuselage for A/V-1 being mated to the forward fuselage in Palmdale. This entire section was a fuel tank, and was constructed of stainless steel honeycomb structure and skins, with only minor use of H-11 steel in some frames. (Boeing via the Tony Landis Collection)

Technicians work on the windshield of A/V-2 during assembly, showing the movable ramp that improved the aerodynamics at high speeds. The black radome under the nose was very production-looking, but there were no antennas behind it. (Boeing via the Gerald H. Balzer Collection)

The splitter plate at the leading edge of the wing just above the air intake being manufactured. A piece of this plate would fail during Flight 1-12 on 7 May 1965, causing Al White and Fitz Fulton a bit more excitement than they expected. (Boeing via the Tony Landis Collection)

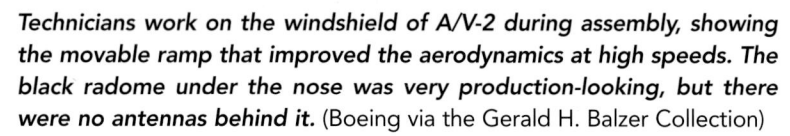

time was very limited, as was the production capacity (rolling, milling, etc.). The Blackbird was never envisioned (except, perhaps, in Kelly Johnson's mind) as a large-scale production project, so the use of a relatively scarce resource was not much of an issue. However, the Air Force would have liked to build a large fleet of B-70s, and each aircraft would have required a significant amount of the material. It is very possible that the Air Force "suggested" that North American find a less strategic material for their construction. The Source Selection Board did note that Boeing had preferred titanium, but it is not known if this detracted from their score.[41]

The dry weight of the XB-70A airframe was approximately 150,000 pounds, a little heavier than a fully loaded Blackbird. The material North American chose for almost 69 percent of this was a PH15-7-Mo stainless steel honeycomb sandwich, and each XB-70A used about 20,000 square feet of the material. The attributes listed by North American were light weight, high strength, aerodynamic smoothness, low heat transfer from the skin to underlying structure at 450–640 degrees Fahrenheit, reliable strength at high temperatures, fatigue resistance, and rigidity. Producibility and relatively low cost were initially thought to be attributes, but these ended up to be very questionable as the program began procuring large amounts of the material.[42]

At least initially, the material suffered from some serious problems. On numerous occasions, pieces of the skin – sometimes large pieces – separated from A/V-1 at high speeds. The worst was when the aircraft lost a triangular section of its wing apex forward of its splitter plate and the debris was sucked into the air intakes, effec-

tively destroying six engines. The aircraft subsequently lost a 40x36-inch piece from the underside of its left wing, and an 8x38-inch strip from its right fuselage section later still. The skin panels separated when thermal expansion and aerodynamic buffeting ballooned a defective area around a small crack in the face sheet. This in turn led to the skin cover separating where the brazings were too thin or poorly formed. Engineers traced the immediate problem to flaws in the manufacturing process and better quality controls were implemented. When a void was detected, North American welded pins between the outer and inner face sheet, through the honeycomb structure. Along with improved fabrication techniques, this essentially eliminated the problem in A/V-2, although a large piece did separate from the upper surface of its right wing during one high-speed flight. North American was certain that the process would eventually be perfected, and the Air Force did not appear overly worried. Still, it is an open question if the material would have been satisfactory in large-scale use over a long period of time.

Although not the primary construction material, three types of titanium nevertheless accounted for approximately 12,000 pounds (8 percent) of the airframe in 22,000 individual parts. A 6Al-4V alloy was used in thickness of 0.030 to 0.070-inch for the skin of the forward 60 feet of the fuselage where temperatures were expected to be 450–550 degrees Fahrenheit. The second alloy was 4Al-3Mo-1V, used primarily for the internal structure of the forward fuselage. The third was 7Al-4Mo, used for various forgings and extrusions. Sheet titanium represented 50 percent of the total; 25 percent was plate 0.75 to 1-inch thick; and the remainder was in the form of forgings and extrusions. A limited amount of René-41 was also used in the engine compartment because of the exotic alloy's very high temperature qualities.[43]

The second major problem encountered during production was fuel tank sealing. At Mach 3, the temperature of the structure surrounding the fuel tanks in the wings could rise above the flash point of the fuel vapors in the ullage space (the empty area above the fuel as it was burned out). In that situation, all that was needed for combustion – and explosion – was sufficient oxygen, so a nitrogen inerting system had to be developed to reduce the oxygen content in the ullage below the point that would support combustion. This was more of a problem with the expected use of HEF-3, but was still an issue with JP-4/6. Why the B-70 program never considered using the JP-7 low-vapor-pressure fuel developed for the J58 engines in the Blackbirds could not be ascertained.

The fuel tanks were integral units, and sealing them became a difficult problem because of the nitrogen head that had to be maintained. The design criteria said that the tanks had to withstand 10 psi with zero leakage – a level that was required primarily to prevent the dissipation of the gaseous nitrogen that was used as the inerting agent. A metal-to-metal seal was provided by welding or brazing the individual panels together. Since the accuracy of the tests to measure leakage was not absolutely precise, an indicated leakage of less than 10 cubic inches per minute was considered acceptable. This was equivalent to allowing one hole the diameter of a human hair in a 3,000-square-foot surface.[44]

To locate leaks, the tanks were either vacuum or pressure checked using various methods, usually involving helium as a pressurant. This was a repetitive operation, with lesser leaks showing up as the larger leaks were eliminated. Leaks that were approximately 0.050-inch in diameter were located by applying a soap solution over the suspect area with incoming air creating bubbles at the leak. An ultrasound device was also used to detect larger leaks by detecting the noise created by the passage of air through an orifice. A staining dye activated by ammonia that was drawn through a hole could outline a small leak. The smallest leaks were located using a helium gas "sniffer" that was carefully moved around each seam in the tank. The engineers and technicians went to extraordinary lengths to ensure the tanks were leak free.[45]

However, when A/V-1 was first tested, the fuel tanks leaked – a lot. Pinhole flaws where the tanks had been welded during construction caused the majority of the leaks. Much of the problem could be traced to a lack of production tooling created when the program was scaled back to only three flight vehicles. Before the end of 1962, the repair technique used a hand-held torch to braze (melt) the area around the seam. This process was critical and time consuming, since no sealing was accomplished if the temperature was too low, and secondary damage to the thin honeycomb panel face sheets occurred if the temperature was too high. Damage of this nature to various fuel tank sections caused a heavy workload at the end of 1962, with almost 3,000 damaged areas needing repair. After various trials and errors, North American developed a new method to seal small leaks. This process consisted of plasma-spraying aluminum over a leaking area, and then applying up to six coats of Viton B cured at 375 degrees Fahrenheit by electric blankets (or even hair dryers in some less accessible areas). This sealing method resulted in minor secondary heat damage but was considerably better than the earlier process. The process was used on each tank, and seemed to work – except on tank No. 5 in A/V-1. This U-shaped tank at the extreme rear of the fuselage was considered too small and too inaccessible to warrant the time necessary to properly correct the leaks so the fuel pumps were removed and the tank rendered inoperative.[46]

A/V-1 being moved into the final assembly hangar where the wings and vertical stabilizers will be installed. The wedge hinges for the verticals are in place on the upper aft fuselage. The four escape hatches in the crew compartment are still missing. (Boeing via the Tony Landis Collection)

Politics

It should be noted that the Viton-B solution was not considered satisfactory for production aircraft; engineers estimated it would have a useful life of only 1,000 hours before it would need to be stripped off and reapplied. However, since the XB-70A flight test program was scheduled to last only 180 flight hours, this was considered adequate. The welds on A/V-2 were subjected to better quality control and the fuel system exhibited significantly fewer leaks. North American was sure they could have perfected the manufacturing techniques for production aircraft, something that would have been greatly aided by having the correct manufacturing jigs and tools.

As with any development effort, there were many component and subsystem tests accomplished before and during construction. One of these involved the cooling system in the airplane. A full-scale mockup of the pressurized area in the forward fuselage was constructed and mounted in a very large chamber heated by hundreds of heat lamps. The object of the program was to check the overall adequacy of the proposed cooling system, which included the place where the crew was going to sit. Obviously, the pilots were interested in the adequacy of this system, so Al White sat in the pilot's seat for the 3-hour duration of the test. Probably the most noticeable

The second airplane was a bit more complete when it was towed over to the final assembly hangar – note the canard and vertical stabilizers are already attached. This is likely because A/V-1 stayed in the final assembly hangar longer than expected trying to seal the fuel tanks, and North American was trying to maintain the completion schedule for A/V-2. (Boeing via the Gerald H. Balzer Collection)

Another angle of A/V-1 being moved into the final assembly hangar. The wedge hinges for the vertical stabilizers show up well here, as does the flat titanium-skinned deck over the engine compartment. (Boeing via the Terry Panopalis Collection)

A/V-1 in the final assembly hangar. The photo in the center shows the wings being moved into position for mating, while the photo at right shows the canard flap to good effect. (Boeing via the Gerald H. Balzer Collection)

effect of the heat came from the windshield; White remembers that "when it got up to stabilized temperature, the radiated heat was like sitting with your face in front of an oven, although the cockpit temperature was somewhere between 80 and 90 degrees. The visor on my helmet helped some, but after a while it got hot also."[47]

The series of program cancellations and restructurings had taken a toll on the production floor that was hard to comprehend. Originally, a series of tools were expected to be procured that would ensure the close assembly tolerances that were required to mate the wing to the wing stubs. However, to conserve funds, most of the wing-joining tools were eliminated during the April 1961 program redirection, and only "contour support" tools were provided. This necessitated matching the wing joint fit of four contoured surfaces along an 80-foot distance to an accuracy of 0.008-inch or better using "optical methods" (i.e., by eye). When this was initially attempted in late 1962, it was found that the support surfaces along the length of the wing could move and that ambient temperature differentials would cause the panels to separate. After several attempts, matching by this technique was abandoned and a fitting was designed to attach to the wing stub to compensate for the inaccuracies in the joint alignment caused by the simplified tooling. Fusion and electron beam welding were used in the wing joining, fusion on the inner weld, and electron beam on the outer. After the inner weld was completed, but prior to beginning the outer weld, the wing joint was X-ray inspected and the fuel tanks pressurized for a leak check. After this the area around the outer joint was cleaned, RTV-77 sealant was applied, and a smooth plate was placed over the sealant to hold the vacuum box and electron beam gun. Initially the welds required a great deal of rework to pass inspection, but this decreased as techniques improved and personnel became more experienced. These problems were unique to the prototypes and would have been overcome in any production vehicles by better tooling.[48]

More Restructuring

At the beginning of 1964, the B-70 program was operating under a set of directives that allowed the completion of three air vehicles. The third vehicle was to be equipped with a four-man crew and a

At left is the left-hand rudder being installed on A/V-1. Oddly, the left-hand wedge hinge was painted when the rudders were installed, but the right-hand one was not (see center photo). At right is an 84-foot-long duct being installed through the fuel tanks and fuselage. This 6.5-inch diameter double-walled duct (the inside pipe was 4 inches in diameter) carried engine bleed air to the environmental control systems located in the intermediate fuselage. The duct could handle up to 300 pounds of air per minute at 165 psi pressure. It was installed remarkably late in the assembly process on both airplanes. (left and center: Boeing Historical Archive; right courtesy of the Gerald H. Balzer Collection)

prototype ASQ-28 bomb-nav system. The initial flight test program with the first two aircraft was to prove the basic handling qualities of the aircraft, define the speed-altitude envelope, and demonstrate the feasibility of sustained Mach 3 operations by a very large aircraft. The third air vehicle was dedicated to demonstrating the functional operation of the ASQ-28, including weapons release at Mach 3. Additional tests on all three aircraft included obtaining Mach 3 data pertaining to flight characteristics, thermal effects, air vehicle subsystem performance, and sonic boom research.[49]

On 25 January 1964, Alexander H. Flax, the Assistant Secretary of the Air Force for Research and Development, chartered a study group to recommend alternatives to the existing XB-70 program. The technical team was chaired by Brigadier General Fred J. Ascani, who was then director of the B-70 Program Office at Wright-Patterson. Paul F. Bikle, the director of the NASA Flight Research Center was also on the team, along with two other Air Force representatives, another NASA member, and two observers from the Federal Aviation Administration (FAA). A separate team, headed by Colonel E. W. Phillips, was char-

The second air vehicle (A/V-2) after wing mate on 12 December 1964. Note the upper skin at the right is still missing, showing some of the internal structure of the wing. (Boeing via the Tony Landis Collection)

The vertical stabilizers on the B-70 hinged at an angle, so they did not rotate left and right like a normal rudder. Instead, they sort of angled in the direction of travel. (Boeing via the Tony Landis Collection)

A/V-2 under construction on 20 January 1965. The drag chute compartment was located between the vertical stabilizers, and is shown here with one door closed and the other missing. The spine of the aircraft carried a myriad of electrical and hydraulic lines, and workers spent many hours installing and testing them. (Boeing via the Tony Landis Collection)

Politics

Various scenes of A/V-1 under construction in Palmdale, culminating with the airplane ready to roll out (bottom of facing page) on the morning of 11 May 1964. (top two this page: Boeing via the Tony Landis Collection; this page bottom: Boeing via the Terry Panopalis Collection; facing page top right: Boeing via the Tom Rosquin Collection; others: Boeing Historical Archives)

Politics

tered to study program costs. The technical team would develop concepts that would then be passed to the cost team for budgeting. The groups only had two weeks to perform their task since Flax wanted a report by 4 February.[50]

The task was to "establish the relative merits of alternate two-aircraft programs in light of long range contributions to the Air Force, DoD, NASA objectives, and the SST program," but was limited by a mandate to stay within the already allocated $1,500 million program budget. The ground rules were that a minimum of two air vehicles would be completed, and these would demonstrate sustained Mach 3 operations during a 50-hour flight test program. Alternatives to be investigated included completing different air vehicles than planned, restructuring the flight test program, or looking at completely new ideas.[51]

The teams met at the North American Los Angeles Division facility from 27 through 31 January 1964 and were divided into groups that studied XB-70 manufacturing and flight test schedules, engine programming, possible follow-on flight test programs, logistics support, and costs.[52]

At this point, North American was still building three flight vehicles. The schedule below shows the dates the program was working towards, and these were assumed the same in all cases for the study.

Vehicle	Rollout	First Flight
A/V-1	7 May 1964	7 July 1964
A/V-2	15 October 1964	30 November 1964
A/V-3	8 January 1965	22 February 1965

Even in the cases where the second airplane was cancelled, the third could not be accelerated significantly because it was being paced by unique structure in the intermediate fuselage. This structure differed from that in the first two air vehicles in order to accommodate the environmental control system, ducting, and plumbing associated with the four-man crew compartment and the electronic equipment cooling systems.[53]

For all the options, it was assumed that only the 31 flyable engines then under contract would be completed. By the time of the study, 21 of these engines had already been delivered, 2 were ready for delivery, and the others would be delivered by 30 April 1964. It had previously been determined that no appreciable cost savings would be gained by reducing the number of engines since all the major components had already been manufactured. Spare parts were available to support up to 150 hours of flight tests; anything beyond that would require the procurement of additional engine spares. In the end, an additional seven engines would be built to support the flight program, for a total of 38 flyable engines.[54]

Eventually seven different alternatives were developed that ran the gamut of possibilities. Alternatives 2 and 4 assumed the completion of A/V-1 to the point it could be used for the Phase II structural proof tests, but would never fly. In Alternative 4, the airframe would be capable of engine ground runs, whereas Alternative 2 assumed the engines would not be run. Alternative 2 showed that A/V-3 would be completed, but not flown; it would be a spare in case something happened to A/V-2 during its 50-hour flight program. Alternatives 1 and 3 assumed all three vehicles would be completed and flown, although

The wing of A/V-1 ready for mating on 22 July 1962. This proved to be one of the more difficult parts of assembly since the "hard" production tooling had been cancelled and the wings ended up being supported by makeshift jigs and alignment tools. (Boeing via the Tony Landis Collection)

The first of 12 wing fold hinges for A/V-1 after it arrived in Palmdale. Aaron Kolom (left) and Bob Dawson from North American are shown admiring what Curtiss-Wright trademarked a "power hinge." These were remarkably powerful for their size. (Boeing Historical Archives)

Alternative 1 only flew A/V-1 for 5 hours before it entered the Phase II structural proof tests and never flew again. Alternative 5 cancelled A/V-2 and flew the other two aircraft. Alternatives 6 and 7 cancelled A/V-3 and differed primarily in the number of flight test hours allocated to the other two vehicles.[55]

Each of the seven alternatives could be accomplished for less than the $1,500 million program cap. The cheapest was $1,419.7 million and cancelled A/V-3 while flying the other two aircraft for 100 hours and 80 hours, respectively. The most expensive was $1,480.7 million and flew all three vehicles for 30 hours, 80 hours, and 60 hours, respectively. The $61 million difference seems trivial in hindsight, but was not at the time. In the end, the study recommended completing all three air vehicles, but it was not to be; A/V-3 would be stillborn. The third air vehicle was officially cancelled on 5 March 1964, and North American used NA-286 as an account to accumulate costs associated with the cancellation.

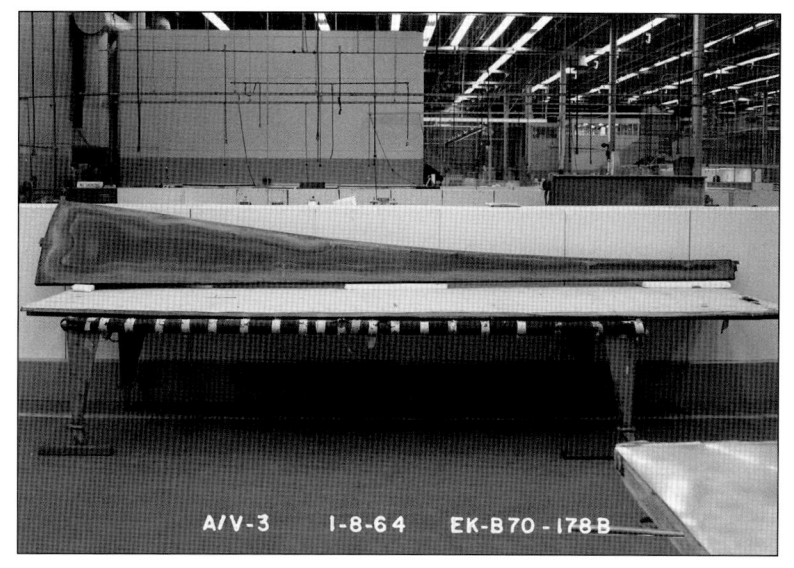

No, we do not know what it is either, although it appears to be the extreme rear part of the fuselage neck where it fairs into the engine deck. It is, nevertheless, one of the few parts identified as being from the cancelled A/V-3. Other parts that were completed include the landing gear bogie beams and the entire canard. (Boeing Historical Archives)

The wing fold hinge line on A/V-2 with the black magnesium-thorium fairing access covers removed. There were six Curtiss-Wright power hinges on each wing. Eight of the A/V-2 hinges were recovered from the crash site and installed on A/V-1 during 1966. (Boeing Historical Archives)

NASA paid the Air Force $263,275 to complete the partially-built canard for A/V-3 so that they could use it in thermal experiments relating to the Supersonic Transport. Here is the canard in a crate when it arrived in December 1966. (NASA Dryden Flight Research Center)

Sukhoi T-4 Sotka

The United States was not the only nation interested in developing a Mach 3 bomber. The Soviet Union began work on a new high-speed medium bomber during the late 1950s, largely in response to the disappointing performance of the original Tupolev Tu-22 Blinder. In 1961, requirements were issued by the Voyenno-Vozdushnye Sily (VVS, the Soviet Air Force) for an aircraft capable of 3,000 kilometers per hour (about 1,900 mph) and a range of 2,000 kilometers (about 1,250 miles). Sukhoi, Tupolev, and Yakovlev responded with proposals, with the Sukhoi design subsequently being selected for development in 1964. The Tushino Machine Building Factory (TMZ) would manufacture the airframes.[56]

The Sukhoi T-4, also known as the Su 100 or Project 100, shared a superficial resemblance to the B-70, but was somewhat smaller. The aircraft was designated Ram H by NATO because it was the eighth unknown aircraft observed at the Soviet test facility at Ramenskoye Airfield, south of Moscow. Reports have indicated that the aircraft was named Sotka ("hundredth") because it had a design weight of 100 metric tonnes (220,000 pounds).

The T-4 design was arguably even more advanced than the B-70. For instance, while the American aircraft used fairly conventional flight control systems, the Sukhoi featured a quad-redundant electrohydraulic fly-by-wire system with full three-axis stability augmentation and autothrottle capability. A mechanical backup system was included, however, just in case. Like the B-70, the T-4 was manufactured largely from titanium and stainless steel (although not the unusual honeycomb used on the American aircraft). Much like the proposed Boeing SST, the T-4 lowered its entire nose to provide visibility during takeoff and landing, and when the nose was up the pilot's had effectively no forward vision, just a small periscope.

The aircraft was 146 feet long and had a wing that spanned just over 72 feet with almost 3,200 square feet of area. In theory, four 35,274-lbf Kolesov RD36-41 turbojets provided sufficient power for a maximum speed of 1,900 mph at an operating altitude of 78,000 feet, with a maximum altitude of 98,000 feet. I fthese would have been attained, this would have made the T-4 the first Mach 3 aircraft in the Soviet Union. A range of 3,700 miles was expected carrying a payload of two large solid-fuel surface-to-air missiles.

Models were tested in various wind tunnels at the Russian Central Aerohydrodynamics Institute (TsAGI) beginning in 1963, and the design evolved considerably from the initial proposal. One of the most notable changes was the deletion of the exposed canopy in favor of the retractable nose found on the prototype. Another change was consolidating all four engines into a single nacelle (like the B-70) instead of two separate two-engine installations (like the B-1). Various flying laboratories were used to test systems for the T-4, including a Tu-16 to evaluate the RD36-41 engines, and a Tu-104B, Tu-22, and An-12 to test the navigation and bombing systems. As was frequently Soviet practice, a sub-scale version of the wing planform was evaluated during actual flight tests, this time using a modified Su-9 interceptor. A mockup of the T-4 was inspected during 1968 and construction of the first two airframes was begun at Series Production Plant 82 in Tushino.

The static test airframe (serial 100S) and a single prototype (serial 101) were completed during 1971 and the test article was sent to TsAGI for complete structural and environmental evaluations. After completing a dozen taxi tests at Ramenskoye, the first flyable T-4 made its maiden flight on 22 August 1972 with test pilot Vladimir Ilyushin, son of aircraft designer S. V. Ilyushin, at the controls and navigator Nikolai Alferov in the back seat. The first five flights were low-speed handling evaluations with the landing gear extended and the results indicated that the aircraft was generally responsive and easy to fly. Reports suggest that 101 completed approximately 11 hours of testing during 9 or 10 flights, reaching Mach 1.28 at 40,000 feet.

Manufacture of the second flyable airframe (102) began in 1969, and by 1972 all of the major assembly had been completed and systems were being installed. This aircraft would have been used for navigation systems tests, followed by 103 for missile tests. Neither aircraft flew before the program was cancelled in late 1973 or early 1974, and three further aircraft were never started. The single flyable prototype was subsequently given to the VVS Museum at Monino where it still resides.

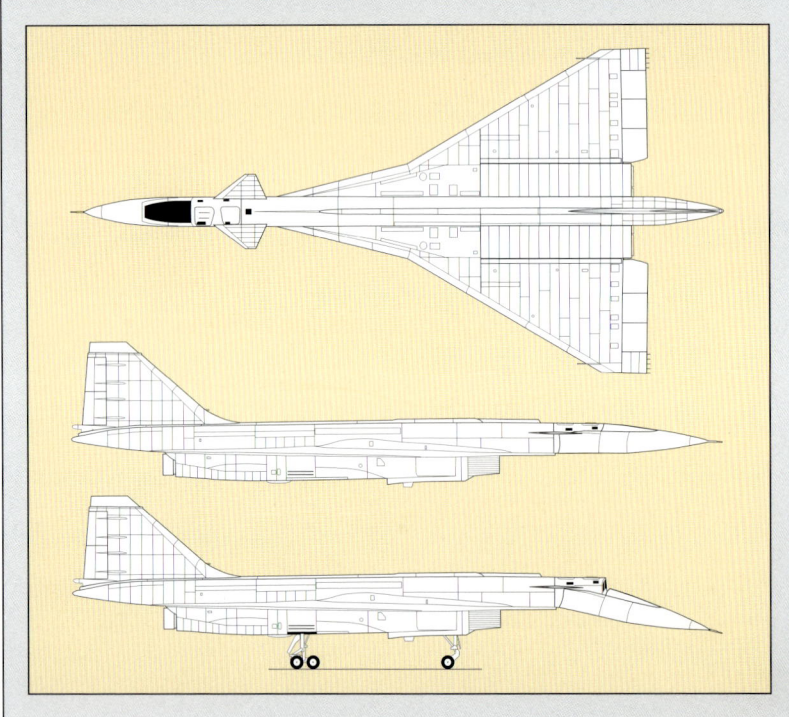

Like many things from the Soviet Union during the Cold War, the T-4 was obviously inspired by a design originating in the West, but was in no way a direct copy of it. (Art by Tony Landis)

Politics

The T-4, showing its similarities and differences from the B-70. Note the four engines, articulating nose, and the number of wheels on the main landing gear. The museum shots are in Monino. (top three and below: Jay Miller; left and above courtesy of the Jay Miller Collection)

Chapter 5   119

Chapter 6

Left: *Program humor before the first flight. Somehow, we do not think this is quite what the designers intended the wingtips to do.* (AFFTC History Office Collection)

Below: *The second air vehicle cruising slow with the wingtips up. On many flights, however, the airplane conclusively demonstrated that it was a Mach 3 cruiser and would routinely exceed 2,000 miles per hour and 70,000 feet altitude.* (AFFTC History Office Collection)

THE FLIGHT PROGRAM
HALF A MILLION POUNDS AT MACH 3

Almost exactly eight years before the maiden flight of the XB-70A, Captain Milburn G. "Mel" Apt took one of the Bell X-2s to Mach 3.196 – the first human to fly three times the speed of sound. Unfortunately, he did not live to tell about it, a victim of the "inertia coupling" phenomenon that plagued the early X-planes. Joseph A. Walker was more fortunate on 12 May 1960 when he took the North American X-15-1 to Mach 3.19 at 77,882 feet, becoming the second man to fly that fast; Walker would become legendary for his 25 flights in the X-15, and would later play a tragic role in the XB-70 program. The most well known of the Mach 3 designs – the Lockheed Blackbird – would first take to the air on 25 April 1962, with Lockheed test pilot Lou Schalk at the controls. A little over a year later, in July 1963, the A-12 would become the first piloted air-breathing aircraft to exceed Mach 3 and the Blackbirds would ultimately log more triple-sonic time than any other manned aircraft. At the same time, North American was getting ready to prove that an aircraft that weighed 20 times more than the X-2 and 4 times more than a Blackbird could sustain Mach-3 flight.

ROLLOUT

The two XB-70As were assembled in a new facility on the north side of Air Force Plant No. 42 in Palmdale, California, although almost all of the major sections were manufactured elsewhere. A/V-1 was rolled out of the hangar on a slightly overcast Monday, 11 May 1964. Just sitting on the ground, the Valkyrie awed the audience, although her actual flight performance was yet to be determined. But just two months later, continuing fiscal problems forced the elimination of the partially-built A/V-3 and a reduction in the flight test program to only 180 hours, hardly enough to really justify the expense of the two remaining vehicles.[1] The flight program was to be run by the Air Force to gather data for military programs, but NASA had already agreed to provide instrumentation for a number of SST-related experiments. The basic instrumentation installed by NASA and North American could record more than 1,000 different parameters at data rates of up to 20,000 bits per second (outstanding for the era). The recorders could accommodate 120,000,000 data points per flight. It was hoped that the Air Force program would be sufficiently successful to justify a follow-on program run by NASA aimed more directly at SST research.[2]

The initial cadre of Valkyrie pilots, from left: Colonel Joseph E. Cotton, Alvin S. White (North American), Van H. Shepard (North American), and Lieutenant Colonel Fitzhugh L. "Fitz" Fulton during the A/V-1 rollout ceremony in Palmdale. (AFFTC History Office Collection)

THE FLIGHT PROGRAM

Various views of the rollout of A/V-1 on a slightly overcast Monday, 11 May 1964. Celebrities attended the event; in the photo at center below is Jimmy Stewart (actor), Joseph A. Walker (NASA test pilot), Warren M. Dorn (Los Angeles County Supervisor), and Brigadier General Irving L. "Twig" Branch (Commander of the Air Force Flight Test Center). Several thousand guests and spectators showed up for the unveiling of what the local press called the "RS-70." (above: via Tom Rosquin; below: AFFTC History Office Collection; bottom; Jeannette Remak Collection)

122   VALKYRIE – NORTH AMERICAN'S MACH 3 SUPERBOMBER

Shortly after rollout, the airplane was towed to the engine run pad for a complete systems checkout program. Since this involved a large number of engine runs, North American test pilots Al White and Van Shepard spent considerable time becoming familiar with the systems and idiosyncrasies of the airplane. Joe Cotton decided that he also wanted an Air Force pilot there any time the engines were running.[3]

Despite the fact that the production program had already been cancelled, and the two airplanes were strictly test vehicles, this was a 24-hour per day, 7-day per week effort. It went so far as to put cots in the maintenance shack where the pilots could rest between tests. During longer delays or maintenance work the pilots would return to their hotel in Lancaster or to their homes at Edwards. Nevertheless, the pilots spent many nights taking naps in the airplane, while maintenance personnel worked on various problems.[4]

Although the Palmdale production plant was located in what was, at the time, a remote region of Los Angeles county, there was still concern about the potential noise from full-throttle testing of the J93 engines. Oddly, it was not humans that would be disturbed. Turkey ranchers were in the area east of the run-up area and the insurance company was concerned that the noise might cause a problem with the birds. A set of large sound abatement chambers were manufactured that could be attached to the engine exhausts, but the problem evidently wasn't as bad as predicted, and the chambers were seldom used.[5]

The most serious problem that surfaced during these early ground tests was with the new 4,000-psi hydraulic system. Due to the vibrations in the engine bays, occasionally a hydraulic line would crack. North American replaced many of the hydraulic lines, added more support brackets and vibration isolators, but it was a persistent problem that continued for most of the flight program. Although the pilots logged long hours in the cockpit, the maintenance and engineering people spent even more hours preparing the airplane; the maintenance supervisor, Mel Beech, was so conscientious that at times he had to be ordered to go home. And while the pilots were clean and dry sitting in marginally comfortable seats, the mechanics working on the hydraulic system inside the airplane were hot, dirty, and being sprayed with hydraulic fluid. But they kept on working.[6]

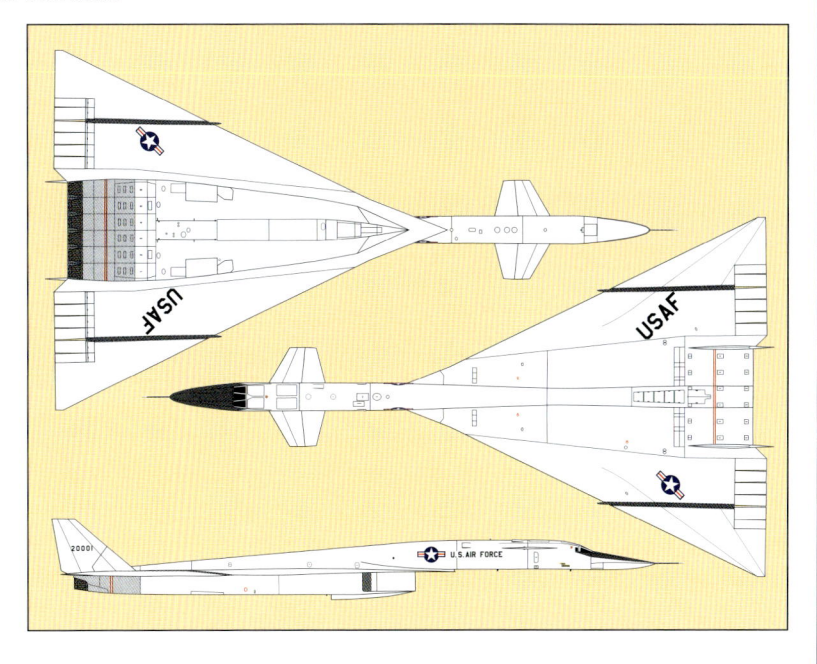

A/V-1 markings at rollout. The natural metal area around the engines would be painted during the layup after Flight 1-4. (Art by Tony Landis)

In early September 1964, the program was ready to conduct the initial taxi tests. This presented some interesting challenges because the pilot of the XB-70 would be steering a nose wheel that was 65 feet behind him. That meant that when he wanted to make a turn from one taxiway to another, he had to run the cockpit about 65 feet past the intersection and then start the turn. Al White measured the distance between the seams in the concrete taxiways, and discovered that they were about 20 feet apart, so he decided to go three seams past the point where he wanted the nose wheel to turn, then apply the rudder. It seemed like a good plan, but nevertheless White was not completely sure of himself. Observers in the North American Mobilcom van kept a close eye on the proceedings and advised White that he was successfully keeping the wheels on the taxiway,

North American built a set of sound abatement chambers to muffle the J93s during engine runs in Palmdale, but they were seldom used during the program. (Boeing Historical Archives)

The Palmdale ground crews put in many long nights getting A/V-1 ready for her first flight. The sound suppression chambers are attached to the airplane, indicating a late-night engine run was being conducted. (Boeing via the Terry Panopalis Collection)

and the procedure soon became routine. The Mobilcom van, which became a familiar sight at all XB-70 flights as it had on the X-15 flights, was equipped with a communications system and carried a flight test engineer and several other specialists that monitored the airplane and its surroundings. It was usually accompanied by a fire truck, a staff car, and sometimes other pieces of ground equipment, just in case.[7]

The initial taxi tests didn't go as smoothly as had been hoped. The first taxi away from the engine run-up pad only went about 100 yards before a hydraulic line broke. The second time it got a little farther, but with the same result. Al White is sure that he left one more puddle of hydraulic fluid on the taxiway before he finally made it to the runway for a real taxi test. He then made one slow taxi down the runway to about 60 knots; success is often made in small steps. The tests revealed that the brakes "chattered" at speeds below about 15 mph, making it difficult to stop smoothly. The brakes were also only marginally effective at medium taxi speeds. In addition, the nose wheel steering could not generate enough torque to turn the airplane at low speeds, requiring higher taxi speeds than were really desirable.[8]

Normally, taxi tests are done up to the speed where the nose wheel lifts off, but Al White objected to doing that in the Valkyrie. The estimated rotation speed of the XB-70 was 160 knots and White figured that the airplane would probably have accelerated to at least 170 knots by the time he got the nose wheel in the air. This would use up more than half of the 10,000-foot runway at Palmdale. White would then have to lower the nose and stop the airplane in the remaining distance. Since the brakes were proving somewhat troublesome even during low-speed tests, and the drag chutes had never been deployed, White made the case that "I had seen several brake systems fail, but never heard of a case where the aircraft failed to rotate when the pilot applied the control."[9] Going as far as nose wheel lift off is mainly for the pilot's benefit because it tells him something about the airplane's response to control input. In this case, White was more concerned about a brake failure than he was of his ability to make a successful takeoff. Eventually, White's conservative argument won the day. During the high-speed taxi test, White accelerated to 110–120 knots, pulled the power off, deployed the drag chutes, and stopped with lots of concrete left in front of him.[10]

THE FLIGHT PROGRAM

FIRST FLIGHT

Before the North American maintenance organization would release the airplane for its first flight, they took it back to the hangar where it had been built and inspected everything. It was put up on jacks in order to cycle the landing gear and verify the hydraulic system. Like many things on the airplane, the landing gear retraction and extension cycles were complex. Each main landing gear was made up of a "bogie beam" with an axle at each end, all attached to the strut by an articulating hinge assembly. Four wheels were mounted on the two axles, and the brake for each axle was between the wheels where it benefited from the air passing over it for cooling. In order to retract into the wheel well, the bogie beam had to rotate 90 degrees and fold up along the strut. Then the whole mechanism retracted rearward into the wheel well. An automatic system applied a small amount of pressure to the brakes in order to stop wheel rotation before the gear entered the wheel well. It all seemed to work in the test rig, but reality would prove somewhat different.[11]

Having the landing gear retract successfully was important because North American would receive a $250,000 bonus if the air-

A soggy day in Palmdale. The second Valkyrie undergoing pre-flight inspections and maintenance before its first flight. (Boeing Historical Archives)

CHAPTER 6 125

Preparing for the first taxi test (left) and successful completion of the run around Plant 42 on 8 September 1964. (AFFTC History Office Collection)

plane went supersonic on the first flight. A $125,000 bonus waited if the airplane first went supersonic on the second flight; there was no bonus on the third flight. If it took more than three flights, there was a $125,000 penalty. Although this seems a little imprudent today, demonstrating supersonic performance on maiden flights was something of a fad during the late 1950s and early 1960s.[12]

As it turned out, there was a problem with the gear retraction during the ground test on 19 September, but the maintenance team worked all night to solve it. The next day the pilots watched the landing gear retract and extend during the final test on the jacks. Al White and Joe Cotton went through the pre-flight briefing one more time so chase pilots Van Shepard and Fitz Fulton – and everyone else – knew the plan. Everything had been practiced repeatedly in the simulator, and the mission had been flown some weeks before with White flying a TB-58 as a surrogate for the XB-70 with Cotton flying chase in another B-58. One set of final checks, then it was time for dinner and bed.[13]

On 21 September 1964, the Valkyrie was ready for its rather spectacular 1.75-hour maiden flight. Since Plant 42 was in a populated area (sort of), White would keep the gear down and the airspeed under 250 knots. However, once the Valkyrie was in the restricted airspace around Edwards AFB, the plan called for retracting the landing gear and accelerating through the speed of sound at 30,000 feet.

The initial flight of any aircraft is a unique source of publicity for the manufacturer, and in the case of the world's largest Mach 3 airplane this was especially true. Hope Ryden, an audio engineer, and Abbot Mills, a cameraman, working for Bob Drew & Associates, had been following White and Cotton and their families for several weeks while producing a film about the first flight. At 04:00 in the morning when White opened the door of his hotel room, floodlights came on to document the beginning of his day.[14]

A little later that morning the ground crew reviewed all the records with White and Cotton. There were a few minor discrepancies that had nothing to do with the first flight plan or flight safety, but the pilots needed to understand them. After this review, White signed the books and accepted the responsibility for the airplane. The chase pilots wished the XB-70 pilots good luck, and then drove to Edwards to get their TB-58 ready. It was still dark when White and Cotton climbed inside A/V-1.

The preflight inspection for the XB-70 was a little different from most other aircraft. The engines and systems were buried inside the airframe high above the ground, so the pilots could not look in the exhausts or into wheel wells, or most of the other things that are traditionally done – consequently the inspection was fairly short. In any case, the ground crew had been out all night getting the airplane ready for this flight, and there was little chance that anything had been overlooked.[15]

At 06:10, White and Cotton climbed aboard the Valkyrie to begin the pre-flight checklist. Engine No. 1 was started and brought up to operating temperature 35 minutes later. In the process of starting the second J93, however, caution lights in the cockpit indicated a failure in the engine's cooling loop. Both engines were shut down. The problem was traced to a tripped circuit breaker and both engines were restarted a few minutes later.

The chase aircraft were alerted. Fulton and Shepard were already in the TB-58 as primary chase and had copies of the XB-70 checklists and emergency procedures so that they were ready to help at any time. Major Don Sorlie was in a T-38 as Chase 2, Major Bob Smith was in another T-38 as Chase 3. John DeLong, the North American cameraman, was in the back seat of one of the T-38s to photograph the flight. Flight surgeon Captain Phil Neal was in a helicopter, ready to assist in case something went horribly wrong. Colonel Jesse Jacobs was already airborne in a C-130, checking out the emergency landing sites north of Edwards. Chase 4 and Chase 5 were two more T-38s flown by Lieutenant Colonel Jake Knight and Major Russ Rogers, ready to fill in if necessary. Captain Paul Balfe was standing by in another helicopter. Everything seemed ready.[16]

Except for A/V-1 – the airplane did not want to cooperate. The No. 2 fuel pump caution light came on, indicating that the pump was not operating. The engine was shut down, and it was determined that the pump needed to be replaced – a procedure that entailed disconnecting the hydraulic systems. Almost miraculously, the ground crew succeeded in replacing the pump within the hour. The chase planes were given an update.[17]

The first two engines were restarted without incident. Engine No. 3 did not start on the first attempt, but did on the second. The remaining engines were started, the generators were brought online, and the ground power units were disconnected. After 2 hours in the cockpit, White and Cotton were finally ready to taxi out at just after 08:00. Frank Munds was the radio contact point in the Mobilcom van. Max Wells was on the radio in Data Control at the North American Flight Test Operations control room at Edwards, along with Walt Spivak, the North American Chief Engineer. Palmdale Tower had also come up on the North American flight test frequency as a courtesy since the pilots already had a heavy workload.[18]

Maiden flight of A/V-1. (AFFTC History Office Collection)

"Mobilcom, Zero-Zero-One [A/V-1] here, how do you read on U2?"
"Reading you five square, Al, how me?"
"Loud and clear"
"Palmdale Tower this is Zero-Zero-One, how do you read?"
"Good morning Zero-Zero-One, Palmdale Tower hears you loud and clear, Al"
"Roger, we're ready to taxi"

"Roger, cleared to Runway Seven via Taxiway Bravo, wind is zero-niner-zero at eight, maximum velocity last two hours has been one-zero knots, cleared for takeoff when ready."
"Roger, thank you, wind's out of the east, huh?"
"Affirmative"
"Great, and we're rolling out"
"Roger, Al, good luck"
"Thanks, Tower"

Al White and Joe Cotton take A/V-1 on her maiden flight on 21 September 1964. The contract had specified that North American would receive a monetary bonus if the airplane exceeded the speed of sound on her first flight, but a faulty hydraulic system ruled out retracting the landing gear and resulted in a slow flight to nearby Edwards AFB. (AFFTC History Office Collection)

The Flight Program

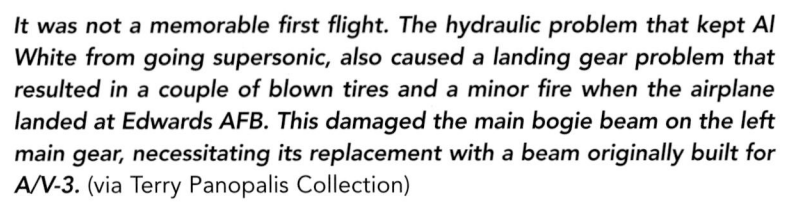

It was not a memorable first flight. The hydraulic problem that kept Al White from going supersonic, also caused a landing gear problem that resulted in a couple of blown tires and a minor fire when the airplane landed at Edwards AFB. This damaged the main bogie beam on the left main gear, necessitating its replacement with a beam originally built for A/V-3. (via Terry Panopalis Collection)

It was well known within the relatively small community that the first flight was imminent, and people had been gathering on both sides of Plant 42 since early morning. Earlier taxi tests had revealed brake chatter during low-speed operations, so White and Cotton exercised caution – the demonstrated braking distance from just 5 mph was 400 feet. White taxied A/V-1 accompanied by the Mobilcom van, a fire truck, some North American executives in a staff car, and a couple of maintenance vehicles. The aircraft stopped on the runway and ground crews made a quick check of the tires, brakes, and flight control surfaces to confirm that all was ready to go. Every journey begins but with a single step.[19]

At 08:24, Al White started to roll in military power (without afterburners), and then lit the afterburners two at a time. Cotton watched the engine instruments while White steered the airplane down the runway. At the 140 knot refusal speed White announced they were going. At 160 knots, the 387,620-pound Valkyrie rotated and A/V-1 came off the ground at 181 knots after using 4,853 feet of runway. Frank Munds informed all stations that the Valkyrie was airborne and climbing out.[20]

The flight plan was to climb to 15,000 feet and verify that there were no problems – in particular, that the hydraulic systems were working satisfactorily since they had been problematic during check-out and taxi tests. Since the landing gear was down, the pilots had to stay below the 250 knots gear limit speed while in full afterburner. This required a rather steep climb, so White pulled the nose up to about 18 degrees and held 220 knots.[21]

After the airplane leveled off at 15,000 feet safely away from Palmdale and everybody was satisfied that the hydraulic systems were okay, the pilots attempted to raise the landing gear. The nose gear came up with no problem. The main gear rotated, but did not fold – the sequence stopped with the two trucks at 90 degrees to the longitudinal axis of the airplane. That ended any idea of going supersonic on the first flight. After consulting with engineers on the ground, Cotton put the gear handle back down. The nose gear came out and locked down, and the main gear rotated back to its normal position. Even after the gear was down and locked, the main landing gear doors did not close like they should have. It was not considered a problem, but it would have an unanticipated effect on the landing.[22]

White and Cotton decided to use a pre-established alternate plan that called for a shorter and slower flight with the landing gear extended. White raised the flaps on the canard, but the indicator malfunctioned and one of the chase pilots had to verify they worked. The pilots of the XB-70 performed some stability work in all three axes, all of which appeared normal. White remembers being disappointed that the airplane had been buffeting from the time it took off. "For some reason I expected that big, sleek-looking machine to be smooth as glass. Later we found that it buffeted, even with gear and flaps up, until we got to somewhere between 0.8 and 0.9 Mach number. From that point on, it was very smooth." It was eventually determined that the buffeting was caused by span-wise flow over the canard, and it is likely that any production aircraft would have featured a modified canard shape to cure the problem.[23]

128   VALKYRIE – NORTH AMERICAN'S MACH 3 SUPERBOMBER

A short while later the No. 3 engine began increasing in RPM – a runaway engine over-speed. When the indicator reached the maximum allowable 108 percent, White shut down the engine. The flight plan changed again. There was a suggestion to gather five-engine performance data, but it was decided instead to conduct a set of slow-speed handling evaluations while preparing to land. White slowed A/V-1 down to 170 knots, which was the predicted flare speed, and found that the airplane handled very nicely. Because of the long neck on the airplane and the predicted nose-up attitude, it was decided to make a low pass down the runway before landing, just to get a feel for the visibility during approach and landing. As it turned out, visibility was not an issue.[24]

One of the major concerns about the landing was the general configuration of the airplane. The main gear was 110 feet behind the cockpit, and it was estimated that the cockpit would be about 40 feet above the surface of the runway at touchdown. Before the flight, White had made a plot assuming a 2.5-degree glide slope and a reasonable angle of attack to find that if he aimed the cockpit at a point 1,000 feet down the runway, and didn't flare at the right time, the wheels would touch down short of the paved surface. Since this would ruin everybody's day, White wisely decided to aim at a point 2,000 feet down the runway. One of the chase planes was calling out the height above the runway (it was not until the 11th flight that White stopped using the chase planes to call out his altitude), but with the ground effect from the large delta wing, it was easy to let the airplane down smoothly onto concrete Runway 04 at Edwards.[25]

However, the first flight's problems were not over. As A/V-1 landed, the left main bogie failed to pivot. (The rear wheels were designed to touch down first, then the bogie would pivot so that the front wheels touched down.) This led to sparks and a minor fire during landing rollout. The XB-70 rolled for 10,800 feet before stopping; the Edwards crash team in hot pursuit. The aircraft remained on the runway for 8 hours while it was defueled and the landing gear was repaired. To make matters worse, the No. 2 engine had ingested debris during the landing, meaning that two engines had to be replaced. Nevertheless, White and Cotton reported that the aircraft had flown well. North American did not collect the bonus.[26]

It was subsequently determined that a 10-port ball valve in the landing gear system had stuck, causing the retraction to fail. A ball bearing in the fuel control valve in the No. 3 engine had come out of its race and jammed the fuel control, leading to the over-speed. The 90-psi brake system that stopped tire rotation before the gear entered the wheel wells on retraction had not released when the gear came back down, so all four brakes were locked on touchdown. Three of them broke loose, but the left rear brake remained locked. No one seemed to associate that particular brake action with the gear doors being open, but it would happen again later in the program.[27]

With the major discrepancies explained, the biggest problem was replacing the bogie beam. This was a large forging that was intricately machined and took a long time to manufacture (a "long lead" item). Many of the components for the now-cancelled A/V-3 had already been manufactured, and fortunately, this was among them; one of the A/V-3 bogie beams was installed on A/V-1.

A Second Try

By early October North American was ready for the second flight. On 5 October 1964, White and Cotton took A/V-1 into the air again with the full intent of going supersonic in order to collect the reduced bonus. The flight plan included determining if the landing gear operated properly, and then obtaining flutter data at 10 different conditions from 260 knots and 16,000 feet to Mach 1.1 and 35,000 feet.

Prior to takeoff, White and Cotton conducted a taxi test to check the newly installed brakes. Following takeoff, with a chase plane on each side, the landing gear was retracted, then lowered, and then retracted again without a problem. About half the flutter data had been gathered when warning indicators for the No. 1 utility hydraulic system indicated that the system had failed while climbing through 27,000 feet. The chase planes could not see any fluid leaking outside the XB-70, but the pressure and quantity indicators confirmed the failure. There was a common point (at the gear actuator) between the Nos. 1 and 2 utility hydraulic systems, and the engineers worried that the 4,000-psi pressure would force fluid from the good system through the metallic seals into the ruptured system, causing a total loss of utility hydraulic power. Since the utility system controlled landing gear extension, the pre-determined procedure was to drop the landing gear immediately if either system failed. Chase pilots reported that the right gear was coming out very slowly and the left gear door had not opened, so White switched to the emergency extension system, and the gear came down. No supersonic flight; no bonus for North American.[29]

A/V-1 undergoes pre-flight checks on the morning of 5 October 1964 prior to its second flight. Al White and Joe Cotton would try again to take the airplane supersonic, and performed several braking tests while taxiing to the runway to verify the brakes and hydraulic system were working. All seemed okay, but the airplane would be temperamental once in the air. (AFFTC History Office Collection)

THE FLIGHT PROGRAM

It was decided to land on a lakebed instead of the concrete runway since it was uncertain if the brakes and drag chutes would work. The actual touchdown on the lakebed was uneventful, and A/V-1 rolled to a stop after 10,000 feet, despite one of the main drag chutes refusing to come out. After an inspection by the ground crew, the XB-70 taxied back to the hard stand under its own power.

The post-flight inspection revealed that a hydraulic line had broken inside the No. 1 fuel tank at the fuel pump. All of the fluid in that system had leaked into the fuel tank, making it impossible for the chase pilots to see, and very difficult for the maintenance crew to find. It was even harder to repair, since the remaining fuel had to be drained, and the tank kept under a nitrogen purge to avoid potential explosions while the hydraulic line was being brazed.[30]

A week later, on 12 October 1964, A/V-1 went supersonic for the first time, reaching Mach 1.11 at 35,400 feet for 15 minutes before decelerating beneath the sound barrier and breaking back through several times to check transonic stability. Since this was the third flight there was no bonus – but also no penalty – for North American. The intent of the flight was to obtain stability data in all three axes, first at high subsonic speeds, and then at Mach 1.1. The flight was, thankfully, uneventful, although once again one of the drag chutes malfunctioned during landing.[31]

The second flight also did not go quite as planned, and a hydraulic leak prompted White and Cotton to land on one of Edwards' lakebeds instead of the concrete runway. Note that the white paint is already beginning to flake off due to the flexing of the airframe during flight. (AFFTC History Office Collection)

The Valkyrie made her first trip past the sound barrier on 12 October 1964 during the third flight. The high-speed dash caused more paint to flake off, and the airplane was no longer the beautiful maiden it had once been. That would be cured after the fourth flight. (Boeing Historical Archives)

130   VALKYRIE – NORTH AMERICAN'S MACH 3 SUPERBOMBER

Despite being generally successful, the third flight did have a minor problem; the white paint had peeled off enough so that the airplane looked like a Dalmatian. The bottom line was that the white paint on the airplane was too thick, although there are several stories circulating about exactly why this was. Al White remembers that many engineers simply thought the manufacturing process was flawed. The more frequent explanation, however, was that during the final stages of building the airplane, large rope-like mesh covers had been used during fuel tank pressure checks and these had rubbed against the skin and marred the paint. Whenever a dignitary came to see the airplane, the scratches were painted over so that the airplane always looked perfect. Regardless of why, the fact was that there was about 1,000 pounds of paint on the airplane for these early flights, and the flexing of the skin during flight caused it to flake off – the phenomenon had first been noticed after the second flight. Although it looked terrible, the paint was not a safety-of-flight issue.[32]

Tragedy struck the program on 19 October 1964 when the planned fourth flight was cancelled when the No. 3 engine experienced a compressor stall during the first part of the takeoff run. Al White successfully stopped the airplane and rolled the Valkyrie onto a taxiway for inspection. The ground crew began pumping the JP-6 fuel out of the airplane when one of the fuel trucks exploded and burned. Ivan Mayo,

The photo is not dated, but this is either the end of Flight 1-3 or the beginning of Flight 1-4 judging by the amount of paint that is missing from A/V-1. The complement of chase planes is fairly normal – a couple of T-38s or F-104s plus the TB-58A. The Hustler could keep up with the XB-70 until the Valkyrie accelerated past Mach 2, then all the chase pilots could do was wait. (AFFTC History Office Collection)

One of the drag chutes did not operate properly on the third flight, shown here with an H-21 helicopter hovering nearby in case there was a problem while the XB-70 rolled-out. The drag chutes would continue to be a problem throughout the flight program. (Boeing Historical Archives)

a 17-year veteran with North American was killed in the explosion and four others were injured. Firefighters quickly dowsed the flames before the XB-70 was damaged.[33]

The fourth flight was rescheduled for 24 October and White and Cotton were at the controls again for a flight that lasted 1 hour and 25 minutes, with A/V-1 reaching Mach 1.42 at 46,300 feet. For the first time, the wingtips were lowered to their 25-degree mid-down position, verifying that they cured a minor directional instability that had been observed on the previous flights with the tips up. The XB-70 remained supersonic for 40 minutes, establishing a new record for sustained supersonic flight. As White became more familiar with the airplane, the airspeeds being used for approach and touchdown seemed a little low. Because the chase planes were reading lower speeds than the XB-70, which meant that A/V-1 was probably going slower than the system indicated, it was decided to increase the speeds about 10 knots. For unexplained reasons, airspeed calibrations were not scheduled until later in the flight program.

The dedicated test article had been cancelled along with the production program, so it was decided to use A/V-1 in a non-destructive proof-loads program after the completion of the initial airworthiness testing. Since this objective was completed with the fourth flight, White and Cotton landed back at Palmdale so the airplane could begin the proof tests. When these tests were finished, North American would perform a thorough inspection of the aircraft which would also undergo major maintenance and various updates. Many of the workers from Plant 42 were out to watch the airplane come back, and, unfortunately, White made what he later described as a "lousy landing." White remembers, "I was landing on Runway 25 at Palmdale. There is 1,000 to 1,500 feet of paved surface

This is how A/V-1 looked when she arrived back at Palmdale after Flight 1-4. Time for a new paint job. (Boeing Historical Archives)

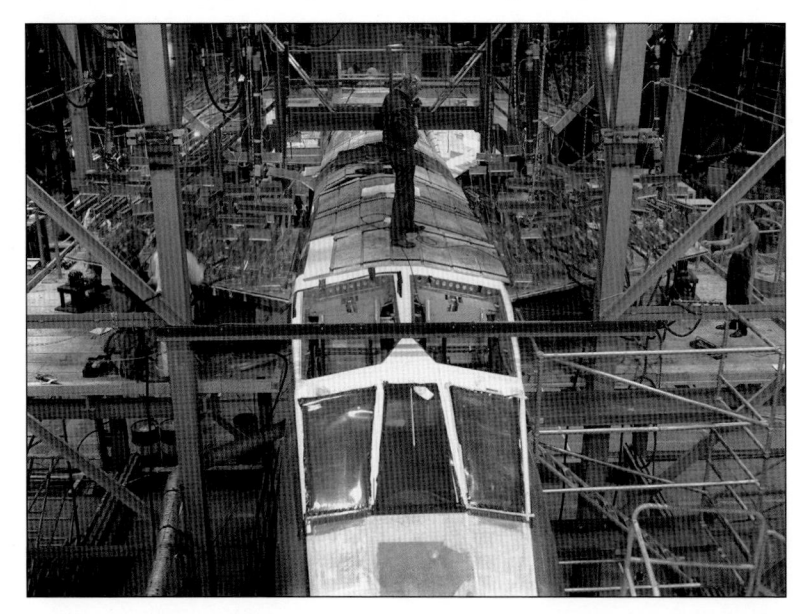

When A/V-1 returned to Palmdale after the fourth flight, the aircraft was stripped of all paint and many subsystems, then put through a series of non-destructive structural tests. These measured the deflection and stresses encountered by various structures, and compared them to values that were calculated using various theories, and also with the results of a series of evaluations that had tested some purpose-built subassemblies to destruction. Major maintenance was also performed, and several modifications were made as everything was put back together. Finally, a nice, thin, consistent coat of gloss white paint was applied, which everybody hoped would cure the flaking problem that had plagued the early flights. A major appearance change was that the bottom of the engine compartment was painted white instead of being left bare metal as it had been. The two photos above and all of the photos on the facing page are from this time in Palmdale. (Boeing Historical Archives, Boeing via the Tom Rosquin, and Boeing via the Gerald H. Balzer Collection)

The Flight Program

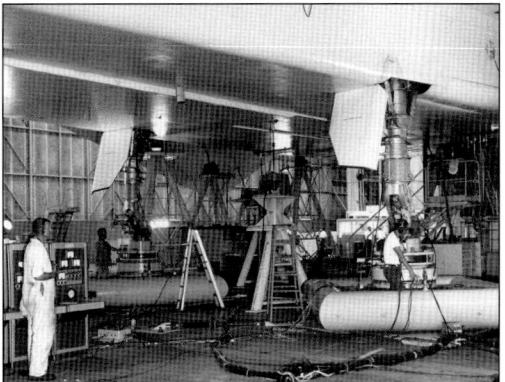

CHAPTER 6

The Flight Program

A full-scale test article of the pressurized area in the forward fuselage was constructed and mounted in a very large chamber heated by hundreds of heat lamps. The object was to check the overall adequacy of the proposed cooling system, which included the place where the crew was going to sit. Obviously, the pilots were interested in the adequacy of this system, so Al White, other pilots, and several engineering volunteers sat in the pilot's seat for the 3-hour duration of the test. Probably the most noticeable effect of the heat came from the windshield; White remembers that "when it got up to stabilized temperature, the radiated heat was like sitting with your face in front of an oven, although the cockpit temperature was somewhere between 80 and 90 degrees. The visor on my helmet helped some, but after a while it got hot also." (Boeing Historical Archives)

short of the runway threshold and as I came from the cooler desert over the hot surface, the airplane started to sink, and I didn't catch it. The runway at Palmdale is 100 feet narrower than the runway at Edwards; so I misjudged my height, and settled in on the overrun about 10 feet short of the threshold. It was something that I should have figured out before the landing, not after." It wasn't pretty, but White got A/V-1 safely on the ground. The maintenance crews began preparing the airplane for the proof loads tests.[34]

These non-destructive tests used A/V-1 since the program had not built a dedicated structural test airframe. During her stay at Plant 42, the airplane was also stripped and repainted with a single thin coat of white paint. A major appearance change was that the bottom fuselage around the engines was now painted white instead of being left natural titanium finish as it had been for the first four flights.

In addition to the proof load tests on A/V-1, the structural test program also used portions of an airframe constructed especially for the effort. Most of these tests had begun prior to the assembly of A/V-1 so that lessons-learned could be incorporated into the flight article. Seven fuselage specimens included approximately one half of the pressurized crew compartment with the fixed windshield panels, escape hatches, and crew entry door. Also tested were a 100-inch-long fuselage section representative of the electronic equipment bay, two longeron-to-honeycomb panel joints representative of the transition region from the conventional forward fuselage to the honeycomb cylindrical tank structure, two upper forward intermediate half-cylinder honeycomb tanks, an aft intermediate fuselage section representative of the air intake duct that extended entirely across the fuselage including simulated wing boxes on each side, and an aft fuselage specimen that was a structurally-complete portion of the engine compartment approximately 140 inches long and the full width of the fuselage with representative wing boxes on each side. The crew compartment tests included jettisoning a hatch and ejecting an escape capsule while the crew compartment was pressurized.[35]

There were also three structural box specimens composed of honeycomb panel covers and corrugated spars representative of critical load areas in the inboard fixed wing. A fourth wing box representative of the highly loaded aft region of the outboard folding wingtip

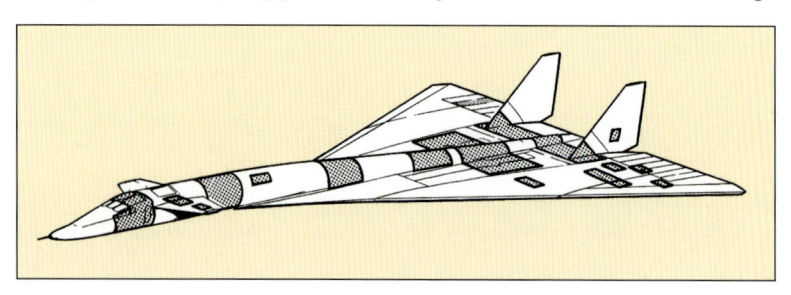

The shaded areas represent portions of an airframe that were constructed for a dedicated structural test program. These pieces were tested to destruction to verify their ultimate strength. (U.S. Air Force)

134   VALKYRIE – NORTH AMERICAN'S MACH 3 SUPERBOMBER

structure was also tested. Another specimen included the wingtip fold joint with its backup honeycomb support structure on each side of the joint. The control surface specimens included two canard structural boxes, one vertical stabilizer main box, and a complete elevon. In general, the four wing boxes were tested to destruction in order to verify their ultimate strength under biaxial loading conditions. The wing folding tip joint was tested to obtain stiffness measurements as well as to obtain the ultimate bending strength. The control surface structural boxes were tested to failure to ascertain their bending strength.[36]

Most of the parts were tested under appropriate environmental conditions, including elevated heating. Not unexpectedly, a variety of premature failures were experienced on some of the specimens. Most of these were repaired, although several new specimens were manufactured and retested to satisfactory load levels. A small number of specimens that failed prematurely were never repaired or replaced since the load levels they failed at were adequate to provide the necessary confidence for the envisioned limited flight test program.[37]

With the proof loads program completed, flight testing began again on 16 February 1965 when Al White and Joe Cotton took the Valkyrie on its fifth flight. For the first time, the wingtips were lowered to the full 65-degree position, and the manual air inlet control system (AICS) throat ramps were cycled. This flight lasted 1 hour and 10 minutes, including 40 minutes at Mach 1.6 and 45,000 feet. Continuing an unhappy trend, the drag chutes again failed to deploy completely, and A/V-1 required 11,100 feet of runway when it landed at Edwards.

The sixth flight, on 25 February 1965, marked the first time someone other than White and Cotton were at the controls. Lieutenant Colonel Fitzhugh "Fitz" L. Fulton, Jr. flew as copilot with Al White, but hydraulic leaks cut the flight short. Despite the problems, on the way back it was decided to perform the initial set of airspeed calibrations. Major William J. "Pete" Knight was flying the chase/pacer off the right wing when he suddenly reported that the right wingtip was coming off! Since the XB-70 program referred to the large folding panels as "wingtips," that comment caused a great deal of concern. Knight soon explained that the small fairing that held the running

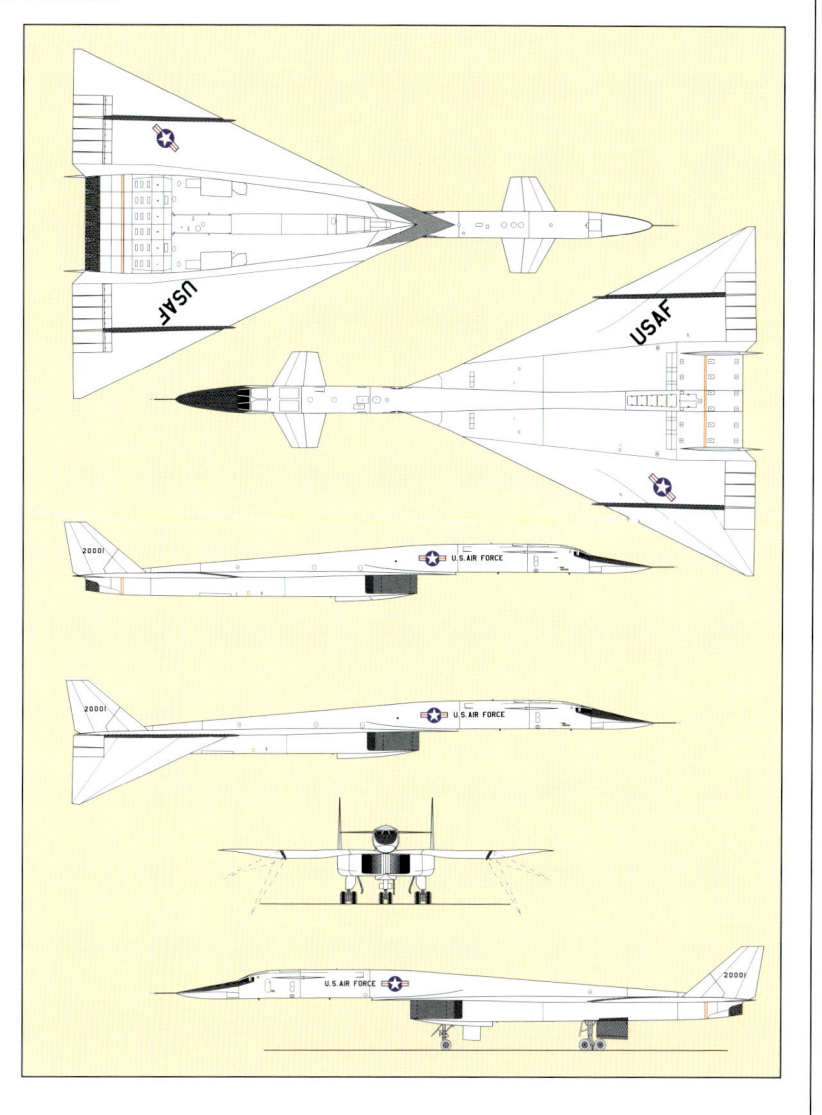

These are the markings that were applied before A/V-1 returned from Palmdale during Flight 1-5. The lower aft fuselage was now painted white instead of being natural metal, and the inside of the air intakes were natural metal instead of being white. All other markings were fairly typical of standard Air Force design for the era. (Art by Tony Landis)

Unsurprisingly, lakebed landings kicked up a lot of dust. Note that one of the drag chutes has not fully deployed, a continuing problem during the early flight program. (Boeing Historical Archives)

light on the right wingtip had come off, probably due to the buffeting being experienced with the gear and flaps down. White and Fulton landed on the lakebed with no difficulty.[38]

On 4 March 1965, the seventh flight had White and Fulton sustaining supersonic flight for 60 minutes, reaching Mach 1.85 and 50,200 feet. North American test pilot Van Shepard made his first flight as copilot during the eighth flight on 24 March, managing Mach 2.14 and 56,100 feet – 40 minutes were spent above Mach 2 and another 34 minutes above Mach 1. This established several aviation records, including the heaviest takeoff (at just over 500,000 pounds) and the longest supersonic flight. The flight was made on an oval-shaped course that began at Edwards and flew just south of Salt Lake City before returning to the

The Valkyrie and her chase planes coming home after Flight 1-10. This was the last flight that Al White routinely used the chase planes to call out his altitude while landing. (Boeing Historical Archives)

high desert. Setting weight, speed, and altitude records would become the norm for the XB-70 as the flight program progressed.[39]

After several flights it was found that the airplane did not need the roll power provided by all six elevon segments on each side of the airplane after the landing gear and flaps were retracted. Al White began positioning the wingtips to the half-down position as soon as practical. This locked the two outboard elevon segments on each wing in the streamlined position, which reduced the roll power and also adverse yaw due to aileron. This procedural change significantly improved the handling qualities of the airplane in this flight regime.[40]

White and Cotton flew the ninth flight, intending to go to Mach 2.25 at 57,500 feet to get flutter and stability data. The airplane was having some engine difficulties, so the pilots decided to use an alternate plan to obtain stability data at Mach 0.8 and 25,000 feet. However, it was one of those rare days at Edwards where the cloud cover was still fairly solid at 25,000 feet, so White decided to go to 35,000 feet. Around the same time, the No. 1 utility hydraulic system failed again, and to make matters worse, the No. 2 hydraulic system quantity was also rapidly decreasing. However, this time the pilots were faced with another set of problems.[41]

To add to the complexity of the situation, Rogers Dry Lake was not dry – it was full of rainwater from the previous night, so the landing had to be made on the concrete runway. White flew the final approach at about 230 knots and touched down at 210 knots weighing 430,000 pounds. Fortunately, the drag chutes came out at 190 knots, and with maximum braking, the airplane stopped before the end of the runway. White taxied off the runway and the pilots shut everything down. The wheels were chocked, and some protective "baskets" were put around the tires to contain fragments in case one of the tires exploded from residual heat. The ground crew was ordered to stay away from the airplane until further notice. About 45 minutes later, one of the tires blew. Although it destroyed the protective basket, nobody was hurt and the airplane – excepting the wheel and tire – was undamaged.[42]

The airplane had now flown faster than Mach 2 and the program was aiming faster, but not everybody was happy. Joe Cotton told Al White that he thought Walt Spivak, the North American Chief Engineer, was pushing too hard to reach Mach 3, and that he had too much influence over the flight program. It was true, but that was Spivak's job, and although he could be very caustic and demanding at times, most people found him to be fair. Nevertheless, White decided to have a talk with Spivak. One of the major topics of the conversation was fixing the hydraulic system. Spivak understood the necessity of finding out why the hydraulic problems had disrupted – to some extent – every flight. A short while later the engineers deduced that if the pilots let the fuel in tank No. 1 run low, the fuel pump would cavitate and the vibration would break the hydraulic line running to it. In response, North American developed flexible hydraulic lines that would withstand that 4,000 psi, greatly reducing the number of hydraulic failures.[43]

Meanwhile, the flight program continued, and Flight 1-11 provided its own excitement, best told by White:

"Shep and I were flying flight 11. I did some flutter pulses at high q [dynamic pressure] at 35,000 feet, and then we moved up to get the stability data at 55,000 and 60,000 feet at Mach 2.4. We got through some duct unstarts, the stability maneuvers at 55,000 feet, and then climbed up to 60,000. In order to get the longitudinal stability point at that altitude and 2.4 Mach, I turned the pitch augmentation off and pulsed the longitudinal control in the nose up direction. The airplane nose never returned to the original position, but just slowly floated up. After nearly 10 seconds, I applied full nose down control, but couldn't arrest it. There's nothing like being up there in strange territory and being out of control – and for another 20 or 30 seconds the airplane was out of control. Shep kept asking me if I wanted him to unstart the ducts. I just yelled at him, "Hell no." Duct unstarts caused a nose up trim change, and that was something I didn't really need at that time. He was trying to stay with the schedule to keep the ducts started. Going through 63,000 feet, when I was just getting ready to roll the airplane to get the nose down, I managed to stop the nose up travel. We topped out at 64,000 feet at 2.2 Mach, and almost immediately, I got full control back.[44]

"At that point, I had no idea what had caused this strange happening, so I decided to go in and land and talk about it on the ground. While I took a quick shower and changed my shorts, the engineers came up with the cause of the event. When I turned the pitch augmentation switch off, it was supposed to turn off the electrical input from the rate gyros (the brains of the system), and also turn off the two solenoid valves that shut off the hydraulic power to the augmentation system (the muscle of the system). Unfortunately, there was a double failure – neither of the solenoid valves closed, and so the augmentation system had hydraulic power but no information to tell it what to do – no electrical power to the system. It had muscle but no brains. It drifted slowly to full nose up control while I was attempting to counteract it. Luckily, one of the valves finally closed and I got control back. This was flight test at its most exciting – I thought, at that time. Little did I know. It was only the second time Shep had been in the airplane so I'm sure it was exciting for him. We came back to Edwards and I landed the airplane without the chase calling out the distances above the surface. I had been curious as to how difficult it might be to land it without assistance, and found that it was very easily done."[45]

The 12th flight, on 7 May 1965 with White and Fulton at the controls, proved even more dramatic. The flight plan called for a practice inlet unstart at Mach 2.4 and 60,000 feet, stability work at Mach 2.5 and 60,000, more stability work at Mach 2.6 and 65,000 feet, and a ram purge test. During climb, the XB-70 encountered turbulence all the way to 65,000 feet, resulting in a higher-than-expected fuel burn. After the unstart at Mach 2.4, engineers on the ground requested that the pilots skip the stability tests at Mach 2.5 to conserve fuel, and to go directly to the tests at Mach 2.6 at 65,000 feet.[46]

One hour and six minutes into the flight, while traveling Mach 2.60 (1,690 mph) at a pressure altitude of 65,000 feet, the right duct began vibrating. Fulton took the normal corrective action and opened the right-duct bypass doors to reposition the shock. Unknown to the pilots, a piece of debris struck all three engines in the right duct, causing a momentary stall and a pronounced unstart signal; the left duct continued to indicate normal operation. Fulton apparently reacted to the unstart signal by continuing to open the bypass doors in the right duct to regain a started inlet condition. Less than a second later, he used the manual control to open the throat and restart the inlet.[47]

After the shock was returned to its started position, Fulton closed the right bypass doors to their original position. However, because of the damage to the engines and the consequent reduction in the engine airflow, it became necessary to set the doors to 11 degrees rather than the original 4-degree setting, to bring the shock to its proper operating position. At the same time, White throttled No. 5 down to military power because of a persistent vibration; all other engines were cut to minimum afterburner and began to exhibit an afterburner instability. The afterburner instability was a persistent problem with the YJ93s, and was not related to the problem generated by the damage to the engines. Two minutes later, all engines except No. 5 were momentarily advanced in power and then retarded to military power as White and Fulton began slowing down and descending.[48]

After White retarded the No. 5 engine an "incipient duct buzz" – essentially a vibration that was not severe enough to cause the warning light to come on – began. As the engine spooled-down, the duct pressure built up because the remaining two engines in that duct could not use all of the air being forced toward them. If the by-pass doors were not opened quickly, the excess pressure would spit the shock wave out the front of the duct (unstart the duct). If the duct was set up to start, the duct ingested the shock waves again, and the cycle repeated about once every 2 seconds. All of this resulted in a yawing oscillation. But White did not know this at the time and thought the yaw dampers had failed so he turned off the augmentation system. In the meantime, Fulton opened the bypass doors slightly to restart the duct, unknowingly relieving the pressure and stopping the unstart cycle, and the yawing oscillation stopped. The pilots later admitted that it was a stressful time, and crew coordination was not as good as it could have been.[49]

Five minutes after the initial indications of a problem, Fulton – aware that some engine damage had probably occurred, but not aware of the magnitude – was not completely satisfied with the response from the bypass-door opening and began closing the bypass doors to see if that would help eliminate the problem. This appears to have initiated a steady-state stall on the mildly damaged Nos. 4 and 6 engines. White finally gave up and shut down all three engines on the right side. This time the yawing oscillations were more severe, and the pressure buildup was strong enough that the duct buzz warning light came on. Fulton immediately opened the bypass doors to relieve the pressure, and things seemed under control, at least for a little while.[50]

In the XB-70, if a duct buzz was allowed to continue for any length of time it could destroy the duct. To make matters worse, the frequency of the buzz cycle was about the same as the natural bending frequency of the fuselage neck and could lead to structural failure if allowed to continue. White and Fulton were aware that they were getting close to that condition and were very relieved when it ceased.[51]

It should be noted that A/V-1 did not have an automatic AICS that would have provided an automatic buzz control. With the manual AICS, a system was provided to warn the copilot of buzz conditions and thereby alert him to eliminate the buzz by manually opening the bypass doors. If the same sequence of events would

From almost any angle, the XB-70 looked imposing. This photo was likely taken as the airplane was ready to leave Palmdale on Flight 1-5. (AFFTC History Office Collection)

This is what caused all the excitement on Flight 1-12 – a three-foot triangular shaped piece of stainless steel honeycomb separated from the apex of the wing and was ingested by the engines. The part was replaced with a solid piece of titanium. (AFFTC History Office Collection)

An expensive day. Five of the six J93s were extensively damaged by the debris from the wing apex. This shows the damage inside the right air duct and engine face. (AFFTC History Office Collection)

have occurred on A/V-2 with its automatic AICS, the buzz, in all likelihood, would have been automatically eliminated. However, the sequence of events did point out what could happen during an emergency after failure of an automatic AICS and subsequent recourse to manual air induction control.[52]

There was another system in the XB-70 that came into play about this time, although neither pilot immediately recognized the fact. An "RPM lock-up system" kept engine rpm at 100 percent to maintain stable airflow, regardless of throttle setting, when the airspeed was above Mach 1.5; this was intended to prevent engine damage, although there was some debate over its necessity. The system could be switched on or off, but the pilots usually left it on based on advice from General Electric. The system automatically disengaged below Mach 1.5 and the engine rpm reverted to throttle control. Above military power, the system varied the afterburner to control thrust. Below military power, throttle movement with the lockup engaged varied the exhaust-nozzle area, which in turn, varied engine thrust. Previous descents had been made at military power until the airplane was well below Mach 1.5, so the system had never come into play before this flight.[53]

After Fulton had eliminated the duct buzz, the crew was still faced with three dead engines on the right side and a rather large display of warning and caution lights. White reduced the three left-side throttles to idle power to counter the yaw created by the asymmetrical thrust. Unknown to White, he had reduced thrust by moving the exhaust nozzles, but had left the engines at 100-percent rpm.[54]

This is where the RPM lock-up system came into play. As the airplane decelerated through Mach 1.5, all three engines on the left side immediately went from 100-percent power to idle because White had pulled the throttles back. With the sudden loss of thrust, White assumed he had lost the other three engines and pushed the nose over to maintain enough speed to keep the engines windmilling, and drive the generator to operate the electric throttles, engine ignitors, radios, instrumentation, and also to attempt an airstart. Actually, it was important to keep all of the engines windmilling enough to drive the hydraulic pumps, otherwise there would be no way to control the airplane. What White failed to realize was that the three left-side engines were operating, only at idle power.[55]

White began the airstart procedure on the No. 3 engine because it powered one of the primary generators, and the engine had been operating okay before. The procedure called for "throttle to idle cut-off – air start switch on – throttle to idle." The unexpected result, however, was that when White moved the No. 3 throttle to idle cut-off, everything got very quiet and very dark, because he had just killed the only engine that was running a primary generator and supplying electrical power. White lowered the windshield so he could see a little better, and after about 10 seconds the emergency generator that ran off the No. 5 utility hydraulic pump on the right side of the airplane kicked in. At least the airplane had electricity again.[56]

Idle power rpm and windmilling rpm were about the same, and – 1 minute and 40 seconds after everything went dark – Fulton finally suspected that engines Nos. 1 and 2 were running in idle, which they were. Around 40,000 feet White brought engines Nos. 1 and 2 up to

All aircraft need weight data, and Edwards is equipped with a large weight and balance hangar just for that purpose. Note the X-21A in the background. (Boeing Historical Archives)

full power while Fulton airstarted No. 3 so all three engines on the left side of the airplane were now operating at full power. White airstarted the No. 5 engine since it appeared to be the best of the engines in the right duct. It started, but at full throttle, it was only running at 85-percent rpm. Jet engines provide very little thrust at less than 100-percent rpm, but this engine also supplied the hydraulic pressure for the emergency electrical generator, so the fact that it was operating at all was comforting to the pilots.[57]

The XB-70 leveled off at 20,000 feet and White brought the wingtips up. By now, the chase planes had joined up with the bomber and reported that a portion of the wing-fuselage apex was missing, but that the airplane looked otherwise intact. When they had Rogers Dry Lake in sight, the XB-70 pilots decided to lower the landing gear. It came down and locked at about 10,000 feet, but the flaps were inoperative, so White headed for lakebed Runway 18. The simulator had said that the no-flap approach speed was 240 knots, so that is how White flew it. The Valkyrie touched down at 210 knots, requiring about half of the available lateral control to compensate for the asymmetric power. The drag chutes would not deploy, and the nose wheel steering did not engage, but the airplane stopped after about 13,000 feet of roll. It was not until now that White realized part of the problem had been the unexpected interference by the RPM lock-up feature.[58]

A group gathered around just in front of the nose wheel of the XB-70 and looked up at the splitter between the inlet ducts. Just above this was where the apex of the wing had been – somehow a triangular 3-foot piece of stainless steel honeycomb had come off and been sucked into the intakes, with the majority of it sucked into the right side. Five of the six engines were seriously damaged and sent back to General Electric for repair; the other was inspected and reinstalled in the airplane. After this flight, the splitter itself was replaced with a single solid piece of titanium alloy in place of the honeycomb unit that had failed. This is when concerns about the integrity of the honeycomb skin began, and the next four flights were used to "heat soak" the skin for sustained periods of time. For the first time, the ability of the XB-70 to reach Mach 3 was being questioned.

Tragedy struck the program again on 9 May when Wilbert J. Lanning was crushed during the cycle test of the main landing gear on A/V-2 in Palmdale. Lanning was inside the wheel well observing a cycle test as the landing gear retracted. Somehow he was not far enough out of the way.[59]

Still, the program aimed higher and faster. Amazingly, despite the damage suffered on Flight 1-12, A/V-1 flew again only five weeks later, essentially repeating the same flight profile. This time things worked much better, but a failure of the No. 2 primary hydraulic system again dictated a lakebed landing. On 1 July 1965, during her 14th flight, A/V-1 recorded Mach 2.85 at 68,000 feet for 10 minutes and flew above Mach 2.5 for 40 minutes. Several sheets of honeycomb skin peeled off the fuselage and upper wing surface, but fortunately none were ingested by the engines. Mach 3 was getting closer, but doubts persisted.[60]

A/V-2 JOINS THE FRAY

Most of the major problems plaguing A/V-1 were cured during the manufacture of A/V-2, which was rolled out on 29 May 1965. In addition to having a functional No. 5 fuel tank, A/V-2 had five degrees of dihedral on the main wing, versus the zero degrees on A/V-1. This change was a result of simulator studies and wind tunnel testing conducted as A/V-1 was being assembled that showed the airplane would have poor roll stability with the wingtips fully lowered. The tradeoff was that, at low speeds with the wingtips up, A/V-2 suffered from a dihedral effect where sideslip caused one wing to drop. The pilot, sensing the low wing but not spotting the sideslip, would use the elevons to bring the wing back up – causing more sideslip, forcing the wing to

With a great deal less fanfare than her sister, A/V-2 was rolled out from the Palmdale hangar on 29 May 1965. (AFFTC History Office)

THE FLIGHT PROGRAM

The first flight of A/V-2, on 17 July 1965, went much smoother than the first airplane's had. Al White lowered the wingtips to full-down and proceeded to Mach 1.41 at an altitude of 42,000 feet on the way to Edwards. (AFFTC History Office Collection)

drop lower. The only solution was for the pilots to closely watch the sideslip indicator. It was expected that any production aircraft would cure this behavior with changes to the stability augmentation system but the austere budget of the demonstration program prohibited this.[61]

Internally, A/V-2 featured a revised hydraulic system to reduce the leaking that continued to trouble A/V-1. This involved better brazing, the use of more supporting brackets to reduce flex, and an increased number of flex-hoses in areas subjected to high vibration levels. The techniques to build the honeycomb skin also improved with experience. An automatic air inlet control system was installed in place of the manual system on the first aircraft. The most visible external difference was that the radome for the non-existent bomb-nav system was black on A/V-2; it was white on A/V-1.

Although greatly improved, A/V-2 wasn't completely trouble free. For instance, the brakes still chattered during low-speed taxiing. It was suspected that this stemmed from the lack of return springs for the brake pads, but no fix was readily apparent. Far more worrisome, however, were glitches in the automatic AICS system, which would inexplicably recycle during supersonic flight, causing a duct "unstart" and its associated problems.

On 17 July 1965, A/V-2 joined the flight test program. With much better luck than had accompanied A/V-1's first flight, the

One of the most noticeable features of the B-70 design was the "variable geometry" wingtips (although this term later took on a different meaning). Each wing was hinged at 60-percent semi-span and could be angled downward into either of two positions to increase directional stability at high speeds. The mid-down position is shown at left, while the full-down position is at right. The aircraft had to be jacked-up for these tests since the wingtip would be below ground level when full-down if the airplane was sitting on its landing gear. These were not small pieces – each wingtip was approximately the size of the wing on a Convair B-58 Hustler medium bomber. (Tony Landis Collection)

wingtips were lowered to full-down, and the airplane reached a top speed of Mach 1.41 at an altitude of 42,000 feet on the flight to Edwards. Al White reported, "The dihedral in the wings was readily apparent during the subsonic and low supersonic flight with the wingtips up and at 25 degrees, but once the wingtips were down to 65 degrees there wasn't too much difference in the feel of the airplane." The second flight of A/V-2 was significant in that it was the first time that Al White was not the pilot-in-command of an XB-70; he and Joe Cotton swapped seats on 10 August 1965 when A/V-2 recorded Mach 1.45 and 41,000 feet.[62]

This provided Al White the chance to learn new things. As the pilot of A/V-1, he had never needed to worry about managing the center-of-gravity (by controlling the fuel system) or controlling the AICS, since that was done from the right seat. But the program had progressed to the point that the other pilots needed to be checked out in the left seat, meaning that White would need to learn the intricacies of operating these systems. It was something that pilots of the now-cancelled production aircraft would never have had to worry about since they would have been automated, but for the two prototypes, their correct operation was essential.

Onward to Mach 3

In the meantime, A/V-1 continued to go faster. The first Mach-3 flight of the program came on 14 October 1965 during the 17th flight of the first airplane with Al White and Joe Cotton at the controls. The XB-70 was – by far – the largest and heaviest air-breathing vehicle to exceed three times the speed of sound.

The preflight went smoothly, and White and Cotton started the first engine at 08:00 – A/V-1 took off from Runway 22 at Edwards 1 hour and 6 minutes later. After raising the gear and flaps, White lowered the wingtips to the mid-down position at 320 knots and began to climb to 32,000 feet at about 450 knots. When level at 32,000 feet, the pilots began accelerating, raising the windscreen as they went supersonic. The air traffic restriction for the initial part of the flight meant that the airplane could not exceed 33,000 feet until further clearance. At Mach 1.3, the wingtips were lowered to the full-down position and the airplane began accelerating to its 575-knot (Mach 1.48) climb speed. Air traffic control cleared the airplane to climb, and White quickly accelerated to Mach 1.7 while passing through 39,000 feet. Al White remembers that maintaining a climb schedule at these speeds was difficult since none of the flight instruments were constant: Mach was increasing, airspeed was decreasing, rate of climb was changing. According to White, "Maintaining the climb schedule was by trial and error. I had to select a pitch attitude, and then see if I went through the next altitude at the right Mach number. If not, I had to make a change in the attitude, and then wait to see if that was right." Nevertheless, this particular climb was more or less on the desired profile and performance was as predicted.[63]

While White was trying to keep the climb on track, Cotton was busy with the fuel management system. As soon as the airplane reached Mach 2, Cotton was going to get even busier controlling the

Some of the things Al White had to learn when he began flying in the right seat. The manual AICS controls at are the top center of the photo. The fuel tank sequence panel just beneath it presented a graphic display of tank sequencing. Dual-colored tapes (white and black) were used to indicate the fuel level in each tank – white indicated fuel; black indicated no fuel. When the display was completely black, the tank was empty. The intertank transfer of fuel to control the center-of-gravity was automated on A/V-2, but was accomplished manually by the copilot on A/V-1. (Boeing Historical Archives)

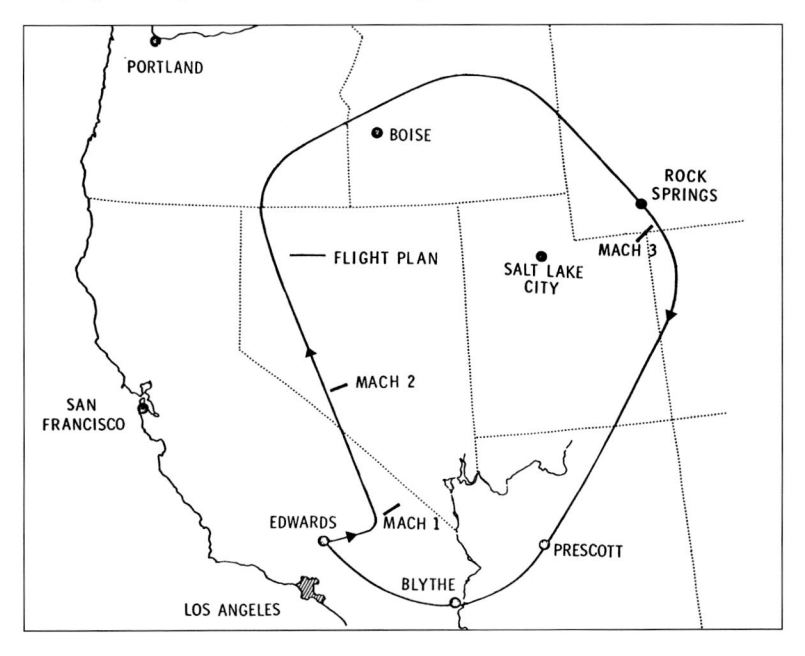

Typical ground track for an XB-70 Mach 3 flight. (U.S. Air Force)

THE FLIGHT PROGRAM

"Mach 2.94 at 69,000, 551 on the temp – things are sure looking good – Mach 2.96 at 69,300, total temperature 567." And then, "Okay, there's that big magic number." The XB-70 had just exceeded Mach 3 for the first time and was still accelerating.[67]

A minute later the total temperature was at 576 degrees – well within the expected value – when White suddenly announced, "just a second, I got a little problem here." It wasn't much of a problem, just a slight nose up trim change at 70,000 feet that caught the pilots by surprise. White assumed that it was the primary shock wave coming under the leading edge of the wing, which may or may not have been the case. It also could have been caused by Cotton moving the bypass doors, which he was doing at the time. They would find out shortly.[68]

White made a small correction in pitch attitude that caused A/V-1 to lose nearly 1,000 feet in altitude. At Mach 3, one degree of pitch attitude change causes a rate of change of altitude of 3,000 feet per minute: 50 feet per second. All of the instruments looked okay and the airplane felt good so White started to climb back up, but at about 69,500 feet there was a loud bang. The XB-70 had been at Mach 3 for almost 2 minutes, reaching a maximum of Mach 3.04, something just over 2,000 miles per hour. Since nobody could identify the source of the bang, both pilots concurred that it was time to slow down; Cotton adjusted the inlets and White began throttling back and descending.[69]

It took a long time to get down, but when the bomber reached 34,000 feet White and Cotton began a series of maneuvers to get performance data for the test card. After the first run, one of the chase planes caught up with A/V-1 and reported that a large strip of skin was missing off the leading edge of the left wing just outboard of the inlet duct. The mystery of the loud bang was solved. It was decided to skip the remaining tests and bring the airplane back to Edwards.[70]

Once the airplane was back on the ground and taxiing towards the hangar, Max Wells made an announcement: "All stations, this is Edwards Data Control. There will be a celebration at the Hideaway

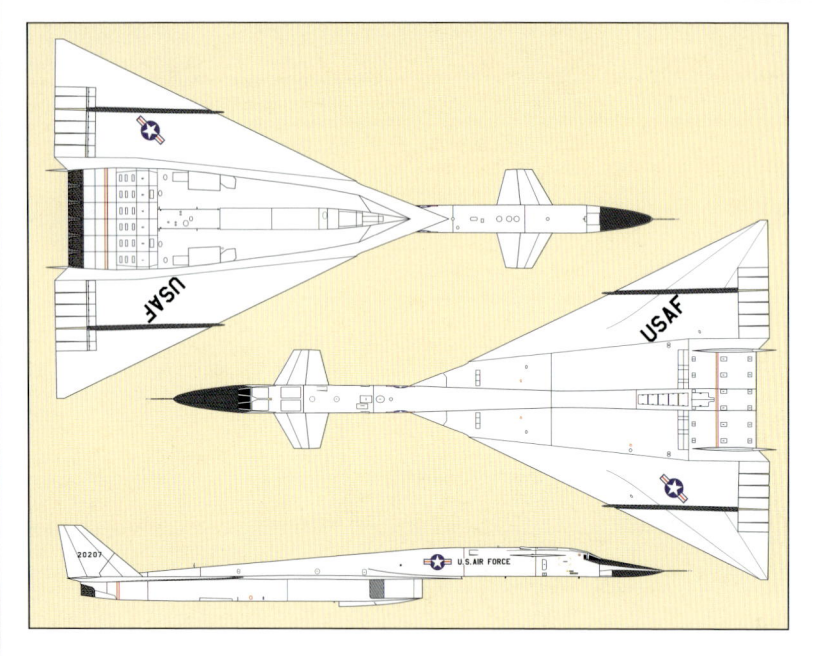

The major appearance items that differentiated A/V-2 from A/V-1 were the black radome under the nose and the white inlet interior (on A/V-1 it was white sometimes and natural metal others). A more subtle – but more important – difference was the five degrees of dihedral on the main wing to cure a minor instability at some speeds. (Art by Tony Landis)

inlet ducts. Just above Mach 2 the airplane entered light turbulence; none of the pilots liked turbulence since the long forward fuselage was not stiff enough to resist the disturbances. White later commented, "It was like we were riding on the end of a big fishing pole. The oscillations were up and down, or side to side, or combinations of both."[64]

Joe Cotton started both intake ducts at Mach 2, but a short time later the left duct indicated an unstart, so White throttled back to 75-percent power. Engineers on the ground worked with Cotton on the problem, restarting the duct several times, only to end up with the unstart indication each time. It was finally decided that the indicator was faulty and the duct was operating properly, so the pilots went back to full afterburner and continued to accelerate and climb.[65]

By the time the airplane was at 62,000 feet, it had accelerated to Mach 2.6, indicating 540 knots, heading toward the Great Salt Lake. The ground track was reviewed to ensure the airplane would not "boom" Salt Lake City, and White slightly adjusted the flight path to pass to the west of the city. At Mach 2.77 and 67,000 feet, the total temperature was 484 degrees Fahrenheit and the fuel remaining was well within the preflight estimate. Everything looked good.[66]

White reported a little buffeting, but nothing serious. At Mach 2.82 and 68,000 feet, the airspeed was indicating 512 knots and the total temperature was 506 degrees. Cotton opened the bypass doors a little, causing a slight nose up trim, but the airplane held steady at Mach 2.9 with a total temperature of 542 degrees. White remembers that "it was apparent that we were going to make it, and I was getting a little excited, and also a little impatient." White called to the ground,

Ground crew stenciling their overalls after hearing A/V-1 had broken Mach 3 briefly on Flight 1-17. (Boeing Historical Archives)

142 VALKYRIE – NORTH AMERICAN'S MACH 3 SUPERBOMBER

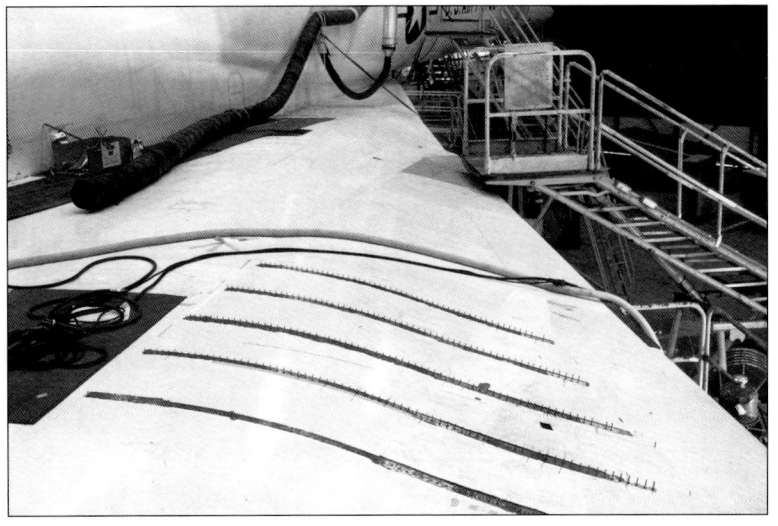

The stainless steel honeycomb panels on A/V-1 suffered structural problems that eventually led to a Mach 2.5 speed limit being placed on the airplane. The skin panels separated when thermal expansion and aerodynamic buffeting ballooned a defective area around a small crack in the face sheet. This in turn led to the skin cover separating where the brazings were too thin or poorly formed. Engineers traced the immediate problem to flaws in the manufacturing process and better quality controls were implemented. When a void was detected, North American welded pins between the outer and inner face sheet, through the honeycomb structure. By the time A/V-1 was turned over to NASA, the skin problems had been solved and the speed limit was raised to Mach 2.6, although the airplane never went that fast. (Tony Landis Collection)

[a local bar] on 110th street and Avenue H, at 15:00 hours this afternoon, to commemorate the B-70's successful accomplishment of Mach-3 flight. All personnel associated in any way with the program are cordially invited." It may have been less than 2 minutes, but it was Mach 3, and the program was ready for a big celebration.[71]

There had been a competition between the two XB-70 ground crews about which airplane was going to get to Mach 3 first. The crew for A/V-1 was prepared; they had made a stencil during the early part of the flight, and when it was announced that the airplane had reached Mach 3, everyone had a sign sprayed on the back of their coveralls that said: "XB-70 – SHIP 1 – MACH 3+" ... it was a happy day all around and the Hideaway did a brisk business.[72]

Just over a year and 17 flights into the test program, A/V-1 had finally reached her goal – but she would never fly at Mach 3 again. Alarmed with the skin separation problem, and hoping that improvements in A/V-2 would eliminate it, the Air Force imposed a Mach 2.5 speed limit on A/V-1, although this would be raised to Mach 2.6 very late in the flight program. Still, for a while A/V-1 was the largest and heaviest aircraft to have ever flown Mach 3, even for 2 minutes.

Nevertheless, not everybody was so happy about large supersonic aircraft. Dignitaries from Las Vegas asked that the Valkyries not "boom" their city because some of their buildings had very expensive glass frontages. With few exceptions the program only flew supersonically in specific "corridors" that attempted to avoid heavily populated areas, so the request was not unreasonable. Nevertheless, somehow the mayor of Boise, Idaho, heard about the Las Vegas request and wrote a letter saying that Boise would welcome the B-70 over their city. Joe Cotton answered the letter, saying that if he had some Idaho potatoes, he could bake them at the temperatures experienced on Mach-3 flights. A little while later, a sack of potatoes arrived, and the crew put them in the weapons bay near the instrumentation package. What everybody seemed to forget was that the instrumentation package was cooled by a massive refrigeration system. When the crew went to recover the "baked" potatoes, they were frozen solid.[73]

Frozen potatoes anybody? (AFFTC History Office Collection)

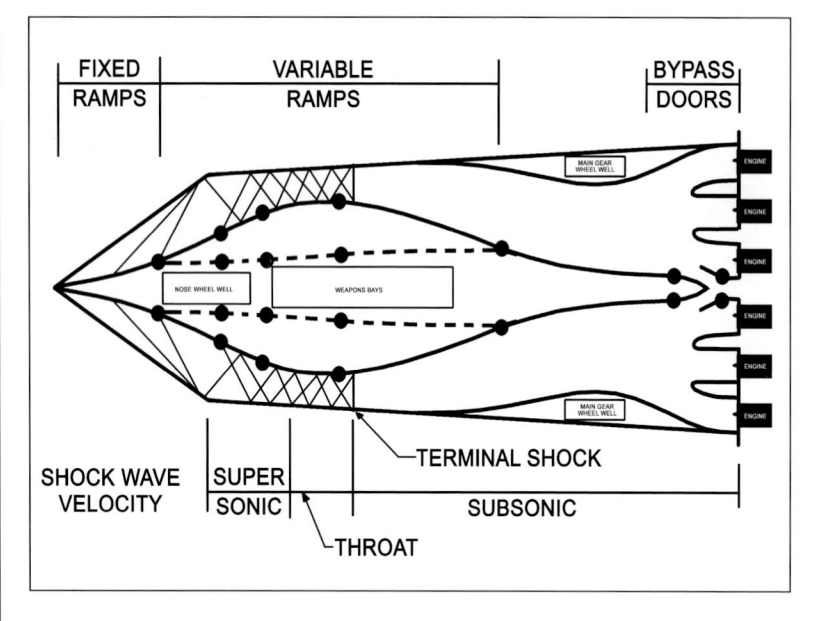

Jet engines want subsonic air entering the compressor. Like most supersonic aircraft, the Valkyrie used a series of shock waves in the inlet to slow down the supersonic air to velocities tolerable to the engines. Keeping the shock waves (the zig-zag lines in the air inlet) in the proper position to slow the supersonic air to subsonic velocities was called "starting" the inlet. If the shock wave bounced outside the front of the inlet, this was an "unstart." (U.S. Air Force)

The normal climb schedule for the XB-70 consisted of a series of accelerations, combined with variations in wingtip, windshield, and air inlet geometry. The landing gear was retracted early before the airplane accelerated faster than 250 knots. Wingtips were lowered to mid-down anywhere from 400 knots to 630 knots to provide extra stability in the transonic region. Steady acceleration to Mach 1.5 at 32,000 feet followed, then the wingtips were lowered to their full-down position. Mach 1.5 was maintained to about 50,000 feet, and then varying rates of acceleration were applied until Mach 3 at 70,000 feet was reached. The best-recorded time to Mach 3 was 25 minutes from rotation.

The rectangular air inlet ramps began to close at Mach 2. As speed increased, their geometry changed to provide the optimum pressure recovery through a series of sequential shocks beginning with an oblique shock from the splitter plate, ending with a terminal shock as the air reached the throat areas. Introducing the initial shock wave was "starting" the inlet ramps. If the shock wave refused to enter, or popped back out of the inlets, it was called an "unstart."

Al White described an unstart at Mach 3 as sudden and violent, accompanied by a large reduction in engine thrust. The aircraft rolled, pitched, and yawed, accompanied by considerable buffeting. Normally one inlet unstarted with a bang and as the pilot was recovering the other inlet would unstart. Similar problems also affected the Lockheed Blackbirds – it was one of the hazards of very high-speed flight. While not particularly dangerous, unstarting was one problem facing supersonic transport designers since it was unlikely that passengers would appreciate the disturbance. There was another potentially more serious problem. Sometimes, speed and throat ramp settings would create a condition where the shock wave was right at the boundary of the inlet, jumping in and out. This "buzz" had to be corrected quickly since the acoustical stresses and vibration could cause structural damage.[74]

The engineers predicted that the most critical transients were associated with an engine loss at Mach 3, an inlet unstart at Mach 3, or a combination of both. This was aggravated by the wingtips being full down since they caused a strong negative dihedral effect. This meant that if the nose of the airplane was yawed in one direction, the relative wind striking that turned down wingtip caused the airplane to roll in the opposite direction. These transients were not too hard to control with the stability augmentation system turned on, but were – naturally – more difficult to control with the augmentation off. During early 1962 North American put considerable effort into evaluating these conditions, and after doing it a few times, Al White developed a technique that worked, at least in the simulator. It remained to be seen if the airplane would react in the same way.

North American continued working in the simulator to develop techniques to control the airplane in emergency situations. The results of these early tests, combined with new wind tunnel data from the NASA Ames Research Center, is what led North American to include 5 degrees of dihedral in the wings of A/V-2 to improve the directional stability, and cancel some of the negative dihedral effect at Mach 3 caused by the folding wingtips. Given that it was not possible to modify A/V-1, North American turned to a bit of trickery to assist during unstarts. A simple lateral bob-weight had been installed in A/V-1 during the layup after Flight 1-4. Mostly at Al White's instance, the bob-weight could be locked prior to flight, and this was the case during the in-flight emergency on Flight 1-12.[75]

Changes in the Cockpit

The program's 32nd flight – the 21st for A/V-1 – marked a milestone of a different sort. For the previous 31 flights, Al White had been in one seat or the other. For this flight, he was in the back seat of the TB-58A chase plane, watching Joe Cotton and Van Shepard fly an airplane to which he had dedicated seven years of his life. However, the pace of the program was picking up, and the pilots would need to trade off more and more – White simply could not make every flight. At least that was the theory. Reality proved somewhat different when five flights were launched between 29 November and 3 December – one per day; somehow, White managed to fly on all of them. This level of activity was somewhat unusual, but not by much; the Valkyries managed to log 10 flights during the first 22 days of December 1965.[76]

During her 15th flight, on 11 December 1965, A/V-2 reached Mach 2.94 briefly, but ran at Mach 2.8 for 20 minutes and spent 41 total minutes above Mach 2.5 without any skin separation. Ten days later, after 7 minutes above Mach 2.9 (and 32 minutes above Mach 2.8), the oil pump for the No. 4 engine failed. Shutting down the engine, White and Cotton headed back to Edwards, when an over-

Two Mach 3 aircraft pose together at Edwards: the first XB-70A and second YF-12A. (Boeing Historical Archives)

The famous "tip toe" landing of A/V-1 on Flight 1-37 after hydraulic problems. The aircraft rolled for three miles on the lakebed before coming to a stop, almost half a mile off the centerline of the runway it landed on. (AFFTC History Office Collection)

temperature indicator came on for the No. 6 engine, which was shut down as well. After landing, it was discovered that, despite the early shutdown, loss of lubrication had destroyed the No. 4 engine; the No. 6 engine was removed and sent to General Electric for repair.[77]

Flight 1-27 had an unusual test requirement. Al White and Joe Cotton were onboard for the 20 December 1965 flight that ultimately reached Mach 1.78 and 42,000 feet. At Mach 1.4 and 41,000 feet, White pushed his seat back and encapsulated himself (but, obviously, did not eject) to demonstrate that an encapsulated pilot could adequately control the airplane. After flying this way for about 10 minutes, White opened the capsule and the flight continued normally. A similar test would later be conducted on Flight 1-39 on 24 March 1966.[78]

Less than six months after her first flight, on 3 January 1966, A/V-2 reached Mach 3 on her 17th flight – coincidentally, the same number of flights A/V-1 needed to accomplish the same feat. A top speed of Mach 3.05 (2,010 mph) was recorded for 3 minutes, with an additional 17 minutes above Mach 2 and 16 more above Mach 1. The post-flight inspection revealed no sign of skin damage. The program was still being cautious, however, and A/V-2 would make two more short flights above Mach 3 before sustaining 2,000 mph at 73,000 feet for 15 minutes during Flight 2-22 on 17 February 1966. The Valkyrie was finally proving to be a true Mach 3+ airplane.

It was also proving to be a fairly reliable airplane given its prototype status, and A/V-1 made two flights on 11 January 1966. The first, Flight 1-31, had Fitz Fulton and Van Shepard at the controls for a 1 hour and 35 minute flight that reached Mach 1.85 and 46,000 feet. After landing to refuel, Joe Cotton and Al White took the aircraft for a 58 minute subsonic flight.[79]

The two aircraft seemed determined to add excitement at the same intervals. Both aircraft had exceeded Mach 3 on their 17th flights. Each of their 37th flights added a different type of drama.

On 7 March 1966 the 37th flight of A/V-1 showed the type of adversity that could be overcome by a pair of experienced test pilots. Van Shepard was the pilot and Joe Cotton was copilot. Halfway through the planned flight, a problem that had been largely overcome came back to haunt the Valkyrie – both hydraulic systems began to fail. Shepard quickly headed for Edwards as Cotton extended the landing gear. No green indicators came on, followed by a call from the chase plane that there was trouble with both main gear. On the left side, the gear had not fully lowered before rotating to meet the direction of travel, leaving the rear wheels higher, rather than lower, than the front set of wheels.[80]

The right side was in worse shape – it had not lowered at all before rotating. Even more alarming, it hadn't completely rotated in line with the direction of travel, although it was close. Neither the backup nor emergency system corrected the problem. After what must have seemed like hours in the cockpit, engineers on the ground called up to the pilots with their plan. Shepard would land the Valkyrie on the dry lakebed. The engineers believed that the weight of the XB-70 touching down would force the left bogie into its level position. As for the right gear … being behind the centerline of the main strut, it was unlikely that the gear would level out, but they hoped that the landing would at least cause the gear to finish swinging into the direction of travel, and the wingtip would still clear the ground, although the right side would be much lower than the left.[81]

Van Shepard set A/V-1 down on the lakebed, and each main gear did what the engineers expected. After touchdown the aircraft wanted to turn sharply to the right, threatening to ground loop. Although probably not fatal to the pilots, this would likely have damaged the aircraft beyond economic repair. Shepard kept applying power to the No. 6 (farthest right side) engine to help keep the XB-70 somewhat straight. After rolling almost 3 miles, the XB-70 came to a stop. The path, when viewed from above, looked like an upside-down letter "J" because the aircraft had swung half a mile to the right and had turned 110 degrees. Only the size of the lakebed allowed this landing to be survivable; it is one major reason the Air Force tests at Edwards. The first commander of the Air Force Flight Test Center, Major General Albert Boyd, once commented that the lakes were nothing less than "God's gift to the U.S. Air Force."[82]

It would be easy to imagine the two scenes above as simply a production B-70 coming home to roost with its B-52 and KC-135 squadron mates. But it was not to be. Instead, this is A/V-2 making a one-time appearance at the Carswell AFB air show. (above: C. Roger Cripliver; top left: Terry Panopalis Collection; others: Boeing Historical Archives)

The Flight Program

A/V-2 configured for speed: wingtips full down, afterburner nozzles fully open. The aircraft would eventually fly for more than 32 minutes at over Mach 3, demonstrating that it was possible to cruise for as long as there was fuel in the tanks. (AFFTC History Office Collection)

The damage was quickly repaired and A/V-1 took to the skies again on 22 March piloted by Cotton and Shepard on a very conservative 2 hour 11 minute hop that only reached Mach 0.97 at 32,000 feet.

The only time an XB-70 traveled somewhere other than Edwards or Palmdale (not counting the last flight to the Air Force Museum) was on 24 March 1966, when Fitz Fulton and Al White took A/V-2 to the Armed Forces Day air show at Carswell AFB, Texas. The Valkyrie spent only 13 minutes at Mach 2.71 before arriving over Fort Worth just 59 minutes after takeoff. For the next half hour, A/V-2 thundered around the skies of Texas before landing at Carswell. Fulton was replaced by Joe Cotton for the return trip two days later, and he and White made a 3 hour trip back to California at subsonic speeds – the only flight during the entire program where performance data was not recorded.[83]

On 12 April 1966 A/V-2 was conducting a flight that had been scheduled to fly at Mach 3 for 30 minutes, but Al White and Joe Cotton decided to cut the high-speed run short after an inlet unstart. The internal shock wave moved forward from its optimum position while the flight crew was experimenting with the manual vernier controls for "fine tuning" the engine inlets to achieve maximum performance. The unstart was aggravated by a turn maneuver, turning always affected inlet airflow, but was usually – on A/V-2 anyway – compensated for by the automatic inlet control system. The unstart was corrected and the airplane spent 20 minutes at Mach 3.08 and 72,800 feet. The purpose of the flight was to expose the airplane to high temperatures, and the maximum free-stream temperature reached 624 degrees Fahrenheit at stagnation points on the wing and inlet leading edges. The highest previous free stream temperature had been 610 degrees Fahrenheit during a 16-minute Mach-3 flight on 8 April. The higher temperature on this flight was attributed to atmospheric conditions and not the duration of the flight.[84]

The TB-58 was the only chase plane at Edwards that could keep up with the XB-70 for any distance – at least up to Mach 2 – and was used on most test flights. (AFFTC History Office Collection)

A Paperclip?

Not to be outdone by her older sister, A/V-2 also experienced a landing gear problem on her 37th flight. On the morning of 30 April 1966, Al White and Joe Cotton took off with the intent of accomplishing a 30-minute Mach-3 flight, but a few seconds after Cotton put the gear handle up, the pilots heard a loud thump. White decided to put the handle back down. The main gear went down to the locked position, but the indicator remained red for the nose gear. By that time, one of the T-38 chase planes caught up and reported that the nose gear was not down – it was jammed against the partially open nose gear door. The door was caught between the two nose wheels, and had sliced into the left tire.[85]

While the engineers on the ground were trying to come up with a solution to this problem, the pilots tried several things to separate the nose gear from the gear door. White first brought the XB-70 around for a touch-and-go, hoping that a hard impact on the main gear would knock the nose gear loose and let it fall to the extended position. Even after a second try, however, the nose gear remained jammed. They tried the emergency gear lowering system with no success, and then they tried pulling g's and side-slipping the airplane, all to no avail. At this point, ejecting and losing the aircraft was becoming the only option. Luckily, there was a lot of fuel so there was time for the engineers to find a solution.[86]

After about 30 minutes, White got a radio call from Bob McDonald, a North American specialist on the landing gear, asking if he had a paperclip. The engineers were fairly sure they had determined what the problem was, and had devised a procedure to get the nose gear down. The hypothesis was that there had been a short-circuit in the landing gear system that had caused a couple of circuit breakers to trip when the crew raised the gear. One of these was a breaker that allowed hydraulic power to be applied to open the door. In this situation, when the circuit was interrupted, the door was just floating whichever way the air stream was blowing it.[87]

During normal landing gear operation, when the gear handle was put in the down position, the first thing that happened was that the gear doors opened. When each door was fully open, it triggered a sequence switch indicating that the door was out of the way of the landing gear. Hydraulic power could not be applied to lower that particular landing gear until the corresponding door was fully open. In this situation when the short occurred, the door drifted in front of the nose gear as it was coming up and was caught between the two tires. The air stream was holding the nose gear against the door so it couldn't open and the gear wouldn't go down until the door *was* open – Catch-22. It was a puzzling situation, but once the engineers figured out what had happened, they asked Cotton to go back into the instrumentation bay and bypass the sequence switch in the door circuit by shorting across two specific connectors on a large terminal board. This would allow hydraulic power to be applied to the gear down actuator.[88]

Joe Cotton carried a variety of equipment in his briefcase on every flight, but he did not have a paperclip; neither did White. Ever resourceful, especially when it came to saving a multi-million dollar airplane, Cotton fashioned a wire from a piece of the clip on his oxygen hose. Equally important, he had a screwdriver, which he needed to remove the cover from the terminal board, and a flashlight. Cotton found the correct terminals and made the connection while White engaged the emergency gear down system. The chase planes reported that the nose gear was lowering into position. Everyone heaved a sigh of relief, but there was still the issue of the blown nose tire.[89]

It was decided to burn fuel until A/V-2 was at the most aft center of gravity. White decided that he would land with enough speed to let the nose wheel down gently, and be ready to go around if he felt he

Flight 2-37 started badly. On the B-70, the gear door was kept closed except when the landing gear was extending or retracting – even when the gear was down the doors were closed. Somehow on this flight the nose gear began to retract before the gear door was fully open. The door got stuck between the two nose wheels, slicing the left tire in the process. Repeated attempts at cycling the gear and hard touch-and-go landings initially only succeeded to separate the outer and inner skin of the door (photo at right). (AFFTC History Office Collection)

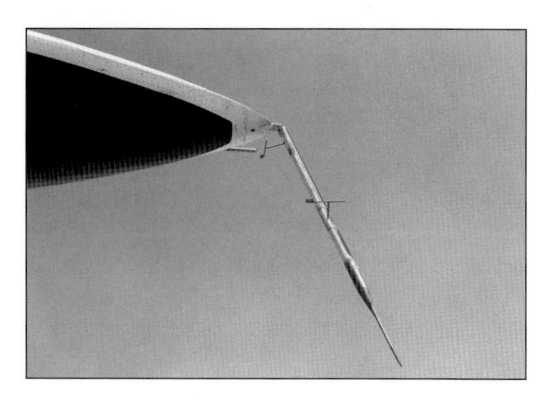

More shots of Flight 2-37. As usual, the crash crews were right there, saving the airplane and pilots from serious harm. (Tony Landis Collection)

could not adequately control the airplane. In that case, they would let the crash crews foam the runway and try again. White made a flat approach, but when the main gear touched down all other options disappeared. The brakes were locked – again – and this time six of the eight main gear tires blew. The tires caught fire, and before A/V-2 could stop, the wheels and both bogie beams were badly damaged. When the nose gear touched down at about 125 knots, the vibration was so severe that it broke the nose boom off the airplane, and the knobs on some of the controls in the cockpit were knocked off.[90]

Fortunately, there were two spare bogie beams available – the second one manufactured for A/V-3, and the one from A/V-1 that had been rebuilt after being badly damaged on the first flight. A little over two weeks later the airplane was ready to fly again, and on 16 May 1966, White and Cotton went up in A/V-2 to do unstarts at speeds above Mach 2 and some stability work. This was also as a general functional check on all the systems in the airplane. If all went well, the program was intending to fly for 30 minutes at Mach 3 on the next flight. Everything checked out and all appeared in order to accomplish the last major requirement of the program.[91]

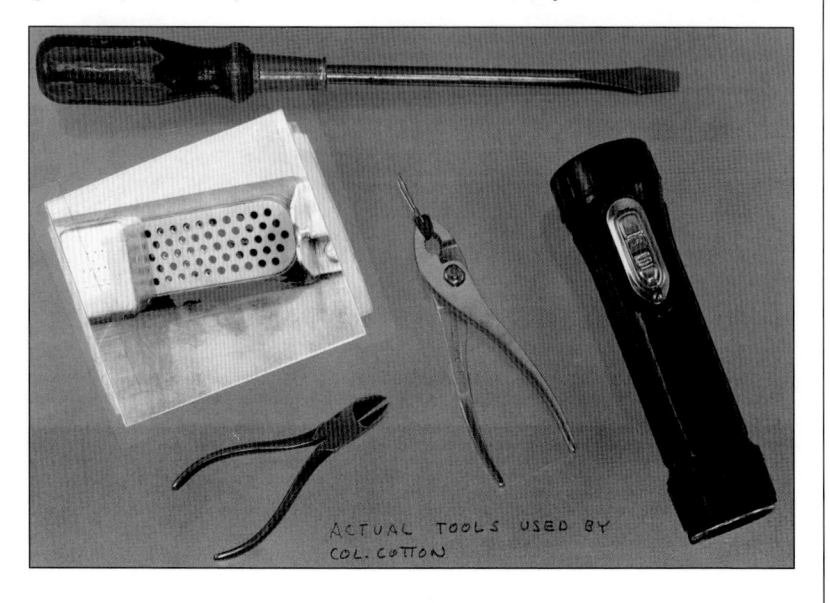

The tools used by Joe Cotton on Flight 2-37. (Boeing Historical Archives)

A great view of the six J93 exhaust nozzles on A/V-2 with A/V-1 in the background. North American ducted bleed air around the engines to cool the structure around the engine compartment. On production bombers this may have helped hide the hot exhaust trail from infrared detection. Note how the fixed wedge hinge on the all-moving vertical stabilizers is angled. (Boeing Historical Archives)

The Flight Program

Artist Ronald Stephano generated this terrific-looking caricature of A/V-2 for this book. (Original artwork by Ronald Stephano, ©2004)

A/V-2 late in its career. Markings for an experiment may be seen on top of the right wing. (Gerald H. Balzer Collection)

Just three days later, on 19 May, White and Cotton were off the ground at 09:00 and heading out to fly the track that Sam Richter had plotted during the morning briefing. Like most modern bombers, the navigation equipment for the B-70 was part of the bombing system, and neither XB-70 was equipped with the IBM ASQ-28 bomb-nav system. For the prototypes, the only navigation equipment in the airplane was a single TACAN set – and it wasn't very reliable. Most XB-70 flights were guided mainly by preflight information and radar tracking by the High Range sites at Edwards, and Beatty and Ely, Nevada.

The track would take A/V-2 over nine states in a long loop that headed north through Nevada and the southeast corner of Oregon.

Three good chutes as A/V-2 lands at Edwards. The TB-58 chase plane can be seen high in the background. (Gerald H. Balzer Collection)

White made a series of turns over Idaho and Wyoming with the airplane reaching Mach 3 near Rock Springs, Wyoming; White throttled back to hold Mach 3.02. The pilots had already learned from previous flights at this speed that it was difficult to hold a constant altitude or a constant Mach number. The altimeter and rate-of-climb instrument were constantly changing due to the rapid changes in the pressure fields the airplane was traveling through, and temperature flares in the atmosphere also affected the Mach indicator. Earlier, technicians had expanded the scale of the attitude indicator to make it easier to read, and preflight planning had moved the target altitude up to 72,500 feet; it helped, but the autopilot and Doppler radar scheduled for production aircraft would have been useful.[92]

One of the contractual requirements on North American was to demonstrate the XB-70 was capable of Mach-3 flight for a minimum of 30 minutes. The engineers had already concluded that this duration would allow all of the structure and systems to get as hot (or cold) as they were going to get; this flight would effectively demonstrate that the airplane was capable of maintaining Mach 3+ until fuel exhaustion. After 32 minutes above Mach 3 – the indicator was actually reading Mach 3.06 at the time – Al White slowly began decelerating. The total temperature had reached 620 degrees Fahrenheit. The Valkyrie traveled over 2,400 miles during the flight – an average speed of more than 1,500 miles per hour, including takeoff and landing. Finally, all remaining concerns about skin separation were laid to rest. In theory, with full internal fuel the B-70 would have been capable of flying almost 2.5 hours at Mach 3 – a true triple-sonic cruiser.[93]

Three days later, A/V-2 thrilled the spectators at the Armed Forces Day show at Edwards, including a couple of supersonic passes over the crowd. Test data on stability and control issues were recorded during the 2-hour and 22-minute flight that reached Mach 1.51 and 36,500 feet.

With all systems tested and the major performance goals demonstrated, NASA was preparing to become more involved in the test

The Flight Program

A good view of the large delta planform of the XB-70. Each engine is numbered on the bottom of the airplane. Note the weapons bay door and its track, although it could not be opened in flight on either prototype. (Boeing via the Jay Miller Collection)

program where extensive sonic boom and handling tests would begin. A/V-2 was refitted with additional instrumentation and data recording equipment; more than a thousand sensors, recording devices, and telemetry equipment were installed. These instruments would give a better look at a number of phenomena that couldn't be thoroughly tested in a wind tunnel including body flex, flutter, and pressure distributions. At the same time, NASA began setting up a large number of ground sensors to precisely measure the effect of sonic booms.

New pilots were also joining the program, including NASA chief test pilot Joseph A. Walker, who had just come from the X-15 program. Walker had flown the X-15 to almost Mach 6 (4,100 mph) in level flight; Mach 3 would seem slow. Also joining the program was Air Force Major Carl S. Cross. At the same time, both Al White and Joe Cotton began to gradually ease out of the program, with White going to work on other programs at North American and Cotton continuing as the Air Force B-70 Program Manager.

After their selection to fly the XB-70, both Carl Cross and Joe Walker began attending ground school and flying the simulator at North American to familiarize themselves with the airplane. Although he was well acquainted with large aircraft, Carl Cross had

The Flight Program

no exposure to deltas, so he logged time in the TB-58A chase aircraft, making six flights for 13.5 hours in March 1966 and two more flights worth another 3.5 hours in May. Joe Walker had flown an early Convair F-102 Delta Dagger for over 34 hours in 1963 but also lacked any large delta-winged time, so he logged several flights in the TB-58A totaling almost 3 hours of time during May 1966. By the beginning of June both Cross and Walker had substantially finished their training and were ready to fly the XB-70 – Cross would get his chance first, on 8 June with Fitz Fulton. Walker would follow two days later with Al White. But fate had other plans.

An unusually humid day at Edwards provides an exciting photograph of A/V-2. Note the position of the canard flaps. (Boeing Historical Archives)

A family portrait with A/V-1 in the background. (Boeing Historical Archives)

An unusual shot of A/V-2 on the ramp with the wingtips half-down. It was not possible to put the wingtips full-down on the ground without jacking the aircraft since they extended below the level of the landing gear. (Boeing Historical Archives)

Both Valkyries could fit into their hangar at the same time, validating claims by North American that the B-70 could be maintained in the same facilities that had been constructed for the B-52 fleet. Note the two small cutouts for the twin vertical stabilizers. (Boeing Historical Archives)

Mid-Air …

On 8 June 1966, Carl Cross was making his first flight in the right seat of A/V-2 for a series of relatively simple tests. As originally planned, the flight had two primary objectives: airspeed calibration runs and familiarization for Cross. The day before the flight, a sonic boom run was added at the request of Air Force Headquarters, and Al White replaced Fitz Fulton as pilot because of a scheduling conflict for Fulton. White started the engines at 06:20, explaining the procedure to Cross but not taking too much time; A/V-2 was scheduled for two flights on this day, so things needed to proceed with some haste. White released the brakes at 07:15 and performed four airspeed calibration runs. The T-38 chase was out of fuel and landed while the Valkyrie prepared for the sonic boom run; another T-38 took off to act as chase. The sonic boom run was completed at approximately 08:30 and everything went according to plan.[94]

Now came the photo session with a Northrop F-5A Freedom Fighter flown by General Electric test pilot John M. Fritz, who had organized the event; a Northrop T-38A Talon piloted by Captain Peter C. Hoag, with Joe Cotton in the rear seat; a McDonnell F-4B Phantom II flown by Navy Commander Jerome P. Skyrud with E. J. Black in the back; and a NASA F-104N (N813NA) flown by Joseph A. Walker. A Gates LearJet (likewise GE-powered) flown by H. Clay Lacy carried the photographers.

The rendezvous for the photo-op was completed at 08:45 on a southwesterly heading away from Edwards at 20,000 feet. The Valkyrie was leading – Walker's F-104N was off the right wing; Fritz's F-5 was outboard and to the rear of Walker; Skyrud's F-4 was off the left wing; Hoag's T-38 was outboard and to the rear of Skyrud. The LearJet was positioned about 600 feet left of the formation. After all the airplanes joined up, Clay was having a little trouble staying with the formation in the Lear because White had to go a little higher than intended to get out of the clouds. The XB-70 was flying a left-hand racetrack pattern at about 25,000 feet and 300 knots between Mojave and Barstow. During this time, Cross took the controls for one circuit of the pattern to get a feel for the Valkyrie. As the photo shoot progressed, the photographers asked several times for the formation to close up until all five aircraft were in close proximity. Around 09:00 an Air Force photo aircraft returning from an unrelated mission with a hundred feet of unexpended film asked for and received permission to photograph the formation. At approximately 09:15 the LearJet was queried about additional time since the 30 minutes originally planned had elapsed. The Lear requested another 15 minutes. At 09:26, the photographers were done, and everyone prepared to break formation and return to Edwards.[95]

While the formation was on the final eastbound leg, White and Cross heard a loud thump and somebody began shouting "mid-air … mid-air … mid-air" over the radio. The F-104N's tee-tail had struck the Valkyrie's drooped right wingtip and rolled sharply left, out of control. The Starfighter then flipped upside down and rolled over the Valkyrie inverted, shearing off part of the bomber's right and most of the left vertical stabilizer. Joe Walker was already dead.

As if nothing had happened, the XB-70 flew straight and level for 16 seconds, both of its vertical stabilizers missing. The airplane started to roll slightly, and when White put in a little aileron to correct the roll, it yawed violently to the right. White pulled all three left throttles to idle, and was trying to advance the right-hand throttles to stop the yaw, but the airplane was out of control. The XB-70 rolled rapidly to the right and, during the second rotation, the left wing separated at the manufacturing splice. Cotton was yelling, "Bail out! Bail out! Bail out!"[96]

Al White remembers,

> "At some time during those violent maneuvers, I encapsulated, which was the first step in the bail out procedure. With that demanding call-out from Cotton, I expected that Carl would have done the same. Unfortunately, during all this thrashing around I failed to pull my right arm in when I encapsulated. The capsule door came down and trapped my arm between the door and the bailout handle. The capsule doors were still open and at that point, if I had fired the rocket to eject, I would have lost my arm.[97]
>
> "The airplane settled into a flat spin and the forces became strong and almost constant, pushing us forward and to the side. I was having a hard time trying to keep my feet back against the heel kickers. I recalled seeing Carl's helmet bobbing around, but once encapsulated with my arm blocking the clamshell door of my capsule, I could not talk to him. During the encapsulation process, the control wheel is automatically stowed forward into the panel, so I could no longer reach the mike button. The designers of the capsule had included a system that automatically turned the interphone to the 'hot mike' when the capsule doors were closed, but I had blocked the door open, so that provision was not available to me either. I knew we were in trouble, but there was nothing I could do to help Carl, and I had my own problem.[98]
>
> "The way the system was set up in this prototype, *only* the capsule occupant could actuate the process of bailing out. Each of us was on his own. It was determined during the accident investigation that, for reasons unknown, Carl had never actuated the encapsulation procedure. Unfortunately, he went down with the airplane, and was fatally injured."

An aneroid device that operated automatically at or below 15,500 feet opened the parachute that brought the capsule down. Fortunately, White was below that altitude when he ejected, so the chute opened almost immediately, and the airplane fell away from him. After the chute opened, the capsule was leaning forward, and swaying back and forth. Even though White was strapped in, he felt like he was going to fall out, so he manually closed the doors. About the same time, he heard the terrible "whomp" when A/V-2 impacted the desert a few miles north of Barstow, California, approximately 1 minute and 52 seconds after the initial impact. The capsule had a small window in the upper door, and White noticed that he was descending very rapidly. Before he could think any more about it, he hit the side of a small rise. The impact was so hard that White's heel prints were embedded in the metal floor of the capsule, and the seat partially collapsed.[99]

THE FLIGHT PROGRAM

The Flight Program

Chapter 6 159

THE FLIGHT PROGRAM

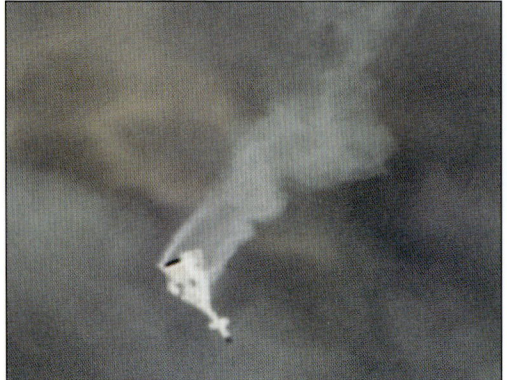

Previous two pages and this page: **A/V-2 accident sequence as photographed from the LearJet.** (AFFTC History Office Collection)

alive." White eventually worked his way out of the capsule, and pulled a jacket out from the back of the seat. This flight had not required wearing pressure suits so White was just wearing a flight suit, helmet, and mask. Even though it was late morning in the summer, White was entering shock and was very cold. He finally managed to stand up, but couldn't get the jacket on, so he pulled the canopy of the parachute around himself to keep warm.[102]

The chase planes scrambled to keep track of the Valkyrie, the one escape capsule, and the pieces of the F-104 so that the rescue teams could find them. A radio broadcast went out, "Attention all stations, this is Edwards Data Control. The XB-70 number 207 has crashed. Emergency condition KILO is established. Crash location is approximately 5 miles Northwest of Barstow. The capsule location is approximately 5 miles North of Lane Mountain." The rescue helicopter arrived about 45 minutes later and transported White to the hospital at Edwards for a checkup. Amazingly, although banged, battered, and bruised, he suffered no broken bones. White returned to flight status just three months later, but he never flew the Valkyrie again.[103]

Carl Cross was not so fortunate. Still in his seat, he impacted the ground with A/V-2 and was killed.

Back at the Flight Research Center, Don Mallick had just landed his F-104N from an aborted chase flight of the X-15 research airplane. Joe Vensel, the NASA chief of operations, assigned Mallick to take a helicopter with flight surgeon Dr. Jim Roman to the crash sites to look for Joe Walker – Mallick was the only helicopter-qualified pilot available. Given the 52 mph speed of the Bell Model 47G, it took a while to get to the area. Mallick and Roman saw the burned remains of the XB-70, and were surprised by how intact the majority of the structure was given the "pancake" landing suffered during the crash. Mallick landed in the small clearing near the XB-70 and was pointed in the general direction of Walker's F-104. After searching for about 5 minutes, Mallick and Roman came across the main wreckage of the F-104 approximately 2.27 miles from the main crash site, but the forward fuselage was missing. A few more minutes of searching yielded the cockpit section with Joe Walker still inside. Doc Roman pronounced Walker dead at the scene, and rescue personnel were notified.[104]

Later, it was calculated that the impact force on the capsule was 44-g, and the impact broke the seat loose from its mounts on the rear capsule wall. Fortunately, breaking that structure attenuated the force on White's body, which was estimated to be about 33-g. White later reported that the impact had "hurt worse than anything I had ever felt. It gave me a severe whiplash, and my whole body hurt. The only things that didn't hurt were my legs."[100]

The capsule had an impact attenuator on the bottom that consisted of a large inflatable bag with blowout patches on the sides. Normally, the bag automatically inflated to cushion the landing shock, but because White had left the airplane with the capsule doors open, the lower door was covering the bag and it did not inflate. There was a manually actuated back-up system to inflate the bag after White shut the doors, but he did not activate it.[101]

After landing, the capsule was lying on its side, and White was trying to kick the doors open. He remembers, "I thought my right arm was really in bad shape because I couldn't move it. Evidently, I was disoriented because the reason I couldn't move my arm was that I was laying on it. I got the doors open far enough to get my head and left arm out just as the T-38 went by. I waved as best I could, and was happy to know that somebody knew where I was, and that I was

The Flight Program

The Investigation

As with any crash, especially a fatal one, the Air Force convened an accident board. There were eight voting members from the Air Force, plus 12 non-voting members, including Don Bellman from the NASA Flight Research Center. Once it had been determined that the accident happened under unusual circumstances (i.e., the photo flight), a "collateral board" was also convened. The accident board was charged with determining the cause of the accident, but not assigning blame (if any existed). The collateral board determined who, if anybody, was responsible for the accident. NASA was not particularly thrilled with this procedure, or with being excluded from voting status on the accident board (it appears that NASA had no representation on the collateral board).[105]

Separately, NASA convened its own inquiry board, mainly to review the role of the F-104 in the accident. The F-104Ns had experienced unexplained pitch transients in flight, although they were rare. NASA began investigating that particular F-104N to see if any anomalies could be found. After reviewing all of the maintenance records and the remains of the flight control system recovered after the accident, nobody could prove there had been anything wrong with the Starfighter.[106]

The Air Force accident board devoted nearly 7,000 man-hours to the investigation and produced over 2,500 pages of testimony and supporting analysis. The board reviewed all of the photographic evidence, data recordings, and witness statements. But Don Bellman was not satisfied with the preliminary explanation of how the accident occurred. Bellman wanted to see the upper surface of the F-104N horizontal stabilizer, which had still not been located. Don Mallick and project engineer Jim Adkins renewed the search for the piece; four days later the pair found the elusive piece a couple of miles from the crash site. On the outer top edge was an imprint of the XB-70's right wingtip navigation light. It appeared that the first part of the F-104N to contact the XB-70 was the top of the horizontal stabilizer, which came up under the right wingtip of the XB-70. Don Bellman began calculating the energy of the wake vortex flow around the B-70 wingtip and found that within about eight feet of the wingtip, the wake vortex was so powerful that it came close to exceeding the control forces available to the F-104N. A computer run at North American validated this conclusion. Once the horizontal stabilizer of the F-104N came up near the bomber, it became "pinned" by the vortex. The F-104N lost its trim and pitched up violently, rolling inverted across the top of the bomber. This data was forwarded to the Air Force accident board.[107]

The findings of the accident board were reported upward through the chain of command to Secretary of the Air Force Harold Brown in early August 1966, and forwarded to Secretary of Defense Robert S. McNamara on 12 August. The final cause of the mid-air was determined to be the inability of Joe Walker in the F-104N to discern that he had gradually closed-in on the XB-70. The accident report noted that "… it is readily apparent that the movement of the F-104 from a position of safe clearance to one of contact was possible through gradual motion without the pilot's awareness … The likelihood is further increased by the fact that at the position of impact of the F-104 horizontal stabilizer with the XB-70 drooped wingtip, the pilot's head was at least 10 ft. below the centerline of the [XB-70] fuselage."[108]

Many books have attempted to relate the accident board findings, and most have also folded in various second-hand accounts or personal opinion. It somehow seems easier to simply reproduce the summary of findings (see Summary Accident Report on the following pages) and let the reader draw their own conclusion.[109]

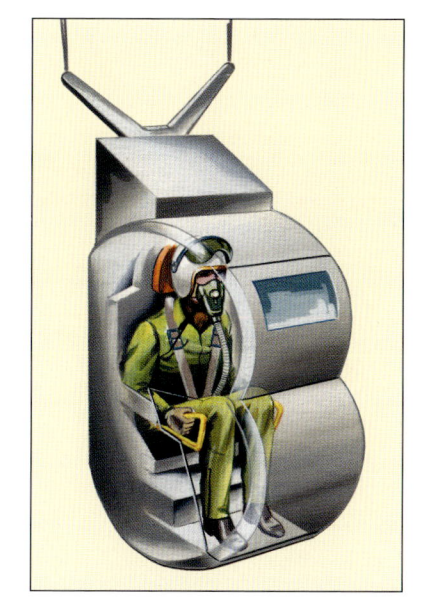

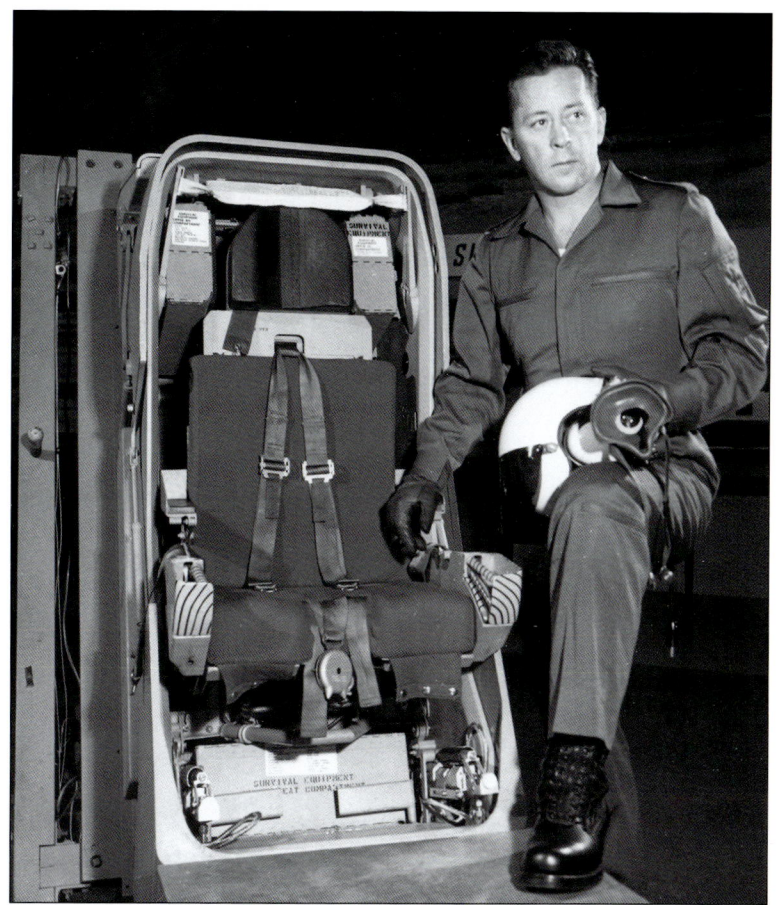

When Al White posed for the photo, he never expected to actually use the capsule to escape from a crippled Valkyrie. (drawing: Jim Tuttle Collection; photo: Gerald H. Balzer Collection)

Chapter 6

Summary Accident Report

All of the pilots in the formation had considerable flying time and had qualified in the particular aircraft involved.

Mr. White, pilot of the XB-70, had logged in excess of 5,900 flying hours as of 8 June 1966 in a variety of aircraft. He has had extensive flight test experience and was fully qualified in the XB-70, having flown the first and some seventy-plus other flights in the two XB-70 aircraft. His total time since 1 July 1965 was approximately 93 hours, a good share of which was in the XB-70.

Major Cross, co-pilot of the XB-70, had flown a total of 8,530 hours. He had gained considerable experience in flight test operations and was experienced in a variety of aircraft, including heavy multi-engine jet aircraft, and was a graduate of the Air Force Test Pilot School. He had undergone ground training on the XB-70 and was, on this flight, having his first familiarization ride in the aircraft preparatory to becoming one of the test pilots in the XB-70 program.

Mr. Walker, pilot of the NASA F-104, had a total of 4,998 hours of flying time. He had extensive background and experience in experimental flight testing, including the X-15 program. His experience included a variety of aircraft, including the F-104 in which he was current and had logged 27 hours and 45 minutes in the 90-day period preceding the accident. Mr. Walker had completed the XB-70 formal ground course having been chosen as the NASA pilot for the continuing XB-70 test program. He had additionally flown as chase pilot on XB-70 test missions on nine occasions, eight of which were flown in an F-104.

Mr. Fritz, pilot of the General Electric F-5, is a former Air Force pilot who had logged considerable flying time as of the date of the accident. He has been a civilian test pilot since 1956.

Commander Skyrud, pilot of the Navy F-4, had logged 4,249 hours flying time. He is also a qualified test pilot having graduated from the Empire Test Pilot School (British).

Colonel Cotton, riding in the T-38, had logged 11,263 flying hours at the time of the accident. Additionally, he is an experimental test pilot of many years' standing, and has flown the XB-70 in the test program numerous times as pilot and co-pilot.

Captain Hoag, pilot of the T-38, had logged 2,452 flying hours, is a graduate of the Aerospace Research Pilots School, and is currently assigned as an experimental test pilot at the Air Force Flight Test Center.

With regard to aircraft condition, the pre-flight mechanical condition of the XB-70 was without discrepancies of significance. Some minor discrepancies were carried on the maintenance records, as is usual with aircraft, but have no relation to the accident which occurred. This is borne out by the XB-70 telemetry analysis of the flight from time of take-off to ground impact.

The pre-flight condition of the F-104 did not exhibit any maintenance deficiencies that would be contributory to the accident occurrence. The NASA system of maintenance follows Air Force practice and uses Air Force type documentation.

The mechanical condition of the XB-70 prior to the collision was determined from the on-board instrumentation with telemetered relay to the ground control. Telemetry was received throughout the flight, including the times immediately prior to and during the collision and until the XB-70 ground impact. For a period of 44 seconds prior to the collision the XB-70 was in essentially straight and level flight. There was no indication of any abnormal condition or operation on any recorded data during this period.

The condition of the F-104 immediately prior to the collision can not be as positively stated as that of the XB-70. Because the airplane was used only for chase and proficiency flying and was not a research vehicle, no on-board instrumentation was available, so that all conclusions must be based on observer reports and the post-accident mechanical analysis of the wreckages. This analysis does not indicate any mechanical failure or malfunction; however, this conclusion must be weighed in light of the severe damage to the aircraft. No indications of impending trouble were noted either visually or aurally by any surviving members of the flight.

In examining the data with respect to the accident, several hypotheses were explored, i.e.:

- Air turbulence causing motion of one of the aircraft.
- Mechanical malfunction in one of the aircraft.
- Physiological problems of one or the other crew.
- Distraction of the F-104 pilot.
- Aerodynamic effects on the F-104 due to airflow near the XB-70.
- Inadvertent movement of the F-104 towards the XB-70 not perceptible to the pilot as a result of the available visual references.

With regard to air turbulence, the XB-70 telemetered traces induced little or no acceleration about any airplane axis, conclusively ruling out any abrupt motion of the XB-70 in pitch, yaw, or roll. The F-5 pilot who was flying in a position close to the F-104 and with the F-104 between his airplane and the XB-70 stated there was no turbulence during this period, nor was it reported by other members of the formation. Since turbulence is not normally confined to an area small enough to affect single aircraft within a flight of five without being felt by any other member of the flight, turbulence can be discounted as a contributory factor in the collision.

As previously discussed, a malfunction in the XB-70 is ruled out. Although the probability of a malfunction of the F-104 being a cause factor is remote, it cannot be eliminated from consideration.

The XB-70 pilot indicated no physiological problem to himself either in testimony or statement. As he was flying the aircraft at impact, physiological problems in the XB-70 crew can be eliminated in cause considerations.

The post-mortem examination of Mr. Walker indicates little or no likelihood of pre-collision coronary problems. Due to the condition of the body, the determination of whether pre-collision dysbarism or hypoxia existed cannot be made with certainty.

No other pilot in the formation noticed any abrupt or unusual movement of the F-104 or Mr. Walker prior to the initial collision. Although this supports to a large extent the possibility that Mr. Walker was not suffering physiological problems, it also is not totally conclusive. Even slight hypoxia, for example, could result in loss of judgment on the part of the pilot and a gradual movement of the F-104 into the XB-70 that might not be sensed by him.

Based on the above analyses, the possibility of physiological problems as the primary cause of the accident is considered remote.

Numerous reasons for the F-104 pilot being distracted can be postulated. One possible reason was a B-58 which was on a sonic boom run and approaching from the opposite direction and above the formation just prior to the collision. This was reported to the flight by radar approach control (RAPCON) approximately 16 seconds prior to collision. Mr. White reported he had the B-58 in sight. Mr. Walker could have diverted his attention from the XB-70 to the B-58, although this is unlikely in the case of a pilot of his experience. Other possibilities for distraction due to occurrences within the cockpit exist but are remote in that an experienced pilot is not likely to divert his attention, except momentarily, from the airplane on which he is flying formation. Also, should he have done this, his head movements and perhaps attendant aircraft movements most likely would have been noticed by the F-5 pilot. In view of the foregoing, it must be concluded that pilot distraction was a possible, but improbable, causative.

The aerodynamic phenomena of a swirling air vortex which emanates from the wing tip and trails behind an aircraft is common to all lifting wing surfaces. The vortex is created by the natural flow at the tip of the wing from the high pressure area below the wing to the low pressure area above the wing. This phenomenon existed with the XB-70; however, analyses indicate that the pressure gradient would not be severe enough to cause loss of control of the F-104, until the latter was within a few feet of the XB-70 wing. Several examples of close chase formation on previous XB-70 flights are apparent in photographic documentation and pilot reports; none of these indicates vortex effects on the chase airplane. The other airflow phenomena of engine wake and underbelly suction could not have affected the F-104 due to its position at the right wing of the XB-70. It can be concluded that airflow effects of the XB-70 on the F-104 did contribute to the collision only after the point was reached where the F-104 tail was so close to the XB-70 that a collision was imminent in any case. Therefore, this must be considered as an indirect contributory factor.

There are no records that would indicate Mr. Walker's recent experience with formation flying of the type involved. Although Mr. Walker had flown the F-104 while chasing the XB-70 on eight previous occasions and a B-58 on another, it is unlikely that he flew in such formation for any extended period during these flights.

The F-5 pilot stated that the F-104 did have a noticeable (but not violent) up and down and fore and aft motion on occasion during the flight. These motions were large enough to cause the F-5 pilot to "work harder" in his formation flying but in his view were not extreme or dangerous. Furthermore, the F-5 pilot was observing the F-104 immediately prior to impact and noticed no sudden motions except after the collision sequence had started. Indications lead to the conclusion that although Mr. Walker's proficiency in close formation could have been less than optimum, it did not result in extreme motions of the F-104 which would account for impact.

A pilot flying formation with his right hand on the control stick and left extended forward to the throttle is almost certain to be looking on a sight line no farther aft than about 30 degrees forward of his left shoulder. Any position of the head farther left than this would be extremely uncomfortable for an extended period of time. This assumption leads to the conclusion that Mr. Walker most likely was holding his position by viewing the XB-70 fuselage someplace between the engine inlets and the nose. In this case, most of the XB-70 wing would have been out of his field of vision. When viewing along this sight line no two separated points on the XB-70 could have been available to Mr. Walker for visually judging alignment. Therefore, a gradual movement of the F-104 either laterally or fore and aft may not have been noticed. The measure of lateral separation must then be based by the pilot on his own judgement of distance from his own position to the points on the fuselage on which he has concentrated. This judgement is degraded with increased distance which in this case would be nearly 70 feet, based on the half-wing span and the leading edge sweep. Viewing the sequence of pictures in the accident analysis from the point of view of the pilot's line of sight to the fuselage, it is readily apparent that the movement of the F-104 from a position of safe clearance to one of contact was possible through gradual motion with the pilot's awareness. The likelihood is further increased by the fact that from the position of impact of the F-104 horizontal stabilizer with the XB-70 drooped wing tip the pilot's head was at least 10 feet below the centerline of the fuselage.

It is concluded that the most probable cause of the accident was that this inadvertent movement of the F-104 caused it to reach a point so near the XB-70 wing tip that contact was inevitable. After initial contact, and in the existing environment, insufficient control existed to separate the aircraft and the process continued to their eventual destruction.

Both the post-mortem examination and the analysis of the collision point to a conclusion that Mr. Walker was most probably killed either when the left vertical stabilizer of the XB-70 severed the F-104 behind the cockpit or subsequently when the forward area of the F-104 struck the left wing of the XB-70. In either case there would have been no opportunity for ejection as the total time from initial impact to the point of contact with the left vertical tail was approximately 2.8 seconds. During the latter part of this period, extreme forces on the pilot were inevitable.

The XB-70 is equipped with an individual escape capsule for each of the two crew members, which can be closed in two manners for completely encapsulated ejection. First, these can be closed manually after the seat is manually moved aft. (Moving the seat aft would be difficult, if not impossible, while under forces directly forward.) The second manner and the one used by the XB-70 pilot is "ballistic" encapsulation. To encapsulate ballistically, the pilot raises either or both armrests and gas pressure from charges moves the seat back and closes the door. When either armrest is raised, a trigger is exposed. Squeezing this trigger completes the ejection sequence. (Should forward forces be greater than the gas pressure could overcome or beyond the limit of the safety burst mechanism, the gas would be lost without seat retraction and escape would be impossible.) After ejection, certain sequences occur automatically, including parachute deployment and pressurization of a gas-filled "attenuation bag" for reducing the landing shock. Emergency handles within the capsule allow operation of some of these post-ejection sequences during descent in case of an automatic sequence failure.

Mr. White reported that he seemed for a period to be unable to move in the capsule due to loads throwing him forward and to the left, even after he heard the call, "Bail out! Bail out! Bail out!" Finally, he pulled the right handle of his escape capsule and encapsulated ballistically. In the excitement and stress of the moment, he failed to keep his right elbow inside the capsule and it became wedged in the door. Mr. White was finally able to free his arm and complete his ejection. (Mr. White had such difficulty on his own part that he could not contact Major Cross or help him physically in any way.) The parachute opened smoothly and since the doors had not fully closed, Mr. White closed them manually. Mr. White had lost the emergency checklist during ejection and, although he was aware that the gas-filled bag for landing shock attenuation was not inflated, he could not recall where the emergency inflation control was. Mr. White sustained minor injury. [When A/V-1 returned to flight after the accident, a decal had been added to each escape capsule identifying the impact attenuator inflation lever, and a light had been added to illuminate the decal.][110]

At the time of the flight, Major Cross had completed ground training for checkout (except for some simulator flying time), including complete coverage of the crew escape system. Although Major Cross did not "grow up" with the system as Mr. White had during its development, there is no reason to believe that he failed to escape due to a lack of understanding its operation. This is most apparent in light of the fact that ballistic encapsulation and ejection requires the two steps of lifting the armrest(s) and squeezing trigger(s) which is common to a majority of Air Force airplanes and therefore completely familiar to a pilot with Major Cross's experience.

Major Cross was not ejected from the crippled XB-70 and apparently died in the crash. The following possibilities were considered in searching for the reason ejection was not accomplished:

- Failure to follow proper ejection procedures.
- Escape system malfunction.
- Forces beyond system capability due to XB-70 motions.
- Major Cross burned or injured during Mr. White's ejection.
- Incapacitation or injury due to violence of XB-70 motion.
- Failure to remove safety pin prior to flight.

Considering the ground training received by Major Cross, his experience in aircraft with ejection seats, and the simplicity of procedures for ballistic encapsulation and ejection (identical to numerous other Air Force ejection systems), the probability of not following procedures as the reason for Major Cross failing to escape is remote.

The materiel analysis of Major Cross' capsule does not indicate any failure in the system. However, the condition of the equipment after impact with the ground makes a positive conclusion impossible. A system failure must therefore be retained as a possible, though reasonably unlikely, cause for failure to eject.

In statement and testimony, Mr. White indicates extreme forces were holding him forward and to the left during the period after loss of control of the XB-70 and until his own ejection was completed. The following three quotes from his statement indicate the severity of these forces:

"For the next few seconds I seemed unable to move in the capsule; the loads being somewhat oscillatory, throwing us forward and to the left."

"During this period of time I tried to talk, thinking that I had a hot mike; but I could only hear myself grunting under the excitement and extreme forces that seemed to be exerted on us and throwing us forward and to the left. While I was trying to free my arm, I did observe Major Cross' head bobbing in the right-hand capsule."

"I was aware that the force was throwing me forward at this time …"

Since it is mandatory for successful completion of ballistic encapsulation and ejection from the XB-70 that the seat be moved to the full aft position, the gas pressure must overcome any forward forces. (Manual encapsulation under these conditions would be extremely difficult, if not impossible.) Capsule analysis indicated that the relief diaphragm which releases the gas overpressure when the seat reaches a full aft position had been ruptured. This could have occurred as the result of gas pressure building to the limit when the system attempted to move the seat back against extreme forward forces. Had the latter occurred, no further opportunity for ballistic encapsulation would have existed. Even though moments of lowered force levels may have allowed successful ejection by one crew member, an unfortunate timing for actuation of the ballistic cycle during this forward force by the other may have resulted in the seat failing to retract precluding further possibility of escape. It should be noted here that the XB-70 remained in a flat spin, which would impose forward forces on the crew, from shortly after loss of control until ground impact.

It is concluded that this was a likely cause for Major Cross' failure to escape.

The possibility that Major Cross was incapacitated due to burns or injury suffered when Mr. White ejected exists since the pilot's capsule was ejected upward by the reaction to downward firing rockets. Since when Mr. White last saw Major Cross, he does not think Major Cross was encapsulated, he would have been burned by the rocket blast or struck by an object propelled by this gas. One static ground test tends to indicate that this effect is not too severe.

Autopsy can neither confirm nor refute this so it must be retained as a possible but improbable reason for failure to escape.

As with the foregoing case, autopsy can neither support nor deny the possibility of incapacitation or injury due to violence of the XB-70 motion. Major Cross was restrained with both a seat belt and shoulder harness. He was wearing protective headgear so that he should have been able to withstand extreme motions and forces without injury. Under the extreme stress of an aircraft in violent maneuvers, pilots have been successful in reaching the ejection handle. Even so, this cannot be entirely discounted as a cause.

Failure to remove the safety pin is not considered a cause as Mr. White observed that Major Cross had removed the safety pin prior to taking the runway for take-off.

THE FLIGHT PROGRAM

The A/V-2 crash site some four miles north-northeast of Barstow, California. Given the utter destruction evident at the site, it is remarkable that some pieces were salvaged and later used on the remaining airplane. (Jim Tuttle and AFFTC History Office Collection)

Al White survived the accident after ejecting in this escape capsule. In the photo at left, the separation rocket motor is in the center, with scorch marks below it, and the unused pressurization cylinder for the impact attenuator is to the left. The center photo shows the attenuator compartment still enclosed in its three support bands. The photo at right shows the open parachute compartment. The small window in the top of the capsule allows the pilot to verify the that parachute functioned correctly. (Jim Tuttle Collection)

The Flight Program

Carl Cross could not eject and perished in the accident. The photo at left is looking in the hatch opening where Cross sat. The center photo shows where the hatch was torn off during the impact with the desert floor. Post-crash analysis showed that Cross had successfully pulled one of the capsule's ejection handles, and that the capsule had apparently tried to initiate the "ballistic encapsulation" mode. The first step in the process was for a gas generator to force the seat backward into the capsule. The seat retractor had blown its relief valve, indicating there was too much forward force (from the aircraft spinning) on the seat for the retractor to succeed. (Jim Tuttle Collection)

The F-104 broke apart when it hit the vertical stabilizer on the XB-70, apparently killing Joe Walker in the process. Very little of the Starfighter remained. (Three above: NASA Dryden Flight Research Center; left: Tony Landis Collection)

The remains of the Valkyrie's left wing. (AFFTC History Office Collection)

166   Valkyrie – North American's Mach 3 Superbomber

In the days before sophisticated computer models, engineers built scale models and made stop-action movies in an attempt to graphically explain what happened. The models were moved into the desired position, a single frame of film exposed, then the models would be moved minutely into a different position. The process continued, painstakingly, until the sequence was complete. Unlike most accidents that take place with very little real-time evidence, this one had photographic and telemetry coverage of the entire sequence of events. The prevailing theory is that Joe Walker inadvertently flew too close to the wingtip of the XB-70 and the vortices around the wingtip were too powerful for the Starfighter to counter – the vortices did not "suck" the F-104 into the bomber as is often reported. These models show the F-104 begin to flip over the XB-70, impacting the top of the right wing, then the right vertical stabilizer. The F-104 probably broke in half at this point, killing Walker. The Starfighter – or at least the fuselage aft of the cockpit – then continued across the Valkyrie impacting the left vertical stabilizer. (Boeing Historical Archives)

THE CONSEQUENCES

At the conclusion of their investigation, the collateral board also reported results to the Secretary of the Air Force and upward to the Secretary of Defense. In addition to the two pilots that perished, others suffered from their roles in organizing, planning, and approving the flight. John Fritz, chief test pilot for General Electric, set the chain of events in motion during early May when he requested permission from North American for the photo shoot. North American initially declined, mostly because the schedule for flight tests of the B-70 was tight and they did not want to interfere with their contractual obligations. Fritz took the request to Joe Cotton, the XB-70 Test Director, who agreed to provide such an opportunity on a non-interference basis after a regularly-scheduled test flight. Cotton believed that General Electric had supported the test program positively and deserved some consideration. However, North American – not knowing Cotton had approved the request – again turned General Electric down, but stated the photo-op could likely be accommodated during the Phase II flight program. Eventually, John S. McCollom, who oversaw the North American contract for the Air Force Systems Command, and Colonel Albert M. Cate, deputy for systems test at Edwards and Cotton's superior, approved the flight. No further approval was sought from higher headquarters.[111]

Cotton made sure a T-38 was scheduled as chase (one normally was), and Fritz requested a Navy F-4 from Point Mugu, which was authorized as a routine training flight. Fritz piloted the F-5A on what was supposed to be a flight to "perform engine airstart evaluations," although these tests were apparently never accomplished. Fritz also tried to arrange for a B-58 to join the formation, but was unsuccessful. Cotton and Fritz asked Walker to provide an F-104, and Walker did so within his authority to schedule NASA chase aircraft.[112]

An Air Force public affairs officer in Los Angeles learned of the photo mission from a commercial photographer two days before the flight. He referred the caller to Colonel James. G. Smith, chief of public affairs at Edwards. Smith had also been unaware of the planned flight, but expressed no concerns once he ascertained that Colonel Cate had approved the mission.

A memorandum from Secretary of the Air Force Harold Brown to Secretary of Defense Robert S. McNamara summarized the formal findings: "the photographic mission would not have occurred if Col. Cotton had refused the General Electric request or at least not caused North American to reconsider its reluctance. It would not have occurred if Col. Cate had taken a more limited view of his own approval authority. It would not have occurred if Col. Smith had advised of the need for higher approval. It would not have occurred if Mr. McCollom had exercised the power he personally possessed to stop the flight. But it did occur."[113]

Secretary Brown went on to state, "these individuals acted in ignorance of prescribed procedures, rather than with intent to violate them." Subsequently, Cate was relieved of command, and Cotton and Smith received formal letters of reprimand. John McCollum was also reprimanded. The Air Force made numerous administrative changes to ensure such flights would not occur in the future without a thorough review.[114]

In addition to the human lives, there was monetary cost associated with the accident. The Air Force listed the total cost of the loss of A/V-2 as $219.5 million, including $209.3 for the airframe, $7.2 million for the six J93s, $1.0 million for various electronics and sensors, and an additional $2.0 million for the NASA-installed instrumentation systems for SST research. NASA calculated the cost of the F-104N as $1,133,053, including $759,929 for the airframe, $161,788 for the J79, $8,570 for an engine kit, and $202,766 for the MH-97 autopilot.[115]

Sonic Booms

A sonic boom is the audible component of the air shocks caused by the aircraft flying faster than the speed of sound. As an object moves through the air it creates a series of pressure waves in front and behind it, similar to the bow and stern waves created by a boat. These waves travel at the speed of sound, and as the speed of the aircraft increases, the waves are forced together because they cannot get out of the way of each other, eventually merging into a single shock wave at the speed of sound.[116]

In normal flight, the shock wave starts at the nose of the aircraft and ends at the tail. There is a sudden rise in pressure at the nose, decreasing steadily to a negative pressure at the tail, where it suddenly returns to normal. This overpressure profile is known as the N-wave due to its shape. The magnitude of the shock wave is dependent on the amount of air that is being sped up, and thus the size and weight of the aircraft. Interestingly, as the vehicle increases speed, the shocks grow tighter around the aircraft and do not become much louder. The length of the boom from front to back is dependent on the length of the aircraft (by a factor of 3:2 not 1:1) and longer aircraft spread out their booms more than smaller ones, leading to a less powerful shock wave hitting the ground.

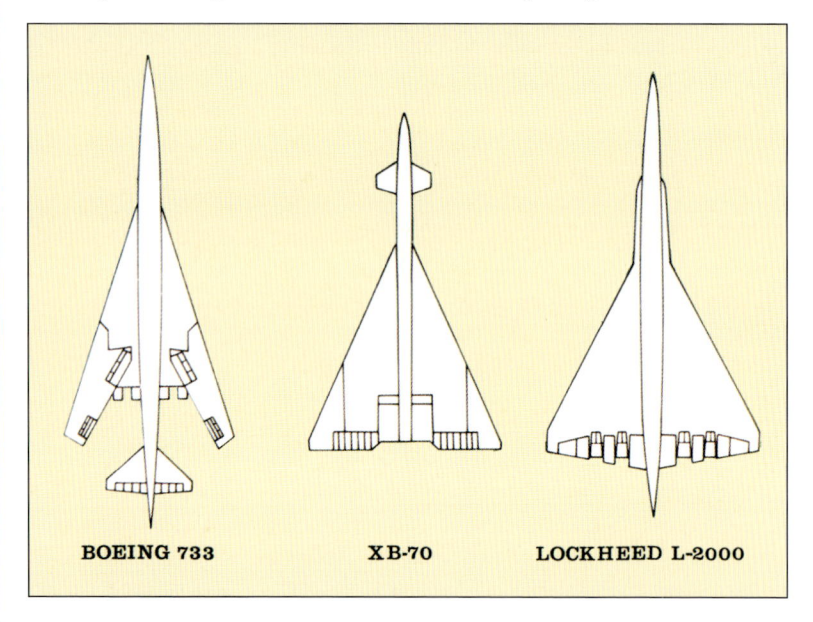

The XB-70 was approximately the same size as the proposed supersonic transports, but weighed considerably more (military systems and fuel being heavier than passengers) – 500,000 pounds versus a predicted weight of about 300,000 pounds for the SSTs. The XB-70 was also considerably faster and longer-ranged, but this had no impact on the testing since the bomber could simply fly the Mach 2.7 profiles expected of the airliner. Unfortunately, the structural materials used in the XB-70 were not what either Boeing or Lockheed proposed to use in the SST, so the Valkyrie was not terribly useful for evaluating that aspect of the upcoming passenger aircraft. (NASA)

Smaller shock waves also form at other points on the aircraft, primarily any convex points or curves such as the wing-fuselage intersection. After travelling some distance these smaller shock waves blend together with the main shocks to create a much more defined N-wave shape, which maximizes both the magnitude and the rise time of the shock, making it seem louder. On most designs the blending distance is about 40,000 feet, meaning that below this altitude the sonic boom will seem softer since all of the shock waves have not converged. However, cruising at supersonic speeds below 40,000 feet is not fuel-efficient and generally places an unacceptable thermal burden on the aircraft.

When sustained supersonic flight became a reality around 1950, its accompanying sonic boom was somewhat unexpected. Aerodynamicists knew about the shock waves associated with supersonic motion, but they did not expect these shock waves to reach the ground. Nevertheless, people heard the booms and wondered what they were. As military aircraft increased the number of supersonic missions over populated areas, there were growing numbers of complaints and damage claims.[117]

In June 1961 a joint committee comprised of the Department of Defense (DoD), National Aeronautics and Space Administration (NASA), and Federal Aviation Administration (FAA) released the Commercial Supersonic Aircraft Report. Also known as the SST Bluebook, the group reported that the development of a commercial supersonic transport was technically feasible, but that a major research and development program would be required to solve many problems associated with such a venture. Sonic booms were one of the major problems and it became essential to understand the level of sonic boom exposures that might be acceptable to the public. The Air Force had data associated with complaints and claims received during 10 years of supersonic operations, but could not correlate what aircraft type or flight condition was associated with each claim. More research was clearly needed.[118]

Several tests were conducted to assess community reaction to measured sonic booms including over St. Louis from November 1961 through January 1962. Subsequent testing was conducted over Edwards AFB in 1963, in Oklahoma City in 1964, and in Chicago during 1965. The areas were exposed to overpressures up to 3 pounds per square foot, and the measured signatures generally matched the predictions. It was found that for a particular boom, exposures inside buildings were lower in intensity, existed for a longer period of time, and were more complex than those outside. Generally, the sonic booms experienced inside structures were less acceptable than those experienced outside – most likely because of the rattling of items and the vibration of the structure. Researchers concluded that there was no one level of overpressure below which acceptance was assured and decided that further testing was necessary.[119]

In response, researchers embarked on a major sonic boom test program at Edwards AFB in an effort to accurately forecast psychological reaction and structural damage associated with overpressures from supersonic transports. The National Sonic Boom Program (NSBP) was set up by the President's Office of Science and

A/V-2 was used for some SST research, including the first two flights of the National Sonic Boom Program, before the aircraft was lost in the 8 June 1966 mid-air collision. (AFFTC History Office Collection)

Technology, and consisted of three principal participants: the Air Force, NASA, and Stanford Research Institute. At its inception, the Air Force and NASA equally funded the program. As with most joint research programs of the era, the Air Force managed the effort and NASA provided technical direction – it was largely the same arrangement that had been used successfully on the X-1 and X-15 research airplane programs.

Initially, the effort used aircraft such as the Lockheed F-104, North American X-15, and Convair B-58 Hustler. But none of these were large enough to provide a meaningful comparison to the proposed SSTs, leading to a desire to use the B-70. Eventually the concept of flying higher to avoid the overpressure wave was proven false, and the XB-70 generated large booms from altitudes of 70,000 feet. This research eventually led to the characterization of the N-wave and Seebass-George subsequently defined a figure-of-merit (FM) to characterize the sonic boom levels of difference aircraft. The FM calculation is the aircraft weight divided by the three-halves of the aircraft length. The lower this value, the less boom the aircraft generates. Using this calculation, the figures of merit for the Concorde was about 1.41 and the theoretic value for the proposed Boeing 2707 was 1.9 (the XB-70, which was designed with no forethought about sonic booms, had a 2.2 figure of merit). Researchers predicted the FM would need to drop below 1.0 to be acceptable, and this eventually doomed most SST projects as public resentment, somewhat blown out of proportion, mixed with politics and eventually resulted in laws that made any such aircraft impractical (flying only over water for instance).[120]

Of course, there were other areas of study important to the supersonic transport besides sonic booms. To support Boeing and Lockheed in their development effort, the NASA Flight Research Center (FRC-now the Dryden Flight Research Center) had several SST studies underway during the early 1960s. Several aircraft in the FRC fleet were actively involved in SST flight tests: a Douglas F5D-1 was used for landing studies, a North American F-100C was modified to simulate SST handling qualities, a North American A-5A was used to simulate an SST for tests of the air traffic control system, and a Lockheed JetStar was modified as an in-flight SST simulator.

NASA first proposed using the XB-70 for SST research in a memo on 3 May 1962. Following initial meetings during 1962 between NASA Administrator James Webb and Secretary of Defense Robert McNamara, NASA funded a program to install instrumentation on the two XB-70 prototypes in support of the SST program. After President John F. Kennedy authorized the development of an American SST in June 1963, NASA proposed that the original plan be revised to expedite the acquisition of data to support the contractor studies. This revision was discussed at meetings of the Tri-Agency [Air Force, FAA, and NASA] Flight Test Planning Group on 23 October and 15 November 1963. The Aeronautics and Astronautics Coordinating Board (AACB) subsequently approved the plan on 9 January 1964. The AACB acknowledged that gathering data in support of the SST was "of sufficient importance to warrant special effort" during the XB-70 test program.[121]

It should be noted that using the B-70 for these tests was not universally supported. Much depended on which community you represented. The air inlet researchers wanted to use a Lockheed YF-12A since its three-dimensional, one-engine-per-inlet configuration more

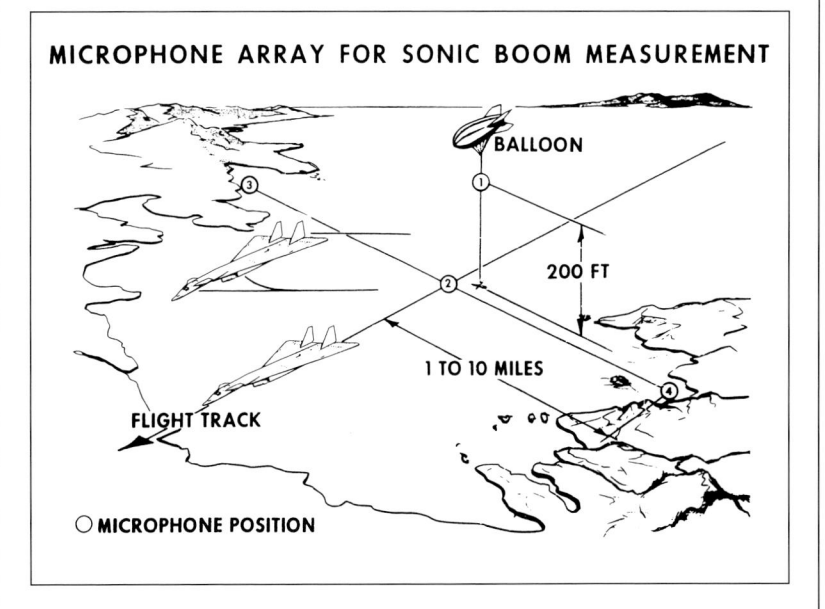

A variety of aircraft were used in the sonic boom tests over the High Desert, but the XB-70 was the major player given its size and weight was closest to the proposed SST. The few tests with the X-15 research airplane – mainly to gather baseline data on a hypersonic aircraft – were less than successful since the pilot of the X-15 could seldom fly precisely enough to directly overfly the microphone arrays. The B-58 and Blackbirds contributed significantly since they were fast aircraft that were routinely flown at Edwards anyway. (NASA)

The Flight Program

closely resembled the anticipated SST configurations. The engine researchers also favored using a Blackbird for much the same reason, but they understood that the YF-12s were not instrumented for thrust measuring (partially because of cost, but largely because of security concerns) whereas the XB-70 was. The airframe researchers were even more torn, wanting to see how a large aircraft performed, but being more interested in the construction methods used on the Blackbirds. There were also those who thought the B-58 was a good compromise, even if it was almost a Mach number slower than the expected SST.[122]

One of the problems, despite the perceived importance of SST research, was that the XB-70s were only scheduled to fly for a maximum of 180 hours. This did not provide enough time to meet even the basic Air Force requirements for testing a prototype aircraft, which would have required 420 flight hours and exceeded the $1,500 million total program cost directed by the Pentagon. Careful planning and coordination between the Air Force, FAA, and NASA resulted in a program that stayed within the planned budget and provided the maximum amount of useful information for each party. For their part, NASA reviewed the instrumentation provided by the Air Force and North American, and supplemented it where necessary to meet FAA and NASA research requirements. Even at this early date it was planned to make sonic boom tests, and NASA noted that no onboard instrumentation was required, but that NASA would provide a "ground instrumentation complex" to measure the overpressures.[123]

The XB-70 seemed to be a perfect platform for sonic boom research since it was the only very-large aircraft capable of flying the Mach 2.7 profiles expected of the new SSTs. Although overpressures of equal peak magnitudes could be obtained with F-104s and B-58s, the duration of the boom itself varied with each aircraft due the shape of the shock waves and the weight of the aircraft. Actually, as it turned out, the XB-70 was a bit too heavy. Ideally, SST researchers wanted an airplane with a gross weight of about 300,000 pounds to produce the sonic booms since this was what the contractors were predicting for the SST. Joe Cotton objected to using the XB-70 at this weight since it left the airplane "somewhat low on fuel" for landing. The researchers indicated they could accept weights up to 315,000 pounds, but Cotton later decided that 317,000 pounds was as low as he could authorize. This gave the XB-70 approximately 50,000 pounds of fuel after the sonic boom runs, allowing an early gear extension and two low approaches prior to landing. Given there was no alternative, the researchers agreed.[124]

It had been decided to use A/V-2 for the SST research mainly since A/V-1 was procedurally limited to Mach 2.5 because of its continual skin-peeling problems. The second airplane also was a bit easier to fly due to the dihedral on the wings and the automated inlet control system. The NASA research flights were to begin in mid-June 1966, once

The first XB-70 poses proudly on the ramp at Edwards during the Armed Forces Day in May 1965. (Robert Cooper)

A/V-1 after the addition of the NASA stripe on the vertical stabilizer. Traditionally, when military aircraft are bailed to NASA, they retain their normal military markings. This gives an excellent view of the underside of the airplane. (Mike Machat Collection)

the North American Aviation Phase I tests were completed, and Joe Walker was selected as the project pilot. While A/V-2 was finishing up its contractor tests, NASA began installing a sophisticated set of instrumentation in the aircraft – hundreds of transducers were mounted throughout the structure with recording equipment located in the forward weapons bay. Although this equipment would provide some data in support of the sonic boom program, most of it was intended to gather more data on high-speed flight in general.

Some 250 sonic boom tests were planned, mostly at overpressures of 1.5 to 3.0 pounds per square foot, but some would reach 4.0 psf. The 250 tests did not equal that many flights since multiple test points could be obtained during a single hour-long flight. The proposed 300,000 pound SST, cruising at Mach 2.7 at 65,000 feet, was expected to generate an overpressure of 2.0 psf. The first flight dedicated to the NSBP was on 6 June 1966 when A/V-2 reached Mach 3.05 at 72,000 feet and recording devices on the ground monitored the overpressure and acoustic signatures. The second NSBP test was on 8 June, but ended in the mid-air collision that destroyed A/V-2, throwing the program into limbo.

Initially, the Air Force and NASA had doubts that the Mach 2.5 speed limitation on A/V-1 would allow the aircraft to conduct meaningful research since the both Boeing 2707 and Lockheed L-2000 SSTs were envisioned as Mach 2.7 aircraft. However, the first XB-70 was undergoing maintenance and modifications at the time of the accident and the ground crew had spent a considerable amount of time checking the skin and repairing any damaged honeycomb they found – they felt they had eliminated the skin-peeling problem. After further consideration, the government felt that given the short duration of the sonic boom tests, even if the problem had not been completely eliminated there was little concern that major chunks of skin would peel off. The Air Force, NASA, and North American decided that once testing of the rudder bob-weight confirmed it provided adequate stability during an inlet unstart, the Mach 2.5 speed limit on A/V-1 would be raised to at least Mach 2.6, and perhaps a bit higher. This would allow

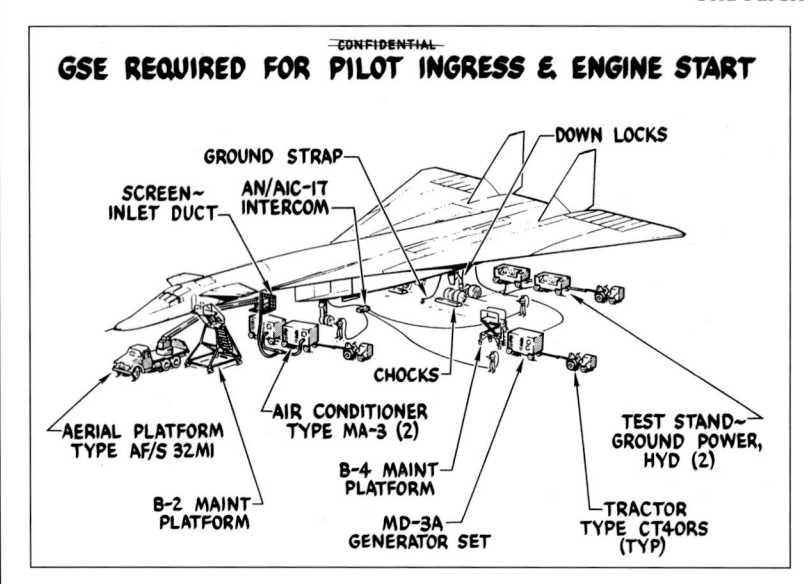

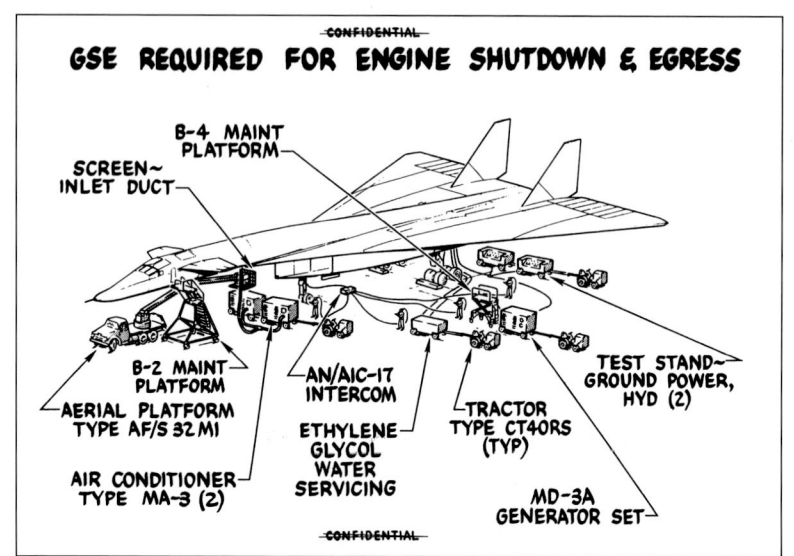

A set of drawings showing the ground support equipment (GSE) usually required for the XB-70 at the beginning and end of each mission. Since the aircraft were only flown at Edwards, the equipment varied based on what was available at the test facility, but this gives a good general idea. What is missing here are the JP-6 fuel tankers and nitrogen trucks that were used to fuel and defuel the airplane. (U.S. Air Force)

meaningful data to be collected for the SST program. By 13 June the various agencies involved had concluded, "that every major goal of the program can be realized through some updating and modification of the #1 aircraft." Interestingly, there was an urgency to the decision, not for research reasons, but because the contracts with North American and General Electric were set to expire on 15 June and needed to be extended if the program was to continue.[125]

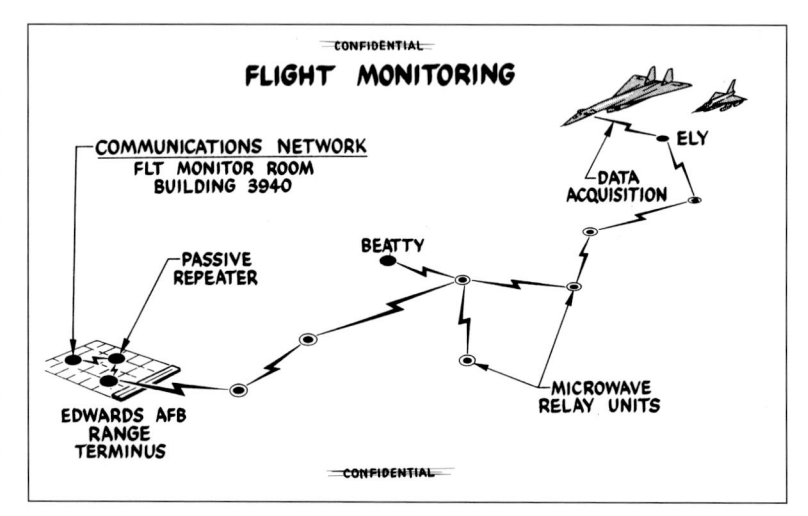

The X-15 was the first research airplane at Edwards that flew further than the local radar and communications could cover, so the Air Force and NASA built the High Range that consisted of radar and telemetry stations at Beatty and Ely, Nevada, as well as equipment at Edwards. Since the B-70 flew over much of the same area, it also used the resources of the High Range. (U.S. Air Force)

After it was decided to use A/V-1 for the sonic boom program, numerous modifications were made to the airplane. Most major was the replacement of eight wing fold hinges with improved models that were salvaged from the wreck of A/V-2, refurbished, tested, and installed on A/V-1. Transducers and recording equipment – some of it also salvaged from A/V-2 – were installed to support the program. The modifications added 5,310 pounds to the empty weight of the airplane. The most urgent problem was the fact that one of the main landing gear bogie beams on A/V-1 had been removed to replace a damaged unit on A/V-2. North American was in the process of repairing the damaged unit from A/V-2, but there was a great deal of concern over whether the repairs would be adequate. Testing up to a gross weight of 561,000 pounds was successful, but doubts persisted and a new bogie beam was subsequently fabricated.[126]

The ninth and final XB-70 flight of the NSBP was on 17 January 1967. Scientists saw little point in continuing the program since the XB-70 flights had already provided sufficient data about large aircraft overpressures. It was found that booms were affected by many factors – temperature inversions, Mach number at altitude fluctuations, unparallel shock waves, and variations in aircraft weight, size, and shape.[127]

NASA Takes Over

As part of the post-accident investigation, Colonel J. C. Holbrook from the Aeronautical Systems Division, conducted a review between 15 and 18 August 1966 to determine if any changes needed to be made to the escape capsules, given the injuries to Al White and death of Carl Cross. The report contained three principal recommendations; shorten the shoulder harnesses; expand the capsule training course; and install dual seat and foot retractors before high-risk flights resumed. A variety of other changes were also recommended. Although Holbrook had recommended the changes be made immediately, higher headquarters decided on 23 September 1966 to hold off on the changes pending a decision on how the entire B-70 flight program would be shaped in the future. This non-decision was reaffirmed on 11 January 1967.[128]

Initially, NASA agreed with the escape capsule modifications, but after more review began to question the usefulness of them. Both Joe Cotton and Fitz Fulton believed that the shortened shoulder harnesses were overly restrictive and recommended against installing them. Cotton and Fulton, however, agreed that other changes needed to be made, including the installation of dual seat retractors (to move the seat aft in preparation for encapsulation), eliminating the electric throttle control and replacing it with an emergency descent control, and deleting various survival items in order to save weight. This last item was especially critical since adding the dual seat retractors put the capsule over is certified weight limit, and five parachute tests during 1967 at an increased weight all failed. Eventually, the liferaft was eliminated from the survival gear, along with some food and other supplies, and the pilots all agreed to keep their individual weights below 190 pounds (13 pounds below the 95-percentile male). Very few of these changes had been made when A/V-1 resumed flying in support of the NSBP, and it appears that some of the changes were only incorporated for the last few flights of the program.[129]

The B-70 flight program was divided into two phases. The first phase began with the maiden flight on 21 September 1964 until the end of North American flight-worthiness demonstrations on 15 June 1966. The Air Force fully funded the Phase I tests, with the exception of unique instrumentation provided by NASA, as part of contract AF33(657)-12535, to which North American assigned the NA-281 internal tracking number. The second phase of the program began on 16 June 1966, with the first flight occurring on 3 November 1966. The Phase II program included the nine flights of the NSBP, plus two additional flights on 25 and 31 January 1967. The Air Force and NASA jointly funded Phase II of the flight program under a Memorandum of Understanding signed on 28 May 1965. Originally, using both aircraft during the Phase II test program was expected to cost each agency (Air Force and NASA) $5.18 million per quarter each. The revised one airplane program would cost between $3.2 and $3.6 million per quarter each. Phase II was covered by contract AF33(657)-15871 with North American using the NA-303 account.[130]

On 31 January 1967 the Air Force announced that the entire XB-70 program would be transferred to NASA as soon as possible. Although NASA would be responsible for all funding after that date, the Air Force agreed to provide $5 million in FY67 for safety-of-flight modifications and other contingencies. NASA had $5,713,000 left of the $12 million originally appropriated for Phase II tests, and those would cover the flight program for the remainder of 1967. NASA awarded contract NAS4-1175 to North American to support the effort and requested an additional $10 million for 1968; the company used NA-303 to represent the effort. Although the Air Force had been spending approximately $2 million per month, NASA was negotiating with the contractors to allow the program to continue for $800,000 per month; $600,000 for North American and $200,000 for General Electric.[131]

The Memorandum of Understanding that transferred the responsibility to NASA was similar to ones that had previously governed the X-15 and other research programs. The MoU transferred full control to NASA on 25 March, and the program was expected to finish at the

Ever wonder what the black lines on various parts of the XB-70 were? They were reference marks to let the chase pilots know when they were in the correct position. The photo above was taken from exactly where a chase plane was supposed to be. (Dryden History Office)

Here the chase location is six feet too high. Notice how the markings on the vertical stabilizers do not line up. (Dryden History Office)

Here the chase location is six feet too far forward. There is a small black marking on the trailing edge of the canard that should line up with the lines on the fuselage, but does not. (Dryden History Office)

THE FLIGHT PROGRAM

A/V-1 did not change much in appearance after the loss of A/V-2, mainly the intakes were again painted white and discrete NASA markings were added. The airplane also gained a significantly better instrumentation system to enable it do conduct the SST research that had been planned for its sister ship before the mid-air collision. (NASA Dryden Flight Research Center)

end of 1968. The remaining aircraft (A/V-1), all engines, and support equipment would be provided to NASA at no charge, which is normal for inter-government transfers. The Air Force would continue to provide a TB-58A for chase and proficiency flights, although the MoU indicated the airplane would not be replaced if it was lost or damaged during the program. Everything would be returned to the Air Force when the program terminated. The MoU stated, "If the aircraft [A/V-1], while in the custody and under the control of NASA, is damaged beyond economical repair, NASA shall not be required to reimburse the Air Force for the aircraft." Interestingly, although

During December 1967 NASA measured engine noise on the XB-70 using an array of microphones around the rear of the airplane. Note the black smoke from the six J93s whenever they were throttled. (Boeing via the Terry Panopalis Collection)

174 VALKYRIE – NORTH AMERICAN'S MACH 3 SUPERBOMBER

things like a multi-million-dollar aircraft and engines were provided at no cost, the MoU specifically indicated that "long distance telephone toll calls" would be charged to NASA.[132]

Between January and April 1967, additional instrumentation designed to measure structural responses to gusts, stability and control, boundary layer noise, and SST simulation was installed. These included wing rakes on the right wing for measuring the boundary layer, microphones in the lower nose section for measuring boundary layer noise, instruments to measure gusts and dynamic response of the airframe, and additional performance instrumentation. FRC director Paul Bikle and Air Force Flight Test Center (AFFTC) commander Major General Hugh Manson created a joint FRC/AFFTC XB-70 Operating Committee on 15 March 1967. The first NASA XB-70 flight occurred on 25 April 1967 with Fulton and Cotton at the controls.[133]

Not all of the excitement during the Phase II program involved the XB-70. As was usual procedure, a TB-58A (55-0662) flew as chase for a XB-70 flight on 2 November 1967. Joe Cotton and Ted Sturmthal were in A/V-1 and Fitz Fulton and Don Mallick were in the TB-58A. Since the TB-58A could not keep up with the XB-70 once it accelerated past Mach 2, the chase plane generally set up a holding pattern in the center of the XB-70 ground track so that it could respond to a problem anywhere it might occur. On this day, unexpectedly, the TB-58A was running low on fuel when it picked up the Valkyrie coming home over Las Vegas. Fulton asked Cotton if the TB-58A could land first after they verified the XB-70 landing gear had come down successfully; although the procedure was unusual, Cotton agreed that it was prudent.[134]

Unfortunately, as Fulton made a nice, smooth landing at Edwards, the crew heard a "pop," although the TB-58A felt fine. As they approached the end of Runway 04, Fulton and Mallick heard the tower radio the Valkyrie to go around. Fulton radioed "zero-zero-one [XB-70], we are clearing the runway shortly and you should be able to land behind us." Edwards Tower immediately responded, "No, zero-zero-one, go around. The B-58 is on fire." This was news to Fulton and Mallick; the tower had not bothered to inform the TB-58A crew that their aircraft had flames coming out of the No. 3 engine. Fulton advised Mallick and the crew chief in the third seat to prepare to abandon the airplane once it stopped. All three crewmembers successfully escaped, and the Air Force crash team managed to get the fire out before it caused major damage to the Hustler. As it turned out, the engine fire and the low-fuel condition were related; a fuel filter clamp had come loose and allowed fuel to leak into the No. 3 nacelle.[135]

Don Mallick got his first chance to fly the XB-70 from the left seat on 13 February 1968; he had already flown four missions in the right seat with Joe Cotton as pilot-in-command. Mallick soon learned the intricacies of taxiing the Valkyrie. The XB-70 was not happy on the ground. As they had since the beginning, the brakes chattered and were mostly ineffectual at low speeds. The nosewheel steering did not provide sufficient torque to turn the aircraft at low speeds and high gross weights. This made it exciting coming out of the parking area since the pilots had to use a significant amount of engine thrust to overcome the inertia of the parked aircraft and then

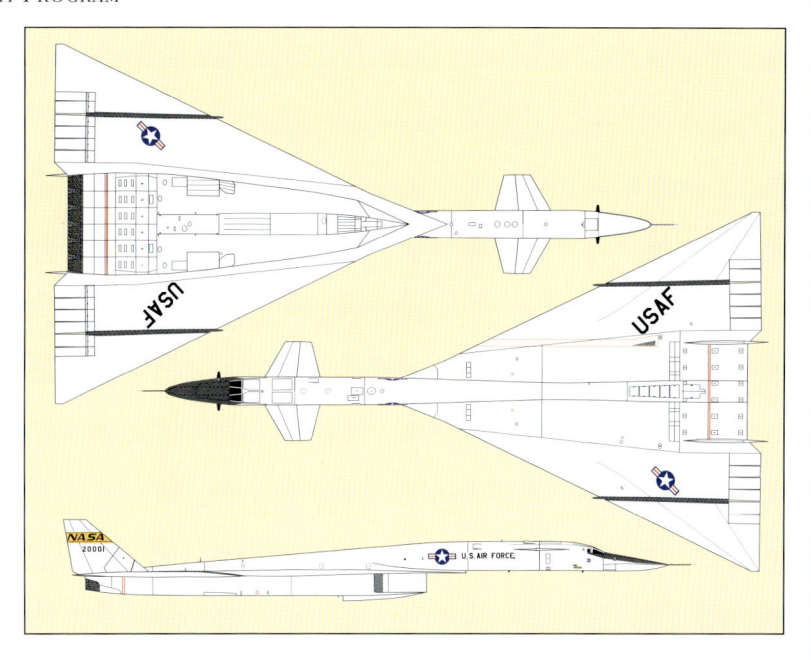

The final markings worn by A/V-1 just before the airplane was retired to the Air Force Museum. Note the rake experiment on the upper wing surface and the ILAF vanes on the forward fuselage. (Art by Tony Landis)

left the power on until a relatively high-speed taxi was attained. Since the aircraft did not have a taxi-speed indicator, the pilots had to rely on radio contact with the ground-support vehicles to maintain a taxi speed between 20 and 25 mph. Slowing down as they approached the runway also proved exciting given the reluctance of the brakes to stop the 500,000-pound airplane.[136]

Lining up on the runway was similar to trying to find the right spot on the taxiways. The pilots had to let the long neck of the air-

Getting into or out of the XB-70 required some help given the height of the entrance door. (SSgt Robert Hoffman)

The Flight Program

Besides supporting the SST program, NASA conducted other research using the XB-70. Here a set of rake probes has been installed on the wing and fuselage to measure the boundary layer pressure. The outline area was done in red and masks a 'No Step' zone for the tubing running across the upper surface of the wing going to the probe. The photos were taken on 16 March 1967. (NASA Dryden Flight Research Center)

plane run past the runway, then turn and try to line up on the centerline. Fortunately, the Edwards runways were wide enough that it was not essential to hit the mark exactly, but pilots being pilots, they always tried. Once the XB-70 was at the end of the runway, the pilots completed the pre-takeoff checklist. Then they advanced the throttles to minimum afterburner on all six engines, released the brakes, and pushed the throttles to full afterburner. Even with almost 180,000-lbf available, the acceleration of the 500,000-pound airplane was leisurely at first. As speed increased to 80 knots or so, the long neck of the Valkyrie began accentuating the roughness of the runway. When 175 knots appeared on the indicator, the pilot pulled back on the yoke and the nose slowly came up. As the B-70 accelerated to 215 knots, the cockpit was about 40 feet above the ground, but the main wheels were still firmly in contact with the runway. Another few knots and the aircraft came off the ground, and the pilots had to make sure to get the gear up before 250 knots.[137]

During a maintenance period that lasted from February through May 1968, A/V-1 was fitted with two small vanes on the extreme

The forward weapons bay of both XB-70s carried an instrumentation package and its associated data recorders and telemetry equipment. The package was installed much like a weapon would have been – suspended from racks – and was easily raised and lowered when needed. The weapons bay doors could not be opened in flight. The photo at left shows the package in A/V-1, probably in 1964 or 1965. The July 1967 photo at right shows the updated equipment installed by NASA. (Left: Boeing Historical Archives; right: NASA Dryden Flight Research Center)

176   VALKYRIE – NORTH AMERICAN'S MACH 3 SUPERBOMBER

forward fuselage as part of the Identically Located Acceleration and Force (ILAF) experiment. This "modal control system" was installed specifically to evaluate its performance potential for the SST over a wide range of operating conditions. Specifically, NASA wanted to determine its ability to improve the "ride qualities" by reducing the acceleration response of the airplane, and also to determine its effectiveness in reducing gust loads. The vanes rotated through an arc of 12 degrees at a rate of up to 8 cycles per second to induce a structural vibration in the XB-70 at a known frequency and amplitude. Accelerometers detected air disturbances and signaled the stability augmentation system to damp out the motion. Some of the pilots were not sure the system would work as planned, but when XB-70 research flights resumed on 11 June 1968 the ILAF proved its ability to reduce the effects of turbulence and atmospheric temperature changes. A similar system was tested on a YF-12A and subsequently installed on the Rockwell International B-1s.[138]

> ## TOTAL COST OF THE B-70 PROGRAM
>
> When it was all said and done, the Air Force had spent $1,477.1 million on the B-70 program, slightly below the $1,500 ceiling placed on the program. These expenditures, by research and development (R&D) and operations and maintenance (O&M) were broken down as (in millions):[139]
>
> | | FY55-61 | FY62 | FY63 | FY64 | FY65 | FY66 | FY67 | FY68 |
> |---|---|---|---|---|---|---|---|---|
> | R&D | 800.00 | 220.30 | 206.80 | 135.78 | 4.02 | 0 | 0 | 0 |
> | O&M | 0 | 0 | 0 | 20.02 | 52.98 | 32.20 | 5.00 | 0 |
>
> In addition, NASA spent $24.32 million on the B-70 program, broken down as (in millions):[140]
>
> | | FY63 | FY64 | FY65 | FY66 | FY67 | FY68 |
> |---|---|---|---|---|---|---|
> | R&D | 0.75 | 0.95 | 0.62 | 0 | 0 | 0 |
> | O&M | 0 | 0 | 0 | 8.00 | 4.0 | 10.0 |

The Identically Located Acceleration and Force (ILAF) experiment added two small vanes to the forward fuselage just below the movable windshield ramp. The last 10 flights of the airplane were made with these installed, although they were subsequently removed at the Air force Museum after the airplane was retired. Each of the vanes could move through an arc of 12 degrees up to 8 times per second. The experiment proved fairly successful at reducing the effects of turbulence and air density. (NASA Dryden Flight Research Center)

THE FLIGHT PROGRAM

There was a lot of high-speed research going on at Edwards during the 1960s, and North American was responsible for much of it. In the photo below, the XB-70-1 and X-15A-2 pose together on 4 August 1967. The rocket-powered X-15 was more than twice as fast as the Valkyrie, but was much smaller and could only fly for a few minutes at a time. The X-15 was carried to altitude and launched by one of the NB-52s operated as motherships. It seemed natural that North American would propose – unsuccessfully – using one of the XB-70s as a follow-on carrier aircraft. (Upper left: Boeing Historical Archives; left: Art by Erik Simonsen; above: Art by Tony Landis; below: NASA Dryden Flight Research Center)

178   VALKYRIE – NORTH AMERICAN'S MACH 3 SUPERBOMBER

The Flight Program

By the end of 1968 the NASA flight program had accomplished the majority of its research goals. The XB-70 was going to require major maintenance in the near future, including a resealing of the fuel tanks – something that had always been expected at 180 flight hours. The XB-70 was also an expensive aircraft to fly and maintain. The Flight Research Center was struggling for funds and several flight programs were competing for what little money there was. A decision was made to terminate the XB-70 flight program at the end of 1968; the X-15 program would be allowed to "expire" at the same time. Thus ended an exciting era. Initially it was thought that the XB-70 would be placed in flyable storage at Edwards pending possible future use by the SST program, but in the end it was decided that the airplane should make one last flight to the Air Force Museum.

A bottom view with the wingtips full-down as the XB-70 prepares to accelerate. (NASA Dryden Flight Research Center)

Vapor trails stream off A/V-1 on 24 August 1967 with Fitz Fulton and Don Mallick at the controls. (AFFTC History Office Collection)

The XB-70 on the lakebed at Edwards, possibly after the first NASA flight on 25 April 1967. (NASA Headquarters)

Retirement

The final XB-70 flight was originally scheduled for 22 January 1969 but was delayed for maintenance reasons. It ultimately took place on 4 February 1969 when Fitz Fulton and Ted Sturmthal made a 3-hour and 17-minute subsonic structural dynamics test flight to Wright-Patterson AFB, Ohio. The 1,880-mile flight was made at Mach 0.92 and 33,000 feet. Fitz Fulton made a single pass over the runway before bringing the XB-70 down for a perfect landing, marking the conclusion of its 83rd flight and the end of the B-70 program. Fulton turned the logbook over to the Air Force Museum's curator and the aircraft became part of the museum's permanent collection.

The first XB-70 made 83 flights totaling 160 hours and 16 minutes, while the second XB-70 logged 46 flights in its brief life, totaling 92 hours and 22 minutes.[141]

On 26 February 1969, the Air Force Chief of Staff sent a telex to the Air Force Museum with directions on displaying the Valkyrie. "The XB-70 now assigned to the AF Museum for public display has both normal USAF aircraft insignia markings and the NASA yellow stripes on the vertical stabilizers. The addition of the NASA insignia during the joint USAF/NASA research flight test program was in accordance with normal practice and was appropriate at the time. Since the aircraft was developed and funded by the Air Force as the B-70 bomber and the Air Force retains ownership, it is now appropriate to restore this aircraft to its original marking configuration as it was before the joint research flight test program. All NASA markings should be completely removed or painted over to avoid confusion by the public." The telex went on to say that "This message should not be misinterpreted to preclude giving NASA full recognition for their many contributions in the fields of supersonic aircraft research or their participation in the joint USAF/NASA XB-70 research program." The exciter vanes were removed at the same time the NASA markings were painted over.[142]

After her arrival at Wright-Patterson, the Valkyrie sat outside at the old museum complex, until she was towed to the new museum with the rest of the collection in October 1970. The airplane sat outside the front entrance of the new complex until the modern flight gallery was constructed, providing an enclosed space for several years. In 2003 the airplane was taken out of the modern flight gallery and towed to the museum annex next to the presidential aircraft exhibit. It currently sits in this hangar along with most of the museum's X-planes, waiting to be moved into the new Cold War Hangar at the main museum complex.[143]

A/V-1's last landing. (Jim Tuttle Collection)

Being deserviced after arrival at Wright-Patterson AFB, Ohio. (Terry Panopalis Collection)

On display at the old museum. Note the NASA markings and ILAF vanes have been removed. (Museum of Flight Collection)

The next bomber design after the B-70 was the B-1. Here, A/V-1 poses with the fourth B-1A at the museum in December 1987. (David Menard)

The Flight Program

Above and below left: *When the new museum opened, the aircraft had to be towed along public roads to the facility.* (Jeannette Remak Collection)

The Valkyrie on display in front of the new museum. It would remain here until the modern flight exhibit opened. (Jeannette Remak Collection)

The XB-70, along with most of the other X-planes, is currently housed in the annex next to the presidential aircraft display on the other side of the field from the main museum. There are plans to move the Valkyrie into the new Cold War Hangar at some point in the future. (Tom Tullis)

Chapter 6   181

Chapter 7

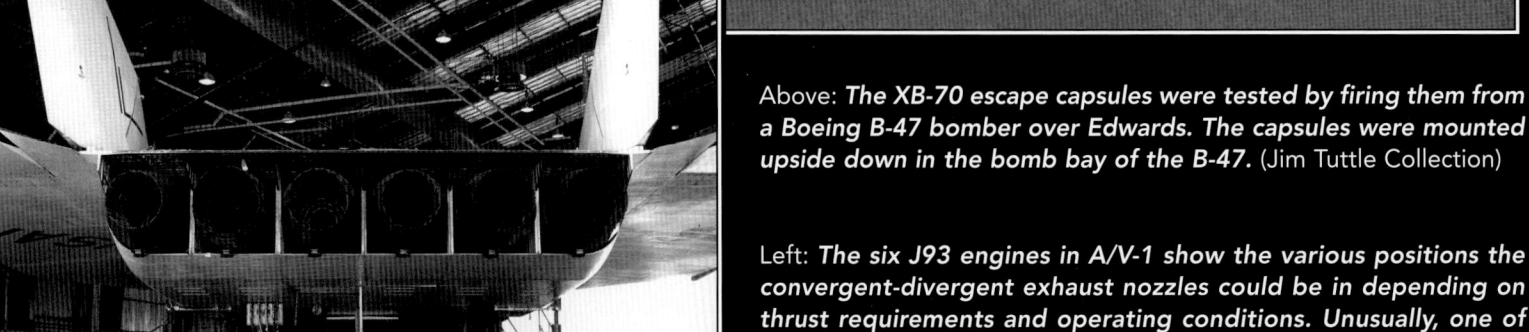

Above: *The XB-70 escape capsules were tested by firing them from a Boeing B-47 bomber over Edwards. The capsules were mounted upside down in the bomb bay of the B-47.* (Jim Tuttle Collection)

Left: *The six J93 engines in A/V-1 show the various positions the convergent-divergent exhaust nozzles could be in depending on thrust requirements and operating conditions. Unusually, one of the main gear doors is open, probably indicating a landing gear test was underway when the photo was taken.* (NASA Dryden Flight Research Center)

1960s STATE-OF-THE-ART
Construction and Systems

As built, the two XB-70As were two-seat high-performance demonstrators, not truly prototype bombardment aircraft. For the most part, the following description applies to the as-built configuration; the differences between the two air vehicles are noted as appropriate. Where they are known, the details of any possible production bomber are also included.

The XB-70 had truly remarkable performance possibilities; the maximum design speed exceeded Mach 3 at altitudes up to 85,000 feet.[1] The maximum taxi weight was 542,000 pounds and the maximum takeoff weight was 535,000 pounds. Maximum landing weight was 524,000 pounds. However, after a main landing gear bogie was repaired on A/V-1, the maximum weights for that aircraft were reduced to 520,000 pounds. It should be noted that the structure had to be designed for much higher loads; the maneuvering flight conditions of the aircraft, coupled with its expected gross weight, produced total airloads in excess of 1,000,000 pounds.[2]

The third air vehicle would have been more representative of the weight projected for the operational vehicles.[3]

Maximum Taxi Weight	542,029 pounds
Maximum Takeoff Weight	542,029 pounds
Maximum Design Landing Weight	524,209 pounds
Normal Design Landing Weight	296,292 pounds
Structural Jacking Weight	240,412 pounds
Structural Jacking Weight (no engines)	207,303 pounds

Fuselage

The XB-70 was characterized by a long forward fuselage neck, with a canard located just aft of the flight deck. At touchdown, the pilot was 30 to 40 feet above the ground and 110 feet ahead of the main landing gear. Given that the delta-wing XB-70 touched down decidedly nose-up (as do all deltas), instead of the level profile used by the B-52, it would have required some major adjustments by operational pilots.[4]

The forward fuselage consisted of three major sections: the nose, crew compartment, and the electronics equipment bay. The unpressurized nose section was essentially empty in the two XB-70s, but would have housed the radar antennas and the stellar inertial platform on production aircraft. The basic structure of the nose section was conventional 6Al-4V titanium alloy sheet metal skins supported by 4Al-3Mo-1V titanium sheet metal frames and machined longerons. The 6Al-4V alloy was chosen because it was tear resistant and could easily sustain multiple pressure cycles. The large nose radome that would have housed the attack and navigation radar antennas was manufactured from laminated Vibran glass-reinforced polyester. The upper portion of the nose contained a large, movable, PH15-7Mo honeycomb windshield ramp and a movable windshield assembly.[5]

The intermediate fuselage consisted of PH15-7Mo steel brazed honeycomb panels used to form the outer moldline skin, the duct walls, the frames, and bulkheads. Large tubular truss members made from PH15-t and H-11 supported the moldline panels over the boundary-layer control ducts and the engine air intake ducts. The forward section of the intermediate fuselage distributed the concentrated longeron loads from the forward fuselage into the honeycomb panels, redistributed the loads from one circular shell to the lower fuselage

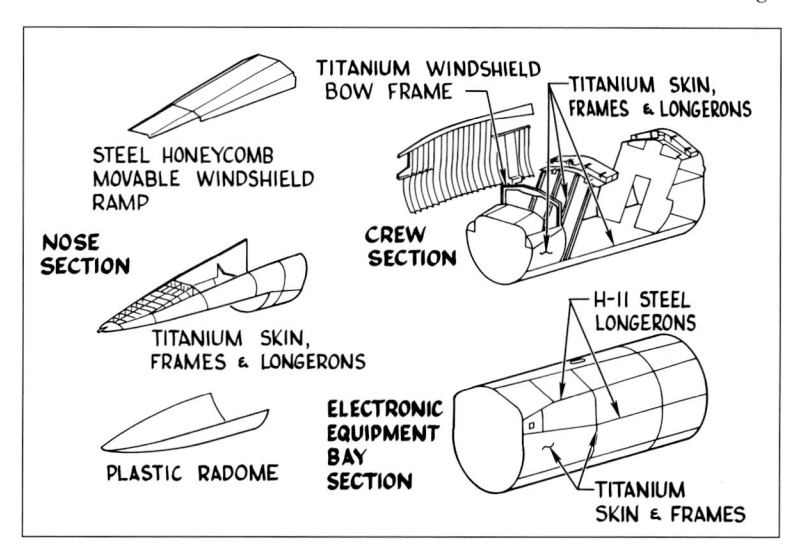

Assembly breakdown of the forward fuselage. (U.S. Air Force)

1960s State-of-the-Art

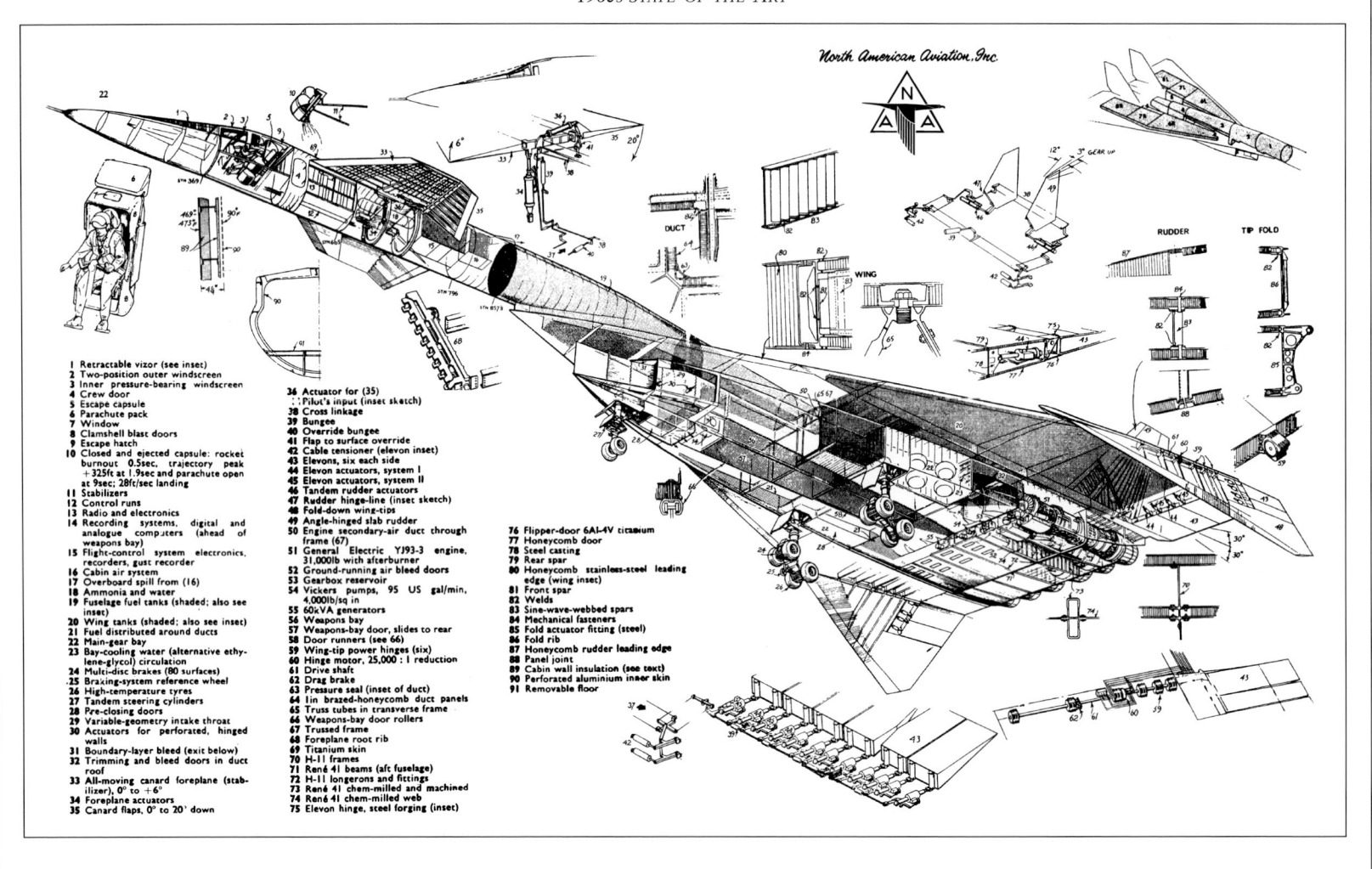

1. Retractable visor (see inset)
2. Two-position outer windscreen
3. Inner pressure-bearing windscreen
4. Crew door
5. Escape capsule
6. Parachute pack
7. Window
8. Clamshell blast doors
9. Escape hatch
10. Closed and ejected capsule: rocket burnout 0.5sec, trajectory peak +325ft at 1.9sec and parachute open at 9sec; 28ft/sec landing
11. Stabilizers
12. Control runs
13. Radio and electronics
14. Recording systems, digital and analogue computers (ahead of weapons bay)
15. Flight-control system electronics, recorders, gust recorder
16. Cabin air system
17. Overboard spill from (16)
18. Ammonia and water
19. Fuselage fuel tanks (shaded; also see inset)
20. Wing tanks (shaded; also see inset)
21. Fuel distributed around ducts
22. Main-gear bay
23. Bay-cooling water (alternative ethylene-glycol) circulation
24. Multi-disc brakes (80 surfaces)
25. Braking-system reference wheel
26. High-temperature tyres
27. Tandem steering cylinders
28. Pre-closing doors
29. Variable-geometry intake throat
30. Actuators for perforated, hinged walls
31. Boundary-layer bleed (exit below)
32. Trimming and bleed doors in duct roof
33. All-moving canard foreplane (stabilizer), 0° to +6°
34. Foreplane actuators
35. Canard flaps, 0° to 20° down
36. Actuator for (35)
37. Pilot's input (inset sketch)
38. Cross linkage
39. Bungee
40. Override bungee
41. Flap to surface override
42. Cable tensioner (elevon inset)
43. Elevons, six each side
44. Elevon actuators, system I
45. Elevon actuators, system II
46. Tandem rudder actuators
47. Rudder hinge-line (inset sketch)
48. Fold-down wing-tips
49. Angle-hinged slab rudder
50. Engine secondary-air duct through frame (67)
51. General Electric YJ93-3 engine, 31,000lb with afterburner
52. Ground-running air bleed doors
53. Gearbox reservoir
54. Vickers pumps, 95 US gal/min, 4,000lb/sq in
55. 60kVA generators
56. Weapons bay
57. Weapons-bay door, slides to rear
58. Door runners (see 66)
59. Wing-tip power hinges (six)
60. Hinge motor, 25,000 : 1 reduction
61. Drive shaft
62. Drag brake
63. Pressure seal (inset of duct)
64. 1in brazed-honeycomb duct panels
65. Truss tubes in transverse frame
66. Weapons-bay door rollers
67. Trussed frame
68. Foreplane root rib
69. Titanium skin
70. H-11 frames
71. René 41 beams (aft fuselage)
72. H-11 longerons and fittings
73. René 41 chem-milled and machined
74. René 41 chem-milled web
75. Elevon hinge, steel forging (inset)
76. Flipper-door 6Al-4V titanium
77. Honeycomb door
78. Steel casting
79. Rear spar
80. Honeycomb stainless-steel leading edge (wing inset)
81. Front spar
82. Welds
83. Sine-wave-webbed spars
84. Mechanical fasteners
85. Fold actuator fitting (steel)
86. Fold rib
87. Honeycomb rudder leading edge
88. Panel joint
89. Cabin wall insulation (see text)
90. Perforated aluminium inner skin
91. Removable floor

An excellent cutaway drawing of the XB-70 showing most of the major systems and structure. The origin of the drawing is uncertain, but it appears to be accurate for the airplane as-built. (Provided courtesy of Jim Tuttle Collection)

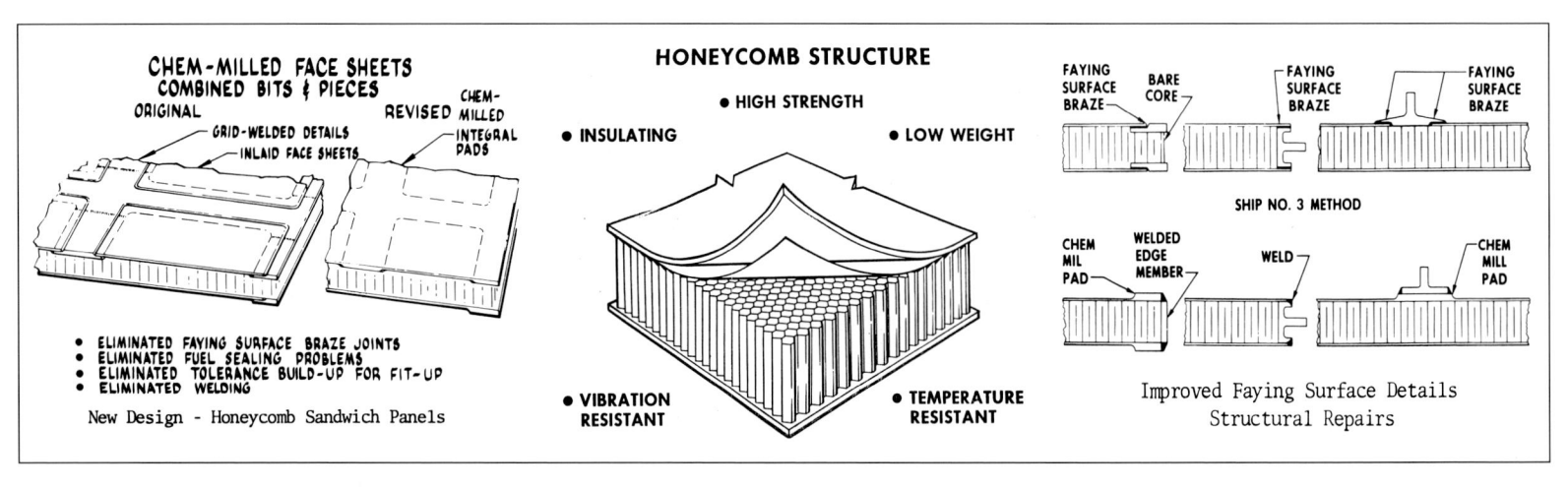

The honeycomb skin was an interesting concept that worked very well once the initial bugs were worked out of the manufacturing process. But it was very labor intensive to manufacture, and even more so to repair. Still, with practice, North American was certain they could make it comparable with other materials. It had the advantages of being heat resistant, relatively light, and a good thermal insulator. (Randy Cannon Collection)

1960s STATE-OF-THE-ART

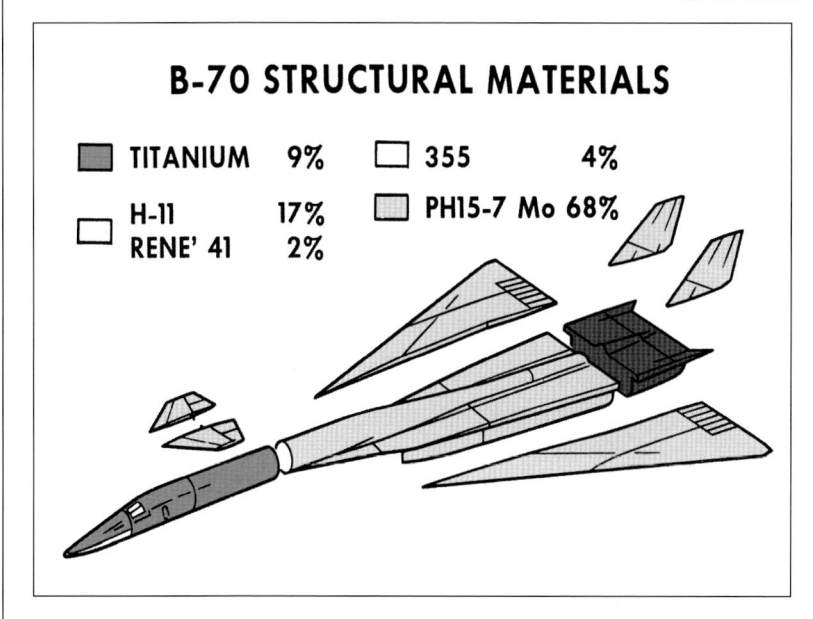

B-70 STRUCTURAL MATERIALS

- TITANIUM 9%
- 355 4%
- H-11 17%
- PH15-7 Mo 68%
- RENE' 41 2%

Materials and construction used in the upper and lower intermediate fuselage. (U.S. Air Force)

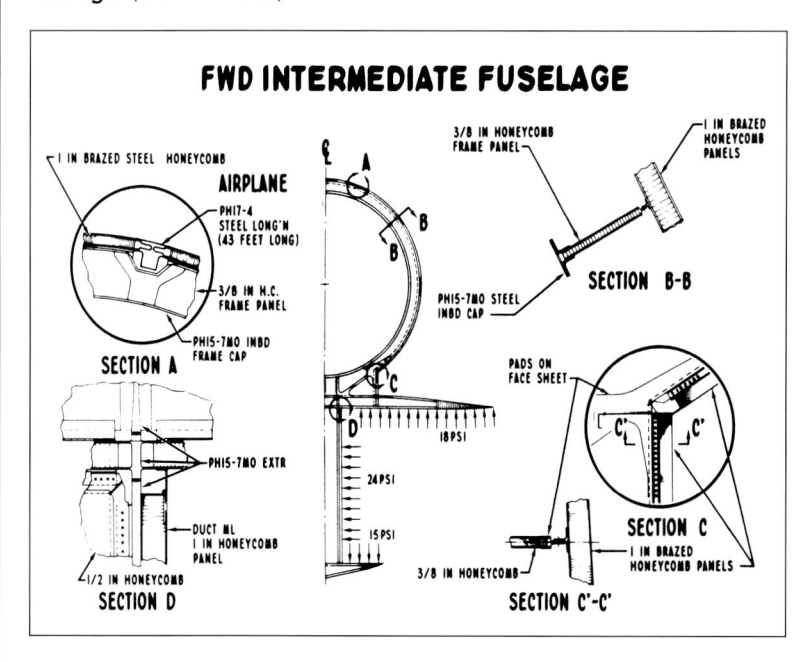

The typical construction technique used for the forward intermediate fuselage. (Randy Cannon Collection)

structure, supported the fuel in the upper forward tanks, and provided the ramps for the engine air intake ducts. The aft section of the intermediate fuselage provided the attachment to the wing structure and served as the carry-through structure for the wing. It also supported the fuel in the aft fuel tanks and distributed the landing gear loads.[6]

The aft fuselage was a conventional structure consisting of H-11 steel (often called "tool steel") frames and longerons, a René-41 internal structure, and titanium skins. The primary loads were imposed by the wing and vertical stabilizers, and consequently were in the cross-ship direction. The frame caps were made from H-11 steel due to the intensity of the axial loads and the high temperature from the engines. For maximum sheer efficiency, the frame webs were made from 4Al-3Mo-1V chem-milled titanium sheet. An integrally machined H-11 steel fitting was used to transmit the loads from the PH15-7Mo steel honeycomb wing skins to the side fuselage frames. The lower fuselage frames were fabricated as a single-piece H-11 steel "I-beam" section because of the high stresses resulting from their restricted depth.[7]

The wing stub structure was a PH15-7Mo steel honeycomb sandwich supported by transverse vertical webs. H-11 steel "Jo-Bolts" attached the cover skins to the fuselage frames. The aft fuselage used 4Al-3Mo-1V and 6Al-4V titanium skins because of their high strength-to-weight ratios at high temperatures. These skins were attached using conventional A286 rivets. The engine divider beams were made from chem-milled René-41 webs supported by vertical René-41 hat sections placed back to back. These parts were subjected to a maximum temperature of 1,100 degrees Fahrenheit due to engine heating, necessitating the use of heat resistant materials.[8]

Cockpit

The crew compartment contained the ejection hatches and the crew entrance door; all were made from titanium sheet metal elements with H-11 attachment fittings.[9]

The pilot and copilot sat side-by-side in individual escape capsules. A/V-3 and operational aircraft would have had offensive and defensive systems operators sitting behind the two pilots. The XB-70s used Type B capsules that were six inches wider than the Type A capsules originally developed for the F-108. This allowed the pilots to wear David Clark Company A/P22S-6 full-pressure suits if needed (usually for flights above 40,000 feet during the test program). Although the extra width undoubtedly helped, tests conducted after the loss of A/V-2 showed that "use of pressure suits compromises the chances of successful escape" and "tests … using B-70 pilots wearing pressure suits showed that encapsulation with an inflated suit is extremely difficult." The escape capsules were fabricated from bonded aluminum honeycomb panels and weighed nearly 1,000 pounds, including the crewmember and all equipment. Each escape capsule had a self-contained oxygen and pressurization system, affording complete crew protection during and following ejection. The capsules could also be closed, if necessary, for crew protection during an in-flight emergency, particularly one that involved the decompression of the crew compartment. Limited control of the aircraft and engines (throttle down only) was possible from inside the closed capsules that had a window that allowed the pilot to see the instrument panel. When the capsules were closed, the crew microphones went "hot" to provide continuous communication. The capsules provided meaningful escape from zero to 90,000 feet and 100 to 2,100 mph. In recognition of the planned low-level interdiction role for the B-70, the capsules could be used up to speeds of Mach 0.95 at altitudes as low as 200 feet.[10]

CREW COMPARTMENT (typical)
CAPSULES NOT SHOWN

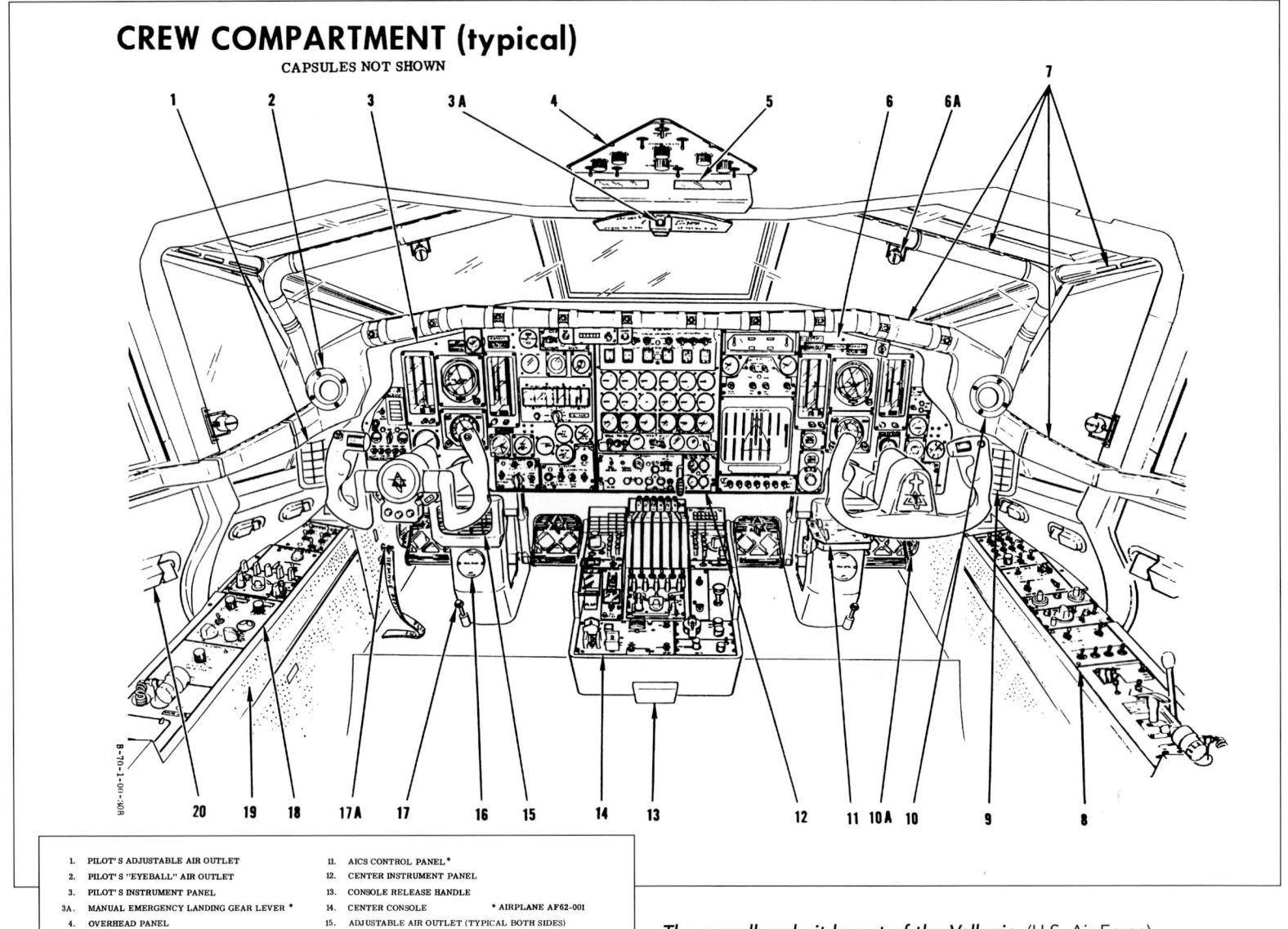

1. PILOT'S ADJUSTABLE AIR OUTLET
2. PILOT'S "EYEBALL" AIR OUTLET
3. PILOT'S INSTRUMENT PANEL
3A. MANUAL EMERGENCY LANDING GEAR LEVER *
4. OVERHEAD PANEL
5. OVERHEAD PANEL FLOODLIGHTS
6. COPILOT'S INSTRUMENT PANEL
6A. DEFOGGING SYSTEM THERMAL SWITCH (TYPICAL)
7. FIXED AIR OUTLETS (TYPICAL)
8. COPILOT'S CONSOLE
9. COPILOT'S ADJUSTABLE AIR OUTLET
10. COPILOT'S "EYEBALL" AIR OUTLET
10A. FIXED AIR OUTLET (TYPICAL BOTH SIDES)
11. AICS CONTROL PANEL *
12. CENTER INSTRUMENT PANEL
13. CONSOLE RELEASE HANDLE
14. CENTER CONSOLE   * AIRPLANE AF62-001
15. ADJUSTABLE AIR OUTLET (TYPICAL BOTH SIDES)
16. RUDDER PEDAL ADJUSTMENT KNOB (TYPICAL BOTH SIDES)
17. CONTROL COLUMN RELEASE PEDAL (TYPICAL BOTH SIDES)
17A. GROUND ESCAPE HATCH INITIATOR MAINTENANCE SAFETY PIN
18. PILOT'S CONSOLE
19. AIR RECIRCULATION TRANSPIRATION WALL (TYPICAL)
20. CONSOLE FLOODLIGHT (TYPICAL)

The overall cockpit layout of the Valkyrie. (U.S. Air Force)

The encapsulation and ejection cycles were controlled by handgrips within the capsules. Interestingly, on the two prototypes, each crewman had to initiate his own ejection – there was no master-command capability. Raising the handgrips automatically encapsulated the crewman, while squeezing a trigger within the handgrip jettisoned the escape hatch and ejected the capsule. A rocket catapult propelled the capsule from the aircraft and clear of the vertical stabilizers, while stabilization booms deployed to prevent the capsule from tumbling. As the capsule descended, barometrically controlled actuators deployed the recovery parachute. As the capsule descended below 15,000 feet, an impact attenuator – essentially a large inflatable bag on the bottom of the capsule with patches designed to blow out during landing – was initially inflated as soon as the parachutes opened by one of the more than 30 pyrotechnic devices located on each capsule. The extended stabilization booms provided the capsule with a self-righting characteristic in the event of water landing, and the capsule was watertight and could float for prolonged periods if necessary. An Air Force volunteer actually survived 72 hours afloat in a Type A F-108 capsule during January 1960.[11]

Survival equipment was provided in four separate kits in each capsule, mounted on the upper left and right walls, and under the capsule floor. The equipment consisted of cold weather clothing, a life raft, sustenance gear, signaling equipment, first aid kit, and rations.

Al White remembers, "These capsules had so much equipment in them that, jokingly, people were asking where the pillows and blan-

1960s State-of-the-Art

The escape capsule open with the seat in the normal flight position (left) and closed with the seat retracted to the back of the capsule. This is a Type B capsule, which was six inches wider than the original Type A capsule designed for the F-108. Note the two windows – the upper one allowed the pilot to view the instrument panel while still in the aircraft, while the lower one let him observe the ground during descent. A third window was located directly above his head so he could verify the parachute had deployed. (Boeing Historical Archives)

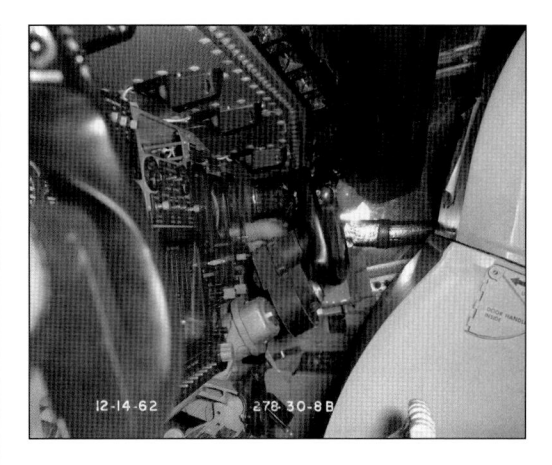

This photo shows the minimal clearance between a closed escape capsule and the instrument panel. When the pilot encapsulated, retractors automatically pulled the control yoke forward and out of the way at the same time as the pilot's feet were pulled back against the seat and the seat was retracted rearward into the capsule. Initially, a single gas generator retracted the seat, but it could fail due to excessive maneuvering of the airplane. After the loss of A/V-2 and death of Carl Cross, a second gas generator was added, giving the pilot two chances to encapsulate. (Boeing Historical Archives)

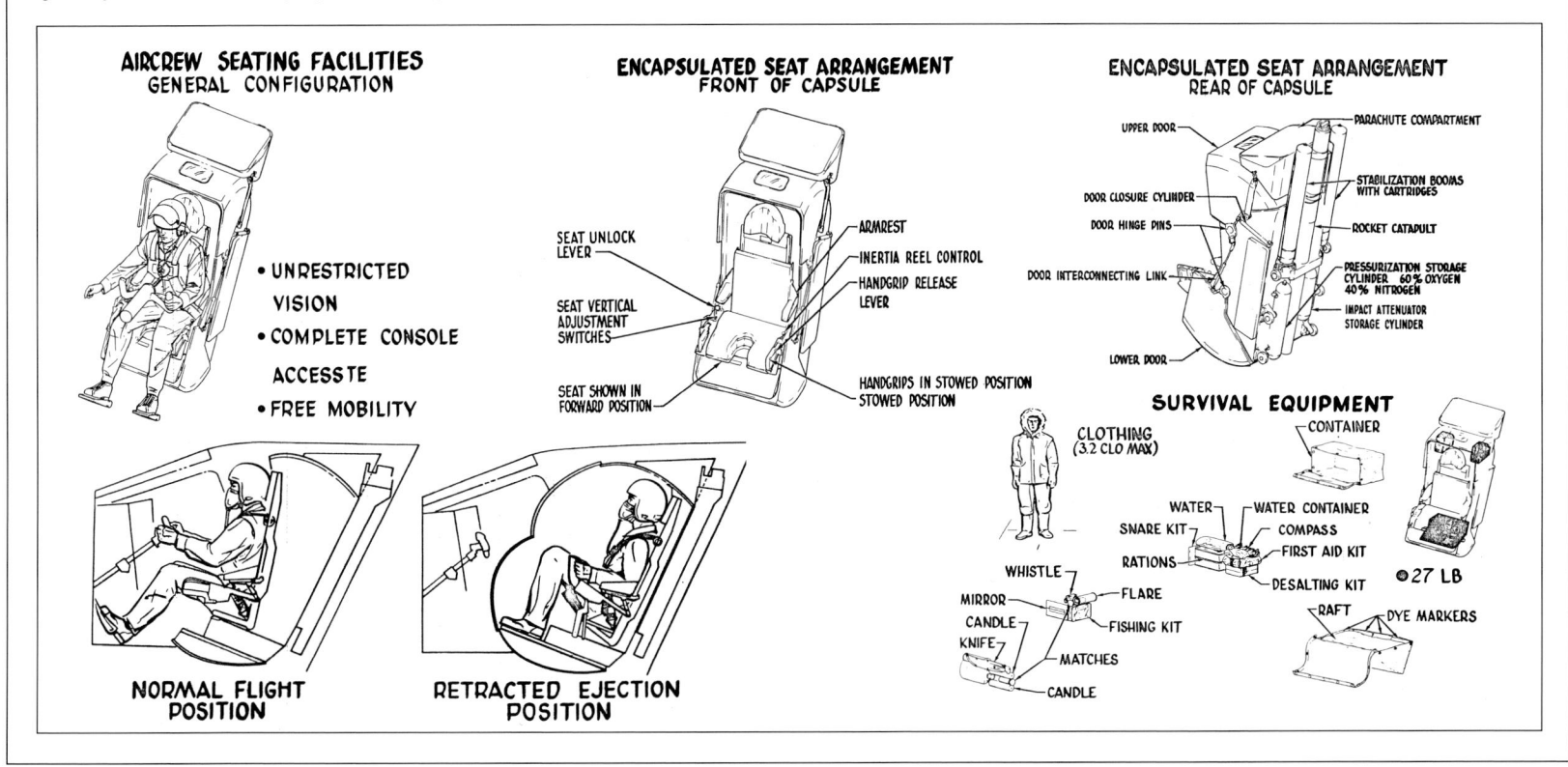

Chapter 7

187

1960s State-of-the-Art

Cut and paste collage showing a capsule test from a B-47 over the Edwards range. In both the B-47 and B-58 tests the capsule was mounted upside down and fired using its rocket motor so that the entire system could be tested. Note that the stabilization booms deploy as soon as the capsule clears its surroundings. (Boeing Historical Archives)

Higher speed ejection tests were conducted from a specially-configured pod under a Convair B-58 Hustler. (Boeing Historical Archives)

Al White poses with an early capsule. The capsule was extensively tested during its development. (Gerald H. Balzer Collection)

The capsule was fitted with nitrogen-inflated flotation bags and would float almost indefinitely if needed. (Jim Tuttle Collection)

The first capsule drop ended when the parachute deployed as expected and the capsule made a soft landing. (Boeing Historical Archives)

The F-108 and B-70 escape capsules were tested from the back of stationary trucks (above and right) and also from mockups of the forward fuselage traveling at high speeds on rocket sleds (left). (Boeing Historical Archives)

1960s State-of-the-Art

GROUND AND LABORATORY TESTS

- CARTRIDGE BREADBOARD AND OPERATIONAL CHECKS
- STATIC STRUCTURAL TESTS
- PRESSURE CHAMBER
  DUMMY, SIMIAN, HUMAN
  18 TESTS
  MAX ALT 100,000 FT
- FLOTATION TESTS
- IMPACT
  DUMMY, HUMAN, LAND, WATER
  17 TESTS
- EJECTION FROM CABIN SECTION
  ONE TEST

Two photos of the capsule being loaded into the modified pod under the B-58 at Edwards. The charts show the number and types of testing accomplished on the capsules prior to the first flight of the XB-70. (Boeing Historical Archives)

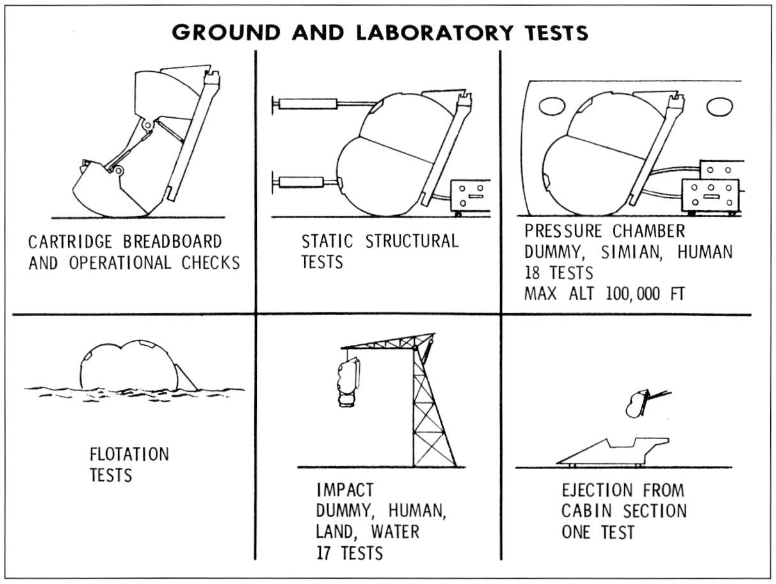

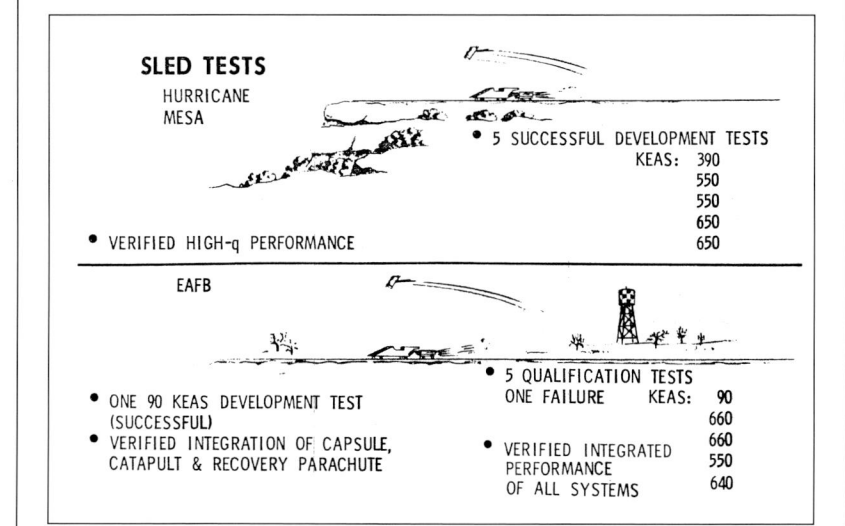

SLED TESTS

HURRICANE MESA

- 5 SUCCESSFUL DEVELOPMENT TESTS
  KEAS: 390
        550
        550
        650
        650
- VERIFIED HIGH-q PERFORMANCE

EAFB

- ONE 90 KEAS DEVELOPMENT TEST (SUCCESSFUL)
- VERIFIED INTEGRATION OF CAPSULE, CATAPULT & RECOVERY PARACHUTE
- 5 QUALIFICATION TESTS
  ONE FAILURE   KEAS: 90
                      660
                      660
                      550
                      640
- VERIFIED INTEGRATED PERFORMANCE OF ALL SYSTEMS

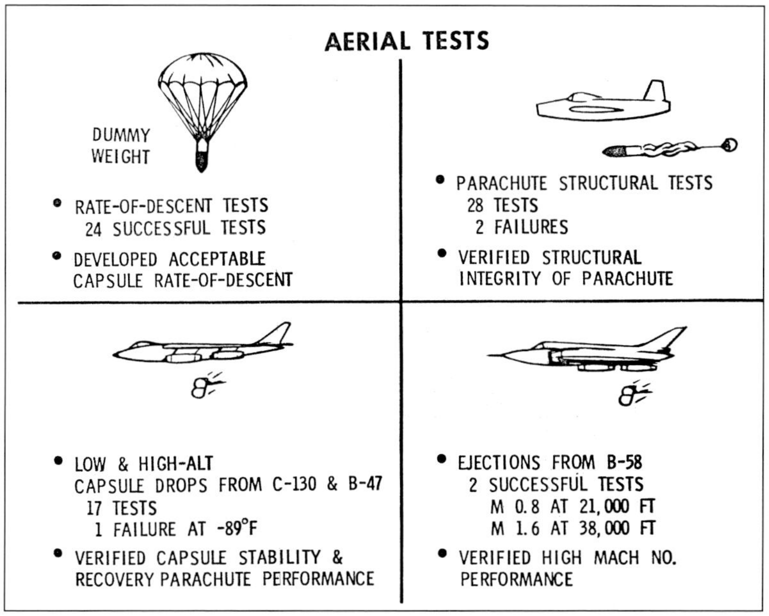

AERIAL TESTS

- RATE-OF-DESCENT TESTS
  24 SUCCESSFUL TESTS
- DEVELOPED ACCEPTABLE CAPSULE RATE-OF-DESCENT

- PARACHUTE STRUCTURAL TESTS
  28 TESTS
  2 FAILURES
- VERIFIED STRUCTURAL INTEGRITY OF PARACHUTE

- LOW & HIGH-ALT CAPSULE DROPS FROM C-130 & B-47
  17 TESTS
  1 FAILURE AT -89°F
- VERIFIED CAPSULE STABILITY & RECOVERY PARACHUTE PERFORMANCE

- EJECTIONS FROM B-58
  2 SUCCESSFUL TESTS
  M 0.8 AT 21,000 FT
  M 1.6 AT 38,000 FT
- VERIFIED HIGH MACH NO. PERFORMANCE

PILOT'S INSTRUMENT PANEL

1. AIRSPEED - MACH NUMBER INDICATOR
2. ATTITUDE DIRECTOR INDICATOR
3. CABIN OVER 42,000 FEET CAUTION LIGHT
4. CREW ENCAPSULATED INDICATOR LIGHT
4A. VERTICAL ACCELEROMETER (SHROUD-MOUNTED)
5. ALTITUDE - VERTICAL VELOCITY INDICATOR
6. MASTER CAUTION LIGHT
6A. NOSE WHEEL STEERING ON INDICATOR LIGHT
7. LETDOWN CHART HOLDER LOCATION (PLUG-IN)
8. TOTAL TEMPERATURE GAGE
9. SIDESLIP INDICATOR
10. ENCAPSULATE CAUTION LIGHT SWITCH
11. BAIL-OUT WARNING LIGHT BUTTON
12. STANDBY ATTITUDE INDICATOR
13. STANDBY ALTIMETER
13A. ENGINE-ADS VIBRATION CAUTION LIGHTS*
14. ENGINE-ADS GEARBOX VIBRATION INDICATORS (TYPICAL)
15. ENGINE-ADS VIBRATION RECORD SELECTOR SWITCH
16. ENGINE -ADS VIBRATION CAUTION LIGHT †
17. ENGINE-ADS VIBRATION INDICATOR TEST BUTTON
18. LIQUID OXYGEN QUANTITY GAGE
19. ELECTRONIC EQUIPMENT COMPARTMENT AIR TEMPERATURE GAGE
20. WATER QUANTITY GAGE
20A. QUANTITY GAGES TEST BUTTON
21. AMMONIA QUANTITY GAGE
22. AIR RECIRCULATING FAN SWITCH
23. AIR RECIRCULATING FAN THERMAL PROTECTION OVERRIDE SWITCH
24. CABIN AIR SWITCH
25. BLEED AIR SWITCH
26. CABIN PRESSURE ALTIMETER
27. STANDBY GYRO FAST ERECT BUTTON
28. ATTITUDE DIRECTOR INDICATOR SELECTOR SWITCH
29. FLIGHT DIRECTOR MODE SELECTOR SWITCH
30. COMMAND CONTROL SWITCH
31. FLIGHT DIRECTOR SYSTEM ALTITUDE HOLD SWITCH
32. CLOCK
33. MARKER BEACON INDICATOR LIGHT
34. HORIZONTAL SITUATION INDICATOR
35. STANDBY AIRSPEED INDICATOR
36. ANALOG TAPE REMAINING INDICATOR
37. AC VOLTMETER
38. INSTRUMENTATION PACKAGE COOLING SYSTEM SELECTOR SWITCH
39. AC VOLTMETER PHASE SELECTOR SWITCH
40. AC VOLTMETER BUS SELECTOR SWITCH
41. CAMERA SWITCH
42. INSTRUMENTATION MASTER SWITCH
43. TELEMETERING SWITCH
44. DIGITAL RECORDER SELECTOR SWITCH
45. DIGITAL TAPE REMAINING INDICATOR
46. RECORDING SYSTEM SELECTOR SWITCH
47. RECORDING RESTART BUTTON
48. DIGITAL RECORD INDICATOR LIGHT
49. ANALOG RECORD INDICATOR LIGHT
50. INTERVAL RECORD SWITCH
51. INSTRUMENTATION CAUTION AND INDICATOR LIGHTS

* AIRPLANE AF62-207
† AIRPLANE AF62-001

COPILOT'S INSTRUMENT PANEL

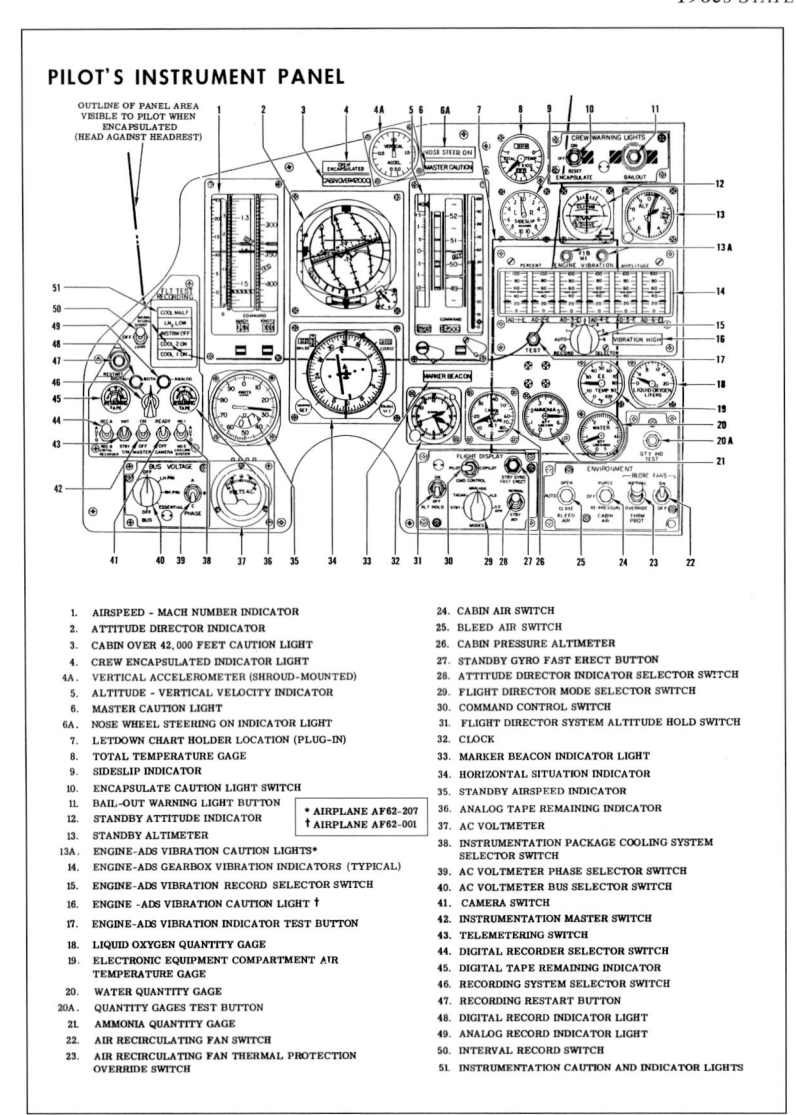

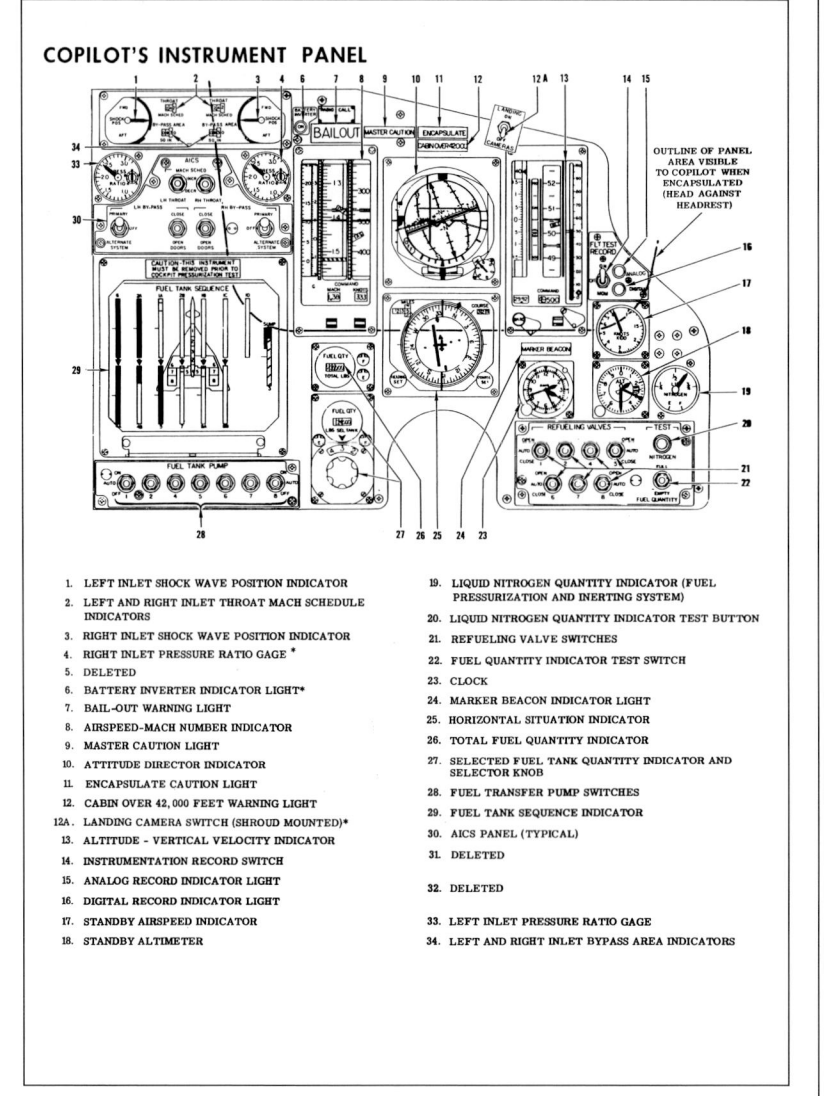

1. LEFT INLET SHOCK WAVE POSITION INDICATOR
2. LEFT AND RIGHT INLET THROAT MACH SCHEDULE INDICATORS
3. RIGHT INLET SHOCK WAVE POSITION INDICATOR
4. RIGHT INLET PRESSURE RATIO GAGE *
5. DELETED
6. BATTERY INVERTER INDICATOR LIGHT*
7. BAIL-OUT WARNING LIGHT
8. AIRSPEED-MACH NUMBER INDICATOR
9. MASTER CAUTION LIGHT
10. ATTITUDE DIRECTOR INDICATOR
11. ENCAPSULATE CAUTION LIGHT
12. CABIN OVER 42,000 FEET WARNING LIGHT
12A. LANDING CAMERA SWITCH (SHROUD MOUNTED)*
13. ALTITUDE - VERTICAL VELOCITY INDICATOR
14. INSTRUMENTATION RECORD SWITCH
15. ANALOG RECORD INDICATOR LIGHT
16. DIGITAL RECORD INDICATOR LIGHT
17. STANDBY AIRSPEED INDICATOR
18. STANDBY ALTIMETER
19. LIQUID NITROGEN QUANTITY INDICATOR (FUEL PRESSURIZATION AND INERTING SYSTEM)
20. LIQUID NITROGEN QUANTITY INDICATOR TEST BUTTON
21. REFUELING VALVE SWITCHES
22. FUEL QUANTITY INDICATOR TEST SWITCH
23. CLOCK
24. MARKER BEACON INDICATOR LIGHT
25. HORIZONTAL SITUATION INDICATOR
26. TOTAL FUEL QUANTITY INDICATOR
27. SELECTED FUEL TANK QUANTITY INDICATOR AND SELECTOR KNOB
28. FUEL TRANSFER PUMP SWITCHES
29. FUEL TANK SEQUENCE INDICATOR
30. AICS PANEL (TYPICAL)
31. DELETED
32. DELETED
33. LEFT INLET PRESSURE RATIO GAGE
34. LEFT AND RIGHT INLET BYPASS AREA INDICATORS

The pilot's (left) and copilot's (right) main instrument panels, noting the differences between A/V-1 an A/V-2 where appropriate. (U.S. Air Force)

kets were going to be stored. Some of the fun-loving guys in our motion picture unit decided to make a little movie parodying this fact. It depicted a capsule on the ground after a bailout. In this film clip, the occupant then got out and reached back in to remove a set of golf clubs and a jug of whiskey. Just then a beautiful, bikini-clad girl strolled by, evidently heading for the beach. The guy abandoned the golf clubs and pulled out a surf board, and headed off after the girl."[12]

An important series of tests that had to be completed before first flight was to verify the escape system would work as planned in the unlikely (they hoped) event it was needed. The capsules and their supporting systems went through a wide variety of tests before they were cleared for use. Initially there were a variety of ground and laboratory tests, including 18 evaluations conducted in a pressure chamber at altitudes up to 100,000 feet. These used anthropomorphic dummies, simians, and humans as test subjects. Various floatation tests, impact tests on land and water, and structural tests were also conducted. Sled testing was done at Hurricane Mesa in Utah and on the long track at Edwards. There were five successful development tests at Hurricane Mesa, at speeds of 390, 550, 550, 650, and 650 knots. These verified the performance of the seat under high dynamic pressures. This was followed by five tests at Edwards at 90, 660, 660, 550, and 640 knots to verify the integration of the capsule, catapult, and recovery parachute.[13]

The main parachutes had already been evaluated using a dummy weight to verify their rate-of-descent; 24 tests were successfully completed. This was followed by parachute structural tests where the chutes were attached to a weight and released at high speeds to verify the structural integrity of the chute; of 30 tests, 28 were considered successful. Next came low and high altitude capsule drops from a C-130 and B-47. Of 18 tests, there was one failure.[14]

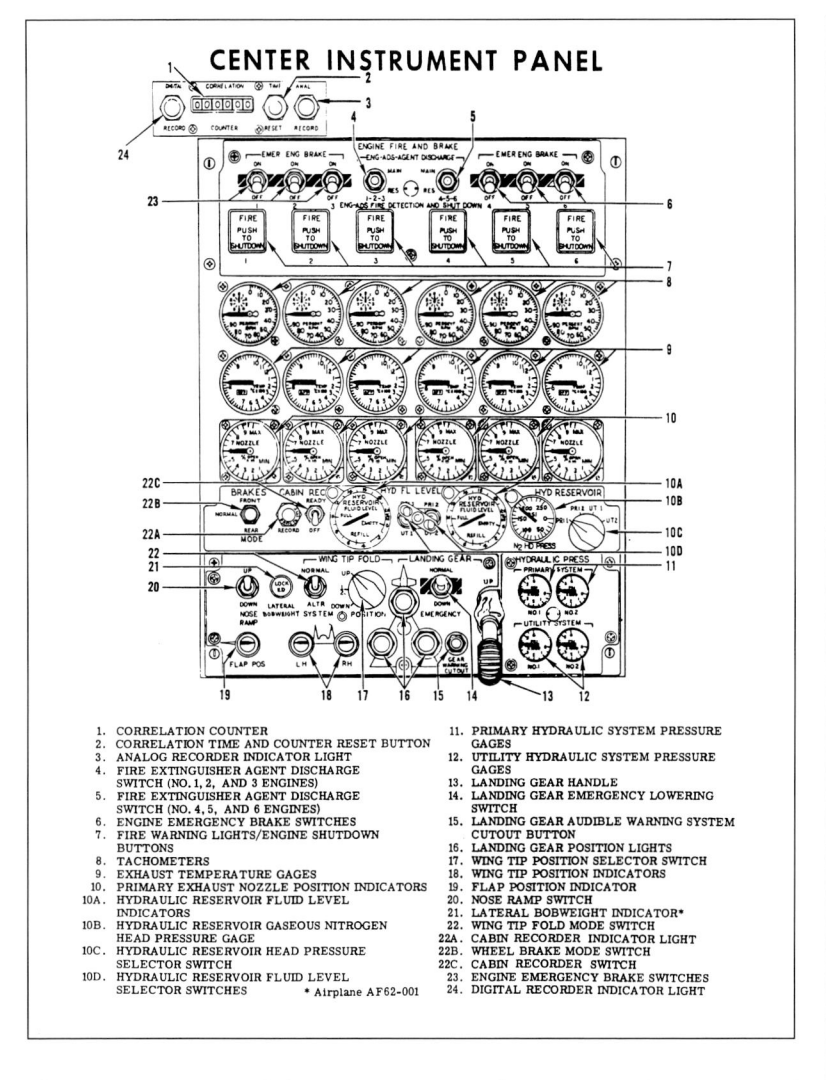

The center portion of the instrument panel containing the majority of the engine instruments. (U.S. Air Force)

Perhaps the most interesting of the tests were two made from a B-58 over Edwards. The capsules would not fit in the cockpit of the Hustler, so Convair modified a pod to hold a single upside-down seat that was ejected downward. In the first test, the capsule was ejected at Mach 0.8 and an altitude of 21,000 feet; the second test was at Mach 1.6 and an altitude of 38,000 feet. As soon as the seat cleared the pod, telescoping steel and aluminum booms deployed that kept the seat from tumbling until a barometric pressure switch released the drogue chutes and main parachutes. The tests were both considered successful. The B-58 pilot for both tests was Major John E. "Jack" Allavie.[15]

The XB-70 instrument panels were a mixture of traditional round instruments and the unique vertical "tape" instruments that found brief favor during the 1960s. The instruments were color-coded and illuminated by white light (the traditional red light washes out any other color). A few digital (using rolling dials like some old alarm clocks) instruments were also used.

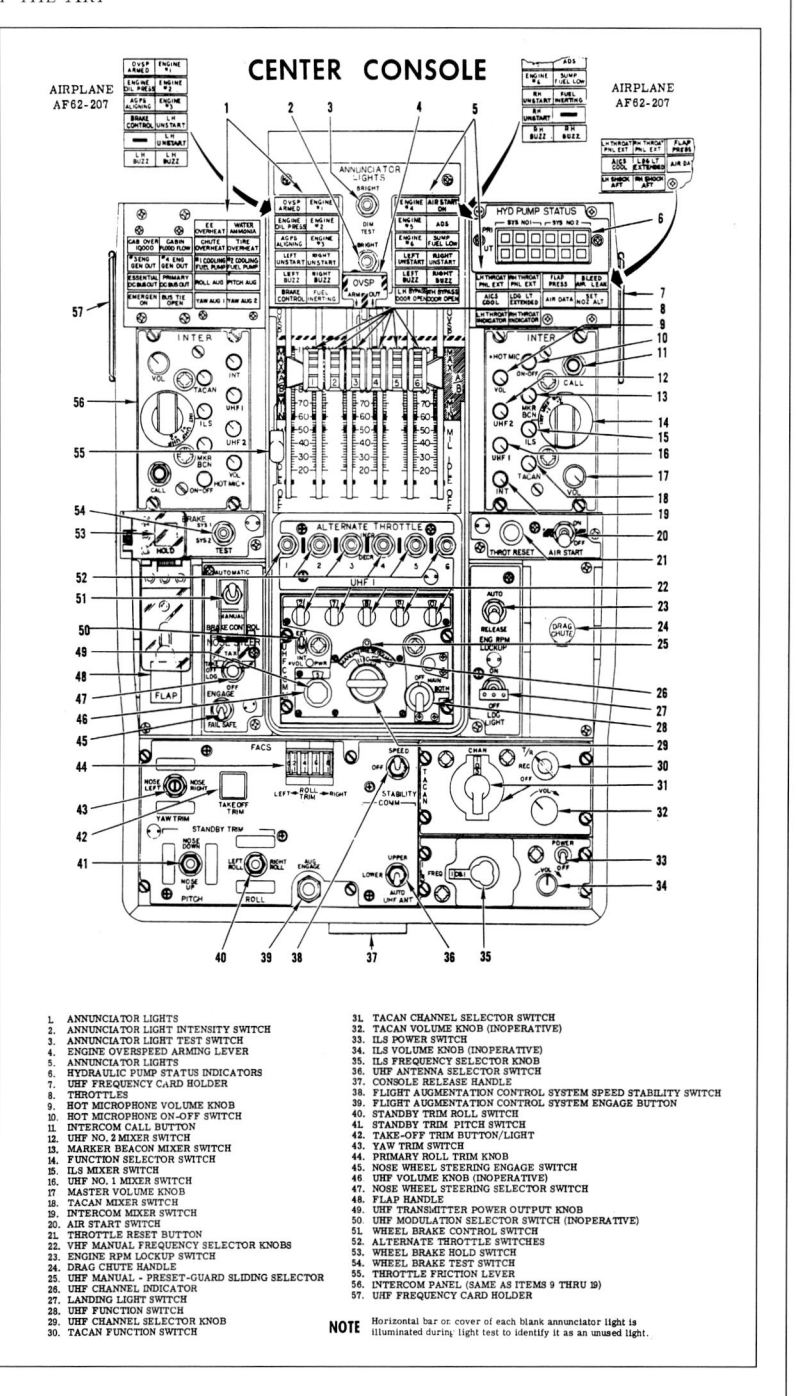

The center console panel located between the two seats. (U.S. Air Force)

In theory, the XB-70s provided a "shirt sleeve" environment, but in fact, many of the test flights were conducted using David Clark Company A/P22S-6 full-pressure suits. The crew compartment temperature could be regulated between 42 degrees Fahrenheit and 105 degrees Fahrenheit, according to crew preferences. A constant pressure altitude of 8,000 feet was maintained under normal circumstances, and an emergency ram air system could maintain a pressure

The instrument panel in A/V-1 on 11 May 1965. Note the B-70 and North American logos on the control columns. (Boeing Historical Archives)

altitude of 40,000 feet (requiring oxygen, but not pressure suits) in the event of a primary system failure.[16]

The main crew entrance was on the left side of the aircraft, forward of the canard. This entrance was 17 feet above ground level and required special access stands for ingress and egress. Care had to be taken to ensure the access stand did not touch the fuselage since rubbing could result in minor surface damage that would be aggravated by Mach 3 flight. There were four separate hatches in the upper fuselage, corresponding to the positions of the expected four-person crew in any future production version. In the XB-70s, the two forward hatches were ballistically removed in the event of crew ejection; the two aft hatches could be ballistically or manually removed for aircrew escape during ground emergencies.[17]

The aircraft had two windshields: a movable outer unit and a fixed inner unit. The movable windshield and ramp assembly consisted of five full-tempered glass panels in a framework structure

1960s State-of-the-Art

The instrument panel in A/V-2 on 1 September 1965. Note the North American logos on the rudder pedals. (Boeing Historical Archives)

that was hinged at the forward end and guided by four frame-mounted roller assemblies. In the full-up position, the slope of the ramp and windshield formed a nose section contour that provided minimal drag. In the full-down position, a 24-degree slope provided increased visibility for low-speed operations. Intermediate positions could be selected as necessary. The movable windshield and ramp assembly was hydraulically operated and electrically controlled. An emergency system was provided that allowed the ramp to be fully lowered in the event the primary system failed. A windshield anti-ice and rain removal system directed high-temperature (≈600 degrees Fahrenheit) engine bypass air through two nozzles on the leading edge of the movable windshield – windshield wipers do not work at Mach 3. The inner fixed windshield consisted of five glass panels in a 78-inch wide, 200-pound 7Al-4Mo titanium forging. A defogging system was provided for the inner surface of both the movable and fixed windscreens.[18]

A view not often seen – the back of the main instrument panel. The unit was surprisingly self-contained compared to many earlier instrument panels that were a maze of wires and tubing. (Boeing Historical Archives)

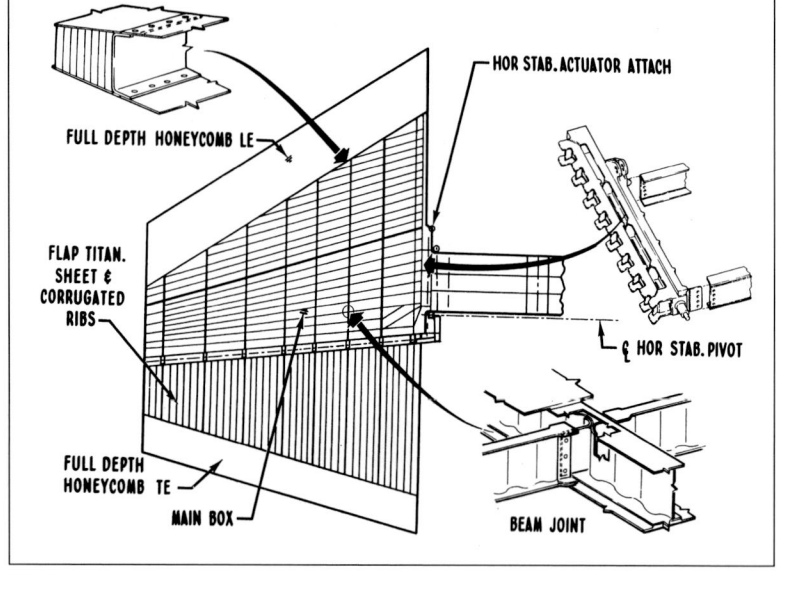

Canard construction (still called a horizontal stabilizer). (U.S. Air Force)

Canards

The B-70 included a canard surface mounted near the top of the fuselage, just behind the cockpit. The canard was a multi-spar thick-skin box structure supported by two pivot bearings mounted in the fuselage bulkhead at FS605.[19] Two hydraulic actuators used an interconnected linkage to ensure simultaneous operation. The canard served primarily as a trimming device, but could be used in conjunction with the elevons for additional pitch control under some circumstances. The entire canard could be deflected from zero to 6 degrees for trim control, and the two-position trailing edge could be lowered 20 degrees to function as a flap. The flap was supported by eight hinge fittings extending aft from the rear beam.[20]

The leading edge sweep was 31.70 degrees with a total area of 265.28 square feet (415.59 square feet including the fuselage portion). The skins were made of heavy 6Al-4Ti plates that were dictated by aerodynamic stiffness requirements. The main box had 10 beams that were continuous from root rib to tip rib. The front and

When the third air vehicle and structural test article were cancelled, NASA decided to fund the completion of the canard that was being manufactured for A/V-3 and use it as a thermal test specimen. The photo at left shows the completed canard in its shipping crate when it arrived at the Flight Research Center in December 1966. At center is one of the thermal reflectors used in the test rig. At right is the test fixture (the canard would be placed between the upper and lower reflectors) during late 1968. Note the two X-15s in the foreground – the X-15 flight program had ended by this time and the two airframes were in storage awaiting their final disposition. (NASA Dryden Flight Research Center)

1960s State-of-the-Art

Midway through the design evolution that led to the B-70, North American decided to use the canard as a trimming device. As such, the entire surface could deflect from zero to six degrees incidence – this photo shows the canard at its extreme nose-up position. (U.S. Air Force)

rear beams were made from flat web 4130 steel and the others were constructed from corrugated titanium. The flap was made from titanium skins and corrugated ribs.[21]

When the canard flaps were raised, the entire surface was used for longitudinal trim, somewhat reducing the overall trim drag. The small amount of drag from the canard reportedly was less than the drag would have been by using the elevons for trimming. In addition, in order to cancel the expected nose down trim change when going supersonic, the canard provided positive lift (up) at the front of the airplane. Without the canard, the elevons would have had to be trimmed up to cancel the transonic nose down trim change, which would cause a down force at the tail of the airplane (negative lift). It was believed that by managing the fuel burn on high-speed long-range flights, the elevons could be maintained in a nearly streamlined position. This reduction in trim drag would improve the aerodynamic efficiency of the airplane, hence increasing the expected range.[22]

Between Mach 0.8 and 0.9, the two XB-70s exhibited some unwanted buffeting that smoothed out as the airplane went supersonic. It was eventually determined that the buffeting was caused by span-wise flow over the canard, and it is likely that any production aircraft would have featured a modified canard shape or fence to cure the problem.[23]

Wings

The wing had an aspect ratio of 1.751:1, with a mean chord of 117.75 feet at the root and 2.25 feet at the tip. The leading edge was swept back at 65.56 degrees and the total area was 6,297.15 square feet. The wing was a multi-spar structure with honeycomb cover panels. The cover panels were fabricated by brazing PH15-7Mo steel face sheets to a 1-inch deep PH15-7Mo steel honeycomb core. The face sheets varied from 0.008 to 0.065-inch thick. The leading edge was a full-depth honeycomb piece attached to the wing by mechanical fasteners on the front spar. The spars were PH15-7 steel using sine wave corrugations with an average spacing of 19 inches. There were three ribs: a fold rib, a root rib, and an intermediate rib located approximately midway between the other two. The ribs were constructed of PH15-7Mo steel consisting of a flat sheet stiffened by corrugated sheet. The folding tips were of similar construction using 0.75-inch deep honeycomb and 12-inch spar spacing.[24]

The first aircraft had no anhedral on the main wing, but A/V-2 featured 5 degrees of dihedral. Both aircraft had a slight aerodynamic twist on the outer panel leading edge. The wing-to-fuselage joint was 80 feet long and both the inner and outer honeycomb face sheets of the upper and lower wing surfaces had to be welded together. The first step welded the inner edge of the honeycomb using a tungsten electrode inserted through a 0.125-inch gap between the outer face sheets. The latter were then joined with a filler strip welded with an electron-beam gun to minimize shrinkage. In all, there were over 6 miles of welding during component assembly and 2.5 miles of welding during final assembly; several of these miles involved the edges of fuel tanks.[25]

The outer 40-percent (span-wise) of each wing could be folded downward to increase directional stability during high-speed flight. Each tip occupied about 500 square feet of area and was driven by six Curtiss-Wright 32,000:1 motor hinges housed under a black magnesium-thorium fairing. On production aircraft, the leading edge of the fairing would have housed an infrared sensor for the defensive avionics. The motor hinges on A/V-2 were a slightly improved design. After the loss of A/V-2, eight of the hinges were recovered from the crash site, refurbished, and installed on A/V-1 in time for Flight 1-50.[26]

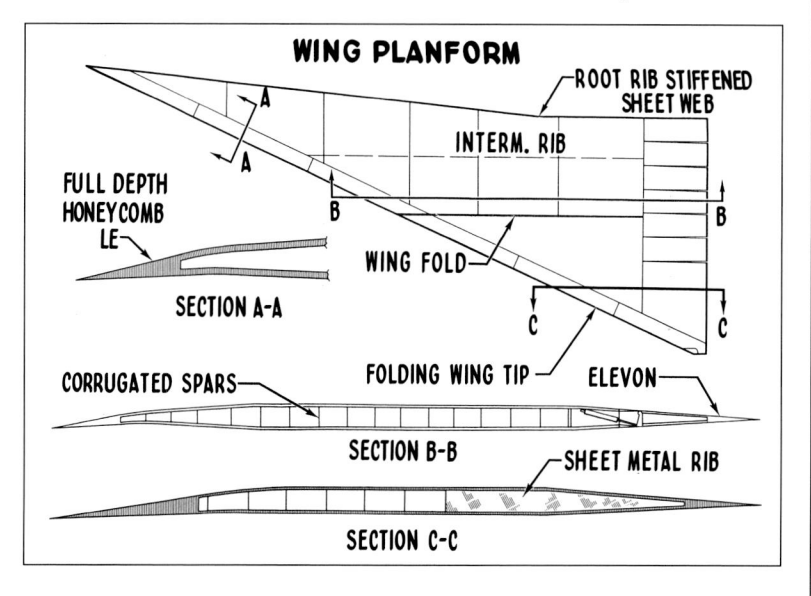

The delta wing on the XB-70 was huge, and the movable wingtips were almost as large as a B-58's entire wing. The fixed portion of the wing held much of the fuel load, and production aircraft would have carried even more fuel outboard in the folding wingtips. (U.S. Air Force)

1960s State-of-the-Art

centerline. Symmetrical movement of the elevons provided basic pitch control; differential movement provided roll control.[28]

A wing fold disengage system was incorporated that automatically locked the outer two elevon sections on each wing (located on the folding wingtip section) at the neutral position and disengaged them from further movement until the wings were unfolded. Weight-on-wheels sensors prevented the wingtips from being folded on the ground since the wingtips would impact the ground in the full down position. An emergency up system was provided in the event the two primary systems failed to return the wingtips to the up position during flight – the airplane could not land with the tips full down, and was procedurally restricted from doing so with them mid-down.[29]

The XB-70s used a flight augmentation control system that used electrical signals in parallel with the mechanical linkage between the control columns and hydraulically actuated flight controls. The actual deflection of the flight control panels was primarily by the mechanical linkage; the electrical control provided a small degree (either the same as, or opposite of the mechanical) of deflection for trim purposes. The augmentation system also provided automatic damping about all three axes. In the pitch mode, the augmentation system only used the elevator mode of the elevons and did not affect the canard.[30]

Vertical Stabilizers

The vertical stabilizers had a leading edge sweep of 51.76 degrees and 233.96 square feet of area. Interestingly, if North American had not opted for the folding wingtips, the vertical stabilizers would have

One of the Curtiss-Wright power hinges being installed. There were six motors on each wing. (Gerald H. Balzer Collection)

The wingtips could be commanded to three positions: UP (parallel to the rest of the wing), 1/2 (25 degrees down on A/V-1 and 30 degrees on A/V-2), and DOWN (64.5 degrees on A/V-1 and 69.5 degrees on A/V-2). The UP position was used for landing, takeoff, and subsonic flight. The 1/2 position was used for transonic and supersonic flight, while the DOWN position was used at very high speeds (Mach 2.5 and up). The use of the folding wingtips provided additional directional stability and allowed a decrease in drag by allowing smaller vertical stabilizers. As an added benefit, when the tips were full down, the shock wave they generated impinged on the bottom surface of the wing, adding about 5 percent more lift to the compression lift already being generated.[27]

Elevons at the wing trailing edge were segmented into six sections per side to prevent binding of the control surfaces due to bending of the wing. (Elevons are combination ailerons and elevators supplying both pitch and roll control.) Two hydraulic actuators powered each elevon segment, which could move 30 degrees up or down from the

Two all-moving vertical stabilizers provided directional stability. These surfaces were much smaller than would have been required if the folding wingtip concept had not been selected. The aircraft was procedurally restricted from high Mach number flight if the wing fold system was inoperative. (Gerald H. Balzer Collection)

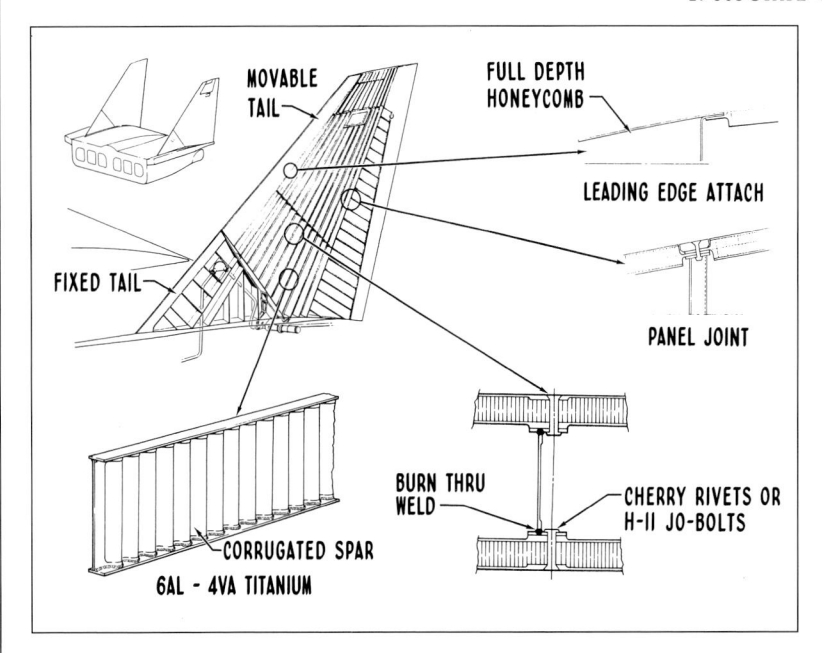

The construction of the vertical stabilizer. Note the wedge-shape "fixed tail" that contained the hinge for the rudder. (U.S. Air Force)

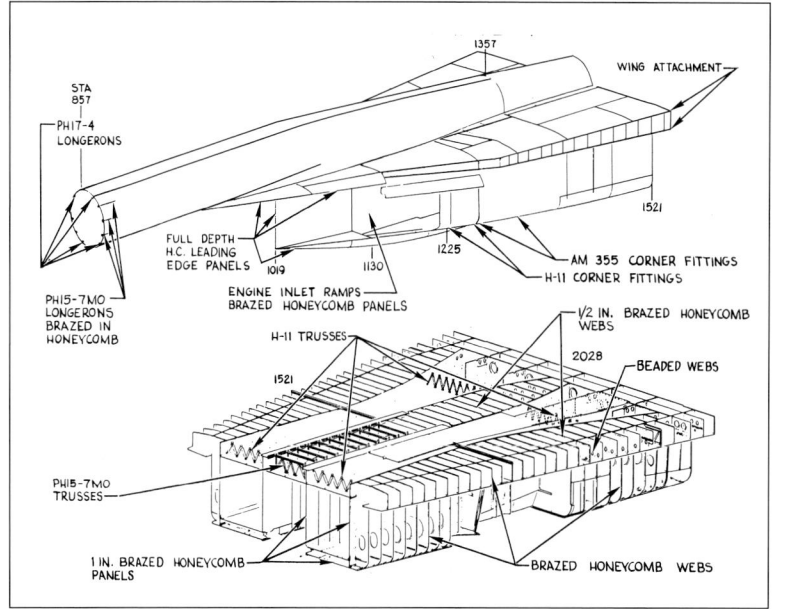

Materials and construction used in the upper and lower intermediate fuselage. (U.S. Air Force)

needed 467.92 square feet to provide equivalent directional stability. Only the forward lower edge (about a third of the area) was fixed; the rest of the surface was used as a rudder driven by dual hydraulic actuators. The hinge line was angled 45 degrees from the vertical and the rudders could deflect 12 degrees either side of center with the landing gear down and 3 degrees with the gear up.[31]

The fixed supporting base was a multi-spar design with PH15-7Mo brazed steel honeycomb skin panels. The panel face sheets were chemmilled to provide pads at the attachments to the corrugated 6Al-4V titanium spars. It was attached to the wing root juncture by mechanical fasteners. The movable rudders were also multi-spar with brazed honeycomb skin panels. The leading and trailing edges were full-depth brazed PH15-7Mo steel honeycomb wedges.[32]

Lower Fuselage

The lower fuselage was a hybrid structure consisting of a variety of different construction techniques. During high-speed flight, the external skin temperatures of certain areas could reach 675 degrees Fahrenheit, while the internal temperatures could exceed 900 degrees Fahrenheit in the aft fuselage due to engine heat. Since the engines occupied most of the last 26 feet of the lower fuselage and the air intakes and weapons bay occupied most of the forward section, North American could not use full-depth transverse framing. In order to carry the wing bending loads across the fuselage, North American used multiple shallow-depth crossbeams to form the upper part of the unit. The side and lower transverse frames supported the engine access doors and were used to complete the unit. The spars were machined from H-11 steel and used titanium webs. At the side of the fuselage, the honeycomb sandwich wing stub was joined to the H-11 frames with high-strength mechanical fasteners. The skin covering the top and sides of the lower fuselage was 6A1-4V titanium alloy riveted in place. The engine compartment doors used 6A1-4V titanium skins over 4A1-3Mo-1V titanium frames.[33]

Although often described as a single 29-foot-long weapons bay, there were in reality two separate 14-foot-long bays covered by a

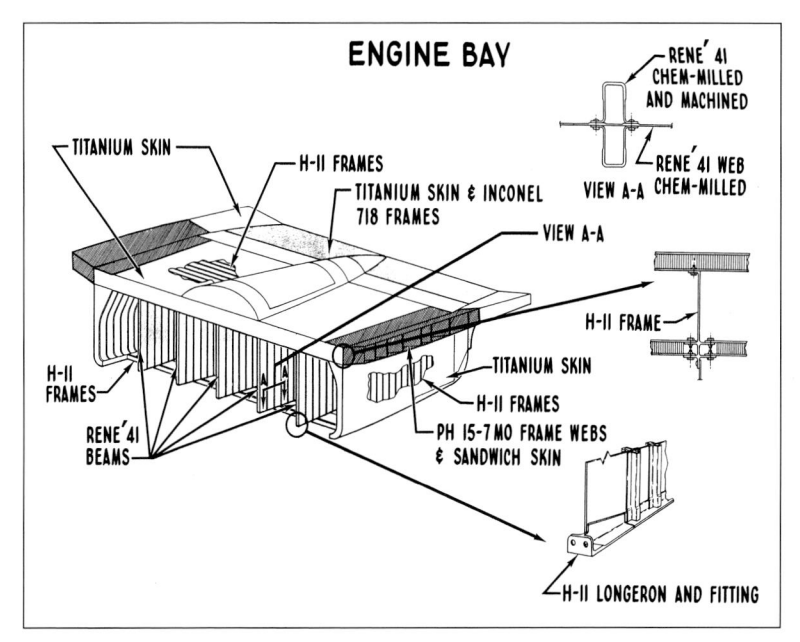

Materials and construction used in the engine bay. (U.S. Air Force)

shared set of doors. The combined bay extended from FS1356 to FS1704. The opening in the bottom of the fuselage was 7 feet above ground level and was covered by two doors operating on a single set of tracks. The length of the track permitted only one door to be opened at a time. Moving both doors aft opened the forward 14 feet of the bay; moving only the aft door opened the rear 14 feet of the bay; the center 1 foot was unusable since the doors never cleared the area.[34]

Air Induction

One of the problems with supersonic airplanes is that nobody has developed a truly workable supersonic jet engine – all engines expect their intake air to be subsonic. North American addressed this with an innovative design that led to a very efficient propulsion system. The concept was validated by several thousand hours in various wind tunnels including NASA Langley and Ames, the Air Force Arnold Engineering Development Center (AEDC), and several private facilities. In addition, there were several hundred hours of operations at AEDC using an actual YJ93 engine.[35]

In the XB-70, two completely separate and independent inlet duct systems were provided, each delivering air to three engines. Each intake was about 7 feet high at the splitter and air was ducted approximately 80 feet back to a plenum chamber just ahead of the engines. The plenum chamber was the size of a small room. The rectangular-section intake was manufactured from brazed stainless steel honeycomb sandwich panels except for H-11 steel sections around the front of the engines. Each duct system incorporated a rectangular variable-geometry inlet, a variable area bypass, a boundary layer bleed air control, and an air inlet control system (AICS). The primary function of the Hamilton Standard AICS was to position the shock waves created at supersonic speeds so that the air entering the engines was subsonic.[36]

The variable-geometry inlet created a series of carefully managed shock waves inside the ducts, beginning with the primary shock wave created by the leading edge of the splitter duct and ending aft of the minimum throat area. Two secondary shocks prior to the duct entrance were caused by breaks in the sweep of the splitter duct. The air followed a circular route in the duct, which caused another series of shocks. The terminal shock to subsonic velocity was the last to occur. Three movable panels, positioned by two hydraulic actuators, opened or closed the throat area to meet engine air requirements; the maximum opening was 48 inches wide (doors set at 25.5 degrees) while the minimum was 19 inches (3.6 degrees).[37]

Bypass Door Setting	Engine Condition
400 square inches (3.6 degrees)	All engines operating normally
700 square inches (7.0 degrees)	One engine shut down
1,100 square inches (13.2 degrees)	Two engines shut down
1,800 square inches (25.5 degrees)	Three engines shut down

Since the speed of air is reduced as it passes through a shock wave, and since pressure increases behind a shock wave, this was an ingenious way to reduce the speed of the air as it entered the engines, and at the same time increase the pressure. In essence, the inlet ducts served as air compressors. At Mach 3 and 70,000 feet, it was estimated that the air pressure at engine face was 30 times that of the ambient pressure outside the airplane. The pressure recovery was estimated at something between 85 and 90 percent. At the same time, the speed of the air was reduced from 2,000 mph to 600 mph at the engine face.[38]

Two views of the inside of one air intake. The left photo is taken from the middle of the intake looking forward; the movable ramps are on the left. The photo at right is from the middle looking aft toward the empty engine locations. (NASA Dryden Flight Research Center)

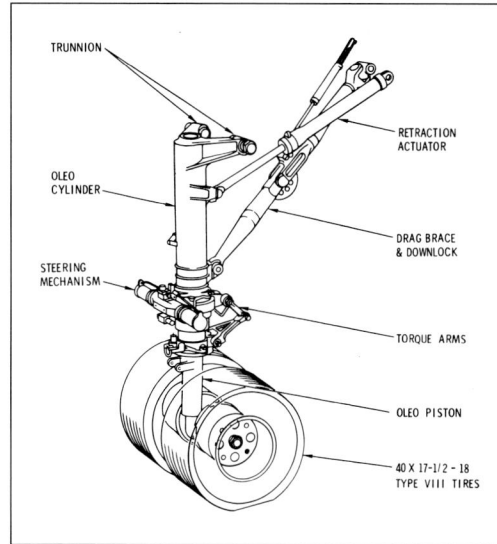

The nose gear on the XB-70 used the same wheels and tires as the main landing gear, something that had also been true with the B-58. The silver finish on the tires was both impregnated into the rubber and painted on. (Photos: NASA Dryden Flight Research Center; drawing: U.S. Air Force)

Ideally, the terminal shock wave would have been at the minimum throat area. However, factors such as gust disturbances could "pop" the shock outside the inlet, resulting in an "unstart" and possible engine flameout. A three-position switch in the cockpit allowed the pilots to choose how far back the terminal shock would be positioned. For maximum range and most efficient air recovery, the shock was positioned forward. On the other hand, if the aircraft was flying through turbulent air or maneuvering, the shock would be positioned further back. The aft position provided the most stable operation and precluded the shock from being expelled through the front of the duct.[39]

Excess inlet air was jettisoned overboard through six pairs of bypass doors located on the upper surface of the wing between and slightly forward of the vertical stabilizers. The six sets of doors were divided into two sets of trimmer doors and four sets of primary doors. Each pair of doors was interconnected (one door opened downward and the other opened upward). The bypass doors provided from zero to 2,400 square inches of bypass area.[40]

The three movable panels in the throat of each inlet were perforated so that slow-moving turbulent boundary layer air was bled to ambient pressure on the other side of the panels into four separate plenums, each bleeding boundary air from a different section of the forward duct. This air was discharged at the rear of the step just aft of the nose wheel well. The remaining boundary layer air was diverted into the engine compartments to provide cooling. This air exited from ducts around the engines. North American believed that ducting inlet bleed air around the engines would also effectively cloak the afterburner from infrared detection. However, little could be done about the miles-long trail of hot gases generated by the six J93s.[41]

Two pairs of unstart sensors were located between the throat panel hydraulic actuating cylinder and the outboard wall of the forward part of the weapons bay. An inlet unstart was "an undesirable condition resulting from the expulsion of the terminal normal shock wave during flight when it is desired to have it located inside the duct." In the two XB-70s, the air induction control system package was located in the aft portion of the weapons bay, complete with its own environmental control system. This equipment would have been relocated in any production version.[42]

Landing Gear

Cleveland Pneumatic manufactured the tricycle landing gear that had dual steerable nose wheels and four wheels on each main gear bogie. The gear retracted into environmentally controlled compartments in the lower fuselage. The movable wheel well doors were kept closed except when the gear was being extended or retracted. The landing gear weighed 12,000 pounds.[43]

The nose gear consisted of a shock strut, drag brace, torque links, actuators, a steering servo actuator, and two 40-inch wheels and 40x17.5-inch 36-ply B.F. Goodrich tires. The wheels were made from steel and incorporated a pressure-reducing device to bleed off excessive tire pressure. The tires had a silver color as a result of a heat-resistant material being impregnated into the rubber during construction and painted on the exterior surface. The nose and main gear wheels and tires were identical. The nose wheels could be steered 58 degrees either side of center at taxi speeds, or 35 degrees either side of center during takeoff or landing. The nose wheel steering was hydraulically powered and electrically controlled via the rudder pedals. At low speeds, the aircraft could make a 180-degree turn in an area approximately 100 feet wide. During mid-1966 A/V-1 had a separate emergency nose-wheel extension system added; it is unclear if A/V-2 had such a system.[44]

1960s STATE-OF-THE-ART

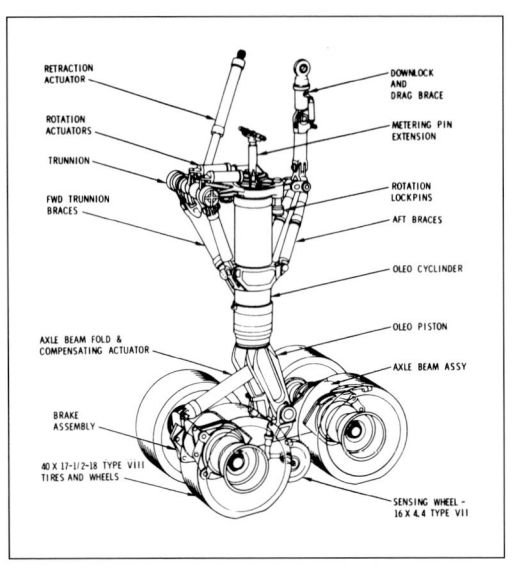

The main landing gear was excessively complex, something necessitated by requiring it to occupy as little space in the fuselage as possible when retracted. In service the main landing gear proved troublesome. (Photos: NASA Dryden Flight Research Center; drawing: U.S. Air Force)

Each of the two main landing gear assemblies consisted of a main shock strut, drag braces, actuators, and a folding bogie assembly with four wheels, two brakes, and a 16x4.4-inch brake reference wheel. The wheels ran on bearings fitted directly to the H-11 forged steel bogie instead of on an axle. Each end of the bogie beam had jacking attach points and could accommodate an aircraft at the maximum taxi weight. The main gear went through a complicated folding and rotation sequence to fit into relatively small compartments while not interfering with the air intakes or the engine plenum chambers.[45]

Throughout the flight program the landing gear exhibited problems during retraction and extension cycles. These were, for the most part, traced to clearances in a ball valve that controlled the

A main landing gear strut is at left. The main gear retraction sequence began with the door opening and the bogie tilting front wheel up until it was flush vertically with the strut. The entire strut rotated 90 degrees, then retracted upward into the fuselage, closing the door behind it. (Left: Boeing Historical Archive; others: NASA Dryden Flight Research Center)

hydraulic system during the cycles. (The valves had a specified clearance of 0.000040-inch, and had failed at 0.000025-inch.) Despite concentrated effort by North American, and later, NASA, the problems were never completely resolved. In late 1968 North American modified two ball valves with increased clearances, and one of them was tested successfully during 10 cycles with the airplane on jacks. The other valve, however, failed its laboratory tests. NASA concluded, "that confidence is lacking that the spool clearance rework is in fact the answer to the problem." NASA also acknowledged that "the general reliability of the landing gear has been somewhat improved, but due to the complicated nature inherent in the gear design, some calculated risk of landing gear malfunction will always be present." Clearly, North American would have had to do something different on any production aircraft.[46]

The brakes were unusual, with a stack of 21 stationary and 20 revolving disks located between opposing wheels and shared between them. The stationary discs were splined on a stator ring cage and the rotating discs splined to the torque tube to which the wheels were attached. Much more efficient cooling was achieved since the brake discs were separated from the wheels. Still, at maximum effort the brake temperatures exceeded 2,000 degrees Fahrenheit and absorbed over 200 million foot-pounds of kinetic energy. An antiskid braking system was incorporated on the main gear wheels, and a small "fifth wheel" on each main bogie provided a speed reference for the antiskid system. The fifth wheel and one main wheel contained speed sensors that sent data to the antiskid computer. The difference in speeds between these two sensors indicated the amount of slippage (since the

Three drag chutes were housed in an environmentally-controlled compartment on top of the aft fuselage. As often as not during the early program only two of the chutes would deploy completely, leading to a change in how they were packed prior to installation starting with Flight 2-5 on 17 September 1965. (Gerald H. Balzer Collection)

fifth wheel had no loads, it was assumed that it always recorded actual speed). If an excessive speed differential existed, the computer then relieved some brake pressure to that bogie. There were four brake computer units, one for each brake. The computers received the output signals from the brake torque sensors, wheel load, reference and main wheel speed sensors, and used this data to compute the optimum settings for the brakes with a goal of eliminating – or at least minimizing – wheel slippage.[47]

Three 28-foot-diameter drag chutes were housed in an environmentally-controlled compartment on top of the fuselage, 18 feet from the rear of the aircraft. The ring-slot nylon chutes deployed simultaneously to reduce the landing roll. A 30-inch-diameter spring-loaded pilot chute pulled an 11-foot-diameter extraction chute that in turn deployed the main chutes. The upward-opening compartment doors were locked in the open position when the pilot commanded the chutes to deploy and could only be closed by the ground crew. The drag chutes could be deployed at speeds as high as 200 knots, after the main gear was firmly on the ground. Early in the flight program the drag chutes tended not to deploy correctly – or at all in several instances – leading North American to make changes to the system beginning with the 20th flight. The riser attachments were relocated from the top of the stowed chute bundle to the bottom, and this largely solved the problem. Adding "ribbons" to eight of the slots in the parachutes themselves reduced the porosity of the chutes and increased the chances they would fully inflate and remain inflated. These changes seemed to work and the chutes functioned well for the latter portion of the flight program.[48]

A good view of the inside of the main landing gear door – not much to look at. The doors were kept closed unless the gear was extending or retracting. (Boeing Historical Archives)

Fuel System

Each XB-70 was equipped with 11 fuel tanks;[49] however, since tank No. 3 was over the center-of-gravity it was used as a sump tank and not for fuel storage. Five of the tanks were located in the aft part of the fuselage neck, and three integral tanks were in the main part of each wing. In all, the tanks held just over 47,000 gallons of fuel. All the tanks were fabricated from brazed stainless steel honeycomb panels joined by welding. Some reports indicate that A/V-3 and production aircraft would have had another fuel tank in each wingtip, but the structural complexity of adding weight into this movable panel might have been extreme. It is likely that the fuel in the wingtip tanks would have been used during climbout, with the tanks remaining empty once the tips were lowered. On A/V-1, tank No. 5 was inoperative due to unresolved leakage problems.[50]

The wing tanks were emptied first. From the main tanks, fuel was fed to the No. 3 sump tank as dictated by engine requirements and center-of-gravity concerns. At cruise power, fuel flowed from tank No. 3 to the engines at 785 pounds per minute. Fueling and defueling were accomplished through a single-point receptacle at a rate of 600 gallons per minute. An adjacent control panel allowed ground crew to select what tanks were to be filled or drained. A fuel tank sequence panel on the copilot's instrument panel presented a graphic display of tank sequencing. Dual-colored tapes (white and black) were used to indicate the fuel level in each tank – white indicated fuel; black indicated no fuel. When the display was completely black, the tank was empty. The intertank transfer of fuel to control the center-of-gravity was automated on A/V-2, but was accomplished manually by the copilot on A/V-1. The third prototype and any production aircraft would have included an aerial refueling receptacle on the upper surface of the nose forward of the articulating windshield.[51]

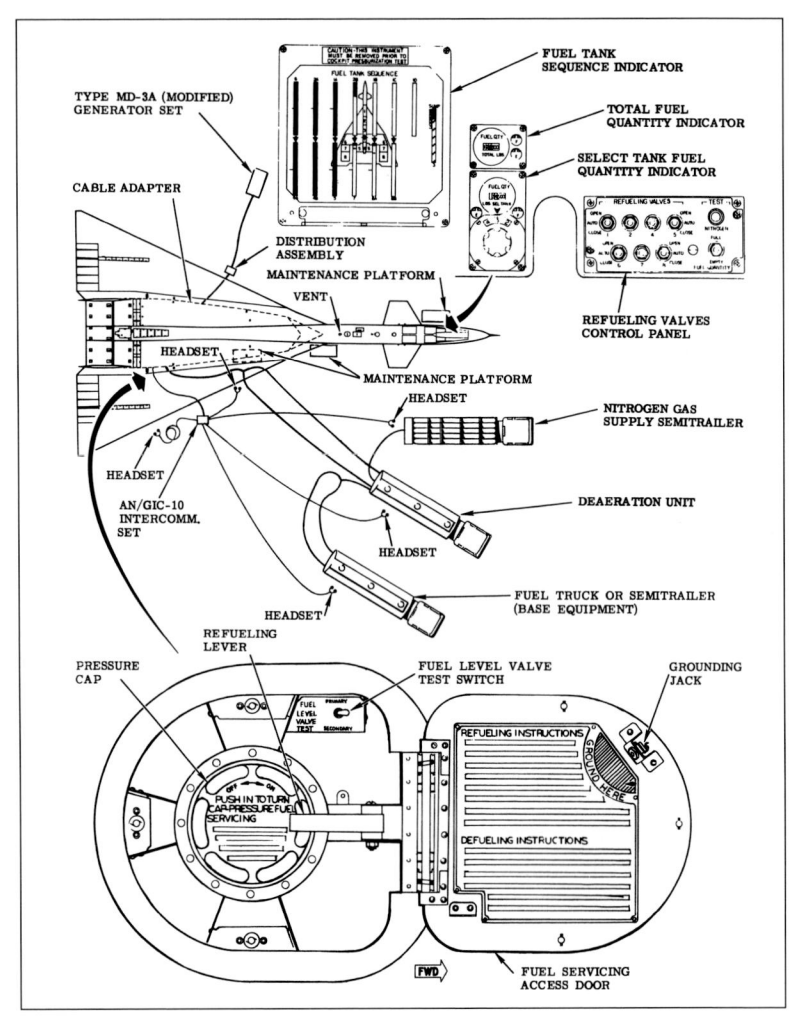

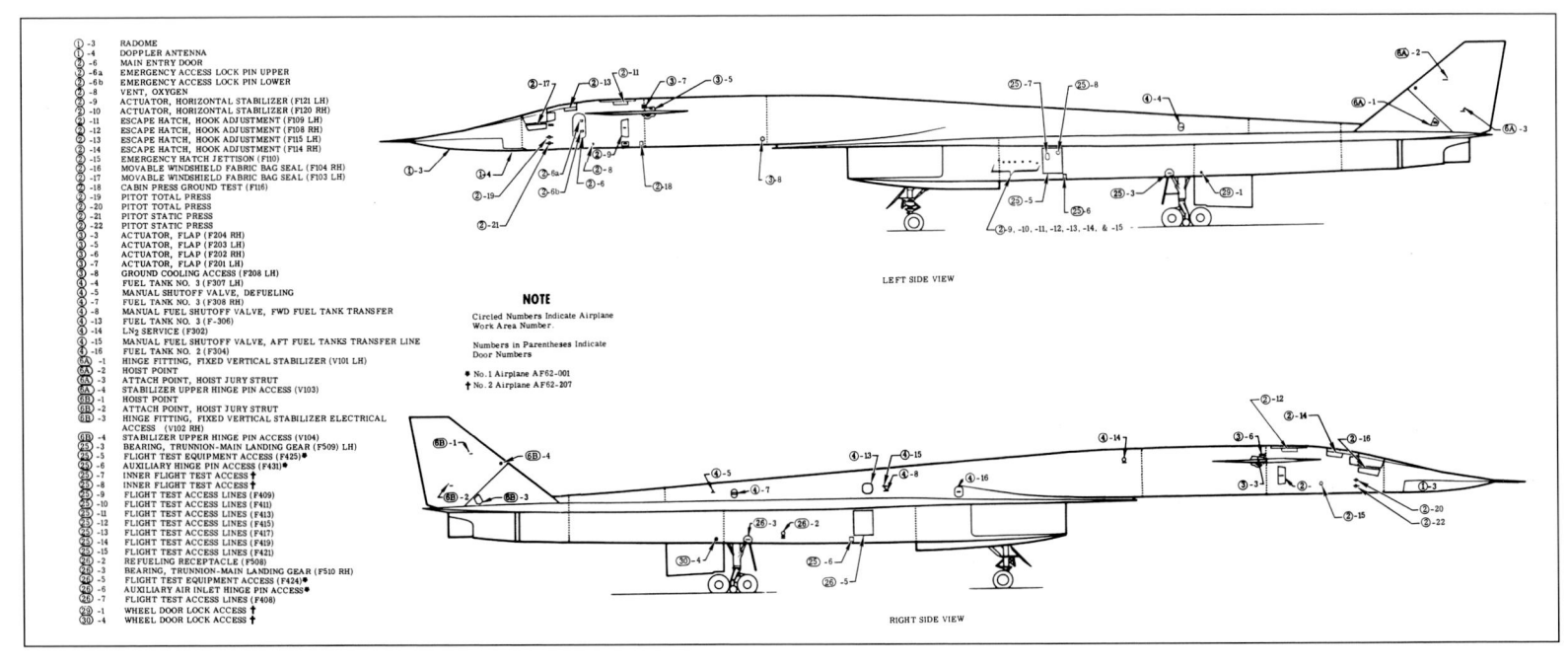

1960s State-of-the-Art

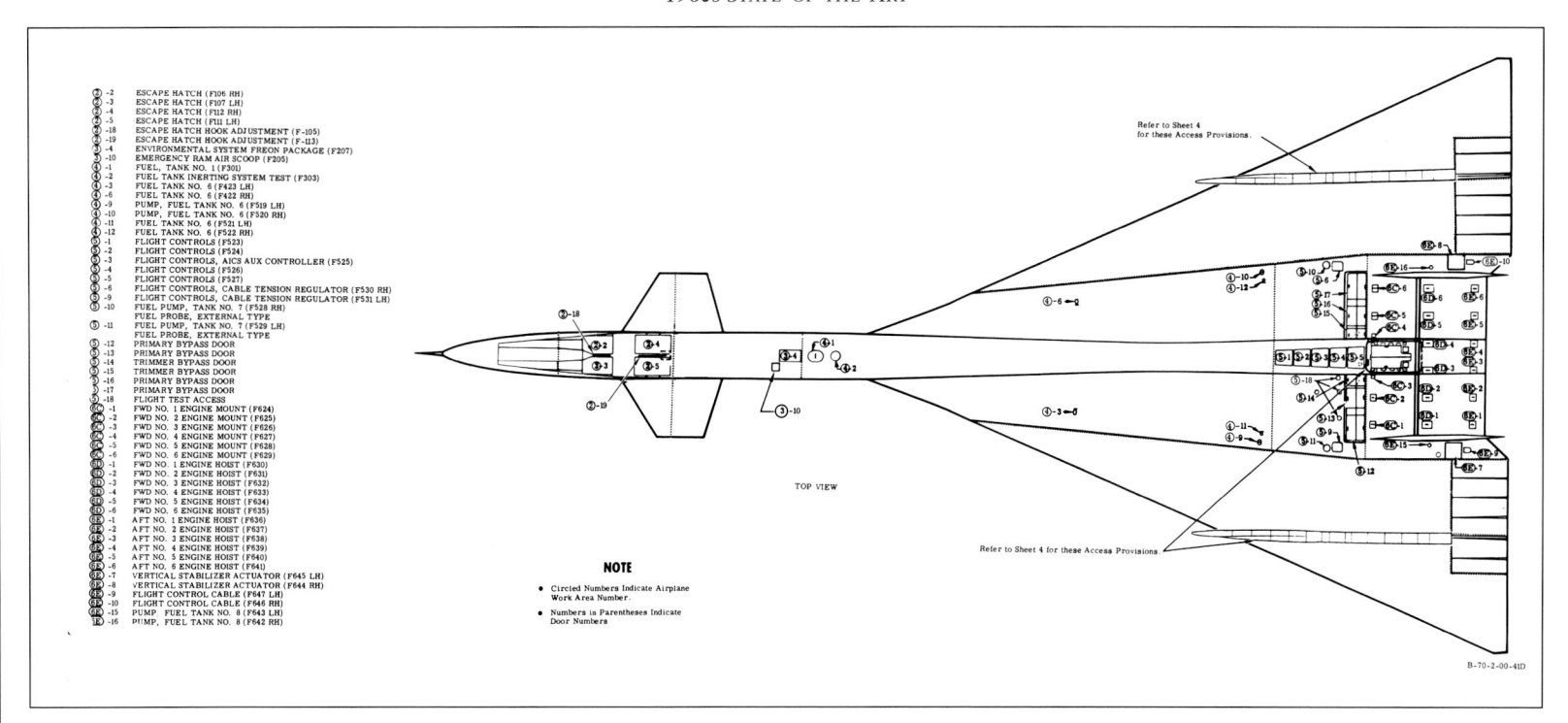

Fuel was used to cool various systems through a series of heat exchangers supplied from the No. 3 sump tank. At Mach 3, the fuel could absorb over 30,000 BTUs per minute from the hydraulic, engine oil, and environmental control systems. However, toward the end of the mission or during periods when the fuel flow was low (such as during in-flight refueling when the engines were throttled back) a secondary cooling method used 4,000 pounds of water that acted as a substitute heat sink. The water was vaporized at a rate of 28 pounds per minute in a boiler by the latent heat from the systems normally cooled by the fuel. At the end of a high-speed flight, the fuel-to-water heat exchanger assured that the fuel delivered to the engines did not exceed 260 degrees Fahrenheit.[52]

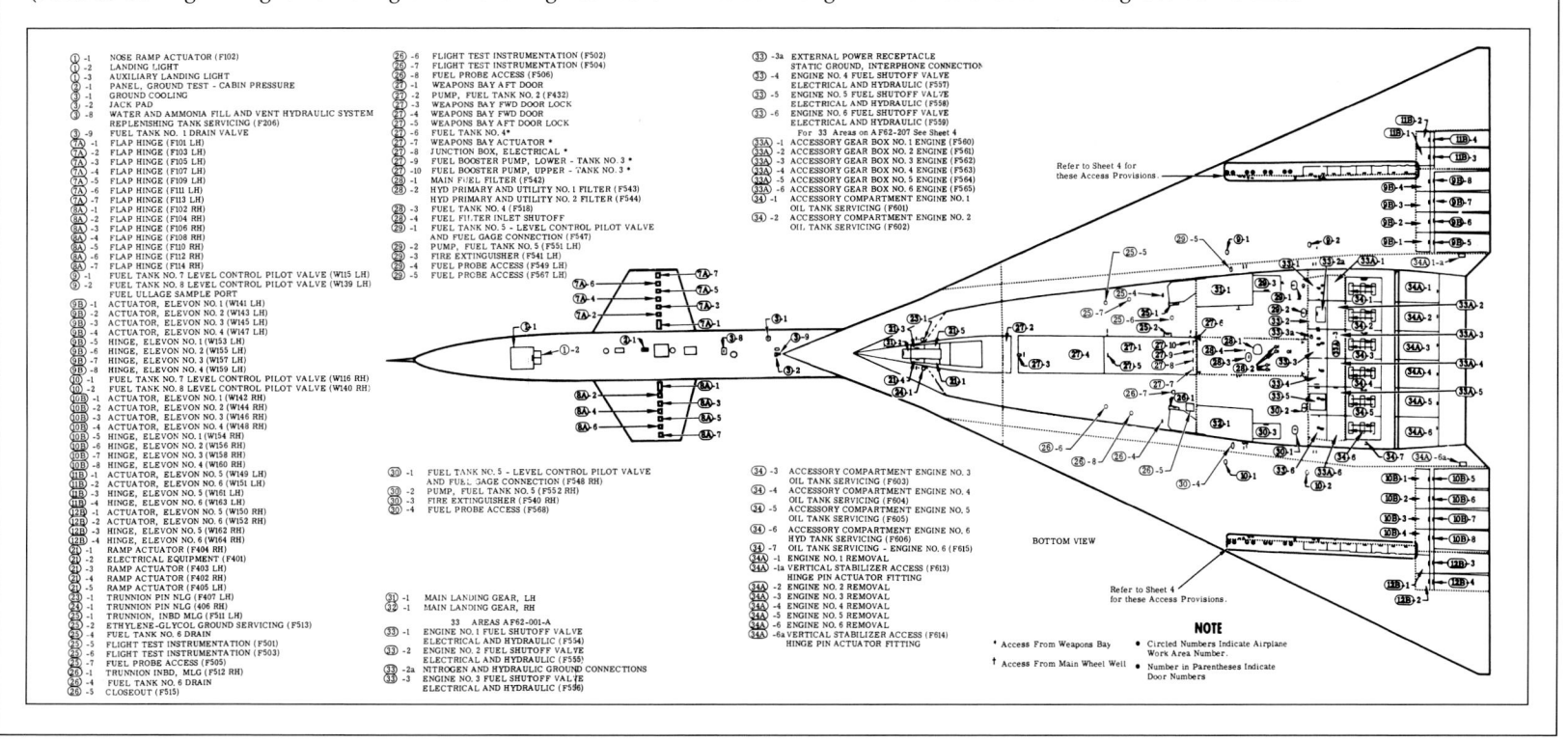

1960s State-of-the-Art

PEAK EXTERNAL SKIN TEMPERATURES
DEGREES FAHRENHEIT

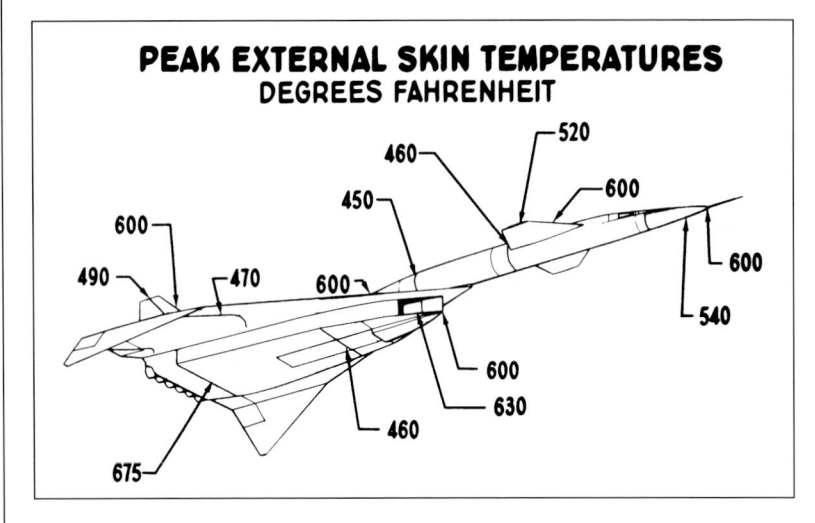

This chart explains why the B-70 used fuel to help keep things cool. Even in the rarified atmosphere at 70,000 feet, the total temperature at 2,000 miles per hour could exceed 600 degrees Fahrenheit. (U.S. Air Force)

Gaseous nitrogen was used for fuel tank pressurization and inerting. Two liquid nitrogen dewars each held 350 pounds of LN2 under 83 psi pressure. A vaporizer circuit converted the LN2 into GN2, which was then supplied to the various fuel tanks and lines under pressure.[53]

Oxygen contamination in the JP-6 was considered detrimental both to the stability of the fuel and to aircraft safety. To help eliminate the oxygen, the fueling process for the XB-70 was somewhat elaborate. A tanker full of JP-6 began by pumping the fuel into a second, empty tanker. At the same time, the second tanker was being pressurized with high-pressure dry nitrogen that was bubbled through the JP-6 as it was pumped in. The dry nitrogen drove out any oxygen in the fuel, and the "clean" JP-6 was pumped into the XB-70 already partially pressurized with nitrogen. This same procedure was also used with the JP-5 alternate fuel.

Hydraulic Systems

During the design of the air vehicle, North American came to realize that using a conventional 3,000-psi hydraulic system would account for almost three percent of the total aircraft weight. After considering various alternatives, it was decided to adopt a 4,000-psi system that ended up using less than two percent of the aircraft weight. The new system allowed the use of small pumps, valves, actuators and also allowed smaller-diameter hydraulic lines. In all, North American estimated that it saved over 10,000 pounds by using the higher pressure system.[54]

Six airframe-mounted accessory drive system (ADS) gearboxes, each shaft-driven by a corresponding engine, were mounted in separate compartments forward of the engines. All six gearboxes drove 4,000-psi hydraulic pumps. The hydraulic pump on No. 5 also drove an emergency electrical generator, and all of the hydraulic pumps could be run "in reverse" to start the engines. Initially, both airplanes had AC electrical generators on the Nos. 3 and 4 gearboxes; a generator was added to the No. 2 gearbox on A/V-1 during mid-1966. Two generators (Nos. 3 and 4 since they were in different inlet ducts) usually were required to power the aircraft, but any of the three was capable of supplying the entire load if required. The constant-speed (8,000 rpm) generators provided 240/416-volt, 3-phase, 400-hertz power through step-down transformers. Having the accessories mounted on the airframe instead of on the engine allowed easier and more rapid engine maintenance, and eliminated building-up different engine configurations (some with AC generators; some without, etc.).[55]

The hydraulic systems in the airplane provided power to operate the flight controls, raise and lower the landing gear, operate the canard and its flaps, power the hydraulic hinges that moved the wingtips, power the hydraulic rams that moved the inlet walls, operate the fuel pumps, and apply the wheel brakes. There were actually four separate systems; two primary systems operated the flight controls and the wingtips, and two utility systems were provided for most other work.[56]

The use of 4,000-psi systems instead of the customary 3,000-psi systems was an attempt to save weight, but led to a considerable number of minor problems. The 30-percent increase in pressure caused the normal B-nut connectors to leak, so most joints in the hydraulic lines were brazed. However, the brazed connectors tended to crack and leak, and were, for the most part, replaced by threaded connectors during the flight program. The extreme vibrations encountered in some parts of the airframe caused the hard-lines to break despite the addition of additional support brackets. North American and its subcontractors embarked on a program to develop flexible hoses which began to be installed during the early flight program. At least partially because of the XB-70 experience, 3,000-psi systems would remain the industry

External servicing carts for the hydraulic system connected to the same locations that would have been used by the alert pod on operational bombers. The engine compartment of the bomber could be reached with fairly low work stands – unlike the forward fuselage that needed 20-foot tall work platforms. (U.S. Air Force via Jerry McCulley)

standard until the Bell V-22 introduced 5,000-psi systems in the late 1990s – again with many problems. All totaled, each XB-70 used 85 linear actuators, 50 mechanical valves, 44 hydraulic motors, and about 400 electrically-actuated solenoid valves. More than a mile of hydraulic tubing contained 3,300 brazed and 600 mechanical joints. To avoid the large weight penalty of providing a cooling system, all of the actuators and valves were designed to withstand high temperatures.[57]

Approximately 220 gallons of a special high-temperature hydraulic fluid called "Fluid 70" (actually named Oronite 70) were used. This fluid could operate continuously at 450 degrees Fahrenheit and intermittently up to 630 degrees Fahrenheit. Although the fluid was much better than the Oronite 8200 that had been selected originally, it still left much to be desired and required constant replacement due to chemical break-down after prolonged exposure to high temperature.[58]

Very late in the flight program a 30-gallon hydraulic replenishing tank was added to A/V-1 to provide an extra measure of redundancy. In the event of a gradual leak in either hydraulic system, the pilot could open valves and replenish the system to prevent pump cavitation. The system was not overly sophisticated, and required that a pilot monitor the hydraulic system fluid levels and manually open the valve (i.e., the system had no automation). Still, it provided some backup in case of a major fluid leak as had happened so often during the flight program.[59]

ELECTRONICS

Because of their demonstrator status, the two XB-70s were very poorly outfitted with avionics. Each airplane was equipped with two AN/ARC-90 UHF command radios that provided 3,500 channels between 225.00MHz and 399.95MHz, and had a built-in guard receiver tuned between 238-248MHz. On A/V-1, only one of the UHF sets was active at a time, the other being in standby mode. On A/V-2, both sets could be used simultaneously. Antennas were located on both the top and bottom of the forward fuselage. An AN/AIC-18 intercom allowed the two pilots to talk to each other. An AN/APX-46 transponder (IFF) set was installed on both aircraft, more for air traffic control (Mode C) purposes than anything else. Again, antennas were located on the top and bottom of the forward fuselage[60]

Each XB-70 was equipped with an AN/ARN-58 instrument landing system and a single AN/ARN-65 TACAN radio navigation system. The TACAN installation was a far cry from the sophisticated bombing-navigation system developed by IBM, and was generally considered only marginally acceptable for test flights. Without the IBM bomb-nav system, the XB-70s did not have an inertial navigation system and were forced to rely totally on dead reckoning and TACAN. Fortunately, the chase planes generally had better navigation systems, and the XB-70s were always under positive radar surveillance by the High Range.

The central air data system provided the flight crew with displays of indicated airspeed, calibrated airspeed, indicated altitude, true altitude, Mach number, maximum safe Mach number, altitude rate (vertical velocity), indicated angle-of-attack, vertical acceleration, and total temperature. Indicated airspeed and altitude were displayed on standby indicators for both the pilot and copilot. Total temperature was displayed to the pilot. The other indications were displayed on vertical scale indicators to both pilots. Since the XB-70s were not equipped with an inertial navigation system, the acceleration data came from the flight test instrumentation package carried in the forward weapons bay.[61]

A 12-foot-long (FS463 through FS605) electronic equipment compartment was located behind the crew and accessed via a door in the rear of the crew compartment. The electronics compartment was pressurized and cooled by a separate system from that used by the crew compartment. The door between the compartments had to remained sealed except for brief periods when crewmembers were transiting between the compartments.[62]

Behind the electronics compartment (FS605 through FS861) was a 21-foot-long environmental control equipment compartment. This compartment could also be accessed in flight through a door in the rear of the electronics compartment. Again, the compartment was pressurized and cooled by a separate system and the connecting door could not remain open for prolonged periods.[63]

SIX PACK

As finally completed, the two XB-70s were each powered by six General Electric YJ93-GE-3 turbojet engines, unofficially called the "six pack." The YJ93-GE-3 was an axial flow, single rotor, afterburning turbojet engine with a flight envelope that extended to Mach 3.2 and maximum operating altitude of 95,000 feet. The engine was designed for optimum performance at Mach 3.0 and 65,000 feet with continuous afterburner operation. The publicized thrust was "in the 30,000-pound class," but the actual figure was never provided for security reasons. In

The J93s were reliable engines given their prototype status, but they did not like foreign object damage. These are two of the engines from Flight 1-12 on 7 May 1965 when the wing apex failed and was ingested into the inlet. (AFFTC History Office Collection)

The exhaust nozzle was a variable area convergent-divergent ejector-type. The primary and secondary nozzles consisted of 16 flaps and 16 seals and were positioned by separate link systems connected to an actuating ring that was moved by four hydraulic actuators. The control system prevented the secondary area from becoming as small as the primary area.[66]

A two-piece heat shield was constructed of longitudinally corrugated René 41 alloy. The inner and outer skins were 0.004-inch thick and the inner corrugation was 0.003-inch thick, forming a sandwich with a total thickness of 0.25-inch. The inner surface was gold plated to prevent loss of reflectivity due to high temperature corrosion, and the outer surface was painted black. When mounted on the engine, the shield encased 10 feet of the entire length, extending from the main combustor (65 inches aft of the forward flange on the compressor) to the forward lip of the secondary nozzle. Rows of overlapping finger seals were attached to the forward lip of the heat shield and the exhaust nozzle shroud. The seals prevented leakage of secondary airflow past a bulkhead at the forward lip of the heat shield, routing secondary airflow into the annulus between the engine surface and heat shield.[67]

The J93 was the first engine to use air-cooled turbine blades and the first to use blades made from titanium alloy. This allowed operating temperatures "several hundred" degrees higher than was normal practice at the time. The blades proved somewhat more fragile than their steel counterparts, and at least 25 engines suffered foreign object damage during the flight test program.

Despite a protracted development effort, the YJ93-GE-3 was completed on schedule and passed its 68-hour preliminary flight-rating test in 1961, in time for the original XB-70 first flight date. By the time the first XB-70 was actually rolled out in Palmdale, the J93 had accumulated over 5,000 hours of test time, including 600 hours at Mach 2 or greater. As part of the engine test program, General Electric built a Mach 3 test facility, and used a similar facility at the Air Force Arnold Engineering Development Center (AEDC) in Tullahoma, Tennessee. Engine inlet tests were also conducted at AEDC and the NASA Lewis Research Center, with 52 hours of tests involving 154 engine starts, 109 engine stalls, and over 200 inlet unstarts. The inlet in these tests was a 0.577-scale model using an actual small jet engine. There had been plans to test the engine in a specially configured centerline pod aboard a B-58 (55-0662) where it could be subjected to Mach 2 under "real world" conditions. The pod was manufactured and the B-58 was displayed carrying the pod at an Edwards air show, but it appears that the engine was never tested during flight.[68]

The YJ93 fuel system consisted of an engine-driven, dual element, constant displacement gear-type pump that incorporated a centrifugal boost element that supplied 32 dual-orifice fuel nozzles in the main combustor. An additional 32 fuel injectors fed the afterburner as needed. The ignition system consisted of a low-tension capacitor discharge unit that housed 4-joule and 20-joule circuits. During normal ground starts, the 4-joule circuit was used; during low-temperature ground starts and for all air starts both the 4- and 20-joule systems were used.[69]

Six airframe-mounted accessory drive system (ADS) gearboxes, each shaft-driven by a corresponding engine, were mounted in sepa-

The first J93 being installed in A/V-1 during construction. The engine was relatively easy to install since all of the accessories were on the airframe. (Boeing via the Tony Landis Collection)

reality, the –3 engine made 28,800 lbf in afterburner at sea level; non-afterburning performance was approximately 19,000 lbf.

The YJ93-GE-3 was 237 inches long and 52.5 inches wide; the intake was 42 inches in diameter. The dry weight of the engine was 5,220 pounds, providing a thrust-to-weight ratio of 6:1 – considered very good for the time but paling in comparison to modern turbofans. The engine used JP-6, which was basically an improved kerosene derivative with improved heat stability and resistance to the formation of solids in the exhaust. When it appeared the program would run out of the limited quantity of JP-6 that had been produced, the J93 was certified for use with JP-5, and it appears that that last dozen or so flights used JP-5, although no conclusive documentation could be located.[64]

The 11-stage compressor was a variable stator unit with a nominal sea-level static pressure ratio of 8.7:1 and airflow of 264 pounds per second at a rated rotor speed of 6,825 rpm. The inlet guide vanes and stators 1 through 3 and 7 through 10 were were scheduled as a function of rotor speed and compressor inlet temperature. Compressor speed was governed by a hydro-mechanical fuel control with an electrical exhaust temperature override at maximum speeds.[65]

rate compartments forward of the engines. All six gearboxes drove 4,000-psi hydraulic pumps. The hydraulic pump on No. 5 also drove an emergency electrical generator, and all of the hydraulic pumps could be run "in reverse" to start the engines. Initially, on both airplanes, the Nos. 3 and 4 gearboxes drove AC electrical generators; a generator was added to gearbox No. 2 on A/V-1 during mid-1966. Two generators (Nos. 3 and 4 since they were in different inlet ducts) usually were required to power the aircraft, but any of the three was capable of supplying the entire load if required. The constant-speed (8,000 rpm) generators provided 240/416-volt, 3-phase, 400-hertz power through step-down transformers.[70]

Moving most accessories to the airframe allowed for a much simpler engine installation than was traditional at the time, but is fairly common today. An engine could be replaced in 25 minutes – a feat demonstrated on several occasions. Each engine was equipped with a 3,500-psi hydraulic pump that was separate from the airframe-mounted 4,000-psi pumps and was used only for engine control. The engine used hydraulic power to move the front and rear variable stators, and the primary and secondary exhaust nozzles.[71]

Because they were prototype engines, and the XB-70 test program was not expected to fly into known icing conditions, the engines were not equipped with anti-icing systems. However, the basic J93 design incorporated all the necessary structural facilities (internal piping for air supply, mounting pads, etc.) for an anti-icing system.[72]

The XB-70 was ahead of its time in providing a "thrust-by-wire" system. The throttle levers in the cockpit sent electrical signals to each engine control system. This in turn provided a mechanical linkage to the engine that integrated the operation of the main fuel control, afterburner fuel control, and primary nozzle area control. In addition to the conventional throttles, emergency thrust control switches were provided on the center aisle console and in each escape capsule. Having electric control of the engines was one of the keys to providing limited aircraft control from within the sealed escape capsules.

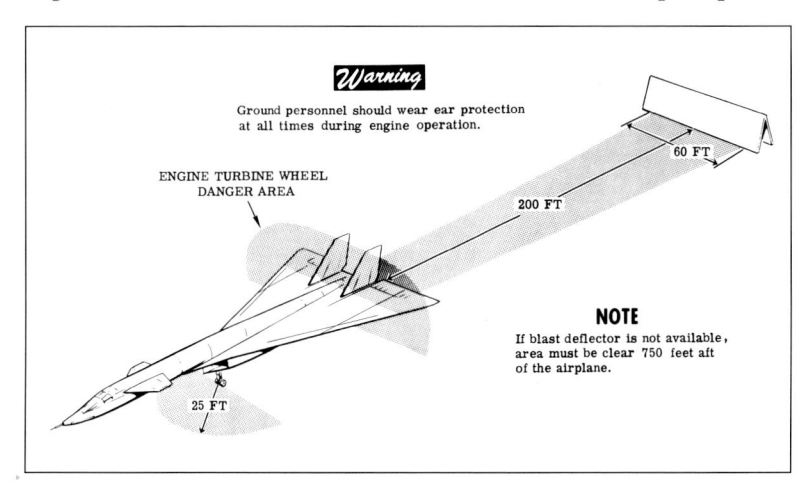

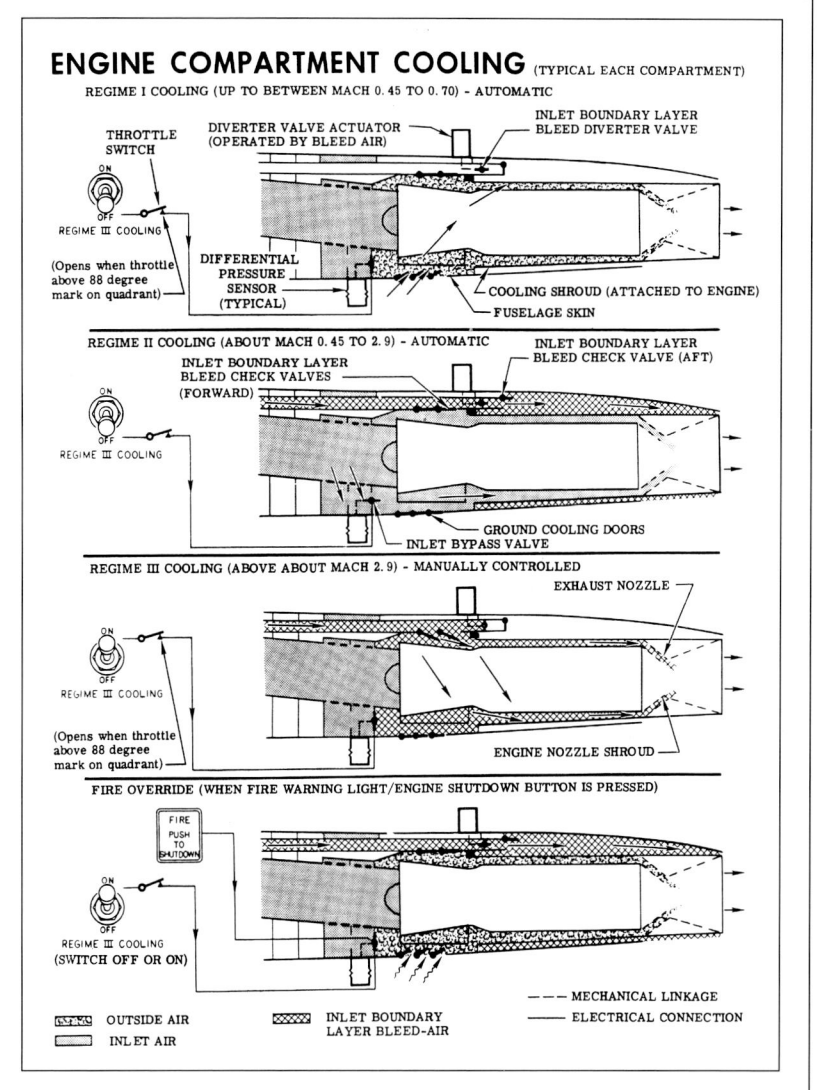

Managing airflow around the engines to keep them cool was a major undertaking. North American also thought that this scheme would help reduce the exhaust's infrared signature on any production version. (U.S. Air Force)

Oddly, the engine thrust could only be reduced from inside the capsule, not increased. The concept was that once the aircraft slowed down and lost altitude, the pilots could open the capsules and control the aircraft normally.[73]

General Electric manufactured 38 YJ93-GE-3 engines. After the cancellation of the J93 project, many of the lessons learned from the engine were applied to the development of the General Electric G4 turbojet designed for the Boeing Supersonic Transport (SST). The first GE4 demonstrator ran on 18 July 1966, and two days later, it achieved its rated RPM. On 23 August, it achieved its design thrust of 40,000 lbf. With afterburning, the engine produced 52,600 lbf. A later version of the engine achieved 63,200 lbf on 19 September 1968, establishing it as the most powerful jet engine in the world at the time.[74]

Major danger areas when the engines were running included (naturally enough) the area within 25 feet of the air intakes and behind the airplane for a considerable distance. (U.S. Air Force via Jerry McCulley)

TABLE II.– GEOMETRIC CHARACTERISTICS OF THE XB-70 AIRPLANES

```
Total wing –
  Total area (includes 2482.34 sq ft covered by fuselage but
    not 33.53 sq ft of wing ramp area), sq ft . . . . . . . . . . .  6297.15
  Span, ft . . . . . . . . . . . . . . . . . . . . . . . . . . . . . . . .  105
  Aspect ratio . . . . . . . . . . . . . . . . . . . . . . . . . . . . .  1.751
  Taper ratio . . . . . . . . . . . . . . . . . . . . . . . . . . . . . .  0.019
                                                          XB-70-1  XB-70-2
  Dihedral angle, deg . . . . . . . . . . . . . . . . . . . .  0        5
  Root chord (wing station 0), ft . . . . . . . . . . . . . . . . . . .  117.76
  Tip chord (wing station 630), ft . . . . . . . . . . . . . . . . . . .  2.19
  Mean aerodynamic chord (wing station 213.85), in. . . . . . . . . . .  942.38
  Fuselage station of 25-percent wing mean aerodynamic
    chord, in. . . . . . . . . . . . . . . . . . . . . . . . . . . . . .  1621.22
  Sweepback angle, deg:
    Leading edge . . . . . . . . . . . . . . . . . . . . . . . . . . . .  65.57
    25-percent element . . . . . . . . . . . . . . . . . . . . . . . . .  58.79
    Trailing edge . . . . . . . . . . . . . . . . . . . . . . . . . . . .  0
  Incidence angle, deg:
    Root (fuselage juncture) . . . . . . . . . . . . . . . . . . . . . .  0
    Tip (fold line and outboard) . . . . . . . . . . . . . . . . . . . .  -2.60
  Airfoil section:
    Root to wing station 186 (thickness-chord ratio,
      2 percent) . . . . . . . . . . . . . . . . . . . . . . . .  0.30 - 0.70 HEX (MOD)
    Wing station 460 to 630 (thickness-chord ratio,
      2.5 percent) . . . . . . . . . . . . . . . . . . . . . . .  0.30 - 0.70 HEX (MOD)
Inboard wing –
  Area (includes 2482.34 sq ft covered by fuselage but
    not 33.53 sq ft wing ramp area), sq ft . . . . . . . . . . . . . . .  5255.47
  Span, ft . . . . . . . . . . . . . . . . . . . . . . . . . . . . . . .  63.44
  Aspect ratio . . . . . . . . . . . . . . . . . . . . . . . . . . . . .  0.766
  Taper ratio . . . . . . . . . . . . . . . . . . . . . . . . . . . . .  0.407
                                                          XB-70-1  XB-70-2
  Dihedral angle, deg . . . . . . . . . . . . . . . . . . . .  0        5
  Root chord (wing station 0), ft . . . . . . . . . . . . . . . . . . .  117.76
  Tip chord (wing station 380.62), ft . . . . . . . . . . . . . . . . .  47.94
  Mean aerodynamic chord (wing station 163.58), in. . . . . . . . . . .  1053
  Fuselage station of 25-percent wing mean aerodynamic
    chord, in. . . . . . . . . . . . . . . . . . . . . . . . . . . . . .  1538.29
  Sweepback angle, deg:
    Leading edge . . . . . . . . . . . . . . . . . . . . . . . . . . . .  65.57
    25-percent element . . . . . . . . . . . . . . . . . . . . . . . . .  58.79
    Trailing edge . . . . . . . . . . . . . . . . . . . . . . . . . . . .  0
  Airfoil section:
    Root (thickness-chord ratio, 2 percent) . . . . . . . . .  0.30 - 0.70 HEX (MOD)
    Tip (thickness-chord ratio, 2.4 percent) . . . . . . . .  0.30 - 0.70 HEX (MOD)
```

TABLE II.– GEOMETRIC CHARACTERISTICS OF THE XB-70 AIRPLANES – Continued

```
  Mean camber (leading edge), deg:
    Butt plane 0 . . . . . . . . . . . . . . . . . . . . . . . . . . . .  0.15
    Butt plane 107 . . . . . . . . . . . . . . . . . . . . . . . . . . .  4.40
    Butt plane 153 . . . . . . . . . . . . . . . . . . . . . . . . . . .  2.75
    Butt plane 257 . . . . . . . . . . . . . . . . . . . . . . . . . . .  2.60
    Butt plane 367 to tip . . . . . . . . . . . . . . . . . . . . . . . .  0
Outboard wing –
  Area (one side only), sq ft . . . . . . . . . . . . . . . . . . . . .  520.84
  Span, ft . . . . . . . . . . . . . . . . . . . . . . . . . . . . . . .  41.56
  Aspect ratio . . . . . . . . . . . . . . . . . . . . . . . . . . . . .  1.658
  Taper ratio . . . . . . . . . . . . . . . . . . . . . . . . . . . . .  0.046
  Dihedral angle, deg . . . . . . . . . . . . . . . . . . . . . . . . .  5
  Root chord (wing station 380.62), ft . . . . . . . . . . . . . . . . .  47.94
  Tip chord (wing station 630), ft . . . . . . . . . . . . . . . . . . .  2.19
  Mean aerodynamic chord (wing station 467.37), in. . . . . . . . . . .  384.25
  Sweepback angle, deg:
    Leading edge . . . . . . . . . . . . . . . . . . . . . . . . . . . .  65.57
    25-percent element . . . . . . . . . . . . . . . . . . . . . . . . .  58.79
    Trailing edge . . . . . . . . . . . . . . . . . . . . . . . . . . . .  0
  Airfoil section:
    Root (thickness-chord ratio, 2.4 percent) . . . . . . . .  0.30 - 0.70 HEX (MOD)
    Tip (thickness-chord ratio, 2.5 percent) . . . . . . . .  0.30 - 0.70 HEX (MOD)
  Down deflection from wing reference plane, deg . . . . . . . . . .  0, 30, 70
  Skewline of tip fold, deg:
    Leading edge in . . . . . . . . . . . . . . . . . . . . . . . . . .  1.5
    Leading edge down . . . . . . . . . . . . . . . . . . . . . . . . .  3
  Wing-tip area in wing reference plane (one side only), sq ft:
    Rotated down 30° . . . . . . . . . . . . . . . . . . . . . . . . . .  472.04
    Rotated down 70° . . . . . . . . . . . . . . . . . . . . . . . . . .  220.01
                                                              Wing tips
                                                              Up     Down
  Elevons (data for one side):
    Total area aft of hinge line, sq ft . . . . . . . . . .  188.45   132.44
    Span, ft . . . . . . . . . . . . . . . . . . . . . . .   20.44    13.98
    Inboard chord (equivalent), in. . . . . . . . . . . . .  116      116
    Outboard chord (equivalent), in. . . . . . . . . . . .   116      116
    Sweepback angle of hinge line, deg . . . . . . . . . .   0        0
    Deflection, deg –
      As elevator . . . . . . . . . . . . . . . . . . . . .  -25 to 15  -25 to 15
      As aileron with elevators at ±15° or less . . . . . .  -15 to 15  -15 to 15
      As aileron with elevators at -25° . . . . . . . . . .  -5 to 5    -5 to 5
      Total . . . . . . . . . . . . . . . . . . . . . . . .  -30 to 30  -30 to 30
Canard –
  Area (includes 150.31 sq ft covered by fuselage), sq ft . . . . . . .  415.59
  Span, ft . . . . . . . . . . . . . . . . . . . . . . . . . . . . . . .  28.81
  Aspect ratio . . . . . . . . . . . . . . . . . . . . . . . . . . . . .  1.997
  Taper ratio . . . . . . . . . . . . . . . . . . . . . . . . . . . . .  0.388
```

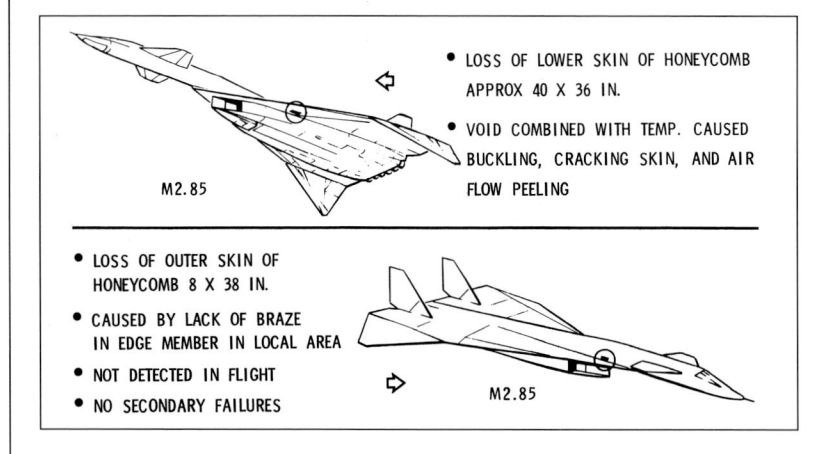

M2.85
- LOSS OF LOWER SKIN OF HONEYCOMB APPROX 40 X 36 IN.
- VOID COMBINED WITH TEMP. CAUSED BUCKLING, CRACKING SKIN, AND AIR FLOW PEELING

M2.85
- LOSS OF OUTER SKIN OF HONEYCOMB 8 X 38 IN.
- CAUSED BY LACK OF BRAZE IN EDGE MEMBER IN LOCAL AREA
- NOT DETECTED IN FLIGHT
- NO SECONDARY FAILURES

M3.00
- LOSS OF LOWER SKIN OF WING LEADING EDGE HONEYCOMB PANEL APPROX 17 X 120 IN.
- ARC SPOT-WELD CRACKS PROPAGATED TO 40-INCH LENGTH
- ARROWHEAD-TO-CORE ATTACH FAILED
- AIRFLOW ENTERED PANEL CAUSING EXCESSIVE INTERNAL PRESSURE WHICH TORE LOWER FACESHEET FROM CORE.

M2.57
- LOSS OF LOWER SKIN OF WING APEX PANEL FORWARD 35 INCHES
- LOSS OF REPAIR PIN ATTACHMENT
- AERODYNAMIC "SHOCK DETACHMENT" PHENOMENON PRODUCED GREATER DOWN LOADS AT M1.3
- AIRFLOW ENTERED PANEL CAUSING LOWER FACESHEET TO PEEL FROM CORE

Despite the well-publicized skin peeling events, there were actually only a few times that major sections of skin separated from A/V-1. The bottom event at right was the most serious. (U.S. Air Force)

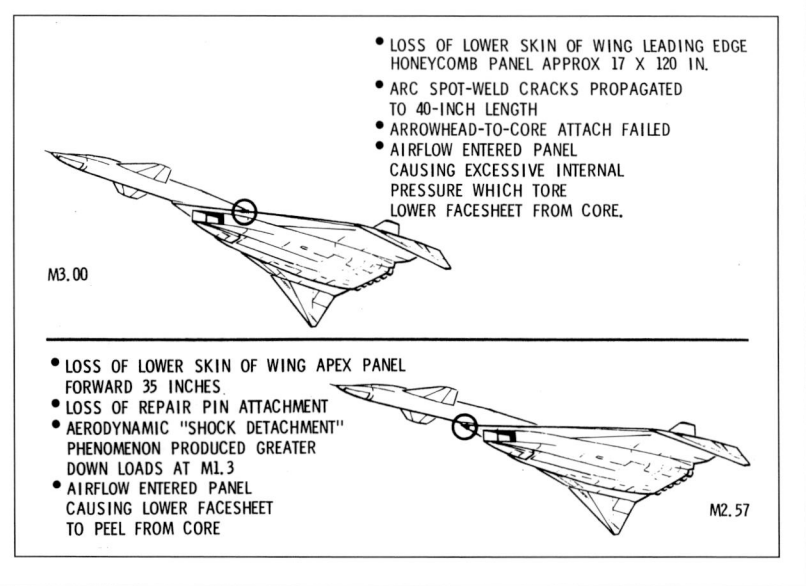

TABLE II. – GEOMETRIC CHARACTERISTICS OF THE XB-70 AIRPLANES – Continued

Dihedral angle, deg	0
Root chord (canard station 0), ft	20.79
Tip chord (canard station 172.86), ft	8.06
Mean aerodynamic chord (canard station 73.71), in.	184.3
Fuselage station of 25-percent canard mean aerodynamic chord	553.73
Sweepback angle, deg:	
Leading edge	31.70
25-percent element	21.64
Trailing edge	-14.91
Incidence angle (nose up), deg	0 to 6
Airfoil section:	
Root (thickness-chord ratio 2.5 percent)	0.34 - 0.66 HEX (MOD)
Tip (thickness-chord ratio 2.52 percent)	0.34 - 0.66 HEX (MOD)
Ratio of canard area to wing area	0.066
Canard flap (one of two):	
Area (aft of hinge line), sq ft	54.69
Ratio of flap area to canard semi-area	0.263
Vertical tail (one of two) –	
Area (includes 8.96 sq ft blanketed area), sq ft	233.96
Span, ft	15
Aspect ratio	1
Taper ratio	0.30
Root chord (vertical-tail station 0), ft	23.08
Tip chord (vertical-tail station 180), ft	6.92
Mean aerodynamic chord (vertical-tail station 73.85), in.	197.40
Fuselage station of 25-percent vertical-tail mean aerodynamic chord	2188.50
Sweepback angle, deg:	
Leading edge	51.77
25-percent element	45
Trailing edge	10.89
Airfoil section:	
Root (thickness-chord ratio 3.75 percent)	0.30 - 0.70 HEX (MOD)
Tip (thickness-chord ratio 2.5 percent)	0.30 - 0.70 HEX (MOD)
Cant angle, deg	0
Ratio vertical tail to wing area	0.037
Rudder travel, deg:	
With gear extended	±12
With gear retracted	±3
Fuselage (includes canopy) –	
Length, ft	189
Maximum depth (fuselage station 878), in.	106.92
Maximum breadth (fuselage station 855), in.	100
Side area, sq ft	939.72
Planform area, sq ft	1184.78
Duct –	
Length, ft	104.84
Maximum depth (fuselage station 1375), in.	90.75
Maximum breadth (fuselage station 2100), in.	360.70

TABLE II. – GEOMETRIC CHARACTERISTICS OF THE XB-70 AIRPLANES – Concluded

Side area, sq ft	716.66
Planform area, sq ft	2342.33
Inlet captive area (each), sq in.	5600
Surface areas (net wetted), sq ft –	
Fuselage and canopy	2871.24
Duct	4956.66
Wing, wing tips, and wing ramp	7658.44
Vertical tails (two)	936.64
Canard	530.83
Tail pipes	340.45
Total	17,294.26
Landing gear –	
Tread, ft	23.17
Wheelbase, in.	554.50
Tire size:	
Main gear (8)	40 x 17.5-18
Nose gear (2)	40 x 17.5-18

MINIMUM TURNING RADIUS AND GROUND CLEARANCE

TURNING RADIUS BASED ON NOSE WHEELS TURNED 58 DEGREES FROM CENTER. (NOSE WHEEL STEERING SWITCH AT TAXI POSITION)

1. PITOT BOOM — 142 FEET
2. NOSE — 134 FEET
3. WING TIP — 97 FEET
4. NOSE GEAR — 54 FEET
5. LEFT MAIN GEAR — 40 FEET
6. RIGHT MAIN GEAR — 17 FEET

15 FT   10 FT   13 FT   7 FT   9 FT   15 FT   16.5 FT

Rings were installed around the J93 nozzles to allow the sound abatement chambers to be connected. (Boeing Historical Archives)

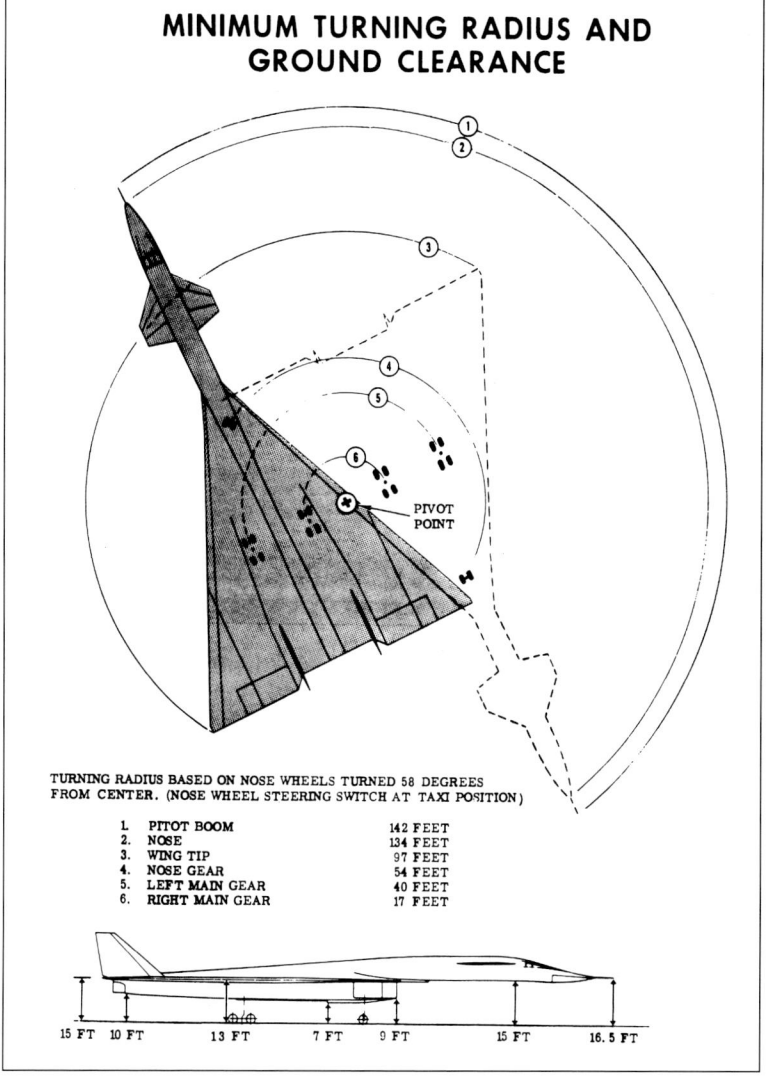

Taxiing the XB-70 was a challenge since the nose wheel was 65 feet behind the pilots. (U.S. Air Force via Jerry McCulley)

Chapter 8

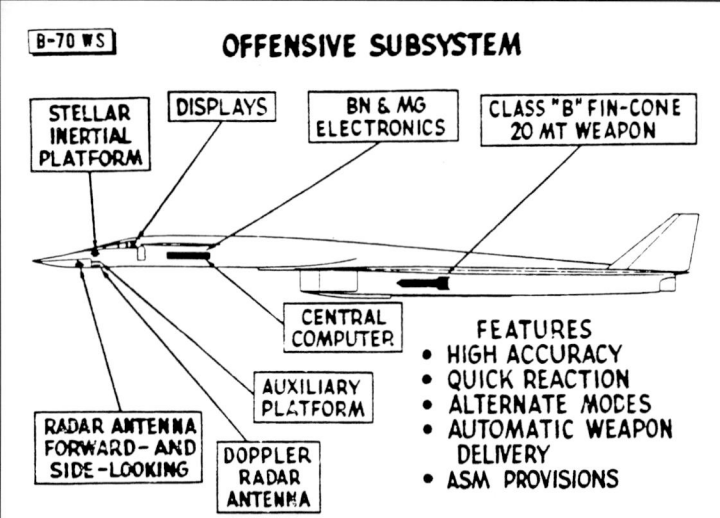

Left: *Production B-70s would have carried the most sophisticated offensive systems of the day, including a new bombing, navigation, and missile guidance (BN&MG) system developed specifically for the Valkyrie.* (U.S. Air Force)

Below: *The Pye Wacket lenticular defensive missile in a wind tunnel at the Air Force Arnold Engineering Development Center. This was one of the more radical proposals for an active defensive system for WS-110A and WS-125A* (Arnold Engineering Development Center)

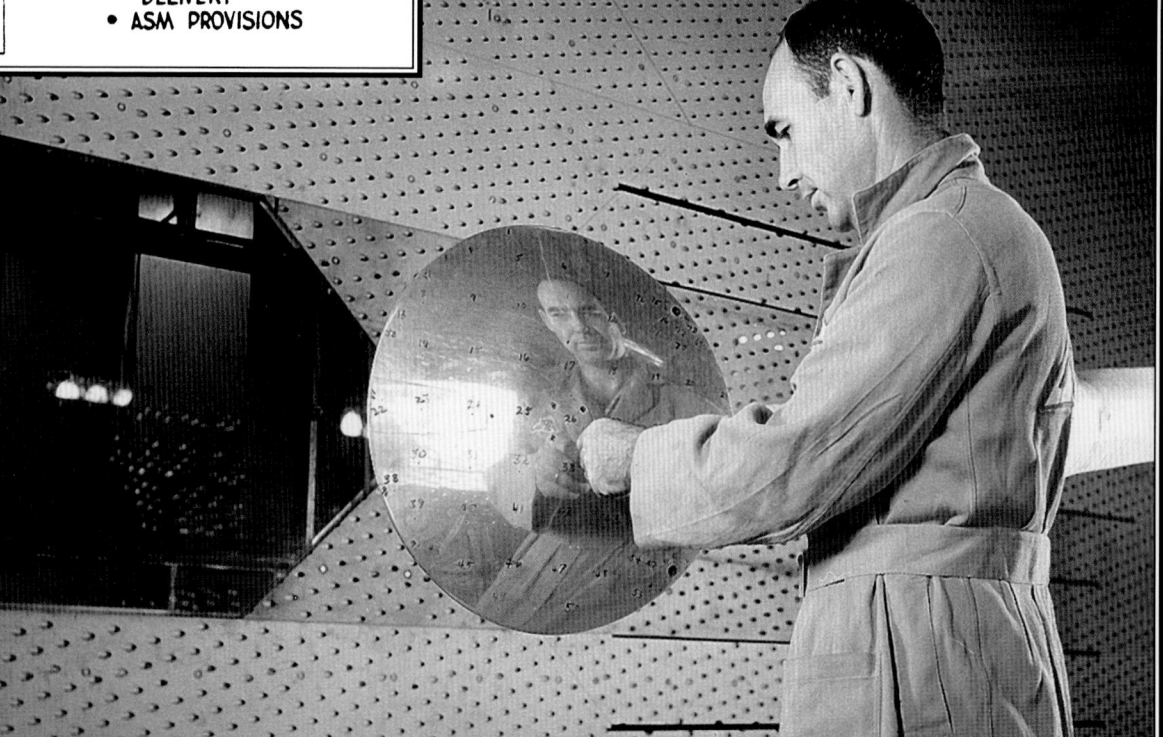

NO APPARENT THREAT
MILITARY SYSTEMS

Because of their purely test roles, the two XB-70As never carried any military systems – no bombsights, defensive weapons, or electronic countermeasures. However, a great deal of time and money was poured into the development of these systems during the early period when it appeared operational B-70s would actually serve with the Strategic Air Command. What follows is a history of that development effort. Not very many pretty pictures, but an interesting story nevertheless.

WEAPONS BAY

Although often described as a single 29-foot long weapons bay, there were in reality two separate 14-foot-long bays covered by a shared set of doors. The combined bay extended from FS1356 to FS1704. Using a pair of sliding doors on a single set of tracks instead of the usual outward-opening snap-action doors solved the problem of opening the weapons bay doors at very high speeds. The length of the track permitted only one door to be opened at a time. Moving both doors aft opened the forward 14 feet of the bay; moving only the aft door opened the rear 14 feet of the bay; the center 1 foot was unusable since the doors never cleared the area. This also meant that weapons longer than about 13 feet could not be carried by the B-70. In the closed position, the leading edge of the forward door was held tight against the step fairing of the fuselage by two interconnected hooks that engaged the fuselage structure. The aft door was locked to the forward door in a similar manner. It should be noted that the weapons bay doors on A/V-1 and A/V-2 were not powered and could not be opened in flight. The forward weapons bay contained the flight test instrumentation package while the aft weapons bay contained the air inlet control system equipment. A/V-3 would have had powered doors, as well as suspension and release equipment in the rear portion of the weapons bay for a single type of weapon for demonstration purposes.[1]

The weapons bay was sized to house a variety of bombs, including thermonuclear devices up to 10,000 pounds each, 20,000-pound conventional bombs, various smaller conventional bombs, chemical and biological weapons, or up to two new air-to-ground missiles. The missiles were to have a range of 300 to 700 nautical miles and an accuracy of less than a mile; conceptually these missiles were much like the later AGM-69A SRAM. Other missiles (probably Douglas GAM-87 Skybolts) were to be carried on external hard points under the wings, along with additional fuel in external drop tanks. Despite some speculative drawings that show what appear to be Skybolts in the weapons bay, the missile was much too large to fit and the door openings would never have allowed such a large weapon to be launched.[2]

THE BOMB-NAV SYSTEM

As early as 1945, the Armament Laboratory at the Wright Air Development Center (WADC) had expressed an interest in navigation techniques based on star tracking. Stellar navigation, unlike radar or optical techniques, grew more accurate as altitude increased, and could – theoretically at least – be accomplished with no Earth

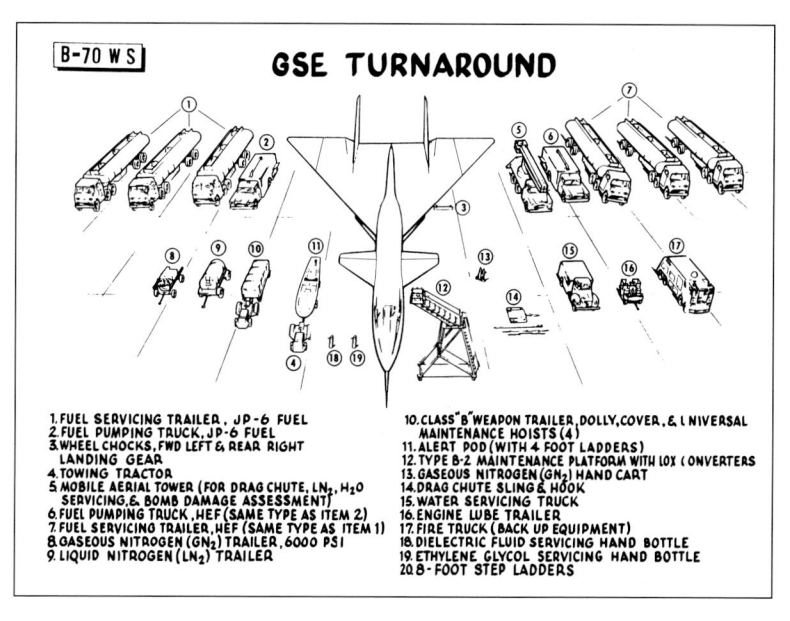

Here is the ground support equipment the Air Force expected to use with operational B-70s. Note the alert pod (number 11). (U.S. Air Force)

reference. Sailors and airmen had been doing it manually for centuries. The trick was to do it quickly enough to be useful at very high speeds. Stellar reference points had known positions with respect to the Earth and made it possible to compute the observer's exact terrestrial position, theoretically allowing solutions to bombing and navigation problems to be obtained automatically. Moreover, the ability to deliver a weapon without reliance on the transmission of radar or radio signals was obviously desirable to the Air Force.[3]

At the same time, the Air Force also looked to the possibilities inherent in the development of inertial platforms, as well as hybrid inertial systems that were monitored and updated by star trackers. Assuming they knew exactly where they started, inertial devices could derive their position entirely by sensing acceleration in all three axes, and therefore were completely self-contained. They were, however, very large and heavy, at least at the time.[4]

Academic Investigations

Since both types of systems seemed to hold promise, the Air Force asked Dr. Charles Stark Draper at the Massachusetts Institute of Technology (MIT) to undertake research in both areas. During 1946, MIT took an important step along the stellar-inertial path under what came to be called Project FEBE (after the Sun god, Pheobus). The preliminary tests of inertial components were so encouraging that MIT abandoned theoretical work on star tracking and attempted to design a pure inertial navigation system – without stellar monitoring – that would give an accuracy of 1 nautical mile after 12 hours of flight at high subsonic speeds.[5]

Based on the promising experimental results, Draper attempted to design, fabricate, and test an experimental inertial unit as part of Project SPIRE (Space Position Inertial Reference Equipment). Progress was excruciatingly slow, and by December 1957, the project had been terminated, although astonishingly good flight test results had been recorded during the final few months. Flight-derived acceleration data had supplied nearly all the information required to compute the actual course, position, and velocity of an aircraft with respect to Earth. This data, if fed into a bombing computer, could be used to compute a bomb release signal. The computer would "know" when flight-derived position data showed the aircraft to be precisely where preflight calculations indicated it should be at the instant of bomb release. Despite the program's untimely cancellation, it had been an outstanding achievement.[6]

Unfortunately, the SPIRE system weighed almost 3,000 pounds, and the gimbal system for its gyroscopes was over 4 feet in diameter. Its control console was also extremely bulky. The experimental system did not have any provisions for allowing the aircraft to fly a "dog-leg" course, and the target could not be changed after the aircraft had taken off. The experimental equipment, installed in a Boeing C-97 transport, was neither pressurized nor insulated, and was not suitable for use in an operational environment. It was expected, however, that these problems could be overcome with further development. Another problem, however, looked insurmountable at the time; the system needed 48 hours of pre-flight gyroscope calibration and alignment before each mission. The enemy would need to give lots of notice to allow SPIRE to be ready.[7]

In early 1955, during the SPIRE tests, Draper began designing a lighter and more flexible inertial system, called SPIRE Jr., that scientists hoped would overcome the shortcomings of the original unit. SPIRE Jr. was flight tested in the same C-97 as its predecessor and was about half its size and weight. Alignment still took two days, but the new unit could be aligned while in the hangar then installed in an aircraft in under 5 minutes. In theory this would allow multiple units to be in varying phases of alignment at all times; when the need arose, the "most ready" unit would be installed in an aircraft. Typical of the test program, on one 6-hour flight, the system generated position errors of 4 miles in range and 1.5 miles in track. This was considered excellent for the era, and was getting to close to what a typical human navigator could manage.[8]

Industry Investigations

Air Force interest in the concept of a "correctable" inertial system, particularly one that used star tracking to compensate for gyro drift error led to a series of study contracts being issued to the AC Spark Plug Division of General Motors, Hughes Aircraft Company, IBM Corporation, North American Aviation, Pacific Mercury Television Manufacturing Company, and the Sperry Gyroscope Company.[9]

One of the earliest was a May 1946 contract awarded to Hughes to develop an experimental red-sensitive automatic star-tracker for use in a stellar-inertial navigation system. The unit was to be capable of detecting and tracking bright stars in full daylight. The goal of the study was to demonstrate the capability of guiding an aircraft over a course between two predetermined points using an inertial device corrected by continuous star sightings. Later that year, Hughes reported that the experimental Mark I star tracker had been successfully tested on the ground, converting daylight star images into useful electrical signals. Next, Hughes modified the design so that it could be mounted on a five-gimbal gyro-stabilized platform that allowed tracking stars while the aircraft was maneuvering. This Mark II device began flight tests in November 1947, but proved to be overly complicated and Hughes began designing a simpler three-axis gimbal platform.[10]

It was a long process, but by February 1950, the simplified model was undergoing flight tests. Within two months, the device had demonstrated destination errors of approximately 5 miles after 4 hours of continuous flight. Although this did not meet the existing specifications for navigation, bombing, or guidance systems, the Hughes equipment had performed sufficiently well to justify continuing the effort. By mid-1951, Hughes had completed two engineering models of the star-tracker itself, and had performed limited experimental work with a smaller telescope that used a refrigerated infrared detector cell that allowed a considerable increase in the number of stars that could be tracked. This smaller telescope proved to be practical and would be used as the basis of further efforts.[11]

Unexpectedly, however, Hughes backed out of the project, explaining that the company did not have sufficient resources to accommodate all of the Air Force contracts that had recently been awarded.[12] The WADC transferred the project – along with most of the hardware already developed by Hughes – to the Pacific Mercury Television Manufacturing Company.[13] However, some project personnel and at least two experimental star-trackers also went to North American where they were used as a basis for the navigation systems ultimately developed for the SM-64 Navaho intercontinental missile program.[14]

Pacific Mercury continued the development work and by mid-1953 had constructed three star trackers employing miniaturized telescopes. However, the Air Force terminated the program because of "excess cost." Mercury Pacific delivered one of the star trackers to Wright Field for further testing, while the others went to the AC Spark Plug Division of General Motors for use in a stellar-inertial bombing system called SIBS.[15]

The AC work had begun several years earlier, and the original specifications called for day and night operation at 60,000 feet with ground speeds as high as 1,050 knots and true air speeds of 800 knots. The first components for the inertial system had been manufactured during August 1951 and ground tests were completed in December 1952. After this, AC constructed one experimental and one preproduction system based on the original MIT-developed SPIRE Jr. design, but incorporated the Pacific Mercury star tracker to monitor the inertial component. The Air Force also anticipated that any operational version of the system would include some type of "precision bomb director" employing either an active radar or optical sight for the final bomb run into the target.[16]

The ultimate goal was the development of a navigation system that operated in five general phases. During the preflight phase the way-points, targets, navigational stars, and primary and alternate routes would be selected. Ground teams would then prepare punched paper tapes containing the information required for the onboard computer. During this phase, the inertial system would be aligned and calibrated, largely through the use of portable instrumentation.[17]

The navigation phase of the mission, which could cover any distance, would be flown using completely automatic stellar-inertial navigation guidance. Some distance from the target, the navigator would briefly switch on the radar and the crosshairs of the bomb-sight would automatically align on a predetermined checkpoint with a maximum uncertainty of 1 nautical mile. The navigator then centered the crosshairs on the checkpoint to reduce the system error to less than 1,000 feet. Under ordinary circumstances, the bombing phase of the mission would be completely automatic and would not require the radar, although it could be used to further improve accuracy. The radar could also be used to perform a damage assessment if desired. Automatic stellar-inertial navigation would then guide the aircraft back to a predetermined recovery base.[18]

Up until this time, the stellar-inertial systems had been intended for both manned aircraft and intercontinental missiles such as the Navaho. In May 1954, the Armament Laboratory separated the stellar-inertial development efforts into two distinct entities and combined all bomber efforts under a single large effort called the "High Altitude Strategic Bombing Components and Techniques" program. The two major goals

After years of academic and industry research, star trackers became a reality, and the upward-pointing lens of the one for the proposed operational B-70 was located just ahead of the windscreen. The in-flight refueling receptacle may be seen on the upper surface of the extreme nose of the B-70 mockup. (Boeing Historical Archives)

were the perfection of a stellar-inertial system that had as many automatic features as possible and the development of a system to launch inertial-guided air-to-surface missiles. The unspecified air-to-surface missile was to have a circular error probable (CEP) of 1 nautical mile "with the entire crew of the launching aircraft incapacitated"; with the crew in attendance, this error was to be reduced to under 1,500 feet.[19]

The overarching program included a number of different projects, including one that called for IBM to modify the then-in-development MA-2 bombing system (that relied on radar) so that it could "align and launch" air-to-surface missiles. By February 1955, IBM was studying alignment and launching techniques and was fabricating experimental components to operate the MA-2 in conjunction with an air-to-surface missile. At this point, the MA-2 was planned for installation on the B-52, and was carried as a backup for the B-58.[20]

At the same time, Sperry Gyroscope Company was in the middle of component development of a three-axis stellar-inertial device called TEMPO. By February 1955, the first two TEMPO systems using infrared star trackers were entering flight test. Sperry, however, reported three major problems: a difficulty in the precision manufacturing required for the gyroscopes and accelerometers, an inability to demonstrate continuously-reliable star detection under flight conditions, and the need to simplify the preflight procedures.[21]

Running concurrently with these developments was extensive inertial and stellar-inertial research at North American. The company had begun investigating inertial systems in 1946 in support of what eventually became the SM-64 Navaho. During 1950, while continuing the Navaho efforts, North American began development of a stellar-inertial guidance system for manned bombers. One of the first efforts was part of BRASS RING, a relatively short-lived attempt to employ B-47s as drone bombers to deliver a massive thermonuclear weapon to targets well beyond the range of existing bombers.[22] North American made extensive use of the work that had been accomplished by Hughes, and even hired some of the Hughes engineering team. In June 1951, North American acquired two of the star-trackers that had been manufactured by Hughes before they had abandoned the program.[23]

By this time, North American had independently developed the X-1 all-inertial system and the X-2 stellar-inertial system. The X-2 was mounted in a truck for its initial tests during early 1951, leading North American to report "the first known successful tracking of dim stars in daylight from a moving vehicle has been accomplished and is consistently repeatable." The X-2 was subsequently flight tested in a C-97, continuing until May 1953. However, the X-1 and X-2 were breadboard models intended solely to demonstrate the basic concept. In 1952, North American began working on an operational version of the X-2 called the XN2B. The XN2B was tested in a T-29 beginning in June 1954 and was installed in an X-10 subscale Navaho in late 1954 for additional tests. North American also developed the N2C version as a back-up guidance system for the Northrop Snark missile.[24]

Coming Together

On 15 April 1955, these semi-independent efforts took on new meaning when the Air Force published SR-22 for a "Piloted Strategic Intercontinental Bombardment Weapon System." The requirements outlined in this document clearly indicated the need for an inertial navigation system with some sort of monitoring and correction capability. Three days before, the Weapons Guidance Laboratory at the WADC had published an "exhibit" (appendix) outlining the functions required for the bombing and navigation system for the new bomber. This was the first time a specific application had been mentioned for the work that had been ongoing at the various companies.

The bombing and navigation system envisioned in SR-22 was to be shared to the maximum extent possible between WS-110A and WS-125A. If a completely common system was not feasible, then as many common components as possible should be shared between the two platforms. The system was to take advantage of the "inherent flexibility" of a manned aircraft and employ automatic features "only to the extent necessary for mission success." A "careful balance between accuracy, reliability, and serviceability" was required, plus "minimum susceptibility to passive detection" and a "high degree of security from jamming." In addition, "enroute [position] fixing and terminal sighting" accuracy in "reference point bombing from distances of up to 200 NM" and "indirect bomb damage assessment" needed to be provided. System component malfunctions were to be minimized "by the use of such techniques as multiple circuitry and modular construction." A 1,500-foot CEP was required for conventional bombing,[25] although this figure could be increased to 5,000 feet "if the loss can be translated into increased reliability and/or improved maintenance characteristics."[26]

Officially, the new equipment was called a bombing-navigation-missile guidance (BNMG) system, but this was generally shortened to bombing-navigation system, or even more simply to bomb-nav. SR-22 required that the bomber had to be able to cover the last 200 nautical miles to the target "without employing radiation devices for guidance." This meant no radar from the bomber. The only known system that could fulfill this requirement was an inertial system. However, in 1955 (indeed, even in 1960), inertial platforms were not accurate enough to solve the bombing and navigation problem by themselves. They seemed to be particularly fallible in providing azimuth data (the heading of the aircraft with respect to north). Time, azimuth, velocity, and altitude were – of course – the critical factors in determining the position of the air vehicle.[27]

Time was relatively easy, sufficiently accurate aircraft clocks having been available for years. The best available method of obtaining accurate azimuth data was thought to be from a star tracker. Experiments had already proven that star trackers could be integrated with inertial platforms, so this quickly became the baseline configuration. The Weapons Guidance Laboratory determined that the best way to obtain velocity data (relative to the Earth) was to employ a Doppler radar to measure slowly varying changes in speed while two accelerometers sensed rapid velocity changes. Altitude was available from air data sources of Doppler radar.[28]

Based on what was known, the desired system appeared to be a stellar-inertial system with a Doppler radar. Now the Weapons Guidance Laboratory had to figure out how to integrate these sensing devices into a workable system. Ideally, this required a digital computer, but one had never been used in a bombing and navigation system. In fact, the only airborne application for such a device in 1955 was the planned use in the highly sophisticated Hughes MX-1179 fire control system being developed for the Convair F-102B (F-106) interceptor.[29]

The storage capacity of a digital computer also played a part in star tracker operation. Obviously, star trackers needed exceedingly accurate data on the location of stars. Star trackers rapidly lost accuracy when scanning through a large area, so the initial attempt to find a specific star should ideally be limited to no more than one-fifteenth of a mile in position and one-tenth of a degree in azimuth. The computer would have to store, before flight, a large number of exact star locations (later set at 100) in order to determine what stars could best be tracked at any time. Furthermore, to provide acceptable navigation at supersonic speeds, the system would require new position information every half second or so, and only a digital computer could accommodate this refresh rate.[30]

Unsurprisingly, IBM was very interested in the new project and was consulted early in the design process. The first estimate of the nascent system provided by IBM indicated that the ultimate device would have some 2,000 transistors, 4,000 diodes, and 600 connectors – considered extremely complex for the time.[31] After one look at this estimate, the Weapons Guidance Laboratory quickly concluded that the reliability of the system would be unacceptably low. As an alternative, it was decided to allow humans to play a much greater role in the system since it was felt that a well-trained operator could monitor the equipment and provide in-flight maintenance to compensate for failures. Because IBM predicted that the computer would probably fail before any of the other components, the laboratory decided to add a contingency computer. It was smaller and less efficient, but supplemented by human intelligence it could do the job if necessary.[32]

In addition, the human operator was to have a direct operational function. Since he could observe a radar scope (optical bombsights were not feasible at the speed and altitude envisioned for the new bomber), the laboratory included a search radar to be used as a conventional bombing instrument and for navigation.[33]

The problem of aligning and calibrating the system remained; the short response time dictated by SR-22 essentially meant the task would have to be accomplished in flight. The Doppler radar provided velocity information, but azimuth and position data was harder to obtain. If each runway was precisely surveyed, then the rough azimuth could be provided during the takeoff roll or early in flight. Based on this data and the Doppler velocity, the gyroscopes could be erected, but the platform would require much more precise data before it could function as designed. Next came the "gyro-compassing phase" where the erected inertial platform was rotated so that it defined a line relative to the axis of the Earth's rotation; this gave a reasonably precise orientation with respect to true north.[34]

The precise position information required by the star tracker was obtained using the search radar scanning for known features on the Earth somewhere near the airfield. This provided a relationship to a known terrestrial location, allowing the computer to supply the star tracker with instructions on which star to seek and approximately where it was located. After the first star was found, a second was located. Thereafter the system could provide accurate azimuth and position data. The entire process took about 30 minutes, by which time the aircraft was several hundred miles from where it started. At a reference point 200 nautical miles from the target (but theoretically any time after alignment), the search radar would take a final position fix to recalibrate the platform. All transmissions then stopped and navigation became completely dependent on the inertial system and star tracker.[35]

The Weapons Guidance Laboratory felt that there was insufficient time to develop an entirely new system, so once the operational technique had been established, the laboratory began looking at what components already under development could be applied to the new system. Funding and scheduling (to ensure the system was synchronized with the overall aircraft schedule) would soon become the dominant factors in the entire WS-110A bomb-nav system effort.[36]

Initial attention was given to various "K-system" components used on earlier bombers such as the B-36 and B-47, as well as the new MA-2 system being developed by IBM for the B-52. Other components included the system (later designated ASQ-42) being developed by Sperry for the Convair B-58 and a modified version of the SPIRE Jr. concept. By August 1955, the laboratory had narrowed the search to an improved MA-2 and the B-58 system, although neither totally met the proposed requirements. Based on its advanced search radar and anti-jamming features, the MA-2 was favored by the laboratory. Despite this apparent decision, in September, the laboratory issued study contracts to IBM, Motorola, and Sperry to investigate other bomb-nav system configurations for both WS-110A and WS-125A.[37]

It quickly became apparent that the new bomb-nav systems needed to be disassociated because the schedules for the two bomber programs were rapidly diverging. The WS-110A was scheduled to enter Phase I development (advanced study) some 13 months before its nuclear-powered WS-125A cousin. During the 1950s, IBM was a favored contractor by the Air Force, mainly because they were perceived as owning the cutting edge, and usually managed to deliver what they promised. Based on the compressed development schedule for WS-110A, the Weapons Guidance Laboratory favored contracting with IBM on a sole source basis. There was little opposition from higher commands, and on 7 December, IBM was awarded a contract for the development of the WS-110A bombing and navigation system. This had the effect of making a modified MA-2 virtually inevitable for WS-110A. At the same time, Bell Telephone Laboratories was awarded a contract for the WS-125A system, although the Air Force hoped it would be largely similar to the IBM WS-110A system.[38]

Almost as soon as the two airframe manufacturers were under contract for the initial WS-110A studies, they began to provide input to the bomb-nav system requirements. North American was essentially in agreement with the Air Force and was planning on using "components ... drawn from existing programs which were well advanced" for the "initial" WS-110A, and proposed to investigate advanced systems for later versions of the airplane. Boeing, on the other hand, favored a completely new bomb-nav system and dismissed the idea of using existing components. The Boeing approach, in the opinion of the Weapons Guidance Laboratory, "might endanger the success of the complete weapon system." The laboratory also questioned the Boeing proposal to rely on side-looking radar in lieu of a conventional forward-looking unit. Side-looking radar increased

The North American Navaho was a Mach 3 intercontinental cruise missile that, like the B-70, fell victim to the ICBM. (Boeing Historical Archives)

No Apparent Threat

system resolution, but was slower in operation (due to processing requirements), posed video display problems (no large CRTs available yet), and was not a proven technique.[39]

On 15 December 1955, the laboratory issued another "exhibit" to SR-22 that established July 1957 as the date for a mockup review of the new bomb-nav system. The same document required that the first prototype be available in April 1960, the first production model in November 1961, and the first fully-capable system would be delivered to SAC a year later. The exhibit also specified that the study had to consider "existing components, components in the advanced states of development, and proven techniques" before proposing anything else.

Once again, reliability was a critical factor, and overall performance had to be at least equivalent to the MA-2.[40]

During the early months of 1956, the Weapons Guidance Laboratory considered extending the IBM contract to cover the atomic-powered WS-125A as well, but the idea was not implemented based largely on not wanting to dilute the WS-110A effort. On 9 March, IBM submitted a technical proposal for the WS-110A bombing and navigation system, and delivered a complete development plan six days later. The laboratory was receptive to the IBM proposal, but the development schedule was six months behind the overall WS-110A timeline.[41]

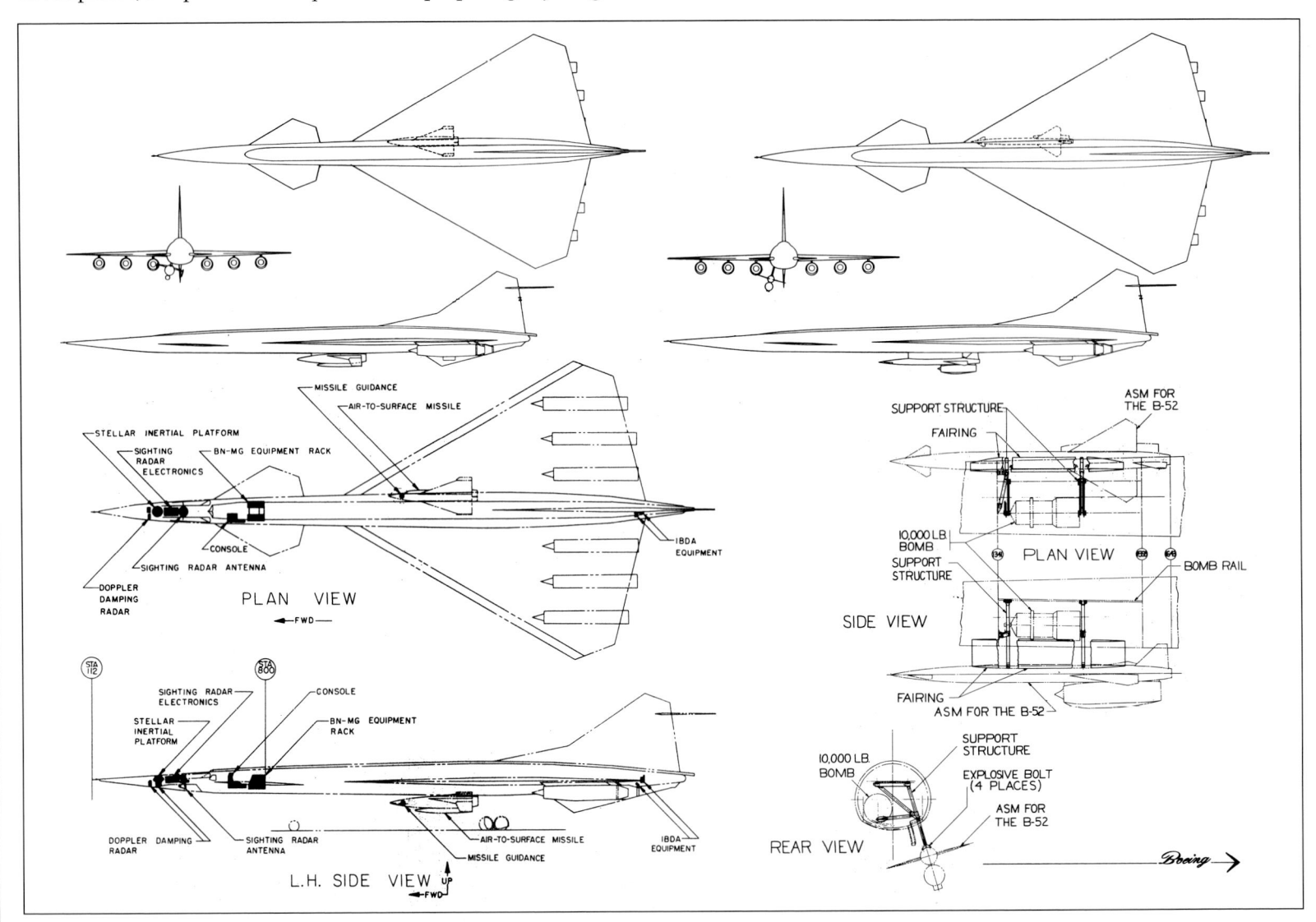

None of the North American WS-110A design studies could be located, but many of the Boeing proposals were retained. Here is the Boeing Model 804-4 showing details of the proposed air-to-surface missile installation. The larger drawing and the top left drawing show a new missile being developed for WS-110A, while the right and top right drawings show the 804-4 carrying a North American GAM-77 (AGM-28) Hound Dog. The GAM-77 was developed for the B-52G/H and was a jet-powered cruise missile developed under WS-131B. For reference, the 9,600-pound Hound Dog was 42 feet 6 inches long, 2 feet 4.5 inches in diameter, and had a wingspan of 12 feet 2 inches. (Boeing Historical Archives)

Further complicating matters was an initiative to accelerate the bomber schedule by a year or more. The Weapons Guidance Laboratory responded by advising the WS-110A Program Office that the new schedule could be met only if the overall system performance requirements were eased. They added that the best bet for the new dates was the MA-2 system modified to incorporate a star tracker and Doppler radar. As things happened, however, the new schedule was a straw in the wind, merely an indication of the rapidity with which the entire program was changing. No program acceleration resulted.[42]

On 30 March 1956, IBM agreed to negotiate a development contract as a follow-on to the existing study contract, and by April, the Weapons Guidance Laboratory had completed its evaluation of the IBM proposal. Although the laboratory judged the proposal "comprehensive and complete," it was not accepted for a number of reasons. One was the schedule disparity; IBM indicated that the prototype system would be at least a year behind the bomber schedule. The laboratory was also still skeptical about the use of side-looking radar, a feature incorporated by IBM largely at the urging of Boeing. The laboratory requested IBM to submit a scaled-down proposal that emphasized free-fall bombing at the expense of missile launching, and without the side-looking radar. Nevertheless, the laboratory asked IBM to provide a system with the "growth potential to meet [the] fully desired performance."[43]

The revised proposal was based on the MA-2 system developed for the B-52 with a (forward looking) High Speed Bombing Radar, and included the North American N2C stellar-inertial platform (developed as a backup for the Snark missile), a General Precision Laboratories APN-96 Doppler radar, and the IBM Dinaboc solid-state digital computer then under development. A Goodyear side-looking radar was provided for use in conjunction with the forward-looking radar but was not given primary emphasis. This concept was presented in briefings on 16 May 1956, and met with general approval.[44]

However, when IBM submitted its formal proposal on 15 June 1956, the laboratory raised new objections. Specifically, the laboratory felt that IBM had "overestimated the scope of the program," "lost sight of objectives," and had shown neither a reasonable management concept nor adequate accounting for the risk associated with the development effort. In addition, the laboratory questioned the estimated $155 million development cost.[45]

By September 1956 Boeing and North American had run out of funding and were authorized to continue the airframe study "on a sustaining basis" only. On 25 October, the Air Force decided to end both studies and four days later announced a decision to reduce the bombing and navigation system effort as well. The fiscal problems led to the entire WS-110A effort being delayed 14 months, changing the first flight date of the initial aircraft from April 1960 to June 1961. IBM was advised of the new schedule and fiscal limitations and submitted a revised proposal on 15 October 1956. Now that more time was available, all parties agreed that it would be possible to include advanced components in the bomb-nav system, although this seemed to ignore the fiscal constraints the program was under. The primary enhancement IBM wanted to incorporate was the High Resolution Side-Looking Radar being designed by Goodyear.[46]

In January 1957, the Air Force dictated a further 11-month schedule slip, pushing first flight out to May 1962 and the first delivery to SAC in November 1964. Around the same time, the IBM effort was formally designated Bombing-Navigation-Missile Guidance System, AN/ASQ-28(V). Nevertheless, the exact character of the program – indeed of the entire WS-110A effort – was more uncertain than ever.[47]

As the WS-110A program continued to slip, the Weapons Guidance Laboratory took the opportunity to expand the functionality of the bomb-nav system. A five-day conference was held at Wright Field in late March, and IBM submitted yet another revised proposal in April. By the end of May 1957, the laboratory began to favor including the side-looking radar into the baseline configuration. In addition, the laboratory directed a comparison between the General Precision APN-96 Doppler radar and the IBM System 14 Doppler radar to determine which was superior. Advanced computers and anti-jamming techniques were also investigated.[48]

At this point, the IBM effort took two separate tracks. The first was essentially what had been originally envisioned: using existing components to build an early capability aimed primarily at demonstrating how well a digital computer would integrate with a stellar-inertial system and Doppler radar. Concurrently, however, IBM now proceeded with the definition and development of an advanced bomb-nav system employing as many improved and new components as possible. The demonstration systems were called experimental models while the advanced systems were called engineering models. IBM was to build two of the former – one for ground tests, the other for flight tests – with the first being available in March 1958. Flight tests were to begin in December 1958. The first engineering model was to be delivered in July 1960 with flight-testing beginning in February 1961.[49]

The experimental models were to use the North American N2C stellar-inertial platform, IBM Dinaboc computer, General Precision APN-96, and the IBM forward-looking High Speed Bombing Radar. The engineering models would incorporate an improved stellar-navigation system (again, probably from North American), the IBM System 14 Doppler radar, high resolution forward-looking and side-looking radars, a faster and higher-capacity computer, some sort of map-matching device, and improved anti-jamming features, probably based on the addition of a traveling wave tube to the radars.[50]

Unexpectedly, in April 1957, Wright Field received notice of a new policy that established guidelines for all future Air Force bomb-nav systems. Originating in the Office of the Deputy Chief of Staff for Development at the Pentagon, the message advised the ARDC and AMC that "after careful consideration, it has been decided that we will no longer develop new BNMGs [bombing-navigation-missile guidance] for each new airplane added to the inventory, especially in view of the present and anticipated limited budgets, together with the missile-manned airplane force structure." Since Air Force Headquarters believed that the ASQ-28 represented the best bet for a system that could be applied to any future manned bomber, the program would be reoriented "toward development of an advanced type BNMG System

This was the radar display for the prototype ASQ-28 radar displays. The left map display had a film transport system and a projector to display where the airplane "should be." The right radar display showed the real world outside the airplane. The radar had a camera on top to record the display during an actual or practice bomb drop. (Jim Tuttle Collection)

that will have sufficient growth potential to be used in any strategic bombardment weapon system built for the 1965–1970 time period." The IBM effort, therefore, took on a new importance.[51]

To provide the most advanced system possible, the Weapons Guidance Laboratory directed IBM to investigate replacing the germanium switching circuits in the Dinaboc computer with silicon transistors and diodes to overcome the excessive weight and cooling problems of the basic design. Furthermore, the laboratory wanted an improved display that included some kind of comparison feature to aid in target identification, but was not ready to authorize the use of the IBM AN/ASB-4 "Topographical Comparator" until the device had passed its acceptance tests. The System 14 Doppler radar was to be improved to allow operation from aircraft flying at 2,500 knots and 100,000 feet, and to incorporate "very narrow pencil beamed widths which are extremely difficult to jam and detect." The side-looking radar was expected to be able to look out either side of the aircraft for a range of 50 miles, and in more narrowly-focused modes provide a resolution of 200 feet. The forward-looking search radar had a range of 250 nautical miles and could track a target at 125 nautical miles.[52]

The publication of the revised GOR-82 on 7 March 1958 coincided with the release of the "Description of Technical Development Program for Weapon System 110A Bombing-Navigation-Missile Guidance Subsystem" by North American. This report reflected the analysis conducted at IBM and Wright Field into possible configurations for the ASQ-28. As the newly contracted weapon system integrator, North American assumed cognizance over the IBM effort and all other component developments for the B-70. As such, the North American description of the system became the new IBM statement of work, effective 1 April 1958.[53]

North American outlined the growth requirements of the system (operation at Mach 3.5 and 110,000 feet), suggested that IBM delete the pencil beam radar study, informed IBM that the radar sighting equipment should be similar in performance to the General Electric APS-75 SABRE, and approved the use of certain components such as the Goodyear Range Gated Filter Processor. The APS-75 high-resolution X-band side-looking radar employed pulse-to-pulse frequency tuning using a traveling wave tube and was considered extremely jam-resistant.[54]

A stellar-inertial platform "equivalent in performance to the N2J," which was a modification of the N2C being developed by the company's new Autonetics Division, was desired by North American. A Doppler radar similar to the IBM System 14 (now designated APN-115) was also required, and further studies into map matching were authorized. As well as expanding the IBM efforts, the support North American requested from the Air Force was extensive. A total of 650 hours of flight time in a Lockheed RC-121 was requested for IBM testing, and North American wanted a T-29 for flight tests by Autonetics, a C-54 and B-57 for General Precision Laboratories, a B-47 or B-66 for the General Electric SABRE tests, and a JB-29 for Goodyear. It appears that most, if not all, of this support was granted.[55]

On 1 May 1958, the IBM contract with the Air Force was terminated, and North American entered negotiations with IBM for a peer-to-peer contract (L861-GX-600013). The Weapons Guidance Laboratory wanted this finalized before September 1958. However, before this could be accomplished, a considerable amount of criticism from the Office of Electronics in the Office of the Secretary of Defense had to be overcome. Most of the complaints centered on the side-looking radar which the electronics office felt would not function beyond 35 nautical miles. The office also expressed doubt about the usefulness of testing the radar portion of the system in a subsonic B-47 and questioned the probability of developing the devices needed for low-level operations. In the view from the Pentagon, the estimated ASQ-28 development cost of $200 million was excessive.[56]

Lieutenant General Samuel E. Anderson, the ARDC commander, responded on 12 September. Although he conceded that "some of the questions" posed by the Office of Electronics were valid, he defended the overall approach as the best way to attack hardened targets such as missile sites. He recognized that the side-looking radar had limitations, but responded "there is no other more promising avenue available immediately and this technique offers growth potential." Anderson noted that the side-looking radar had already demonstrated a 38 nautical mile range during testing, and that this was acceptable if the full 50 nautical mile range proved unattainable. Regarding the flight tests, Anderson stated that the B-47 would provide an adequate platform for initial tests, and that a B-58 could be used for later tests if found necessary. The low-level requirements, he conceded, were open to debate.[57]

North American artist concept of an operational B-70 launching an unidentified air-to-surface missile. (Boeing Historical Archives)

Anderson defended the cost estimates, and concluded by advising the Pentagon that the program was "under constant evaluation by ... the most highly qualified technical teams available within ARDC." Still, he did not deny that the program was "faced with many technical problems, the immediate optimum solutions to which are not now available" and welcomed "any constructive comments as to how these technical problems can be overcome." This seemed to settle the matter.[58]

By this time, component development was well under way. Tests of the APN-115 had begun, and IBM was planning to begin tests of the improved computer in October. It was at this point that the immense complexity of the computer and its relatively low reliability induced IBM and the Weapons Guidance Laboratory to seriously consider the installation of a backup computer. Goodyear was making progress with their high-resolution radar data processor and happily announced that the component count had been reduced from 12,000 to 8,000. General Electric expected to begin flight tests of the SABRE radar in June 1959 and North American had begun tests of the N2J in a T-39.[59]

However, Washington was again raising issues, and on 27 November, Air Force Headquarters notified ARDC of its "concern with the manner in which the B-70 program is developing." Specifically, the Pentagon felt that there were "areas in which time and money may be saved through judicious use of currently available equipments, better utilization of the flight test inventory, and reduced over-all complexity of subsystems." On that basis, the Pentagon directed a study into the feasibility of reducing "the sophistication of the bombing and navigation subsystem."[60]

In response, IBM and North American proposed six hypothetical bomb-nav systems to be reviewed in terms of cost and performance, with a system comprising only existing components at one end of the spectrum, and the ASQ-28 system (as the most sophisticated) at the other. During January 1959, the resulting analysis was discussed in meetings with all concerned. All parties finally agreed that the Air Force was getting the most for its money with ASQ-28, and the Pentagon later approved this view.[61]

Surprisingly, this study provided about 10 months of unimpeded development time for the bomb-nav system, and considerable progress was made. With the Pentagon seemingly satisfied, the program just had to worry about the technical problems. On 12 January 1959, North American proposed substituting the newly developed N3B stellar-inertial platform for the N2J. The N3B was based on the same general principles, but was half the size, was capable of more precise operation, and included dual 2-degree-of-freedom gyroscopes compared to the three single-degree-of-freedom units in the N2J. The use of beryllium and titanium instead of steel in the motor promised a further reduction in gyro drift rate. Another benefit was that major components from the N3B were to be used on the Minuteman ICBM (WS-133A), and the Weapons Guidance Laboratory supported the commonality aspects of adopting the new unit. Flight tests were to begin in November 1959.[62]

In June 1959, the B-70 Program Office disapproved a plan to use a B-58 as a testbed for components of the bomb-nav system. The Program Office felt that the tests were scheduled too late during development to be of much use, and specifically recommended "early flight test of a completely integrated system was mandatory in order to provide effective and timely engineering data for production

The proposed offensive operator's station for the operational B-70 bomber. Note the ASQ-28 map and radar displays in the center of the panel. The panel above the radar display contained the controls for the air-to-surface missile. (Boeing Historical Archives)

design." Moreover, the WS-110A Program Office also did not agree with North American's plan to use only a single early YB-70 for operational tests. Instead, they recommended using a subsonic vehicle for the initial tests, then having two YB-70s participate at a later date.[63]

Throughout the summer of 1959, fiscal problems continued to influence the B-70 program. This was particularly the case with the requirement for a low altitude interdiction capability. North American submitted a proposal for terrain avoidance equipment and related items in July, but on 5 August, the Program Office informed the contractor that "in view of the current austerity budget ... proposals to implement a low altitude capability for the B-70" would have to be deferred. Nevertheless, planning for a low-level capability continued for at least another year.[64]

Some three months later, the Air Force decided to compress the development program – and cut costs – by freezing the design as early as possible. The time was ripe for such a decision in the case of the ASQ-28 because it had been "developed to the point that the design concepts are clear and design techniques have been defined." However, this was not to mean that changes necessary to meet performance specifications or altered Air Force requirements were prohibited. The design would be frozen on 1 February 1960.[65]

Unfortunately, in November 1959 the Air Force cancelled all plans for producing the B-70 as a strategic bomber, and reduced the flight program to a single prototype XB-70. On 27 November, the Pentagon informed the ARDC that the contracts for the development of defensive, mission and traffic control, and bomb-nav systems were to be terminated. In response, North American terminated the IBM subcontract on 2 December 1959. At this point IBM had essentially completed the experimental model, and the design for the engineering model was scheduled to be complete in May 1960; the subcontract was judged 89 percent complete. Part of the termination order was for IBM to catalog the "vast amount of inventory that had been acquired" so that it could be placed in storage and eventually disposed of.[66]

Nevertheless, the Weapons System Laboratory was reluctant to sacrifice all of the work that had gone into the ASQ-28. On 15 December 1959, IBM presented a complete status report, along with proposals to continue some efforts. At this juncture, IBM tests of an experimental system in an RC-121 were providing important data on the compatibility of components, and IBM had fabricated the first model of the secondary computer. A total of 58 RC-121 flights totaling 216 hours had been completed. General Electric was in the midst of B-66 tests with the SABRE radar, with satisfactory results so far during 20 flights for 45 hours. Testing of the APN-115, 46 flights for 225 hours in a C-54 and B-57, was not so satisfactory, but General Precision was fabricating a transistorized version. Goodyear flight tests (40 flights for 183 hours using a modified B-29 and C-97) of the range gated Doppler data processor for the side-looking radar had demonstrated azimuth resolution of better than 250 feet at 20 miles. North American had completed 94 T-29 flights totaling 342 hours during tests of the stellar-inertial platform.[67]

Based on these results, IBM recommended that the Air Force complete one entire prototype ASQ-28 and continue work on system integration and reliability. Specifically, IBM stated that if approval was forthcoming by 1 February 1960, the end of 1961 could provide a functional ground-test, with a flight unit following a year later. The ARDC took this proposal to Air Force Headquarters, and was pleasantly surprised when it was approved. A series of meetings and intervention by several general officers resulted in $5 million being allocated on 26 January 1960 for an "Experimental Bomb-Nav System for the XB-70." This did not, however, include funds for the side-looking radar or the map matching system. Another $1 million was added on 2 February 1960, despite the fact that the XB-70 was to have "no offensive or defensive capability," only the potential to accept a bomb-nav system.[68]

On 3 March 1960, North American advised IBM to suspend cataloging and disposing of the ASQ-28 inventory pending further direction. This was forthcoming a few weeks later when the Air Force issued contract AF33(600)-41253 to continue a portion of the bomb-nav system development effort known as the C-121 program since it was being tested on a Constellation.[69]

When the YB-70 program was initiated in October 1960, the IBM prime contract with the Air Force was again terminated, and North American issued another subcontract (L1E1-YJ-600221) for IBM to continue the C-121 program concurrently with the design, development, and delivery of 12 flight test models of the ASQ-28. On 3 April 1961, the flight test models were deleted after the YB-70s were cancelled. Nevertheless, the prototype effort continued for use on A/V-3.[70]

By the end of January 1963, a breadboard ASQ-28 had completed a series of tests in an RC-121 and the prototype system intended for A/V-3 was scheduled to be completed on 10 April 1964. The intent was to conduct a 90-hour flight program spread over nine months to evaluate the bomb-nav system. However, on 6 March 1964, the development program was terminated for the convenience of the government. IBM and its subcontractors disposed of approximately 30,000 line items of parts that had been purchased for the systems.[71]

Despite the fact that the prototype ASQ-28 was virtually complete, it was never installed in either of the XB-70A prototypes, which remained toothless for their entire careers. The ASQ-28, however, formed the basis of the early proposals for the B-1A bomb-nav system.[72]

THE DEFENSIVE SYSTEM

During World War II, bomber defenses had consisted of machine guns and cannon mounted in turrets and open blisters around the aircraft. These had grown steadily more formidable and complex, culminating in the sophisticated remote turret system installed on the Convair B-36. However, the next wave of jet-powered bombers could not afford the manpower, weight, or drag associated with this type of defensive armament, and most relied upon speed as their primary defense, with a tail turret in case somebody did manage to catch up with them. As defenders began relying more heavily on radar to guide interceptors to the bombers, electronic countermeasures (ECM) were developed to provide a passive defense. Despite ever increasing speed and more sophisticated ECM, the ability of the B-47, B-52, B-58, and

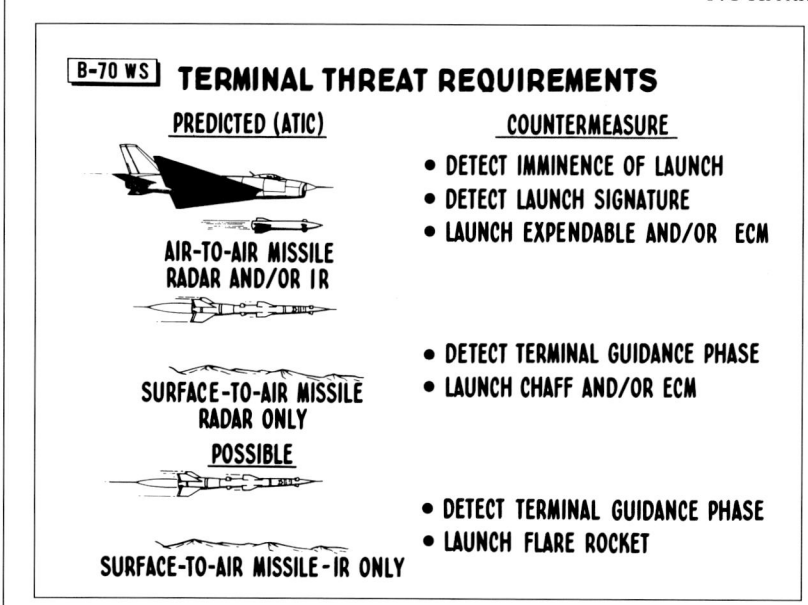

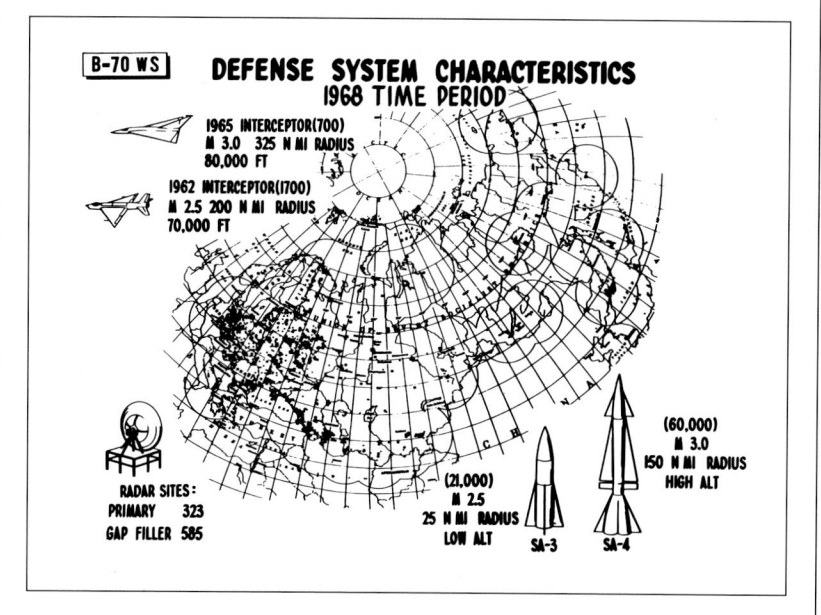

Two charts for a briefing describing the threat environment expected to be faced by the operational B-70 in the mid-1960s. (U.S. Air Force)

B-70 to defend themselves against the growing surface-to-air missile (SAM) threat was called into question during the late 1950s.[73]

Researchers at Wright Field – and their contractors – concerned with protecting bombers against hostile forces were seeking new ways to defend bombers and spacecraft that had not yet been envisioned. Engineers in Dayton had been doing basically the same thing for 30 years. In the immediate post-war period, the "new ways" were generally limited to better methods to aim and fire the cannon that equipped the bombers. In 1947, however, Wright Field began to look at the possibility of providing future bombers with a defensive missile capability to actively strike the attacking interceptor. General Electric received a study contract to investigate the problem, although the effort was soon transferred to Hughes where the MX-904 Falcon program was begun. This missile was subsequently used to arm a generation of manned interceptors, but in the end did nothing to protect the bombers. In September 1952, the Air Force initiated an effort by McDonnell to develop a jet-vane-controlled guided bomber defense missile for the Convair B-58, but the program ran into technical difficulties and was cancelled sometime during 1956.[74]

In early 1955 ARDC Headquarters became more concerned with the active bomber defense program and began two design studies that it hoped would lead to development efforts. The first, System 126A, was to be an interim missile for the Boeing B-52. The second, System 126B, would be "an optimum bomber defense missile for operational use with advanced strategic bombers of the 1963–1966 era." It was hoped that the second missile could be used to destroy interceptor aircraft and SAMs at extremely long ranges before they could initiate an attack on the bombers. The differences in requirements for the two efforts were actually fairly minor, but significant. For instance, a nuclear warhead was "desired" for the interim missile, but "required" for the latter.[75]

As a separate effort, on 22 February 1955, Boeing was authorized to survey the capabilities of existing air-to-air missiles and fire control systems, and study their applicability to the B-52. By the end of 1955, Sperry had received a contract to begin the System 126A project, with the nuclear-powered WS-125A aircraft scheduled to be the first recipient; General Electric and the Raytheon Manufacturing Company were working on competing System 126A designs for the B-52. Two contractor teams, General Electric–McDonnell, and Republic–Westinghouse, were selected to study the more advanced System 126B (soon redesignated System 132A) for the upcoming WS-110A program.[76]

By early 1956, the contractor teams had begun analysis of the problems associated with a bomber defense missile, but fiscal restrictions almost immediately crippled the program. The Sperry version of System 126A was eliminated early because of a very limited projected range. It mattered little; by September 1956 the entire System 126A effort had been cancelled after it was determined that the modifications necessary to the B-52 to carry any defensive missile would be too extensive.[77]

On 28 November 1956, the WADC Weapons Guidance Laboratory held meetings at ARDC Headquarters to discuss the "Active Bomber Defense Technical Development Program" for FY57. Everybody concurred that there was a need for "additional technical development effort to provide techniques necessary for a bomber missile capability." Since the previous projects had not provided any encouragement that similar techniques would succeed, the laboratory began looking for new ideas. In early March, the WADC published a study on a defensive system designed to destroy or negate attacking interceptors before they came within lethal range of the bomber using "some type of weapon utilizing hitherto unexploited principles." Requests for bids for further study were sent out, and 13 responses were received by the 29 March 1956 deadline.[78]

**INBOARD PROFILE
MODEL 713-1-133**

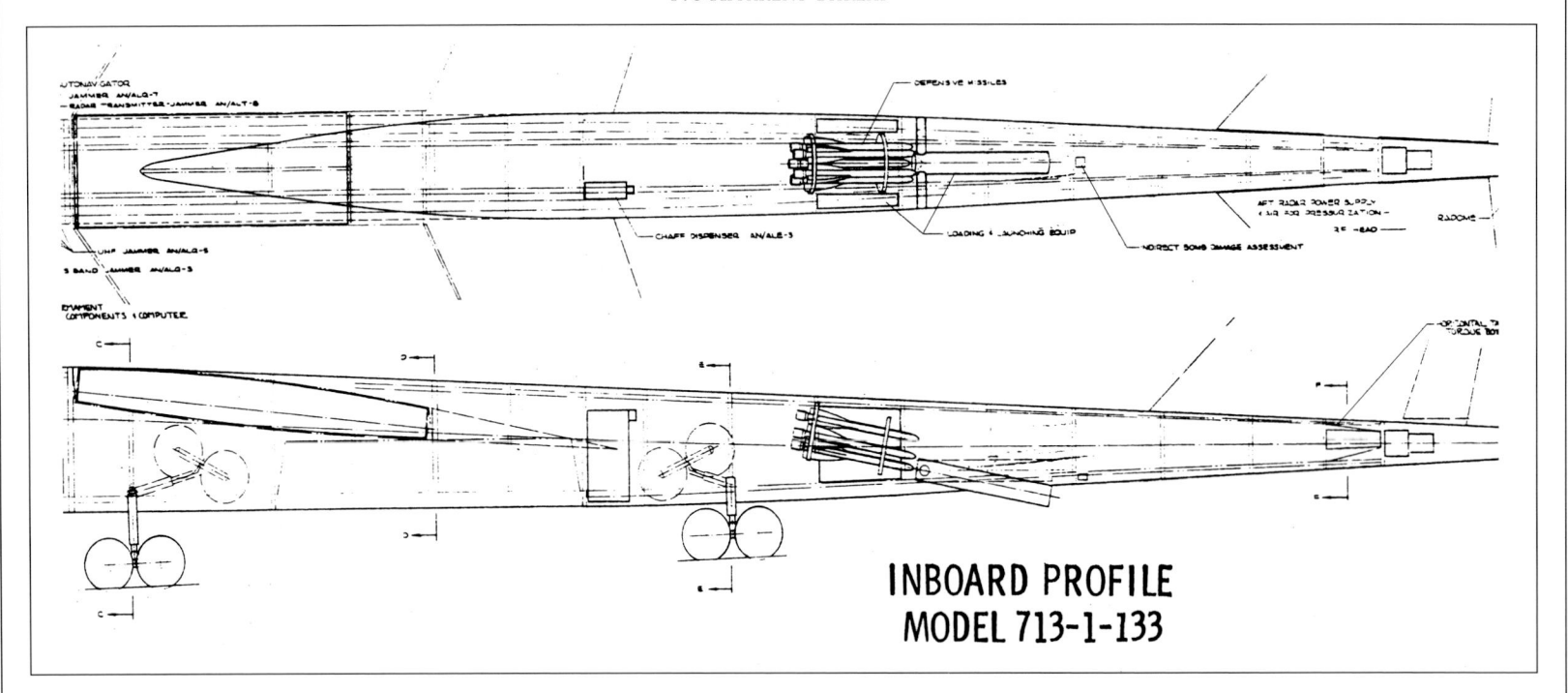

Many of the early Boeing (and presumably North American) design studies included provisions for carrying bomber defense missiles. This Model 713-1-133 shows the installation of a rotary launcher in the aft fuselage. (Boeing Historical Archives)

In July 1957, General Electric, the Crosley Corporation in Cincinnati, and the Stavid Engineering Company[79] received contracts for a series of studies for the Defensive Anti-Missile Subsystem (DAMS). A new concept, developed by Roman Szpur in the Weapons Defense Branch of the Weapons Guidance Laboratory, was based on the contention that a missile could be "deflected or destroyed by a lethal barrier thrust into its path at a safe distance from the bomber." The barrier would contain a large number of high-energy particles or pellets that could be shot from the rear of the bomber in a number of ways. These "pellets" could be chemical agents that would erode the missile, or physical objects such as sand or gravel that could penetrate or shatter the target. Forward hemisphere protection would rely on guided missiles capable of dispensing the same ingredients.[80]

Passive surveillance systems were supposed to look 12 to 15 nautical miles to the rear and 20 to 25 nautical miles forward, and feature tracking, automatic threat evaluation, and the optimum selection of defensive measures. Such a system would, theoretically, "provide bombers with spherical coverage against missiles without invoking the intricate, heavy equipment associated with fire control systems." Somehow, it seemed so simple.[81]

Needless to say, the concept received an enthusiastic reception at the Strategic Air Command during a presentation on 27 August. The same presentation was given to ARDC Headquarters on 1 October and at the Pentagon the following day. Lieutenant General Samuel E. Anderson, the commander of ARDC, had missed the meeting in Baltimore and had a private briefing on 18 October. All agreed the program should proceed as quickly as possible.[82]

In November, General Electric was eliminated from the competition for a "lack of originality" in their program. By this time, Crosley and Stavid had been issuing monthly status reports that took on the look of science fiction, but seemed promising. Crosley were concentrating on tungsten particles shot at high velocity towards the target, and also on an application of the "granite state" theory: that liquid metals, applied in various combinations, even in the minutest quantities, would cause structural failure of the metals contacted. Exactly how the material would be carried or delivered, or the effects on the carrier aircraft if damaged, were not discussed. Stavid's approach was equally interesting, concentrating on highly corrosive chemical agents that could be dispensed to erode the attacking interceptors. Again, how the chemicals would be carried was not discussed.[83]

By the end of the year, the Weapons Guidance Laboratory had received approval to continue the studies, but requested additional funds to further expand the investigation and for field tests. The first of these occurred on 18 December, at Eglin AFB when single-grain tungsten pellets were fired at approximately 3,000 fps at a stationary GAR-1 Falcon missile. Approximately 10 pellets penetrated the missile out of the 23 fired at it. The pellets had not penetrated to the projected depth and had not expanded in size after impact as expected. Still, the results were encouraging since it was felt that the missile would have been either destroyed or deflected from its course by the impacts.[84]

The DAMS concept was beginning to receive consideration from the WS-110A Program Office, as well as the B-52 and B-58 communities. There was also some interest in applying similar techniques to anti-ballistic missile defense systems, and it appeared that the Soviets

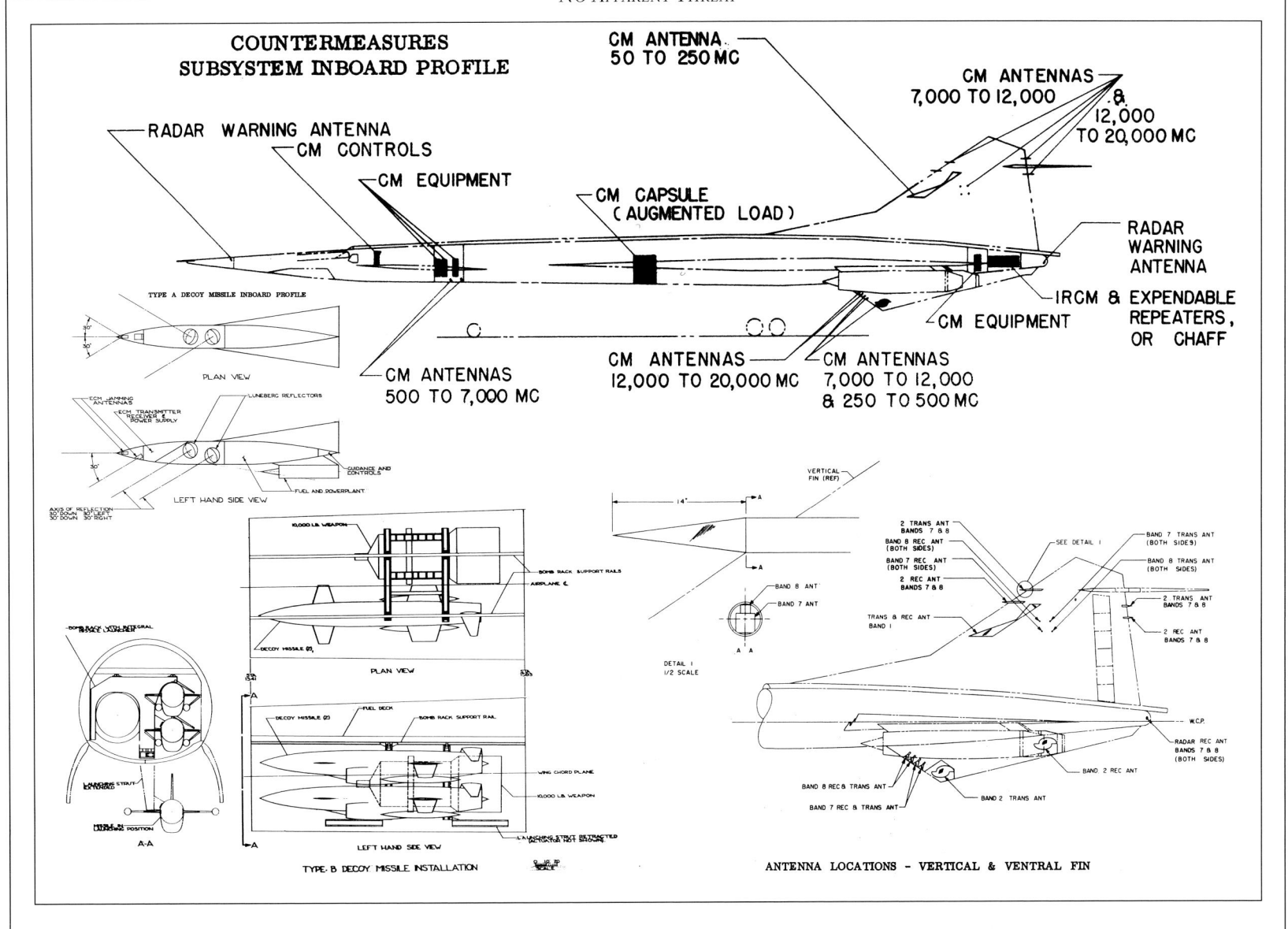

Things had evolved considerably by the time the Boeing Model 804-4 was proposed. The bomber defense missiles were history, replaced by a sophisticated electronic countermeasures system and decoy missiles. Note that the two weapons bays were side-by-side, with one carrying a thermonuclear device and the other housing decoy missiles. (Boeing Historical Archives)

were working on similar theories. On 13 June 1957, the laboratory received unofficial word from an officer in Omaha (who had been informed by a friend in New York City) that two Hungarian refugees who had worked on the Soviet bomber defense project were living in Connecticut. It sounded like a bad movie script. The laboratory immediately asked the Air Technical Intelligence Center to question the men. The interrogation revealed that the DAMS concept had been under investigation behind the Iron Curtain since 1953. By September 1957, the intelligence service had determined that corrosive liquid metals or pellets might well face American interceptors as early as 1962.[85]

Beginning in early 1958, multi-grain pellets were being fired at Falcon missiles at Eglin with more satisfying results. In September, a series of pellet firings began against Sidewinder missiles launched at Mach 2 from a rocket sled at Hurricane Mesa, Utah.[86] The results were more conclusive. The pellets, fired from a tube, impacted with sufficient force against the nose of the missile to destroy the guidance system. By the end of the year, additional data had been gathered that showed a two-grain pellet could destroy the guidance section of any missile at a closing rate of 5,000 to 6,000 fps. Overall, the laboratory felt the technique had been established. Of course, the tests were set up so that the pellet could hardly miss; it proved the basic concept but ignored the larger question of how to actually use the weapon.[87]

A lack of funds forced the cancellation of further work on the use of corrosive chemicals in mid-1958. Still, the granite state theory remained under investigation and additional tests were conducted at Hurricane Mesa during September. Particles containing a liquid metal fluid designed to destroy the granular structure of the interceptor were fired against Sidewinders. The results were considered satisfactory insofar as the action of the liquid metal was concerned, but the techniques for its application were elusive and the program was cancelled in mid-1959.[88]

With the effectiveness of the pellet technique established in their minds, the laboratory engineers attempted to gain approval for a large development program leading to an engineering model of a limited anti-missile defensive subsystem. They envisioned this being a 30-mm version of the T-171 (M61) Gattling cannon, firing 45 to 50 rounds per minute at a target in the rear hemisphere of the bomber. Each 30-mm round would contain approximately 150 pellets. Later, a Dardick breechless, multi-chamber weapon, capable of firing 2,000 rounds per minute, was to be substituted for the modified T-171. However, adequate funds were not available and further work on the pellet technique was terminated in mid-1959. Project Mongoose was an attempt to salvage the program by linking it to the B-52 and using product improvement funds. It did not last long before being cancelled.[89]

Pye Wacket

In February 1958 the pellet program – and all other lethal portions of DAMS – had been lumped together under the title "Barrier Defense Techniques." Within this category, the Weapons Guidance Laboratory began working on a lenticular missile that was shaped like a flying saucer. Whereas the laboratory classified the pellet program as a "limited" defense, the Lenticular Defense Missile was to provide total defense against attacks from any direction. The Air Proving Ground Center at Eglin AFB began the development of the lenticular missile under Project Pye Wacket.[90] The Weapons Guidance Laboratory had to figure out how to provide the guidance and control system necessary to turn the device into a "defending missile with omni-directional launch capability" and was supporting using a nuclear warhead based on the "neutron dudding" technique as the most effective method of countering an attack.[91]

In March 1959, North American had performed an "Active Defense Feasibility Study" to discover "whether active defense was feasible, whether it could be efficiently installed in the airplane, and how it would affect performance and the probability of mission success." The B-70 Program Office needed this type of data to develop a realistic assessment of the potential of various active defense concepts in order to prioritize funding requests. Unfortunately, the study was conducted under less than ideal conditions. The formal B-70 defensive subsystem evaluation was being held at the time the study was made, and several of the firms involved in the bidding could not be contacted while the evaluation was in progress. Additionally, procurement policies limited the amount of information that could be released to the various companies.[92]

Notwithstanding such problems, North American obtained and evaluated a considerable amount of information on the most advanced active defense systems then under development or study. Three basic missiles were included in the study: a "lenticular defense missile," a "cylindrical defense missile," and a modified Hughes GAR-9 (later AIM-47) being designed for the F-108. North American found that the lenticular missile's "unique shape and light weight" provided:

"… performance capabilities which the more conventional missiles are hard put to equal. It can be launched in any direction since the drag is, in effect, the same no matter what its orientation is to the relative wind. While a conventional missile must be launched with its nose pointed forward and turned to attack a target in the rear hemisphere, the LDM [lenticular defense missile] may be headed in the right direction at launch and all of its boost used to propel it toward the target."[93]

By early 1959, there had been a surprising amount of testing of the missile shape at both Eglin and in the Gas Dynamics Facility at the Arnold Engineering Development Center outside Tullahoma, Tennessee. The shape was found to be stable up through Mach 6, although the control surfaces were proving to be harder to define than expected. The missile was 70 inches in diameter, 9 inches deep, and weighed 510 pounds. An infrared seeker was installed in the nose with a jettisonable cover to protect it at launch. A maximum speed of 4,500 mph (Mach 6.5) was provided by two solid rocket motors that provided 10,200 lbf. The range was approximately 72 nautical miles. Assuming it was headed in the proper direction at launch, the missile would generally follow a preprogrammed inertial trajectory until burnout. During this phase the missile nose was not necessarily pointed at the target "since the best path is a function of the velocity vectors," but at burnout a set of spoilers was "differentially actuated to turn the LDM [lenticular defense missile] so that the target will be within the cone of view of the IR seeker." The bomber maintained a radio link to the missile and could point the missile at the most important target. Once the seeker had acquired the target, the missile became autonomous.[94]

North American thought the missile held promise, but worried that its early state of development made it premature to include in the B-70 weapon system. Although North American was impressed with the "center post mounting and ejection method of the LDM," the company was concerned about the "very uniqueness" of the missile and wanted "further detailed study." The mounting system was certainly unusual, and was designed to "fully exploit the unique stacking quality of the shape and also to position [orient] the missile properly at launch." Posts were mounted vertically in the bomb bay and the missiles screwed to them "by means of the center threaded hole which engages an Acme-type thread in the post." The post rotated to accept the missile. Two rows of five missiles could be accommodated. According to North American,

"… at launch, the inner threaded post will rotate to translate the missile downward to the launch position, whereupon the entire shaft will rotate to turn the missile into the desired launch heading. The door will then open and the missile will be ejected by means of a percussion ejector. Rocket motors will not be ignited until the missile is safely clear of the aircraft."[95]

Pye Wacket – the name and the concept – was one of the more bizarre development efforts undertaken by the Air Force. A great deal of time and effort was expended by the Arnold Engineering Development Center, the armament development organization at Eglin AFB, and various contractors on this proposed bomber defense missile. This is a 1959-60 version of Pye Wacket in a wind tunnel at AEDC. (Arnold Engineering Development Center)

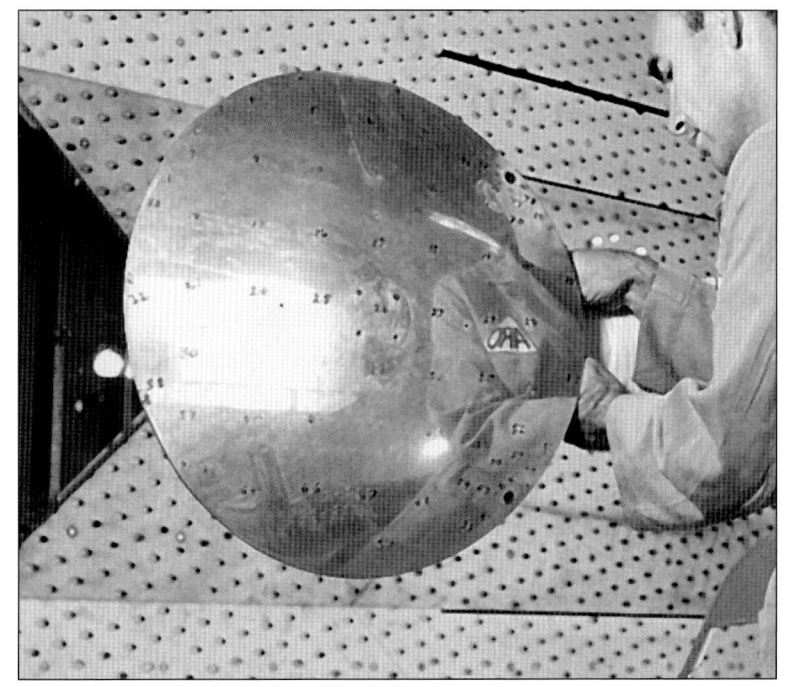

In June 1959, the Air Force awarded contract AF08(635)-542 to the Pomona Division of Convair to study the lenticular missile. This was a general feasibility study to determine the stability, control, and maneuverability of the lenticular configuration. As a result of this study, the basic shape that had been developed by the Air Proving Ground Command was extensively modified. The improved version, called the Model III, had the maximum thickness located at the extreme aft end of the body. This provided a rearward shift (to 43-percent chord) in the dynamic center of pressure, greatly simplifying the problem of controlling the missile in flight. Another advantage of the asymmetrical shape was a large reduction in the supersonic drag because of the blunt trailing edge. This resulted in a higher lift-to-drag ratio, resulting in an increased range and maximum speed. Despite these improvements, however, the new shape largely negated the originally-perceived advantage of its symmetrical shape that could be launched in any direction.[96]

Although there were no immediate applications for the Pye Wacket vehicle – the B-70 program had long since declined to consider it as a part of the defensive systems – the overall concept still held promise. The Air Force issued a Phase II contract (AF08(635)-1168) to Convair to continue the studies. The aerodynamic evaluation was expanded to determine the omni-directional launch characteristics of the vehicle, since these were one of the perceived benefits of the lenticular shape although the asymmetrical refinements had largely eliminated the advantage. To accomplish this, two large wind tunnel models were built, one instrumented for force measurements and one instrumented for pressure measurements. The latter model also included provisions for simulating the power-on condition of four pitch-roll reaction control thrusters.[97]

The lenticular shape was investigated for uses other than bomber defense missiles. Some early space station resupply vehicle concepts used the shape, and the Flight Research Center at Edwards AFB proposed building a low-speed handling evaluation vehicle as part of the lifting-body program. This artist concept shows (from left) the M2-F1, M1-L half-cone, and Langley Lenticular Body shapes. Only the first one was actually built and flown. (NASA Dryden Flight Research Center)

All of the data showed that the lenticular shape was essentially unstable in all axes – a good characteristic for a highly maneuverable vehicle, assuming a means to control it can be developed. In March 1960, a contract was awarded to Crosley to investigate autopilots, and Convair also continued to work on the problem as part of their Phase II contract. It was quickly discovered that the required autopilot not only had to stabilize and control the vehicle, but it had to do so in a manner that fully exploited the unique properties of the configuration. It was determined that at least four control motors would be required to produce pitch moments and four others to produce roll moments. This placed an unacceptable burden on the space available inside the vehicle, so it was decided to position four thrusters so that creative firings would produce the desired pitch and/or roll responses. Two separate thrusters would provide yaw control.[98]

Eventually, over 80 hours were accumulated in the wind tunnels at AEDC including tests at speeds as low as Mach 0.6, and as high as Mach 5. This led to a sled-launched Feasibility Test Vehicle that was 60 inches in diameter with a 0.21 thickness-to-chord ratio. Three Thiokol M58A2 solid-rocket motors, aligned parallel to the missile longitudinal axis, would provide the main propulsion. This was the same motor used in the Falcon series of air-to-air missiles and the trio produced almost 14,000 lbf. The 425-pound test vehicle would be constructed mostly of cast magnesium since it was very stiff and lightweight and reasonably easy to work with.

Reaction controls consisted of a nitrogen pressure-fed hypergolic bipropellant system using six nozzles (four pitch/roll nozzles and two yaw nozzles) producing 500 lbf each. The vehicles would be launched from a twin rail launcher on a high-speed rocket sled at Hurricane Mesa or Edwards AFB. The launcher rails slid into two longitudinal cylinders on either side of the booster motors and could be aimed in any relative direction, as well as elevated up to 90 degrees. This would provide a meaningful demonstration of the omni-directional capability of the missile.[99]

The lenticular missile was designed to maneuver with extreme violence, being slammed by its thrusters into bank attitudes that would produce tremendous accelerations and fantastic rates of turn. Preliminary reports referred to typical accelerations of 60 g, with rates over 250 g being possible at Mach 3 and above. Launched from a B-70 traveling at Mach 3 at 70,000 ft, the operational version of Pye Wacket was expected to be 48 inches in diameter, carry a 50-pound warhead, and be capable of Mach 6 velocities.

Convair noted that the lenticular configuration would be useful as a strike missile to be launched from manned bombers on low-altitude penetration runs. Able to fly laterally and make supersonic terminal maneuvers, the missile could attack SAM sites or other targets close to the bomber's flight path. Convair also decided the lenticular shape held promise as a reentry vehicle to demonstrate controlled lifting reentry. Convair recommended that the Air Force procure 12 test vehicles for the high-speed sled tests, but no documentation can be found that indicates this ever happened. Pye Wacket likely made it no further than the wind tunnel.[100]

The basic lenticular shape was resurrected by the NASA Langley Research Center during the early 1960s. Plans were made to test it along with several other lifting-body shapes as possible candidates for reentry vehicles, but the lenticular vehicle never got past some artist concepts.[101]

OTHER ACTIVE DEFENSES

The March 1959 North American study had investigated weapons other than the lenticular missile. Specifically, it considered a modified GAR-9 from the F-108 program and a cylindrical defense missile with a forward canard. The missile was designed to follow a programmed launch course and employed command midcourse and terminal infrared homing guidance. However, no other descriptive information could be found.

North American concluded "the cylindrical missile appeared to be the most attractive for the B-70. It weighed less than either Pye Wacket or the GAR-9, had a longer range, and employed superior guidance techniques. Moreover, it was attractive because it was 'not a radical departure' from existing programs and because 'little risk would apparently be attached to its development.'" Several of these conclusions seem difficult to imagine, especially that any smaller missile could have a range superior to the GAR-9. In addition, since the GAR-9 and its fire control system were already a funded development effort, it would have seemed to present less risk than a completely new missile.[102]

The study had been predicated that defensive measures would only have to be provided against forward-hemisphere attacks since the speed of the B-70 was thought to preclude attacks from the rear. The most likely threats were a Mach 3 interceptor carrying a GAR-9-type missile (the eventual MiG 25 and R-40/AA-6 Acrid), area defense surface-to-air missiles, and point-defense surface-to-air missiles. Multiple intercepts seemed probable, implying the need for a "multiple target capability" and "some capability against salvo attack." Based on these factors, North American determined that five to eight missiles would have to be carried.[103]

The missiles could provide a "sizable improvement in survival if the system could be installed with no range penalty." As it happened, however, installing either the cylindrical or GAR-9 missiles would involve a 675-nautical-mile range loss, while the lenticular missile would cost 780 nautical miles, both based primarily on the additional weight of the system. Using a highly-unlikely 99-percent kill probability and 90-percent reliability, North American estimated that the missiles would add about 10 percent to the penetration effectiveness of the bomber. "This improvement," said the report, was "too small … to warrant … the addition of an active defense system at this time." The report added, however, that *if* means could be devised for realizing the projected kill probability and reliability rates *without* incurring a significant range penalty "there would be a significant increase in survival probability and penetration effectiveness," particularly for deep penetrations. It was this potential improvement in penetration effectiveness that encouraged North American to recommend continuing study of active defense systems for the B-70. Nevertheless, the range penalties involved led the company to recommend against including active defense to the B-70 "at this time."[104]

A second report was published in August 1959 that noted the cost performance and effectiveness of active defense could not be usefully evaluated without concurrent consideration of other penetration aids, particularly, electronic countermeasures (ECM) and decoy missiles. Additional effort would need to be expended on a new study considering all three technologies. This second report, however, did look a little more deeply at the issues surrounding active defenses. One of the concerns was that "moderately accurate ranging on targets at distances to about 100 nautical miles is essential for active defense of the B-70." Since conventional active radar with this capacity (such as the ASG-18 from the F-108) would weigh an estimated 1,000 pounds, the engineers investigated 10 passive methods of ranging. Overall, none were particularly encouraging, but a radar technique called PADAR and an infrared method were characterized as potentially "promising."[105]

The PADAR employed a time-difference measurement based on the correlation of a direct echo from the target with an echo of radiation bounced from the surface of the Earth to the target and back to the bomber. The solution of the range problem was essentially a matter of triangulation, a relatively simple matter even for the primitive computers then available. Complications arose from the necessary

The operational B-70 would have had the most sophisticated electronic countermeasures system yet devised, and in some respects was years ahead of its time. For instance, both Boeing and North American put great emphasis on infrared detection and countermeasures. The defensive systems operator also was responsible for the mission and traffic control (M&TC) system that included the IFF and ATC transponders. (above: U.S. Air force; right: Boeing Historical Archives)

reliance on an advanced pulse Doppler radar, new antennas, new radomes, and a variety of other technical considerations.[106]

An "infrared power ratio ranging" technique made use of the inverse-square distance relationship by comparing the intensity of received radiation of two measurements spaced by a known time. Although North American was not sure that an accurate range could be determined from the technique, the company considered it worthy of further investigation.[107]

North American noted that many other unknowns could not be resolved during the study. These included the potential warhead effectiveness (and the required "miss distance" the missile would need to achieve), the effect of aerodynamic heating on infrared sensors, and the primitive state of airborne computers. Problems that could be solved by North American, but that were not addressed in detail, included the placement of the active defense radar antenna. The logical place for a forward hemisphere antenna was in the nose of the airplane, but this would displace the aerial refueling receptacle already located there in the preliminary design.[108]

What North American had accomplished in publishing the second report on active defense was to highlight some of the problems that required resolution before any positive step toward developing an active defense system could effectively begin. There was no contention that any or all of the obstacles were so massive as to preclude the development of an active defense system for the B-70 if such a system became essential. However, at the same time, the report reemphasized the accepted premise that very significant advances in technology would be necessary before the objections to installation of an active defense system could be overcome. Moreover, the key question remained: did the B-70 *need* active defense? As had been true since the program began, degradation of the passive defensive system or substantial enhancement of the Soviet defensive potential could cause a change in the situation at virtually any moment.[109]

SR-197

The concept of active defenses for the B-70 had launched other parallel investigations. On 18 November 1958, the Air Force initiated SR-197, "Penetration Aids for Manned Bombers," specifically to review active defenses for the B-70. The study seemed to wander aimlessly for a few months, but a revision of the requirements published in July 1959 asked if an integrated defensive system "would significantly increase the possibility of mission success." The study requirement was at once straightforward and of sufficiently wide scope to cover virtually all possible contingencies. Interestingly, only one of the 17 items to be studied made any direct reference to active defenses.[110]

In June 1959, the Air Force awarded study contracts to Bendix, Boeing, Lockheed, North American, Raytheon, and RCA. The reports were submitted around the end of the year, and were elaborate, detailed, and voluminous. All were evaluated by the WADC, the Institute of Air Weapons Research at the University of Chicago, RAND Corporation, SAC, and several other Air Force agencies.[111]

The reports covered virtually every facet of the B-70 defense problem. Most of the contractors – North American excepted – saw a need for penetration aids, but there was disagreement on how to provide them. North American believed that the aircraft, as designed, could survive and operate effectively in the anticipated threat environment. The reviewers divided into three camps: one did not totally agree with North American but was skeptical of the need for penetration aids; another felt that penetration aids were absolutely essential; and the third thought the entire matter should be studied again. The B-70 Program Office, in particular, expressed disappointment with the quality of the contractor studies, and at least one reviewer added that most of the reports looked more like sales brochures.[112]

Outspoken objections to the philosophy of the B-70 defensive system had been voiced earlier by the WADC organization that was charged with the "physical defense" aspects of the general bomber defense problem. The members of that organization, originally called the Physical Defense Branch of the Weapons Guidance Laboratory, but later the Lethal Defense Branch of the reorganized Navigation and Guidance Laboratory, generally urged the addition of a bomber defense missile to the B-70.[113]

The organization was reluctant to accept the premise upon which North American had considered the active defense needs for the B-70. Although the company considered a Mach 3 interceptor to be the prime threat to the B-70, or at least the prime threat to the complete effectiveness of the passive defensive system, the Physical Defense Branch believed that infrared-guided surface-to-air missiles with nuclear warheads were the major threat. (Ironically, the intelligence services did not expect an infrared-guided nuclear-tipped Soviet SAM to be operational during the B-70's service career.) Citing a variety of sources, the Physical Defense Branch indicated that a 10- to 100-megaton warhead detonated at 70,000 feet would cause "immediate crew incapacitation" on all aircraft within a 30- to 100-mile radius. Left unspoken was the amount of damage such a weapon would do to Soviet forces nearby.[114]

The group felt that a bomber defense missile employing its own nuclear warhead could theoretically take advantage of a technique to render the opposing warhead inoperative without exploding it by using the "neutron effect" of detonating a small nuclear device in close proximity to the opposing warhead. This meant that the B-70 crew would be exposed only to the radiation from the defensive missile, and the laboratory cited figures to show that a relatively low-yield warhead could be exploded as close as 15,000 feet from the B-70 without generating dangerous levels of radiation.[115]

Moreover, if the kill range could be reduced (meaning the bomber defense missile could intercept the incoming SAM closer to the bomber), then the weight and complexity of the associated fire control system and radars could also be reduced. From the point of view of the active defense advocates in the Weapons Guidance Laboratory, the technique seemed well suited to providing an active defense for the B-70, even if it was not tailored for the aircraft. In hindsight, the entire concept of nuclear fratricide seems incredible.[116]

Overall, there was only slight support for the Physical Defense Branch within the Air Force, and almost none within North American. This changed somewhat in July 1959 when a report from the RAND Corporation indicated that the proposed technique held promise. RAND felt that infrared SAMs, rather than manned interceptors, would be the major threat to the B-70, and did not believe the Soviets could design an interceptor missile fuze that would be immune from the "neutron kill" technique. Despite their apparent show of support, however, RAND did not have any plans to study active defenses specifically for the B-70, or even generally for any aircraft.[117]

In fact, only two of the study contractors had investigated active defense missiles with any seriousness. RCA had briefly looked at the missiles and concluded that other penetration aids were more attractive. RCA concluded that, because of weight and power requirements, incorporating the missiles in the B-70 would penalize system performance more than it increased penetration effectiveness. North American had also looked at the missiles, and indicated they were "a high-cost penetration aid with good utility at the expense of approximately 500–nautical-miles range penalty for 10 missiles per aircraft."[118]

The WADC released a response to the SR-197 results on 5 February 1960. One of the six sections of the response dealt exclusively with the bomber defense missile; a second section considered the bomber defense missile as a part of the whole defensive system. The remaining sections discussed infrared, radar reflectivity, chaff, and ECM.[119]

The Physical Defense Branch reviewers thought that RCA had evaluated the defensive missile based on incorrect blast and radiation damage criteria, thus invalidating their own analysis. In their opinion, North American's use of a 65-foot miss-distance criterion was unrealistic because it did not allow for "much state-of-the-art improvement in guidance systems in this time period." Because of this large miss-distance, North American had used a bomber defense missile with a 0.75-kiloton warhead and the Physical Defense Branch believed that a more accurate missile with a smaller warhead would have provided much more favorable results. They also noted "in spite of the ... conservative guidance accuracy, the North American study rates active defensive missiles essentially the same as decoys."[120]

On the whole, active bomber defense missiles had not fared particularly well in the SR-197 studies. The Physical Defense Branch reviewers felt that the potential of bomber defense missiles had been inadequately emphasized in the ground rules for the study, and that the bad showing was largely due to this lack of emphasis. The rebuttal urged further study of missiles as penetration aids, specifically focusing on chaff dispensing vehicles, infrared and radar-guided track-break missiles, and bomber defense missiles. The report also recommended further investigation of ECM systems.[121]

One of the major disagreements between the Physical Defense Branch reviewers and the other agencies dealing with SR-197 concerned differing points of view on the "30-degree cone" problem. Essentially, the contractors in SR-197 and the other WADC reviewers agreed that the most likely attack on a Mach 3 bomber would be from a 30-degree cone directly ahead of the airplane. As the Physical Defense Branch saw things, the key danger to the B-70 was from an interceptor (manned or unmanned) that managed to break through the countermeasures screen around the airplane and attack from almost directly abeam.[122]

The Strategic Air Command did not believe that any of the SR-197 study items presented "a basis for change" in the ongoing B-70 program. The command favored a continual program to improve the penetration ability of the B-70 by whatever means seemed necessary to counter the anticipated Soviet threat. However, SAC did not seem particularly concerned.[123]

The various studies were also reviewed by the Institute of Air Weapons Research, which was run under government contract by the University of Chicago and was essentially a think-tank where concepts and theories were evaluated. The institute noted that the key problem lay in uncertainties regarding the possible Soviet defensive environment. While providing no specific recommendations, the institute noted that infrared vulnerability seemed to be a major issue that had not been treated extensively in the studies, and that only one contractor spent much effort on looking at chaff to defeat radars.[124]

On the other coast, the RAND Corporation disagreed with the value of chaff, and tended to discount it as a penetration aid. They did, however, agree that the B-70 would need "extensive help in penetrating a modern air defense system during its operational lifetime." Uncertainty concerning possible Soviet defense techniques warranted a variety of approaches, and RAND suggested the Air Force consider adopting a dual-function air-launched "lethal decoy." Track-breaking missiles and saturation decoys appealed to the RAND team, with active defense seen as a necessary technique. Furthermore, RAND criticized the North American study as being too optimistic about the ability of the basic bomber to penetrate

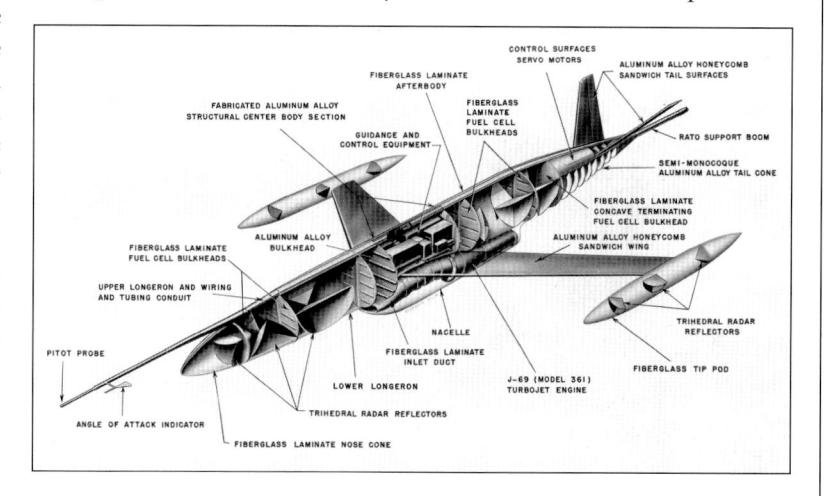

The Convair MX-2223 was an attempt to develop a long-range ground-based decoy that would be launched ahead of the B-36 or B-47 bomber formations to deceive or saturate enemy defenses. A much faster and more capable decoy would have been needed to mask the B-70. (Convair)

Soviet defenses, and suggested that North American should be more open to using additional penetration aids.[125]

The reviewer in the Air Force Chief of Staff's office summed up the results by saying they showed "considerable disagreement as to the most likely characteristics of an enemy air defense system in 1968." In his opinion, "it would certainly not be appropriate to seize upon one possible state of the enemy defense as that against which our offense should be optimized, without carefully considering other likely possibilities as well." Nevertheless, given the austere budget environment, his general conclusion was that development programs that could be deferred "without jeopardy to an important program" should be.[126]

The Aerospace Technical Intelligence Center was likely the closest to being right, noting that the conclusions affecting the survival potential of the B-70, as projected in the several studies, were largely determined by the "particular methodology chosen by each SR-197 participant." The center felt that "B-70 survivability" probably lay somewhere between the extremes postulated by North American at the good end, and the other study contractors (who were, largely, trying to secure new contracts) on the other end.[127]

The final WADC summary of the SR-197 results, published in April 1960, took the middle ground.[128] The summary noted that even if the radar reflectivity and infrared emissivity of the B-70 were significantly reduced, Soviet defenses "within their technical state-of-the-art and budgetary capabilities" could impose heavy losses on the bombers unless the B-70 was supported by "additional effective penetration aids." The summary noted that a bomber defense missile would require "sensory equipment beyond the state-of-the-art and ... extremely high performance ... [and] so does not appear feasible [at this time]." Instead, the summary urged further study of track-breaking missiles and air-launched decoys, both to be carried internally.[129]

In any event, the direction of the B-70 program had been changed very slightly – if at all – by the SR-197 studies. For all practical purposes, no effort was being expended in the development of an active defensive subsystem for the aircraft, and the contentions regarding the advantages or disadvantages of one technique or another remained largely academic. The position of the B-70 Program Office was that when an active defense became both essential and technically feasible, its development would begin. Until that time, the requirements stated in 1958 would remain essentially unchanged.[130]

Electronic Systems

The original SR-22 and GOR-82 indicated that the WS-110A was to "incorporate electromagnetic defense media, and [that] its protective armament" was to provide "the best active defense feasible against omni-directional attacks by both manned and unmanned interceptors." The requirement further stated that such active defenses were to ensure the destruction of the interceptor before it got close enough to "kill" the bomber. Additionally, the GOR specified a provision to carry decoys, radar seeking missiles, and bomber defense missiles.[131]

In April 1956, the Lockheed Missile Systems Division in Van Nuys was issued a study contract for Penetration System No. 1 (PS-1) for use by both WS-110A and WS-125A. This system would include new air-launched decoy and anti-radar missiles, as well as advanced ECM systems; General Electric and Raytheon provided consulting services on the ECM systems. By late 1956, the WS-110A program was being reevaluated and little was accomplished for the next 12 months.[132]

Air Force Headquarters issued revised requirements in March 1958 calling for a five-element defensive system embodying active and passive warning devices, threat evaluation equipment, electronic countermeasures, infrared countermeasures, and chaff dispensing rockets. In addition, the requirements stated that "when an active defense system against air-to-air and ground-to-air missile threats becomes available, it will be incorporated into the system."[133]

Six weeks later, the concept was amended, clarifying many details, but also including some significant requirements. One of these was adding "expendable countermeasures" (chaff and flares) as well as radar-seeking and decoy missiles to the armament load "to the maximum extent feasible."[134]

North American responded to these requirements by preparing a preliminary set of performance specifications for the defensive armament subsystem. Its function was "to sense and interpret external electromagnetic and thermal emissions, program all radiation subsystems of the air vehicle to prevent mutual interference, and initiate appropriate countermeasures against hostile environments." The expected threats included early warning radars, ground-based and airborne intercept radars, ground-control "intercept complexes," and infrared search and track devices. The defensive system was to consist of a Central Intelligence Control (CIC) that included a computer and various displays and controls, an electronic countermeasures section, thermal surveillance and countermeasures, and chaff countermeasures.[135]

The CIC was an advanced concept for the time and was intended to integrate all the "electromagnetic radiating systems" on the aircraft to prevent mutual interference in addition to controlling expendable countermeasures and queuing active defenses. This has long been the utopia for ECM designers, and has largely remained elusive even on the B-1B in 2004. The CIC would also prioritize the threats and record all electromagnetic activity. Frequency surveillance equipment would detect when the aircraft was being illuminated, then locate and categorize the specific threat. The thermal surveillance equipment would perform the same function for heat-emitting sources. Infrared sensors would indicate the "intensity, azimuth, elevation, intensity rate of change, and angular rate of change" of the approaching threat.[136]

The ECM equipment would be capable of noise jamming, deception jamming 30 threat radars operating simultaneously, and track-breaking 10 radars simultaneously. The system covered virtually all radars operating in the 50- to 16,000-megacycle (megahertz) spectrum. Although both the Air Force and North American anticipated that the aircraft would eventually carry some sort of active defense system (i.e., missiles), none were specified in the contract, and none were listed in the contractor report.[137]

Independently, the Air Force had contracted with Sperry for the AN/ALQ-27 Defensive Subsystem for installation in later B-52 models. Given the lack of progress on the Lockheed PS-1, the Air

DEFENSIVE SUBSYSTEM INSTALLATION

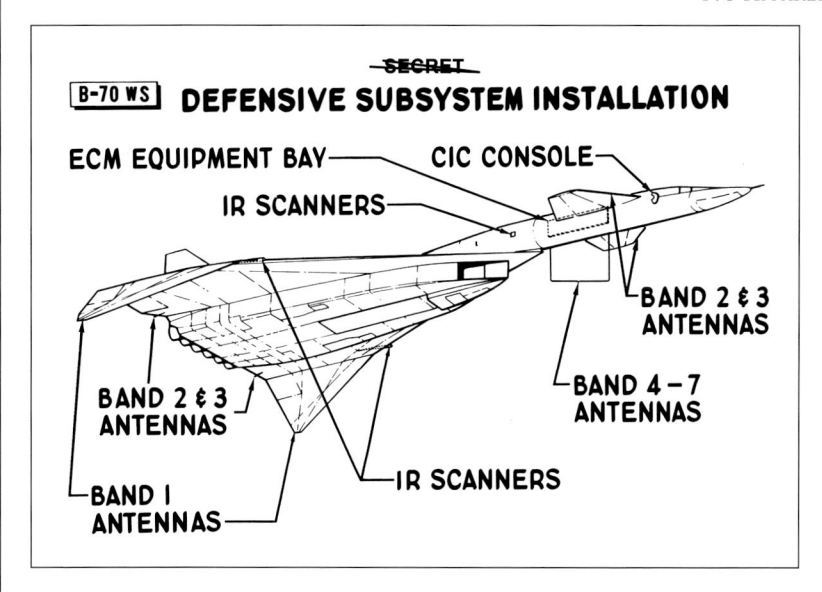

The operational airplane would have had a variety of defensive system antennas and infrared detectors. Interestingly, although the infrared detectors looked to the sides and forward, none looked to the rear – perhaps the J93 exhaust gases would have masked any incoming threat. (U.S. Air Force)

Force asked North American to investigate using the ALQ-27 on the B-70. However, the physical and operating environmental differences between the B-52 and the B-70 were so great that it appeared unlikely that one system could be used on both. On 21 May 1958, the B-70 Program Office notified the Pentagon that very little of the B-52 defensive subsystem "beyond basic circuits, some specialized electronic tubes, and basic contractor know-how" could be profitably applied to the B-70.[138]

At the same time, the B-70 Program Office advised North American to "draw from present technical development programs such as the ALQ-27" in defining the B-70 defensive subsystem. North American produced a detailed specification for the B-70 defensive system and issued a request for proposals to industry. This progress notwithstanding, in April 1959 the B-52 and B-70 program offices agreed to the "use of ALQ-27 information and hardware" for the B-70 program.[139]

Despite the situation with the ALQ-27, North American spent much of 1958 evaluating the proposals from the companies for the B-70 defensive system. On 7 January 1959 North American decided that the Westinghouse Air Arm Division offered the best hope of developing the system primarily based on their "advanced engineering concept" and a subcontract (L961-GX-600124) was finalized on 6 April 1959. Both Westinghouse and North American realized that the giant leap required for the B-70 defensive system would require a combination of techniques beyond the capability of any single contractor, and it was intended to use the "countermeasures industry to the fullest extent" possible. Nevertheless, the Air Force insisted that Westinghouse list all of their second-tier subcontractors so that the government could ensure that "maximum possible use of existing technical knowledge" was made. A detailed survey was completed in November 1959 to aid in the selection of lower tier suppliers.[140]

Development had not progressed very far when the Air Force decided to limit the B-70 program to a single air vehicle on 1 December 1959. Given that this aircraft was not scheduled to carry any offensive or defensive systems, the Westinghouse subcontract was cancelled on 3 December for the convenience of the government.[141]

After the program picked up again during august 1960, Westinghouse was issued a new subcontract (L1E1-YZ-600320) on 29 October 1960 to "conduct analytical, design, test, and other necessary studies." One of these included another complete evaluation of the ALQ-27 and its applicability to the YB-70. Unfortunately – as had been discovered earlier – the basic technique employed in the ALQ-27 relied on the use of specific traveling wave tubes that could not be applied to the B-70 airframe configuration, necessitating a major redesign of the ECM system. The study was completed on 16 January 1961 and the modifications were beginning to be developed when the effort was cancelled on 31 March. Unlike the IBM bomb-nav system, which continued as part of a low-level development program, the Westinghouse ECM system was cancelled outright. The defensive system operator planned to be carried by the third B-70 air vehicle would have nothing to do.[142]

SIGNATURE REDUCTION

One of the complaints frequently voiced against the B-70 was that it was a large target. The concept of "stealth" (a term not yet applied to the idea) was not far advanced in 1960, but engineers at Lockheed and North American both understood that reducing the radar and infrared signature of strategic aircraft would at least delay their detection by the enemy. The shape and materials used by Lockheed in the Blackbird were specifically intended to lower its radar signature. Although not as widely acknowledged, several detailed studies into the signature of the B-70 were made, and provided a basis for reduction attempts.[143]

During the very short YB-70 development period, the Air Force had directed North American to investigate means to reduce the probability of the B-70 being detected. Preliminary investigations were made into applying various radar absorbing materials (RAM) to the airframe, particularly the insides of the air intakes. However, most of the North American effort appears to have concentrated on reducing the infrared (IR) signature of the aircraft.

Exhausting cool air around the J93 engines was one means of reducing the IR signature of the B-70. The basic design of the B-70 inherently provided some reduction in the infrared signature of the engine exhaust because bypass air from the intake was ducted around the engines to keep the surrounding structure cool. This relatively cool air was discharged all around the convergent-divergent exhaust nozzles, creating a cool "tunnel" of air around the hot exhaust. Of course, the exhaust quickly mixed with the cooler air, but the net effect was a reduction in the temperature of the exhaust.

Of course, the airframe itself was a thermal target because of the frictional heat generated during Mach-3 flight. As part of its research,

North American developed a "finish system" (i.e., paint) that provided a low emittance at wavelengths used by Soviet infrared detecting devices, while radiating most of the excess heat from the surface of the airframe in wavelengths not normally under surveillance. The finish used a low emittance basecoat with an organic topcoat that was transparent to energy in the 1 to 6 micron range. The top coating was strangely opaque and highly emissive at wavelengths between 6 and 15 microns. This finish was relatively invisible to infrared detecting equipment, while still allowing the skin to radiate excess heat overboard to maintain its structural integrity.[144]

The first attempt at defining the finish system brought new meaning to the term "gold plated," literally. A gold substrate was applied by electro-deposition to the aircraft; where the gold was applied directly over titanium, it would be baked on at high temperatures under infrared lamps. This was followed by an overlay of Kel-F No. 800 resin coating, and the entire aircraft was baked under infrared lamps. The coating demonstrated some reduction in emittance from the treated test panels, leading North American to believe they were on the right track, but obviously better coatings would need to be found. The gold substrate was only 0.00002-inch thick, but given that there was 17,000 square feet of surface area on the B-70, it still would take 31.7 pounds of the precious metal to cover the entire aircraft. Even at the official $32 per troy ounce price in effect at the time, this equaled $12,173 per aircraft, per treatment. An additional 15 pounds of nickel plating was used in areas that could not be covered with gold, and 187 pounds of Kel-F No. 800 topcoat were used.

By 1961, two improved coatings had been developed, one for areas that reached a maximum of 485 degrees Fahrenheit, the other for areas up to 630 degrees Fahrenheit. The first (logically, called Type I) consisted of Englehard Industries Hanovia Ceramic Metallic Coating No. 2 0.004 mils thick. Over this was applied a 1-mil-thick mixture of 85-percent Ferro Enameling No. AL-8 Frit and 15-percent Hommel No. 5933 Frit. The Type II basecoat was a mixture of 40-percent Hanovia Silver Resinate and 60-percent Hanovia L. B. Coating No. 6593 applied 0.004-mil thick. The topcoat was a mixture of 74-percent 3M Kel-F No. 2140, 24-percent 3M Kel-F No. 601, and 2-percent Al_2O_3 applied 1-mil thick. The Type I coating was actually test flown on the vertical stabilizer of the X-15 research airplane. No observable physical changes occurred during the Mach 4.43 flight, but no attempt was made to measure its effectiveness. In most probability, the topcoats would have been opaque silver instead of the white finish used on the two XB-70A prototypes.[145]

The finish system was somewhat difficult to apply to an aircraft as large as the YB-70s, but the engineers expected that further development would yield improvements in the process. The most difficult problem was that the underlying surface had to be highly polished prior to applying the basecoat. In addition, the basecoat of both finishes had to be cured at 750 degrees Fahrenheit, while the topcoat of the Type II finish had to be cured at 1,000 degrees Fahrenheit (creating almost a ceramic finish). Accelerated environmental tests indicated the surface would prove durable on the stainless steel sections of the aircraft, but its long-term adhesion to titanium appeared to be weak and additional work would be needed to cure this problem. Both finishes were relatively immune to exposure to hydraulic fluid, fuels, oils, and other substances expected to be encountered during operational service, and each could be readily cleaned with soap and water.[146]

Alert Pod

One of the more interesting systems being designed for the operational B-70 was the Alert Pod developed by Beech Aircraft. This was envisioned as a means to provide the B-70 with a self-sufficient ground power system during deployments to relatively austere bases. One of the operational requirements laid down by SAC was that the B-70 should be ready for takeoff in less than 3 minutes after the crew entered the aircraft. In order to accomplish this, many of the B-70 systems would have to have already been powered-up to maintain them at correct operating temperatures. This would require external power.

Instead of relying on transport aircraft to carry external power carts for the B-70, a decision was made to design all of the necessary systems into a streamlined pod that could be carried by the B-70 itself, at least during subsonic flight. The pod would provide all necessary hydraulic, electrical, and pneumatic power to the aircraft while it was on ground-alert status, and during maintenance activities.[147]

The pod was designed to attach to the centerline of the lower fuselage behind the weapons bay, roughly under engines Nos. 3 and 4, and was equipped with its own retractable wheels that were used after it was detached from the aircraft. While sitting on its wheels, the pod was approximately 6 feet high and 30 feet long. Three built-in hoists (two at front and one rear) allowed the pod to be mated to

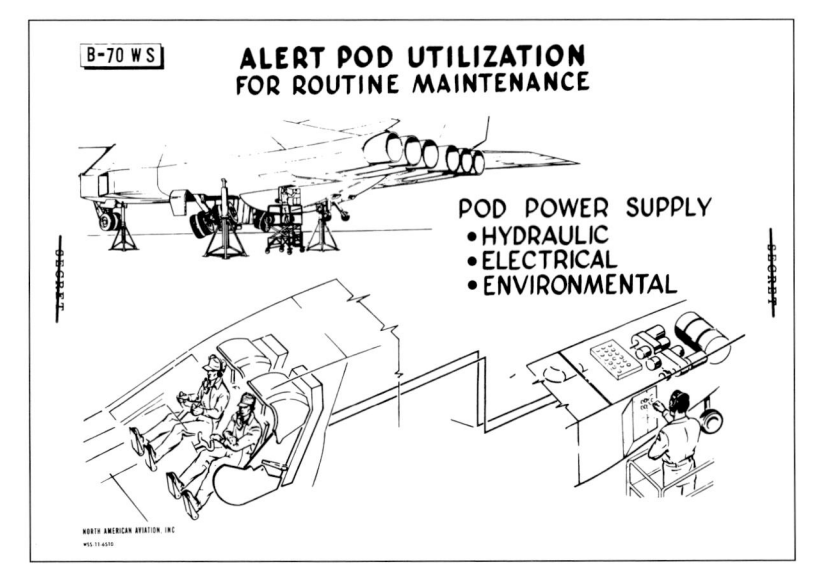

Opposite page and above: *The alert pod was an interesting concept that would have, theoretically, allowed the B-70 to be self-deploying to austere airstrips. As complicated as the B-70 systems were, it is hard to believe that the airplane would have deployed anywhere other than well-equipped SAC bases.* (Beech Aircraft via the Jay Miller Collection)

B-70 WS A NEW APPROACH TO GROUND POWER

INTEGRATED AIRBORNE UNIT
- SIMULTANEOUS POWER DELIVERY
  HYDRAULIC
  ELECTRICAL
  PNEUMATIC
- ALERT
- MAINTENANCE
- DISPERSAL

B-70 WS ALERT POD FEATURES

REAR HOIST, STORAGE AREA, HYDRAULIC DUMPS, HYDRAULIC RESERVOIR, FWD HOISTS, GENERATORS, ACCESSORY DRIVES, POWER TRANSFER PANEL, FUEL HEAT EXCHANGER, GAS TURBINE ENGINES, STARTER PANEL, HOIST CONTROL PANEL, CONTROL PANEL

B-70 WS ALERT POD

10 FT
6 FT

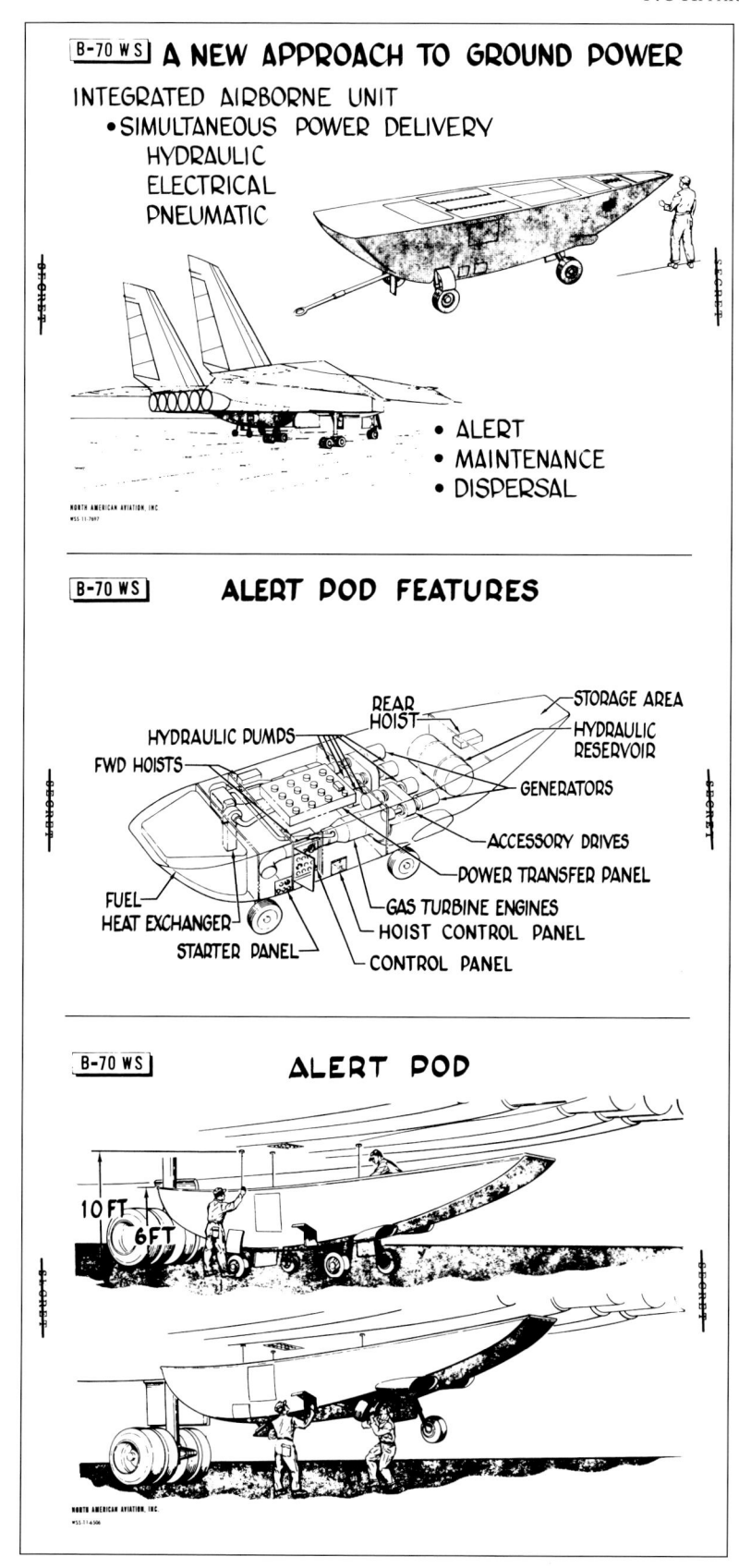

the B-70. The pod contained two small gas turbine engines that drove six hydraulic pumps (one for each J93) and two generators. The hydraulics allowed each of the accessory drives on the B-70 to be powered in order to start the J93s. The pod could also cool and/or heat the B-70 crew compartment and equipment bays as needed. An area in the rear of the pod allowed the ground crew to store tools and minor parts, while a large JP-6 fuel tank at the front was sufficient for 9 hours of unrefueled operation of the turbines. The pod could be controlled locally by the ground crew, or from the crew compartment at the copilot's station.[148]

It was expected that each operational B-70 would have its own alert pod procured for it. Beech and 14 other companies submitted proposals to North American on 27 October 1958, and North American awarded Beech a subcontract (L961-GX-600124) on 6 April 1959. Although the subcontract was announced in a press release, the pod was considered classified and was described only as "a special power device." The Beech contract included detailed design and the construction of a mockup, but did not cover producing any real hardware. The mockup was inspected and approved on 1 August 1959, but all further activity was terminated when the subcontract was cancelled on 3 December 1959 along with the rest of the B-70 work.[149]

When work resumed on the short-lived YB-70, Beech was awarded a new subcontract (L001-YZ-600227) that covered the manufacture of a prototype unit that was supposed to be completed by 1 October 1961. Production units were to be available beginning in August 1963. Beech was in the early stages of design and development when the subcontract was terminated for the convenience of the government on 31 March 1961, with only 4.5 percent of the work having been completed.[150]

Skybolt

The B-70 was always scheduled to carry an unspecified air-launched ballistic missile, and the bomb-nav system acknowledged this in its official name – bombing, navigation, and missile guidance system. When WS-110A and WS-125A were conceived, it was expected that they would both carry the same missile. As the development of the two new weapon systems lagged, the Air Force initiated the development of the improved B-52 (G and H models) with the expectation that at least the latter model would also carry the air-launched ballistic missile. The missile subsequently went through five separate sets of requirements, three demonstration programs, and two program reevaluations.

The development of the WS-138A air-launched ballistic missile (ALBM) began in 1958 following feasibility studies that had determined that a ballistic-type missile could be successfully deployed from the air. Since fixed land-based missiles were vulnerable to attack, a ballistic missile that could be dropped from high altitude then guided toward its target was strategically desirable. The missile was to replace the unsuccessful GAM-63 Rascal air-to-surface missile and serve as a follow-on to the 500-mile range GAM-77 Hound Dog cruise missile carried on the B-52G. Air Force Chief of Staff General

No Apparent Threat

Thomas D. White argued that an air-launched ballistic missile gave bombers a flexibility that could not be matched by submarine-based missiles, a very important policy statement when the rival military services were seeking funding appropriations.

The Air Force issued a request for proposals in early 1959, and Douglas Aircraft was awarded the GAM-87 development contract on 26 May 1959. Subcontracts were awarded to the Nortronics Division of Northrop (guidance systems), Aerojet-General (solid rocket motor), and General Electric (Mk 7 reentry vehicle). The missile would carry a Lawrence Livermore W59 nuclear warhead.[151]

On the other side of the Atlantic, the Royal Air Force had begun developing an air-launched intermediate-range ballistic missile in 1954 for use by the Victor and Vulcan bombers. By 1956, contracts had been issued to Avro (airframe), Armstrong-Whitworth (propulsion), and Elliot Brothers (guidance) for the Blue Steel missile. The missile was developed relatively quickly given the advances in technology required, and full-scale flight tests began over the Woomera range in Australia during the summer of 1960. The missile began arriving at operational squadrons during September 1962, and 617 Squadron was declared operational with the weapon in February 1963. Blue Steel

Speculative artist concept of a fleet of B-70s launching Skybolt missiles. It is highly unlikely that the bombers would attack in formation, and even more improbable that they launch missiles while maneuvering; still, it makes for good art. (Boeing Historical Archives)

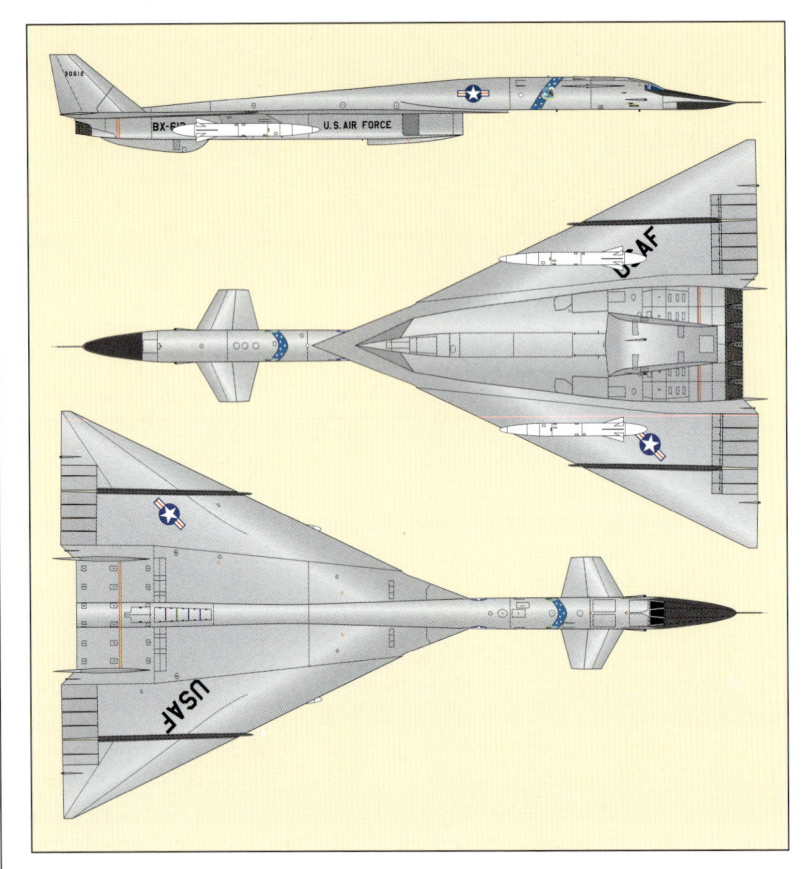

remained in operational service until 30 June 1969, when Britain's nuclear deterrent passed to the Royal Navy's Polaris submarines.[152]

However, even as Blue Steel was entering its development phase, the RAF became interested in the WS-138A program. In 1959, it appeared that the WS-138A missile would be an excellent replacement for Blue Steel and would extend the RAF deterrent role until the mid-1970s. As in the United States, the rivalry between the air force and the navy was intense, and the prestige of carrying the deterrent banner was enormous. In March 1960, a deal was struck between Prime Minister Harold MacMillan and President Dwight D. Eisenhower that would allow the RAF to purchase 100 Skybolts. This was an outright purchase of missiles (but not of warheads) and the United Kingdom was not a party to the development effort.[153]

This agreement was unpopular in both countries, but for different reasons. Some in the United States objected that the Air Force was picking up all of the development costs, while the British objected to purchasing a critical piece of their independent nuclear force from another government. Overall cost was another issue: it was estimated that 1,000 missiles for the U.S. and 100 for the U.K. would cost over $2,500 million. Despite the rhetoric, development continued.[154]

Initial missiles would be carried on the B-52H, which would carry two missiles on an inverted Y-shaped pylon under each wing. While on the pylon, the Skybolt was fitted with a tail cone to reduce aerodynamic drag. When the missile was dropped from the pylon, the tail cone was ejected and the first stage ignited. After first stage burnout, the Skybolt coasted for a while before the second stage ignited. First stage control was by movable stabilizer clusters around the rear of the missile, while the second stage was equipped with a gimbaled nozzle. The maximum velocity of the missile was 9,500 mph.[155]

Speculative drawing of a B-70 with GAM-87 Skybolt missiles. The silver finish is the infrared signature reduction finish developed by North American. Note the ECM antennas on the wing trailing edge and forward fuselage. The alert pod is shown for reference. (Art by Tony Landis)

At least two concepts were investigated for carrying the missile on the B-70. The first used a strengthened version of the same inverted Y-shaped pylon used on the B-52, one under each wing on the hardpoint that had been added to carry the missile or fuel. This would allow each B-70 to carry four missiles but the clearances between the missile and B-70 fuselage were very tight and deemed unacceptable. A simpler solution carried just a single missile on each pylon. The bomber would likely have been restricted to high subsonic speeds until after the missile had been launched and the pylon discarded.

Although development was proceeding well, Skybolt had several major technical problems that still needed to be worked out, and perhaps the major one was shared by the Polaris missile. In order to hit its target 1,000 nautical miles away, the missile needed to know exactly where it was when it was launched. This was a major technical challenge during the late 1950s since the crude inertial platforms of the day were notoriously inaccurate. The Navy had the luxury of a relatively large, slow moving submarine to house an inertial platform that could update the Polaris just before launch. Creating a version of this platform small enough to fit in a B-52 (or B-70 or Vulcan) was not a simple task.[156]

As finally developed, the Douglas GAM-87 Skybolt was a two-stage, solid propellant, air-launched ballistic missile. Skybolt was 38.25 feet long, spanned 5.5 feet across its stabilizers, and was 35 inches in diameter. Launch weight was approximately 11,000 pounds. The missile was designed with a range of 600 nautical miles while carrying a 1,600-pound warhead, or 1,000 nautical miles with a 700-pound warhead. General Electric considered using the same reentry vehicle that it was designing for the Minuteman ICBM, but this was considered too risky since the Minuteman development was not as far along as Skybolt. One idea that was briefly investigated was the CLAW (clustered atomic warhead) concept where multiple warheads were carried in a single reentry vehicle and released like shotgun pellets over the target area. During the spring of 1960, it was decided that the XW59 nuclear warhead was appropriate for use on the missile because it was lightweight (700 pounds) and had a high yield. Alternately, the 1,600-pound XW43 could be carried. By late September, General Electric had been directed to stop work on the heavier reentry vehicle and concentrate on one suitable for the W59 warhead.[157]

This was made official on 6 January 1961, when the Air Force formally asked the Atomic Energy Commission to assign the Lawrence Livermore W59 design to the Skybolt. The first production warhead was to be delivered by 1 July 1963. This was a variation of the same warhead that would be used by the Minuteman I ICBM. However, the Mk 7 reentry vehicle designed by General Electric was much more sophisticated than the Mk 5 used on Minuteman I. The reentry vehicle had a variable altitude fuzing system, and was set up so that if the missile should malfunction prior to launch, it could be used as a free-fall bomb. An even more advanced Mk 7A reentry vehicle that included a reduced radar cross-section and the ability to launch decoys during reentry was under development. The arming and fuzing sequence was initiated by signals from the missile computer indicating a proper trajectory after the second stage fired. Thrust reversal ports were opened to separate the second stage from the reentry vehicle, which then con-

Four Douglas GAM-87 Skybolt missiles on a B-52H. The missile was developed for use on the B-52H and RAF Vulcan, but was also planned for use on the B-70 and possibly a dedicated missile carrier such as the long-abandoned CAMAL concept. (Boeing Historical Archives)

tinued a ballistic trajectory. Upon reentry, deceleration forces would complete the arming and fuzing sequence to explode the warhead at a preset altitude. The XW59-X1 warhead for Skybolt was 47.9 inches long, 23.75 inches in diameter, and weighed 565 pounds. The Mk 7 reentry vehicle, including the warhead, weighed 812 pounds. Full-scale nuclear tests of the Mk 59 Mod 0 warhead later deployed on Minuteman I were conducted during Operation Dominic in 1962; no Skybolt warheads were ever manufactured.[158]

The first unpowered drop tests of inert Skybolt missile shapes began during early 1961 over the Gulf of Mexico. The first five live launches, conducted during 1962, were all considered failures, but each for a different reason. The program was learning from its mistakes and correcting each problem as it materialized. Unfortunately, this string of failures left an unfavorable impression on the new Secretary of Defense, Robert S. McNamara, who recommended the program be cancelled. Ironically, Brigadier General David C. Jones announced the first successful launch of the GAM-87 over the Atlantic Test Range on 22 December 1962; on the same day, President John F. Kennedy announced the cancellation of the program. Although Kennedy had informed Prime Minister MacMillan of his decision prior to the announcement, the move came as a severe blow to Anglo-American relations with the British, seeing this as a breach of faith and a means of preventing the RAF from having a viable nuclear capability.[159]

Limited flight tests with the remaining GAM-87A missiles continued from B-52Hs after program cancellation, and in June 1963, the GAM-87A was redesignated AGM-48A. In total, Douglas built less than 100 Skybolt missiles.[160]

Appendices

Right: *Valkyrie painting used by North American.* (Boeing Historical Archives)

Below: *The pilots may get all of the publicity, but they are but a few of the many. Below is a group photo of some of those involved in the design, development, manufacture, operations, and maintenance of the two XB-70 Valkyries.* (Tom Rosquin Collection)

APPENDIX A
129 FLIGHTS OF THE MAIDENS

The following flight log was excerpted from the "XB-70 Flight Log" compiled by Mrs. Betty J. Love at the NASA Flight Research Center and distributed to members of the XB-70A team on 7 May 1969, and North American Aviation report "XB-70A #1 & 2 Flight Hours Log and Flight Summary," prepared by the Engineering Flight Test Department, 1 July 1969. The "Flt. No." column identifies which aircraft and the flight number for that aircraft. The columns marked "Sub Sonic" and "Mach" identify the hours and minutes spent at each speed on each flight; the "Total Super" column is the total supersonic time (in hours and minutes) on that flight and the "Total Flight" column gives the total flight time (in hours and minutes) for the flight. The "Max Values" columns give the maximum Mach Number (Mn), speed (in mph) and altitude (in feet) for each flight. The "Takeoff" and "Landing" columns each contain three pieces of data: weight (in pounds), runway distance used (in feet), and speed (in KIAS). The "Purpose and Notes" column contains information relevant to that flight. In these columns, "Lakebed" indicates that the flight landed on one of the dry lakes at Edwards, while "Chutes" indicates one or more of the drag chutes failed to deploy. Information in italics was estimated by the pilots or engineers, not actual measured values.

Flt.	Date	Flt. No.	Pilot	Copilot	Sub Sonic	Mach 1.0–1.9	Mach 2.0–2.5	Mach 2.5–2.9	Mach 3.0	Total Super	Total Flight	Mn	mph	Feet	Takeoff lbs/ft/knots	Landing lbs/ft/knots	Purpose Notes
1	21 Sep 64	1-1	White	Cotton	1 07	- -	- -	- -	- -	- -	1 07	0.50	360	16,000	387,604 / 4,853 / 181	307,340 / 10,800 / 181	Handling qualities and characteristics. Main gear rotated but did not fold. No. 3 engine shut down. LH brakes locked.
2	5 Oct 64	1-2	White	Cotton	0 55	- -	- -	- -	- -	- -	0 55	0.85	600	28,000	411,940 / 6,750 / 186	342,040 / *10,000* / 192	Flutter, S&C, and power control tests. U1 hydraulic leak. Landing gear extended using emergency system. Lakebed. Chutes.
3	12 Oct 64	1-3	White	Cotton	1 20	0 15	- -	- -	- -	0 15	1 35	1.11	725	35,400	428,630 / 6,800 / 185	308,530 / 9,900 / 173	Flutter, S&C, and power control tests. Gear recycled after takeoff. First supersonic flight. Chutes.
4	24 Oct 64	1-4	White	Cotton	0 45	0 40	- -	- -	- -	0 40	1 25	1.42	945	46,300	435,700 / 7,350 / 193	301,450 / 7,950 / 167	Wing fold to 25°, S&C, flutter, ram purge. Cabin did not repressurize after ram purge. Landing at Palmdale. Chutes.
5	16 Feb 65	1-5	White	Cotton	0 30	0 40	- -	- -	- -	0 40	1 10	1.60	1,060	45,000	414,630 / 5,300 / 198	295,230 / 11,100 / 179	Wing fold to 65°, AICS, S&C, airspeed cal. Landing at Edwards. Chutes.
6	25 Feb 65	1-6	White	Fulton	0 53	- -	- -	- -	- -	- -	0 53	0.79	655	35,000	464,140 / 7,170 / 202	385,810 / *10,000* / 185	Airworthiness, S&C, AICS, ram purge. Instrumentation failed. U1 hydraulic leak. Right wingtip light. Lakebed.
7	4 Mar 65	1-7	White	Fulton	0 37	1 00	- -	- -	- -	1 00	1 37	1.85	1,200	50,200	492,030 / 8,243 / 217	302,320 / 10,750 / 168	S&C, AICS, airstarts, ram purge tests. Gear recycled after takeoff. Sonic boom test (1.7 psf @ M1.82 and 50,000 feet).
8	24 Mar 65	1-8	White	Shepard	0 26	0 34	0 40	- -	- -	1 14	1 40	2.14	1,365	56,100	501,600 / 7,679 / 210	302,800 / 12,200 / 185	Flutter pulses, S&C, AICS, and ram purge. Cabin would not repressurize. Chutes.

129 Flights of the Maidens

Flt.	Date	Flt. No.	Pilot	Copilot	Sub Sonic	Mach 1.0–1.9	Mach 2.0–2.5	Mach 2.5–2.9	Mach 3.0	Total Super	Total Flight	Mn	mph	Feet	Takeoff lbs/ft/knots	Landing lbs/ft/knots	Purpose Notes
9	2 Apr 65	1-9	White	Cotton	0 54	- -	- -	- -	- -	0 54	0.95	630	34,500	501,700 7,990 210	419,820 11,800 210	Heavyweight takeoff and landing. U1 and U2 hydraulic leaks. Engines Nos. 3 and 5 power control malfunction.
10	20 Apr 65	1-10	White	Cotton	0 28	0 24	0 50	- -	- -	1 14	1 42	2.30	1,485	58,500	499,130 10,400 210	299,850 10,500 177	Flutter pulses, AICS, S&C, windshield ramp. Recycled gear after takeoff. Chutes.
11	28 Apr 65	1-11	White	Shepard	0 27	0 19	0 57	- -	- -	1 16	1 43	2.45	1,570	64,300	508,730 9,760 212	300,090 9,900 177	AICS, flutter pulses, S&C. Lost fuel indication. Chutes. Three tires blew following brake tests after the flight.
12	7 May 65	1-12	White	Fulton	0 27	0 25	0 26	0 07	- -	0 58	1 25	2.60	1,690	65,000	513,070 8,230 210	314,640 12,100 210	AICS and performance tests. Wing apex failed and ingested by engines. Flaps up landing. Lakebed. Chutes.
13	16 Jun 65	1-13	White	Cotton	0 22	0 25	0 28	0 22	- -	1 15	1 37	2.60	1,700	65,000	517,080 9,740 207	300,190 12,000 181	AICS, S&C tests. Indicated slow leak in P2 hydraulics. Initial lateral bobweight operation. Lakebed.
14	1 Jul 65	1-14	White	Shepard	0 25	0 29	0 19	0 40	- -	1 19	1 44	2.85	1,900	68,000	515,870 9,878 212	288,920 10,790 175	Flutter pulses, AICS, S&C (bobweight free). Lost wing and fuselage skin facesheets.
15	17 Jul 65	2-1	White	Cotton	0 52	0 21	- -	- -	- -	0 21	1 13	1.41	935	42,000	393,270 6,200 181	294,970 12,400 171	S&C, wingtips full down. Windshield tests. Low speed handling. Nose gear malfunction after landing.
16	27 Jul 65	1-15	White	Fulton	0 38	0 22	0 07	0 36	- -	1 05	1 43	2.82	1,900	66,000	516,390 9,249 212	289,040 11,296 178	Performance and heat soak. Soaked for 20 minutes at 510°F. No. 1 UHF radio failed.
17	10 Aug 65	2-2	Cotton	White	0 56	0 31	- -	- -	- -	0 31	1 27	1.45	950	41,000	472,510 10,250 221	314,240 11,400 183	Pilot checkout, S&C, performance. Pilot oxygen malfunction. No repressure after ram purge test.
18	18 Aug 65	2-3	Shepard	White	1 14	0 44	- -	- -	- -	0 44	1 58	1.45	950	46,000	483,250 9,330 205	298,520 15,600 196	Pilot checkout, S&C, performance. No. 1 engine air start tests. U2 hydraulics down to 90 percent.
19	20 Aug 65	2-4	Fulton	White	1 23	0 41	- -	- -	- -	0 41	2 04	1.44	950	42,000	495,170 10,060 214	296,290 11,500 168	Pilot checkout, S&C, performance. No. 1 engine air start tests.
20	17 Sep 65	2-5	White	Fulton	0 55	1 00	- -	- -	- -	1 00	1 55	1.83	1,200	50,500	491,370 8,280 206	287,040 ? ?	S&C, AICS. Tower flyby with wingtips half down. Modified chute configuration. Worked.
21	22 Sep 65	1-16	White	Cotton	0 40	0 21	0 07	0 49	- -	1 17	1 57	2.83	1,900	67,000	515,740 10,050 208	289,820 12,000 175	AICS, S&C, performance, heat soak. Soaked for 18 minutes at 508°F.
22	29 Sep 65	2-6	White	Shepard	1 12	0 27	0 05	- -	- -	0 32	1 44	2.23	1,460	54,000	507,230 8,700 203	331,340 ? ?	AICS, S&C, performance. No. 6 engine shutdown. Subsonic 5-engine cruise back. Lakebed.
23	5 Oct 65	2-7	White	Shepard	1 09	0 22	0 09	- -	- -	0 31	1 40	2.30	1,520	55,000	507,440 10,090 202	340,300 12,650 197	AICS operation. No. 2 engine overtemp, shutdown.
24	11 Oct 65	2-8	White	Shepard	0 37	0 25	0 53	- -	- -	1 18	1 55	2.34	1,550	57,500	508,220 10,500 207	284,620 10,850 178	AICS operation, performance, ram purge. No. 5 engine airstart tests unsatisfactory.
25	14 Oct 65	1-17	White	Cotton	0 37	0 24	0 22	0 22	0 02	1 10	1 47	3.02	2,000	70,000	512,530 8,000 206	305,270 11,110 176	Mach 3 performance at 70,000 feet. Only time A/V-1 would fly at Mach 3.
26	16 Oct 65	2-9	White	Fulton	0 31	0 25	0 47	- -	- -	1 12	1 43	2.43	1,600	59,500	514.680 8,995 206	295,200 10,315 176	AICS, performance, S&C.
27	26 Oct 65	2-10	White	Fulton	0 56	0 28	0 43	- -	- -	1 11	2 07	2.46	1,620	59,000	512,370 8,640 204	286,160 11,255 163	AICS, performance, S&C. Engine airstarts.

129 Flights of the Maidens

Flt.	Date	Flt. No.	Pilot	Copilot	Sub Sonic	Mach 1.0–1.9	Mach 2.0–2.5	Mach 2.5–2.9	Mach 3.0	Total Super	Total Flight	Max Values Mn	mph	Feet	Takeoff lbs/ft/knots	Landing lbs/ft/knots	Purpose / Notes
28	2 Nov 65	2-11	White	Cotton	0 34	0 34	0 46	- -	- -	1 20	1 54	2.45	1,610	59,000	507,520 / 9,910 / 208	284,590 / 11,000 / 170	AICS, performance, S&C. No. 3 airstart tests.
29	4 Nov 65	1-18	Fulton	White	0 47	1 17	- -	- -	- -	1 17	2 04	1.86	1,230	46,000	517,690 / 8,590 / 200	292,530 / 11,025 / 175	Propulsion, performance, AICS, airstarts. Flaps up landing.
30	8 Nov 65	1-19	Cotton	White	1 37	0 46	- -	- -	- -	0 46	2 23	1.89	1,250	45,500	516,150 / 10,510 / 220	288,630 / 11,075 / 180	Propulsion, performance, AICS, airstarts. Airspeed calibration.
31	12 Nov 65	1-20	Shepard	White	1 49	0 36	- -	- -	- -	0 36	2 25	1.84	1,220	46,000	518,060 / 9,245 / 212	291,490 / 11,090 / 169	Performance and airspeed calibration. No. 4 generator failed 30 minutes after takeoff.
32	18 Nov 65	1-21	Cotton	Shepard	1 12	0 50	- -	- -	- -	0 50	2 02	1.88	1,240	47,000	507,930 / 8,500 / 205	299,030 / 12,375 / 179	Performance, AICS, propulsion. Airspeed calibration.
33	29 Nov 65	2-12	White	Fulton	2 19	- -	- -	- -	- -		2 19	0.53	380	15,200	524,300 / 8,080 / 205	295,830 / 11,000 / 175	Performance, propulsion, S&C. Airspeed calibration with landing gear down.
34	30 Nov 65	1-22	Fulton	White	0 47	0 19	0 53	- -	- -	1 12	1 59	2.34	1,540	56,000	511,120 / 7,540 / 199	291,710 / 11,330 / 163	Performance, propulsion, S&C. Airstarts at subsonic speeds with new J93 fuel nozzle.
35	1 Dec 65	2-13	White	Fulton	0 38	0 25	0 31	0 28	- -	1 24	2 02	2.67	1,765	64,000	522,890 / 7,980 / 205	283,430 / 10,690 / 173	S&C, performance, AICS tests at Mach 2.6.
36	2 Dec 65	1-23	Cotton	White	0 29	0 48	0 34	- -	- -	1 22	1 51	2.46	1,620	60,000	502,690 / 8,355 / 214	295,010 / 8,740 / 168	S&C, performance, and AICS tests. Engine airstarts at Mach 2.4 and 60,000 feet.
37	3 Dec 65	2-14	White	Cotton	0 41	0 23	0 11	0 40	- -	1 14	1 55	2.87	1,900	69,000	526,040 / 10,000 / 215	292,820 / 8,215 / 172	AICS, S&C, performance, ram purge tests. Touch & go landing.
38	7 Dec 65	1-24	Shepard	Fulton	1 46	0 18	0 22	- -	- -	0 40	2 26	2.45	1,600	62,000	504,610 / 8,177 / 210	289,370 / 11,495 / 179	AICS and performance tests. No. 6 engine windmilled due to engine oil loss.
39	10 Dec 65	1-25	Fulton	Shepard	1 23	0 55	- -	- -	- -	0 55	2 18	1.82	1,200	50,700	508,200 / 9,825 / 214	291,270 / 10,090 / 167	AICS, propulsion, and performance tests. Multi-engine airstarts.
40	11 Dec 65	2-15	White	Shepard	0 47	0 23	0 12	0 41	- -	1 16	2 03	2.94	1,940	70,600	531,040 / 10,000 / 215	283,620 / 10,000 / 170	AICS, performance. Heat soak for 20 minutes above Mach 2.8. Touch & go landing.
41	14 Dec 65	1-26	Shepard	Fulton	2 10	- -	- -	- -	- -		2 10	0.95	670	20,000	506,850 / 7,565 / 207	323,430 / 10,305 / 181	Performance, S&C, airspeed calibration. Poor weather conditions.
42	20 Dec 65	1-27	Cotton	White	0 47	1 11	- -	- -	- -	1 11	1 58	1.78	1,190	42,000	510,060 / 8,375 / 218	286,830 / 12,140 / 172	Performance and propulsion tests. Encapsulated flight control evaluation.
43	21 Dec 65	2-16	White	Cotton	0 29	0 18	0 13	0 49	- -	1 20	1 49	2.95	1,945	72,000	532,600 / 9,580 / 213	294,330 / 11,000 / 170	AICS, performance. Heat soak for 32 minutes above Mach 2.8. Land with engines Nos. 4 and 6 shut down.
44	22 Dec 65	1-28	Shepard	Cotton	2 21	0 14	- -	- -	- -	0 14	2 35	1.42	950	34,000	508,800 / 9,500 / 210	289,430 / 10,000 / 170	S&C, performance, and propulsion tests.
45	3 Jan 66	2-17	White	Cotton	0 30	0 16	0 17	0 46	0 03	1 22	1 52	3.05	2,010	72,000	533,520 / 7,910 / 208	291,390 / 10,500 / 170	Mach 3 performance at 70,000 feet.
46	3 Jan 66	1-29	Fulton	Shepard	2 41	- -	- -	- -	- -		2 41	0.94	655	26,000	508,650 / 7,740 / 205	314,930 / 10,000 / 168	Performance, propulsion, AICS, S&C tests. Engine airstarts and airspeed calibration.

APPENDIX A

129 Flights of the Maidens

Flt.	Date	Flt. No.	Pilot	Copilot	Sub Sonic	Mach 1.0–1.9	Mach 2.0–2.5	Mach 2.5–2.9	Mach 3.0	Total Super	Total Flight	Mn	Max Values mph	Feet	Takeoff lbs/ft/knots	Landing lbs/ft/knots	Purpose Notes
47	6 Jan 66	1-30	Shepard	Fulton	3 40	-	-	-	-	-	3 40	0.94	655	33,000	503,410 / 7,775 / 209	287,830 / 11,000 / 168	Subsonic cruise performance. Environmental tests.
48	11 Jan 66	1-31	Fulton	Shepard	0 49	0 46	-	-	-	0 46	1 35	1.85	1,220	46,000	448,480 / 8,900 / 195	286,830 / 10,500 / 169	Performance and propulsion tests. Engine airstart and nose ramp evaluations. Two flights in one day!
49	11 Jan 66	1-32	Cotton	White	0 58	-	-	-	-	-	0 58	0.95	650	27,000	455,730 / 7,770 / 207	374,530 / 11,000 / 170	Performance and propulsion tests. U2 hydraulic pressure lost during flight. Two flights in one day!
50	12 Jan 66	2-18	White	Cotton	0 24	0 21	0 09	0 50	0 04	1 24	1 48	3.06	2,020	72,000	522,480 / 8,170 / 209	286,000 / 10,000 / 170	Mach 3 performance at 70,000 feet. AICS evaluation.
51	15 Jan 66	1-33	Fulton	White	0 37	0 50	-	-	-	0 50	1 27	1.85	1,220	47,000	455,230 / 6,785 / 198	286,800 / 10,000 / 170	Propulsion and S&C tests.
52	7 Feb 66	2-19	Shepard	Cotton	1 08	1 03	-	-	-	1 03	2 11	1.44	960	42,000	522,930 / 8,380 / 204	288,590 / 10,000 / 170	S&C and performance tests.
53	9 Feb 66	2-20	White	Cotton	0 40	0 21	0 17	0 26	0 05	1 09	1 49	3.04	2,000	70,800	538,190 / 9,290 / 210	302,810 / 10,000 / 170	Mach 3 performance at 70,000 feet. Duct unstart - restart at Mach 3.
54	16 Feb 66	2-21	White	Cotton	3 04	0 02	-	-	-	0 02	3 06	1.10	720	32,000	538,240 / 9,170 / 212	282,150 / 10,000 / 170	S&C, performance, ground effects. Airspeed calibration. Instrumentation inop above 8,000 feet.
55	17 Feb 66	2-22	White	Cotton	0 24	0 18	0 15	0 35	0 15	1 23	1 47	3.04	2,000	73,000	538,310 / 9,105 / 207	294,790 / 10,000 / 170	Mach 3 performance at 70,000 feet. Landed with No. 4 engine shut down.
56	26 Feb 66	1-34	Shepard	Fulton	2 22	-	-	-	-	-	2 22	0.92	650	20,000	508,610 / 7,500 / 205	323,020 / 11,000 / 170	Tuft survey, performance, S&C tests.
57	3 Mar 66	1-35	Fulton	Shepard	2 42	-	-	-	-	-	2 42	0.55	395	15,000	519,630 / 8,000 / 205	291,770 / 10,000 / 170	Tuft survey, S&C tests. Flap up pressure malfunction.
58	4 Mar 66	1-36	Fulton	Shepard	1 39	0 36	0 12	-	-	0 48	2 27	2.02	1,330	56,000	525,640 / 8,000 / 205	284,700 / 10,000 / 170	AICS, performance, propulsion, S&C tests.
59	7 Mar 66	1-37	Shepard	Cotton	1 17	0 46	0 16	-	-	1 02	2 19	2.22	1,450	57,000	520,320 / 8,000 / 204	274,600 / 19,000 / 172	AICS, performance, propulsion, S&C tests. U1 and U2 hydraulics failure. Emergency landing. Lakebed. Chutes.
60	10 Mar 66	2-23	White	Fulton	0 31	0 31	0 15	0 39	-	1 25	1 56	2.76	1,820	67,000	537,700 / 8,000 / 205	298,320 / 10,000 / 173	AICS and performance tests. Mach 2.7 duct evaluation. Chutes.
61	15 Mar 66	2-24	White	Fulton	0 26	0 22	0 10	1 01	-	1 33	1 59	2.85	1,880	69,500	533,670 / 8,000 / 205	284,620 / 10,000 / 170	AICS, performance, S&C, ram purge tests.
62	17 Mar 66	2-25	Fulton	White	0 25	0 18	0 19	0 50	-	1 27	1 52	2.85	1,880	70,350	532,630 / 8,000 / 205	287,860 / 10,000 / 170	AICS, performance, S&C tests. Lakebed.
63	19 Mar 66	2-26	White	Shepard	0 27	0 29	0 17	0 53	-	1 30	1 57	2.93	1,930	74,000	528,880 / 8,000 / 205	287,290 / 10,000 / 170	AICS, performance, S&C tests. Lakebed.
64	22 Mar 66	1-38	Cotton	Shepard	2 11	-	-	-	-	-	2 11	0.97	650	32,000	518,040 / 7,900 / 205	323,460 / 10,000 / 172	Performance, S&C tests. Lost cabin pressurization.
65	24 Mar 66	2-27	Fulton	White	0 45	0 18	0 10	0 19	-	0 47	1 32	2.71	1,600	64,000	499,050 / 8,000 / 205	323,160 / 9,000 / 170	Performance tests. Ferry flight from Edwards to Carswell AFB.

129 Flights of the Maidens

Flt.	Date	Flt. No.	Pilot	Copilot	Sub Sonic	Mach 1.0–1.9	Mach 2.0–2.5	Mach 2.5–2.9	Mach 3.0	Total Super	Total Flight	Max Values Mn	mph	Feet	Takeoff lbs/ft/knots	Landing lbs/ft/knots	Purpose Notes
66	24 Mar 66	1-39	Shepard	Cotton	0 54	0 45	0 21	- -	- -	1 06	2 00	2.42	1,600	60,000	517,740 / 8,000 / 205	286,410 / 10,000 / 172	AICS, S&C, propulsion, performance tests. Encapsulated descent tests.
67	26 Mar 66	2-28	Cotton	White	3 09	- -	- -	- -	- -	- -	3 09	0.94	620	36,000	513,000 / 8,000 / 205	290,000 / 9,000 / 170	Ferry flight from Carswell AFB to Edwards. No data recorded.
68	28 Mar 66	1-40	Shepard	Cotton	0 20	0 49	0 32	- -	- -	1 21	1 41	2.43	1,600	65,000	516,540 / 8,000 / 205	281,690 / 10,000 / 176	AICS, S&C, propulsion tests.
69	29 Mar 66	2-29	Shepard	White	0 26	1 25	- -	- -	- -	1 25	1 51	1.65	1,090	48,000	533,740 / 8,000 / 205	287,560 / 9,000 / 170	Performance, propulsion, S&C tests. AICS malfunction.
70	31 Mar 66	2-30	Shepard	White	0 50	0 18	0 12	0 50	- -	1 20	2 10	2.95	1,950	72,000	535,940 / 8,000 / 205	280,860 / 9,000 / 170	AICS, performance, S&C, ram purge tests. 32 minutes above Mach 2.9.
71	1 Apr 66	1-41	White	Fulton	0 54	0 55	0 20	- -	- -	1 15	2 09	2.45	1,620	58,800	519,540 / 8,000 / 205	278,040 / 10,000 / 170	AICS, propulsion, S&C tests
72	4 Apr 66	2-31	Cotton	White	0 27	0 21	0 19	0 50	- -	1 30	1 57	2.95	1,940	73,000	528,060 / 8,000 / 205	284,660 / 9,000 / 170	AICS, performance, S&C tests. 31 minutes above Mach 2.9.
73	5 Apr 66	1-42	Fulton	Shepard	0 49	0 24	0 48	- -	- -	1 12	2 01	2.43	1,600	61,000	519,980 / 8,000 / 205	288,980 / 10,000 / 170	AICS, propulsion, S&C tests.
74	8 Apr 66	2-32	Fulton	White	0 56	0 19	0 10	0 24	0 16	1 09	2 05	3.07	2,020	73,000	534,240 / 8,000 / 205	294,860 / 9,000 / 170	Mach 3 performance at 70,000 feet. 16 minutes at Mach 3.
75	12 Apr 66	2-33	White	Cotton	0 32	0 24	0 11	0 22	0 20	1 17	1 49	3.08	2,025	72,800	537,230 / 8,000 / 205	296,930 / 9,000 / 170	Mach 3 performance at 70,000 feet. 20 minutes at Mach 3.
76	13 Apr 66	1-43	Shepard	Cotton	0 58	0 18	0 12	0 35	- -	1 05	2 03	2.60	1,700	62,500	509,410 / 8,000 / 205	288,190 / 10,000 / 169	Performance, propulsion, S&C tests. Handling qualities tests.
77	16 Apr 66	2-34	White	Cotton	0 58	0 20	0 08	0 34	0 01	1 03	2 01	3.03	2,000	71,000	532,720 / 8,000 / 205	296,040 / 9,000 / 170	Mach 3 performance at 70,000 feet. No. 3 engine overtemp.
78	19 Apr 66	1-44	Shepard	Fulton	1 12	- -	- -	- -	- -	- -	2 12	0.58	415	17,000	522,190 / 8,000 / 2000	287,620 / 10,000 / 169	Low speed handling quality tests. Airspeed calibration. Landing gear malfunction.
79	21 Apr 66	1-45	Shepard	Fulton	0 42	0 21	0 59	- -	- -	1 20	2 02	2.42	1,600	61,000	523,360 / 8,000 / 204	287,260 / 9,000 / 170	S&C, performance, and propulsion tests.
80	23 Apr 66	2-35	White	Cotton	0 39	0 21	0 21	0 40	- -	1 22	2 01	2.73	1,800	66,000	535,480 / 8,000 / 205	286,540 / 9,000 / 170	AICS unstart investigations.
81	25 Apr 66	1-46	Fulton	Shepard	0 55	0 20	0 44	0 08	- -	1 12	2 07	2.55	1,680	63,000	522,700 / 8,000 / 204	282,640 / 10,000 / 170	S&C, AICS, performance, propulsion tests.
82	26 Apr 66	2-36	Fulton	Cotton	0 48	0 27	0 39	0 11	- -	1 17	2 05	2.65	1,760	65,500	534,000 / 8,000 / 205	290,000 / 9,000 / 170	Performance, S&C tests. No. 2 engine windmill brake.
83	27 Apr 66	1-47	White	Fulton	2 33	0 08	- -	- -	- -	0 08	2 41	1.50	1,010	31,000	522,880 / 8,000 / 204	296,760 / 10,000 / 170	S&C, propulsion, and handling qualities.
84	30 Apr 66	2-37	White	Cotton	2 16	- -	- -	- -	- -	- -	2 16	0.58	415	16,000	534,000 / 8,000 / 205	309,000 / 8,000 / 170	Performance, S&C tests. Nose gear jammed into gear door. Paperclip flight. Lakebed.

129 Flights of the Maidens

Flt.	Date	Flt. No.	Pilot	Copilot	Sub Sonic	Mach 1.0–1.9	Mach 2.0–2.5	Mach 2.5–2.9	Mach 3.0	Total Super	Total Flight	Max Mn	mph	Feet	Takeoff lbs/ft/knots	Landing lbs/ft/knots	Purpose / Notes
85	3 May 66	1-48	White	Fulton	1 22	- -	- -	- -	- -	- -	1 22	0.64	445	23,000	511,840 / 8,000 / 204	333,860 / 10,000 / 175	Propulsion tests. U2 hydraulic leak. Landing gear failed to retract.
86	9 May 66	1-49	White	Fulton	2 16	- -	- -	- -	- -	- -	2 16	0.54	390	15,000	524,000 / 8,000 / 204	315,000 / 10,000 / 175	AICS and handling quality tests. Landing gear extension on electrical emergency system.
87	16 May 66	2-38	White	Cotton	0 58	0 25	0 19	0 27	- -	1 11	2 09	2.75	1,800	65,000	531,000 / 8,000 / 205	290,000 / 9,000 / 170	AICS, flutter, S&C tests.
88	19 May 66	2-39	White	Cotton	0 28	0 18	0 11	0 29	0 32	1 30	1 58	3.06	2,015	72,500	531,000 / 8,000 / 205	287,000 / 9,000 / 180	Mach 3 performance at 70,000 feet. 32 minutes at Mach 3. Data obtained after engine shutdown.
89	22 May 66	2-40	Fulton	Cotton	1 57	0 25	- -	- -	- -	0 25	2 22	1.51	960	26,500	532,000 / 8,000 / 205	290,000 / 9,000 / 170	S&C tests. Armed Forces Day Air Show flight.
90	25 May 66	2-41	Shepard	Cotton	1 34	0 49	- -	- -	- -	0 49	2 23	1.63	1,065	42,000	532,000 / 8,000 / 205	290,000 / 9,000 / 170	Performance, S&C tests.
91	27 May 66	2-42	Shepard	Cotton	0 51	0 38	0 33	0 06	- -	1 17	2 08	2.53	1,640	62,000	535,000 / 8,000 / 205	293,000 / 8,000 / 170	Performance, AICS, S&C tests. Performance landing with moderate braking.
92	31 May 66	2-43	Shepard	Fulton	0 50	0 50	0 22	- -	- -	1 12	2 02	2.23	1,455	57,000	533,000 / 8,000 / 205	295,000 / 8,000 / 170	Performance, AICS, S&C tests.
93	4 Jun 66	2-44	Shepard	Cotton	0 45	0 26	0 28	0 26	- -	1 20	2 05	2.93	1,930	70,000	538,000 / 8,000 / 214	295,000 / 8,000 / 170	Performance, AICS, handling qualities. Sonic boom tests.
94	6 Jun 66	2-45	Shepard	Cotton	0 45	0 22	0 12	0 32	0 09	1 15	2 00	3.05	2,000	72,000	533,000 / 8,000 / 213	290,000 / 8,000 / 170	Performance, ram purge tests.
95	8 Jun 66	2-46	White	Cross	1 59	0 14	- -	- -	- -	0 14	2 13	1.41	940	32,000	530,000 / 8,000 / 205	— / — / —	Airspeed calibration, sonic boom tests. Photo mission. Mid-air collision. A/V-2 destroyed.
96	3 Nov 66	1-50	Cotton	Fulton	1 26	0 22	0 12	- -	- -	0 34	2 00	2.10	1,385	60,000			Functional evaluation, airspeed calibration. Sonic boom tests. Low approaches.
97	10 Nov 66	1-51	Fulton	Cotton	0 27	0 40	0 19	0 13	- -	1 12	1 39	2.52	1,660	60,000			Sonic boom signatures at Mach 1.5 and 2.5. P2 hydraulic system leak. Replenishment system used to lower landing gear.
98	23 Nov 66	1-52	Shepard	Cotton	0 32	0 44	0 13	0 09	- -	1 06	1 38	2.51	1,655	61,000			Sonic boom signatures at Mach 1.5 and 2.5. Airspeed calibrations. No. 3 engine high exhaust gas temperature.
99	12 Dec 66	1-53	Fulton	Shepard	0 56	0 29	0 23	0 09	- -	1 01	1 57	2.52	1,660	60,000			Sonic boom signatures at Mach 1.5 and 2.5. Low speed S&C. Tuft survey tests.
100	16 Dec 66	1-54	Shepard	Fulton	0 53	0 34	0 19	0 08	- -	1 01	1 54	2.55	1,680	60,300			Sonic boom signatures at Mach 1.5 and 2.5. Airspeed calibrations. Tuft survey tests. Crack in No. 1 engine gear case.
101	20 Dec 66	1-55	Cotton	Shepard	0 45	0 28	0 28	0 04	- -	1 00	1 45	2.53	1,640	60,800			Sonic boom signatures at Mach 1.8 and 2.5. Low speed S&C with gear and flaps down. Tuft survey tests.
102	4 Jan 67	1-56	Fulton	Shepard	0 47	0 22	0 27	0 08	- -	0 57	1 44	2.53	1,670	60,400			Sonic boom signatures at Mach 1.8 and 2.5. Low speed S&C and airspeed calibrations. Tuft survey tests. First internal engine failure.
103	13 Jan 67	1-57	Cotton	Fulton	0 46	0 22	0 29	0 09	- -	1 00	1 46	2.57	1,695	61,000			Sonic boom signatures at Mach 1.8 and 2.5. Low speed S&C with gear and flaps down.

129 Flights of the Maidens

Flt.	Date	Flt. No.	Pilot	Copilot	Sub Sonic	Mach 1.0–1.9	Mach 2.0–2.5	Mach 2.5–2.9	Mach 3.0	Total Super	Total Flight	Mn	Max Values mph	Feet	Takeoff lbs/ft/knots	Landing	Purpose Notes
104	17 Jan 67	1-58	Cotton	Shepard	0 43	0 23	0 34	0 04	-	1 01	1 44	2.56	1,690	60,200			Sonic boom signatures at Mach 1.8 and 2.5. ILS approaches. Ground effects evaluations.
105	25 Jan 67	1-59	Fulton	Shepard	0 41	0 51	-	-	-	0 51	1 32	1.40	930	35,000			S&C and handling quality evaluations. No. 1 engine airstart tests.
106	31 Jan 67	1-60	Fulton	Cotton	0 43	0 49	-	-	-	0 49	1 32	1.40	925	27,000			S&C and handling quality evaluations. No. 1 engine airstart using JP-5. Last Air Force flight.
107	25 Apr 67	1-61	Cotton	Fulton	1 07	-	-	-	-	-	1 07	0.43	310	17,000			Functional test after maintenance. Entrance door came open in flight. Gear down flight. Lakebed.
108	12 May 67	1-62	Fulton	Cotton	2 17	-	-	-	-	-	2 17	0.44	315	16,500			S&C, handling qualities. Airspeed calibration with landing gear down. Landing gear failed to retract 2nd time.
109	2 Jun 67	1-63	Cotton	Shepard	1 41	0 42	-	-	-	0 42	2 23	1.43	945	43,000			S&C, handling qualities. Airspeed calibration.
110	22 Jun 67	1-64	Fulton	Mallick	0 57	0 57	-	-	-	0 57	1 54	1.83	1,205	54,000			S&C, bypass airflow calibration. Airspeed calibration. Pilot checkout.
111	10 Aug 67	1-65	Cotton	Sturmthal	2 29	-	-	-	-	-	2 29	0.92	660	15,500			S&C, handling qualities, airspeed calibration. Pilot checkout. Instrument pack cool failed. Frayed tires. Lakebed.
112	24 Aug 67	1-66	Fulton	Mallick	0 33	0 56	0 23	-	-	1 19	1 52	2.24	1,480	57,700			S&C, handling qualities, airspeed calibration. Inlet unstart tests. Frayed tires. Lakebed.
113	8 Sep 67	1-67	Cotton	Sturmthal	0 40	0 24	0 51	-	-	1 15	1 55	2.30	1,515	61,000			S&C, handling qualities. Inlet unstart tests. P1 hydraulic failure. Lakebed.
114	11 Oct 67	1-68	Fulton	Mallick	0 28	0 24	0 47	-	-	1 11	1 39	2.43	1,605	58,000			S&C, nose ramp tests. Inlet unstart tests.
115	2 Nov 67	1-69	Cotton	Sturmthal	0 42	0 27	0 10	0 37	-	1 14	1 56	2.55	1,680	64,000			S&C, nose ramp tests. Inlet unstart tests. TB-58 emergency. Concrete runway closed. Lakebed.
116	12 Jan 68	1-70	Fulton	Mallick	0 53	0 19	0 13	0 29	-	1 01	1 54	2.55	1,685	67,000			S&C, performance, handling qualities. Fuselage bending evaluation. Touch & go landing.
117	13 Feb 68	1-71	Mallick	Cotton	2 27	- 16	-	-	-	0 16	2 43	1.18	780	41,000			S&C, handling qualities, airspeed calibration. Fuselage bending evaluation. Engine airstart. No. 1 engine overtemp on A/B light.
118	28 Feb 68	1-72	Fulton	Sturmthal	1 51	-	-	-	-	-	1 51	0.41	295	18,500			S&C, landing approaches, longitudinal speed. Touch & go landing. Landing gear failed to retract.
119	21 Mar 68	1-73	Cotton	Fulton	2 32	-	-	-	-	-	2 32	0.29	310	15,500			Ground effects maneuvers, performance. Handling qualities. Gear down flight.
120	11 Jun 68	1-74	Mallick	Fulton	1 11	-	-	-	-	-	1 11	0.30	319	9,500			Functional test. Exciter vane aero test. U1 hydraulic malfunction. Gear down flight. Lakebed.
121	28 Jun 68	1-75	Sturmthal	Cotton	2 21	0 18	-	-	-	0 18	2 39	1.23	810	39,400			Exciter vane tests, aeroelasticity evaluation. S&C evaluations, canard loads. Skin friction.
122	19 Jul 68	1-76	Mallick	Fulton	1 07	0 48	-	-	-	0 48	1 55	1.62	1,070	42,000			Exciter vane tests, canard loads. Performance evaluations. Touch & go landing.

129 Flights of the Maidens

Flt.	Date	Flt. No.	Pilot	Copilot	Sub Sonic	Mach 1.0–1.9	Mach 2.0–2.5	Mach 2.5–2.9	Mach 3.0	Total Super	Total Flight	Max Mn	Max mph	Max Feet	Takeoff Landing lbs/ft/knots	Purpose Notes
123	16 Aug 68	1-77	Fulton	Sturmthal	1 00	0 21	0 34	– –	– –	0 55	1 55	2.47	1,630	63,000		ILAF and AICS tests. Inlet unstart tests. No. 6 engine failed. AICS cooling malfunction.
124	10 Sep 68	1-78	Mallick	Fulton	0 44	0 29	0 35	– –	– –	1 04	1 48	2.50	1,650	62,800		ILAF, exciter vane, and inlet tests. S&C evaluations. Runway noise survey.
125	18 Oct 68	1-79	Sturmthal	Fulton	1 02	0 41	0 13	– –	– –	0 54	1 56	2.18	1,440	52,000		ILAF and ILAF/exciter vane tests. Performance evaluations. Skin friction.
126	1 Nov 68	1-80	Sturmthal	Fulton	1 20	0 48	– –	– –	– –	0 48	2 08	1.62	1,070	41,000		ILAF/exciter vane tests. S&C evaluations. AICS cooling malfunction.
127	3 Dec 68	1-81	Fulton	Mallick	1 02	0 56	– –	– –	– –	0 56	1 58	1.64	1,080	39,400		ILAF/exciter vane tests. S&C evaluations. Performance tests.
128	17 Dec 68	1-82	Fulton	Sturmthal	0 33	0 31	0 27	0 14	– –	1 12	1 45	2.53	1,670	63,500		ILAF/exciter vane tests. Skin friction. Ozone measurements.
129	4 Feb 69	1-83	Fulton	Sturmthal	3 17	– –	– –	– –	– –	– –	3 17	0.92	625	29,000		ILAF/exciter vane tests. Ferry flight to Wright-Patterson AFB. Last flight of program.

Total Flight Time for both air vehicles: 145 28   55 50   28 41   20 51   1 48   107 10   252 38

Air Vehicle No. 1 logged 160 hours and 16 minutes during 83 flights
Air Vehicle No. 2 logged 92 hours and 22 minutes during 46 flights

It appears that NASA did not retain records of the takeoff and landing data used here.

AICS = air inlet control system
ILAF = Identically Located Acceleration and Force experiment
ILS = instrument landing system
S&C = stability and control

Flight Hours by Pilot

Name	Affiliation	Number of Flights Pilot / Copilot	Subsonic H:M	Mach 1.0–1.9	Mach 2.0–2.4	Mach 2.5–2.9	Mach 3.0	Total Flights
Colonel Joseph E. Cotton	United States Air Force	19 / 43	24 37 / 43 32	7 35 / 17 40	3 37 / 8 50	1 44 / 10 23	– – / 1 32	119 30
Major Carl S. Cross	United States Air Force	0 / 1	1 59	0 14	– –	– –	– –	2 13
Fitzhugh L. "Fitz" Fulton, Jr.	(total of USAF and NASA)	31 / 32 40	35 48 / 46 11	15 30 / 34 6	7 28 / 50 3	3 05 / 08	0 16 / –	124 25
Lt. Colonel Fulton	United States Air Force	16 / 22 28	18 22 / 41 7	7 59 / 14 4	4 18 / 59	2 01 / 2 59	0 16 / –	76 49
Mr. Fulton	NASA Flight Research Center	15 / 10	17 26 / 12 05	7 31 / 4 20	3 10 / 1 51	1 04 / 0 09	– – / –	47 36
Mr. Donald L. Mallick	NASA Flight Research Center	4 / 5	5 29 / 3 53	1 33 / 3 32	0 35 / 1 23	– – / 0 29	– – / –	16 54
Mr. Van H. Shepard	North American Aviation	23 / 23	30 19 / 25 24	12 00 / 10 25	5 01 / 6 59	2 46 / 2 47	0 09 / –	95 50
Lt. Colonel Emil "Ted" Sturmthal	United States Air Force	3 / 7	4 43 / 10 32	1 47 / 1 43	0 13 / 2 02	– – / 0 51	– – / –	21 51
Mr. Alvin S. White	North American Aviation	49 / 18	44 32 / 18 22	17 25 / 10 42	11 47 / 2 37	13 16 / 3 13	1 23 / 0 16	123 33
Mr. Joseph A. Walker	NASA Flight Research Center	0 / 0	– –	– –	– –	– –	– –	– –

APPENDIX B
THE VALKYRIE PILOTS

Colonel Joseph E. Cotton
(AFFTC History Office Collection)

Major Carl S. Cross
(AFFTC History Office Collection)

Fitzhugh L. "Fitz" Fulton, Jr.
(AFFTC History Office Collection)

Mr. Donald L. Mallick
(Dryden Flight Research Center)

Mr. Van H. Shepard
(Boeing Historical Archives)

Lt. Colonel Emil "Ted" Sturmthal
(Terry Panopalis Collection)

Mr. Joseph A. Walker
(Dryden Flight Research Center)

Mr. Alvin S. White
(AFFTC History Office Collection)

APPENDIX C
A PILOT'S PERSPECTIVE
Al White

Air Vehicle (A/V) No. 1 was delivered to the North American Aviation Flight Test Department on 10 May 1964. For the next three months, certain manufacturing items were completed, systems received operational evaluations, and Phase I proof load tests were conducted. North American and Air Force inspections were completed on 7 August 1964. The first three taxi tests were conducted on 9, 16, and 24 August, and were considered unsatisfactory due to hydraulic line failures. Repairs were undertaken overnight, and a successful taxi test (the fourth) was performed on 25 August. Two additional taxi tests (5 and 6) were conducted on 14 September, and first flight occurred on 21 September 1964.

The XB-70A represented a significant departure in both design and performance from other aircraft of its era. One of the frequent questions is "how did it fly?" It seems easier to let one of the pilots that flew it answer that question. It must be remembered that the two air vehicles that were built were not representative of any operational aircraft – many systems were either not installed, not thoroughly tested, or were placeholders for advanced systems that were cancelled when the aircraft were relegated to test vehicles.

The remainder of this chapter is excerpted from North American report NA-66-1138, "XB-70A Flight Test Summary Report, Contract AF33(657)-12395", prepared in late 1966 by Chief Test Pilot Al White, but never published. A few typographic errors, misspellings, and the like have been corrected, and the meaningless (for this use) official paragraph numbers have been deleted, but otherwise it is taken directly from the report.

This section summarizes pilot opinion of flying the XB-70A. All comments herein were extracted directly from XB-70A PILOTS SUMMARY REPORT written by Mr. A. S. White, Chief Test Pilot. Detailed PILOT FLIGHT REPORTS may be found in the FLIGHT TEST MONTHLY PROGRESS REPORTS, NA-66-360-1 through NA-66-360-23.

Summary: The XB-70 has proven itself to be a very remarkable airplane. It has accomplished every milestone that was set down for it. No aerodynamic changes were required in order to achieve the objectives but in spite of its tremendous performance, the XB-70 is an unfinished airplane. It was operated in a completely new speed and altitude range, but with off-the-shelf navigation equipment and flight instrumentation that were obsolete for this type of flight operation. This pilot believes that with normal development, including some aerodynamic refinement, some system changes, and better instrument navigational equipment, this would be a truly outstanding airplane.

General: In reading this pilot's summary report, consideration should be given to the fact that the combination of this airplane's size, weight, and speed ranges compares to no other airplane in existence; and that the program was primarily a research program with ground rules that allowed only those changes which were necessary to safely accomplish the test objectives. In the normal sequence of development to an operational airplane, many of the opinions and recommendations expressed herein would have been made after the initial airworthiness flights. They are presented now, for the record, and for consideration if improvements can be made for follow-on programs.

In general terms the XB-70A was an interesting airplane to fly. It had some peculiarities due to size, weight, and configuration that were different from most other airplanes. The movable tips introduced some new characteristics in the airplane that had not been experienced before, such as the wide variation in directional stability, roll power, and dihedral effect.

The airplane had a tremendous performance capability and was a thrill to fly from that standpoint, but this capability combined with the fact that the airplane was climbed and cruised very near the boundary of the allowable flight envelope quicker and easier than any other airplane this pilot has flown. The duct pressure limits and the low allowable "g" aggravated the recovery. All this adds to the pressure on the pilot by requiring greater concentration on his part. This was acceptable in a research program of this nature, but would certainly not be acceptable in an operational vehicle. The potential for a great airplane is here but some refinements are required. More specifically, the pilot's opinions and recommendations are as follows:

Ground Handling Qualities: Taxiing the airplane was not a difficult operation. Turns from one narrow taxiway to another narrow taxiway were made with acceptable accuracy. However, parking the airplane in a precise location was difficult because of the restricted visibility, configuration of the airplane, and lack of repeatability of the nosewheel steering system, i.e., the nosewheel steering rate varied with the load on the nose gear so that full rudder pedal application did not consistently give the same turning rate. Ground observers were required for parking, but their inputs were sometimes valueless due to the steering system's inability to follow their directions. *Cooper Rating of 3.5*

Originally the braking system was unsatisfactory at very low speeds, but with development, the system became marginally satisfactory. The airplane could be stopped without brake chatter as long as the pilot anticipated far enough in advance to be able to apply very light braking to make the stop. If an abrupt stop was required at low speeds, heavy brake chatter occurred. *Cooper Rating 4.5*

Low Speed In-Flight Handling Qualities: The pitch control in low speed flight regime was very good. Some lack in airplane response could be detected during abrupt pitch maneuvers; however, the response was satisfactory in all of the normal maneuvers used in flying the airplane. The long period of the short-period oscillation was different from most other airplanes, but did not cause difficulty in controlling the airplane. The damping in pitch was good in the subsonic flight regime. *Cooper Rating of 2.5*

The main difficulty in flying the XB-70 was caused by a combination of characteristics in the lateral-directional sense. These characteristics were: First, that the period of the short-period oscillation was very long as compared to most other airplanes, secondly, the side force per degree of sideslip was low in this airplane. This combination made it difficult for the pilot to sense inadvertent sideslips. In addition to those characteristics, the airplane had a marked positive dihedral effect (particularly A/V-2) and it had excessive adverse yaw due to ailerons. Considering these four characteristics together, if an inadvertent sideslip occurred without the pilot's knowledge (busy with other systems' operation), the airplane rolled due to the dihedral effect. Instinctive reaction of the pilot was to counteract the roll with aileron; however, the aileron input increased the sideslip because of the high adverse yaw due to aileron. This increased sideslip, caused more roll away from the aileron input, and aggravated the situation. The solution was that the pilot had to fly the sideslip or yaw indicator religiously throughout the flight regime. This general characteristic of the XB-70 was most predominant with the wingtips up. *Cooper Rating of 4.5*

Placing the wingtips in the one-half position reduced the tendency for the situation explained in the previous paragraph, because lowering the wingtips reduced the roll power by approximately 50%, therefore reducing yaw due to aileron. In addition, the tips down configuration reduced the positive dihedral effect. *Cooper Rating of 4.0*

The longitudinal trim system was very good. *Cooper Rating of 2.0*

The lateral trim system was also very good, except that the primary lateral trim control was difficult to operate with a high degree of accuracy when the pilot was wearing heavy gloves. *Cooper Rating of 3.0*

The directional trim system was very good after the gear had been retracted. It was too sensitive with the gear down, which caused the pilot to over control when attempting to trim out directionally. Occasionally some difficulty was encountered when engaging the nosewheel steering system due to the inability of finding the neutral directional trim position.

For instance, the pilot would trim out directionally prior to putting the gear down; however, the trim system would not be exactly centered at this time. When the gear was lowered, this minor out-of-trim condition was amplified by a ratio of four to one. Due to turbulence and low speed flight characteristics, this out-of-trim condition would go undetected until after landing when the rudders were released and the nosewheel steering engaged which resulted in an abrupt transient in the steering system. It was recommended that consideration be given to reducing the directional trim rate and incorporating a rudder position indicator. *Cooper Rating of 3.0*

The compatibility of the roll and pitch force gradients was satisfactory; however, due to the large differences in the moments of inertia, the airplane responded much quicker in roll than in pitch or yaw. This was not considered to be a discrepancy against the airplane, but a characteristic of a very long and narrow configuration. It required some getting used to by the pilots in order not to overcontrol in roll, particularly with the tips up. A change should not be made in the response characteristics, but something should be done to reduce the adverse yaw due to ailerons. This would eliminate the primary objectionable characteristics in the airplane. If the pilots were not concerned about generating yaw with aileron inputs, the fighter-like roll response would not be objectionable. *Control force compatibility Cooper Rating of 3.0*

The trim change while operating the landing gear was negligible. The trim change while operating the wingtips was small and occurred at such a slow rate that it was hardly noticeable to the pilot since he took care of it in the normal trimming of the airplane. The trim change due to operation of the flaps was large, but easily manageable with the trim system. Although the trim system did take care of the trim change, when the flaps were lowered the control column moved very near the forward end of its travel leaving very little usable down elevon for maneuvering, go-around, or flying in turbulent air. This could be extremely hazardous in the instance where the CG was farther aft than normal.

It was recommended that a design change be made whereby more down elevon control would be available with flaps down.

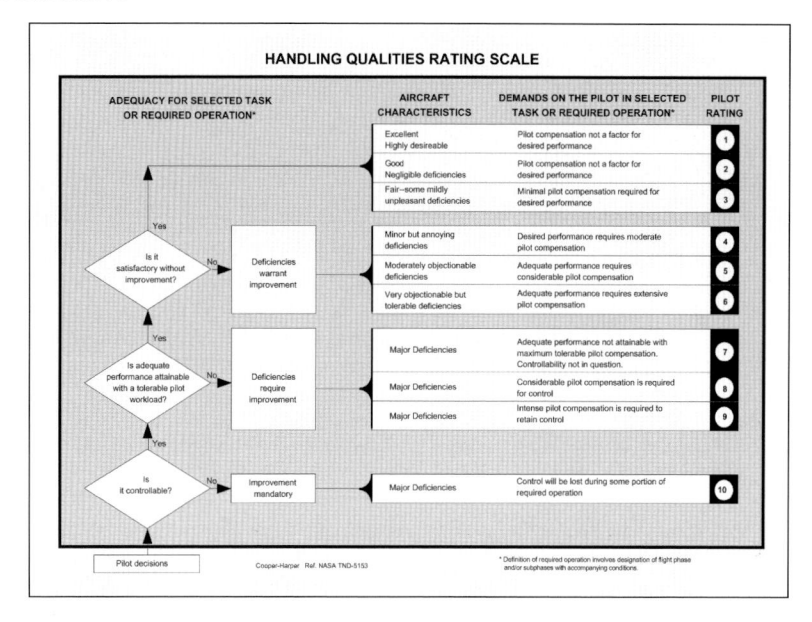

The Cooper-Harper scale is a standard method of measuring the pilot workload of an aircraft. A low score is good; a high score is bad. For the most part Al White rated the aircraft towards the low end of the scale. Given that it was a prototype vehicle, this is a tribute to its basic design. If the aircraft would have entered production, it would undoubtedly have been improved. (NASA)

The airplane had moderate buffet at low speeds with the gear and flaps down. There was a minor change in the buffet level as the gear and flaps were raised. Some buffet persisted and a high aerodynamic noise level existed until the airplane accelerated to 0.87 Mn or above, at which time the buffet completely disappeared and the noise was reduced to at least half of the low-speed level.

High Speed In-Flight Handling Qualities: Pitch control during the transonic acceleration and low supersonic speed ranges was very good. Above Mach 2.0 it became evident that there was some deterioration in the effectiveness of the pitch control. At speeds above 2.5 Mn, the force level required to maneuver the airplane was excessive due to this deterioration and due to the action of the "g" bellows. *Cooper Rating of 3.5*

The directional control was adequate to take care of three engines out on one side, but was much less effective in producing yaw than were the ailerons. Considering the capability of the rudders alone, they were considered adequate. Cooper Rate of 3.0. However, the powerful capability of the ailerons in producing yaw was considered the most objectionable characteristic in the airplane. *Cooper Rating of 4.5*

The roll response of the airplane in the supersonic flight regime was good. The roll response did not seem to deteriorate at the same rate as pitch response, and therefore there was less compatibility in the response of the airplane between Mach 2.0 and 2.7 than in other areas. As the airplane approached Mach 3, the roll response deteriorated and the yaw due to aileron input was reduced; therefore the handling qualities of the airplane in roll were better at Mach 3 than at any other supersonic speed. *Cooper Rating for the roll control system was 3.5*

Although there were minor differences in the flight characteristics between Mach 1.4 and Mach 3 with all augmentation off, the general characteristics were the same. The short-period oscillations in pitch and yaw were 4 to 6 seconds in length and the damping in pitch and yaw was relatively poor. The airplane could be flown at all speeds with the augmentation off, except that extreme care had to be used in the use of ailerons because of the strong tendency to excite lateral-directions oscillations with the ailerons. This was due to a high roll rate in the unaugmented case and because of the excessive level of yaw due to ailerons. When the pilots left the ailerons alone, the yawing oscillations would damp. *Unaugmented supersonic flight Cooper Rating of 5.0*

In-Flight Visibility: The visibility with the windshield down was satisfactory. Although some forward visibility was lost after the rotation at takeoff and during the initial part of the climbout, the remainder of the subsonic flight was satisfactory. The visibility for landing was considered good. At no time was the pilot aware of any loss of the runway visibility during approach, flare, and touchdown: *Cooper Rating of 3.0*

Visibility with the windshield in the up position was unsatisfactory. The pilot cannot see the horizon ahead and must make the flight almost entirely with reference to the pitch attitude indicating system and the poor quality of the heading information precise heading, climb schedule, and altitude flying were extremely difficult. In addition images of light-colored ground such as snow and sandy desert areas reflected badly in the windshield during turns, at times causing vertigo. *Cooper Rating of 5.0*

In-Flight Unstarts: The inadvertent inlet unstarts encountered in the flight test program varied in intensity from mild to severe. They were breathtaking to say the least. In the case of a severe unstart, it jarred the airplane rather violently and was followed by heavy buffeting, intense aerodynamic noise, and minor trim changes. At Mach 3, the primary trim change was in roll, but usually did not persist since the other inlet would normally unstart within a few seconds. If the inlet system did not effect an immediate restart, the inlet would go into buzz. The buzz cycle was immediately recognizable to the pilot since it was almost purely a lateral oscillation at about the natural frequency of the fuselage. If it was not corrected, it built up in intensity to a very disturbing, if not destructive magnitude. In spite of the severity of the transients caused by inlet unstarts airplane control was considered good.

Landing: The XB-70 was not a difficult airplane to land. Some care had to be used due to the distance between the pilot and the main gear and due to the crew station height above the main gear at touchdown. Because of these dimensions, it was easy to undershoot the runway. After some practice, all pilots were able to make satisfactory landings without external assistance from chase aircraft.

The wing of the XB-70 experienced a strong ground effect in the proximity of the runway which helped considerably in making relatively smooth landings. The secret to a good landing, like in most airplanes, was a good stabilized approach using a rather low rate of descent (2 to 3 degrees glide scope).

Crosswind landings in the XB-70 were not as difficult as was predicted. The relatively shallow bank angle per degree of sideslip made the wing-down technique rather easy to use with the XB-70.

Landing in turbulent air required additional pilot concentration, primarily due to the previously mentioned relationship between inadvertent sideslip, dihedral effect, and yaw due to ailerons. The pilot was required to watch the yaw indicator very closely in making an approach so as not to get into this inadvertent sideslip condition close to the ground. *Landing Cooper Rating was 3.5*

Escape Capsule: The pressure seals in the capsule doors were torn loose many times when the pilots entered the capsules. Entering the capsule, particularly when wearing the pressure suit, was very difficult due to the lack of space. The seals should be guarded so that they are not damaged in this way.

The original installation of the capsule handgrip seat pins included a lanyard and a take-up reel which were installed behind the pilot's shoulder. A large percentage of the time the take-up reel did not operate; and when it did operate, the pin was extremely hard to reach to reinstall after flight. A temporary fix was made by cutting the lanyard, thereby eliminating the take-up reel. This worked satisfactorily, except for the minor inconvenience of not having a place to stow the pin.

The emergency parachute and riser cutter handles and the hinge split handle were difficult to see when encapsulated. When the pilot raised his head to see the handles with his helmet on, he had to raise his helmet with his hand in order to see past the bow of the helmet. This was particularly true when the pilot was wearing a pressure suit and was aggravated under the dynamic conditions encountered after ejection.

The pressurization and capsule oxygen gages were particularly hard to see once in the capsule. The safety belt was almost impossible to adjust after it had been fastened. The seal deflate button was very difficult to actuate due to its location when the pilot was wearing a pressure suit.

The hot mike interphone capability during encapsulation was operable only after the capsule doors were closed. It appears wise, after the experience of the recent ejection, that the hot mike be actuated in another way in addition to the door closure. It should be connected to the handgrips so that when encapsulation is made, the hot mike interphone is available even if the doors are not closed. [This refers to the fact that the microphone was not hot while Carl Cross was trying to eject, so no record of what happened was available to the accident investigation board.]

The manual impact attenuator inflation device was extremely difficult to get to while encapsulated. It was recommended that some thought be given to relocating this device between the pilot's knees for easier access.

The Secondary Nozzle Rheostat: This rheostat is in a poor location considering the number of times it was used during flight. It would be desirable to move it forward in the area near the oxygen and visor heater switches.

Hydraulic Pump Status Indicators: The hydraulic pump status indicators became almost useless in view of the number of times the pump status indicators showed yellow with the pumps operating properly.

Nosewheel Steering System: The nosewheel steering engage button ideally should be mounted on the control wheel. Originally this was not done because of lack of space on the wheel. The pilots believed that the augmentation disengage switch should have the priority location on the wheel. The experience gained in the flight test program indicates that it would be satisfactory to move the augmentation disengage switch to the same area as the augmentation engage button on the console and put the nosewheel steering engage switch on the control wheel.

TACAN: The TACAN instrumentation on the XB-70 was only marginally satisfactory. Early in the program the pilots were requested to list the minimum equipment with which they could accomplish the mission, and one TACAN was suggested for navigation. Experience has now shown that without radar tracking and the occasional assistance of the FAA centers, some of the missions would have been extremely difficult to complete satisfactory due to the quality of this equipment and installation.

Attitude and Heading Information: The attitude and heading information were marginally satisfactory. This added to the pilots' difficulty in navigating the airplane. In view of the above two conditions, it was highly desirable to have a more reliable navigation system. An inertial platform was highly recommended.

AICS Controls: The AICS controls were satisfactory for the development stages, although the controls in A/V-1 were minimally satisfactory. It was highly recommended that this system be reviewed for future use.

Flaps: The flap system was marginally satisfactory. Because of a design problem, the flaps were to be raised for the taxi and lowered just prior to takeoff in order to ensure that they would retract in flight. Occasionally they would not extend for landing, and occasionally they would not retract after landing. The result was that the pilots lost confidence in the flap system. It was recommended that a design change be made to eliminate the necessity of the intricate procedure that was required to operate the flap system.

Map Case: The map case was almost inaccessible to the pilots. In most cases the pilot had to get out of his seat to get the equipment from the map case. Although the map case was of little use to the pilots, it was the only place in the cockpit that extra material could be stored. Check lists and pilots data cards had to be strapped to the pilot's legs to be of any use. Some consideration should be given to a more convenient stowage space for let-down charts, handbook, and additional maps, particularly if this airplane is to be used for cross-country work in the future.

Wingtip-Selector Switch: If the flaps are lowered for landing prior to raising the wingtips to the up position, it would be possible to lose control of the airplane. It was recommended that a safety device be installed to prevent lowering the flaps when the tips were not in the up position.

APPENDIX D
LESSONS FOR A SUPERSONIC TRANSPORT
FITZ FULTON

Fitz Fulton presented the following paper at the 21st annual International Air Safety Seminar in Anaheim, California, on 7-11 October 1968. The paper was written prior to the completion of the flight program, so some of the numbers do not reflect the final total. The figures references in the text have not been reproduced here, but the entire paper is available in PDF form at the Dryden web site (http://www.dfrc.nasa.gov).

LESSONS FROM THE XB-70 AS APPLIED TO THE SUPERSONIC TRANSPORT

By Fitzhugh L. Fulton, Jr.
NASA Flight Research Center
Edwards, Calif.

INTRODUCTION

The lessons from the XB-70A program that have been selected for discussion are only a few of the things that have been learned during the program. These things will certainly apply to the supersonic transport (SST). In some cases they will apply to any large airplane, and in a few cases they will apply to almost any airplane. The XB-70 is a very valuable research airplane; there is no other airplane in the world of similar size that can fly in the same speed environment. Many of its design features were pushing the state of the art; therefore, both positive and negative results were obtained, providing validation or correlation of design prediction techniques. It also provided information on operational factors applicable to a large supersonic aircraft. The program has been expensive in money, time, and personal sacrifice, but if the knowledge gained from the XB-70A test program makes it possible to avoid even one catastrophic SST accident, the program will more than pay for itself.

DESCRIPTION OF AIRPLANE AND TEST PROGRAM

The XB-70A is a large, delta-wing, supersonic airplane with dual vertical tail surfaces, a movable canard surface with trailing-edge flaps, and a movable nose ramp to provide acceptable visibility at low speed and reduced drag at high speed. The airplane has retractable landing gear and wing tips that are folded downward to improve directional stability at transonic and supersonic speeds. It is 189 feet long with a wing span of 105 feet. The maximum taxi weight is 542,000 pounds, and the takeoff gross weight for most flights is approximately 532,000 pounds. The airplane is crewed by two pilots on experimental or research flights, which have been flown at speeds up to Mach 3.0 and altitudes above 70,000 feet.

The flight program began on September 21, 1964, under U. S. Air Force direction and funding. Since March 29, 1967 a joint NASA-USAF program has been directed and primarily funded by NASA. Flight support has been provided by the contractors, North American Rockwell and General Electric, since the beginning of the program.

The breakdown of flights and flight hours is shown in the following table:

	Airplane 1	Airplane 2	Both
Flights	78	46	124
Flight hours	149:13	92:22	241:35
Supersonic flight hours	55:41	47:17	102:58
Flight hours at Mach 2.0 or above	23:08	27:18	50:2 6
Flight hours at Mach 2.5 or above	5:55	16:34	22:29
Flight hours at Mach 3.0 or above	:02	1:46	1:48

The test programs covered many areas of interest. Some of the most significant are: Stability and control, airplane handling characteristics on the ground and in flight, performance of airplane, engines, inlet, and systems, structural loads on airplane and landing gear, noise and sonic boom, ground effects during takeoff and landing, response to turbulence, modal control and gust alleviation, and operational characteristics.

DISCUSSION

Realism in Design and Operation

One of the most significant lessons from the XB-70 should be the need for conservative realism in designing and operating the SST. The XB-70 was originally conceived as having intercontinental range. The operational experience to date in conjunction with onboard recorded data indicates that the design range may have been missed by more than 25 percent; the reasons are many. Using the then best available methods of interpreting wind-tunnel data, the contractor along with some Air Force and NASA people overestimated the lift-to-drag ratio, underestimated the transonic drag, and overestimated the inlet performance that could be obtained under practical operational conditions. Also, there were necessary but unplanned increases in airplane empty weight. The result was a large reduction in performance.

Flight Characteristics Versus Wind-Tunnel Predictions

Although agreement between flight and predicted airplane stability and control characteristics was realized in most instances, some of the stability characteristics and handling qualities were unlike the wind-tunnel predictions. For example, the airplane exhibits excessive adverse yaw due to aileron input at all flight conditions, but this characteristic was not predicted for a large portion of the flight regime. Large sideslip angles can be inadvertently generated at some speeds, and the pilot may not be aware of them because under some conditions the transverse accelerations in the cockpit are low, making the pilot relatively insensitive to directional motions. Also, the airplane riding qualities are less than desirable under turbulent-air conditions. Much additional wind-tunnel testing has been done by NASA during the XB-70 test program in an attempt to correlate wind-tunnel data with the flight-test results. Some differences between the model and the airplane are the result of aeroelasticity. Other differences are due to scale effect. Correction factors validated during the test program have brought these data into closer agreement. Hopefully, as a result of these studies, there is now a better basis upon which to make predictions for the SST. Since it appears that the profit margin for the SST will not be high enough to afford large errors in predictions, even with improved methods of prediction it seems that some allowances must be made for minor miscalculations and for the unknown factors that always influence a new airplane.

Enroute Atmospheric Predictions

Another thing that is not new but has certainly been well illustrated is the need for accurate atmospheric predictions along the flight route and especially in the acceleration area. On the most recent XB-70 flight the temperature at the acceleration altitude was estimated to be 8°C to 10°C warmer than standard-day conditions. Inflight data and the performance obtained indicated that the temperature predictions were very close and the fuel usage was considerably higher than had been originally planned, using charts for standard-day conditions. Figure 2 shows the standard-day fuel-usage predictions versus the actual conditions for a segment of the flight. As can be seen, the fuel remaining was 14,000 pounds low at the northwest turning point and the speed was only Mach 2.40 instead of the predicted Mach 2.52. Temperatures warmer than those for a standard day are bad enough when known and accounted for as on this flight, but if they occur without being predicted, there is a good likelihood that fuel reserves will be dangerously low at the destination. In addition, turbulence has been encountered even at altitudes above 60,000 feet, and turbulence is a significant factor in reducing supersonic performance. The predictions of turbulence encounters have not been accurate on many flights.

Variable-Position Nose Ramp

The XB-70A nose ramp (fig. 3) can be operated at indicated airspeeds of up to 560 knots. This has been found to be extremely valuable. It provides the pilot an opportunity to have forward visibility and reduces the possibility of collision. Therefore lessening anxiety during any subsonic operation and even during supersonic speeds. The airplane has been flown to speeds in excess of Mach 2.50 on numerous flights with the windshield ramp down (best visibility). There is a small performance penalty caused by the lower climb-speed schedule in this configuration, 560 KIAS versus the normal 575 KIAS, and by the increase in windshield drag. The improved view of the natural horizon with the nose ramp down is a big aid in flying the airplane and gives the pilot more time to devote to cockpit duties other than instrument flying. The capability of rapidly operating the XB-70A nose ramp up or down over most of the flight envelope is very desirable. It enables an occasional "quick look" when desired. Certainly some reduction in visibility is acceptable to obtain less drag and improved performance at high speed, but those who feel that forward visibility is completely unnecessary during acceleration and cruise are not in agreement with the XB-70 pilots.

Cockpit Instruments

The XB-70 has vertical-tape flight instruments and round-dial engine instruments. It would be nice to say that the XB-70 pilots have concluded that vertical-tape flight instruments are better than round-dial flight instruments; however, that is not the case. The pilots seem to be about evenly split in their preferences between tapes and round dials. I have flown tapes in simulators, an experimental F-102, C-141s, and the XB-70 and have flown round dials in B-52s, B-58s, F-l04s, C-130s, and many other types of airplanes. A satisfactory job can be done with either type, but I prefer round dials, since trends are more easily recognized and possibly because of past experience and training. A feature of the XB-70 and some other airplanes is the digital readout of airspeed and altitude. This is extremely helpful in precise instrument flying. A digital readout of Mach number should also be provided. One of the very desirable engine instruments is an exhaust gas temperature (EGT) gage with a warning light on the face to call attention to an over-temperature condition. Early in the test program the EGT gages installed did not have this warning-light feature, and several engines had to be removed for inspection when pilots failed to immediately see an over-temperature condition. Since the installation of gages with warning lights, there have been numerous occasions of over-temperature alerts to the pilots. The gages have paid for themselves many times over. A yaw or sideslip instrument will probably be required as will a total temperature gage. If the design cruise speed causes the total temperature to always be near the limiting temperature, a warning light or bell will have to be provided. Prolonged exceeding of the limiting temperature is probably as critical as exceeding the limiting speed.

There have been several publicized statements to the effect that "it is very difficult to hold a constant altitude at high speeds in the XB-70." The airplane does not have an autopilot, and there is no question about it being more difficult to maintain altitude with the XB-70 than with a subsonic jet transport, because small angular changes in pitch attitude result in large rates of altitude change. At Mach 3.0 and 70,000 feet altitude, an attitude change of 1° causes the rate of climb to change approximately 3000 feet per minute. The difficulty in holding altitude is probably due in part to the longitudinal control system inasmuch as the trace of elevator force during a sonic-boom run (fig. 4) shows that a high frequency of small inputs was required by the pilot. The same figure also shows that altitude was being held relatively constant at Mach 2.51. The improved altitude holding capability was attributed primarily to installation of an attitude director indicator with a pitch scale of doubled sensitivity. The original instrument was difficult to read within 1/4°; whereas, a more sensitive instrument (fig. 5) provided greater resolution and ease of maintaining altitude. A cockpit modification (fig. 6) has been made recently to allow in-flight selection of attitude indicator sensitivities ranging from 2:l (2° on the instrument versus 1° outside) up to 5:l. Only a few flights have been flown with the modified instrument, but preliminary results indicate that a selection in the sensitivity range between 3:l and 4:l will probably be more satisfactory for high-speed flying. The attitude director indicator (fig. 5) also has a 10:l vertical pitch scale to the left of the attitude ball, but that appears to be oversensitive.

Overspeed Operation

The problem of overspeeds deserves serious consideration. To obtain optimum performance, most supersonic airplanes will need to operate near maximum placard speeds during the climb, cruise, and descent. The XB-70 is normally accelerated to and then climbed at 560 KIAS (nose ramp down) or 575 KIAS (nose ramp up). The pilot is faced with the task of keeping the speed near maximum placard to improve performance, but not above placard because of design considerations. The planned climb schedule has been inadvertently exceeded from 5 to 10 knots indicated airspeed on a number of XB-70 flights. Although deviations are small, it is virtually impossible to hold an exact climb schedule. The most frequent excursions occur at the completion of the constant-altitude transonic acceleration and during the initial transition to a constant indicated airspeed climb schedule. Most pilots begin a gradual pullup to phase into the climb when 15 to 20 KIAS below the desired climb speed, but overspeeds still sometimes occur. No warning device is installed on the XB-70, but for an SST it seems that the warning bell or light should be set at least 10 to 15 KIAS and Mach 0.05 below the placard limit speeds or the maximum speed will be exceeded and cause the warning to be triggered on numerous flights.

Inlet Operation

The XB-70 uses a system of movable inlet panels and airflow bypass doors to control the air being supplied to the engines. These inlet panels and bypass doors provide a means of bringing the normal shock wave inside the inlet at speeds above Mach 2.0 to improve inlet efficiency. With the normal shock inside the inlet, it is considered to be "started;" when the normal shock moved outside the inlet, it is considered to be "unstarted." The normal shock position is sensitive to speed, angle of attack, sideslip, and engine speed. The method of controlling the shock position with the XB-70 is semiautomatic and the switches, controls, and gages (figs. 7 and 8) require much attention from the copilot. When an inlet "unstart" occurs, the XB-70 experiences airframe buffet which ranges from light at Mach 2.2 to heavy at speeds above Mach 2.7. Sometimes the airframe buffet is accompanied by engine stalls and/or possible inlet buzz. Many "unstarts" have been experienced during the test program. Some were planned and others were unintentional. It usually takes from 5 to 10 seconds for the copilot to "restart" the inlet; therefore, the flight crew endures the buffet for a short time. The paying passenger is not likely to willingly endure that type of buffet more than once. The SST inlet control and inlet "restarting" systems must be reliable, automatic, and very fast in returning an inlet to normal operation after an "unstart."

Flying Qualities

The XB-70 has some undesirable flying qualities, such as the yaw due to aileron, development of excess yaw under certain conditions, and the negative dihedral effect at high speeds, but the airplane has excellent longitudinal and directional restoring characteristics. Turning off the augmentation (dampers) results in a deterioration of flying qualities; however, the system can be safely turned off in any flight regime. All takeoffs and landings on the early flights were made with the augmentation off. Intentional sideslips, releases from sideslips, pitch pulses, and wind-up turn stability maneuvers have been routinely accomplished at speeds as high as Mach 2.90 with all the augmentation off. On several recent flights, after the pitch augmentation was turned off, the airplane was flown "hands off" during phugoid tests for periods of over 5 minutes at Mach 2.50 and approximately 62,000 feet. The pilot controlled minor banking tendencies through the rudder pedals, with left rudder to command right rolls and right rudder to command left rolls because of the negative dihedral effect at that speed. Using reasonable pilot effort, the SST should be capable of flight with all augmentation off throughout its entire speed envelope.

Deceleration and Descent

The importance of proper planning and execution of the deceleration and descent from high-speed cruise should not be underestimated. The slowdown and descent from a Mach 2.70 cruise flight will start 200 nautical miles or more from the destination in order to become subsonic at the proper distance and altitude to allow integration with the subsonic jet traffic. Receipt of the traffic clearance and the initiation of the slowdown and descent cannot be delayed. With a speed of approximately 27 nautical miles per minute, the pilot does not have the opportunity to "standby" while awaiting the clearance. He should have that clearance well before reaching the deceleration point. The flight path must be flown in a manner to minimize sonic booms, which means that the speed will probably be at Mach 1.10 or below by the time an altitude of 35.000 feet is reached. I flew a fairly typical deceleration and descent in the XB-70 during a 59-minute flight from Edwards AFB, California, to Carswell AFB, Texas. The slowdown started from Mach 2.70 at 64,000 feet altitude over Lubbock, Texas, and the airplane arrived over Carswell AFB at 5,000 feet above the ground. The sequence of events for the flight was as follows:

Time to Carswell Minutes	Speed	Altitude	Remarks
:16	2.70 Mach	64,000	Lubbock, Texas – 238 n.mi. To Carswell AFB. Thrust reduced from afterburner to military power
:12	2.00 Mach	50,000	Decelerating
:09	1.50 Mach	50,000	Decelerating and descending
:08	1.40 Mach		Thrust reduced below military power
:05.5	1.00 Mach	30,000	Decelerating and descending. 50 n.mi. from Carswell AFB
:02.5	0.90 Mach	20,000	Descending. 25 n.mi. from Carswell AFB
:00	400 KIAS	5,000	Over Carswell AFB

The XB-70 has certain engine and inlet restrictions that prevent reducing power to idle thrust at high Mach numbers. The SST may not be faced with such restrictions and may be provided with deceleration devices such as air brakes or in-flight thrust reversers. These will improve the slowdown capability, but the slowdown will still remain a maneuver that requires proper planning and execution.

Landing-Gear Reliability

Experience has shown that the SST landing gear should be relatively simple in design and operation. The landing gear on the number 1 XB-70 has failed to retract or has incurred malfunctions that prevented retraction on 7 of the 78 flights. The number 2 XB-70 had a similar record of malfunctions. There have been flights on which the landing gear did not retract completely on the first attempt, but on one or more subsequent attempts it did lock up and allow the flight to continue as planned. There have been slower-than-normal retraction cycles and there have been cases where usage of the emergency landing-gear extension system was required in order to get the landing gear "down and locked." Since the time of the early XB-70 flights, there have been special emergency switches installed to allow bypassing certain protective relays, and a special hydraulic system has been added to provide redundancy to the nose-gear extension system. The XB-70 cannot be landed without probable catastrophic failure if the nose gear fails to extend; therefore, bailout would be required. Obviously, bailout is not the solution to a serious SST landing-gear malfunction. If possible, the retraction system should use simple mechanical linkages and avoid large numbers of sequence valves and micro-switches that can get out of adjustment and prevent retraction. An even more important requirement is to have a reliable landing-gear extension system. The emergency extension system should utilize the "free fall" method, since even dual hydraulic systems can fail and cause landing-gear problems, as when both XB-70 utility systems failed (fig. 9) and a "tiptoe" landing resulted. The emergency system should also have a pneumatic or hydraulic backup capability and be one in which crew members have high confidence.

Hydraulic-System Operation

There have been numerous hydraulic-system leaks or failures during the test program. Initially there were hydraulic pressure gages but no hydraulic quantity gages in the cockpit. There was strong pilot insistence on the quantity gages, and they were installed before the first flight. They have proved invaluable by providing cockpit knowledge of hydraulic leaks or fluid transfer between hydraulic systems. After several leaks were experienced, a 30-gallon hydraulic reservoir, an electric pump, and a hydraulic replenishing system were installed to allow in-flight reservicing of a low hydraulic system. The system has been used several times to prevent depletion of a hydraulic system and the resulting cavitation of the hydraulic pump and contamination of the hydraulic system. It also reduces the need for an emergency landing. The system was paid for on its first usage, since the cost of overhauling the hydraulic pumps in a failed system is approximately equal to the cost of installing the replenishing system. The present hydraulic panel is shown in figure 10. The SST should have hydraulic quantity gages and some type of replenishing system in addition to the normal pressure gages.

Approach and Landing

The XB-70 is not a difficult airplane to land under the ideal circumstances provided at Edwards Air Force Base. It has excellent speed stability on the final approach and has a very strong ground cushion. The speed stability and the rapid engine response provided through the electric throttle system allows airspeed to be held easily within 2 knots of aim speed. It can be and has been landed from a 3° approach path but is more comfortable when flown on a 1.5° to 2.0° slope. The normal light-gross-weight approach speed of approximately 200 knots is much too high for an SST and causes some apprehension when maneuvering from an offset approach to line up with the runway. Judgment of flare and touchdown altitude is more difficult because of the pilot's height above the ground and because of the high approach speed. The lower the approach and landing speed of the SST, the easier will be the landing task. The XB-70 responds adversely to turbulence, and the pilot's workload increases significantly when landing under turbulent conditions.

Concluding Remarks

The North American Rockwell XB-70 is a very valuable research vehicle that has allowed important data to be gathered by NASA and the U. S. Air Force that are particularly applicable to the SST program. Its combination of high speed and large size is unmatched anywhere in the world. The extremely reliable J93 General Electric engines, although never previously flown, have been a strong factor in the success of the program. The items covered in this paper represent only a small part of the knowledge gained from the test program. Many reports have already been published on the program and NASA has other reports being prepared for publication. The Boeing Airplane Company and the Federal Aviation Agency have worked closely with the XB-70 test team throughout the program and have full access to all XB-70 data.

Right: *With more than a passing resemblance to the B-70, Northrop proposed this supersonic transport using an innovative Laminar Flow Control technique on the wings and tail surfaces. Northrop believed that the application of LFC would reduce the weight of the aircraft by approximately 60,000 pounds.* (Northrop via Tony Chong)

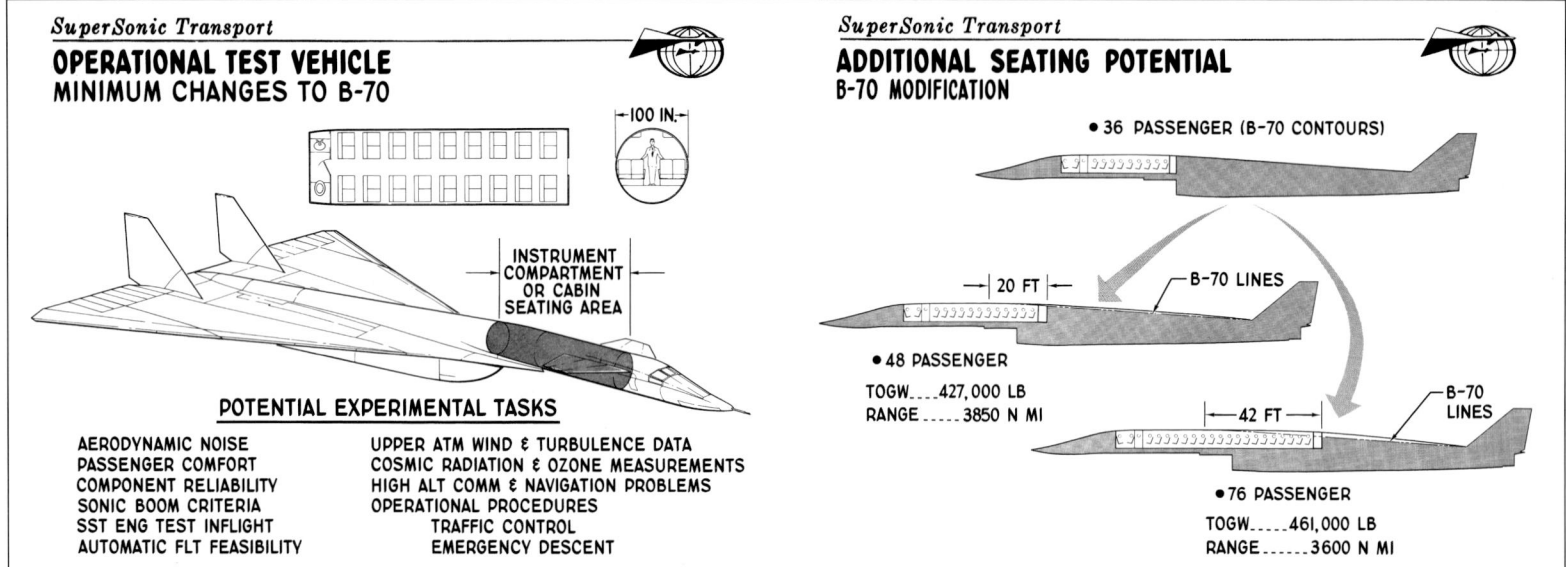

On 7 July 1961 North American released the results of a study into possible development plans for an early American supersonic transport (SST). (Please see Jenkins and Landis, XB-70A Valkyrie, WarbirdTech Volume 34, Specialty Press, for a further description of this proposal). North American proposed modifying an additional B-70 airframe into to a limited passenger configuration by removing the military electronics and fuel from the upper fuselage ("neck") and replacing it with a small passenger compartment. Without changing the mold line of the upper fuselage, a total of 36 passenger could be accommodated in 4-abreast seating. The internal diameter of the fuselage was only 100 inches – four feet narrower than the contemporary Boeing 707. Two other configurations were also proposed that slightly changed the outer mold line, but provided more realistic passenger counts. The first extended the passenger compartment by 240 inches, resulting in seating for 48 passengers. This version had a gross takeoff weight of 427,000 pounds and could fly 3,850 miles while cruising at Mach 3. The other version increased the passenger compartment another 264 inches (for a total stretch of 504 inches) to seat 76 passengers. The gross takeoff weight increased to 461,000 pounds, but range was reduced to only 3,600 miles at Mach 3. Neither modification changed the overall length of the fuselage, but rather resulted in a more pronounced "hump" in the rear part of the neck. The expected effect on stability was thought to be negligible, but given the marginal directional stability of the XB-70 in any case, the modifications would probably have necessitated an increase in vertical stabilizer area. (San Diego Aerospace Museum Collection)

APPENDIX E

INTERESTING FACTS

FROM VARIOUS NORTH AMERICAN AND GENERAL ELECTRIC PRESS RELEASES

Authors' Note: The following were put together by the North American and General Electric public affairs departments, and the authors have no comment as to their relevance or accuracy.

More than 47 linear miles of drawings have been used to build the B-70.

More than 15 acres of drawings have been used to build the B-70.

A pickup truck could fit in each of the giant air intake ducts of the B-70.

There are 70 miles of high temperature wire in the B-70.

Thirty-three thousand individual wire segments had to be cut and numbered for the B-70 electrical system.

There is one mile of stainless steel plumbing in the B-70, with 3,300 separate fittings.

Three average three-bedroom houses could fit under the vast expanse of the B-70 wings.

The air used to cool the B-70 engines is twice as hot as an average home oven.

On a 2,000 mph flight, friction of the 13-mile-high air passing over the skin of the B-70 develops enough heat to keep a 300-room hotel well warmed for 40 hours.

On a normal flight, the B-70 hydraulic fluid becomes as hot as the cooking oil in a deep fryer.

In a single stop, the B-70 brakes must absorb kinetic energy equivalent to the used in stopping 800 medium-sized American automobiles from a speed of 100 miles per hour.

The heat developed in the B-70 brakes during normal landings reaches 1,800 degrees Fahrenheit – enough to melt some grades of steel.

The power developed by the B-70's six J93 engines at cruising speed is more than that of one-thousand 200-horsepower automobiles.

The power requirements of the B-70 engine compressors, if converted to electrical power, would be equivalent to that used by a city the size of Louisville, Kentucky.

The heat available in the engine exhaust for one mission would heat 12 average homes for one year.

The B-70 converts fuel to power 36-percent more efficiently than the most efficient present-day propeller-driven airliner.

The B-70 engine airflow would evacuate all of the air in an average size home in 2.5 seconds.

During a normal cruise condition, the B-70 engines pump sufficient air to supply breathing air for the combined populations of Montana, Nevada, New Mexico, and Wyoming. (Federal Census of 1950)

The environmental control system compartment behind the crew cabin. This view is looking forward toward the cockpit. Production aircraft would have had a great deal more equipment here to cool the military systems and avionics. (Boeing Historical Archives)

Interesting Facts

At cruise the B-70 engines pump enough air to supply 6,230,000 people with air for breathing.

An amount of gasoline equivalent to the amount of fuel carried by the B-70 would enable all the automobiles produced last year (4,000,000) to travel 1/10 mile. Or, 25 automobiles could travel around the Earth.

The maximum fuel consumption of the B-70 is equivalent to that of 14,000 automobiles @ 12 miles per gallon at 100 miles per hour.

The amount of heat absorbed by the fuel during one supersonic design mission is sufficient to heat 100 three-bedroom homes for about 40 hours.

The equivalent horsepower developed by the B-70 engines is equal to 34-percent of that developed by Boulder Dam.

The total impulse developed by the B-70 powerplants is equivalent to that required to send an automobile to the moon and return.

The equivalent horsepower developed by the B-70, if converted to electrical power, would satisfy the normal domestic needs for 2,580,000 Americans, or the total needs for the entire country of Ireland.

The total fuel energy used by the B-70 on the design mission is equivalent to that released by a 1.5-kiloton nuclear bomb.

It would take the equivalent of three and one-half railroad tank cars to fuel the B-70 for a single flight.

The power developed by the B-70 secondary power system exceeds the total engine horsepower of a B-25 bomber.

The B-70 develops enough power to drive an oceanliner.

The hydraulic pumps in the B-70 develop 2,000 horsepower – enough to power a diesel locomotive.

The 33,000 to 1 gear ratio in the B-70 wing fold mechanism transfers enough power to lift a ten-ton truck from each wingtip.

The B-70 wing fold mechanism develops 26,600 pounds force at the tip.

In Mach 3 flight, the B-70 develops more horsepower (370,000) than the new aircraft carrier "America."

The power capacity of the B-70 environmental control system could satisfy the electrical needs for 63 residential houses.

In flight, the B-70 can produce 50 times the propulsive horsepower that can be produced by the current piston engine airliners.

The tensile strength of steels used in the B-70 is such that a rod of this material less than 5/32-inch in diameter could support the weight of an average late model car … or, a bar of this material one-inch-square will support the weight of 75 cars.

Each B-70 engine develops 85 percent of the horsepower of a single Hoover Dam generator.

Converted to electrical energy, the power generated by the B-70 engines would be sufficient to light more than 4 million 100-watt light bulbs.

Cartoon from the North American employee newspaper. The XB-70 was the highest flying airplane of its day, but not quite that high flying! (Jerry McCulley Collection)

The Mobilcom van, which became a familiar sight at all XB-70 flights as it had on the X-15 flights, was equipped with a communications system and carried a flight test engineer and several specialists that monitored the airplane and its surroundings. Note A/V-1 in the background with only two good chutes. (AFFTC History Office Collection)

APPENDIX F

NOTES AND CITATIONS

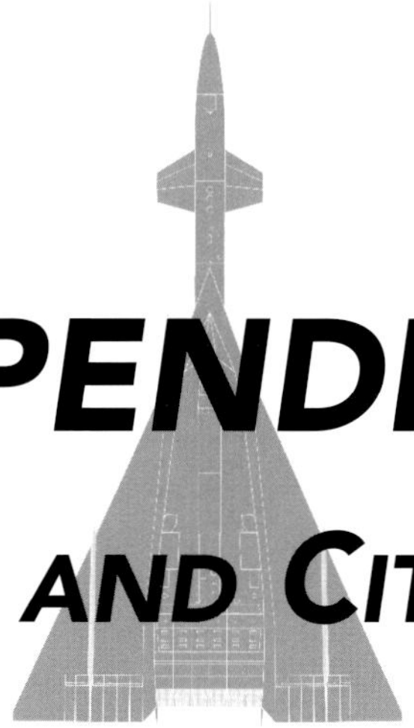

Chapter 1 – An Expensive Diversion

1. *See also*, Carolyn C. James, "The Politics of Extravagance: The Aircraft Nuclear Propulsion Project," *Naval War College Review*, Newport Papers, 2000.
2. Engineering Division, Air Service Technical Command, "Proposed Air Engineering Development Center," 10 December 1945.
3. R. W. Bussard and R. D. DeLauer, *Fundamentals of Nuclear Flight*, (New York: McGraw Hill, 1965), p. 1; J. A. Conner, Jr., "Aerospace Nuclear Power Safety Considerations," *Aerospace Engineering*, May 1960, pp. 26-58; J. S. Butz, Jr., "Navy Aims at Low Power Atom Seaplane," *Aviation Week*, 15 April 1957, pp. 30-32.
4. U.S. Comptroller General, *Report to the Congress of the United States: Review of Manned Aircraft Nuclear Propulsion Program, Atomic Energy Commission and Department of Defense* (Washington: General Accounting Office, February 1963), p. 15.
5. Bussard and DeLauer, *Fundamentals of Nuclear Flight*, p. 1; Conner, "Aerospace Nuclear Power Safety Considerations," pp. 26-58; David M. Carpenter, *NX-2: Convair Nuclear Propulsion Jet*, (Jet Pioneers of America, 2003).
6. President's Air Policy Commission, *Survival in the Air Age: A Report by the President's Air Policy Commission* (Washington: U.S. Government Printing Office, 1 January 1948), p. 80.
7. Susan M. Stacey, *Proving the Principle*, (Washington: U.S. Government Printing Office, 2000), p. 118.
8. Walter G. Whitman, et. al., "Review of the Manned Aircraft Nuclear Propulsion Program," (Washington: U.S. Government Printing Office, 1963). By law, only the AEC could conduct reactor research. The Navy and Air Force, therefore, funded only the remaining systems, such as the airframe and the conventional portions of the engines. This was significant, since it meant that over half the cost of ANP (over half a billion dollars) was to be borne by the AEC.
9. Bussard and DeLauer, *Fundamentals of Nuclear Flight*, p. 1; Carpenter, *NX-2*.
10. Bussard and DeLauer, *Fundamentals of Nuclear Flight*, p. 1; Conner, "Aerospace Nuclear Power Safety Considerations," pp. 26-58.
11. Gunnar Thornton, "Comprehensive Technical Report, General Electric Direct Air-Cycle Aircraft Nuclear Propulsion Program," 28 June 1962.
12. Bussard and DeLauer, *Fundamentals of Nuclear Flight*, p. 1; Conner, "Aerospace Nuclear Power Safety Considerations," pp. 26-58.
13. U.S. Comptroller General, p. 17.
14. The direct-cycle reactor, since it heated air directly, did present fewer technological difficulties, but it had the fundamental weakness that air does not absorb heat as well as liquid metal. In an indirect cycle, the surface needed for heat transfer to liquid metal is many times smaller than that needed to heat air, resulting in a smaller and lighter reactor. Overall engine weight is greater, but a single reactor can power multiple engines. The result for the direct cycle was that a larger amount of air had to go through the reactor, which also had to be larger to create enough energy to produce sufficient engine thrust. The direct cycle also, by necessity, being less compact, would require considerably more shielding than would the more efficient indirect-cycle plant, adding even more weight. Advocates of the indirect cycle thus argued that long-term considerations favored the indirect cycle.
15. http://www.megazone.org/ANP/atomair.shtml, accessed on 20 March 2003.
16. William A. Tesch, "Nuclear Aircraft Presentation to Washington Chapter of Institute of Aeronautical Sciences, April 14, 1959," in Joint Committee on Atomic Energy, *Aircraft Nuclear Propulsion Project: Hearing before the Subcommittee on Research and Development*, 86th Congress, 1st session, 23 July 1959, pp. 154-158.
17. Thornton, "Comprehensive Technical Report."
18. The concept was actually developed by the Sparland Corporation, which was subsequently taken over by Pratt & Whitney.
19. Unlike the Soviets, the United States never favored the operational use of liquid metal reactors. To date, all military reactors with the exception of one liquid sodium reactor on the attack submarine USS *Seawolf* (SSN-575) have been of the pressurized water reactor (PWR) type. Even the *Seawolf* experienced enough problems that the liquid sodium reactor was replaced with a PWR design after 21 months of service.
20. Convair report XM-566, "Short History of the Design and Development of the Nose Section and Crew Compartment Mock-Up for the XB-36H," 20 March 1956; *Convairiety*, 12 September 1951, p. 1; "Convair Development Department Fourth Annual Report," 8 September 1955, p. 19.
21. Technically this was Government Aircraft Plant No. 4, but it had been designed for and operated by Convair since it was constructed during World War II.
22. Convair report XM-566; *Convairiety*, 12 September 1951, p. 1; "Convair Development Department Fourth Annual Report," 8 September 1955, p. 19; Thornton, "Comprehensive Technical Report."
23. Convair report XM-566.
24. *Convairiety*, 25 August 1954, p. 1; "Convair Development Department Fourth Annual Report," 8 September 1955, p. 19.
25. See Dennis R. Jenkins, *Magnesium Overcast: The Story of the Convair B-36*, for further details of the B-36 in general.
26. "Convair Development Department Fourth Annual Report," 8 September 1955, p. 20.
27. *Conclusion of B-36 Aircraft Phase-Out*, Historical Monograph Nr. 1, Headquarters, San Antonio Air Materiel Area, Kelly AFB, Texas, March 1960.
28. For a more complete description of the X-6 aircraft, please see Jay Miller, *The X-Planes, X-1 to X-45* (Hinckley, England: Midland Publishing, April 2001).
29. Miller, *The X-Planes*, pp. 106-111.
30. Thornton, "Comprehensive Technical Report."
31. W. Henry Lambright, *Shooting Down the Nuclear Plane*, Inter-University Case Program 104 (Indianapolis: Bobbs-Merrill, 1967), p. 9.
32. Tesch, "Nuclear Aircraft Presentation." pp. 7-8.
33. U.S. Comptroller General, p. 134.
34. Butz, "Navy Aims at Low Power Atom Seaplane," pp. 30-32; Harry S. Baer, Jr., "Power for Aircraft: Though Many Problems Still Exist, the A-Powered Plane's Future Looks Brighter," *Flying*, June 1957, p. 65.
35. One of these advisors, Edwin M. McMillan, asserted, "It would be sensible to fly one nuclear airplane [that is, the Air Force variant] before getting deluged with others." General Advisory Committee of the Atomic Energy Commission, minutes of Meeting 46, 21-23 September 1955, p. 28.
36. For an excellent history of the nuclear projects in Idaho, see Susan M. Stacey, *Proving the Principle*, (Washington: U.S. Government Printing Office, 2000), p. 120.
37. The installation was owned by the Atomic Energy Commission (AEC) and operated, at the time, by Phillips Petroleum Company. The installation is now known as the Idaho National Engineering and Environmental Laboratory (INEEL) of the Department of Energy (DoE).
38. Stacey, *Proving the Principle*, p. 114.
39. Ibid, p. 116.
40. Thornton, "Comprehensive Technical Report."
41. Stacey, *Proving the Principle*, p. 121.
42. Thornton, "Comprehensive Technical Report;" Stacey, *Proving the Principle*, p. 121.
43. Stacey, *Proving the Principle*, p. 122.
44. Ibid.
45. *Science News Letter*, 13 August 1960, p. 105; Butz,"Navy Aims at Low Power Atom Seaplane," pp. 30-32.
46. Thornton, "Comprehensive Technical Report;" Butz, "Navy Aims at Low Power Atom Seaplane," pp. 30-32.
47. Walter G. Whitman, et. al., "Review of the Manned Aircraft Nuclear Propulsion Program," (Washington: U.S. Government Printing Office, 1963).
48. Ibid.
49. For similar reasons the panel also met with representatives of the Navy, Air Force, and AEC; in addition, it visited the Pratt & Whitney plant at Middletown, Connecticut, and the General Electric offices in Evendale, Ohio. Robert F. Bacher et al., Memorandum for J. R. Killian, Jr., 11 February 1958, pp. 1-2, EPL. Among the earlier studies cited were those of the Littlewood group (April 1957), the Canterbury board (May 1957) and the Mills board (June 1957).
50. Robert F. Bacher et al., Memorandum, pp. 1-8, EPL. Among the earlier studies cited were those of the Littlewood group (April 1957), the Canterbury board (May 1957) and the Mills board (June 1957).
51. Stacey, *Proving the Principle*, p. 125.
52. Thornton, "Comprehensive Technical Report."
53. Carpenter, *NX-2*; Thornton, "Comprehensive Technical Report." Each X211 engine weighed 15,745 pounds and the reactor weighed 11,900 pounds.
54. Thornton, "Comprehensive Technical Report."
55. Ibid.
56. AFSC Historical Publication 61-51-2, "Development of Airborne Armament, 1910–1961," October 1961, p. I-129.
57. "Soviets Flight Testing Nuclear Bomber," *Aviation Week*, 1 December 1958, p. 27.
58. Ford Eastman "Soviet Nuclear Plane Possibility Conceded," *Aviation Week*, 19 January 1959, p. 29; Herbert F. York, *Race to Oblivion*, (New York: Simon and Schuster, 1970), p. 70; AFSC Historical Publication 61-51-2, "Development of Airborne Armament, 1910–1961," October 1961, p. I-129.
59. Herbert F. York, *Race to Oblivion*, p. 69; Susan M. Stacey, *Proving the Principle*, (Washington: U.S. Government Printing Office, 2000), p. 126.
60. Stacey, *Proving the Principle*, p. 126.
61. Whitman, et. al., "Review of the Manned Aircraft Nuclear Propulsion Program," p. 176; Stacey, *Proving the Principle*, p. 264. Although there were three HTRE experiments, there were only two reactors; HTRE-2 had been modified from HTRE-1.

Chapter 2 – Technical Voodoo

1. It is possible to argue that the B-36 was the only true intercontinental bomber to ever serve; all subsequent bombers have needed aerial refueling to give them the required range. The B-36 did it unrefueled, albeit very slowly. See Dennis R. Jenkins, *Magnesium Overcast: The Story of the Convair B-36* (North Branch, MN: Specialty Press, 2001) for a detailed history of the B-36 program.
2. LeMay was born in 1906 and died on 3 October 1990.
3. Air Force Biography, General Curtis Emerson LeMay, in the files of the Air Force History Office.
4. Ibid.
5. Ibid.
6. On 17 March 1943, the Consolidated Aircraft Corporation merged with Vultee Aircraft, Inc., becoming the Consolidated Vultee Aircraft Corporation. This name is often truncated to "Convair," although this did not become official until 29 April 1954, when Consolidated Vultee Aircraft Corporation became the Convair Division of the General Dynamics Corporation after the two companies merged. In between Convair referred to itself alternately as CVAC, or CONVAIR (all caps). This book will use Convair since that is the commonly accepted usage.
7. Colonel Michael Norman Wright McCoy was a legendary bomber pilot. Among his greater feats, he piloted the *Lucky Lady* B-50 on the first non-stop around-the-world flight. McCoy was killed in a B-47 accident at Pinecastle AFB in November 1957. On 7 May 1958 Pinecastle was renamed McCoy AFB in his honor. Today the base is the Orlando International Airport, still using the ICAO identifier MCO.
8. Letter, Brigadier General John W. Sessums, Jr., Dep/Dev, ARDC, to the Commander ARDC, subject: Strategic Bomber/Recon Weapons Systems Development Program, 28 February 1952.
9. *Report of the Preparedness Investigating Subcommittee of the Committee on Armed Services*, United States Senate, 86th Congress, Second session, "The B-70 Program" (Washington: Government Printing Office, 1960), p. 3.
10. This involved a good deal of extrapolation. Chuck Yeager took the XS-1 rocket-plane on its first supersonic flight on 14 October 1947; the bomber being studied was many times larger than the small rocket plane used by Yeager.
11. Air Force Development Directive 00034, 26 February 1952.
12. Letter, Colonel Victor R. Haugen, Chief of the Weapons Systems Division, WADC, to the Commander ARDC, subject: Strategic Bomber/Recon Weapons Systems Development Program, 8 October 1952.
13. Letter, Major General T. S. Power, Vice Commander SAC to the Director of Requirements, USAF, subject: Requirement for Long Range Strategic Bombardment Aircraft, 30 March 1953.
14. See Chapter 1 for more discussion.
15. Marcelle Size Knaack, *Post-World War II Bombers*, (Washington: Office of Air Force History, 1988), pp. 559–560.
16. Chuck Hansen, *U.S. Nuclear Weapons*, (Arlington, Texas: Aerofax, Inc., 1988), pp. 43–50 and 146–153.
17. Letter, Major General Albert Boyd, Commander, WADC, to Commander, ARDC, Subject: Advanced Strategic Bomber Studies, 9 July 1954; letter, Major General A. Boyd, Commander, WADC to Commander, ARDC, Subject: Increment of Nuclear Powered Weapon System Studies to Begin in October 1954, 9 July 1954.
18. Letter, Brigadier General Benjamin S. Kelsey, Acting Director for Research and Development, USAF, to Commander ARDC, Subject: Strategic Weapon System Studies, 21 July 1954.
19. GOR-38, 14 October 1954; *Report of the Preparedness Investigating Subcommittee*, p. 47.
20. Letter, Brigadier General Benjamin S. Kelsey, Acting Director for Research and Development, USAF, to Commander ARDC, Subject: Strategic Weapon System Studies, 21 July 1954.
21. ARDC System Requirement 22, 15 April 1955. There seems to be a debate about exactly what date SR-22 was issued: 18 February or 15 April. Most official documentation says 15 April, and the SR-22 paperwork itself does not have a date. It is likely that 18 February was the date the document was approved for release, the bureaucracy taking a while to actually process it.
22. ARDC System Requirement 22, 15 April 1955.
23. ARDC System Requirement 22, 15 April 1955.
24. Circular Error Probable (CEP): the circle around a target within which 50 percent of released ordnance is statistically expected to land. Essentially, it is a measure

of statistical accuracy of a bomber or missile.
25. ARDC System Requirement 22, 15 April 1955.
26. This preference had saved the B-36 program on more than one occasion. In all, it is a logical argument: what good is speed if you lack the range to get to your target?
27. ARDC System Requirement 22, 15 April 1955; Knaack, *Post-World War II Bombers*, pp. 560–561.
28. Knaack, *Post-World War II Bombers*, p. 561.
29. GOR-82, 22 March 1955; SR 22, 15 April 1955; Knaack, *Post-World War II Bombers*, pp. 560–561.
30. Letter, Brigadier General Howell M. Estes, Jr. Director of Weapon Systems Operations, WADC, to the Commander ARDC, Subject: Chemically Powered Strategic Bomber Program, 7 April 1955; Letter, Major General Francis H. Griswold, Vice Commander SAC to the Commander ARDC, Subject: System Requirement 22, 19 April 1955; *Report of the Preparedness Investigating Subcommittee*, p. 47.
31. Convair was developing the Atlas ICBM; Douglas the Thor IRBM; and Martin the Titan ICBM.
32. AFSC Historical Publication 61-51-2, "Development of Airborne Armament, 1910–1961," October 1961, p. I-129.
33. "Development of Airborne Armament, 1910–1961," p. I-129; *Report of the Preparedness Investigating Subcommittee*, p. 48; Knaack, *Post-World War II Bombers*, pp. 560–562.
34. *Report of the Preparedness Investigating Subcommittee*, p. 48.
35. Memorandum, Colonel J. C. Maxwell, Chief Bombardment Aircraft Division, ARDC, Subject: Selection of Engine for System 110A, 15 June 1956.
36. Memorandum, E. C. Phillips, Technical Director, Power Plant Laboratory, WADC, to Chief 110A WSPO, ARDC, Subject: Selection of Engine for System 110A, 25 June 1956.
37. TWX, RDZ-1-31909, Dir/SM to DC/WS, ARDC, 24 August 1956.
38. Boeing report D2-2371, "Boeing Weapon System 110A (model 804)," 26 December 1957; North American report NA-56-825, "Strategic Bomber Weapon System 110A Summary Briefing," 30 July 1956.
39. C. E. "Bud" Anderson, "Aircraft Wingtip Coupling Experiments," a paper prepared for the Society of Experimental Test Pilots, passim.
40. Ibid; telephone conversations between the author and Bud Anderson, various dates.
41. Ibid.
42. "Convair Development department Fourth Annual Report," 8 September 1955, p. 22.
43. Some reports say as many as 50 hookups were made, but no confirmation of this could be found.
44. Knaack, *Post-World War II Bombers*, p. 563.
45. Boeing report D2-2371, p. 1.
46. Boeing report D2-2371, pp. 38–39.
47. Boeing report D2-2371, pp. 2-3.
48. Boeing report D2-2371, pp. 4–6. *See also* Boeing report D-16382A, B, and C.
49. Boeing report D2-2371, pp. 7–9. *See also* Boeing report D-16794.
50. Boeing report D2-2371, pp. 9–10. *See also* Boeing report D-16794.
51. Boeing report D2-2371, pp. 10–11.
52. Boeing report D2-2371, pp. 12–14 and 38-39.
53. Boeing report D2-2371, pp. 15–17. *See also* Boeing report D-17597.
54. Boeing report D2-2371, pp. 15–17. *See also* Boeing report D-17597.
55. Boeing report D2-2371, pp. 15–17. *See also* Boeing report D-17597.
56. Boeing report D2-2371, pp. 18–20. *See also* Boeing reports D-17597-1 and D2-1100.
57. Boeing report D2-2371, pp. 18–20. *See also* Boeing reports D-17597-1 and D2-1100.
58. Boeing report D2-2371, pp. 18–20. *See also* Boeing reports D-17597-1 and D2-1100.
59. Boeing report D2-2371, pp. 21–23. *See also* Boeing report D-17597-2.
60. Boeing report D2-2371, pp. 24–25 and 38–39. *See also* Boeing report D-17738.
61. North American report TSP65-3933, "Evolution of the B-70," undated, but sometime in 1965, pp. 3–4.
62. North American report TSP65-3933, pp. 5–8.
63. North American report TSP65-3933, pp. 9–14.
64. North American report TSP65-3933, pp. 9–14.
65. *Report of the Preparedness Investigating Subcommittee*, p. 4; Knaack, *Post-World War II Bombers*, p. 563.
66. *Report of the Preparedness Investigating Subcommittee* p. 48; "Development of Airborne Armament, 1910–1961," p. I-134/135.
67. Knaack, *Post-World War II Bombers*, p. 564.
68. Memorandum, T. H. Goss, Assistant Chief, 110A WSPO, to Chief, Power Plant Laboratory, WADC, Subject: Acceleration of System 110A/L Development, 26 March 1956.
69. Letter, Major General D. L. Putt, Deputy Chief of Staff for Development, to Commander ARDC, Subject: USAF Turbine Engine Development Program, 7 May 1957; TWX, RDTAP-5-7-E, Commander ARDC to Commander WADC, 17 May 1957.
70. "Development of Airborne Armament, 1910–1961," p. II-316; Knaack, *Post-World War II Bombers*, p. 564.
71. Boeing report D2-2371, pp. 26–27. *See also* Boeing report D2-1417.
72. Boeing report D2-2371, pp. 28–30 and 38–39. *See also* Boeing report D2-1433.
73. Boeing report D2-2371, pp. 28-30. *See also* Boeing report D2-1433.
74. Boeing report D2-2371, pp. 28–30. *See also* Boeing report D2-1433.
75. Boeing report D2-2371, pp. 31–33. *See also* Boeing report D2-1433-1.
76. Boeing report D2-2371, p. 34. *See also* Boeing report D2-2364.
77. Boeing report D2-2371, pp. 34–36. *See also* Boeing report D2-2055.
78. Boeing report D2-2371, pp. 34–36. *See also* Boeing report D2-2055.
79. Boeing report D2-2371, p. 37. *See also* Boeing reports D2-2411, D2-2412, D2-2413, and D2-2451.
80. Walter A. Spivak, "XB-70A Mach 3 Design and Operating Experience," a paper presented at the Society of Automotive Engineers' National Aeronautic Meeting, New York City, 25-28 April 1966; North American report TSP65-3933, p. 15. The reference to Harrison Storms comes from Alvin S. White, *The Times of My Life: A Pilot's Story*, (Tucson, AZ: Al White, 2003), a prereleased typescript that was not page numbered was used by the authors.
81. The National Advisory Committee for Aeronautics (NACA; always pronounced en-aay-cee-aay, never "naka") became the nucleus of the National Aeronautics and Space Administration on 1 October 1958.
82. Alfred J. Eggers and Clarence A. Syverston, *Aircraft Configurations Developing High Lift/Drag Ratios at High Supersonic Speeds*, (Ames Research Center, CA: NACA, 5 March 1956), NACA research memorandum RM-A55105, passim.
83. Walter A. Spivak, "XB-70A Mach 3 Design and Operating Experience," a paper presented at the Society of Automotive Engineers' National Aeronautic Meeting, New York City, 25-28 April 1966.
84. *Report of the Preparedness Investigating Subcommittee*, p. 29.
85. Spivak, "XB-70A Mach 3 Design and Operating Experience."
86. For the first time in an Air Force procurement, the using command (SAC, in this case) was allowed to participate in the evaluation. Previously this had been limited to the Air Research and Development Command and the Air Materiel Command. Due to the success of the three-team evaluation group, the Air Force changed its source selection procedures, the using command becoming an integral part of the selecting process.
87. "Development of Airborne Armament, 1910–1961," p. I-140; *Report of the Preparedness Investigating Subcommittee*, p. 49; Knaack, *Post-World War II Bombers*, pp. 564–566.
88. Ibid.
89. ARDC Weapon System Requirements, strategic Bombardment Weapon System, WS-110A, 7 January 1958.
90. "Development of Airborne Armament, 1910–1961," p. I-143.
91. Ibid.
92. White, *The Times of My Life*. Heat buildup is the major limited factor for high-speed flight. Heat, caused by friction with the airstream, limits the top speed of modern aircraft such as the F-15 far more than power (the canopy on the F-15 begins to go soft). Beyond Mach 2.5, friction increases at an ever-growing rate (for comparison, an SR-71 operating at Mach 2.2 heats up to about 275 degrees Fahrenheit, but at Mach 3.2, skin temperatures rise to almost 900 degrees Fahrenheit). The same aerodynamics that gave the XB-70 so little drag also helped minimize heat buildup. The hottest portions of the Valkyrie, her nose and horizontal splitter, reached a temperature of about 650 degrees Fahrenheit during Mach 3 flight, with the majority of skin temperatures below 450 degrees Fahrenheit.
93. "Development of Airborne Armament, 1910–1961," p. I-141.
94. Knaack, *Post-World War II Bombers*, p. 566.
95. "Development of Airborne Armament, 1910–1961," p. I-144; Knaack, *Post-World War II Bombers*, p. 566
96. Letter, E. A. Thomas, Acting Manager of Marketing, Jet Engine Department of General Electric, to Commander ARDC, Subject: WS-110A Programming, 13 January 1958; Memorandum, B-70 WSPO to DC/WS ARDC, Subject: Engine Interchangeability F-108/B-70, 3 July 1958; Letter, General E. W. Rawlings, Commander AMC to Deputy Chief of Staff for Materiel, no subject, 17 June 1958; Directive, Brigadier General B. H. Warren, Deputy Director for Procurement, to various AMC offices, Subject: B-70/F-108 Weapon Systems—J93 Engine Program, 12 September 1958.
97. Valkyries (from the Old Norse Valkyrjr, "choosers of the slain") in Norse mythology were the daughters of the principal god Odin, and were often called Odin's Maidens. At his bidding, they flew on their horses over the fields of battle to choose the souls of the heroic dead, which they carried off to Valhalla, Odin's banquet hall in the heavenly realm of Asgard. There the warriors became members of the Einherjar, Odin's companions, and fighting band. The Valkyries were depicted as young, beautiful, but fierce women who dressed splendidly in full armor and swords when riding their horses. Valkyries also had the power to determine who would be the victors and who the defeated in such conflicts. Belief in the existence of magic horsewomen from heaven was widespread in Scandinavia and Germanic cultures, although they were called by different names.
98. Al White remembers "the expressions that popped out of the mouths of visitors when they saw it for the first time was almost unanimous. It led to most of us calling it the 'Savior.' "
99. Knaack, *Post-World War II Bombers*, pp. 566–567.

Chapter 3 – The Elusive Mach 3 Fighter

1. The Lockheed YF-12A is arguably the last interceptor *developed* by the Air Force, but it is likely the airplane was never intended to go into the operational inventory. Every interceptor used since the F-106 was retired – primarily McDonnell Douglas-Boeing F-15s and General Dynamics-Lockheed F-16s – have been slightly-modified versions of tactical fighters, not dedicated interceptors.
2. The theory was that bombers would get Weapon System designations in the 100-series, fighters in the 200-series.
3. AFSC Historical Publication 61-51-2, "Development of Airborne Armament, 1910–1961," October 1961, p. III-540. The actual development contract with Hughes was not signed until October 1950.
4. Jim Upton, *Lockheed F-104 Starfighter* (WarbirdTech Volume 38), (North Branch, MN: Specialty Press, 2003), p. 7.
5. "Development of Airborne Armament, 1910–1961," Volume III, passim and p. IV-591.
6. Convair had intended to use the Wright J67 (a license-built version of the Bristol Olympus) in the F-102; however, development problems led to a decision to use a Westinghouse J40 in early aircraft pending the delivery of the J67. Eventually, all production F-102s used the Pratt & Whitney J57.
7. Called the "Double Cycle Propulsion System" by Republic.
8. Republic Aviation Report ED-AP57-909, *Descriptive Brochure of the Republic XF-103 Interceptor*, 20 June 1952, pp. 15–16.
9. This is different from how the Lockheed Blackbirds handled the problem. The Blackbird partially unloaded the compressor using a bleed-bypass cycle, effectively reducing the compressor exit temperature. The XF-103 completely removed the turbojet engine from the equation.
10. Republic Aviation report ED-AP57-909, *Descriptive Brochure of the Republic XF-103 Interceptor*, 20 June 1952, pp. 20–21.
11. Air Force report 51S-43239-A, *Technical Evaluation - MX-1554, Republic Model AP-57*, 27 March 1951, II-19; ED-AP57-909, pp. 15–16.
12. 51S-43239-A; ED-AP57-909, pp. 9–12. Things have certainly changed. In 1975 a modified McDonnell Douglas F-15A named *Streak Eagle* climbed to 65,620 feet (20,000 meters) in 122.94 seconds: just over 2 minutes. The airplane eventually went to 98,430 feet (30,000 meters) in 207.80 seconds.
13. Marcelle Size Knaack, *Post-World War II Fighters, 1945–1973*, (Washington: Office of Air Force History, 1986), p. 329.
14. ED-AP57-909, pp. 23–24.
15. Ibid., pp. 24–32.
16. Ibid., pp. 33–35. The concept of fly-by-wire had not been invented yet, which meant that all of the controls would need to be mechanically or hydraulically linked to the capsule. This would probably have been a maintenance nightmare.
17. The FFAR was developed jointly by North American and the Navy, and was based on the World War II German R4 rocket and equipped most U.S. interceptors beginning with the North American F-86D Sabre.
18. ED-AP57-909, pp. 36-37.
19. This is not completely unreasonable; to withstand the heat, the aluminum aircraft would need to use very thick skins, increasing the weight past that of the relatively thin skins used on the stainless steel aircraft.
20. ED-AP57-909, pp. 41-42.
21. Knaack, *Post-World War II Fighters*, p. 330.
22. Ibid., p. 329.
23. ED-AP57-909, pp. 43–44.
24. James W. Cortada, *Historical Dictionary of Data Processing*, (New York: Greenwood Press, 1987), pp. 333–334; "A Sentry Goes on Guard for America," *Business Machines*, 3 August 1956, pp. 4–5; IBM Press Release, "IBM-Built Computer is Heart of Electronic Air Defense," 30 June 1956; IBM brochure, "The SAGE Computer," undated (but sometime in the late 1950s).
25. http://history.acusd.edu/gen/20th/sage.html, accessed 28 February 2003. Computers before SAGE relied on printed output, not real-time displays.
26. "A Sentry Goes on Guard for America," pp. 4–5; IBM Press Release, "IBM-Built Computer is Heart of Electronic Air Defense," 30 June 1956; IBM brochure, "The SAGE Computer," undated (but sometime in the late 1950s).
27. http://www.mitre.org/pubs/showcase/sage/sage_feature.html, accessed on 28 February 2003.
28. http://history.acusd.edu/gen/20th/sage.html, accessed 28 February 2003.
29. The Northeast Air Command (NEAC) was activated on 1 October 1950 to integrate administrative and operational control of all U.S. forces in Canada and Greenland. The command was disbanded in 1957 with its component forces going to the Air Defense Command and the Strategic Air Command, as appropriate.
30. "Development of Airborne Armament, 1910–1961," p. IV-624.
31. The War Department established an Air Defense Command on 26 February 1940, but by mid-1944, when the threat of air attack seemed negligible, this organization was disbanded. Subsequently, no real air defense organization existed until the second Air Defense Command was established on 21 March 1946. The ADC became a subordinate element of Continental Air Command on 1 December 1948, and was disestablished on 1 July 1950. It was reestablished as a major command on 1 January 1951. The organization was renamed the Aerospace Defense Command on 15 January 1968, to reflect its growing interest in outer space. The ADC declined after the Air National Guard and Air Force Reserve gradually assumed more and more of the air defense mission, and on 31 March 1980, the remaining ADC resources were divided between Tactical Air Command and Strategic Air Command.
32. "Development of Airborne Armament, 1910–1961," p. IV-625.
33. "Development of Airborne Armament, 1910–1961," p. IV-625. 20 kilotons is a large weapon – the same destructive power as the Hiroshima bomb. The atomic warheads that were ultimately fielded were much smaller.
34. "Development of Airborne Armament, 1910–1961," pp. III-573 and IV-626. Emphasis in the original.
35. Ibid., p. IV-627.
36. Ibid., p. IV-628.
37. Ibid., p. IV-629. Emphasis in the original.
38. Letter, General Benjamin W. Chidlaw, Commander/ADC, to General Nathan F. Twining, Chief of Staff/USAF, 6 March 1954, no subject.
39. "Development of Airborne Armament, 1910–1961," p. IV-632.
40. Gerald H. Balzer and Mike Dario, *Northrop F-89 Scorpion* (Datagraph #8), (Arlington TX: Aerofax Inc., 1993), pp. 29, 35, and 38; *See also* Joe Mizrahi, "Playing the Proposal Game," in *Airpower*, Volume 21, No. 3, May 1991, pp. 36-49.
41. Ibid., pp. 29, 35, and 38.
42. Ibid., pp. 29, 35, and 38.
43. See Kevin Keaveney, *McDonnell F-101B/F* (Minigraph #5) (Arlington TX: Aerofax Inc., 1984) for a more detailed discussion of the two-seat Voodoo.
44. Ibid.
45. "Development of Airborne Armament, 1910–1961," p. IV-633.
46. Ibid., p. IV-633.
47. Ibid., p. IV-636.
48. Ibid., p. IV-639.
49. Ibid., p. IV-639.
50. Ibid., p. IV-641.
51. Ibid., p. IV-642.
52. Ibid., p. IV-643.
53. Ibid., p. IV-645.
54. Ibid., p. IV-645.
55. Ibid., p. IV-646.
56. Ibid., p. IV-647.
57. Ibid., p. IV-647.
58. Ibid., p. IV-648.
59. Ibid., p. IV-649.
60. The board also included Major Generals James Ferguson, Hugh A. Parker, and Kenneth P. Berquist, Colonel J. F. Mocenry, and Dr. C. D. Perkins.
61. "Development of Airborne Armament, 1910–1961," p. IV-651. The radius was further defined in the accompanying documentation as 350 nautical miles at supersonic speed or 1,000 nautical miles at the optimum subsonic speed.
62. North American assigned "model numbers" (which were really project control numbers) to a contract, not necessarily to an individual design. This is why all the variations of the F-108 were simply NA-257.
63. "Development of Airborne Armament, 1910–1961," p. IV-654.
64. Ibid., p. IV-655.
65. Ibid., p. IV-658.
66. Standard Aircraft Characteristics, "Pre-Mockup, North American F-108A," May 1958; North American report NA-57-916-7, "Long Range Interceptor, Weapon System 202A, Monthly Status Report for January 1958."
67. Ibid.
68. North American report NA-57-916-18, "Long Range Interceptor, Weapon System 202A, Monthly Status Report for December 1958." It should be noted that Lockheed has never acknowledged that they received any insight into titanium fabrication from any of the programs (X-15, XF-103, etc.) that had gone before the Blackbirds. With no disrespect to Lockheed, it is highly unlikely that they had not been briefed on the lessons learned from these earlier programs.
69. North American report NA-57-916-10, "Long Range Interceptor, Weapon System 202A, Monthly Status Report for April 1958."
70. North American report NA-57-916-9, "Long Range Interceptor, Weapon System 202A, Monthly Status Report for March 1958."
71. NA-57-916-10; North American report NA-57-916-12, "Long Range Interceptor,

Weapon System 202A, Monthly Status Report for June 1958;" North American report NA-57-916-13, "Long Range Interceptor, Weapon System 202A, Monthly Status Report for July 1958;" North American report NA-57-916-18, "Long Range Interceptor, Weapon System 202A, Monthly Status Report for December 1958." Convair F-106s were modified with an inflight refueling capability after they were manufactured.

72. NA-57-916-7.
73. NA-57-916-7; NA-57-916-9; NA-57-916-18. Pratt & Whitney originally developed the JT9 series engine for the stillborn Lockheed CL-400 aircraft. The J58 was essentially an 80-percent scale JT9, and initial versions of the engine carried various JT9 designations before being changed to JT11. Several commercial engines that powered the 747 and DC-10 also used the basic JT9 core. In November 1958, North American evaluated the JT11C-31C and JT11C-35C versions of the J58. The –35C was a full-scale J58 with a reduced-size afterburner and airflow throttled to the F-108A inlet capacity. The –31C was a similar engine with the first stage of the compressor removed and throttled to the F-108A inlet capacity. North American also looked at the JT11C-33 and –37 engines, which were identical to the –31C and –35C except with thrust reversers. (The Lockheed Blackbirds used various subvariants of the JT11D-20 with thrust ranging from 32,000 lbf to 35,000 lbf.)
74. NA-57-916-9; "Development of Airborne Armament, 1910-1961," p. IV-660; interview with Jim Eastham by the authors, 15 May 2004.
75. NA-57-916-13; Standard Aircraft Characteristics, "Pre-Mockup, North American F-108A," 1 October 1958.
76. NA-57-916-13; NA-57-916-18; Standard Aircraft Characteristics, "Pre-Mockup, North American F-108A," 1 October 1958.
77. "Development of Airborne Armament, 1910–1961," p. IV-659.
78. NA-57-916-18; "Development of Airborne Armament, 1910–1961," p. IV-660. There seems to be some disagreement over the weight of the ASG-18, with some documents showing it at 1,400 pounds and others at 2,098 pounds. The original specification weight was 2,075 pounds, so 1,400 seems very low unless this was not all-inclusive, or perhaps represents the "developed" version used by the Lockheed YF-12A.
79. NA-57-916-16, "Long Range Interceptor, Weapon System 202A, Monthly Status Report for October 1958."
80. Ibid.
81. North American report NA-57-916-17, "Long Range Interceptor, Weapon System 202A, Monthly Status Report for November 1958"; North American report NA-57-916-24, "Long Range Interceptor, Weapon System 202A, Monthly Status Report for June 1959."
82. NA-57-916-18; North American report NA-57-916-19, "Long Range Interceptor, Weapon System 202A, Monthly Status Report for January 1959;" North American report NA-57-916-20, "Long Range Interceptor, Weapon System 202A, Monthly Status Report for February 1959"; NA-57-916-24. The term "irdome" never made it into popular culture, but was used frequently during the 1950s to refer to the infrared-transparent cover for an IR sensor.
83. NA-57-916-18. The XM59 designation was made official in January 1959.
84. NA-57-916-18.
85. Ibid.
86. NA-57-916-18; NA-57-916-19; North American report NA-57-916-23, "Long Range Interceptor, Weapon System 202A, Monthly Status Report for May 1959;" thanks to Scott Lowther for tracking down the designation of the Lockheed motor.
87. NA-57-916-13.
88. NA-57-916-16.
89. Standard Aircraft Characteristics, "Mockup, North American F-108A," 15 December 1958; NA-57-916-17.
90. Standard Aircraft Characteristics, "Mockup, North American F-108A," 15 December 1958.
91. NA-57-916-16.
92. NA-57-916-19.
93. Ibid.
94. NA-57-916-9; NA-57-916-19; Knaack, *Post-World War II Fighters*, p. 330; North American press release, "U.S. Air Force F-108 Rapier," May 1959.
95. NA-57-916-9; NA-57-916-19; Knaack, *Post-World War II Fighters*, p. 330. Various sources, including some Standard Aircraft Characteristics, list thrust reversers on earlier designs, but this was the first engineering model that included them.
96. NA-57-916-16.
97. NA-57-916-19; North American report NA-57-916-21, "Long Range Interceptor, Weapon System 202A, Monthly Status Report for March 1959."
98. NA-57-916-17; NA-57-916-21.
99. "Development of Airborne Armament, 1910–1961," p. IV-661.
100. North American report NA-57-916-8, "Long Range Interceptor, Weapon System 202A, Monthly Status Report for February 1958; NA-57-916-13; NA-57-916-20; NA-57-916-23; interview with Jim Eastham by the authors, 15 May 2004.
101. NA-57-916-23.
102. NA-57-916-16; NA-57-916-20; "Development of Airborne Armament, 1910–1961," p. IV-660.
103. NA-57-916-24.
104. NA-57-916-23; NA-57-916-24; Standard Aircraft Characteristics, "Mockup, North American F-108A," 12 June 1959.
105. "Development of Airborne Armament, 1910–1961," p. IV-661.
106. Ibid., p. IV-663.
107. *Report of the Preparedness Investigating Subcommittee of the Committee on Armed Services*, United States Senate, 86th Congress, Second session, "The B-70 Program" (Washington: Government Printing Office, 1960), p. 51.
108. NA-57-916-20; NA-57-916-23; North American report NA-57-916-25, "Long Range Interceptor, Weapon System 202A, Monthly Status Report for July 1959."
109. NA-57-916-20.
110. NA-57-916-14; NA-57-916-18; NA-57-916-20.
111. "Development of Airborne Armament, 1910–1961," p. IV-664.
112. NA-57-916-25.
113. Interview with Jim Eastham by the authors, 15 May 2004.

Chapter 4 – Another Diversion

1. AFSC Historical Publication 61-51-2, "Development of Airborne Armament, 1910–1961," October 1961.
2. The WADC Power Plant Laboratory and Propeller Laboratory were combined into the Propulsion Laboratory on 17 June 1957.
3. Ray Wagner, *American Combat Planes*. Third edition, (Garden City, NY: Doubleday & Company, 1982).
4. "What You Don't Know Can Hurt You: Pentaborane," E. Floyd Phelps, no date.
5. "What You Don't Know Can Hurt You: Pentaborane," E. Floyd Phelps, no date.
6. "What You Don't Know Can Hurt You: Pentaborane," E. Floyd Phelps, no date.
7. "What You Don't Know Can Hurt You: Pentaborane," E. Floyd Phelps, no date.
8. The eventual boron-based high-energy fuels included: HEF-1, ethyl diborane; HEF-2, propylpentaborane; HEF-3, ethyl decaborane; HEF-4, methyldecaborane; and HEF-5, ethylacetylenedecaborane.
9. Memorandum, E. A. Wolfe, Chief of Plans, Power Plant Laboratory, to Director of Weapon System Operations, WADC, Subject: Review of Strategic Bomber Capabilities, 27 June 1955; Memorandum, Chief of the Power Plant Laboratory, to Director of Weapon System Operations, WADC, Subject: Work Statement for Design Competition for Chemically-Powered Strategic Bomber System 110A, 6 June 1955.
10. A joint effort composed of American Potash and Chemical, the Food Machinery and Chemical Corporation, and the National Distilleries and Chemical Corporation.
11. Boron oxide melts at about 900 degrees Fahrenheit, and is a viscous fluid to temperatures over 3,000 degrees Fahrenheit.
12. "Report of the Committee for Manned Aircraft," September 1956, pp. 10 and 17.
13. Directive, D. M. Ross Chief Operations Office, Propulsion Laboratory, WADC, to Chief 110A WSPO, Subject: Use of HEF-3 in WS-110A, 30 November 1956; WADC Tech Note 57-123, March 1957.
14. Letter, Colonel E. R. Lawrence, Assistant Director for Research and Development, USAF, to Commander ARDC, Subject: Air Force Engine Program for High Energy Fuel, 1 July 1957.
15. Directive, T. H. Goss, Assistant Chief, 110A WSPO, to Chief, Operations Division, WADC, Subject: HEF Program, 28 January 1958.
16. Letter, G. C. Rapp, Manager, J93 Aircraft Programs, GE, to Commander ARDC, Subject: J93 All HEF Feasibility Program, 16 June 1958; Letter, Harrison A. Storms, Chief Engineer, North American Aviation, to Commander AMC, Subject: All HEF B-70, 1 April 1959; Memorandum Colonel E. L. Bishop, Chief, B-70 WSPO, to Chief, Turbojet and Ramjet Engine Branch, Propulsion Laboratory, WADC, Subject: All HEF Turbojet Engine Feasibility Investigation, 13 April 1959.
17. TWX, RDZSSL-30725-E, Director of Systems Management, ARDC, to Chief of Staff USAF, 28 May 1958.
18. WADC Weekly Tech Info report, 7 July 1958.
19. B-70 HEF Program Summary, 28 November 1958
20. TWX, LMSA-4-1183, Commander AMC, to North American Aviation, 30 April 1959.
21. Letter, General T. S. Power, Commander-in-Chief SAC, to Chief of Staff USAF, Subject: Application of High Energy Fuel to the B-70, 25 May 1959.
22. "B-70 HEF Program Summary," 28 November 1958.
23. Memorandum, E. A. Wolfe, Chief of Plans, Power Plant Laboratory, to Director of Weapon System Operations, WADC, Subject: Review of Strategic Bomber Capabilities, 27 June 1955.
24. Systems Management Division (ARDC) Weekly Activity Report, 24 July 1959; TWX, AFMTPEO-6-2294, Chief of Staff USAF, to Commander ARDC, 10 August 1959.
25. *Aviation Week*, 17 August 1959; *Aviation Week*, 31 August 1959; *Aviation Week*, 7 September 1959; *New York Times*, 12 August 1959.
26. A turbofan or bypass engine is essentially a turbojet engine with a larger fan mounted on the front that ducts some of the airflow around the combustor section.
27. Memorandum, T. H. Goss, Assistant Chief, 110A WSPO, to Chief, Power Plant Laboratory, WADC, Subject: Acceleration of System 110A/L Development, 26 March 1956.
28. Memorandum, Colonel J. C. Maxwell, Chief Bombardment Aircraft Division, ARDC, Subject: Selection of Engine for System 110A, 15 June 1956.
29. Memorandum, E. C. Phillips, Technical Director, Power Plant Laboratory, WADC, to Chief 110A WSPO, ARDC, Subject: Selection of Engine for System 110A, 25 June 1956.
30. Memorandum, Colonel J. B. Calderbank, Chief of Power Plant Laboratory, WADC, to Chief, 110A WSPO, ARDC, Subject: Financial Requirement for System 110A Propulsion Development, 17 July 1956.
31. Memorandum, D. M. Ross, Chief of the Operations Office, Power Plant Laboratory, WADC, to 110A WSPO, ARDC, Subject: Selection of Engine for System 110A, 16 November 1956.
32. Letter, Major General W. F. McKee, Vice Commander, AMC, to Deputy Chief of Staff for materiel, USAF, Subject: Industrial Impact Resulting from Non-Award of Engine Development Contracts for Calendar Year 1957, 21 February 1957.
33. Letter, Major General D. L. Putt, Deputy Chief of Staff for Development, to Commander ARDC, Subject: USAF Turbine Engine Development Program, 7 May 1957; TWX, RDTAP-5-7-E, Commander ARDC to Commander WADC, 17 May 1957.
34. TWX, Chief, Bombardment Aircraft Division, ARDC, to Colonel M. F. McNickle, ARDC, 26 August 1957.
35. Letter, Lieutenant General S. E. Anderson, Commander ARDC, to Vice Chief of Staff USAF, Subject: WS-110A Engine Program, 17 September 1957.
36. Letter, Major General J. E. Smart, Assistant Chief of Staff USAF, to Commander ARDC, Subject: Engine Program for WS-110A and WS-125A, 6 November 1957.
37. Memorandum, Colonel M. F. McNickle, Assistant for Aircraft Systems, ARDC, to Deputy Chief of Staff for Development USAF, Subject: Engine Program for WS110A and WS125A, 13 January 1958; TWX, RDZSBL-30179-E, Assistant Chief B-70 WSPO to Commander ARDC, 11 February 1958.
38. "History of the Wright Air Development Center," July–December 1956, Volume II, pp. 592–594; Letter, Lieutenant General D. L. Putt, Deputy Chief of Staff for Development, to Commander ARDC, Subject: Propulsion System for Improved Weapon System 110A, 17 February 1958.
39. Letter, E. A. Thomas, Acting Manager of Marketing, Jet Engine Department of General Electric, to Commander ARDC, Subject: WS-110A Programming, 13 January 1958.
40. Memorandum, B-70 WSPO to DC/WS ARDC, Subject: Engine Interchangeability F-108/B-70, 3 July 1958; Letter, General E. W. Rawlings, Commander AMC to Deputy Chief of Staff for Materiel, no subject, 17 June 1958.
41. Directive, Brigadier General B. H. Warren, Deputy Director for Procurement, to various AMC offices, Subject: B-70/F-108 Weapon Systems, J93 Engine Program, 12 September 1958.
42. TWX, Chief of the Air Vehicle Section, B-70 WSPO, to Commander ARDC, 27 March 1958.
43. North American Aviation report NA-58-1423, Subject: J93 Engine Module Concept, 11 November 1958; Minutes of the J93 Engine Concept Conference, 13 November 1958 and 31 March 1959.
44. Letter, Colonel J. R. V. Dickson, Assistant Director for Research and Development, USAF, to Commander ARDC, no subject, 29 December 1958.
45. Ibid.
46. Alvin S. White, *The Times of My Life: A Pilot's Story*, (Tucson, AZ: Al White, 2003).
47. Untitled report, J93 Engine Section, Turbojet-Ramjet Branch, Propulsion Laboratory, WADC, 19 August 1959.
48. http://www.airbp.com/airbp/public/generalinterest/jethistory.html, accessed on 6 January 2004.
49. Kirk S. Irwin, minutes of the XB-70 Flight Readiness Board Meeting, 1 November 1966. In the files of the NASA History Office.
50. This gave the Air Force and General Electric two different cancellations to negotiate; the –1 program had already been redirected to the –5 configuration and a settlement had not been reached.

Chapter 5 – Politics

1. Iain Pike, "B-70 State-of-the-Art Improver," *Flight International*, 25 June 1964, p. 1,059.
2. Alvin S. White, *The Times of My Life: A Pilot's Story*, (Tucson, AZ: Al White, 2003), a prereleased typescript that was not page numbered was used by the authors.
3. Pike, "B-70 State-of-the-Art Improver," p. 1,059.
4. North American report TSP65-3933, "Evolution of the B-70," undated but sometime in 1965, p. 16.
5. Letter, Colonel E. R. Lawrence, Assistant Director for Research and Development, USAF, to Commander ARDC, Subject: Air Force Engine Program for High Energy Fuel, 1 July 1957.
6. The dual-fuel system required 300 pounds and each engine would add 220 pounds because of a heavier afterburner requirement.
7. "B-70 HEF Program Summary," 28 November 1958.
8. North American report NAA-58-984, "Estimated performance Record for the B-70 Air Vehicle Powered with Six (6) General Electric J-93 Turbojet Engines," 15 August 1958; TSP65-3933, pp. 17-18.
9. TSP65-3933, pp. 19-22; North American report NA-59-268, "Estimated Performance and Drag Substantiation Report for B-70 Primary Air Vehicle," 27 February 1959; White, *The Times of My Life*.
10. Since the entire canard could now deflect 6 degrees, plus another 20 degrees for the flap, the effective deflection was 26 degrees.
11. TSP65-3933, pp. 19-22; NA-59-268; White, *The Times of My Life*; Walter A. Spivak, "XB-70A Mach 3 Design and Operating Experience," a paper presented at the Society of Automotive Engineers' National Aeronautic Meeting, New York City, 25-28 April 1966.
12. Marcelle Size Knaack, *Post-World War II Bombers*, (Washington: Office of Air Force History, 1988)), p. 567.
13. The Douglas GAM-87 Skybolt was an air-launched ballistic missile that would have been carried on the B-52H and B-70A. Armed with a W59 nuclear warhead in a Mk. 7 re-entry vehicle; development was initiated in the late 1950s. The decision to proceed with the Skybolt was made in February 1960, with initial deployment projected for 1964. In June 1960, the Royal Air Force ordered 100 Skybolts to be carried by the Avro Vulcan. However, in December 1962, President Kennedy cancelled the Skybolt missile for political and economic reasons.
14. Letter, Harrison A. Storms, Chief Engineer, North American Aviation, to Commander AMC, Subject: Contract AF33(600)-38669, B-70 Weapon System Configuration Status, 15 May 1959; Letter, Harrison A. Storms to Commander AMC, Subject: B-70 Weapon System Configuration Review, 12 June 1959; North American report NA-59LA-3927A, "Configuration Analysis," 3 March 1959; *Report of the Preparedness Investigating Subcommittee of the Committee on Armed Services*, United States Senate, 86th Congress, Second session, "The B-70 Program" (Washington: Government Printing Office, 1960), p. 50.
15. Letter, Colonel J. R. V. Dickson, Assistant Director for Research and Development, USAF, to Commander ARDC, no subject, 29 December 1958.
16. The nuclear-powered bomber, after overshadowing the chemically-powered aircraft for years, began to suffer from financial malnutrition in 1956. By mid-1959, decisions within the Administration and Department of Defense had put the program into almost total eclipse. The project's downfall was bound to impede the B-70 program since the cost of several B-70 subsystems were to be developed by the nuclear-powered bomber program, which was finally cancelled by the Kennedy Administration in March 1961.
17. Knaack, *Post-World War II Bombers*, p. 567.
18. Ibid, p. 567.
19. Ibid, p. 568.
20. *Report of the Preparedness Investigating Subcommittee*, pp. 1 and 42; Knaack, *Post-World War II Bombers*, p. 568.
21. DoD Subcommittee, House appropriations hearings, 14 January 1960, 86th Congress, Second session, Part I, p. 134.
22. *Report of the Preparedness Investigating Subcommittee*, p. 2.
23. White, *The Times of My Life*.
24. *Report of the Preparedness Investigating Subcommittee*, p. 43; North American Rockwell report SD-72-SH-0003, "B-70 Aircraft Study, Final Report, Volume I," April 1972, prepared under NASA contract NAS9-12100, p. 31; Knaack, *Post-World War II Bombers*, p. 568.
25. White, *The Times of My Life*.
26. Ibid.
27. Ibid.
28. Knaack, *Post-World War II Bombers*, pp. 568, 569.
29. Ibid, p. 569.
30. SD-72-SH-0003, p. 31.
31. The two XB-70s were represented by various monikers during their test series: A/V-1, AV/1, and XB-70-1 all represented the first aircraft, while A/V-2, AV/2, and XB-70-2 represented the second. For consistency, this publication will use the A/V-x form.
32. The 1,575 serial numbers beginning immediately after A/V-3 were assigned to the GAM-83A (AGM-12B) Bullpup air-to-ground missiles.
33. "XB-70A's Research Role will Contribute Mach-3 flight Data for SST Development," *Aviation Week & Space Technology*, 18 May 1964, pp. 26, 27.
34. SD-72-SH-0003, p. 31.
35. Knaack, *Post-World War II Bombers*, pp. 569, 570.
36. Some documentation refers to this as the RSB-70. Neither designation was truly official, but RS-70 seems more likely.
37. SD-72-SH-0003, p. 31; Knaack, *Post-World War II Bombers*, p. 570; Richard West, "Technologically, Craft Goes Far Beyond B-58, B-52 or Even the X-15,"

Los Angeles Times, 18 June 1962, p. 8; Donn A. Byrnes and Kenneth D. Hurley, *Blackbird Rising*, (Los Lunas, NM: Sage Mesa Publications, 1999), pp. 19-40. Interestingly, during 1962 the Southern California press always – and incorrectly – used the RS-70 moniker when talking about the B-70 program.
38. White, *The Times of My Life*.
39. Ibid.
40. North American press release, 11 May 1964.
41. SD72-SH-0003, p. II-237.
42. Ibid.
43. "XB-70A's Research Role will Contribute Mach-3 flight Data for SST Development," *Aviation Week & Space Technology*, 18 May 1964, pp. 26, 27; Pike, "B-70 State-of-the-Art Improver," p. 1,060.
44. SD72-SH-0003, p. II-237; White, *The Times of My Life*.
45. SD72-SH-0003, p. II-237.
46. Ibid, p. II-238.
47. White, *The Times of My Life*.
48. SD72-SH-0003, p. II-238.
49. Air Force report 64-ASV-31, "XB-70 Program Study," 3 February 1964, pp. 8, 9.
50. Memorandum, Alexander H. Flax/SAFRD to Brigadier General Fred. J. Ascani/B-70 WSPO, subject: Charter for XB-70 Program Study, 25 January 1964; Air Force report AF64-ASV-31, "XB-70 Program Study," 3 February 1964, p. 9.
51. AF64-ASV-31, pp. 2 and 5.
52. Ibid, p. 3.
53. Ibid, p. 4.
54. Ibid, pp. 5, 6.
55. Ibid, pp. 10, 11.
56. Vladimir Antonov. Jay Miller. et. al. *OKB Sukhoi: A History of the Design Bureau and its Aircraft*, (Arlington, TX: Aerofax, Inc., 1996), pp. 206-213.

Chapter 6 – The Flight Program

1. The basic engineering drawing release for A/V-3 was completed on 31 October 1963, and all raw materials had been purchased. A few subassemblies for A/V-3 had been completed, but no major structural assembly had occurred. In addition, the prototype IBM bomb-nav system and radars had been completed.
2. Walter A. Spivak, "XB-70A Mach 3 Design and Operating Experience," a paper presented at the Society of Automotive Engineers' National Aeronautic Meeting, New York City, 25-28 April 1966; "XB-70A's Research Role will Contribute Mach-3 flight Data for SST Development," *Aviation Week & Space Technology*, 18 May 1964, pp. 26, 27.
3. Alvin S. White, *The Times of My Life: A Pilot's Story*, (Tucson, AZ: Al White, 2003), a prereleased typescript that was not page numbered was used by the authors.
4. Ibid.
5. Ibid.
6. Ibid.
7. Ibid.
8. Ibid.
9. Actually, the early tail-sitter Messerschmitt Me 262 prototypes suffered from this problem, but it is highly unusual.
10. Ibid.
11. Ibid.
12. Ibid; There seems to be some question over the amount of the proposed bonus payment. Al White remembers it being $500,000, but most other sources claim it was $250,000 for a supersonic first flight. Unfortunately, a copy of the contract could not be located.
13. Ibid.
14. Ibid.
15. Ibid.
16. Ibid.
17. Ibid.
18. Ibid.
19. Ibid.
20. Marcelle Size Knaack, *Post-World War II Bombers*, (Washington: Office of Air Force History, 1988), pp. 572, 573; "XB-70 Flight," *Aviation Week & Space Technology*, 28 September 1964, pp. 25, 26; White, *The Times of My Life*.
21. White, *The Times of My Life*.
22. Ibid.
23. Ibid.
24. Ibid.
25. Ibid.
26. Knaack, *Post-World War II Bombers*, pp. 572, 573; "XB-70 Flight," *Aviation Week & Space Technology*, 28 September 1964, pp. 25, 26; XB-70 Flight Log compiled by Betty Love, DFRC, 7 May 1969.
27. White, *The Times of My Life: A Pilot's Story*, (Tucson, AZ: Al White, 2003).
28. "XB-70 Flight," pp. 25, 26.
29. White, *The Times of My Life*.
30. Ibid.
31. Ibid.
32. Ibid.
33. "Five Injured in Explosion as XB-70 Defuels, *Los Angeles Times*, 19 October 1964; "XB-70A fuel truck explosion fatal to Lancaster man; 4 others hurt," *Ledger gazette*, 20 October 1964; "Worker Hurt in XB-70 Defueling Blast Dies," *Los Angeles Times*, 21 October 1964.
34. White, *The Times of My Life*.
35. North American report NA66-858, "B-70 Program Review," August 1966, no page numbers.
36. NA66-858.
37. Ibid.
38. White, *The Times of My Life*.
39. "Heavyweight XB-70 Sets Speed Records," *Ledger Gazette*, 24 March 1965.
40. White, *The Times of My Life*.
41. Ibid.
42. Ibid.
43. Ibid.
44. Ibid.
45. Ibid.
46. A Ibid.
47. Chester H. Wolowicz, NASA TM-X-1195, "Analysis of an Emergency Deceleration and Descent of the XB-70-1 Airplane Due to Engine Damage Resulting from Structural Failure," March 1966, p. 5.
48. Ibid, p. 6; White, *The Times of My Life*.
49. Wolowicz, NASA TM-X-1195, p. 6; White, *The Times of My Life*.
50. White, *The Times of My Life*.
51. Ibid.
52. Wolowicz, NASA TM-X-1195, p. 7.
53. Wolowicz, NASA TM-X-1195, p. 3; White, *The Times of My Life*.
54. White, *The Times of My Life*.
55. Ibid.
56. Ibid.
57. Wolowicz, NASA TM-X-1195, p. 7; White, *The Times of My Life*.
58. White, *The Times of My Life*.
59. "B-70 worker loses life in accident," *Ledger Gazette*, 10 May 1965; "Mechanic dies in test," *Los Angeles Times*, 10 May 1965.
60. White, *The Times of My Life*.
61. NA66-858.
62. White, *The Times of My Life*.
63. Ibid.
64. Ibid.
65. Ibid.
66. Ibid.
67. Ibid.
68. Ibid.
69. Ibid.
70. Ibid.
71. Ibid.
72. Ibid.
73. Ibid.
74. Ibid.
75. Wolowicz, NASA TM-X-1195, p. 2; White, *The Times of My Life*. Al White mentions that he considered the rudder bob-weight a "useless" gimmick.
76. White, *The Times of My Life*.
77. NA66-858.
78. "Capsule Operation Demonstrated on XB-70A Flight," *Los Angeles Times*, 29 December 1965.
79. "XB-70A-1 Flies, Lands, Takes Off in Historic Flights," *Los Angeles Times*, 14 January 1965.
80. NA66-858.
81. Ibid.
82. http://www.edwards.af.mil/history/docs_html/center/lakebeds.html, accessed 25 January 2002; Michael H. Gorn, *Expanding the Envelope: Flight Research at NACA and NASA*, (Lexington, Kentucky: The University Press of Kentucky, 2001), p. 204.
83. White, *The Times of My Life*. As related in the accident report after A/V-2 was lost, this appearance took explicit approval from the Air Force Director of Information and the Assistant Secretary of Defense (Public Affairs). The initial plans had included a high-speed fly-over during the air show, but this was specifically excluded by higher command. See Memorandum, Secretary of the Air Force Harold Brown to Secretary of Defense Robert S. McNamara, 12 August 1966.
84. "XB-70A Inlet Unstart," *Aviation Week & Space Technology*, 25 April 1966, p. 99; XB-70 Flight Log compiled by Betty Love, DFRC, 7 May 1969.
85. White, *The Times of My Life*.
86. Ibid.
87. Ibid.
88. Ibid.
89. Ibid.
90. "Inflight Repairs Overcome XB-70 Malfunction," *Aviation Week & Space Technology*, 8 May 1966; White, *The Times of My Life*.
91. White, *The Times of My Life*.
92. Ibid.
93. Ibid.
94. Memorandum, Secretary of the Air Force Harold Brown to Secretary of Defense Robert S. McNamara, 12 August 1966; North American Aviation Pilot's Flight Report for 2-46, 8 June 1966; Air Force Accident/Incident Report and accompanying file of data, supplied by Louie F. Alley, Air Force Safety Center, Holloman AFB, New Mexico.
95. Memorandum, Secretary of the Air Force Harold Brown to Secretary of Defense Robert S. McNamara, 12 August 1966.
96. White, *The Times of My Life*.
97. White, *The Times of My Life*; Air Force Accident/Incident Report and accompanying file of data, supplied by Louie F. Alley, Air Force Safety Center, Holloman AFB, New Mexico.
98. White, *The Times of My Life*.
99. North American Aviation report NA-63-360-22, "Escape and Survival," prepared in response to the A/V-2 accident; White, *The Times of My Life*; Air Force Accident/Incident Report and accompanying file of data, supplied by Louie F. Alley, Air Force Safety Center, Holloman AFB, New Mexico.
100. White, *The Times of My Life*.
101. Ibid.
102. Ibid.
103. North American Aviation, Sequence of Events – Flight 2-46, an attachment to Memorandum, Secretary of the Air Force Harold Brown to Secretary of Defense Robert S. McNamara, 12 August 1966; White, *The Times of My Life*; Air Force Accident/Incident Report and accompanying file of data, supplied by Louie F. Alley, Air Force Safety Center, Holloman AFB, New Mexico. Jeannette Remak, author of an excellent book on the B-70, reports that the correct coordinates of the XB-70A crash site are: 35.0629 North, 117.0243 West; the F-104N impacted at 35.0806 North, 117.0580 West.
104. Don Mallick, *The Smell of Kerosene: A Test Pilot's Odyssey*," NASA SP-4108, 2003, pp. 133-135.
105. Memorandum, Secretary of the Air Force Harold Brown to Secretary of Defense Robert S. McNamara, 12 August 1966; Air Force Accident/Incident Report and accompanying file of data, supplied by Louie F. Alley, Air Force Safety Center, Holloman AFB, New Mexico.
106. Mallick, *The Smell of Kerosene*, p. 137.
107. Memorandum, Secretary of the Air Force Harold Brown to Secretary of Defense Robert S. McNamara, 12 August 1966; Mallick, *The Smell of Kerosene*, pp. 140-141.
108. Memorandum, Secretary of the Air Force Harold Brown to Secretary of Defense Robert S. McNamara, 12 August 1966; "XB-70 Crash Findings Reported By Air Force Investigating Board," *Aviation Week & Space Technology*, 22 August 1966, p. 18; Air Force Accident/Incident Report and accompanying file of data, supplied by Louie F. Alley, Air Force Safety Center, Holloman AFB, New Mexico.
109. "Analysis of the XB-70 Accident," Attachment A to Memorandum, Secretary of the Air Force Harold Brown to Secretary of Defense Robert S. McNamara, 12 August 1966.
110. Decal and light data from "XB-70A 001 Flight 1-50 Configuration Status" briefing charts.
111. Memorandum, Secretary of the Air Force Harold Brown to Secretary of Defense Robert S. McNamara, 12 August 1966.
112. Mallick, *The Smell of Kerosene*, pp. 141-142.
113. Memorandum, Secretary of the Air Force Harold Brown to Secretary of Defense Robert S. McNamara, 12 August 1966; "XB-70 Crash Findings Reported By Air Force Investigating Board," *Aviation Week & Space Technology*, 22 August 1966, p. 18.
114. Memorandum, Secretary of the Air Force Harold Brown to Secretary of Defense Robert S. McNamara, 12 August 1966; Mallick, *The Smell of Kerosene*, pp. 142-143.
115. Air Force Accident/Incident Report and accompanying file of data, supplied by Louie F. Alley, Air Force Safety Center, Holloman AFB, New Mexico. Whereas the cost data from the Air Force was typed on an official form, the data from NASA was a hand-written note attached to the file.
116. http://www.free-definition.com/Sonic-boom.html, accessed 3 June 2004.
117. Christine M. Darden, NASA Langley Research Center, "Acceptable Supersonic Flight: Is it Near?," a paper in the 16th International Session in 40th Aircraft Symposium, Yokohama Kaikou-Kinen Kaikan, Yokohama, Japan, 9-11 October 2002.
118. Ibid.
119. Ibid.
120. Ibid.
121. Background material prepared for James Webb's use during Congressional Hearings on the FY68 budget; James A. Martin, "The NASA XB-70/SST Flight Research Program," a paper presented to the NASA Steering Committee for the Task Group for Future Programs, 20 July 1964.
122. See, for example, Memorandum, William Schweikhard and Donald R. Bellman (FRC) to Paul F. Bikle (Director of FRC), "Flight performance and propulsion research on vehicles operating in the SST flight regime," 1 August 1966.
123. James A. Martin, "The NASA XB-70/SST Flight Research Program," a paper presented to the NASA Steering Committee for the Task Group for Future Programs, 20 July 1964.
124. Kirk S. Irwin, minutes of the XB-70 Flight Readiness Board Meeting, 1 November 1966.
125. Ibid; memorandum, Charles W. Harper, NASA/RA/Director, to R/AA for Advanced Research, 13 June 1966.
126. Memorandum, Charles W. Harper, NASA/RA/Director, to R/AA for Advanced Research, 13 June 1966; memorandum, Weldon E. Kordes, FRC/Scientist, to Paul F. Bikle, FRC/Director, 29 July 1966.
127. "NASA Assumes XB-70 Research Effort," *Aviation Week & Space Technology*, 13 February 1967, p. 38.
128. Memorandum for the record, James A. Martin, "XB-70 Escape Systems Mods," 9 November 1967.
129. Ibid; "Minutes of the XB-70 escape capsule DEI held at EAFB," 6 September 1967; Minutes of the XB-70 Flight Readiness Review, 23 May 1968.
130. Memorandum, Charles W. Harper, NASA/RA/Director, to R/AA for Advanced Research, 13 June 1966; Memorandum of Understanding, "Principles for Use of XB-70 Aircraft in Support of the National Supersonic Transport Program," 28 May 1965; Memorandum for the record, Robert C. Seamans, Jr. (Deputy Administrator), "XB-70 Flight research Program Procurement," 16 February 1967; Memorandum of Understanding, "Provisions for the Use of the XB-70 Aircraft in a Jointly Sponsored NASA-DOD (USAF) Flight Research Program," 15 March 1967.
131. Memorandum for the record, Robert C. Seamans, Jr. (Deputy Administrator), "XB-70 Flight research Program Procurement," 16 February 1967.
132. Memorandum of Understanding, "Provisions for the Use of the XB-70 Aircraft in a Jointly Sponsored NASA-DOD (USAF) Flight Research Program," 15 March 1967.
133. "NASA Assumes XB-70 Research Effort," *Aviation Week & Space Technology*, 13 February 1967, p. 38; Mallick, *The Smell of Kerosene*, p. 144; Fact Sheet FS-2003-07-084, XB-70, NASA Dryden Flight Research Center, 15 July 2003.
134. Mallick, *The Smell of Kerosene*, pp. 156-157.
135. Ibid, pp. 157-158.
136. Ibid, pp. 151-152.
137. Ibid, p. 152.
138. Minutes of the XB-70 Flight readiness Review, 23 May 1968; Letter, Boyd C. Myers, II, FRC, to Major General Otto J. Glasser, USAF, no subject, 14 May 1968; Fact Sheet FS-2003-07-084, XB-70, NASA Dryden Flight Research Center, 15 July 2003.
139. Letter, Calvin B. Hargis, Jr. USAF/Deputy for Development, to Charles W. Harper, NASA, 7 April 1967.
140. Memorandum, James A. Martin, FRC, to A. J. Evans, FRC, 10 April 1967.
141. Fact Sheet FS-2003-07-084, XB-70, NASA Dryden Flight Research Center, 15 July 2003.
142. TWX 0580513Z, 26 February 1969. In the files of the AFFTC History Office.
143. Thanks to Jeannette Remak for supplying the dates of the moves around the museum.

Chapter 7 – 1960s State-of-the-Art

1. The actual performance of the airplane was classified, which is why all flights seemed to reach "2,000 mph." DD Form 254, Section 15, Note 3, issued by the Flight Research Center on 1 March 1968, stated that "Air Vehicle test data of speed/velocity or altitude … are classified CONFIDENTIAL." The Air Force concurred with this classification, and reiterated its appropriateness in a letter from Albert J. Evans to James A. Martin on 8 April 1968.
2. North American report NA-66-901, "Operational Limitations of the XB-70A Air Vehicle," prepared under NASA contract NAS4-1175, 30 August 1966; Walter A. Spivak, "XB-70A Mach 3 Design and Operating Experience," a paper presented at the Society of Automotive Engineers' National Aeronautic Meeting, New York City, 25-28 April 1966.
3. North American report NA-61-858, "Ground Loads for the B-70 Prototype Air Vehicle Six Engine Turbojet Bomber (NAA Designation NA-278) Air Force Designation XB-70, Contract AF33(600)-42058," 22 October 1962, p. 17.
4. XB-70-2-1, "Development Program Manual, General Airplane, USAF Series XB-70A Aircraft," 30 July 1966, changed 31 March 1967, p. 1-1.
5. NA66-858; Spivak, "XB-70A Mach 3 Design and Operating Experience."
6. NA66-858.
7. Ibid.

8. Ibid.
9. Ibid; Alvin S. White, *The Times of My Life: A Pilot's Story*, (Tucson, AZ: Al White, 2003).
10. Memorandum, James A. Martin, FRC, to Paul F. Bikle and James E. Love, FRC, "Ad Hoc Committee Report on Flight Readiness of the XB-70 Following Modification Layup Prior To Flight 1-74," 10 June 1968; XB-70-2-1, p. 1-2; White, *The Times of My Life*.
11. XB-70-2-1, pp. 2-2 and 2-3; White, *The Times of My Life*.
12. White, *The Times of My Life*.
13. NA66-858.
14. Ibid.
15. Ibid; Air Force Aeronautical Systems Division press release 63-19, 5 February 1963.
16. XB-70-2-1, p. 2-13.
17. Ibid, pp. 1-2 and 2-2.
18. Ibid, pp. 1-2, 2-15, 2-18, and 2-19.
19. The Cartesian coordinate system used on the XB-70 was generally the same as used by almost all aircraft. The coordinate system used X, Y, and Z to designate the axis; subscript F was used for the fuselage, W for the wing, etc. In the case of the Valkyrie, the zero coordinate of the fuselage was located 128 inches ahead of the nose; i.e., the nose (ignoring the pitot boom) was at YF128. "Fuselage station" (FS) 605 was the same as YF605; i.e., it was 605 inches from the zero coordinate or 477 inches from the nose.
20. NA66-858.
21. Ibid.
22. White, *The Times of My Life*.
23. Ibid.
24. NA66-858.
25. XB-70-2-1, p. 1-1; Iain Pike, "B-70 State-of-the-Art Improver," *Flight International*, 25 June 1964, p. 1,062.
26. XB-70-2-1, pp. 1-1, 2-33, and 2-34; Kirk S. Irwin, minutes of the XB-70 Flight Readiness Board Meeting, 1 November 1966.
27. XB-70-2-1, pp. 1-1, 2-33, and 2-34.
28. Chester H. Wolowicz, NASA TM-X-1195, "Analysis of an Emergency Deceleration and Descent of the XB-70-1 Airplane Due to Engine Damage Resulting from Structural Failure," March 1966, p. 2; XB-70-2-1, pp. 1-1 and 2-33.
29. XB-70-2-1, pp. 2-34, and 2-35; "XB-70A's Research Role will Contribute Mach-3 flight Data for SST Development," *Aviation Week & Space Technology*, 18 May 1964, pp. 26, 27.
30. Wolowicz, TM-X-1195, p. 3; XB-70-2-1, pp. 2-35 and 2-36.
31. Richard L. Schleicher, "Structural Design of the XB-70," a paper presented at the Institute of Aeronautical Sciences in 1967.
32. NA66-858; Chester H. Wolowicz, NASA TM-X-1195, "Analysis of an Emergency Deceleration and Descent of the XB-70-1 Airplane Due to Engine Damage Resulting from Structural Failure," March 1966, p. 3.
33. Schleicher, "Structural Design of the XB-70."
34. North American report "XB-70 Program Engineering Effort to be Accomplished on Contract 42058 (31 July 1962 through 30 June 1964), 9 August 1962; XB-70-2-1, p. 1–4.
35. Spivak, "XB-70A Mach 3 Design and Operating Experience."
36. XB-70-2-5, "Development Program Manual (Propulsion Related Systems), USAF Series XB-70A Aircraft," 30 July 1966, changed 21 November 1966, pp. 7-1 through 7-10.
37. Wolowicz, TM-X-1195, p. 6.
38. White, *The Times of My Life*.
39. T. O. 1B-70(X)A-1, "Interim Flight Manual, USAF Series XB-70A Aircraft," 31 August 1964, changed 25 June 1965; "XB-70A's Research Role will Contribute Mach-3 flight Data for SST Development," *Aviation Week & Space Technology*, 18 May 1964, pp. 26, 27.
40. XB-70-2-5, "Development Program Manual (Propulsion Related Systems), USAF Series XB-70A Aircraft," 30 July 1966, changed 21 November 1966, pp. 7-1 through 7-10.
41. XB-70-2-5, pp. 7-1 through 7-10; Pike, "B-70 State-of-the-Art Improver," p. 1,060.
42. XB-70-2-5, pp. 7-1 through 7-10.
43. XB-70-2-1, pp. 1-2 and 2-17.
44. NA-61-858; XB-70-2-1, pp. 2-16 and 2-17; Internal Letter, D. K. Kramer/North American, to LAD System Safety Committee Members, Subject: Information on Crash of XB-70 No. 2, 2 August 1966.
45. XB-70-2-1, pp. 2-16 and 2-17; Pike, "B-70 State-of-the-Art Improver," p. 24.
46. Minutes of the XB-70 Flight readiness Review, 23 May 1968; memorandum, James A. Martin, FRC, to Paul F. Bikle and James E. Love, FRC, "Ad Hoc Committee Report on Flight Readiness of the XB-70 Following Modification Layup Prior To Flight 1-74," 10 June 1968.
47. NA-61-858, p. 6; XB-70-2-1, pp. 2-16 and 2-17; Pike, "B-70 State-of-the-Art Improver," p. 24.
48. XB-70-2-1, pp. 1-2, 2-18, and 2-19; North American report NA-66-901, "Operational Limitations of the XB-70A Air Vehicle," prepared under NASA contract NAS4-1175, 30 August 1966, p. 2; T. O. 1B-70(X)A-1; Spivak, "XB-70A Mach 3 Design and Operating Experience."
49. There were 11 physical tanks; however, most technical documentation for the XB-70A says there were eight tanks. This is because the two corresponding wing tanks were considered one logical unit since they were controlled simultaneously to maintain the center of gravity. These tanks were designed Nos. 6 left/right, 7 left/right, and 8 left/right. The fuselage tanks were designated Nos. 1 through 5.
50. Spivak, "XB-70A Mach 3 Design and Operating Experience."
51. XB-70-2-1 pp. 1-2, 2-8, 2-9, and 2-10.
52. Ibid, pp. 2-11 and 2-14.
53. Ibid, pp. 2-11 and 2-14.
54. Spivak, "XB-70A Mach 3 Design and Operating Experience."
55. XB-70-2-1, pp. 1-2 and 2-19; Internal Letter, D. K. Kramer/North American, to LAD System Safety Committee Members, Subject: Information on Crash of XB-70 No. 2, 2 August 1966; Air Force Accident/Incident Report and accompanying file of data, supplied by Louie F. Alley, Air Force Safety Center, Holloman AFB, New Mexico.
56. White, *The Times of My Life*.
57. "XB-70A's Research Role will Contribute Mach-3 flight Data for SST Development," *Aviation Week & Space Technology*, 18 May 1964, pp. 26-27; Pike, "B-70 State-of-the-Art Improver," p. 20.
58. "XB-70A's Research Role will Contribute Mach-3 flight Data for SST Development," pp. 26-27; Pike, "B-70 State-of-the-Art Improver," p. 20.
59. Memorandum, James A. Martin, FRC, to Paul F. Bikle and James E. Love, FRC, "Ad Hoc Committee Report on Flight Readiness of the XB-70 Following Modification Layup Prior To Flight 1-74," 10 June 1968
60. XB-70-2-1, pp. 2-37 and 2-38.
61. Ibid, p. 2-21.
62. Ibid, p. 1-4.
63. Ibid, p. 1-4.
64. Kirk S. Irwin, minutes of the XB-70 Flight Readiness Board Meeting, 1 November 1966.
65. Air Force report AEDC-TDR-64-162, "Testing of a YJ93-GE-3 Turbojet Engine Equipped With a Modified XB-70 Aircraft Heat Shield in an Altitude Test Cell," August 1964, p. 2.
66. Ibid, p. 3.
67. Ibid, p. 3.
68. Pike, "B-70 State-of-the-Art Improver," p. 1,060.
69. XB-70-2-1, p. 2-4.
70. Ibid, pp. 1-2 and 2-19; Internal Letter, D. K. Kramer/North American, to LAD System Safety Committee Members, Subject: Information on Crash of XB-70 No. 2, 2 August 1966; Air Force Accident/Incident Report and accompanying file of data, supplied by Louie F. Alley, Air Force Safety Center, Holloman AFB, New Mexico.
71. XB-70-2-1, p. 2-5.
72. Ibid, p. 2-6.
73. Ibid, pp. 2-6 and 2-7.
74. *Jane's All the World's Aircraft*, 1970–1971 edition, (London: Jane's Yearbooks, 1971), pp. 765, 766.

Chapter 8 – No Apparent Threat

1. North American report "XB-70 Program Engineering Effort to be Accomplished on Contract 42058 (31 July 1962 through 30 June 1964), 9 August 1962; XB-70-2-1, "Development Program Manual, General Airplane, USAF Series XB-70A Aircraft," 30 July 1966, changed 31 March 1967, p. 1–4.
2. AFSC Historical Publication 61-51-2, "Development of Airborne Armament, 1910–1961," October 1961, pp. I-108–160.
3. Ibid, p. I-108.
4. Ibid, p. I-108.
5. Progress Report, Engineering Division/WADC, July 1946; Minutes of the Army Air Force Technical Committee meetings of 29 April and 30 July 1947; http://www.draper.com/corporate/profile/docslab.php, accessed on 29 May 2004.
6. "Development of Airborne Armament," p. I-109. It is important to note here that the actual bomb dynamics and mission profile were computed prior to flight, and that the inertial data was used to provide an offset to the precomputed data. At the time, airborne computers were incapable of real-time profile computations.
7. Ibid, p. I-110.
8. Ibid, p. I-110.
9. Ibid, p. I-111.
10. Ibid, p. I-111.
11. Ibid, p. I-112.
12. Among other things, Hughes was heavily involved in developing most of the interceptor radar/fire control systems for the Air Force, as well as several of the air-to-air missiles that armed the interceptors.
13. This company built television sets from at least 1950 through 1964 under a variety of names (Mercury Television, Pacific Mercury, etc.) but nothing could be found regarding their ultimate fate.
14. "Development of Airborne Armament," p. I-112.
15. "WADC Weekly Technical Information Report," 3 July 1953.
16. Letter, Brigadier General A. A. Kessler, Jr. director of Procurement and Industrial Planning, to Commander/AMC, 7 November 1949, subject: Stellar Inertial Bombing Systems.
17. Paper tape – about an inch wide and as long as needed – was a popular way to program computers and other devices during the 1950s (and well into the 1980s in some cases). In addition, it needs to be recognized that the use of the term "computer" here does not infer the sort of general-purpose digital devices that are used to today. These were usually hard-wired analog machines capable of very limited computations of very specific data.
18. "Development of Airborne Armament," p. I-114.
19. Ibid, p. I-114.
20. Ibid, p. I-115.
21. Ibid, p. I-116.
22. A human crew would be in the bomber for takeoff, and possibly for the first stages of flight. The crew would then bail out over friendly territory and automatic guidance systems would take the bomber to the target. Using unmanned aircraft also seemed desirable at the time since the general expectation was that the then-untested thermonuclear bomb would invariably destroy any aircraft within many miles of the blast.
23. "Development of Airborne Armament," p. I-116.
24. Ibid, p. I-117.
25. In this use, "conventional" refers to free-fall bombing as opposed to the air-to-surface missile. The free-fall bombs could be either nuclear or chemical high explosives.
26. ARDC System Requirement 22, 15 April 1955; WADC Exhibit WCLG-785, "Bombing Navigation System" 12 April 1955.
27. "Development of Airborne Armament," p. I-123.
28. Ibid, p. I-124.
29. Ibid, p. I-124.
30. Ibid, p. I-125.
31. By comparison, a Pentium 4 microprocessor from 2004 has between 55 million and 178 million transistor-equivalents.
32. "Development of Airborne Armament," p. I-125.
33. Ibid, p. I-126.
34. Ibid, p. I-127.
35. Ibid, p. I-128.
36. Ibid, p. I-128.
37. North American report SD72-SH-0003, "B-70 Aircraft Study, Final Report," Subcontractor Matrix, WBS Code: 2.24.1, p. II-195; "Development of Airborne Armament," p. I-128.
38. "Development of Airborne Armament," p. I-130.
39. Ibid, p. I-130.
40. Ibid, p. I-131.
41. Ibid, p. I-132.
42. Ibid, p. I-132.
43. Ibid, p. I-133.
44. Ibid, p. I-133.
45. Ibid, p. I-134.
46. Ibid, p. I-134.
47. Ibid, p. I-135.
48. Ibid, p. I-136.
49. Ibid, p. I-137.
50. Ibid, p. I-137.
51. Ibid, p. I-138.
52. Ibid, p. I-139.
53. North American report (no number), "Description of Technical Development Program for Weapon System 110A Bombing-Navigation-Missile Guidance Subsystem," 7 March 1958, no page numbers.
54. Ibid.
55. "Development of Airborne Armament," p. I-147.
56. SD72-SH-0003, p. II-195; "Development of Airborne Armament," p. I-148.
57. Letter, Lieutenant General Samuel E. Anderson, Commander/ARDC to Director of Research and Development/DCS, 12 September 1958, subject: Comments on B-70 Bombing-Navigation System.
58. Ibid.
59. "Development of Airborne Armament," p. I-152.
60. Ibid, p. I-152.
61. Ibid, p. I-153.
62. Ibid, p. I-154.
63. Ibid, p. I-156.
64. Ibid, p. I-157.
65. Ibid, p. I-157.
66. SD72-SH-0003, p. II-195; "Development of Airborne Armament," p. I-158.
67. "Development of Airborne Armament," p. I-159.
68. Ibid, p. I-161.
69. SD72-SH-0003, p. II-196.
70. SD72-SH-0003, p. II-196.
71. Air Force report 64-ASV-31, "XB-70 Program Study," 3 February 1964, Chart 1-24.
72. "Development of Airborne Armament," p. I-161.
73. Many people consider jamming an "active" defense, but the literature of the period seems to call all electronic measures "passive" and uses the term "active" to mean missiles and other "weapons" that were fired at an enemy interceptor. In addition, the term "interceptor" as used by the bomber defense groups was meant to encompass manned interceptors, surface-to-air missiles, and any other physical object that might potentially endanger the bomber.
74. "Development of Airborne Armament," p. II-355.
75. Ibid, p. II-356.
76. Ibid, p. II-356.
77. Ibid, pp. II-314 and II-356.
78. Ibid p. II-357.
79. In 1959, the Lockheed Aircraft Company acquired the Stavid Engineering Company, a small but versatile military electronics firm, and merged it with its own electronics division to form the Lockheed Electronics Company.
80. "Development of Airborne Armament," p. II-358.
81. Ibid, p. II-358.
82. Ibid, p. II-359.
83. Ibid, p. II-359.
84. Ibid, p. II-361.
85. Ibid, p. II-360.
86. The Hurricane Mesa site, located near Virgin, Utah, was acquired by the Air Force in 1955, as the Hurricane Mesa Supersonic Research Site and included approximately 3,500 acres. The property consisted of a supersonic test track and support facilities on the mesa top and an area below the mesa used as an impact area. In 1962, the Air Force returned approximately 2,800 acres to the Bureau of Land Management and to the State of Utah Land Trust. Today, portions of the site are owned by the Bureau of Land Management and the State of Utah; the mesa top still supports a supersonic sled track operated by BF Goodrich Aerospace.
87. "Development of Airborne Armament," p. II-361.
88. Ibid, p. II-361.
89. Ibid, p. II-362.
90. The story goes that a secretary in the Project Office did not think "lenticular defense missile" was imaginative enough and came up with Pye Wacket, the name of the cat in the book and movie, *Bell, Book, and Candle*.
91. "Development of Airborne Armament," p. II-363.
92. North American report (not numbered), "B-70 Air Survival Improvement Active Defense Feasibility Study," March 1959.
93. "Development of Airborne Armament," p. II-363.
94. Ibid, p. II-364.
95. Ibid, p. II-365.
96. Air Force report APGC-TR-60-25, "Pye Wacket Lenticular Rocket Feasibility Study," May 1960.
97. Air Force report ASD-TR-61-34, "Pye Wacket Feasibility Test Vehicle Study" (prepared by Convair as part of AFSC Project 3811), 15 February 1961.
98. ASD-TR-61-34.
99. Air Force report AEDC-TN-61-27, "Investigation of Static Stability and Aerodynamic Effects of Control Jets on a 1/3-Scale Pye Wacket Missile at Supersonic Speeds," March 1961; Air Force report AEDC-TN-60-219, "Investigation of Static Stability and Aerodynamic Effects of Control Jets on a 1/3-Scale Pye Wacket Missile at Transonic Mach Numbers," December 1960; ASD-TR-61-34; http://www.ufx.org/rvs/pyewacket.htm, accessed on 10 February 2003.
100. AEDC-TN-61-27; AEDC-TN-60-219; ASD-TR-61-34; http://www.ufx.org/rvs/pyewacket.htm, accessed on 10 February 2003.
101. Dennis R. Jenkins, *Space Shuttle: The History of the National Space Transportation System*, (Cape Canaveral, FL: Specialty Press, 2001), p. 34.
102. "Development of Airborne Armament," p. II-321.
103. North American report NA-59-206, "B-70 Air Survival Improvement Active Defense Feasibility Study," March 1959, no page numbers.
104. Ibid.
105. Ibid.
106. Ibid.
107. Ibid.
108. Ibid.
109. Ibid.
110. "Development of Airborne Armament," p. II-335.

Notes and Citations

111. Ibid, p. II-336.
112. Ibid, p. II-336.
113. Ibid, p. II-339.
114. Ibid, p. II-340.
115. Ibid, p. II-341.
116. Ibid, p. II-342.
117. Ibid, p. II-344.
118. Ibid, p. II-346.
119. WADC report (not numbered), "Comments on SR-197 Study Reports by Weapons Guidance and Aerial Reconnaissance Laboratory," 5 February 1960, no page numbers.
120. Ibid.
121. Ibid.
122. "Development of Airborne Armament," p. II-349.
123. Ibid, p. II-349.
124. Ibid, p. II-350.
125. Ibid, p. II-351.
126. Ibid, p. II-351.
127. Ibid, p. II-353.
128. Actually, by this time the Wright Air Development Center (WADC) had been merged (on 15 December 1959) with the ARDC Directorate of Systems Management and been renamed the Wright Air Development Division (WADD). I continue to use WADC here for convenience.
129. WADD report (not numbered), "SR-197, Penetration Aids for the B-70 Manned Bombers," April 1960.
130. "Development of Airborne Armament," p. II-353.
131. ARDC System Requirement 22, 15 April 1955.
132. Lockheed report MSD-1720, "Penetration System No. 1, Progress Report for April," 16 May 1956; AFSC Historical Publication 61-51-2, "Development of Airborne Armament, 1910–1961," October 1961, p. II-315.
133. Air Force report (not numbered), "Tentative (B-70) Operational Concept," 13 March 1958.
134. Air Force report (not numbered), "Tentative (B-70) Operational Concept," 28 April 1958
135. North American report (not numbered), "Preliminary Performance Specification, Defensive Subsystem for the B-70 Air Vehicle, Weapons System B-70, Contract AF33(600)-36599, 4 April 1958.
136. Ibid.
137. Ibid.
138. "Development of Airborne Armament," p. II-330.
139. Memorandum, G. W. Bollinger, B-52 WSPO, to B-70 WSPO, 11 August 1959, subject: Utilization of AN/ALQ-27 Development.
140. SD72-SH-0003, p. II-196; "Development of Airborne Armament," p. II-332.
141. SD72-SH-0003, p. II-197.
142. SD72-SH-0003, p. II-197.
143. See, for example, North American report NA-59-53-1, "Thermal Radiation Characteristics of the B-70 Weapon System," 31 July 1959 and North American report NA-59-1887, "B-70 Radar Cross Section, Infrared Radiation, and Infrared Countermeasures," 31 December 1959.
144. North American report NA61-295 "Development of Coating Materials for Reduction of the Infrared Emission of the YB-70 Air Vehicle," 16 March 1961, page numbers not readable on microfilm printout.
145. Ibid.
146. Ibid.
147. North American briefing, "B-70 Weapon System Alert Pod," undated.
148. Ibid.
149. SD72-SH-0003, p. II-196; North American news release, 23 April 1959.
150. Ibid.
151. http://www.globalsecurity.org/wmd/agency/oo-alc.htm, accessed 1 June 2004.
152. Kev Darling, *Avro Vulcan* (WarbirdTech volume 26), (North Branch, MN: Specialty Press, 1999), pp. 69–74.
153. Ibid, pp. 74, 75.
154. Dennis R. Jenkins and Brian Rogers, *Boeing B-52G/H Stratofortress* (Aerofax Datagraph 7), (Arlington, TX: Aerofax, Inc., 1990), p. 34.
155. http://www.designation-systems.net/dusrm/m-48.html, accessed 12 May 2004.
156. Darling, *Avro Vulcan*, pp. 74, 75.
157. Chuck Hansen, *U.S. Nuclear Weapons*, (New York: Orion Books, 1988), p. 184.
158. Ibid, p. 185.
159. Jenkins and Rogers, *Boeing B-52G/H Stratofortress*, p. 34; http://www.zianet.com/jpage/airforce/weapons/ordnance/gam-87.html
160. http://www.designation-systems.net/dusrm/m-48.html, accessed 1 June 2004.

The black radome on A/V-2 (foreground) contrasts with the white unit on A/V-1 in the background. This photo also illustrates how the air intakes were painted differently, at least for a while during the flight program. (Boeing Historical Archives)

APPENDIX G
INDEX

1954 Interceptor, *See* Convair: F-102

A-12, *See* Lockheed: Blackbird
A/V-1, 87-89, 102-111, 114, 116-117, 121-132, 134-135, 137, 139-144, 146-148, 150-151, 155, 164, 170-176, 179-180, 182-183, 190, 192, 195-196, 199, 202, 204-208, 211, 238, 252
A/V-2, 88, 103, 106, 108, 110, 113, 116-117, 138-144, 146-154, 156-157, 160, 165, 167, 169-172, 174, 185, 187, 190, 193, 195-196, 199, 202, 205, 211, 242, 252
A/V-3, 103-104, 116-117, 117 (ill.), 128-129, 150, 177, 194 (ill.), 220, 231
AC Spark Plug Division of General Motors, 212-213
Active Defense Feasibility Study, 224
ADC, *See* United States Air Force: Air Defense Command
AEC, *See* Atomic Energy Commission
AF08(635)-1168 (contract), 235
AF08(635)-542 (contract), 235
AF33(038)-2664 (contract), 15
AF33(038)-21250 (contract), 15
AF33(600)-2961 (contract), 78
AF33(600)-3367 (contract), 79
AF33(600)-3702 (contract), 73
AF33(600)-31801 (contract), 19, 30
AF33(600)-31802 (contract), 19
AF33(600)-35605 (contract), 58
AF33(600)-35824 (contract), 33, 85
AF33(600)-36599 (contract), 40
AF33(600)-42058 (contract), 101
AF33(616)-2070 (contract), 16
AF33(657)-15871 (contract), 173
AFN, Inc., 79
AGM-28A Hound Dog, *See* North American: GAM-77 Hound Dog
AGM-48A Skybolt, *See* Douglas: GAM-87 Skybolt
AIM-47 (missile), *See* Hughes: Falcon missile
Air Defense Command, *See* United States Air Force: Air Defense Command
Air Force Museum, *See* United States Air Force: Museum
Air Materiel Command, *See* United States Air Force: Air Materiel Command
Air Research and Development Command, *See* United States Air Force: Air Research and Development Command
Aircraft Nuclear Propulsion Program, 2, 4, 7-9, 11, 16, 82
Aircraft Shield Test Reactor, 3-4, 3 (ill.), ; *See also* Convair: NB-36H
alert concept (SAC), 34, 40, 86
alert pod, 98, 204, 211, 232-234
Allison Division of General Motors, 1, 80, 84
Allison: J71, 55
Allison: J89, 19, 33, 82-84
Allison: PD24, 85
ALQ-27, *See* Sperry: ALQ-127
AMC, *See* United States Air Force: Air Materiel Command
American Potash and Chemical Corporation, 79
Ames Aeronautical laboratory, *See* National Advisory Committee on Aeronautics: Ames Aeronautical Laboratory
AN/ALQ-27 Defensive Subsystem, 230
Anderson, Major Clarence E. "Bud" , 20
Anderson, Lieutenant General Samuel E., 85, 218, 222
ANP, *See* Aircraft Nuclear Propulsion Program
APL, *See* Johns Hopkins Applied Physics Laboratory
Applied Physics Laboratory, *See* Johns Hopkins Applied Physics Laboratory
Arco, Idaho, *See* National Reactor Test Site
ARDC, *See* United States Air Force: Air Research and Development Command

Armed Forces Day, 148, 152, 170, 242
Arnold Engineering Development Center, United States Air Force: Arnold Engineering Development Center
Ascani, Brigadier General Fred J., 112
ASG-18 (fire control system), *See* Hughes: ASG-18
ASQ-28 (bomb-nav system), *See* IBM: ASQ-28
ASTR, *See* Aircraft Shield Test Reactor
Astronautics Coordinating Board, 169
Atlas ICBM, viii, 17 (ill.),
Atomic Energy Commission, 1-2, 5, 8, 11, 235

B-36, *See* Convair: B-36
B-47 Strotojet, *See* Boeing: B-47 Stratojet
B-52 Stratofortress, *See* Boeing: B-52 Stratofortress
B-58 Hustler, *See* Convair: B-58 Hustler
B-70 (production aircraft), *See* North American: B-70 Valkyrie
B-70 (WS-110A) Program Office, 19, 79, 85-86, 96, 112, 217, 220, 222, 231
B-70B, *See* North American: B-70B
Balfe, Captain Paul, 126
Bausch & Lomb, 48
Beech Aircraft Company, 232
Bell Telephone Laboratories, 215
Bellman, Donald R., 161
Bendix, 44
Bikle, Paul F., 112, 175
Black, E. J., 157
Blackbird, *See* Lockheed: Blackbird
Blackburn, Al "Blacky", 105
Boeing Airplane Company, 9, 15-16-17, 19, 21-24, 33-34, 36, 39, 41, 56, 79, 83, 169, 228
    B-47 Stratojet, 14, 14 (ill.), 21, 54, 75
    B-52 Stratofortress, viii, 13-14, 14 (ill.), 16, 18, 21, 32 (ill.), 33, 77, 213, 221, 231, 234-235, 235 (ill.)
    Model 713, 21-22, 24 (ill.) 25 (ill.), 26 (ill.), 222 (ill.)
    Model 722, 21, 26 (ill.),
    Model 724, 22-23, 22 (ill.), 23 (ill.), 27 (ill.), 29, 34-35,
    Model 725, 27 (ill.), 28 (ill.), 29, 34-35,
    Model 804, 34 (ill.), 36, 36 (ill.), 37 (ill.), 38 (ill.), 38, 100 (ill.), 216 (ill.), 223 (ill.)
    Supersonic Transport, 100, 169, 171, 207
bomber defense, cannon, 31
bomber defense, electronic countermeasures, 220
bomber defense, missiles, 21-23, 221-222
boron fuels, *See* high-energy fuels
Boyd, Major General Albert, 56, 58, 147
brakes, problems with, 124, 128, 140
Branch, Brigadier General Irving L. "Twig", 122 (ill.)
Brown, Harold, 161, 167
Bruckman, B. W., 88 (ill.)
BuAer, *See* United States Navy: Bureau of Aeronautics
Burke, Admiral Arleigh A., 5

Callery Chemical Company, 78
CAMAL, 8, 9
canard, debate over B-70 use, 91-92, 195
CANEL, *See* Connecticut Aircraft Nuclear Engine Laboratory
Carswell AFB, Texas, vii, 4, 105, 147 (ill.), 148, 240-241, 251
Cate, Colonel Albert M., 167
Chance-Vought Aircraft Company, 41, 44
Charyk, Joseph V., Dr., 82
chemically-augmented nuclear-powered aircraft, 17-18
Chidlaw, General Benjamin W., 55-57
Combs, Vice Admiral Thomas S., 5

compression lift, theory, 38-39, 96
Connecticut Aircraft Nuclear Engine Laboratory, 3
Continental Aviation, 1
Convair , 3, 7, 9, 11, 14-15, 17, 19, 44, 60, 73, 225-226
    B-36, viii, 3-5, 8, 10-11, 13-15, 13 (ill.), 20-21, 32 (ill.), 33, 215, 220, 229
    B-58 Hustler, 9, 15, 16 (ill.), 57, 62, 73-76, 80 (ill.), 88, 104-105, 126, 131 (ill.), 140, 144, 154, 169, 174-175, 189 (ill.), 190, 213
    F-102 Delta Dagger, 42, 44-45, 55, 58, 61, 77
    F-106 Delta Dart, 43-44, 51, 63 (ill.), 77, 214
    Generalized Bomber, 15 (ill.)
    NB-36H, 3-4, 3 (ill.), 6, 11,
    Nuclear Engine Bomber, 3
    X-6, 3-5, 4 (ill.), 7-8
Cooper rating of XB-70, 246-248
CORONA (satellite), 19, 40
Cotton, Colonel Joseph E., vii, x (ill.), 88 (ill.), 98 (ill.), 106, 121 (ill.), 126-129, 132, 135-137, 141-144, 146-150, 152, 162, 167, 170, 173, 175, 244 (table), 245 (ill.)
Crosley Corporation, 222
Cross, Major Carl S., ix, 153-154, 157, 160, 162-163, 166, 172, 187, 244 (table), 245 (ill.)

David Clark Company A/P22S (pressure suit), 70, 185, 191
Defensive Anti-Missile Subsystem, 222-224
DeLong, John, 126
Delta Scorpion, *See* Northrop: Delta Scorpion
Department of Defense, 2, 5, 11, 86, 88, 96, 101, 105, 168
direct-cycle (powerplant), 2
Double Voodoo, 55
Douglas Aircraft Company, 7, 9, 17, 19, 44, 56, 234
Douglas: GAM-87 Skybolt, 93, 211, 234-235, 234-235 (ill.), 257
Douglas, James H., 39
Draper, Charles Stark, 212

Eastham, Jim, 75
Eggers, Alfred J., 38
Eisenhower, President Dwight D., 7, 19, 97, 234
electronic countermeasures, *See* bomber defense, electronic countermeasures
Electronic Specialty Company, 73
Elliot Brothers, 234
Empire Test Pilot School, 162
escape capsule, 47 (ill.), 49, 60, 60 (ill.), 67, 70, 160, 161 (ill.), 163, 165 (ill.), 172-173, 182 (ill.), 185-186, 187-189 (ill.), 190
Esenwein, August C., 3
Estes, General Howell, 19
Ethyl Corporation, 79

F-101 Voodoo, *See* McDonnell: F-101
F-102 Delta Dagger, *See* Convair: F-102
F-104 Starfighter, *See* Lockheed: F-104 Starfighter
F-106 Delta Dart, *See* Convair: F-106
F-108 Rapier, *See* North American: F-108
F-89 Scorpion, *See* Northrop: F-89 Scorpion
Fairchild Engine & Airplane Company, 1, 80
Falcon (missile), *See* Hughes: Falcon missile
Federal Aviation Agency/Administration, 112, 153, 168, 170
Fermi, Enrico, 1
Firth Sterling, Incorporated, 80
Flader Corporation, 1
Flax, Alexander H., 112, 116
Flight Engine Test Facility, 5, 6
flight log, XB-70, 237-244

Appendix G   261

Index

floating wing panels, 20, 22-23, 22 (ill.), 23 (ill.), 29, 29 (ill.), 30 (ill.), 32(ill.), 33
Fly Early (ANP concept), 7, 8
Fly First (ANP concept), 5, 8
folding wingtips, 38-39, 196
Fritz, John M., 157, 162, 167
Fulton, Lieutenant Colonel Fitzhugh L. "Fitz", vii, vii (ill.), 88 (ill.), 106, 121 (ill.), 126, 135-139, 146, 148, 153-154, 157, 173, 175, 180, 244 (table), 245 (ill.)

GAM-77 Hound Dog, *See* North American: GAM-77 Hound Dog
GAM-87 Skybolt, *See* Douglas: GAM-87 Skybolt
GAR-1 (missile), *See* Hughes: GAR-1 Falcon
GAR-9 (missile), *See* Hughes: Falcon missile
GAR-X (missile), *See* Hughes: Falcon missile
GEBO, *See* Convair: Generalized Bomber
General Electric, 1-3, 6, 10, 19, 41, 44, 78-81, 84-88, 139, 167, 172, 220-222, 230, 234-235
   J47, 6
   J79, 15, 16 (ill.), 19, 33, 87
   J79 on HEF, 79, 79 (ill.), 88,
   J87, 9
   J93, 33, 41, 59, 61, 67, 69, 72, 76 (ill.), 80, 82-83, 85-86, 85 (ill.), 87-89, 87 (ill.), 89 (table), 92, 96, 104, 182 (ill.), 205-207, 206 (ill.)
   J93 with thrust reverser, 68 (ill.), 69-70, 72,
   TF31, 82
   X24, 15
   X39, 6, 9
   X40, 3-5, 8-9
   X207, 19, 82
   X211, 9
   X275, 19, 22-23, 30-31, 33, 83
   X279, 29, 33, 35-36, 38
   XNJ140E, 9
General Precision Laboratories, 217-218
   APN-96, 217
Gerrity, Major General Tom, 20
Glenn L. Martin Company: P6M-1 Seamaster, 5, 77
Go Slow (ANP concept), 7,
Goodmanson, Lloyd T., 21-22, 35
Goodyear Aircraft Corporation, 60, 219
GOR-38, 17, 19
GOR-82, 19, 41, 79, 92, 230
GOR-96, 18
GOR-114, 51, 57
Graves, Douglas E., 22
Gray, Edward Z., 34

Hamilton Standard, 73, 198
Harmony Borax Works, 77
Haugen, Colonel Victor R., 255
Haynes Stellite Company, 80
Heat Transfer Reactor Experiment, 6-9, 11
HEF Guidance Committee, 81
HEF-3, *See* high-energy fuel
high-energy fuel, 17, 29, 31-33, 41, 60, 77-82, 81 (ill.), 88-89, 92, 96, 109
Hoag, Captain Peter C., 157, 162
Holbrook, Colonel J. C., 172-173
Horan, John, 6
HTRE, *See* Heat Transfer Reactor Experiment
Hughes Aircraft Company, 44, 51, 56, 58-59, 61, 62, 71, 212, 221
   ASG-18, 61-63, 62 (ill.), 64-65 (ill.), 66, 69, 73-75, 227
   Falcon missile, 22, 43 (ill.), 44, 51, 54-56, 58-59, 61-62, 66, 68 (ill.), 71, 73-75, 74-75 (ill.), 224-227
   GAR-1 Falcon, 44, 49, 51, 55, 222
   MA-1, 44, 49 (ill.), 50
   X-3 IRST, 61-63, 62 (ill.), 66, 68 (ill.)
Hurricane Mesa Supersonic Research Site, 259
hydraulic system, problems with, 124, 129-130, 136, 140, 204

International Business Machines Corporation, 53, 212, 215, 218, 221
   ASQ-28, 41, 97, 102, 112, 152, 217-218, 218 (ill.), 219-220
   MA-2, 213, 215, 217
ICBM, *See* Intercontinental Ballisc Missile. *See also* Atlas ICBM, Titan ICBM.
Idaho potatoes, 143
Identically Located Acceleration and Force experiment, 175 (ill.), 176-177, 177 (ill.)
ILAF, *See* Identically Located Acceleration and Force experiment
indirect-cycle (powerplant), 2, 10,
infared search and track system (for F-108), *See* Hughes: X-3
infrared signature reduction efforts for B-70, 231-232
inlet/engine temperature, 45
intercontinental ballistic missile, development of, 16-17, 19, 53, 97
intercontinental bomber, discussion of, 13, 17
International Nickel Company, 80
IRST (for F-108), *See* Hughes: X-3 IRST

J47 (engine), *See* General Electric: J47

J58 (engine), *See* Pratt & Whitney: J58
J67 (engine), *See* Wright: J67
J71 (engine), *See* Allison: J71
J75 (engine), *See* Pratt & Whitney: J75
J79 (engine), *See* General Electric: J79
J87 (engine), *See* General Electric: J87
J89 (engine), *See* Allison: J89
J91 (engine), *See* Pratt & Whitney: J91
J93 (engine), *See* General Electric: J93
Jacobs, Colonel Jesse, 126
Johns Hopkins Applied Physics Laboratory, 1, 80
Johnston, Leonard E. "Bill", 5
Jones, Brigadier General David C., 235
JP-4 (fuel), 31, 33, 92, 94, 96, 109
JP-5 (fuel), 88
JP-6 (fuel), 61, 72, 82, 88, 92, 96, 109, 131, 233
JP-TS (fuel), 88

Kartveli, Alexander, 44, 46-49
Keirn, General Donald J., 1, 5
Kelsey, Brigadier General Benjamin S., 17
Kennedy, President John F., 11, 102, 169, 235
Knight, Lieutenant Colonel Jake, 126
Knight, Major William J. "Pete", 135

Lacy, H. Clay, 157
landing gear, problems with, 125, 128-129, 128 (ill.), 147, 149-150, 149 (ill.), 150 (ill.), 200-201
Lanning, Wilbert J., 139
LeMay, General Curtis E., viii, 1, 9, 13-14, 13 (ill.), 17-18, 33, 41
Lenticular Defense Missile, 224, 259. *See also* Pye Wacket.
Lewis Flight Propulsion Laboratory, *See* National Advisory Committee on Aeronautics: Lewis Flight Propulsion Laboratory
Lexington Report, 2, 11
Lincoln Laboratory, 53
Linde Company, 80
Lippisch, Alexander, 44
Livermore Laboratory, 11, 234
Lockheed Aircraft Company, 7, 9, 11, 17, 19, 41, 44, 50, 56-57, 169, 228, 230
   Blackbird, 39-40, 49, 60, 83, 86, 88, 96, 106, 108, 121, 144
   F-104 Starfighter, 44, 57, 157, 160-163, 166 (ill.), 169
   PS-1, 230
   YF-12A, 65, 73-77, 75 (ill.), 145 (ill.), 169
Long-Range Interceptor, 51, 54, 57
Los Alamos Laboratory, 16
Love, James E., 259
low-level penetration using B-70, 99-100
LRI-X, *See* Long-Range Interceptor. *See also* North American: F-108
Lycoming, 1

MA-1 (fire control system), *See* Hughes: MA-1
MA-2 (bomb-nav system), *See* International Buisiness Machines: MA-2
Macauley, John B., 82
MacMillan, Prime Minister Harold, 234
Manhattan District, 1
Mallick, Donald L., vii, x (ill.), 160-161, 175, 244 (table), 245 (ill.)
Manson, Major General Hugh, 175
Marquardt, 80
Martin Aircraft, 9, 17, 19, 56, 60. *See also* Glenn L. Martin Company
Massachusetts Institute of Technology, 2, 53, 212
Mayo, Ivan, 131
McCollom, John S., 167
McCoy, Colonel Michael N. W., 14
McDonald, Bob, 149
McDonnell Aircraft Company, 56
McDonnell: F-101, 54-56, 61, 77, 79 (ill.), 88
McNamara, Robert S., 102, 104, 161, 167, 235
Menasco Manufacturing, 1
mid-air collision of A/V-2, 157-167, 158-160 (ill.)
mid-air collision of A/V-2, monetary cost, 167
Minuteman ICBM, 95, 219, 235
MIT, *See* Massachusetts Institute of Technology
Model 713, *See* Boeing: Model 713
Model 722, *See* Boeing: Model 722
Model 724, *See* Boeing: Model 724
Model 725, *See* Boeing: Model 725
Model 804, *See* Boeing: Model 804
Munds, Frank, 127-128
MX-601, 21, 44. *See also* Hughes: Falcon missile
MX-798, 44. *See also* Hughes: Falcon missile
MX-904, 44, 221. *See also* Hughes: Falcon missile
MX-1022, 15
MX-1179, 44-45, 48, 56, 58, 63, 214. *See also* Hughes: MA-1
MX-1554, 44-45
MX-1589, 3
MX-1712, 15
MX-1847, 21
MX-1964, 15
MX-1965, 15

MX-2145, 17, 21
MX-2223, 229 (ill.)

N-126, *See* Northrop: Delta Scorpion
NA-236, *See* North American: NA-236
NA-257, *See* North American: NA-257
NA-264, *See* North American: NA-264
NA-267, *See* North American: NA-267
NA-274, *See* North American: NA-274
NA-278, *See* North American: NA-278
NA-281, *See* North American: NA-281
NA-286, *See* North American: NA-286
NA-303, *See* North American: NA-303
National Advisory Committee on Aeronautics: Ames Aeronautical Laboratory, 33
National Advisory Committee on Aeronautics: Lewis Flight Propulsion Laboratory, 78-79 (ill.), 80
National Aeronautics and Space Administration: Ames Research Center, 97, 144, 198
National Aeronautics and Space Administration: Flight Research Center, 112, 117, 160-161, 166, 169, 174, 176-179, 182, 194, 198-200, 226, 237, 244-245, 249
National Aeronautics and Space Administration: Langley Research Center, 198, 226
National Aeronautics and Space Administration: Lewis Research Center, 80, 206
National Laboratories, 1-2, 11, 14, 16-17, 71
National Reactor Test Site, 5
National Sonic Boom Program, 168-169, 171
Naval Reactors Facility, 6
Navy Bureau of Aeronautics, 78
Neal, Captain Phil, 126
NEBO, *See* Convair: Nuclear Engine Bomber
North American Aviation, 9, 19, 29-31, 33-34, 38-39, 41, 44, 50, 57, 59, 71, 79, 81-84, 86, 91, 99, 108, 116, 144, 171-172, 212, 217-218, 224, 228, 231
   B-70, first Mach 3 flight, 141-142, 146
   B-70, cancellation of, 97, 102
   B-70, alternate flight programs review, 116-117
   B-70, as carrier for X-15, 178 (ill.)
   B-70, evolution of, 92-94, 92-93 (ill.)
   B-70, external stores, 94
   B-70, first supersonic flight, 130
   B-70, flight log, 237-244
   B-70, maiden flight, 126, 127 (ill.), 140, 140 (ill.)
   B-70, mockup inspection, 93
   B-70, retirement of, 180
   B-70, rollout, 121, 122 (ill.), 139, 139 (ill.)
   B-70, total cost of, 177 (table)
   B-70B, 103
   Columbus Division, 73, 99
   F-108, 41, 42 (ill.), 58-73, 58-73 (ill.), 96, 185
   F-108, cancellation of, 72
   GAM-77 Hound Dog, 216 (ill.), 233
   NA-236, 57-58
   NA-257, 58-59
   NA-264, 93
   NA-267, 94
   NA-274, 101
   NA-278, 103
   NA-281, 173
   NA-286, 117
   NA-303, 173
   RS-70, 104, 122
   YB-70, 101-103, 231-233
   YF-108, 58
Northrop Aircraft Corporation, 1, 56-57
   Delta Scorpion, 54-56, 55 (ill.)
   F-89 Scorpion, 43, 54
   Nortronics Division, 234
NRTS, *See* National Reactor Test Site
NTA, *See* Convair: NB-36H
Nuclear Aircraft Research Facility, 4, 11
Nuclear Test Aircraft, *See* Convair: NB-36H
nuclear weapons, getting larger/smaller, 14, 16
NX-2, 7, 10 (ill.)

Oak Ridge National Laboratory, 1-2
Olds, Colonel Robin, 69
Olin Mathieson Chemical Corporation, 78, 81
Operation Wiener Roast, 6, 6 (ill.)

P&W, *See* Pratt & Whitney
P-1 propulsion system, 4
P-3 propulsion system, 7
P6M-1 Seamaster, *See* Glenn L. Martin Company: P6M-1 Seamaster
Pacific Mercury television Manufacturing Company, 212-213
paperclip flight, 149-150
Parson-Macco-Liewitt, 5
Partridge, General Earle E., 57, 59

Penetration System No. 1, *See* Lockheed: PS-1
polar navigation, discussion of, 67
Power Plant Laboratory, *See* United States Air Force: WADC: Power Plant Laboratory
Power, Lieutenant General Thomas S., 18
Powerplant Laboratory, 83
Pratt & Whitney, 3, 10, 80, 87, 96
  J58, 33, 38, 41, 61, 84, 84 (ill.), 86-87, 96, 109
  J75, 19, 77, 82
  J91, 19, 33, 82-83, 85
President's Scientific Advisory Committee, 8
pressure suits, 70, 185, 191
Price, Melvin, Representative, 10
Project DASH, 78
Project Mongoose, 224
Project Pluto, 2
Project Rover, 2
Project ZIP, 78
Project ZOOM, 79
PS-1 (defensive system), *See* Lockheed: PS-1
Pye Wacket, 210 (ill.), 224-226, 225 (ill.)

R-1 reactor, 4-5
radar effectiveness against high-speed targets, 15
Ramenskoye Airfield, 118
Ramo-Wooldridge, 58
RAND Corporation, 228-229
Rapier, origin of name, 72
Raytheon Manufacturing Company, 221
Reaction Motors, 80
Republic Aviation Corporation, 20, 44, 49, 56
  XF-103, 42, 44-52, 44-52 (ill.), 55, 58, 82
Richter, Sam, 152
Rogers Dry Lake, 136, 139
Roman, Dr. Jim, 160
RS-70, *See* North American: RS-70
Ruffner, Benjamin F., 21, 29
Russell, Rear Admiral James S., 5
Russell, Senator Richard B., 9

SAC, *See* United States Air Force: Strategic Air Command
SAGE, *See* Semi-Automatic Ground Environment
Santa Susana (test site), 87-89
Schleicher, Richard L., 259
Schriever, General Bernard A., 99, 104
Seamans, Robert C., Jr., 258
Semi-Automatic Ground Environment, 53 (ill.), 53, 55-56, 58,
Sessums, Brigadier General John W., Jr., 14
Shepard, Van H., vii, 100, 105, 121 (ill.), 123, 126, 135-136, 144, 146-148, 244 (table), 245 (ill.)
simulators, 60, 60 (ill.), 99-102
skin separation problems, *See* stainless steel honeycomb, problems with and repairing of
Skyrud, Commander Jerome P., 157, 162
Smith, Colonel James G., 167
Smith, Major Bob, 126
Smith, Major General Frederic H, Jr., 54
Snoopy (B-58), 73-75, 73-74 (ill.). *See also* Convair: B-58 Hustler
sonic boom research, 157, 168-169, 169 (ill.)
Sperry Gyroscope Company, 41, 44, 56, 58, 212-213
Sperry: ALQ-127, 230-231
SPIRE Jr., 212-213, 215
Spivak, Walt, x (ill.), 98 (ill.), 127, 136
split-mission scenario, 33-34
Sputnik I, 7
SR-22, 18-19, 215, 230
SR-56, 19
SR-71, *See* Lockheed: Blackbird
SR-197, 228-230
stainless steel honeycomb, problems with and repairing of, 108, 110, 137-139, 140, 184 (ill.), 208 (ill.)
Stauffer Chemical Company, 79
stealth efforts for B-70, 231-232
Stock, Alfred, Dr., 77-78
Storms, Harrison A. "Stormy", 38, 98 (ill.)
Structural testing, 132-135
Sturmthal, Lieutenant Colonel Emil "Ted", vii, 175, 180, 244 (table), 245 (ill.)
Sukhoi T-4 Sotka, 118, 119 (ill.)
Supersonic Transport, 29, 100, 116-117, 121, 144, 168-172, 207, 249-252
Syverston, Clarence A., 38
Szpur, Roman, 222

Talco Engineering Company, 60
TAN, *See* Test Area North
Tate, Colonel Albert M., 167
Tea Bag (Boeing study), 34-35
Test Area North, 5
thermal environment at Mach 3, 40, 148, 152, 197

thrust reverser (for J93 engine), *See* General Electric: J93 with thrust reverser
Thurlow, D. W., 29
TIP TOW, 20-21, 20 (ill.)
Titan ICBM, viii
TJ32C4 (engine), *See* Wright: J67
Tom-Tom, 20-21
total cost of B-70 program, 177 (table)
total hours flown, 244
Townsend, Colonel Guy, 88 (ill.)
Tupolev Tu-95, 11
Twining, General Nathan F., 55-56, 97

Ultimate Interceptor, *See* Convair: F-106
Union Carbide Corporation, 80
United States Air Force, 2, 8, 78, 171
  Air Defense Command, 43, 51, 54-58, 60, 71,
  Air Force Flight Test Center, 72-73, 122, 147, 162, 175
  Air Force Headquarters, 16-19, 55-57, 79-80, 82, 84-85, 219, 230
  Air Force Systems Command, 104, 167
  Air Force Weapons Board, 82
  Air Materiel Command, 13, 39, 46, 56, 81-88, 217
  Air Proving Ground Command, 225
  Air Research and Development Command, 9, 14, 17-18, 21, 39, 56, 58-59, 69, 82, 88, 99, 217
  ARDC: Headquarters, 19, 55, 157, 219, 221-222
  Air Staff, 33, 39, 41
  Air Technical Intelligence Center, 223
  Arnold Engineering Development Center, 46, 76, 83, 83 (ill.), 88-89, 91, 198, 206, 210, 224-225
  Museum, vii, ix, 180, 181 (ill.)
Northeast Air Command, 54
Strategic Air Command, vi, 1, 9, 13-14, 16, 39, 41, 55, 82, 86, 211, 222
Wright Air Development Center, 14-15, 17-18, 55-58, 77-78, 80-81, 86-87, 211, 213, 229-230
  WADC: Armament Laboratory, 211, 213
  WADC: Power Plant Laboratory, 77-78
  WADC: Weapons Guidance Laboratory, 214-215, 217-222, 228
United States Navy, 2, 5, 8, 11, 41, 78, 84-85
  Bureau of Aeronautics, 5, 78, 80
University of Chicago, 228-229
Upson, Colonel Linus F., Jr., 69

Valkyrie, origin of name, 41
Vitro Corporation, 79
Vogt, Richard, Dr., 20
Vultee Aircraft, Inc., 255

WADC, *See* United States Air Force: Wright Air Development Center
Walker, Joseph A., 121, 122 (ill.), 153-154, 157, 160, 162, 167, 171, 244 (table), 245 (ill.)
weapons system designations, 44
weapons system integrator, 44
Webb, James, 169
Wells, Max, 127, 142
Westinghouse, 1, 44
White Sands Missile Range, 75
White, Alvin S., vi, vi (ill.), vii, x (ill.), 88 (ill.), 98 (ill.), 99, 102, 105, 110-111, 121 (ill.), 123, 124, 126-130, 132, 135-139, 141-142, 144, 146, 148-150, 152-154, 157, 160, 162-163, 165 (ill.), 186-187, 188 (ill.), 244 (table), 245 (ill.)
White, General Thomas D., 41, 97, 234
Whitman, Walter G., Dr., 2
Whitten, Major General Lyman P., 54
Wickham, J. M., 21
Wilson, Charles, 7
Wilson, Lieutenant General R. C., 86
Witchell, Arthur S. "Doc", 4
Withington, H. W. "Bob", 35
Wolowicz, Chester H., 258-259
Wood, Brigadier General Floyd B., 56
Wright Aeronautical Corporation, 1, 44-45, 80, 84
Wright: J67, 18, 44, 44 (ill.), 45-47, 51, 55, 77, 82
Wright: XRJ55, 45-47, 45 (ill.), 51
Wright Air Development Center, *See* United States Air Force: Wright Air Development Center
Wright Field, 1, 9, 19-20, 82, 213, 217-218, 221
WS-110A, 9, 13, 16, 18-19, 21, 24, 29-30, 32-34, 36, 39-40, 59-60, 79, 81, 85, 91, 97, 210, 214-218, 221-222, 230, 233
WS-110A Program Office, *See* B-70 Program Office
WS-110A/L, *See* WS-110A and WS-110L
WS-110A, bidders conference, 19
WS-110A, LeMay's comment, 33
WS-110A, redirection, 33, 79
WS-110A, winner, 39
WS-110L, 18-19, 30, 40,
WS-125A, viii, 7. 9, 11, 18-19, 59, 210, 214-215, 221, 230, 233
WS-125A: bidders conference, 19
WS-138A, 233-234
WS-201A, 44
WS-202A, 58, 61, 85
WS-204A, 45
WS-217A, 55. *See also* McDonnell: F-101
WSPO, *See* B-70 (WS-110A) Program Office

X-6, *See* Convair: X-6
X24 (engine), *See* General Electric: X24
X39 (atomic engine), *See* General Electric: X39
X40 (atomic engine), *See* General Electric: X40
X84 (engine), *See* General Electric: TF31
X207 (engine), *See* General Electric: X207
X211 (engine), *See* General Electric: X211
X275 (engine), *See* General Electric: X275
X279 (engine), *See* General Electric: X279
XB-70 Valkyrie, *See* North American: XB-70 Valkyrie. *See also* A/V-1 and A/V-2
XF-103, *See* Republic: XF-103
XF-108, *See* North American: F-108
XJ93 (engine), *See* General Electric: J93
XNJ140E (powerplant), *See* General Electric: XNJ140E
XRJ55 (engine), *See* Wright: XRJ55

YB-70 Valkyrie, *See* North American: YB-70 Valkyrie
YF-108 Rapier, *See* North American: YF-108
YF-12A, *See* Lockheed: YF-12A. *See also* Lockheed: Blackbird
YJ93 (engine), *See* General Electric: J93
York, Herbert F., 11, 255

ZIP fuels, *See* high-energy fuels

A Convair B-58 Hustler was used as a surrogate for engine noise measurements before the XB-70 began its pre-flight tests in Palmdale. Note the sound abatement chambers behind the B-58 that were built to placate local turkey farmers.
(Boeing Historical Archives)

(Boeing Historical Archives)

THE END

We hope you enjoyed this book ...

With over 500 titles available in our warehouse, we're sure you'll find additional books that will intrigue and interest you. For a free catalog listing all our historical, military, naval, spaceflight, and civil aviation books, please call, write, or visit us online at:

Specialty Press
39966 Grand Avenue
North Branch, MN 55056

Toll Free: 1-800-895-4585
Tel: (651) 277-1400
Fax: (651) 277-1203
www.specialtypress.com

specialtypress
PUBLISHERS AND WHOLESALERS

UK and Europe distribution by

Midland Publishing
4 Watling Drive
Hinkley, LE10 3EY, UK
Tel: (+44) 01455 254 450
Fax: (+44) 01455 233 737

www.midlandcountiessuperstore.com

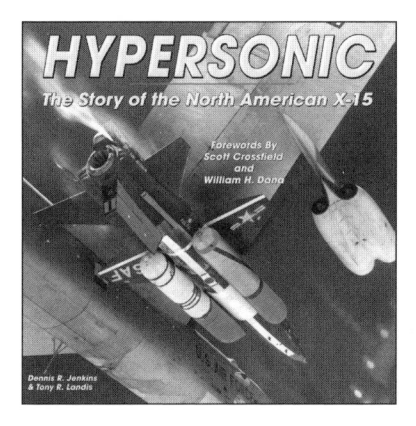

Hypersonic: The Story of the North American X-15 by Dennis R. Jenkins and Tony R. Landis. The result of years of research including correspondence with many of the program principals, this book is the most detailed accounting of what is generally considered the most successful flight research program ever undertaken. In addition of the X-15 itself, this book traces the modifications of the NB-52 carrier aircraft, developing the High Range, and surveying the dry lakebeds. A technical description and a detailed flight log are also included. 10 x 10 inches, 276 pages, 450 B&W and 60 color photos. Hardbound with dust jacket. *Item SP068, ISBN 1-58007-068-X.*

Magnesium Overcast: The Story of the Convair B-36 by Dennis R. Jenkins. The author did extensive original source-material research in various archives around the country, uncovering new and previously unpublished details about the B-36 and its derivatives. This material includes new photos of the never-flown second prototype YB-60, and the devastating 1952 Carswell AFB tornado that almost wiped out a good part of the existing B-36 fleet. Coverage includes a look at weapons, decoys, and electronics. 10 x 10 inches, 276 pages, 500 B&W and 53 color photos. Hardbound with dust jacket. *Item SP042, ISBN 1-58007-042-6.*

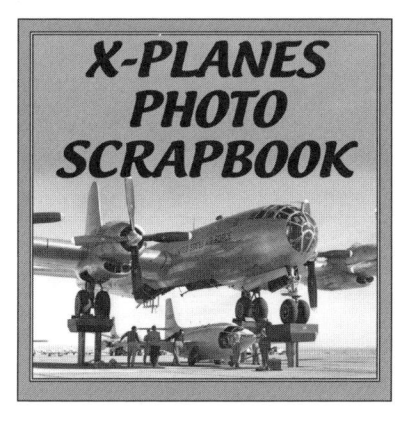

X-Planes Photo Scrapbook. The X-Planes conjure up images of Chuck Yeager first breaking the sound barrier in the X-1 or of the black, bullet-shaped X-15 streaking through the skies at over Mach 6. This book does not limit itself to the formal X-series of aircraft, but instead covers many of the experimental aircraft used by the U.S. military and NASA for flight research. Hundreds of photos – many in color and many never-before-seen – detail the modern history of experimental flight. 9 x 9 inches, 144 pages, 300 B&W and 100 color photos. Softbound. *Item SP076, ISBN 1-58007-076-0.*

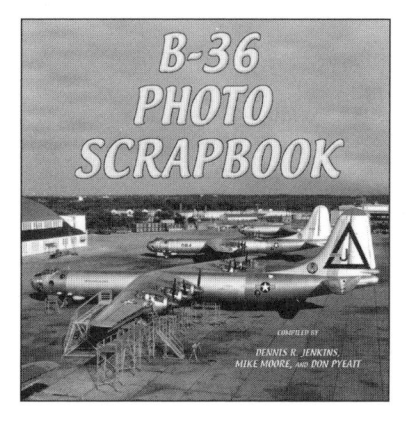

B-36 Photo Scrapbook compiled by Dennis R. Jenkins, Mike Moore, and Don Pyeatt. While doing research for his two books on the B-36, Dennis R. Jenkins ran across several excellent sources of photos, hundreds of which appeared in *Magnesium Overcast*. Other sources and had access to additional unpublished, significant photos of this magnificent icon of the early Cold War. Many of these have been assembled into the *B-36 Photo Scrapbook*. 9 x 9 inches, 108 pages, 300 B&W and 50 color photos. Softbound. *Item SP075, ISBN 1-58007-075-2.*

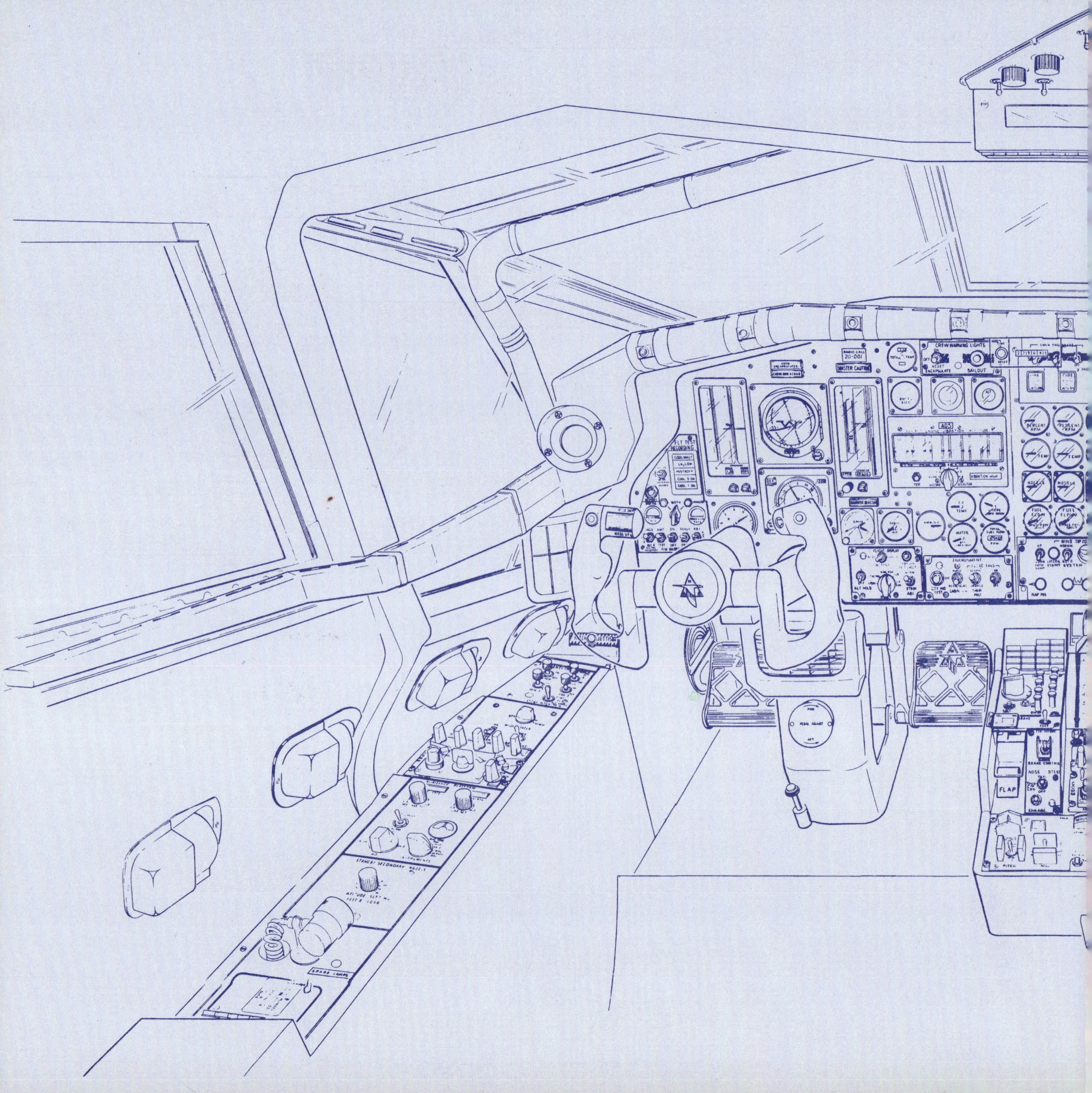
CREW WARNING LIGHTS
BAILOUT
MASTER CAUTION
FLAP
SPARE LAMPS